The **Rough Guide** to

Rajasthan, Delhi & Agra

written and researched by

Daniel Jacobs and Gavin Thomas

www.roughguides.com

Contents

Forts and palaces of Rajasthan colour section following p.208

Rajasthani crafts colour section following p.304

◀◀ Flock of pigeons, Jaipur ◀ "The Blue City" of Jodhpur

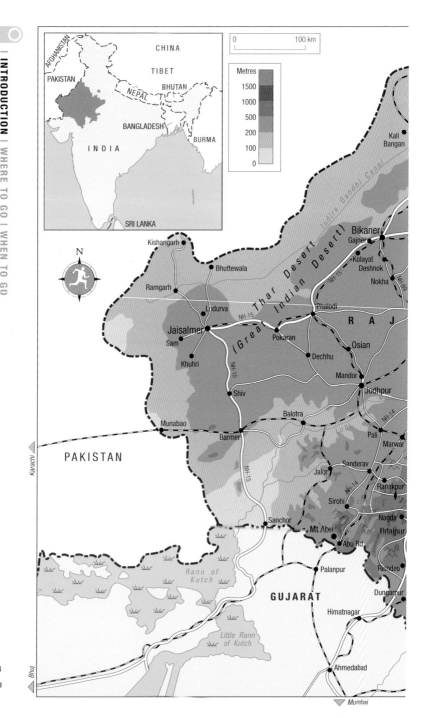

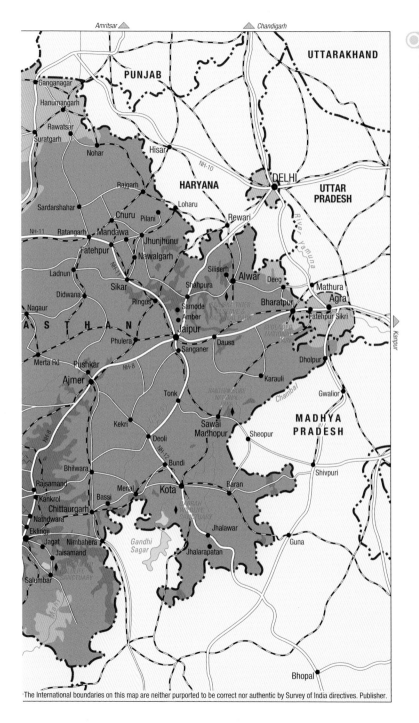

Introduction to

Rajasthan, Delhi and Agra

The most colourful state in the world's most colourful country, Rajasthan is majestic in scale, its huge forts towering over a rugged desert landscape. It was once a patchwork of princedoms, each ruler trying to outdo his rivals in the magnificence of their palaces and patronage of the arts. Moreover, Rajasthan is within easy striking distance of the two greatest cities of India's mighty Mughal Empire: Delhi, still the nation's capital, and one of the most vibrant cities on earth, and Agra, home to the incomparable Taj Mahal. The region as a whole fulfils every romantic expectation of India, with picturesque crowds of men in top-heavy turbans and women in vibrantly coloured saris; crowded bazaars overflowing with sumptuous embroidered fabrics and exquisite jewellery; and even the vivid orange flash of a tiger or leopard seen padding quietly through the undergrowth of a national park. All together, the area's myriad attractions are a recipe for delicious Subcontinental sensory overload.

Many of Rajasthan's sights rank among India's most spectacular and memorable: the Taj Mahal and Islamic monuments of Agra and Delhi; Udaipur's romantic lakeside palaces and Jaisalmer's remote desert fortress; the bazaars of Jaipur's Pink City and the mighty Meherangarh Fort at Jodhpur. In addition there are countless less-heralded places to seek out, and even repeated visits to the region are unlikely to exhaust its extraordinarily rich array of attractions.

Elephant with painted face, Jaipur

Where to go

Most visitors to the region arrive in **Delhi**, and pretty much everyone spends at least a few days exploring India's historic capital, although you could spend weeks wandering the city's countless monuments, museums and bazaars, including the soaring Qutb Minar, erected by the city's first Muslim ruler, the Mughal-era Red Fort (Lal Qila) and Jama Masjid, and the grandiose imperial creations of the British.

From Delhi it's a short train journey south to **Agra**, home to an astonishing collection of Mughal monuments, including the superlative Taj Mahal, and also conveniently close to the remarkable abandoned city of **Fatehpur Sikri**. West of Agra lies the bustling city of **Jaipur**, the third point of the famous "Golden Triangle", and the capital of the state of Rajasthan, home to an intriguing collection of monuments and bazaars.

Jaipur is also the starting point for forays into eastern Rajasthan. Immediately north of Jaipur, the fabulous painted havelis (mansions) of the **Shekhawati** region are attracting increasing numbers of foreign visitors, though the region is best known for **Keoladeo National**

Fact file

• **Rajasthan**, with 66.7 million people (89 percent Hindu, 8.5 percent Muslim, 1.4 percent Sikh, 1.2 percent Jain), is India's largest and eighth most populous state. It came into existence following Independence in 1947, formed from a union of nineteen princely states, plus Ajmer, which had been under direct British rule. The main languages are Hindi and Rajasthani. Rajasthan is ruled by the Congress Party, who wrested control from the opposition BJP in state elections in 2008. The economy is mainly agricultural, along with copper and zinc mines, and quarries for sandstone and marble.

• **Delhi**, India's federal capital and second-largest city (after Mumbai) is home to 15 million people (82 percent Hindu, 12 percent Muslim, 4 percent Sikh, and around one percent Jain and one percent Christian). Not part of any state, it has its own legislative assembly and Capital Territory status, and is ruled by the Congress Party. Most employees work in the public sector, but IT, telecommunications and the media are important industries.

• **Agra**, populated by 1.7 million people (predominantly Hindu, but with a large Muslim minority), is the third-largest city in the state of Uttar Pradesh (UP). Its politics are dominated by the largely local, socialist Samajwadi Party, which promotes the rights of the lower castes and religious minorities.

7

Bundi bazaar

Park at Bharatpur, one of the world's finest bird-spotting destinations, and **Ranthambore National Park**, one of the easiest places on the planet to see tigers in the wild.

West of Jaipur, the pretty little town of **Pushkar** is famous for its astonishing annual camel fair, and has long been Rajasthan's principal backpacker hangout. By contrast, surprisingly few tourists venture out to the historic nearby city of **Ajmer**, Rajasthan's most important Muslim settlement. West of Ajmer, **Jodhpur** also remains relatively overlooked by travellers, despite boasting arguably Rajasthan's most spectacular fort.

Beyond Jodhpur, the Thar Desert begins in earnest, its rolling, scrub-covered sands enveloping Rajasthan's two remotest cities. The first, **Bikaner**, is renowned for its superb Junagarh fort and for the unique Karni Mata shrine, or "rat temple", at Deshnok. The second, **Jaisalmer**, is one of the archetypal Rajasthan destinations: a fairy-tale walled city marooned amid the sands of the Thar, its narrow streets lined with fantastically carved havelis and ornate temples.

In stark contrast to the deserts of western Rajasthan, the southern part of the state is notably green and hilly. The main attraction here is the beautiful city of **Udaipur**, with its romantically tangled skyline of palaces and havelis strung

Jaisalmer Lake, Rajasthan

out around the sylvan waters of Lake Pichola. North of Udaipur, the massive **Kumbalgarh** fort and the superb Jain temples at **Ranakpur** are both easily visited as a day-trip, while there are further spectacular Jain temples west of Udaipur at the engaging little hill station of **Mount Abu**.

Rajasthan's ethnic minorities

Like most Indian states, Rajasthan has a number of "tribal" peoples who live outside the social mainstream. Many are nomadic, and often called "Gypsies" – indeed the Romanies of Europe are thought to have originated among these Rajasthani Gypsy tribes. The most prominent are the **Kalbeliyas**, found largely in Pushkar. The Kalbeliyas discovered how to charm snakes, and they used to sing and dance for royalty, as they now do for tourists, but living on the margins of society, they suffer much the same sort of discrimination as their brethren in Europe.

Similarly, the **Bhopas** are a green-eyed tribe of nomads who used to work as entertainers to the maharajas, and to this day they make a living as itinerant poets and storytellers. They are asked to perform particularly where someone is sick, as their songs are believed to aid recovery.

In the Jodhpur region, many tourists take an excursion into the countryside to visit the **Bishnoi** (see p.278), a religious rather than strictly ethnic group, whose tree-hugging beliefs chime with those of Western hippies. Living in close proximity to them, though with a very different lifestyle, are the **Bhils**, great hunters who used to hire themselves out as soldiers in the armies of the Rajput kingdoms. They have their own language and religion, and their dances have become very popular, especially at Holi.

Heading east from Udaipur, the superb fort at **Chittaurgarh** is among the most spectacular and historically important in the state, while further east the city of **Kota** is one of Rajasthan's most heavily industrialized, but compensates with some outstanding murals at its grand city palace. Even finer examples of Rajasthani painting can be seen nearby at the small town of **Bundi**, whose laidback charms are attracting increasing numbers of Western visitors.

When to go

R
ajasthan's **climate** reaches the extremes common to desert regions; in general, the western half of the state is drier and hotter than the eastern and southern areas. The **best time to visit** is between October and March, when daytime temperatures hover around the 25°C mark, though night-time temperatures can fall to near freezing, and mornings can be chilly. However, hotels tend to get booked up during this period and room rates are at their highest. During the **summer**, from April to September, average daytime temperatures push up into the mid-30s, and can top 45°C in May and June. On the plus side, hotel rates fall significantly at many places from around April to September, and pretty much everywhere has vacancies. The **monsoon** arrives, and temperatures fall, in July and August (in theory,

▼ Market, Pushkar

at least – rainfall in recent years has been sporadic and unpredictable, with widespread drought in parts of the state and catastrophic flooding in others). **Delhi** and **Agra** enjoy a similar climate to Rajasthan, though without ever quite reaching the extremes of heat experienced in western Rajasthan.

Average temperatures (in °C) and rainfall (in mm)

	Jan	Feb	Mar	Apr	May	Jun	Jul	Aug	Sep	Oct	Nov	Dec
Agra												
Max/min	22/7	26/10	32/16	38/22	42/27	41/29	35/27	33/26	33/25	31/19	29/12	24/8
Rainfall	16	9	11	5	10	60	210	263	151	23	2	4
Bikaner												
Max/min	22/8	25/11	32/16	38/23	42/28	42/29	38/28	37/27	37/26	36/22	30/14	24/9
Rainfall	6	6	5	4	14	30	81	90	32	4	2	4
Delhi												
Max/min	21/7	24/10	30/15	36/21	41/27	40/29	35/27	34/26	34/25	35/19	29/12	23/8
Rainfall	25	22	17	7	8	65	211	173	150	31	1	5
Jaipur												
Max/min	22/8	25/11	31/15	37/21	41/26	39/27	34/26	32/24	33/23	33/18	29/12	24/9
Rainfall	14	1	8	9	4	10	54	193	239	90	19	4
Jaisalmer												
Max/min	24/8	28/11	33/17	38/21	42/25	41/27	38/27	36/25	36/25	36/20	31/13	26/9
Rainfall	2	1	3	1	5	7	89	86	14	1	5	2
Jodhpur												
Max/min	25/9	28/12	33/17	38/22	42/27	40/29	36/27	33/25	35/24	36/20	31/14	27/11
Rainfall	7	5	2	2	6	31	122	145	47	7	3	1
Udaipur												
Max/min	24/8	28/10	32/15	36/20	38/25	36/25	31/24	29/23	31/22	32/19	29/11	26/8
Rainfall	9	4	3	3	5	87	197	207	102	16	6	3

18

things not to miss

It's not possible to see everything that Rajasthan, Delhi and Agra have to offer in a single trip – and we don't suggest you try. What follows is a selective taste of the region's highlights: outstanding monuments, memorable wildlife and spectacular festivals. Attractions are arranged in five colour-coded categories with a page reference to take you straight into the Guide, where you can find out more.

01 **Taj Mahal** Page **158** • Magical, mysterious and completely unforgettable: Shah Jahan's immortal monument to love is, quite simply, the most sublime building on the planet.

02 **Shekhawati havelis** Page **216** • North of Jaipur, the Shekhawati region is home to an extraordinary collection of crumbling havelis decorated with murals, featuring everything from religious scenes to depictions of European society.

04 **Mughlai cooking, Agra** Page **171** • A taste of imperial Mughal culinary splendour, with dishes cooked in rich, cream- and curd-based sauces, accompanied by pulao rice dishes and milky sweets such as *kheer*.

03 **Camel trekking in the Thar** Pages **289** & **300** • Climb aboard a camel and sally forth into the rolling sands of the Thar Desert, one of India's quintessential wilderness experiences.

05 **Red Fort, Delhi** Page **116** • The centrepiece of Mughal Delhi, the Red Fort (Lal Qila) offers an absorbing insight into the public pageantry and private life of its creator, Shah Jahan, and his imperial successors.

06 Humayun's Tomb, Delhi Page **121** • Delhi's finest Mughal monument – an imposing, Persian-style mausoleum, erected in honour of the second Mughal emperor, Humayun.

07 Baha'i Temple, Delhi Page **128** • Delhi's answer to the Sydney Opera House – a remarkable modernist temple, in the form of a giant unfolding lotus.

08 Chittaurgarh Fort Page **342** • The quintessential Rajput fort, its magnificent collection of temples, palaces and monuments bear witness to the city's glorious, and often gruesome, history.

09 **Fatehpur Sikri** Page 174 • The enigmatic abandoned capital of the great emperor Akbar – a hauntingly deserted showcase of Mughal architecture.

10 **Karni Mata Temple, Deshnok** Page 307 • The "rat temple" of Karni Mata, just outside Bikaner, is one of India's weirder religious experiences, revered for its population of sacred rodents.

11 **Keoladeo National Park, Bharatpur** Page 238 • India's most famous ornithological hotspot, its wetlands attracting vast flocks of migrant birds from across Asia and beyond – drought permitting.

12 **Jain temples at Ranakpur** Page 330 • Tucked away in the hills north of Udaipur, this small temple complex provides a stunning example of the exquisitely detailed carving typical of Jain shrines throughout the region.

13 Pink City, Jaipur

Page **192** • The original heart of old Jaipur, and still Rajasthan's most vibrant commercial district, with streets full of imposing pink mansions, crammed with colourful bazaars.

14 Pushkar Camel Mela

Page **265** • Held annually in November, the largest livestock market on earth sees over two hundred thousand-odd Rajasthani camel herders converging on Pushkar to trade dromedaries.

15 Udaipur

Page **314** • The most romantic city in India, with a spectacular array of ornate palaces and havelis clustered around – or floating amid – the peaceful waters of Lake Pichola.

17 Ranthambore National Park Page **240** • Rajasthan's most popular national park is probably the easiest place in the world to spot wild tigers – an unforgettable experience, despite the crowds.

16 Jaisalmer Page **280** • Honey-coloured city deep in the Thar Desert, its streets crammed full of extravagantly carved temples and havelis.

18 Meherangarh Fort, Jodhpur Page **272** • The epitome of Rajput military might, its sheer-sided ramparts towering high above the labyrinthine, blue-painted streets of old Jodhpur.

Basics

Basics

Getting there

The easiest way of getting to India from abroad is by plane. The region's principal international airport is at Delhi, which is served by direct flights from London, New York, Los Angeles and Toronto, as well as numerous points in Asia. If you're already in India, internal flights are usually the quickest way to reach the region, but it's also worth considering the train, particularly the Rajdhani and Shatabdi express services which run to Delhi, Jaipur and Agra from major cities nationwide.

International **airfares** vary slightly with the **season**. In the northern hemisphere, you'll usually get the best fares in January and February, when fewer people are travelling, higher fares around July and August, and the highest over Christmas, Easter and Diwali (usually Nov). From the southern hemisphere, fares are usually lowest in July and August, rising over the summer (Nov to March), and peaking during Christmas, Easter and Diwali. Prices quoted below are inclusive of tax.

It's worth shopping around for the most convenient **arrival times**; nearly all of the cheaper flights land in the middle of night and it can be worth shelling out a little extra to arrive in the morning, particularly if this is your first trip to India.

A large number of operators run **package holidays** to the region, ranging from standard "Golden Triangle" tours of Delhi, Agra and Jaipur through to specialist tours focusing on wildlife, crafts, religion or old steam locomotives (such as the luxury Palace on Wheels and Royal Rajasthan on Wheels train journeys – see p.29). Many companies can also arrange **tailor-made tours** customized to your own interests.

Flights from the UK and Ireland

London's Heathrow is the only airport in the UK with **direct flights** to Delhi, currently operated by BA, Air India, Virgin Atlantic and Jet Airways. Flying time is around 7 hours 30 minutes outbound, slightly longer coming back. There are also over a dozen airlines offering **indirect flights** from London to Delhi, changing planes either in Europe (including Lufthansa, Swiss, Austrian, Air

France and KLM) or the Gulf (Emirates, Etihad, Qatar Airways and Gulf Air). From elsewhere in the UK or Ireland, you'll either have to make your way to London or take an indirect flight, changing planes in Europe or the Gulf.

If you're heading straight to Rajasthan and want to avoid having to travel overland from Delhi, there are frequent internal **domestic flights** from Delhi and Mumbai to **Jaipur**, **Udaipur** and **Jodhpur** (and there is a new airport also scheduled to open at **Jaisalmer** in 2010). There are also flights from Delhi to **Agra**. See the list of operators on p.31, and also check the "Moving on" sections at the end of the various city accounts. There are a few **international flights** to **Jaipur**, although this currently only has limited connections with the Gulf (to Muscat with Oman Air, and Sharjah with Air Arabia).

Return fares from London to Delhi usually start at around £400.

Flights from the US and Canada

If you live on the East Coast it's quicker to go via Europe, while from the West Coast it's roughly the same distance whether you fly via Europe or the Pacific. Whichever way you fly, it's a long haul: fourteen hours direct to Delhi from New York or Toronto, and twenty hours from Los Angeles.

There are **direct flights** to Delhi from New York (with Air India and Continental/United), Chicago (with Jet Airways/American Airlines) and Houston (with Continental). There are no direct flights from Canada. From any other airport in North America you'll have to take an **indirect flight**, changing at either New York or Chicago, or in Europe, the Middle

East or Asia. Round-trip fares from New York to Delhi start at around $1000.

Flights from Australia and New Zealand

There are no nonstop flights to Delhi from Australia or New Zealand. Flying from **Australia**, you'll have to change planes at least once in Asia; one-stop flights are available from Sydney, Melbourne, Perth, Adelaide and Brisbane with Singapore Airlines (via Singapore), Thai Airways (via Bangkok), Malaysia Airlines (via Kuala Lumpur), Cathay Pacific (via Hong Kong) and Qantas/Jet Airways (via Singapore). Fares from Sydney to Delhi start at around A$1500 and the flight typically takes a minimum of around seventeen hours. From **New Zealand**, it's a similar story, except that the choice of carriers is more limited, and you may need to change more than once. Fares start from around NZ$2000.

RTW flights

If north India is only one stop on a longer journey, you might want to consider buying a **Round the World** (RTW) ticket. Some travel agents can sell you an "off-the-shelf" RTW ticket that will have you touching down in about half a dozen cities; others will have to assemble one for you, which can be tailored to your needs but is likely to be more expensive. Figure on around £1800/US$3500 for an "off-the-shelf" ticket including Delhi. Some tickets allow for arrival at Delhi and departure out of Mumbai or Kolkata (Calcutta), travelling overland in between. If you plan to arrive in Delhi and travel southwards through Rajasthan, ending up at Mount Abu or Udaipur, then it may well suit you to continue down to Mumbai and fly on from there.

Six steps to a better kind of travel

At Rough Guides we are passionately committed to travel. We feel strongly that only through travelling do we truly come to understand the world we live in and the people we share it with – plus tourism has brought a great deal of **benefit** to developing economies around the world over the last few decades. But the extraordinary growth in tourism has also damaged some places irreparably, and of course **climate change** is exacerbated by most forms of transport, especially flying. This means that now more than ever it's important to **travel thoughtfully** and **responsibly**, with respect for the cultures you're visiting – not only to derive the most benefit from your trip but also to preserve the best bits of the planet for everyone to enjoy. At Rough Guides we feel there are six main areas in which you can make a difference:

- Consider what you're contributing to the **local economy**, and how much the services you use do the same, whether it's through employing local workers and guides or sourcing locally grown produce and local services.
- Consider the **environment** on holiday as well as at home. Water is scarce in many developing destinations, and the biodiversity of local flora and fauna can be adversely affected by tourism. Try to patronize businesses that take account of this.
- Travel with a purpose, not just to tick off experiences. Consider **spending longer** in a place, and getting to know it and its people.
- Give thought to how often you **fly**. Try to avoid short hops by air and more harmful night flights.
- Consider **alternatives to flying**, travelling instead by bus, train, boat and even by bike or on foot where possible.
- Make your trips "**climate neutral**" via a reputable carbon offset scheme. All Rough Guide flights are offset, and every year we donate money to a variety of charities devoted to combating the effects of climate change.

Flights from elsewhere in India

India's burgeoning number of domestic airlines (see the list on p.31) now cover virtually every part of the country, with regular, reliable services. Delhi itself is easily reached by plane from just about everywhere, while **Jaipur** has connections with over ten other Indian cities (plus a couple of places in the Gulf). There are also flights from Delhi and Mumbai to **Jodhpur**, **Udaipur** and (starting in 2010, possibly) **Jaisalmer**, as well as from Delhi to **Agra**; Ⓦwww.travelocity.co.in is a good place to explore the myriad routes and fares currently available.

Trains

Getting to **Delhi** by train is usually straightforward enough, though journeys from the south and east can take well over a day. There are fast Rajdhani and Shatabdi express services from Mumbai, Chennai, Kolkata (Calcutta) and Guwahati to Delhi, as well as direct express and mail services from major cities nationwide. **Agra** and **Rajasthan** are less well connected than Delhi, although **Agra** and **Jaipur** are both easily reached by train from Delhi, Mumbai and Kolkata. For full details of all train services, plus fares, see the Indian Railways **website** at Ⓦwww.indianrail.gov.in.

There are two **international train services** currently running into India from Pakistan. At the time of writing it appears that only Indian and Pakistani nationals were being allowed to use these services – though this may of course change in the future. The **Samjhauta Express** leaves Lahore twice weekly (usually either Mon & Thurs or Tues & Fri) at 8am, arriving at 3pm in Amritsar. Political tensions sometimes affect the running of this service, however, and there may be extended delays at the border. Security may also be a concern: in February 2007, 68 passengers were killed when terrorists bombed the train. The **Thar Express** leaves Karachi every Friday at 11pm, arriving Jodhpur around 9.30pm on Saturday. For the latest news, check Ⓦwww.seat61.com/Pakistan.htm.

For further information on train reservations and rail passes, see pp.26–29.

Buses

Buses comes a poor third to plane and train as a way of reaching the region, although you might be forced to take a bus if approaching Delhi from northern parts of India, such as Kashmir, Himachal Pradesh and Uttarakhand, where the rail network doesn't reach. There are also comfortable express bus services to southern Rajasthan from Mumbai and Gujarat.

Airlines, agents and operators

Airlines

Aer Lingus Ⓦwww.aerlingus.com.
Air Canada Ⓦwww.aircanada.com.
Air France Ⓦwww.airfrance.com.
Air India Ⓦwww.airindia.com.
Alitalia Ⓦwww.alitalia.com.
American Airlines Ⓦwww.aa.com.
Asiana Airlines Ⓦwww.flyasiana.com.
British Airways Ⓦwww.ba.com.
Cathay Pacific Ⓦwww.cathaypacific.com.
China Airlines Ⓦwww.china-airlines.com.
Continental Airlines Ⓦwww.continental.com.
Delta Ⓦwww.delta.com.
Emirates Ⓦwww.emirates.com.
Etihad Ⓦwww.etihadairways.com.
Gulf Air Ⓦwww.gulfairco.com.
Jet Airways Ⓦwww.jetairways.com.
Kingfisher Ⓦwww.flykingfisher.com.
KLM Ⓦwww.klm.com.
Lufthansa Ⓦwww.lufthansa.com.
Malaysia Airlines Ⓦwww.malaysia-airlines.com.
Qantas Ⓦwww.qantas.com.
Qatar Airways Ⓦwww.qatarairways.com.
Singapore Airlines Ⓦwww.singaporeair.com.
Swiss Ⓦwww.swiss.com.
Thai Airways Ⓦwww.thaiair.com.
Virgin Atlantic Ⓦwww.virgin-atlantic.com.

Tour operators

Adventure Center US & Canada ☎1-800/228-8747, Ⓦwww.adventurecenter.com. General Golden Triangle and Rajasthan itineraries, plus wildlife and "Mughal Highlights" tours.
Audley Travel UK ☎01993/838300, Ⓦwww.audleytravel.com. Privately guided, tailor-made itineraries including several good Rajasthan options, and Palace on Wheels train tour (see p.29).
Bales UK ☎0845/057 1819, Ⓦwww.balesworldwide.com. Upmarket escorted tours

including a fourteen-day "Palaces of Rajasthan" tour, and a thirteen-day "Classic India" tour spent mainly in Delhi, Agra and Rajasthan.

Blazing Trails UK ☎01902/894009, ⊛www .blazingtrailstours.com. Adventure motorbike trips across India, including a 15-day tour of Rajasthan.

Butterfield & Robinson US & Canada ☎1-866/551-9090, ⊛www.butterfield.com. Refreshingly off-the-beaten-track cycling and walking trips, including a varied nine-day tour of Rajasthan by bike.

Cox & Kings UK ☎020/7873 5000, ⊛www .coxandkings.co.uk, US ☎1-800/999-1758; ⊛www.coxandkings.com. Established in India in 1758. Upmarket group and private tours, many featuring Rajasthan and Agra, plus the *Palace on Wheels*.

Equine Adventures UK ☎0845/130 6981, ⊛www.equineadventures.co.uk. Good selection of riding holidays in Rajasthan, either off-the-shelf or tailor-made.

Exodus UK ☎0845 863 9600, Ireland ☎01/804 7153, US ☎1-800/843 4277, Canada ☎866/338 8735, Australia ☎1300 655 433, New Zealand ☎0800 838 747; ⊛www.exodus.co.uk. Several options including cycling through Rajasthan and more mainstream Golden Triangle tours.

Explore Worldwide UK ☎0845/013 1537, US ☎1-800/486-9096, Australia ☎02/8913 0700, New Zealand ☎09/524 5118; ⊛www.explore .co.uk. Wide range of small-group adventure holidays including a 21-day Rajasthan tour and a nine-day "Mughal Highlights" itinerary.

Geographic Expeditions US ☎1-800/777-8183, ⊛www.geoex.com. Inventive Indian itineraries, including an unusual thirteen-day "Villages of Rajasthan" tour.

Greaves India UK ☎020/7487 9111, US & Canada ☎1-800/318-7801, ⊛www.greavesindia.com. Upmarket Indian specialist. Trips include a two-week "Essence of Rajasthan" tour, featuring a few off-beat sites alongside Delhi, Jaipur and Udaipur.

Imaginative Traveller UK ☎0845/026 1788, ⊛www.imaginative-traveller.com. Good range of tours, including a deluxe 21-day "Amongst the Maharajahs" tour and a more adventurous 22-day Rajasthan safari.

Indus Tours UK ☎020/8901 7320, ⊛www .industours.co.uk. Specialists in tailor-made tours,

also offering a number of excellent off-the-shelf North India options including an unusual 16-day "Hidden Rajasthan" trip.

Insider Tours UK ☎01233/811771, ⊛www .insider-tours.com. Some of the most original, "hands-on" and ethical itineraries on the market, including extended trips through Delhi and Rajasthan.

Mountain Travel/Sobek US & Canada ☎1-888/831 7526, UK ☎0808/234 2243; ⊛www .mtsobek.com. Adventure travel firm offering a 15-day "Royal Rajasthan Trek", plus an 8-day tour of Rajasthan and Agra.

Peregrine UK ☎00844/736 0170, Australia ☎03/8601 4444; ⊛www.peregrineadventures .com. Trekking specialists with a wide range of tailored group and individual tours including several featuring Rajasthan, Delhi and Agra.

Pettitts India UK ☎01892/515966, ⊛www .pettitts.co.uk. Tailor-made holidays off the beaten track, and off-the-shelf itineraries including an inventive 19-day "Rural Rajasthan" tour, as well as more mainstream itineraries.

Trans Indus Travel UK ☎020/8566 3739, ⊛www.transindus.co.uk. Indian specialists, offering a particularly good range of group and private tours.

Voyages Jules Verne UK ☎0845/166 7003, ⊛www.vjv.co.uk. Upmarket cultural tour operator with several Rajasthan options including the *Palace on Wheels* (see p.29).

Western & Oriental Travel UK ☎0845/277 3355, ⊛www.westernoriental.com. Award-winning, upmarket agency with tailor-made itineraries and several excellent Rajasthan tours.

Wilderness Travel US & Canada ☎1-800/368-2794, ⊛www.wildernesstravel.com. Three Rajasthan tours, featuring visits to the Nagaur and Pushkar fairs, and a journey on the *Royal Rajasthan on Wheels* heritage train.

Worldwide Quest Adventures US & Canada ☎1-800/387-1483, ⊛www.worldwidequest.com. Sightseeing plus trekking, cycling, camel safaris and cultural tours.

Indian Railways sales agents abroad

UK SD Enterprises, 103 Wembley Park Drive, Wembley, Middlesex HA9 8HG ☎020/8903 3411, ⊛www.indiarail.co.uk.

Entry requirements

Almost everyone needs a visa before travelling to India. The only permanent exceptions are citizens of Nepal and Bhutan. A one-year pilot scheme was introduced in 2010 allowing visitors from New Zealand, Singapore, Finland, Luxembourg and Japan to be issued with a thirty-day visa on arrival if landing at Delhi, Mumbai, Chennai or Kolkata (Calcutta) airports – it's possible that this scheme will eventually be extended to citizens of other countries, though citizens of the UK and US are unlikely to be included.

If you're going to Delhi, Rajasthan or Agra on business or to study or work, you'll need to apply for a special student or business visa; otherwise, a standard **tourist visa** will suffice. These are valid for six months from the date of issue (**not of departure from your home country or entry into India**), and usually cost £30/US$75. You're asked to specify whether you need a single-entry or a multiple-entry visa, and as the same rates apply to both, it makes sense to ask for the latter just in case you decide to go back within six months. Note, however, that a new ruling introduced in late 2009 now (in theory at least) prevents visitors on a tourist visa (or visas) from re-entering India within two months of their last visit except in exceptional circumstances, and with pre-arranged clearance from your local embassy or consulate – although, again, whether or not this ruling is likely to be strictly enforced remains unclear at the time of writing. For details of other kinds of visas, check the websites on p.24.

Visas in the UK, US, Canada and Australia are no longer issued by Indian embassies themselves, but by various third-party companies – see p.24 for details. The various websites give all the details about applying for a visa. Read the small print carefully and always make sure you've allowed plenty of time to get your visa. Applying in person, you may be able to get a visa by the following working day. Postal applications will take a minimum of ten working days plus time in transit, and often longer. Elsewhere, visas are still issued by the relevant local embassy or consulate, though the same caveats apply. Bear in mind too that Indian high commissions, embassies and consulates observe Indian public holidays as well as local ones, so always check opening hours in advance. In addition, embassies in India's neighbouring countries often drag their feet, demanding letters of recommendation from your embassy, or making you wait and pay for them to send your application to Delhi.

In many countries it's possible to pay a **visa agency** (or "visa expediter" – see list on p.24) to process the visa on your behalf, which typically costs £60–70/$100–120, plus the price of the visa. This is an option worth considering if you're not able to get to your nearest Indian high commission, embassy or consulate yourself. Prices vary a little from company to company, as do turnaround times. Two weeks is about standard, but you can get a visa in as little as 24 hours if you're prepared to pay premium rates. For a full rundown of services, check the company websites on p.24, from where you can usually download visa application forms.

Visa extensions

It is no longer possible to **extend a tourist visa** in India, though exceptions may be made in special circumstances.

Indian embassies, consulates and visa-processing centres abroad

Australia c/o VFS Global (⊛ www.vfs-in-au.net). Offices in all states except Tasmania and NT; see the website for contact details.

Canada c/o VFS Global (⊛ http://in.vfsglobal.ca). Nine offices countrywide – see the website for details.

Duty-free allowances

Anyone over 17 can bring in two litres of wine or spirits, plus 200 cigarettes, or 50 cigars, or 250g tobacco. You may be required to register anything valuable on a tourist baggage re-export form to make sure you can take it home with you, and to fill in a currency declaration form if carrying more than $5,000. For full details, see ⓦwww.cbec.gov.in/travellers.htm.

Ireland Embassy: 6 Leeson Park, Dublin 6 ☏01/497 0843, ⓦwww.indianembassy.ie.
Nepal c/o Indian Visa Service Centre (IVSC), House no. 296, Kapurdhara Marg, Kathmandu ☏01/400 1516, ⓦwww.indianembassy.org.np.
New Zealand High Commission: 180 Molesworth St, PO Box 4045, Wellington ☏04/473 6390, ⓦwww.hicomind.org.nz.
South Africa 852 Schoeman St (corner of Eastwood St), PO Box 40216, Arcadia 0007, Pretoria ☏012/342 2593, ⓦwww.indiainsouthafrica.com; 1 Eton Rd, Parktown, PO Box 6805, Johannesburg 2000 ☏011/482 8484 to 9, ⓦwww.indconjoburg .co.za; The Old Station Building (4th floor), 160 Pine St, PO Box 3276, Durban 4001 ☏031/307-7020, ⓦwww.indcondurban.co.za.

Sri Lanka High Commission: 36–38 Galle Rd, Colombo 3 ☏011/232 7587, ⓦwww.hcicolombo .org. Consulate: 31 Rajapihilla Mawatha, PO Box 47, Kandy ☏081/222 4563.
UK c/o VFS Global (ⓦhttp://in.vfsglobal.co.uk). Offices in London, Birmingham, Manchester, Cardiff, Edinburgh and Glasgow – see the website for contact details.
US c/o Travisa (ⓦhttps://indiavisa.travisa outsourcing.com). Offices in Washington, New York, San Francisco, Chicago and Houston – see the website for contact details.

Visa agencies

CIBT US ☏1-800/929-2428, ⓦwww.cibt.com. UK ☏0844/736 0211, ⓦwww.uk.cibt.com.
India Visa Office UK ☏0844/8004018, ⓦwww .indiavisaheadoffice.co.uk.
India Visa Company UK ☏020/8582 1117, ⓦwww.skylorduk.com/gle_visa.htm.
India Visa 24 ☏0800/084 5037, ⓦwww .indiavisa24.co.uk
Travel Document Systems US; Washington ☏1-800/874 5100, New York ☏1-877/874 5104, San Francisco ☏1-888/874 5100; ⓦwww .traveldocs.com.
Visa Connection US & Canada ☏1-866/566-8472, ⓦwww.visaconnection.com.
Visa Link Australia ☏03/9673 1500, ⓦwww.visalink.com.au.

Getting around

Local transport in India may not be the fastest or the most comfortable in the world, but it's cheap, comprehensive, and generally gives you the option of train or bus – and sometimes even plane. Transport around town comes in even more permutations, ranging from cycle rickshaws and old-fashioned Ambassador taxis to – in Delhi – a sparkling modern metro system.

By rail

Travelling by train is one of India's great experiences. Trains are often late of course, often by hours rather than minutes, but they're cheap and much more comfortable than buses, and serve almost everywhere you might want to go in the region. The main exceptions are Pushkar and Mount Abu,

which don't have their own railway stations, but which are a short bus ride away from the stations at Ajmer and Abu Road respectively.

On longer journeys (Udaipur or Jaisalmer to Jaipur or Delhi, for example), an **overnight train** can save you a day's travelling and a night's hotel bill. Between 9pm and 6am anyone with a bunk reservation is entitled to exclusive use of their bunk as a bed, but before 9pm, the middle and lower bunks may be used as seats: the upper bunk has the advantage that you can stretch out on it at any time. When travelling overnight, it's a good idea to padlock your bag to your bunk; an attached chain is usually provided beneath the seat of the lower bunk.

Indian Railways do have a relatively high **accident rate**, with four to five hundred crashes nationwide every year, and seven to eight hundred fatalities, making it the most dangerous rail network in the world. Train passengers, however, can take solace in the fact that travelling by rail is considerably safer than using **buses** (see p.30).

Routes and types of train

There are three basic types of passenger train in India. You're most likely to use long-distance **inter-city trains** (called "express" or "mail") along with the speedier "**super-fast**" air-conditioned trains – these include the various "Rajdhani" expresses, which link Delhi with cities nationwide, and "Shatabdi" expresses, daytime trains that connect major cities within an eight-hour travelling distance (the only Shatabdi routes relevant to this book are between New Delhi, Jaipur and Ajmer, and New Delhi and Agra). There are also painfully slow local "**passenger**" trains, which stop everywhere, and which you'll only use if you want to get right off the beaten track.

In addition to these three basic types of train, there are also a few dedicated **tourist trains**, such as the famous Palace on Wheels – see p.29 for more.

Classes of train travel

Indian Railways distinguishes between no fewer than nine **classes** of travel. Different types of train carry different classes of carriage, though you'll seldom have more than four to choose from any one service. The simplest and cheapest class, used by the majority of Indians, is **second-class unreserved** (or "second seating", abbreviated to "II"). These basic carriages have hard wooden seats and often become incredibly packed during the day – bearable for shortish daytime journeys, but best avoided

for longer trips and (especially) overnight travel, unless you're exceptionally hardy or unusually poor. On the plus side, fares in second class unreserved are so cheap as to be virtually free. It also represents a way of getting on a train at the last minute if you haven't been able to secure a reserved seat.

Far more civilized, and only around fifty percent more expensive, is **second-class sleeper** ("sleeper class"; abbreviated to "SL", or "2S" for daytime journeys), consisting of carriages of three-tiered padded bunks that convert to seats during the day. All seats in these carriages must be booked in advance even for daytime journeys, meaning that they don't get horrendously overcrowded like second class unreserved, although there's usually still plenty going on, with itinerant chai- and coffee-sellers, travelling musicians, beggars and sweepers passing through the carriages. Overnight trips in second-class sleeper compartments are reasonably comfy. **First class** (FC) consists of non-air-conditioned seating in comfortable if ageing compartments of two to four berths, though this class is being phased out and is now found on relatively few trains.

The other four classes are all air-conditioned (available only on intercity and superfast trains). **A/c chair car** (CC) is found almost exclusively on superfast services and consists of comfortable reclining seats; they're really designed for daytime travel, since they don't convert to bunks, and aren't generally found on overnight services. A posher version of the a/c chair car is the **executive chair-car** (EC; although this class doesn't currently show up on the Indian Railways website). Shatabdi expresses are made up entirely of a/c and executive chair car carriages.

There are three classes of air-conditioned sleepers. The cheapest, **third class a/c** (3A), has open carriages with three-tier bunks – basically the same as second-class sleeper, except with air-conditioning. Less crowded (and found on more services) is **second class a/c** (2A), which has two-tier berths. Most comfortable of all is **first-class a/c** (1A), which consists of two-tier bunks in two- or four-person private compartments, complete with carpeting and relatively presentable bathrooms – although fares can

Distance chart (in km)

	Agra	Ajmer	Alwar	Bharatpur	Bikaner	Chittaurgarh	Delhi
Agra	–	388	172	56	665	579	195
Ajmer	388	–	272	332	233	191	392
Alwar	172	272	–	116	462	463	163
Bharatpur	56	332	116	–	497	523	251
Bikaner	665	233	462	497	–	424	470
Chittaurgarh	579	191	463	523	424	–	583
Delhi	195	392	163	251	470	583	–
Jaipur	232	138	143	175	354	345	259
Jaisalmer	853	490	762	822	333	657	882
Jodhpur	568	205	477	537	243	372	597
Kota	453	200	383	418	432	158	504
Mount Abu	737	375	647	707	569	297	767
Nawalgarh	370	207	164	280	239	398	292
Sawai Madhopur	230	252	228	233	485	283	484
Udaipur	637	274	551	581	506	112	664

work out only slightly cheaper than taking a plane.

Note that bed linen is provided free on most air-conditioned services, while bottled water, snacks and simple meals are included in the ticket price of Rajdhani and Shatabdi services. **Ladies' compartments** exist on all overnight trains for women travelling on their own or with other women; they are usually small and can be full of noisy kids, but can give untold relief to women travellers who otherwise have to endure incessant staring in the open section of the carriage. They can be a good place to meet Indian women, particularly if you like (or are with) children. Some stations also have ladies-only waiting rooms.

For more detailed descriptions, along with photographs of seats and carriages in the different classes, plus good advice and information on train travel, visit the Man in Seat 61's India pages at Ⓦ www.seat61.com /India.htm.

Timetables and tickets

Easily the most convenient place to check **timetables** is online at Ⓦ www.indianrail .gov.in, which also has comprehensive information about fares and availability. Alternatively, Indian Railways' *Trains at a Glance* (Rs30; updated twice a year; also available online at Ⓦ www.indianrailways.gov.in/tag /index.htm) contains timetables of all intercity and superfast trains and is available from information counters and newsstands at all main stations.

All rail fares are calculated according to the exact **distance** travelled. *Trains at a Glance* prints a chart of fares by kilometres, and also gives the distance in kilometres of stations along each route in the timetables, making it possible to calculate what the basic fare will be for any given journey.

Each individual train has its own **name and number**, prominently displayed in station booking halls.

Reserving tickets

It's important to plan your train journeys in advance, as demand often makes it impossible to buy a long-distance ticket on the same day that you want to travel (although the new Tatkal quota system – see p.29 – has made life a little easier). Travellers following tight itineraries tend to buy their

Jaipur	Jaisalmer	Jodhpur	Kota	Mt Abu	Nawal-garh	Sawai Mad	Udaipur
232	853	568	453	737	370	230	637
138	490	205	200	375	207	252	274
143	762	477	383	647	164	228	551
175	822	537	418	707	280	233	581
354	333	243	432	569	239	485	506
345	657	372	158	297	398	283	112
259	882	597	504	767	292	484	664
–	543	317	242	465	138	164	347
543	–	285	690	572	540	742	545
317	285	–	404	326	347	457	260
242	690	404	–	455	407	161	270
465	572	326	455	–	582	580	185
138	540	347	407	582	–	306	481
164	742	457	161	580	580	–	395
347	545	260	270	185	185	395	–

departure tickets from particular towns the moment they arrive to avoid having to trek out to the station again. At most large stations, it's possible to reserve tickets for journeys starting elsewhere in the country. You can even book tickets for specific journeys before you leave home, with Indian Railways representatives abroad (see p.22) or online (see below). Bookings are accepted up to six months in advance.

When **reserving a ticket** in person at a railway station, the first thing you'll have to do is fill in a little form at the booking office stating your name, age and sex, your proposed date of travel, and the train you wish to catch (giving the train's **name and number**, which should be displayed on a timetable in the booking hall). Most stations have computerized booking counters and you'll be told immediately whether or not seats are available. **Reservation offices** in the main stations are generally open from Monday to Saturday from 8am to 8pm, and on Sunday to 2pm. In larger cities, major stations have special tourist sections to cut queues for foreigners, with helpful English-speaking staff. Elsewhere, buying a ticket can often involve a longish wait, though

women can often bypass this by simply walking to the head of the queue and forming their own "ladies' queue" (men may often find ladies pushing in front of them on the same principle). Some stations also operate a number system of queuing, allowing you to repair to the chai stall until your number is called.

A good alternative to queuing yourself is to get someone else to buy your ticket for you. Many **travel agents** will do this for a small fee (typically around Rs30–50). Alternatively, an increasing number of **guesthouses** can arrange railway bookings, usually charging a modest fee, and saving you an awful lot of hassle.

It's now also possible to **book train tickets online**. The official Indian Railways portal is at ⓦwww.irctc.co.in. You can book up to sixty days in advance and, having booked your travel, you can then print out your own e-ticket, taking this along with some photo ID, such as a passport, when you board the train. Note that you're limited to a maximum of ten bookings per month through this site. Unfortunately, the site only works during Indian opening hours and can be frustratingly difficult to use. The payment section of the website is particularly incomprehensible: you'll be presented with a long list of India-based banks through which to process your payment. This doesn't mean you need to have an account with any of these banks – they simply serve as payment agents (or "gateways") for your card. CitiBank is often suggested as the most reliable "gateway", though in practice payments are often rejected for no apparent reason, and there's not a lot you can do about it, apart from contacting a reliable travel agent (or guesthouse offering travel services) and getting them to do it for you.

Alternatively, tickets can be booked through the independent ⓦwww.cleartrip .com. Booking tickets through this website incurs an additional Rs100 surcharge, but it's far more user-friendly, and well worth the extra cash. Alternatively, a third website, ⓦwww.makemytrip.com, had also begun offering online railway bookings at the time of going to print, and may be worth checking out if the two more established options fail.

If there are no places available

If there are no places available on the train you want, you have a number of choices. First, some seats and berths are set aside as a "**tourist quota**" – ask at the tourist counter if you can get in on this, or else try the stationmaster. This quota is available in advance but usually only at major or originating stations. Failing that, other special quotas, such as one for "emergencies", only released on the day of travel, may remain unused – however, if you get a booking on the emergency quota and a pukka emergency or VIP turns up, you lose the reservation. Alternatively, you can stump up extra cash for a **Tatkal** ticket (see opposite), which guarantees you access to a special ten percent quota on most trains, though certain catches and conditions apply.

RAC – or "Reservation Against Cancellation" – tickets are another option, giving you priority if sleepers do become available – the ticket clerk should be able to tell you your chances. With an RAC ticket you are allowed onto the train and can sit until the conductor can find you a berth. The worst sort of ticket to have is a **wait-listed** one – identifiable by the letter "W" prefixing your passenger number – which will allow you onto the train but not in a reserved compartment; in this case go and see the ticket inspector as soon as possible to persuade him to find you a place if one is free: something usually is, but you'll be stuck in unreserved if it isn't. Wait-listed ticket holders are not allowed onto Shatabdi and Rajdhani trains. You could **travel unreserved**, but if the train is full (as it

Delhi–Jaipur: comparative fares

For comparison, here are the fares for different forms of transport between Delhi and Jaipur, a journey of just under 260km by road, or 308km by rail.

Train

2nd class unreserved (3E)	Rs99	2nd class sleeper (2S)	Rs175
A/C three-tier	Rs290	A/C chair class (Shatabdi)	Rs450
A/C two-tier	Rs551	Executive chair class (Shatabdi)	Rs860
A/C first	Rs869	Rajdhani	Rs1225

Bus

Ordinary state bus	Rs165
Deluxe private bus	Rs130–150
Private sleeper bus	Rs200
Silver Line (deluxe)	Rs300
Silver Line (A/C deluxe)	Rs400
Volvo Gold Line (A/C deluxe)	Rs550

Plane

Economy	Rs4000	Business class	Rs20,000

will be on major routes) travel in second class will be extremely uncomfortable. If you get on where the train starts its journey, **baksheesh** may persuade an official to "reserve" you an unreserved seat (or even a luggage rack) where you can stretch out for the night (station porters may be able to act as middlemen in this regard, taking a cut themselves, of course). You could even fight your way on with everybody else and try to grab a seat yourself, but your chances are slim. For short journeys, or on minor routes where trains are not so crowded, you won't need to reserve tickets in advance.

Another possibility is to try for a **Tatkal** ticket (Ⓦ www.indianrail.gov.in/tatkal.html). A quota of ten percent of places on the more important intercity services is reserved under this scheme, bookable at any computerized office. Tickets are released from 8am two days before the train departs, and there's a surcharge of Rs75–150 in sleeper or chair car class, and Rs200–300 in first or air-conditioned sleepers, depending on the standard fare. The real catch, however, is that you also have to pay for the entire length of the journey from originating to terminating station, however much or little of the ride you do, meaning that Tatkal obviously isn't worth it if, for instance, you want to get from Jaipur to Bikaner on the Howrah Express from Kolkata (Calcutta). If you're covering most of the route, though, you're pretty well guaranteed to find a place, especially if you get in the day before, as a lot of resident Indians have been put off by the price hike.

Indrail passes

Indrail passes, sold to foreigners and Indians resident abroad, cover all fares and reservation fees for periods ranging from half a day to ninety days, but are considerably more expensive than buying tickets individually. The pass is designed for nationwide travel, so if you only use it between Delhi, Agra and the cities of Rajasthan, you won't be getting your money's worth. The pass does, however, save you queuing for tickets, and it allows you to make and cancel reservations with impunity (and without charge), and generally smooths your way in. For example, if you need to find a seat or berth on a "full" train, passholders get priority for tourist quota

places. Indrail passes are available in sterling or US dollars, at main station tourist counters in India, and outside the country at IR agents (see p.22) and sometimes at Air India offices. A seven-day pass costs US$80 in second class, US$135 in first, and US$270 in AC class. There's a full list of prices at Ⓦ www .indianrail.gov.in/intert.html.

Tourist trains

Inspired by the Orient Express, Indian Railways offers holiday packages aboard luxury **tourist trains** – with exorbitant prices in dollars to match. The flagship of the scheme is the **Palace on Wheels** (Ⓦ www .palaceonwheels.net), with sumptuous ex-maharajas' carriages updated into modern air-conditioned coaches, still decorated with the original designs. An all-inclusive, eight-day whistle-stop tour (Sept–April weekly) starts from Delhi and travels through Jaipur, Chittaurgarh, Sawai Madhopur, Udaipur, Jaisalmer and Jodhpur, returning via Bharatpur and Agra; prices start at US$2350 per person for the full trip, with discounts off-season (Sept & April). Note that the train is often booked up for months ahead, so early reservations are advised.

The Palace on Wheels has proved so popular that it has spawned a number of similar heritage trains. Launched in late 2009, **Royal Rajasthan on Wheels** (Ⓦ www.royal palaceonwheels.com) follows the same itinerary as the Palace on Wheels in an even more lavishly decorated train, complete with on-board spa. Rates are US$4255 per person (or US$5760/person in one of the train's "super-deluxe staterooms"). A less expensive second service, **Heritage on Wheels** (Ⓦ www.palaceonwheels.net/new /heritage.htm), offers a three-day trip from Jaipur to Bikaner and Shekhawati starting at US$450 per person.

All three trains can be booked through the Rajasthan Tourism Development Corporation (RTDC), Bikaner House, Pandara Road, New Delhi 110011 (☎011/2338 1884, Ⓦ www .rajasthantourism.gov.in). Or you can call toll-free in North America (☎888/463-4299), the UK (☎0800/8456 201), Australia (☎1800/156 671), New Zealand (☎0800/442 510), or book online at Ⓦ www.palaceon wheels.net or www.indiarailtours.com.

One final option is the **Fairy Queen**, driven by the oldest working steam engine in the world, which takes a two-day trip through eastern Rajasthan to Alwar and the Sariska tiger reserve (Oct–Feb; twice monthly; US$165/person). The train was not running at the time of writing, though it may return to service in the future. You should be able to make bookings through the Rajasthan Tourism Development Corporation in Delhi (see p.145), the Government of India Tourist Office, 88 Janpath, New Delhi (☎011/2332 0005), or online at ⓦwww.indiarailtours.com.

Cloakrooms

Most stations in India have **cloakrooms** (sometimes called parcel offices) for passengers to leave their baggage. These can be extremely handy if you want to go sightseeing in a town and move on the same day. In theory, you need a train ticket or Indrail pass to deposit luggage, but staff don't always ask; they may, however, refuse to take your bag if you can't lock it. Losing your reclaim ticket causes problems; the clerk will be assumed to have stolen the bag if he can't produce it, so

there'll be untold running around to obtain clearance before you can get your bag without it. Make sure, when checking baggage in, that the cloakroom will be open when you need to pick it up. The standard charge is usually Rs10 per 24 hours.

By bus

Buses go almost everywhere in Rajasthan, and are generally more frequent (and sometimes faster) than trains, albeit generally less comfortable and not as safe. According to official statistics, an average of 85,000 people die on India's roads every year.

Services vary somewhat in price and standards. The state transport companies – Delhi Transport Corporation (DTC; ⓦdtc.nic .in) in Delhi, the Rajasthan State Road Transport Corporation (RSRTC; ⓦwww .rsrtc.gov.in) in Rajasthan, the Uttar Pradesh State Road Transport Corporation (UPSRTC; ⓦwww.upsrtc.com) in Uttar Pradesh, which includes Agra – cover most routes. RSRTC have ordinary and express buses, bog-standard in terms of comfort, as well as deluxe "silver line" and air-conditioned "gold line" buses, which are a good deal more comfortable (and expensive). Popular routes are also usually covered by **private buses**, which tend to be more comfortable than the ordinary state services. Whichever you choose, try to avoid the back seats, which can be very bumpy indeed.

Luggage travels in the hatch of private buses. On state-run buses, you can usually squeeze it into an unobtrusive corner, or under your seat, though it may get dirty there, or you may sometimes be requested to put it in the hold or up on the roof; in the latter case, check that it's well secured (ideally, lock it there) and not liable to get squashed. Whether on the roof or in the hold, baksheesh is in order for whoever puts it there for you.

Buying a bus ticket is usually less of an ordeal than buying a train ticket, although at large city bus stations there may be several counters, assigned to different routes. You can always get on ordinary state buses without a ticket, and at bus stands outside major cities you can usually only pay on board, so you have to be sharp to secure a seat. Prior booking is usually available and preferable for express and private services. You can often pay on board private buses too, though doing so reduces your chances of a seat.

It's also a good idea to check when you buy your ticket exactly where your bus will leave from – many towns in Rajasthan have multiple **bus stands**, usually with separate departure points for government and private services.

By air

There are currently passenger airports at Delhi, Agra, Jaipur, Jodhpur and Udaipur, while a new passenger terminal is scheduled to open at Jaisalmer in 2010. Direct flights connect all four cities with one another and with many other places in the country. You won't save much time travelling from, say, Jaipur to Delhi or Jaipur to Jodhpur by plane, but flying from Delhi to Jodhpur or Udaipur offers a quick alternative to a long train or bus journeys. Current flight times and frequencies are listed in the "Moving On" sections at the end of each Guide chapter, but be aware that schedules and carriers are constantly changing – Kingfisher Airlines, Jet Airways and Indian are the main

carriers at present. **Fares** are generally good value by international standards – tickets start from around Rs4000 (£55/US$90) for a one-way ticket between any of the region's four airports. For latest information and fares, check ⓦwww.expedia.co.in or www.travelocity.co.in.

Domestic airlines

Air India ⓦwww.airindia.com.
Air-India Express ⓦwww.airindiaexpress.in.
GoAir ⓦwww.goair.in.
Indian ⓦwww.airindia.com.
IndiGo Air ⓦbook.goindigo.in.
Jet Airways ⓦwww.jetairways.com.
JetLite (formerly Air Sahara) ⓦwww.jetlite.com.
Kingfisher Airlines ⓦwww.flykingfisher.com.
SpiceJet ⓦwww.spicejet.com.

By car

Driving in India is not for beginners. If you do drive yourself, expect the unexpected, and expect other drivers to take whatever liberties they can get away with. Traffic circulates on the left, but don't expect anybody to obey road regulations. Lane discipline is nonexistent, and almost nobody bothers to indicate when turning. Overtaking is willy-nilly on either side. Generally the vehicle in front seems to have right of way, so at busy intersections or roundabouts (rotaries) drivers try and get out in front as soon as possible. Another unstated law of the road is that might is right.

Traffic in the **cities** is heavy and undisciplined; vehicles cut in and out without warning, and pedestrians, cyclists and cows wander nonchalantly down the middle of the road. In the **country** the roads are narrow, in terrible repair, and hogged by overloaded "Tata" trucks that move aside for nobody, while something slow-moving like a bullock cart or a herd of goats can take up the whole road. To **overtake**, sound your horn (an essential item on Indian roads) – the driver in front will signal if it is safe to overtake; if not, he will wave his hand, palm downwards, up and down. A huge number of potholes don't make for a smooth ride either. Furthermore, during the monsoon roads can become flooded. Ask local people before you set off, and proceed with caution, sticking to main highways if possible.

You should have an **international driving licence** to drive in India, but this is often overlooked if you have your licence from home. **Insurance** is compulsory, but not expensive. Car **seat belts** are compulsory in Delhi and Rajasthan, and strongly recommended in any case. Accident rates are high, and you should be on your guard at all times. It is particularly dangerous to drive at night – not everyone uses lights, and bullock carts don't have any. If you have an **accident**, it might be an idea to leave the scene quickly and go straight to the police to report it; mobs can assemble fast, especially if pedestrians or cows are involved, and drivers involved in accidents with local people are frequently roughed up.

Fuel is reasonably cheap (around Rs50 a litre for leaded or unleaded petrol, Rs35 for diesel), but the state of the roads will take its toll on your car, and mechanics are not always very reliable, so some knowledge of vehicle maintenance is handy, as is a checkup every so often. Luckily, if you get a flat tyre, puncture-wallahs can be found almost everywhere.

The classic Indian automobile is the Hindustan Ambassador (basically a Morris Oxford), nowadays largely superseded by more modern vehicles such as the Maruti Suzuki. Renting a car, you'll probably have a choice of these two or others.

It's much more usual for tourists to be driven in India than it is for them to drive themselves. **Cars with driver** can be easily arranged either through your hotel or a local travel agent. Costs are around £18–25/US$30–40 per day; air-contioning, unlimited mileage and an English-speaking driver tend to push prices up.

By motorbike

Riding a motorbike around India has long had a strong appeal, but is not without its hazards. Besides the appalling road conditions (see p.31), **renting a motorbike** can be a bit of a nightmare, unless you're well versed in maintenance, with breakdowns often in the most inconvenient places. Motorbike rental is available in some tourist towns and useful for local use, but the quality of the bikes is never assured. Helmets are best brought from home.

A few tourists buy themselves a motorbike in India, and aficionados of classic bikes love the Enfield Bullet (350 model), an Indian-made version of an old British model, the Royal Enfield. Motorcycles of various sorts can easily be bought new or secondhand. In Delhi, the Karol Bagh area is renowned for its motorcycle shops. For a short stay, buying a bike when you arrive and selling it again when you leave seems like a lot of trouble, but given the right bargaining skills, it's possible to buy a used bike and sell it again later for a similar price to a dealer or by advertising it in hotels and tourist hangouts. A certain amount of bureaucracy is involved in transferring vehicle ownership, but a garage should be able to put you on to a broker ("auto consultant") who, for a modest commission (around Rs500), will help you find a seller or a buyer, and do the necessary paperwork.

It's worth noting that a motorbike can be taken in the luggage car of a **train** for the same price as a second-class passenger fare (get a form and pay a small fee at the station luggage office).

By bicycle

For getting around between cities, a bicycle is in many ways the ideal form of transport, offering total independence without loss of contact with local people. You can camp out, though there are cheap lodgings in almost every town – and take your bike into your room with you. And, if you get tired of pedalling, you can always put the bike on top of a bus as luggage, or transport it by train.

Bringing a bike from abroad requires no carnet or special paperwork, but spare parts and accessories may be of different sizes and standards in India, and you may have to improvise. Bring **basic spares** and **tools**, and a **pump**. Panniers are the obvious thing for carrying your gear, but fiendishly inconvenient when not attached to your bike, and you might consider sacrificing ideal load-bearing and streamlining technology for a backpack you can lash down on the rear carrier.

Buying a bike in India presents no great difficulty, and there are cycle shops in all big towns. The advantages of a local bike are that spare parts are easy to get, locally produced tools and parts will fit, and your bike will not draw a crowd every time you park it. Disadvantages are that Indian bikes tend to be heavier and less state-of-the-art than ones from abroad; mountain bikes are beginning to appear in cities and bigger towns, though quality is still low. Selling should be quite easy: you won't get a tremendously good deal at a cycle market, but you may well be able to sell privately, or even to a rental shop.

Bicycles can be **rented** in most towns, usually for local use only: this is a good way to find out if your legs and bum can survive the Indian bike before buying one. Around Rs50 per day is the going rate, occasionally more in tourist centres, and you may have to leave a deposit, or even your passport, as security. One or two of the tour operators listed on pp.21–22 offer bicycle tours of Rajasthan.

City transport

Transport around towns takes various forms. If you want to see a number of different places around town, it's usually worth hiring a taxi, cycle rickshaw or auto-rickshaw **for the day**. Find a driver who speaks English reasonably well and agree a price beforehand. This usually works out cheaper and a lot more convenient than picking up transport as you go, while a good driver will invariably act as a guide and source of local knowledge.

The most useful form of city transport for casual visitors is the **auto-rickshaw**, that most Indian of vehicles, perfect for nipping in and out of heavy traffic – rickshaw rides can occasionally be nerve-jangling, and drivers are sometimes reckless, but that's all part of the experience. Always agree a fare beforehand (some autos are fixed with a meter, but it's virtually impossible to find drivers who are willing to use them). Naturally, it helps to have an idea in advance what the fare should be, so check at your hotel before setting off, and remember that any figures quoted in this or any other book should be treated as being the broadest of guidelines only. Drivers will occasionally try to increase the fare during the journey or at the end – either ignore them (and don't give them a tip) or just threaten to get out of the rickshaw there and then without paying. Several train stations and

bus stands in major cities, including central Delhi and Jodhpur, now have **pre-paid auto stations** where you buy a ticket to your destination in advance from a kiosk rather than paying your auto-wallah on arrival, enabling you to get a much cheaper fare than would otherwise be the case.

In major tourist centres, auto-wallahs may hustle people for business on the street, usually with the aim of overcharging them, or taking them to commission-paying shops en route to their destination. It's invariably better to hail an auto yourself rather than go with a driver who hustles for business, and it's also worth avoiding autos that hang around outside hotels.

Slower and cheaper still is the **cycle rickshaw** – basically a glorified tricycle. Foreign visitors often feel uncomfortable about travelling this way, as rickshaw-wallahs are invariably emaciated pavement dwellers who earn only a pittance for their pains. In the end, though, to deny them your custom on those grounds is spurious logic; they'll earn even less (and be even more emaciated) if you don't use them – and of course you're always free to be generous when tipping. Tourists in any case usually pay a bit more than locals, so your custom will be more than welcome. As with autos, it's best to hail a rickshaw yourself rather than go with a rickshaw-wallah who hustles for a ride. It's also worth remembering that cycle rickshaws can be painfully slow compared to autos, and are best avoided if you're in any sort of hurry.

A faster option is to hire a **taxi** – these can usually be arranged through your hotel, while in Delhi and Jaipur there are radio taxis, and in Delhi cabs can be flagged down on the street (though you'll have to haggle over the fare in the likely event that the driver is unwilling to use his meter). Some stations and most airports operate prepaid taxi schemes with set fares that you pay before departure.

All the major cities in the region – Delhi and Jaipur in particular – have extensive **city bus networks**, though routes are difficult to work out and vehicles can get unbelievably crowded, so beware of pickpockets, razor-armed pocket-slitters, and "Eve teasers" (see p.61).

Health

You hear a lot of scare stories about the health risks of travelling in India, but coming down with a serious tropical illness is very much the exception rather than the rule. Risks do exist, and yes, travellers do sometimes come down with malaria, dysentery, hepatitis or even typhoid, but generally speaking, such diseases can be avoided by taking elementary precautions, and if you're careful, you should be able to get through with nothing worse than a mild dose of "Delhi belly". It is important, however, to keep your resistance high and to be aware of the health risks of untreated water, mosquito bites and undressed open cuts.

What you **eat** and **drink** is crucial: a poor diet lowers your resistance. Meat and fish are obvious sources of protein for non-vegetarians in the West, but not necessarily in India: eggs, pulses (lentils, peas and beans), rice, *paneer* and curd are all protein sources, as are nuts. Overcooked vegetables lose a lot of their vitamin content, but eating plenty of peeled fresh fruit helps keep up your vitamin and mineral intake. It's also important to drink plenty of water. And make sure you eat enough (an unfamiliar diet may reduce the amount you eat), and **get sufficient sleep** and rest: it's easy to get run-down if you're on the move a lot, especially in a hot climate.

If you do fall ill, and can't get to a doctor, it's worth knowing that almost any medicine can be bought over the counter without a prescription, though heavy-duty drugs such as antibiotics should not be taken without medical advice, except perhaps in the case of dire emergency.

Precautions

The lack of sanitation in India can be exaggerated. It's not worth getting too worked up about it or you'll never enjoy anything, but a few **common-sense precautions** are in order, bearing in mind that things such as bacteria multiply far more quickly in a tropical climate, and your body will have little immunity to Indian germs.

For details on the **water**, see box opposite. When it comes to **food**, be particularly wary of prepared dishes that have to be reheated – they may have been on display in the heat and exposed to flies for some time. Anything that is boiled or fried (and thus sterilized) in your presence is usually all right, though meat can sometimes be dodgy if the electricity supply (and thus refrigerators) is unreliable. Anything that has been left out in the open for any length of time is definitely suspect. Unpeeled fruit and vegetables should always be viewed with suspicion, and it's usually best not to eat salads unless sterilized with iodine or potassium permanganate. Wiping down a plate before eating is sensible, as is avoiding straws as they are often dusty or second-hand. As a rule of thumb, stick to cafés and restaurants that are doing a brisk trade, and where the food is thus freshly cooked, and you should be fine.

Be vigilant about **personal hygiene**. Wash your hands often, especially before eating, keep all cuts clean, treat them with iodine or antiseptic, and cover them to prevent infection. Be fussier than usual about sharing things like drinks and cigarettes, and never share a razor or toothbrush. It is also inadvisable to go around barefoot – best to wear flip-flops even in the shower.

Advice on avoiding **mosquitoes** is offered under "Malaria". If you do get bites or itches try not to scratch them: it's hard, but infection and tropical ulcers can result if you do. Tiger balm and even dried soap may relieve the itching.

Finally, especially if you are going on a long trip, have a **dental checkup** before you leave home – you don't want to go down with unexpected tooth trouble in the middle of rural Rajasthan. If you do, and it feels serious, head for Delhi, and ask a foreign consulate to recommend a dentist, or try Delhi Dental Centre (see p.143).

Vaccinations

No **vaccinations** are legally required for entry into India, but meningitis, typhoid and hepatitis A jabs are recommended, and it's worth ensuring that you are up to date with tetanus, polio and other boosters. All vaccinations can be obtained in Delhi if necessary; just make sure the needle is new. If you're arriving in India from a country infected with Yellow Fever (which mainly means tropical Africa), you'll be asked for an inoculation certificate.

Hepatitis A is not the worst disease you can catch in India, but the frequency with which it strikes travellers makes a strong case for immunization. Transmitted through contaminated food and water, or through saliva, it can lay a victim low for several months with exhaustion, fever and diarrhoea, and may cause liver damage. The Havrix vaccine has been shown to be extremely effective; though expensive, it lasts for up to ten years. The protection given by gammaglobulin, the traditional serum of hepatitis antibodies (now rarely used), wears off quickly and the injection should therefore be given as late as possible before departure: the longer your stay, the larger the dose. Symptoms by which you can recognize hepatitis include a yellowing of the whites of the eyes, nausea, general flu-like malaise, orange urine (though dehydration could also cause that) and light-coloured stools. If you think you have it, avoid alcohol, and get lots of rest. More serious is **hepatitis B**, passed on like HIV through blood or sexual contact. There is a vaccine, but it is generally only given to those planning to work in a medical environment.

Typhoid, also spread through contaminated food or water, is endemic in India, but rare outside the monsoon. It produces a persistent high fever with malaise, headaches and abdominal pains, followed by diarrhoea. Vaccination can be by injection (two shots

What about the water?

One of the chief concerns of many prospective visitors to India is whether the water is safe to drink. To put it simply, it's not, though your unfamiliarity with Indian microorganisms is generally more of a problem than any great virulence in the water itself.

As a rule, it is not a good idea to drink **tap water**, although in big cities such as Delhi and Jaipur it is usually chlorinated. However, you'll find it almost impossible to avoid untreated tap water completely: it is used to make ice, which may appear in drinks without being asked for, to wash utensils and so on.

Bottled water, available in all but the most remote places these days, may seem like the simplest and most cost-effective solution, but it has some major drawbacks. The first is that the water itself might not always be as safe as it seems. Independent tests carried out in 2003 on major Indian brands revealed levels of **pesticide** concentration up to 104 times higher than EU norms. Top sellers Kinley, Bisleri and Aquaplus were named as the worst offenders.

The second downside of bottled water is the **plastic pollution** it causes. Visualize the size of the pile you'd leave behind you after getting through a couple of bottles per day, and imagine that multiplied by millions, which is the amount of non-biodegradable landfill waste generated each year by tourists alone.

The best solution from the point of view of your health and the environment is to purify your own water. **Chemical sterilization** is the cheapest method. **Iodine** isn't recommended for long trips, but **chlorine** is completely effective, fast and inexpensive, and you can remove the taste using neutralizing tablets or lemon juice.

Alternatively, invest in some kind of **purifying filter** that uses chemical sterilization to kill even the smallest viruses. An ever-increasing range of compact, lightweight products is available these days at outdoor shops and large pharmacies, but anyone who's pregnant or suffers from thyroid problems should check that iodine isn't used as the chemical sterilizer.

are required, or one for a booster), giving three years' cover, or orally – tablets are more expensive but easier on the arm.

Cholera, spread the same way as hepatitis A and typhoid, causes sudden attacks of watery diarrhoea with cramps and debilitation. It only appears during periodic epidemics. If you get it, take copious amounts of water with rehydration salts and seek medical treatment. There is currently no effective vaccination against cholera.

Some medical authorities recommend vaccination against **meningitis** too. Spread by airborne bacteria (through coughs and sneezes, for example), this illness attacks the lining of the brain and can be fatal. The symptoms appear at first to be similar to those of a cold, but they progress rapidly to include (not necessarily all at once) fever, a severe headache, vomiting, intolerance to light, stiffness in the neck and in some cases a rash, whose spots do not lighten when pressed against a glass; note that the rash may be hard to spot if you have dark skin. If you suspect that you have meningitis, it is vital to seek medical help quickly, as it can be fatal if left untreated.

You should have a **tetanus** booster every ten years whether you travel or not. Tetanus (or lockjaw) is picked up through contaminated open wounds and causes severe muscular spasms; if you cut yourself on something dirty and are not covered, get a booster as soon as you can.

Assuming that you were vaccinated against **polio** in childhood, only one (oral) booster is needed during your adult life. Immunizations against **mumps**, **measles**, **TB** and **rubella** are a good idea for anyone who wasn't vaccinated as a child and hasn't had the diseases.

Rabies is a problem in India. The best advice is to give dogs and monkeys a wide berth, and not to play with animals at all, no matter how cute they might look. A bite, a scratch or even a lick from an infected animal could spread the disease; wash any such wound immediately but gently with soap or detergent, and apply alcohol or iodine if possible. Find out what you can about the animal and swap addresses with the owner (if there is one) just in case. If the animal might be infected or the wound begins to tingle and fester, act immediately to get treatment – rabies is invariably fatal once symptoms appear. There is an (expensive) vaccine, which serves only to shorten the course of treatment you need, and is only effective for a maximum of three months.

Medical resources for travellers

For up-to-the-minute information, make an appointment at a **travel** clinic. These clinics also sell travel accessories, including mosquito nets and first-aid kits. Highly recommended for travel to India and other tropical countries is the *Rough Guide to Travel Health* by Dr Nick Jones.

A travellers' first-aid kit

Below are items you might want to carry with you, especially if visiting remote areas of Rajasthan. All are available in India at a fraction of what you might pay at home:

- Antiseptic cream
- Insect repellent and cream such as Anthisan for soothing bites
- Plasters/band aids
- A course of Flagyl antibiotics
- Water sterilization tablets or water purifier
- Lint and sealed bandages
- Knee supports
- Imodium (Lomotil) for stop-gap diarrhoea treatment
- Paracetamol or aspirin
- Multi-vitamin and mineral tablets
- Rehydration sachets
- Hypodermic needles and sterilized skin wipes
- Condoms
- Iodine or potassium permanganate solution

Malaria

Protection against **malaria** is absolutely essential. The disease, caused by a parasite carried in the saliva of female **anopheles mosquitoes**, is endemic in India, though less so in Delhi, Agra and Rajasthan than in areas further south. One of the biggest killers in the Indian Subcontinent, malaria has a variable incubation period of a few days to several weeks, so you can become ill long after being bitten. Programmes to eradicate the disease by spraying mosquito-infested areas and distributing free preventative tablets have proved disastrous; within a short space of time, the anopheles develop immunities to the insecticides, while the malaria parasite itself constantly mutates into drug-resistant strains, rendering the old cures ineffective.

It is vital for travellers to take **preventative tablets** according to a strict routine, and to cover the period before and after your trip. The drug used is **chloroquine** (trade names include Nivaquin, Avloclor and Resochin), usually two tablets weekly, but India has chloroquine-resistant strains, and you'll need to supplement it with daily **proguanil** (**Paludrine**) or weekly **Maloprim**. In India chloroquine is easy to come by but proguanil isn't, so stock up before you arrive. An alternative is the highly effective weekly anti-malarial **Larium** (**Mefloquine**), which can be bought over the counter in India, but note that this can cause horrible side effects in some people (see below), and should not be used without medical advice unless you have used it before and are sure that you will not suffer an adverse reaction. Australian authorities are now prescribing the antibiotic **Doxycycline** instead of Mefloquine, and there is another drug called **Malarone** which can also be used as an alternative. As the malaria parasite can incubate in your system without showing symptoms for more than a month, it is essential to continue taking preventative tablets for at least four weeks after returning home. Most people who catch malaria as a result of foreign travel do so because they forget to keep taking the pills when they get home – don't join them. If you go down with a fever within three months of getting home, be aware that it could be malaria, and seek medical help quickly if you suspect that it may be.

Side effects of anti-malaria drugs may include itching, rashes, hair loss and sight problems. In the case of Larium some people may experience disorientation, depression, sleep disturbance and even delusions; if you're intending to use Larium you should begin to take it two weeks before you depart to see whether it will agree with your metabolism, though normally you only need to begin taking anti-malaria medication a week before your departure date.

Malarial symptoms

The first **signs of malaria** are remarkably similar to a severe flu, and may take months to appear: if you suspect anything go to a hospital or clinic for a blood test immediately. The shivering, burning fever and headaches come in waves, usually in the early evening. Malaria is not infectious, but certain strains can be fatal if not treated promptly, in particular, **cerebral malaria**. This virulent and lethal strain of the disease, which affects the brain, is treatable, but has to be diagnosed early. Erratic body temperature, lack of energy and aches are the first key signs.

Preventing mosquito bites

The best way of combating malaria is of course to stop yourself getting bitten: malarial mosquitoes are active from dusk until dawn and during this time you should use **mosquito repellent** and take all necessary precautions. Sleep under a **mosquito net** if possible – one which can hang from a single point is best (you can usually find a way to tie a string across your room to hang it from), burn **mosquito coils** (widely available in India, but easy to break in transit) or electrically heated repellents such as All Out. An Indian brand of repellent called Odomos is widely available and quite effective, though most travellers bring their own from home, usually one containing the noxious but effective compound **DEET**. DEET can cause rashes, and a strength of more than thirty percent is not advised for people with sensitive skin, though they should still use DEET on clothes and nets. Mosquito "buzzers" – plug-in contraptions that make a noise that supposedly deters mosquitoes – are pretty useless, but wrist and ankle bands are as effective as spray and a good alternative for sensitive skin. Though active from dusk till dawn, female anopheles mosquitoes prefer to bite in the evening, so be especially careful at that time. Wear long sleeves, skirts and trousers, avoid dark colours, which attract mosquitoes, and put repellent on all exposed skin, especially ankles and feet.

Dengue fever

Another illness spread by mosquito bites is **dengue fever**, whose symptoms are similar to those of malaria, plus aching bones. However, unlike malaria, which is spread by the anopheles mosquito, dengue is spread by the aedes "tiger" mosquito (identifiable by its black and white body), which tends to bite in daylight hours, especially early morning and late afternoon. There is no vaccine available and the only treatment is complete rest, with drugs to assuage the fever.

Intestinal troubles

Diarrhoea is the most common bane of travellers. When mild and not accompanied by other major symptoms, it may just be your stomach reacting to unfamiliar food. Accompanied by cramps and vomiting, it could well be food poisoning. In either case, it will probably pass of its own accord in 24 to 48 hours without treatment. In the meantime, it is essential to replace the fluids and salts you're losing, so drink lots of water with **oral rehydration salts** (commonly referred to as ORS, or called Electrolyte in India). If you can't get ORS, use half a teaspoon of salt and eight of sugar in a litre of water, and if you are too ill to drink, seek medical help immediately. Travel clinics and pharmacies sell double-ended moulded plastic spoons that measure the exact ratio of sugar to salt.

While you are suffering, it's a good idea to avoid greasy food, heavy spices, caffeine and most fruit and dairy products. This can be surprisingly difficult in India – you quickly become aware of just how much food is fried in ghee with heavy spices. Bananas and pawpaws are good, as are plain rice or *kitchri* (a simple dhal and rice preparation) and rice soup and coconut water, while curd or a soup made from Marmite or Vegemite (if you happen to have some with you) are forms of protein that can be easily absorbed by your body when you have the runs. Drugs like Lomotil or Imodium simply plug you up – undermining the body's efforts to rid itself of infection – though they can be useful if you have to travel. If symptoms persist for more than a few days, a course of antibiotics may be necessary; this should be seen as a last resort, following medical advice.

Sordid though it may seem, it's a good idea to look at what comes out when you go to the toilet. If your diarrhoea contains blood or mucus and if you are suffering other symptoms including belches and rotten-egg farts, the cause may be **dysentery** or giardia. With a fever, it could well be caused by **bacillic dysentery**, and may clear up without treatment. If you're sure you need it, a course of antibiotics such as tetracycline should sort you out, but they also destroy "gut flora" in your intestines (which help protect you – curd can replenish them to some extent). If you start a course, be sure to finish it, even after the symptoms have gone. Similar symptoms, without fever, indicate **amoebic dysentery**, which is much more serious, and can damage your gut if untreated. The usual cure is a course of Metronidazole (Flagyl) or Fasigyn, both antibiotics that may themselves make you feel ill, and must not be taken with alcohol. Symptoms of **giardia** are similar – including frothy stools, nausea and constant fatigue – for which the treatment is again Metronidazole. If you suspect that you have either of these, seek medical help, and only start on the Metronidazole (750mg three times daily for a week for adults) if there is definitely blood in your diarrhoea and it is impossible to see a doctor.

Finally, bear in mind that oral drugs, such as malaria pills and the contraceptive pill, are likely to be largely ineffective if taken while suffering from diarrhoea.

Bites and creepy crawlies

Worms may enter your body through skin (especially the soles of your feet) or food. An itchy anus is a common symptom, and you may even see them in your stools. They are easy to treat: if you suspect you have them, get some worming tablets such as Mebendazole (Vermox) from any pharmacy.

Biting **insects** and similar animals other than mosquitoes may also aggravate you. The obvious suspects are bed bugs – look for signs of squashed ones around beds in cheap hotels. Head and body **lice** can also be a nuisance; you can buy medicated shampoo to treat them, but more effective for head lice is to apply a thick hair conditioner and comb thoroughly with a metal fine-tooth comb, repeating this daily for a week (or else have your head shaved). You should also change all sheets and pillowcases. Avoid scratching bites, which can lead to infection. Bites from ticks and lice can spread typhus, characterized by fever, muscle aches, headaches, and, later, red eyes and a measles-like rash. If you think you have it, seek treatment (tetracycline is usually prescribed).

Snakes are unlikely to bite unless accidentally disturbed, and most are actually harmless in any case. If you do get bitten, remember what the snake looked like (kill it if you can), try not to move the affected part, and seek medical help immediately: antivenoms are available in most hospitals.

Scorpions can also be a problem in much of Rajasthan. They usually live under stones and in crevices, but they come out at night. Be particularly wary if camping (don't sleep directly on the ground, and shake your shoes out before putting them on in the morning). If you do get stung, follow the same procedure as for a snake bite; you can also put a cold compress on the area if you have one at hand.

Black widow **spiders** are also found in Rajasthan. Only the shiny black female is venomous. The bite itself is not painful and may pass unnoticed, but the reaction, including abdominal pain, cramps and nausea, can lay you out for some days, though it is not usually fatal in adults. First-aid procedures are the same as for a scorpion sting.

The sun and the heat

The sun and the heat can cause a few unexpected problems. Many people suffer a bout of **prickly heat** rash before they've had time to acclimatize. A cool shower, zinc oxide powder (sold in India) and loose cotton clothes should help. **Dehydration** is another possible problem, so make sure you're drinking enough fluids; if you want to optimize water absorption by your body, add rehydration salts (see p.38). The main danger sign for dehydration is irregular urination (only once a day, for instance); dark urine definitely means you should drink more, though it could also indicate hepatitis.

As well as the obvious dangers of sunburn, the **sun** can also cause sunstroke, and a high-factor sun block is vital on exposed skin, especially when you first arrive; pay attention to areas newly exposed by haircuts or changes of clothes. A light hat is also a very good idea, especially if you're doing a lot of walking around in the sun.

Finally, be aware that overheating can cause **heatstroke**, which is potentially fatal. Signs are a very high body temperature, without a feeling of fever but accompanied by headaches and disorientation. Lowering body temperature (taking a tepid shower, for example) and resting in an air-conditioned room is the first step in treatment; also take in plenty of fluids, and seek medical advice if the condition doesn't improve after 24 hours.

HIV and AIDS

The rapidly increasing presence of **HIV/AIDS** has only recently been acknowledged by the Indian government as a national problem. The reluctance to address the issue is partly due to the disease's association with sex, a traditionally closed subject in India. As yet, only NGOs and foreign agencies such as the World Health Organization have embarked on awareness and prevention campaigns. As elsewhere in the world, high-risk groups include prostitutes and intravenous drug users. It is extremely unwise to contemplate casual sex without a condom – carry some with you (preferably brought from home as Indian ones may be less reliable; also, be aware that heat affects the durability of condoms), and insist on using them if you do have sex with a new partner.

Should you need an injection or a transfusion, make sure that new, sterile equipment is used; any blood you receive should be

Ayurvedic medicine

Ayurveda, a Sanskrit word meaning the "knowledge for prolonging life", is a five-thousand-year-old holistic medical system that is widely practised in India. Ayurvedic doctors and clinics in large towns deal with foreigners as well as their usual patients, and some **pharmacies** specialize in Ayurvedic preparations, including toiletries such as soaps, shampoos and toothpastes.

Ayurveda assumes the fundamental sameness of self and nature. Unlike the allopathic medicines of the West, which depend on finding out what's ailing you and then killing it, Ayurveda looks at the whole patient: disease is regarded as a symptom of **imbalance**, so it's the imbalance that's treated, not the disease. Ayurvedic theory holds that the body is controlled by three forces, which reflect the forces within the self: *pitta*, the force of the sun, is hot, and rules the digestive processes and metabolism; *kapha*, likened to the moon, the creator of tides and rhythms, has a cooling effect, and governs the body's organs; and *vata*, wind, relates to movement and the nervous system. The healthy body is one that has the three forces in balance. To diagnose an imbalance, the Ayurvedic **vaid** (doctor) responds not only to the physical complaint but also to family background, daily habits and emotional traits.

Imbalances are typically treated with herbal remedies designed to alter whichever of the three forces is out of whack. Made according to traditional formulae, using indigenous plants, Ayurvedic medicines are cheaper than branded or imported drugs. In addition, the doctor may prescribe various forms of yogic cleansing to rid the body of waste substances. To the uninitiated, these techniques will sound rather off-putting – for instance, swallowing a long strip of cloth, a short section at a time, and then pulling it back up again to remove mucus from the stomach.

from voluntary rather than commercial donor banks. If you have a shave from a barber, make sure he uses a clean blade, and don't undergo processes such as ear-piercing, acupuncture or tattooing unless you can be sure that the equipment is sterile.

Getting medical help

Pharmacies can usually advise on minor medical problems, and most doctors in India speak English. Also, many hotels keep a doctor on call; if you do get ill and need medical assistance, take advice as to the best facilities around. Basic medicaments are made to Indian Pharmacopoea (IP) standards, and most medicines are available without prescription (always check the sell-by date). Hospitals vary in standard: **private clinics** and mission hospitals are often better than state-run ones, but may not have the same facilities. Hospitals in the big cities, including university or medical-school hospitals, are generally pretty good, and cities such as Delhi boast state-of-the-art medical facilities, but at a price. Many hospitals require patients (even emergency cases) to buy necessities such as medicines, plaster casts and vaccines, and to pay for X-rays, before procedures are carried out. Remember to keep receipts for insurance reimbursements.

However, **government hospitals** provide all surgical and after-care services free of charge, and in most other state medical institutions charges are usually so low that for minor treatment the expense may well be lower than the initial "excess" on your insurance. You will, however, need a companion to stay, or you'll have to come to an arrangement with one of the hospital cleaners, to help you out in hospital – relatives are expected to wash, feed and generally take care of the patient. Beware of scams by private clinics in tourist towns such as Agra where there have been reports of overcharging and misdiagnosis by doctors to claim insurance money. Addresses of foreign consulates in Delhi (who will advise in an emergency) can be found on p.143, and addresses of clinics and hospitals can be found in the "Listings" sections for major towns in this book.

Accommodation

On the whole, accommodation, like so many other things in India, provides good value for money, though in Delhi especially, luxury establishments with Western-style comforts and service also charge international prices.

Inexpensive hotels

While accommodation prices are generally on the up, there's still an abundance of **cheap hotels**, catering for backpacking tourists and less well-off Indians. Most charge Rs250–500 for a double room, and some in rural and small-town Rajasthan have rooms for less than Rs200 ($4.25/£2.65/€3). The rock-bottom option may be in a dormitory of a hostel or budget hotel, where you'll usually be charged Rs100–150 for a bed. Budget accommodation varies from filthy fleapits to homely guesthouses and, naturally, tends to be cheaper the further you get off the beaten track; it's most expensive in Delhi, where prices are at least double those for equivalent accommodation elsewhere. Many budget hotels, especially at the bottom of the scale, lack hot running water, though cold showers are not too much of a hardship in summer, and even the cheapest places will supply hot water in a bucket. Bathroom facilities may well be shared, and it's always wise to check out the state of the bathrooms and toilets before taking a room. A room with its own private bathroom is known as an "**attached**" room in India. Bed bugs and mosquitoes are other things to check for – blood spots on the sheets and on the walls where people have squashed them are tell-tale signs.

If a taxi driver or auto- or rickshaw-wallah tells you that the place you ask for is full, closed or has moved, it's more than likely because he wants to take you to a hotel that pays him commission, which will often be added to your bill. Hotel touts likewise work by getting commission from the hotels they take you to; they usually operate at New Delhi station, among other places (see p.86). Never let touts attach themselves to you and accompany you to a hotel, and don't accept alternative hotels offered by taxi, auto- or rickshaw-wallahs who are unwilling to take you to the place you've asked for; either insist that they take you there (and make sure it really is the same place), or ask to be dropped off nearby. Indeed, it's a wise policy not to allow a taxi driver or rickshaw-wallah to accompany you into a hotel in any case.

Mid-range hotels

These often have large clean rooms, with a freshly made bed, your own spotless (often

---

Accommodation price codes

Accommodation price levels in this book are **coded** using the symbols below. The codes are based on the ordinary high-season price (including tax) of double rooms when the book was researched.

Delhi, Agra and Rajasthan don't really have a **tourist season** as such, though certain resorts and some spots on established tourist trails do experience some variation and will be more expensive, or less negotiable, when demand is at its peak, which tends to be in the winter months, with particularly high prices around Christmas.

❶ Rs299 and under	❹ Rs1000–1499	❼ Rs4000–6999
❷ Rs300–599	❺ Rs1500–2499	❽ Rs7000–9999
❸ Rs600–999	❻ Rs2500–3999	❾ Rs10,000 and above

Be a royal guest in the land of forts & folklore

Rajasthan, with its colourful, vibrant cities and the splendour of the Thar desert, is romantic India at its best.
With Mahindra Homestays, experience its local flavour guided by your host and savour experiences that nobody else can offer.

Mahindra Homestays offers you the authentic experience of staying with a Rajasthani family in their home that has been selected for its comfort, cleanliness, safety and originality.

Visit desert tribes on camelback, learn to cook a curry, get your host to bargain at the colourful bazaars or get invited to a wedding while you explore the land of royalty. Mahindra Homestays is dedicated to providing you with comfortable, safe and enriching experience of 'The Real India'.

Choose from the following destinations
• Jaipur • Jodhpur • Udaipur • Ajmer

Types of homestays
• Palaces • Havelis • Heritage Homes
• Modern Homes • Farm Stays

Visit www.mahindrahomestays.com
or call
UK No. 02031408422
INDIA No. 1800–425–2737
for booking assistance.

mahindra
homestays

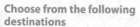

STAY IN FAMILY HOMES – EXPERIENCE THE REAL INDIA

sit-down) toilet, and hot and cold running water, all for around Rs500–1000 ($10.50–21/£6.50–13/€7.50–15). You'll pay more for a TV, a balcony, and, above all, **air conditioning** (a/c). This is not necessarily the advantage you might expect – in some hotels you can find yourself paying double for a system that is so dust-choked, wheezy and noisy as to preclude any possibility of sleep – but providing it entitles a hotel to consider itself mid-range. Some also offer a halfway-house option known as **air-cooled** – noisy and not as effective as full-blown air conditioning, but better than nothing in severe heat. Non-air-conditioned rooms should otherwise have a fan, and you won't need air conditioning in winter – indeed you may want to take a room with heating.

Rajasthan's state government runs its own hotels, similar to private mid-range establishments, but often also offering pricier air-conditioned rooms and cheaper dorms, though they tend to be rather run-down. We've indicated such places throughout this guide by including the state acronym RTDC (Rajasthan Tourist Development Corporation).

Upmarket hotels

Most **luxury hotels** in India fall into one of two categories: old-fashioned institutions brimming with class, and modern jet-set chain hotels, largely confined to large cities and tourist resorts.

The faded grandeur of the **Raj** lingers on in a few former imperial hangouts such as Delhi's *Maidens* hotel (see p.95). In Rajasthan, however, where most of the Rajputs remained substantially independent of British rule, there are some magnificent **old forts** and **palaces** (*thikanas*) from feudal estates, and **havelis**, the former homes of aristocratic families, now designated **heritage hotels**.

Modern deluxe establishments – slicker, brighter, faster and far more businesslike – tend to belong to **chains**. Some of these, such as the Taj and Oberoi hotels, along with the India Tourist Development Corporation's Ashok chain, are Indian-owned, while others are international. Double rooms at these five-star establishments start at around Rs10,000, and can go up to over five times that, but in Rajasthan's palaces and heritage hotels you'll still get excellent value for money, with rates only just beginning to approach those of their counterparts in Europe.

Note that when it comes to five-star and other high-end hotels, it's worth shopping around online, as some websites provide access to rates that may be far lower than the standard rack rates you'll be quoted over the phone or if you walk in. Upmarket tour operators at home may also be able to organize a package including the hotel of your choice at a lower price than you would pay if you book the room yourself.

Other options

Many **railway stations** have "**retiring rooms**" where passengers can sleep. These rooms can be particularly handy if you're catching an early-morning train, though tend to get booked up well in advance. They vary in price, but generally charge roughly the same as a budget hotel, and have large, clean, if somewhat institutional rooms; dormitories, where you can bank on being woken at the crack of dawn by a morning chorus of throat-clearing, are often available. Occasionally you may come across a main station with an air-conditioned room, in which case you will have found a real bargain. Retiring rooms cannot be booked in advance and are allocated on a first-come-first-served basis; just turn up and ask if there's a vacancy, but note that you normally need to have a train ticket to use the station retiring rooms.

In one or two places, it's possible to rent rooms in people's **homes**. In Rajasthan, the tourist office runs a "**paying guest house**" scheme to place tourists with families offering lodging. There are also two private schemes: Rajputana Discovery (Ⓦwww .rajputanadiscovery.com) and Mahindra Homestays (Ⓦwww.mahindrahomestays .com). Also, Servas (Ⓦjoomla.servas.org), established in 1949 as a peace organization, is now devoted to providing homestays; you have to join before travelling by applying to your local Servas secretary, and you will be interviewed to check you are suitable. You then get a list of hosts to contact in the place you are visiting. Some people provide free accommodation, others are just day

Accommodation practicalities

Check-out time is often noon, but confirm this when you arrive: some hotels expect you out by 9am, but many others operate a 24-hour system, under which you are simply obliged to leave by the same time as you arrived. Some places let you use their facilities after the official check-out time, sometimes for a small charge, others won't even let you leave your baggage after check-out unless you pay for another night.

Unfortunately, not all hotels offer **single rooms**, so it can often work out more expensive to travel alone; in hotels that don't, you may be able to negotiate a slight discount. However, it's not unusual to find rooms with three or four beds – great value for families and small groups.

In cheap hotels and hostels, you needn't expect any additions to your basic bill, but as you go up the scale, you'll find **taxes** and **service charges** creeping in. Service is generally ten percent; taxes are determined by state governments, but in Rajasthan this varies between eight and twelve and a half percent; in Delhi, it's always twelve and a half percent, and in Agra five percent.

Like most other things in India, the price of a room may well be open to **negotiation**, especially off-season. If you think the price is too high, or if all the hotels in town are empty, try haggling. You may get nowhere – but nothing ventured, nothing gained.

hosts. There is no guarantee a bed will be provided – it's up to the individual.

Camping is possible too, though it's hard to see why you'd want to be cooped up in a tent overnight when you could be sleeping on a cool *charpoi* (Indian bed) on a roof terrace for a handful of rupees – let alone why you'd choose to carry a tent around in the first place. It's not usual to simply pitch a tent in the countryside, though hotels occasionally allow camping in their grounds.

There are HI **youth hostels** in Delhi, Jaipur, Mount Abu, Jaisalmer, Bikaner and Alwar, and also at Shahpura, 70km west of Bundi, but with accommodation so cheap anyway, there's probably no reason for staying in them. We've included the most useful one in Delhi (p.96). Some, such as Delhi, are open to HI members only, but most are open to all. Further information can be found on ⓦwww.yhaindia.org, or by calling the youth hostel in Delhi on ⓣ011/2611 6285.

Occasionally, and especially if you have a particular interest in religion, you may be able to stay in a Hindu, Sikh or Jain **temple**, for which a donation may be expected, and is certainly appreciated.

Food and drink

Rich, aromatic and of course spicy, Indian food has a well-deserved reputation across the globe. If you're a vegetarian, you've come to the right place, as around half of India's restaurants are vegetarian ("veg"), and even non-veg restaurants offer plenty of vegetarian options. In northern India, and particularly in old Mughal centres like Delhi and Agra, there is a strong tradition of non-veg cuisine, while Rajasthan has two parallel traditions – meat dishes, particularly "mutton" (which in India means goat), eaten by the warrior Rajput class, and strictly vegetarian dishes eaten by Brahmins and Jains, the merchant class.

Restaurants

The cheapest kind of restaurant in India is a **dhaba**, or roadside diner, or a **bhojanalaya** (sometimes called a "hotel", though it does not have accommodation); to a large extent the two terms are interchangeable, though *dhaba* suggests somewhere a little more basic than *bhojanalaya*. Food in *dhabas* and *bhojanalayas* is simple – usually just a veg curry with dhal and bread or perhaps rice – but it's often good and invariably cheap. Some *dhabas* and *bhojanalayas* are spotlessly clean; others can be quite grubby, so give them a once-over before you commit yourself to eating there. In general, they are not used to catering for foreigners, but they'll often have a menu in English tucked away somewhere; if not, you'll have to ask what they've got, or just point to what you want.

Proper **restaurants** vary in price and quality, and can be veg or non-veg, offering a wide choice of dishes much like Indian restaurants anywhere else in the world. They'll always have a menu in English, and the best ones will usually specialize in a particular type of cuisine, be it Punjabi, Mughlai, tandoori or whatever, though some will be "multi-cuisine" with standard Indian dishes plus "Continental" (which tends to mean Western in general) and Chinese dishes, of a sort. In places with a large contingent of foreign tourists – Jaisalmer, Pushkar, Delhi's Paharganj or Agra's Taj Ganj, for example, you'll find eating places catering specifically for that market, with pancakes, toast and fruit salad. They may well miss the mark by a long way, and they are not of course authentically Indian, but

they can offer a break from fried and spicy food, especially if you've got tummy troubles. **Deluxe restaurants** such as those in five-star hotels can be very expensive by Indian standards, but they offer a chance to try classic Indian cooking of very high quality: rich, subtle, mouthwatering. Try to have a meal in one at least once.

Following the Sikh tradition of offering hospitality to all and sundry, Sikh **gurudwaras** (temples) serve a simple meal of rice and dhal twice a day, and all visitors to the *gurudwara*, regardless of their religion, are welcome to partake.

Veg and non-veg

Because so many people in India are **vegetarian**, a large proportion of restaurants serve only vegetarian food, and all restaurants offer vegetarian options. Most religious Hindus don't eat meat, fish or eggs, while some orthodox Brahmins will not eat food cooked by anyone outside their household (or onions or garlic, as they are considered to inflame the baser instincts). Jains are even stricter, eschewing not only animal products (apart from dairy), but also all root and tuber vegetables such as onions, potatoes and carrots. **Veganism** is not common, however, and though vegetarian food in India usually excludes eggs, it does not exclude dairy products, and particularly ghee (clarified butter), in which most things are fried. In fact, one of the most common ingredients in Indian veg cooking is **paneer**, a mild cheese made without rennet.

All eating places in India specify whether they are **veg** or **non-veg**, though meat-eaters

For advice on **drinking water** in India, see p.35.

should exercise caution even when meat is available – its quality is not assured except in the best restaurants, and you won't get much in a dish anyway. Hindus, of course, do not eat beef and Muslims shun pork, so you probably won't find those anywhere, except perhaps in the odd European or Chinese restaurant.

Indian food

What Westerners call a **curry** covers a variety of wet dishes (that is, dishes in a sauce, or "gravy"), each made with a different mix of spices, or masala. Curry powder is not used in India, the nearest equivalent being *garam masala* ("hot mix"), a combination of dried ground black pepper and other spices, in theory added to a dish at the last stage of cooking to spice it up, but often used as a substitute for other aromatics. Commonly used **spices** include chilli, turmeric, garlic, ginger, cinnamon, cardamom, cloves, coriander – both leaf and seed – cumin and even saffron. These are not all added at the same time, and some are used whole, so beware of chewing on them. Fenugreek, the spice that gives ready-made curry powder its distinctive taste, is actually used much more sparingly in India.

It's the Indian penchant for **chilli** that alarms many Western visitors. The majority of foreigners develop a tolerance for it; if you don't, you'll just have to stick to mild dishes such as korma and biryani where meat or vegetables are cooked with rice, and eat plenty of chapati. Indians tend to assuage the effects of chilli with chutney, *dahi* (a type of yoghurt, commonly referred to as curd) or *raita* (curd with mint and cucumber, or other herbs and vegetables). Otherwise, **beer** is one of the best things for washing chilli out of your mouth; the essential oils that cause the burning sensation dissolve in alcohol, but not in water.

Vegetarian curries are usually identified (even on menus in English) by the Hindi names of their main ingredients (see pp.405–407 for a food and drink glossary), such as *alu gobi* for potato and cauliflower.

Terms like "curry" and "masala" don't really tell you what to expect; meat curries are more often given specific names such as korma or dopiaza, to indicate the kind of masala used or the method of cooking.

A main dish – which may be a curry, but could also be a dry dish such as a kebab, or a tandoori dish without a masala – is usually served with dhal (lentils) and bread such as chapatis or naan. Rice is usually an optional extra in north India. Many restaurants offer a set meal or **thali**. This is a stainless-steel tray with a number of little dishes in it, containing a selection of curries, a chutney and a sweet. In the middle you'll get bread and usually rice. In many places, waiters will keep coming round with refills until you've had enough.

Many people in India prefer to eat with their fingers (to feel the food as well as taste it) and in some cheap places you may have to ask for cutlery. Avoid getting food on the palm of your hand by eating with the tips of your fingers, and wash your hands both before and after eating. Wherever you eat, remember to use only your right hand.

In north India, food is usually served with bread, which comes in a number of varieties, all of them flatbreads rather than loaves. **Chapati** is a generic term for breads, but tends to refer to the simplest, unleavened type. It's usually made from wheat flour, but in Rajasthan you may come across chapatis made from millet. The term **roti** is likewise generic, and a roti can be exactly the same as a chapati, but the term tends to refer more to a thicker bread baked in a tandoor. In Rajasthan you get quite a variety of rotis, made with different flours and spices. **Naan** is a leavened bread, thick and chewy, and invariably baked in a tandoor; it's a favourite in non-veg restaurants as it best accompanies rich meaty dishes. You may also come across fried breads, of which **paratha** (or parantha) is rolled out, basted with ghee, folded over and rolled out again several times before cooking, and often stuffed with ingredients such as potato (*alu paratha*); it's popular for breakfast. Less common in the region, **puri** balloons out like a puffball when fried, and needs to be served immediately. **Poppadum** (papad) is a crisp wafer made from lentil flour and is typically served as an appetizer.

Mughlai and tandoori cuisine

The classic cuisine in Delhi and Agra is **Mughlai**, the food of the Mughals, mostly non-veg and extremely rich, with ingredients such as cream, almonds and saffron. A Mughlai meal is usually accompanied by **makhania** dhal, which is made with cream. **Korma** is a Mughlai dish of meat (or vegetables) cooked in curd, usually quite mild in terms of spices. Also typical of Mughlai cooking is **biryani**, in which rice and meat are cooked together. A **pulao** is very similar, except that the meat and gravy are added to the rice at a later stage (and pulaos tend to be wetter than biryanis). **Kebabs** also feature strongly in Mughlai cuisine, particularly *seekh kebab* (minced lamb grilled on a skewer) and *shami kebab* (small minced lamb cutlets). Another classic Mughlai dish is **rogan josh**, a rich mutton curry with tomatoes and saffron. Although in principle Mughlai cuisine is non-veg, vegetarian versions of most Mughlai dishes are available, often made with *paneer*. Mughlai food is typically eaten with naan. A *mughlai masala* normally indicates a mild, creamy one. *Mughlai paratha* is a *paratha* with egg.

The other big (and mainly non-veg) north Indian style of cooking is **tandoori**, which you'll find right across Rajasthan, Delhi and Agra, though the region with which it is most strongly associated is **Punjab**. The name refers to the deep clay oven (tandoor) in which the food is cooked. **Tandoori chicken** is marinated in yoghurt, herbs and spices before cooking. Boneless pieces of meat, marinated and cooked in the same way, are known as **tikka**. Tandoori meats may be served in a medium-strength masala, one thickened with almonds (**pasanda**), or in a rich butter sauce – if chicken is involved, this is known as **murg makhani** or butter chicken. Breads such as naan and roti are also baked in the tandoor. Though tandoori food is most often chicken (wags have it that tandoori chicken is Punjab's national bird), it can also be made with mutton, *paneer* or even fish.

Rajasthani food

Rajasthan's ruling Rajput class, as warriors, have always eaten a largely non-veg cuisine, very similar to that of the Mughals. The merchant class however, largely Brahmin and Jain, have traditionally eschewed meat in favour of strictly vegetarian cooking.

The most popular of all Rajasthani dishes is **dhal bati churma**, which consists of *bati* (a baked wheatflour ball with a tough crust), dhal (as ever, a soupy lentil stew) and *churma*, a sweet made of coarse-ground wheatflour cooked with ghee and sugar. The three are served as a thali, sometimes with other veg curries to accompany them.

Another vegetarian Rajasthani speciality is **gatta**, small dumplings of gram flour (made from ground chickpeas) cooked in a masala- or yoghurt-based sauce. *Gatta* recipes vary across the state, but the best known is *govind gatta*, in which the dumplings are round and quite large. *Gatta ki sabji* is *gatta* with vegetables. There is also a lentil-flour dumpling called **mangodi**, most typically served in a curry with potatoes (*alu mangodi*), though it can come with fenugreek leaves (*methi mangodi*) or onions (*mangodi piaza*).

A couple of delicious but unfamiliar **vegetables** that you may come across in Rajasthan are **sangri**, the long pods of the *khejri* tree, and **kair** (or *kher*), the caper-like fruit of a shrub that grows in the same region. The two are typically cooked and served together in villages of the Bishnoi people, to whom the *khejri* tree is sacred (see p.278).

Among meat dishes, Rajasthan's pride is **lal maas** or laal maans ("red meat"), a spicy dish of lamb marinated in chilli. A less fiery alternative is **safed maas** ("white meat") – mutton in a mild cashew, curd and cream curry. *Sula* (or *maas ka sula*) is a Rajasthani tandoori kebab, whose distinctive marinade includes kachri, a vegetable that tenderizes the meat.

Food from other regions of India

Along with Rajasthani, Mughlai and Punjabi food, you'll also come across restaurants specializing in cuisine from other parts of India. **Gujarati cuisine**, from the state adjoining Rajasthan, is generally spicy, often quite tangy, and mainly vegetarian. In Rajasthan, Delhi and Agra, it most commonly appears in the form of a Gujarati thali, which is generally a good way to sample it.

For a **glossary** of food items, see
pp.405–407.

South Indian food is even more popular,
and you'll find south Indian restaurants all
over the place. South Indian curries are very
spicy and served with rice. More commonly,
however, you'll come across light meals
based on either *dosa*, *iddli*, *uttapam* or *vada*.
Dosa is a crispy rice-based pancake which,
when filled with a lightly spiced potato mix, is
called a **masala dosa**, and served with a
coconut chutney, and with **sambar**, a tangy
vegetable soup containing tamarind and
asafoetida. Sambar is also commonly served
with **iddli**, a steamed rice cake. **Uttapam** is
likewise made of rice, but thinner and flatter
than iddli, more like a pancake, while **vada** is
a doughnut-shaped fried lentil cake.

Snacks and street food

Snack food (**chaat**) is ubiquitous, and
should be approached with caution when
sold on the street. The guiding principle is
that frying will sterilize anything, but leaving it
out for any length of time allows germs to
breed, so stick to freshly cooked food and
steer clear of items that have been lying in
the open for hours.

Favourite snack foods include **samosas**,
pastry triangles filled with meat or potato.
There's even a sweet version (*mawa
samosa*) that's filled with a kind of milk fudge
and drizzled with syrup. A speciality of

Jodhpur is **mirchi bada**, a large chilli fried in
a thick batter of wheatgerm and potato.

Puris may appear in the form of **chana
puri**, served with a chickpea curry, or **bhel
puri**, a speciality of Mumbai that you may
nonetheless run across in Delhi, Agra or
Rajasthan, consisting of a mix of puffed
rice, deep-fried vermicelli, potato, and
crunchy puri with tamarind sauce. **Gol
gappa** is a kind of stuffed puri. Similar but
larger is **raj kachori**, a crisp shell usually
filled with chickpeas and doused in curd
and sauce, a mix of flavours that explodes
inside your mouth.

Also popular, and more portable, are
namkeens, the dry snacks that make up
what is known in the West as "Bombay mix".
In India these are available individually or in
various combinations, with or without
masala seasoning. Bikaner in particular is
known for them, and especially for **Bikaneri
bhujia** – thin, vermicelli-like sticks made
from gram and lentil flour, which are
supposed to be extra crisp in Bikaner
because of the dry climate.

International food

Delhi has a wide choice of international
cuisines, including Thai, Japanese, Italian
and French, particularly in upmarket restaurants in South Delhi, and in five-star hotels.
In Agra and Rajasthan, you'll find **Chinese
food** on the menu in a surprising number of
places, though it isn't what you'd call
authentic. **Western** ("Continental") **food** is

Paan

You may be glad to know that the red stuff people spit all over the streets isn't
blood, but juice produced by chewing **paan** – a digestive, commonly taken after
meals, and also a mild stimulant.

Paan consists of chopped or shredded nut (called betel nut, though in fact it
comes from the areca palm), wrapped in a leaf (which does come from the betel
vine) that is first prepared with ingredients such as *katha* (red paste), *chuna* (slaked
lime), *mitha masala* (a mix of sweet spices, which can be ingested) and *zarda*
(chewing tobacco, not to be swallowed on any account). The triangular package
thus formed is wedged inside your cheek and chewed slowly, and in the case of
zarda paans, spitting out the juice as you go.

Paan, and *paan masala* (a mix of betel nut, fennel seeds, sweets and flavourings),
are sold by paan-wallahs, often from tiny stalls squeezed between shops. Paan is
an acquired taste; novices should start off, and preferably stick to, the sweet
(*mitha*) variety, which can safely be swallowed.

variable, but you can get some decent pasta dishes on occasion, and even fish and chips. In big cities, you'll also find the usual junk food franchise chains. Tourist centres such as Pushkar, Udaipur, Agra's Taj Ganj and Delhi's Paharganj offer a fair choice of Western and also Middle Eastern (Israeli) food, often including some quite passable hummus. The same places will also serve what has become the international fare of backpackers across Asia, such as porridge, toast, omelettes, banana pancakes, and fruit salad with yoghurt, which can be especially welcome at **breakfast** time. Indian breakfasts include *chana puri* or *alu paratha* with dhal, but these can be a little spicy for some. Alternatives include South Indian snacks such as masala dosa or *iddli sambar*.

Sweets

Many Indians have a sweet tooth and Indian **sweets**, usually made of milk, can be very sweet indeed. Of the more solid type, **barfi**, a kind of fudge made from milk which has been boiled down and condensed, varies from moist and delicious to dry and powdery. It comes in various flavours from plain creamy white to *pista* (pistachio) in livid green and is often sold covered with silver leaf (which you eat). Round, smoother-textured **penda** and thin diamonds of cashew paste called **kaju katli** are among many other sweets made from **chhana** or boiled-down milk. Gelatinous **halwa** (not to be confused with the sesame sweet of the Middle East) originates in Sindh, now in Pakistan, but has become popular across the Subcontinent. **Ladoo** is a ball of wheat or gram flour with sugar, and often other ingredients such as raisins. A lot of sweets in Rajasthan are made with **mawa** (solidified condensed milk), and you can even get *mawa* samosas and *mawa* kachoris. Bikaner is best known for its sweets, but confectionery is generally good throughout Rajasthan.

Getting softer and stickier, **jalebis** are syrup-filled, deep-fried batter tubes, and are as sickly as they look. Other syrup-laden sweets tend to be Bengali in origin, but some towns in Rajasthan have made quite a name for their own versions. **Gulab jamuns** are deep-fried cream cheese sponge balls soaked in syrup (though in Rajasthan you may also come across a savoury dish of the same name, made with *mawa*), and **rasgullas** are rosewater-flavoured cream cheese balls floating in syrup. **Ras malai** is similar but soaked in cream instead of syrup.

Western-style ice cream is not great in India (and stay away from street ices unless you have a seasoned constitution), but do try **kulfi**, a pistachio- and cardamom-flavoured frozen sweet which is India's answer to ice cream and extremely delicious, even in its mass-produced versions. Kheer, a wonderfully aromatic rice pudding, is also a popular dessert.

Fruit

What **fruit** is available varies with region and season, but there's always a fine choice. Ideally, you should **peel** all fruit including apples, or soak them in strong iodine or potassium permanganate solution for half an hour. Roadside vendors sell fruit which they often cut up and serve sprinkled with salt and even masala – don't buy anything that looks like it's been hanging around for a while.

Mangoes of various kinds are usually on offer, but not all are sweet enough to eat fresh – some are used for pickles or curries. Indians are picky about their mangoes, which they feel and smell before buying; if you don't know the art of choosing the fruit, you could be sold the leftovers. Among the species appearing at different times in the season, which lasts from spring to summer, look out for alphonso and langra. Bananas of one sort or another are also on sale all year round, and oranges and tangerines are generally easy to come by, as are sweet melons and thirst-quenching watermelons.

Among less familiar fruit, the *chiku* (sapodilla) looks like a kiwi and tastes a little bit like a pear. It comes from the tree whose sap was originally used to make chewing gum. The watermelon-sized jackfruit, whose spiny green exterior encloses sweet, slightly rubbery yellow segments, each containing a seed, is sometimes sold in individual segments at roadside stalls.

Tea and coffee

India sometimes seems to run on **chai** (tea), sold by chai-wallahs on just about every street corner, but although it was introduced from China by the East India Company in 1838, its consumption was only popularized by a government campaign in the 1950s.

Chai is usually made by putting tea dust, milk and water in a pan, boiling it all up, straining it into a cup or glass with lots of sugar and pouring back and forth from one cup to another to stir. Ginger and/or cardamoms are sometimes added. If you're quick off the mark, you can get them to hold the sugar. English tea it isn't, but most foreign visitors get used to chai. "Think of it as a drink in its own right rather than tea," advise some. From time to time, especially in tourist spots, you might get a pot of European-style "tray" tea, generally consisting of a tea bag in lukewarm water – you'd do better to stick to the pukka Indian variety.

Coffee is all too frequently instant, but sleek cafés selling espresso, cappuccino, frappés and the like have sprung up in Delhi and other large towns, and filter coffee is sometimes available.

Soft drinks

Sodas (known as cold drinks in India) are ubiquitous. Coca-Cola and Pepsi returned to India in the early 1990s after being banned from the country for seventeen years and have taken over most of the indigenous brands such as Thums Up and Limca. In parts of Rajasthan there has been controversy over Coca-Cola plants accused of depleting the local water table.

Plain soda, served alone or with lime juice, is much more refreshing than straight water (see also p.35), either treated, boiled or bottled, and reports have revealed high concentrations of pesticides in bottled water (see p.35). There are also cartons of Frooti, Jumpin, Réal and similar brands of fruit juice drinks, which come in mango, guava, apple and lemon varieties. If the carton looks at all mangled, it is best not to have it as it may have been "recycled". At larger stations, there will be a stall on the platform selling apple juice from the state of Himachal Pradesh. Street stalls often sell delicious freshly pressed sugar-cane juice, but be choosy where you get it from, as not all of them are tremendously hygienic.

India's greatest cold drink, **lassi**, is made with beaten curd and drunk either sweetened with sugar, or salted, or mixed with fruit. It varies widely from smooth and delicious to insipid and watery, and is sold at virtually every café, restaurant and canteen in the country. Salted lassi is surprisingly good, and a lot more refreshing than the sweet variety. In some places, lassi may be spiced – sweet lassi with cardamom or saffron, salted lassi with cumin. In western Rajasthan, and particularly Jodhpur, you'll get deliciously rich makhania lassi, made with saffron and cream. Bhang lassi contains cannabis, and should be approached with caution (see p.57).

Freshly made milkshakes are commonly available at establishments with blenders. They'll also sell you what they call a fruit juice, but which is usually fruit, water and sugar (or salt) liquidized and strained. With all such drinks, exercise **caution** in deciding where to buy them: consider in particular where the water is likely to have come from.

Alcohol

Prohibition, once widespread in India, still applies in Pushkar. Even in the rest of Rajasthan, bars other than those in hotels can be few and far between, but in practice, restaurants in many guesthouses serve alcohol, though strictly speaking it is illegal. There are also "dry" days when alcohol cannot be bought or served; in Rajasthan and Agra only three days are dry, namely Republic Day (Jan 26), Independence Day (Aug 15), and Gandhi Jayanti (Oct 2), but Delhi has no less than 21 dry days in its annual calendar. The minimum legal age for buying alcohol is eighteen in Rajasthan, but 25 in Delhi and Agra. Despite the lower drinking age, Rajasthani society remains conservative in its attitude to alcohol, which is seen as a low-life pursuit, but among the wealthier classes in Delhi, on the other hand, a pub culture not dissimilar to that of the West has taken root. Alcohol is usually cheaper in Delhi than it is in Rajasthan or Agra.

Kingfisher is the leading brand of **beer**, but there are plenty of others. Bar prices are Rs80–200 for a 650ml bottle. All lagers tend to contain chemical additives including glycerine, but they are palatable enough if you can get them cold. In certain places or on "dry" days, beer may be sold in the form of "special tea" – a teapot of beer, which you pour into and drink from a teacup to disguise what it really is.

Spirits usually take the form of "Indian Made Foreign Liquor" (IMFL), although the recently legitimized foreign liquor industry is expanding rapidly. Some Scotch, such as Seagram's Hundred Pipers, is now being bottled in India and sold at a premium, as is Smirnoff vodka, among other known brands. Some of the brands of Indian whisky are not too bad and are affordable in comparison; gin and brandy can be pretty rough, while Indian rum is sweet and distinctive. Steer well clear of *arak*, which is distilled illegally and often contains methanol (wood alcohol) and other poisons. A look through the press, especially at festival times, will soon reveal numerous cases of blindness and death as a result of drinking bad hooch (or "spurious liquor" as it's called). Unfortunately, the Indian **wine** industry, though slowly improving with vineyards such as Grovers, is not up to scratch and the wines are pricey, while foreign wine available in upmarket restaurants and luxury hotels comes with an exorbitant price tag.

The media

Though few people in India speak English at home, most literate people can speak it, and a lot of the media, particularly print media, is in English, which makes it very easy to keep up with Indian and foreign news while you are in the country.

Newspapers and magazines

There are a large number of English-language daily newspapers; most prominent of the nationals are the *Times of India* (Ⓦtimesofindia.indiatimes.com), *The Hindu* (Ⓦwww.hinduonline.com), *The Statesman* (Ⓦwww.thestatesman.net), the *Hindustan Times* (Ⓦwww.hindustantimes.com), the *Economic Times* (Ⓦeconomictimes.india times.com) and the *Indian Express* (Ⓦwww .indianexpress.com; usually the most critical of the government). All are pretty dry and sober, and concentrate mainly on Indian news, often with Delhi or Rajasthan editions that have sections devoted to regional news too. Online, the *Times of India*, *The Hindu* and the *Hindustan Times* provide the most up-to-date and detailed news services. India's press is the freest in Asia, and attacks on the government are often quite outspoken. However, as in the West, most papers can be seen as part of the political establishment, and are unlikely to print anything that might upset the "national consensus", particularly on topics such as Kashmir.

In recent years, a number of *Time/Newsweek*-style **news magazines** have hit the market, the best being *India Today* (Ⓦindiatoday.intoday.in) and *Frontline* (Ⓦwww.frontline.in), published by *The Hindu*. Others include *Outlook* (Ⓦwww .outlookindia.com), plus there are magazines and periodicals in English covering all sorts of popular and minority interests, so it's worth checking newsstands to see what's available.

Foreign publications such as the *International Herald Tribune*, *Time*, *Newsweek*, *The Economist* and the international edition of the British *Guardian* can be found in the main cities. The *Guardian* has an excellent archive of articles on India on its website at Ⓦwww.guardian.co.uk/india.

For a read through the American press in Delhi, try the American Information Resource Center (see p.136).

Radio

India's national **radio** service, All India Radio, runs the popular Vividh Bharati Seva station, with a mix of music (mainly *filmi*), comedy and news in several languages, including English, though most of its talk shows are in Hindi. It can be picked up on medium wave throughout the region, broadcasting on 819kHz, 666kHz and 1017kHz (280m, 366m and 450m) in Delhi, 1530kHz (196m) in Agra, 1476kHz (203m) in Jaipur, and several AM and FM frequencies in different parts of Rajasthan (see Ⓦallindiaradio.org /schedule/freq_nr.html for full details). Recent years have seen a plethora of independent FM stations spring up following a relaxation of government restrictions on radio broadcasts. Delhi in particular is well blessed with music stations, some of them, like Radio One (94.3MHz), offshoots from stations originally established in Mumbai. Others, such as Adlab Radio's Big FM (92.7MHz), are home-grown. The Entertainment Network of India's channel, Radio Mirchi (98.3MHz), broadcasts in Jaipur as well as Delhi. All play a mix of Indian and foreign pop hits. Others include Red FM (93.5MHz), Hit FM (95.0MHz) and Fever FM (104.0MHz).

If you want to hear **foreign news stations**, BBC World Service radio (Ⓦwww.bbc.co.uk/worldservice) can be picked up on medium wave (AM) at 1413kHz (212m), or on short wave, where frequencies include 15.31MHz (19.6m), 17.79MHz (16.9m) and 9.74MHz (30.1m). The Voice of America (Ⓦwww.voa.gov) can be found on 15.75MHz (19m) and 75.75MHz (39.5m), among other frequencies. Radio Canada (Ⓦwww.rcinet.ca) broadcasts in English on 6165 and 7255kHz (48.6 and 41.3m) at 6.30–7.30am and on 9635 and 11,975 kHz (31 and 25m) at 8.30–9.30pm.

Television

The government-run **TV** company, Doordarshan, which broadcasts a sober diet of edifying programmes, has now been swept aside by a wave of new digital channels broadcasting in Hindi, English and local languages. These include Rupert Murdoch's Star TV, which broadcasts largely in English, Zee TV (with Z News), a progressive blend of Hindi-oriented chat, film, news and music programmes, and NDTV, which has a number of news and entertainment channels. In addition there are the usual international broadcasters, including the BBC and CNN, and of course sports and music channels, which concentrate on cricket and Indian pop respectively.

Festivals and holidays

Virtually every temple in every town or village has its own festival. The biggest and most spectacular in Rajasthan include the camel fair at Pushkar in November, and the Gangaur festival in March or early April. While many festivals are religious in nature, merrymaking rather than solemnity is generally the order of the day, and onlookers are usually welcome. Indeed, if you are lucky enough to coincide your visit with a local festival, it may well prove to be the highlight of your trip.

Hindu, Sikh, Buddhist and Jain festivals follow the Indian **lunar calendar** and their dates therefore vary from year to year against the plain old Gregorian calendar. Determining them more than a year in advance is a highly complicated business best left to astrologers.

Each lunar cycle is divided into two *paksa* (halves): "bright" (waxing) and "dark" (waning), each consisting of fifteen *tithis* ("days" – but a *tithi* might begin at any time of the solar day). The *paksa* start respectively with the new moon (*ama* or *bahula* – the first day of the month) and the full moon (*purnima*). Lunar festivals, then, are observed on a given day in the "light" or "dark" side of the month. The lunar calendar adds a leap month every two or three years to keep it in line with the seasons. Muslim festivals follow the **Islamic calendar**, whose year of exactly twelve lunar months loses about eleven days per annum against the Gregorian. Islamic festival dates are only approximate as they depend on the actual sighting of the new moon at the start of each month.

You may, while in the region, have the privilege of being invited to a **wedding**. These are jubilant affairs with great feasting, always scheduled on auspicious days. A Hindu bride dresses in red for the ceremony, and marks the parting of her hair with red *sindhur* and her forehead with a *bindi*. She wears gold or bone bangles, which she keeps on for the rest of her married life. Although the practice is officially illegal, large dowries often change hands. These are usually paid by the bride's family to the groom, and can be contentious; poor families feel obliged to save for years to pay for their daughters to get married.

Festivals

The festivals are listed below under the Hindu calendar months (in brackets) in which they occur as most of the festivals listed are Hindu, and in any case, Sikhs, Buddhists and Jains use the same months.

Jan–Feb (Magha)

H Vasant Panchami (20 Magha; Feb 8, 2011; Jan 28, 2012; Feb 15, 2013; Feb 4, 2014; Jan 24, 2015): One-day spring festival in honour of Saraswati, the goddess of learning, celebrated with kite flying, the wearing of yellow saris, and the blessing of schoolchildren's books and pens by the goddess.

N Nagaur Fair (22–25 Magha): One of Rajasthan's biggest cattle fairs, held at Nagaur, with sales of steers, horses and camels, plus camel racing, tug-of-war games and general celebrations.

Key: B = Buddhist; C = Christian; H = Hindu; J = Jain; M = Muslim; N = non-religious; S = Sikh; R = public holiday in Rajasthan; D = public holiday in Delhi; A = public holiday in Agra.

H Baneshwar Fair (11–15 Magha): Held where the Mahi and Som rivers meet near Dungarpur, this is the main Bhil festival of the year, celebrated with acrobatics and magic shows, and a silver image of Mavji, one of Vishnu's incarnations, carried in procession on horseback.

N Jaisalmer Desert Festival (28–30 Magha): A three-day cultural display, with Gair tribal dancers, fire dancers, and even a turban-tying contest.

H Makar Sankranti/Uttarayan (Jan 14): The passing of the sun into Capricorn marks its move into the astrological northern hemisphere, and is celebrated with competitive kite flying.

N Republic Day (Jan 26): A military parade in Delhi typifies this state celebration of India's republic-hood, followed on Jan 29 by the "Beating the Retreat" ceremony outside the presidential palace in Delhi. (RDA)

M Mawlid (approximately Feb 15, 2011; Feb 4, 2012; Jan 24, 2013; Jan 13, 2014; Jan 3 & Dec 23, 2015): Birthday of the Prophet Mohammed, celebrated with feasting, processions and gatherings to discuss the life and deeds of the Prophet. (RDA)

Feb–March (Phalguna)

N Bharatpur Braj Festival (Feb 2–4): Singing and dancing in the streets mark this festival in honour of Lord Krishna, in particular the Raslila dance depicting the story of Krishna and his consort Radha.

N Taj Mahotsav (Feb 18–27): A ten-day craft fair with music and dance held at the Shilpgram crafts village in Agra (see www.tajmahotsav.org).

H Shivratri (14 Phalguna; March 3, 2011; Feb 20, 2012; March 10, 2013; Feb 28, 2014; Feb 17, 2015): Anniversary of Shiva's tandav (creation) dance, and his wedding anniversary. Popular family festival but also a sadhu festival of pilgrimage and fasting. (A)

H Holi (15 Phalguna): Hugely popular water festival held during Dol Purnima (full moon) to celebrate the beginning of spring. Expect to be bombarded with water, paint and coloured powder (which can permanently stain clothing, so don't go out in your Sunday best). (RDA)

N Jaipur Elephant Festival (15 Phalguna): Held on Holi, and featuring parades of elephants, naturally, plus elephant-back polo and even a people vs. elephants tug-of-war.

March–April (Chaitra)

H Cheti Chand (1 Chaitra; April 4, 2011; March 23, 2012; April 11, 2013; March 31, 2014; March 21, 2015): Lunar new year, more popularly celebrated in the south of India. (A)

H Gangaur (3–4 Chaitra): Rajasthani festival in honour of the goddess Parvati, marked with singing, dancing and processions bearing an image of Parvati in her manifestation as Gauri, goddess of marital happiness. Jaipur, Jodhpur, Jaisalmer, Bikaner, Udaipur and Nathdwara have the biggest processions; around Bundi, Kota and Jhalawar the goddess is festooned with garlands of opium poppies.

H Kaila Devi Fair (12 Chaitra): Held at the village of Kaila, 24km southwest of Karauli, in honour of the goddess Laxmi, as worshipped at the local temple.

H Ramanavami (9 Chaitra): Birthday of Rama, the hero of the Ramayana, celebrated with readings of the epic and discourses on Rama's life and teachings. (RDA)

N Tilwara Cattle Fair (11–26 Chaitra): One of the biggest cattle fairs in Rajasthan, and barely a tourist in sight. See p.279.

J Mahaveerji Fair (24 Chaitra): A festival in honour of the 24th Jain *tirthankara*, held at a temple dedicated to him in the village of Chandangaon, 29km north of Karauli, with a procession carrying his image in a golden chariot hauled by four bullocks to the river to be bathed.

C Good Friday (movable): Crucifixion of Jesus. (RDA)

April–May (Vaisakha)

HS Baisakhi (April 13 or 14): To Hindus, it's the solar new year, celebrated with music and dancing; to Sikhs, it's the anniversary of the foundation of the Khalsa (Sikh brotherhood) by Guru Gobind Singh.

H Parshuram Jayanti (3 Vaisakha; May 5, 2011; April 24, 2012; May 13, 2013; May 2, 2014; April 22, 2015): Birthday of Parshuram, the sixth avatar of Vishnu. (A)

J Mahavir Jayanti (13 Vaisakha): Birthday of Mahavira, the founder of Jainism. The main Jain festival of the year, observed by visits to sacred Jain sites, and with present-giving.

N Mount Abu Summer Festival (13 Vaisakha; May 15, 2011; May 4, 2012; May 23, 2013; May 12, 2014; May 2, 2015): Folk and classical music recitals, plus tribal dancing for this three-day carnival celebrating the arrival of summer.

B Buddha Purnima (15 Vaisakha): The holiest day in the Buddhist calendar, as according to tradition Buddha was not only born on this day, but achieved enlightenment and also died on the same date. (RDA)

June–July (Ashadha)

M Urs Ajmer Sharif (6 Rajab; approximately June 7, 2011; May 27, 2012; May 16, 2013; May 5, 2014; April 25, 2015): Muslim pilgrims from all over India come to pay homage at the tomb of Ajmer's Sufi saint. Poems are recited, Sufi chants are performed, and huge vats of *kheer* (a kind of milk pudding) are cooked up.

July–Aug (Shravana)

H Teej (3 Shravana; Aug 2, 2011; July 22, 2012; Aug 9, 2013; July 30, 2014; Aug 17, 2015): Festival

in honour of Parvati, to welcome the monsoon. Celebrated particularly in Jaipur.

H Raksha Bandhan/Narial Purnima (15 Shravana): Festival to honour the sea god Varuna. Brothers and sisters exchange gifts, the sister tying a thread known as a *rakhi* to her brother's wrist. Brahmins, after a day's fasting, change the sacred thread they wear. (RA)

N Independence Day (Aug 15): India's biggest secular celebration, on the anniversary of independence from Britain. (RDA)

M Ramadan or Ramzan (first day approximately Aug 1, 2011; July 20, 2012; July 9, 2013; June 28, 2014; June 18, 2015): The holy month during which Muslims may not eat, drink, smoke or have sex from sunrise to sunset.

Aug–Sept (Bhadrapada)

H Kajli Teej (3 Bhadrapada; Aug 15, 2011; Aug 4, 2012; Aug 22, 2013; Aug 12, 2014; Aug 31, 2015): Bundi's celebration of Teej, half a month later than everyone else's.

H Janmashtami (8 Bhadrapada; Sept 2, 2010; Aug 22, 2011; Aug 10, 2012; Aug 28, 2013; Aug 17 2014; Sept 5, 2015): Krishna's birthday, an occasion for fasting and celebration, especially in Agra. (RDA)

M Id ul-Fitr (approximately Sept 9, 2010; Aug 30, 2011; Aug 19, 2012; Aug 8, 2013; July 28, 2014; July 17, 2015): Feast to celebrate the end of Ramadan, after 28 days of fasting. Fatehpur Sikri is one of the best places to celebrate this. (RDA)

Sept–Oct (Ashvina)

H Dussehra (9–10 Ashvina; Oct 15, 2010; Oct 4, 2011; Oct 22, 2012; Oct 12, 2013; Oct 2, 2014; Oct 21, 2015): Two days' public holiday (with an eight-day run-up) associated with vanquishing demons, in particular Rama's victory over Ravana in the Ramayana, and Durga's over the buffalo-headed Mahishasura. Dussehra celebrations include performances of the *Ram Lila* (life of Rama). Celebrated particularly in Kota and Alwar. (RDA)

H Marwar Festival (14–15 Ashvina): Music and dance festival celebrated in the region around Jodhpur.

N Mahatma Gandhi's Birthday (Oct 2): Solemn commemoration of Independent India's founding father. (RDA)

Oct–Nov (Kartika)

M Id ul-Zuha or Bakr Id (10 Duhl-Hijja; approximately Nov 16, 2010; Nov 6, 2011; Oct 26, 2012; Oct 15, 2013; Oct 4, 2014; Sept 23, 2015): Pilgrimage festival to commemorate Abraham's preparedness to sacrifice his son Ismail. Celebrated with slaughtering and consumption of sheep. (RDA)

N Pushkar Camel Fair (7–15 Kartika; Nov 13, 2010; Nov 2, 2011; Nov 20, 2012; Nov 9, 2013; Oct 30, 2014; Nov 18, 2015): Camel herders don their finest attire for this massive livestock market on the fringes of the Thar Desert.

H Chandrabhaga Fair (14 Kartika): Held by the Chandrabhaga River at Jhalawar, pilgrims come to bathe while cattle are brought to be traded.

H Diwali or Deepavali (15 Kartika; Oct 26, 2011; Nov 13, 2012; Nov 3, 2013; Oct 23, 2014; Nov 11, 2015): Festival of lights, and India's biggest, to celebrate Rama and Sita's homecoming in the Ramayana. Festivities include the lighting of oil lamps and firecrackers, and the giving and receiving of sweets and gifts. Diwali coincides with Kali Puja, celebrated in temples dedicated to the wrathful goddess. (RD one day; A two days)

J Jain New Year (15 Kartika): Coincides with Diwali, so Jains celebrate alongside Hindus.

S Nanak Jayanti (16 Kartika): Guru Nanak's birthday marked by prayer readings and processions. (RDA)

Nov–Dec (Margashirsha, or Agrahayana)

M Muslim New Year (1 Muharram; approximately Dec 7, 2010; Nov 26, 2011; Nov 15, 2012; Nov 5, 2013; Oct 25, 2014; Oct 14, 2015).

M Ashura (10 Muharram; approximately Dec 16, 2010; Dec 5, 2011; Nov 24, 2012; Nov 14, 2013; Nov 3, 2014; Oct 23, 2015): Festival to commemorate the martyrdom of the (Shi'ite) Imam, the Prophet's grandson and popular saint, Hussain. (RDA)

Dec–Jan (Pausa)

C Christmas Day (Dec 25): Birth of Jesus. (RDA)

N Bikaner Camel Festival (14 Pausa; Jan 18, 2011; Jan 8, 2012; Jan 26, 2013; Jan 15, 2014; Jan 4, 2015): Camels dressed up in colourful costumes, ridden by proud Rajasthanis in all their finery.

Sports and outdoor activities

Camel trekking

The way to experience the desert in style is from the top of a camel. The one-humped Arabian camel, or dromedary, common in desert regions of Rajasthan, is well adapted to the terrain, with long double eyelashes to keep sand out of its eyes, nostrils that it can close, and broad, soft, padded feet that are ideal for walking on sand. Riding on a camel is smoother than riding on a horse because the camel moves its left and then right legs together, rather than front and then back legs like a horse, giving it a more rolling gait. They are usually docile, good-tempered animals, but the male goes into rut in spring, when it becomes rather grumpy and can kick and bite, and spit its regurgitated stomach contents in anger.

Camel treks can be arranged at Jaisalmer (see p.289), Bikaner (see p.300), Khuhri (see p.295) and also at Mandawa in Shekhawati (see p.223). In fact, arriving in Jaisalmer, you can barely move for touts trying to sell you a camel safari, but dodgy operators abound, so beware.

Some treks stick to the beaten track, and take you to the popular tourist sights. Others specialize in heading off deep into the desert for a feeling of isolation and remoteness. Typically, camel treks include two days in the saddle and a night spent camping in the desert, but you can opt for longer or shorter trips. For more on camel trekking, see box, p.289 & p.300.

Horseriding

Udaipur is Rajasthan's main centre for horse-riding, followed by Mount Abu, while several places in Shekhawati, Udaipur (see p.327) and around Bundi also offer horseriding activities. Other places include Rohet Garh near Jodhpur (see p.271) and Roop Niwas in Nawalgarh (see p.215); the same company also offers horse safari packages (see Ⓦwww.royalridingholidays.com), as do Equitours in the US (Ⓦwww.ridingtours.com).

Spectator sports

Cricket is by far the most popular spectator sport in India, and a fine example of how something quintessentially British (well, English) has become something quintessentially Indian. Travellers to India will find it hard to get away from the game – it's everywhere. Expectations are high and disappointments acute; India versus Pakistan matches are especially emotive.

Test matches are a rare event, so if you want to see a game live, interstate cricket is your best bet. States (plus some city and occupational teams) compete between October and March for the Ranji Trophy, the country's most prestigious award, equivalent to England's County Championship or Australia's Pura Cup.

Horse racing can be a good day out, especially if you enjoy a flutter. The course at Delhi has races every Tuesday (see p.137). Other spectator sports include **polo**, originally from upper Kashmir, but taken up by the British to become one of the symbols of the Raj. A number of Rajasthani cities, including Jodhpur and Mount Abu, still have polo grounds, as does Delhi, and the sport remains hugely popular among upper-class Rajasthanis. The Maharaja of Jodhpur's website (ⓦ www.maharajajodhpur.com) has a section devoted to polo.

Golf is extremely popular and relatively inexpensive in India, and Delhi has several golf courses and plenty of enthusiasts.

One indigenous sport you may see is **kabadi**, played on a small (badminton-sized) court, and informally on any suitable open area. The game, with seven players in each team, consists of a player from each team alternately attempting to "tag" as many members of the opposing team as possible in the space of a single breath (cheating is impossible; the player has to maintain a continuous chant of kabadikabadikabadikabadi etc), and getting back to his/her own side of the court without being caught. The game can get quite rough, with slaps and kicks in tagging allowed, and the defending team must try to tackle and pin the attacker so as not to allow him or her to even touch the dividing line. Tagged victims are required to leave the court. Although still an amateur sport, kabadi is taken very seriously with state and national championships, and now features in the Asian Games.

Popular with devotees of the monkey god, Hanuman, Indian **wrestling**, or **kushti**, has a small but dedicated following. Wrestlers are known as *pahalwaans* or "strong men" and can sometimes be seen exercising early in the morning with clubs and weights along river ghats.

Crime and personal safety

In spite of the crushing poverty and the yawning gulf between rich and poor, India is, on the whole, a safe country to travel in, and that includes not only Rajasthan and Agra, but also Delhi, despite its size and metropolitan character. As a tourist, however, you are an obvious target for thieves (who may include some of your fellow travellers), and stand to face serious problems if you do lose your passport, money and ticket home. Common sense, therefore, suggests a few precautions.

If you can tolerate the encumbrance, carry valuables in a money belt or a pouch around your neck at all times. In the latter case, the cord should be hidden under your clothing and not be easy to cut through. Beware of **crowded locations**, such as packed buses or trains, in which it is easy for pickpockets to operate – slashing pockets or bags with razor blades is not unheard of, and even itching powder is sometimes used to distract the unwary. Thieves often work in teams, one member distracting your attention – for example by bumping into you – while another swipes your bag. In hotels, don't leave valuables lying around in your room. Upmarket establishments will have a room safe; budget hotels will often have a safe at reception to keep them in.

A **padlock** can be used to secure the doors of cheap hotel rooms, and you can also use them to lock your bag to seats or racks in trains. Don't put valuables in your

Drugs

Rajasthan, and particularly the region around Chittaurgarh and Kota, is a major centre for the legitimate production of **opium**, which is used to make medicines for the pharmaceutical industry. Traditional use of opium is ingrained in Rajasthani culture: Rajputs used to take a dose before battle to assuage fear, or in case of injury or pain; their wives took it before committing *sati*. Even today, in many Rajasthani villages, opium is commonly offered as a sign of hospitality. The drug makes you drowsy, and is pleasurable but addictive. If you are offered some on a village tour and don't want to fall under its effects, you could accept a very small token crumb of it just to be polite, though it is of course illegal and you are quite within your rights to refuse it outright. In Rajasthan, it is not smoked, but drunk in the form of a tea. It is also used medicinally. Some people do become addicts, and opium addiction can be a social problem, particularly if the family's main bread-winner spends all his income on the drug and all his time under its influence. Heroin ("brown sugar") is not widespread in rural communities, but it's an increasing problem among the urban poor. In central Delhi particularly, you may well see homeless people smoking it on the street.

Cannabis comes in three forms. **Bhang** (marijuana leaf, usually boiled and pounded) is used in religious celebrations and is legal. It is most commonly stirred into drinks, though it can also be made into sweets, and it is sold in licensed bhang shops at several places in Rajasthan. Cafés and restaurants in places like Pushkar and Udaipur may also serve bhang lassis. Because of its legal status, you may be tempted to try bhang, but if you are not used to the effects of cannabis, beware: the drug does not agree with everybody, and when eaten (bhang is not usually smoked), the dosage is notoriously difficult to gauge, and the effects can last for some hours, occasionally causing intense paranoia and psychological distress. Also be aware that potentially dangerous adulterants such as datura or even tranquillizer pills are sometimes added to bhang drinks to increase their effect.

The other two varieties of cannabis – **ganja** (marijuana bud) and **charas** (cannabis resin, hashish) – are generally mixed with tobacco and smoked in a pipe called a chillum, which was originally the bowl of a hookah. Both drugs are illegal, though sadhus (religious mendicants) are allowed to smoke ganja as part of their religious devotion to Shiva, who is himself apparently partial to a smoke.

Aside from such religious use, and the festive consumption of bhang, the use of cannabis is considered a low-life habit (if you see anyone in a movie smoking a chillum, you can be sure it's the baddie), and the **law** against it is harsh. Anyone arrested with less than five grams that they can prove is for their own use is liable to a maximum of six months in prison, but cases can take years to come to trial (two is normal, and eight not unheard of). For more than five grams, you can expect a hefty prison sentence. "Paying a fine now" may be possible on arrest (though it will probably mean all the money you have), but once you are booked in at the station, your chances are slim; most of the foreigners languishing in Indian jails are there on drugs charges. Police raids on budget hotels in Delhi's Paharganj area are not unknown (though we haven't heard of any in recent years), and in Pushkar, where hippy tourism is still the order of the day, the police also keep a sharp eye out. If you are arrested, expect no sympathy from your consulate. Best advice is to steer clear of all illegal drugs including charas and ganja.

luggage for bus or plane journeys: keep them with you at all times. If your baggage is on the roof of a bus, make sure it is well secured. On trains and buses, the prime time for theft is just before you leave, so keep a particular eye on your gear then, beware of deliberate diversions, and don't put your belongings next to open windows. Druggings leading to theft and worse are rare but not unheard of, and so you are best advised to politely **refuse food and drink** from fellow passengers or passing strangers, unless you are completely confident it's the family picnic you are sharing or have seen the food purchased from a vendor.

However, don't get paranoid; the best way to enjoy your visit is to stay relaxed but have your wits about you. Crime levels in India are a long way below those of Western countries, and violent crime against tourists in Rajasthan, Delhi and Agra is extremely rare. Few of the people who approach you on the street intend any harm: most want to sell you something (though this is not always made apparent immediately), some want to practise their English, others (if you're a woman) to chat you up, while more than a few just want to add your address to their book or have a picture taken with you. Just a few (especially around Connaught Place in Delhi) are touts trying to lure you into an overcharging travel agent's office or (and this includes anyone offering wonderful-sounding moneymaking schemes) work some con on you.

If you do feel threatened, it's worth looking for help. Tourism police are found sitting in clearly marked booths in main railway stations, some bus stations and major tourist centres throughout Rajasthan, and in Delhi and Agra.

Be wary of **credit card fraud**; a credit card can be used to make duplicate forms to which your account is then billed for fictitious transactions, so don't let shops or restaurants take your card away to process – insist they do it in front of you or follow them to the point of transaction.

It's not a bad idea to keep US$100 or so separately from the rest of your money, along with your travellers' cheque receipts, insurance policy number and phone number for claims, and a photocopy of the pages in your passport containing personal data and your Indian visa. This will cover you in case you do lose all your valuables.

If the worst happens and you get robbed, the first thing to do is **report the theft** as soon as possible to the local police. They are very unlikely to recover your belongings, but you need a report from them in order to claim on your travel insurance. Dress smartly when you go to the police, and expect an uphill battle – city cops in particular tend to be jaded from too many insurance and travellers' cheque scams.

Losing your passport is a real hassle, but does not necessarily mean the end of your trip. First, report the loss immediately to the police, who will issue you with the all-important "complaint form" that you need to be able to travel around and check into hotels, as well as claim back any expenses incurred in replacing your passport from your insurer. A complaint form, however, will not allow you to change money or travellers' cheques. If you've run out of cash, your best bet is to ask your hotel manager to help you out (staff will have seen your passport when you checked in, and the number will be in the register). The next thing to do is telephone your nearest embassy or consulate in the region. Normally, passports have to be applied for and collected in person, but if you are stranded, it is usually possible to arrange to receive the necessary forms in the post. However, you still have to go to the embassy or consulate to pick up your new passport. "Emergency passports" are the cheapest form of replacement, but are normally only valid for the few days of your return flight. If you're not sure when you're leaving the country, you'll have to obtain a more costly "full passport" from your country's embassy in Delhi.

Culture and etiquette

Western visitors will find that cultural differences in India extend to all sorts of things. While allowances will usually be made for foreigners, those unacquainted with Indian customs may need a little preparation to avoid causing offence or making fools of themselves. The list here is hardly exhaustive: when in doubt, watch what Indian people are doing and follow suit.

Eating and the right-hand rule

In Rajasthan, Delhi and Agra, cutlery is usually supplied in eating places, but sometimes you may have to eat the traditional way – with your fingers. In such cases, the rule is that you should **eat with your right hand only**. In India, as right across Asia, the left hand is for wiping your bottom, cleaning your feet and other unsavoury functions (you also put on and take off your shoes with your left hand), while the right hand is for eating, shaking hands, and so on.

People nowadays, especially in Delhi, don't tend to be too strict about this (washing hands before and after eating is more of an issue), but especially in rural areas, it is best to follow the rule. While you can certainly hold a cup or utensil in your left hand, and use both hands to tear your chapati, you should not pass food or put it into your mouth with your left hand. Best to keep it out of sight below the table.

In theory, this rule extends beyond food too. In general, it is best to avoid passing things to people with your left hand, or pointing at people with it, and the same applies to putting it in your mouth.

The other rule to beware of when eating or drinking is that your lips should not touch other people's food – *jhuta* or sullied food is strictly taboo. Don't, for example, take a bite out of a chapati and pass it on. When drinking out of a cup or bottle to be shared with others, don't let it touch your lips, but rather pour it directly into your mouth. It is customary to wash your hands before and after eating.

Temples and religion

Religion is taken very seriously in India; it's important always to show due respect to religious buildings, shrines, images, and people at prayer. When entering a temple or mosque, remove your shoes and leave them at the door (socks are acceptable). Some temples – Jain ones in particular – do not allow you to enter wearing or carrying leather articles, and forbid entry to menstruating women. Sikh temples do not allow you to enter with alcohol, tobacco or any other drug, and a couple of Hindu temples in Delhi that are popular with tourists require you to deposit cameras and mobile phones at the entrance. When entering a religious establishment, dress conservatively (see below), and try not to be obtrusive.

In a mosque, you won't normally be allowed in at prayer time and women are sometimes not allowed in at all. In a Hindu temple, non-Hindus may be asked not to enter the inner sanctum, and it is not usually permitted to take **photographs** of images of deities inside temples. Indeed, it's best not to wield your camera inside a temple at all without at least checking with someone beforehand. In some cases you will have to leave your camera at the door, so it may be best not to bring it with you. Never take photos of funerals or cremations.

Dress

Some Indian people can be quite conservative about **dress**. This is not so much true in cities, and particularly among the upper and middle classes, but in the countryside women usually dress modestly, with legs and shoulders covered. Trousers are acceptable for women, but wearing shorts and short skirts is rather risqué – no problem in a Delhi nightclub perhaps, but definitely not the done thing if visiting a village in rural Rajasthan, while men should not wander around in public without a shirt. These rules go double in temples and mosques. Cover your head with a cap or cloth when entering a *dargah* (Sufi shrine) or Sikh *gurudwara*; women in particular are also required to cover their limbs. Men are similarly expected to dress appropriately with their legs and head covered. Caps are usually available on loan, often free, for visitors, and sometimes cloth is available to cover up your arms and legs.

In general, Indians find it hard to understand why rich Westerners should wander round in ragged clothes or imitate the lowest ranks of Indian society, who would love to have something more decent to wear. Staying well groomed and dressing "respectably" vastly improves the impression you make on local people, and reduces sexual harassment too.

Drinking and smoking

While lots of Indian men smoke anything from bidis to chillums, it is not the done thing for women to smoke, especially in public, and doing so will give a very bad impression, and lead some to regard you as a loose woman, which means a potential target for harassment.

Drinking alcohol is also to some extent considered a low-life occupation, for members of both sexes, but especially for women. This is not so much the case at the upper end of the market – and in Delhi particularly, you will find plenty of upmarket bars where both men and women can quite happily drink without fear of opprobrium – but women in particular do not frequent low-class bars if they are respectable, and this is especially true in Rajasthan, where hotel bars are usually your best bet if you are female.

Other possible gaffes

Kissing and **embracing** are regarded in India as part of sex: do not do them in public. In more conservative areas (ie outside westernized parts of big cities), it is not even a good idea for couples to hold hands, though Indian men can sometimes be seen holding hands as a sign of "brotherliness".

Be aware of your **feet**. When entering a private home, you should normally remove your shoes (follow your host's example); when sitting, avoid pointing the soles of your feet at anyone. Accidental contact with one's foot is always followed by an apology.

Meeting people

Westerners have an ambiguous status in Indian eyes. In one way, they represent the rich sahib, whose culture dominates the world, and the old colonial mentality has not completely disappeared. On the other hand, as non-Hindu, they are outcaste, their presence in theory polluting to an orthodox or high-caste Hindu, while to members of all religions, Western morals and standards of spiritual and physical cleanliness are suspect.

As a traveller, you will constantly come across people who want to strike up a **conversation**. English not being their first language, they may not be familiar with the conventional ways of doing this, and thus their opening line may seem abrupt if at the same time very formal. "Excuse me good gentleman, what is your mother country?" is a typical one. Many people will simply come up to you and demand to know your name or nationality, but while this may seem an odd way to begin, they are merely trying to start a conversation. Straight questions about your name, origin, family and occupation are considered polite conversation between strangers in India, and help people place one another in terms of social position. Indian English can be very formal and even ceremonious. Indian people may well call you "sir" or "madam", even "good lady" or "kind sir". At the same time, you should be aware that your English may seem rude to them. In particular, swearing is taken rather seriously in India, and casual use of the F-word is likely to shock.

Things that Indian people are likely to find strange about you are lack of religion (you could adopt one), travelling alone, leaving your family to come to India, being an unmarried couple (letting people think you are married can make life easier), and travelling second class or staying in cheap hotels when, as a foreign tourist, you are obviously relatively rich. You will probably end up having to explain the same things many times to many different people; on the other hand, you can ask questions too, so you could take it as an opportunity to ask things you want to know about India. English-speaking Indians, and members of the large and growing middle class in particular, are usually extremely well informed and well educated, and often far more *au fait* with world affairs than Westerners.

Sexism and women's issues

India is not a country that provides huge obstacles to women travellers. In the days of the Raj, upper-class eccentrics started a tradition of lone women travellers, taken up enthusiastically by the flower children of the hippy era. Plenty of women keep up the tradition today, but few get through their trip without any hassle, and it's good to prepare yourself to be a little bit thick-skinned.

Indian streets are almost without exception male-dominated – something that may take a bit of getting used to, particularly if you find yourself subjected to incessant staring, whistling and name calling. This can usually be stopped by ignoring the gaze and quickly moving on, or by firmly telling the offender to stop looking at you. Most of your fellow travellers on trains and buses will be men, who may start up most unwelcome conversations about sex, divorce and the freedom of relationships in the West. These cannot often be avoided, but demonstrating too much enthusiasm to discuss such topics can lure men into thinking that you are easy about sex, and the situation could become threatening. At its worst in larger cities, all this can become very tiring. You can get round it to a certain extent by joining women in public places, and you'll notice an immense difference if you join up with a male travelling companion. In this case, expect Indian men to approach him (assumed, of course, to be your husband – an assumption it is sometimes advantageous to go along with) and talk to him about you quite happily as if you were not there. Beware, however, if you are (or look) Indian with a non-Indian male companion: this may well cause you harassment, as you might be seen to have brought shame on your family by adopting the loose morals of the West.

In addition to staring and suggestive comments and looks, **sexual harassment**, or "Eve teasing" as it is bizarrely known, is likely to be a nuisance, but not generally a threat. Expect to get groped in crowds, and to have men "accidentally" squeeze past you at any opportunity. It tends to be worse in cities than in small towns and villages, but anywhere being followed can be a real problem.

In time you'll learn to gauge a situation – sometimes wandering around on your own may attract so much unwanted attention that you may prefer to stay in one place until you've recharged your batteries or your male fan club has moved on. It's always best to dress modestly – a *salwar kameez* is perfect, as is any baggy clothing – and refrain from smoking and drinking in public, which only reinforces prejudices that Western women are "loose" and "easy".

Returning an unwanted touch with a punch or slap is perfectly in order (Indian women often become aggressive when offended), and does serve to vent a little frustration. It should also attract attention and urge someone to help you, or at least deal with the offending man – a man transgressing social norms is always out of line, and any passer-by will want to let him know it. If you feel someone getting too close in a crowd or on a bus, taking off and brandishing your left shoe in his face can be very effective.

To go and watch a Bollywood movie at the cinema is a fun and essential part of your trip to India but, at cheap cinemas especially, such an occasion is rarely without hassle. If you do go to the cinema, it's best to go to an upmarket theatre, or at least to go with a group of people and sit in the balcony area, where it's a bit more expensive but the crowd is much more sedate.

Violent sexual assaults on tourists are extremely rare, but the number of reported cases of rape is rising, and you should always take precautions: avoid quiet, dimly lit streets and alleys at night; if you find a trustworthy rickshaw/taxi driver in the day, keep him for the night journey; and try to get someone to accompany you to your hotel whenever possible. While Indian women are still quite timid about reporting rape – it is considered as much a disgrace to the victim as to the perpetrator – Western victims should always report it to the police, and before leaving the area try to let other tourists, or locals, know, in the hope that pressure from the community may uncover the offender and see him brought to justice.

In Delhi there's a police helpline for women in distress (☎1091 or 011/2331 7004), and a special police unit to deal with crimes against women, and the women's organization JAGORI lists Delhi helpline numbers on their website at ⓦjagori.org/resources /helplines. Rajasthan does not have such resources, but if you prefer to contact a women's group rather than go straight to the police, you could try VIVIDHA on ☎0141/276 2932.

The **practicalities of travel** take on a new dimension for lone women travellers. Often you can turn your gender to your advantage. For example, on intercity buses the driver and conductor will often take you under their wing, and there will be countless other instances of kindness wherever you travel. You'll be more welcome in some private houses than a group of Western males, and may find yourself learning the finer points of Indian cooking round the family's clay stove. Women frequently get preference at bus and railway stations where they can join a separate "ladies' queue", and use ladies' waiting rooms. On overnight trains the enclosed ladies' compartments are peaceful havens (unless filled with noisy children); you could also try to share a berth section with a family where you are usually drawn into the security of the group and are less exposed to lusty gazes. In hotels watch out for "peep-holes" in your door (and in the common bathrooms), and be sure to cover your window when changing and when sleeping.

Lastly, bring your own supply of **tampons**, which are not widely available outside main cities.

Toilets

A visit to the loo is not one of India's more pleasant experiences: toilets can be filthy and stink. They are also major potential breeding grounds for disease. And then there is the squatting position to get used to; the traditional Asian toilet has a hole in the ground and two small platforms for the feet, instead of a seat. Paper, if used, often goes in a bucket next to the loo rather than down it. Indians use instead a jug of water and their left hand, a method you may also come to prefer, but if you do use paper, keep some handy – it isn't usually supplied, and it might

be an idea to stock up before going too far off the beaten track as it is not available everywhere. Travelling is especially difficult for women as facilities are limited or nonexistent, especially when travelling by road. However, toilets in the air-conditioned carriages of trains are usually kept clean, as are those in mid-range restaurants. In tourist areas, most hotels offer Western-style loos, even in budget lodges.

Baksheesh

As a presumed-rich sahib or memsahib, you will, like wealthy Indians, be expected to be liberal with the **baksheesh**, which takes three main forms.

The most common is **tipping**: a small reward for a small service, which can encompass anyone from a waiter or porter to someone who lifts your bags onto the roof of a bus or keeps an eye on your vehicle for you. Large amounts are not expected – ten rupees should satisfy all the aforementioned. Taxi drivers and staff at cheaper hotels and restaurants do not necessarily expect tips, but always appreciate them, of course, and they can keep people sweet for the next time you call. Some may take liberties in demanding baksheesh, but it's often better just to acquiesce rather than spoil your mood and cause offence over trifling sums.

More expensive than plain tipping is paying people to **bend the rules**, many of which seem to have been invented for precisely that purpose. Examples might include letting you into a historical site after hours, finding you a seat or a sleeper on a train that is "full", or speeding up some bureaucratic process. This should not be confused with bribery, a more serious business with its own risks and etiquette, which is best not entered into.

The last kind of baksheesh is **alms giving**. In a country without a welfare system, this is an important social custom. People with disabilities and mutilations are the traditional recipients, and it seems right to join local people in giving out small change to them. Kids demanding money, pens, sweets or the like are a different case, pressing their demands only on tourists. In return for a service it is fair enough, but to yield to any request encourages them to go and pester others.

Shopping

So many beautiful and exotic souvenirs are on sale in Rajasthan, Delhi and Agra, at such low prices, that it's sometimes hard to know what to buy first. On top of that, all sorts of things (such as made-to-measure clothes) that would be vastly expensive at home are much more reasonably priced here. Even if you lose weight during your trip, your baggage might well put on quite a bit – unless of course you post some of it home.

Rajasthan in particular is well blessed with all kinds of wonderful crafts, while Delhi, as the nation's capital, has emporiums full of goods from all over India, and also from neighbouring countries such as Tibet. For more information on shopping in Rajasthan, see the *Rajasthani crafts* colour section.

Where to shop

Quite a few items sold in tourist areas are made elsewhere and, needless to say, it's more fun (and cheaper) to pick them up at source. Best buys are noted in the relevant sections of the Guide, along with a few specialities that can't be found outside their regions. India is awash with **street hawkers**, often very young kids. Although they can be annoying and should be dealt with firmly if you are not interested, do not write them off completely as they sometimes have decent souvenirs at lower than shop prices and are open to hard bargaining.

Virtually all the state governments in India run handicraft "**emporiums**", and most of them have branches in Delhi, where there is also a **Central Cottage Industries Emporium** (Ⓦ www.cottageemporium.in), selling goods made by artisans from across India. Goods in these places are generally of a high quality, even if their fixed prices are a little expensive, and they are worth a visit to get an idea of what crafts are available and how much they should cost.

Rajasthan is particularly known for its textiles, but there's also the blue ceramicware of Jaipur, as well as jewellery, miniature paintings and leatherware. In **Agra**, the top souvenir is marble inlay work in the same style as that in the Taj Mahal. The *Rajasthani crafts* colour section has more

detail about what's available in the way of arts and crafts, but there are plenty of more everyday goods that are worth buying, including books (cheaper here than at home), DVDs (especially Hindi films with English subtitles), Bollywood film posters, stainless-steel tiffin boxes, tea from Assam or Darjeeling, spices, essential oils and joss sticks.

Buying metals and gemstones

Among precious metals, **silver** is generally a better buy than gold but is difficult to distinguish from cheap white metal often palmed off as silver in curio shops. **Gold** is usually 22 carat and very yellow, but relatively expensive due to taxes (smuggling from the Gulf to evade them is rife) and to its popularity as a form of investment – women traditionally keep their wealth in this form, and a bride's jewellery is an important part of her dowry. Silver varies in quality, but is usually reasonably priced, with silver jewellery generally heavier and rather more folksy than gold. Gold and silver are usually sold by weight, the workmanship costing very little.

Buying **gemstones** can be something of a minefield; scams abound, and you would be most unwise to even consider buying gems for resale or as an investment without a basic knowledge of the trade. That said, some precious and semiprecious stones can be a good buy in Rajasthan, particularly those which are indigenous to India, such as garnets, black stars and moonstones. Jaipur is a major centre for gems, but also for con tricks, so tread carefully.

Finally, things **not to bring home** include ivory and anything made from a rare or protected species, including snakeskin and turtle products. As for drugs, don't even think about it.

Bargaining

Whatever you buy (except food and cigarettes), you will almost always be expected to **haggle** over the price. Bargaining is very much a matter of personal style, but should always be lighthearted, never acrimonious. There are no hard and fast rules – it's really a question of how much something is worth to you. It's a good plan, therefore, to have an idea of how much you want to pay. Bid low and let the shopkeeper argue you up. If he'll settle for your price or less, you have a deal. If not, you don't, but you've had a pleasant conversation and no harm is done.

Don't worry too much about the first quoted prices. Some people suggest paying a third of the opening price, but it really depends on the shop, the goods and the shopkeeper's impression of you. You may not be able to get the seller much below the first quote; on the other hand, you may end up paying as little as a tenth of it. If you bid too low, you may be hustled out of the shop for offering an "insulting" price, but this is all part of the game, and you'll no doubt be welcomed as an old friend if you return the next day.

"Green" tourists are easily spotted, so try and look like you know what you are up to, even on your first day, or leave it till later; you could wait and see what the going rate is first.

Haggling is a little bit like bidding in an auction, and similar rules apply. Don't start haggling for something if you know you don't want it, and never let any figure pass your lips that you are not prepared to pay – having mentioned a price, you are obliged to pay it. If the seller asks you how much you would pay for something, and you don't want it, say so.

Sometimes rickshaw-wallahs and taxi drivers stop unasked at shops; they get a small commission simply for bringing customers. In places like Jaipur and Agra where this is common practice, tourists sometimes even strike a deal with their drivers – agreeing to stop at five shops and splitting the commission for the time wasted. If you're taken to a shop by a tout or driver and you buy something, you pay around fifty percent extra. Stand firm about not entering shops and getting to your destination if you have no appetite for such shenanigans. If you want a bargain, shop alone, and never let anybody on the street take you to a shop – if you do, they'll be getting a commission, and you'll be paying it.

Travelling with children

Indians are very tolerant of children so you can take them almost anywhere without restriction, and they always help break the ice with strangers, but the attention they receive can be relentless, and sometimes a problem in itself.

Foreign children in some parts of India can be a novelty, and lots of people will want to pick them up and have their picture taken with them. This is especially the case in places where foreigners are less common. Often, these approaches can be extremely intrusive; people may simply pick up your child without asking permission. If your child is comfortable with it, then you may as well go with the flow, but if not, then you will need to be firm, and preferably avoid crowds and perhaps less touristy places.

Extra protection is needed from the sun, unsafe drinking water, heat and unfamiliar food. Chilli in food may also be a problem, if they're not used to it. Remember, too, that diarrhoea, perhaps just a nuisance to you, could be dangerous for a child: rehydration salts (see p.38) are vital if your child goes down with it. Make sure, if possible, that your child is aware of the dangers of rabies; keep them away from animals, and consider a rabies jab before you go. Children should also be made aware that monkeys can be dangerous if teased.

For babies, **nappies** (diapers) are available in most large towns at similar prices to the West, but it's worth taking an additional pack in case of emergencies, and bringing sachets of Calpol, which aren't easily available in India. A changing mat is another necessity. And if your baby is on powdered milk, it might be an idea to bring some of that: you can certainly get it in India, but it may not taste the same. Dried baby food could also be worth

taking – any café or chai-wallah should be able to supply you with boiled water.

For touring, hiking or walking, child-carrier backpacks are ideal; some even come with mozzie nets these days. When it comes to **luggage**, bring as little as possible. If your child is small enough, a fold-up buggy is also well worth packing, even if you no longer use a buggy at home, as kids tire so easily in the heat.

On Indian Railways, children under five **travel free**, and those aged between five and twelve pay half the adult fare. On a plane, children under twelve pay half fare, unless they are under two and sharing a seat with an adult, in which case they pay ten percent of the adult fare.

Travel essentials

Costs

For visitors to Rajasthan, Delhi and Agra, a little foreign currency can go a long way.

The costs we give below are only an approximation of what you can expect to spend on a daily basis. On a good day, you may spend very little, but it's always worth making room for unexpected expenses, such as the odd splurge, or buying souvenirs.

As a foreigner in the region, you are penalized by double-tier entry prices to museums and historic sites as well as in upmarket hotels, all of which are levied at a higher rate and in dollars. Even at the lower end of the market, you will generally be paying more for goods and services than Indian people would pay. Some tourists resent this, but to be fair, even a budget traveller is far better off than most Indians, and it's worth bearing this in mind and accepting the surcharge with good grace.

What you spend depends on where you are: Delhi is rather more expensive than most places for both accommodation and food. Pushkar, on the other hand, is cheaper, particularly for accommodation. On a budget

of as little as Rs800 (US$17/£10.50/€12) per day, you'll manage if you stay in cheap budget accommodation, eat in local *dhabas* and don't move about too much. On Rs1500 ($32/£20/€22) a day, you'll be able to afford mid-range hotels, as well as meals in smarter restaurants, regular rickshaw or taxi rides and entrance fees to monuments. If you're happy spending around Rs2000 (US$42.50/£26.50/€30) per day, however, you can really pamper yourself; to spend much more than that, you'd have to be doing a lot of air-conditioned travelling, flying instead of taking trains, staying in swish hotels and eating in top restaurants.

Generally speaking, you can usually find an inexpensive hotel for around Rs250 (US$5.30/£3.30/€3.70) per person per night, and a basic veg meal for less than half that, while a mid-range hotel will cost around Rs750 (US$16/£10/€11) per person and a good meal in a moderately priced restaurant shouldn't set you back much more, even if you throw in a beer or two. Even in a classy restaurant, you'll be hard pushed to pay more than Rs1500 for a meal. Bear in mind that service is often added to the bill (usually ten percent), along with 12.5 percent VAT. For typical transport costs, see box, p.28.

If service isn't included, ten percent is an acceptable **tip** in a restaurant. Tourists usually tip taxi drivers and auto- or rickshaw-wallahs, often very generously, but it should not be expected, and certainly not demanded. In a hotel, you might tip the porter Rs10–20.

Disabled travellers

Disability is common in India; many conditions that would be curable in the West, such as cataracts, are permanent disabilities here because people can't afford the treatment. Disabled people are unlikely to get jobs, and the choice is usually between staying at home to be looked after by your family, and going out on the street to beg for alms.

For the **disabled traveller**, this has its advantages and disadvantages: disability doesn't get the same embarrassed reaction from Indian people that it does from some able-bodied Westerners. On the other hand, you'll be lucky to see a state-of-the-art wheelchair or a disabled loo, and the streets are full of all sorts of obstacles that would be hard for a blind or wheelchair-bound tourist to negotiate independently. Kerbs are often high, pavements uneven and littered, and ramps nonexistent. There are potholes all over the place and open sewers. Some of the more expensive hotels have ramps for the movement of luggage and equipment, but if that makes them accessible to wheelchairs, it is by accident rather than design. Nonetheless, the 1995 Persons with Disabilities Act specifies access for all to public buildings, and is sometimes enforced. A visit to Delhi by the wheelchair-bound astrophysicist Stephen Hawking resulted in the appearance of ramps at several Delhi tourist sights including the Red Fort, Qutub Minar and Jantar Mantar. Following a 1997 court case, Delhi airport has also been made a lot more accessible for chair users. Meanwhile, Delhi's new metro system has been deliberately designed for accessibility, and has step-free access from street to platform at every station.

If you walk with difficulty, you will find India's many street obstacles and steep stairs hard going. Another factor that can be a problem is the constant barrage of people proffering things (hard to wave aside if you are, for instance, on crutches), and all that queuing, not to mention heat, will take it out of you if you have a condition that makes you tire quickly. A light, folding camp-stool is one thing that could be invaluable if you have limited walking or standing power.

Then again, Indian people are likely to be very helpful if, for example, you need their help getting on and off buses or up stairs. Taxis and rickshaws are easily affordable and very adaptable; if you rent one for a day, the driver is certain to help you on and off, and perhaps even around the sites you visit. If you employ a guide, they may also be prepared to help you with steps and obstacles.

If complete independence is out of the question, going with an able-bodied companion might be on the cards. Contact a specialist organization for further advice on planning your trip. In Delhi, Timeless India (T011/2617 4205 or 4206, W www.timeless excursions.com) offers accessible tours for wheelchair-bound visitors, which can cover Delhi, Agra and Jaipur. Otherwise, some package tour operators try to cater for travellers with disabilities – Bales and Somak among them – but you should always contact any operator and discuss your exact needs with them before making a booking. You should also make sure you are covered by any insurance policy you take out.

For more information about disability issues in India, check the Disability India Network website at W www.disabilityindia.org.

Electricity

India's electricity supply is 230V 50Hz AC. Most sockets are triple round-pin (accepting European-size double round-pin plugs). British, Irish and Australasian plugs will need an adaptor, preferably universal; American and Canadian appliances may need a transformer too, unless multi-voltage. Power cuts and voltage variations are very common; voltage stabilizers should be used to run sensitive appliances such as laptops.

Gay and lesbian travellers

Homosexuality is not generally open or accepted in India, but in a landmark decision in July 2009, the High Court declared unconstitutional the Victorian ban on gay sex between consenting adults, as a result of which it is now legal. Prejudice is still ingrained however, especially in conservative areas such as Rajasthan.

For **lesbians**, making contacts is difficult; even the Indian women's movement does not readily promote lesbianism as an issue that needs confronting. The only public faces of a hidden scene are the organizations in Delhi listed below. For **gay men**, homosexuality is no longer solely the preserve of the alternative scene of actors and artists, and is increasingly accepted by the upper classes, but Mumbai remains much more a centre for gay life than Delhi, let alone traditionalist Rajasthan. Following the High Court ruling however, there are now gay nights in several Delhi clubs, and *Time Out Delhi* has a section on gay and lesbian events.

One group of people you may come across are **hijras**, who look like transvestites and are accepted as a transitional "third sex" between male and female. Pukka hijras are born with genitals that are neither fully male nor female, but some are eunuchs who undergo castration to become hijras because they are transsexuals (physically male but psychologically female). They live in their own "families" and have a niche in Indian society, but not an easy one. At weddings, their presence is supposed to bring good luck, and they are usually given baksheesh for putting in a brief appearance. Generally, however, they have a low social status, face widespread discrimination, and many make a living by begging or prostitution.

Gay and lesbian contacts and resources

You will need to contact the following places in advance for information as most addresses are PO boxes:

Campaign for Lesbian Rights (CALERI)/Shakhi PO Box 3526, Lajpat Nagar, New Delhi 110065 Ⓔ caleri@hotmail.com. Collective working for lesbian rights.

Gay Delhi Weekly social meetings and other events for gay men in Delhi; for information send a blank email to Ⓔ gaydelhi-subscribe@yahoo.groups.com.

Humsafar Trust Ⓦ www.humsafar.org. Set up to promote safe sex among gay men, but the website has lots of links and up-to-date information.

Indian Dost Ⓦ www.indiandost.com/delhigay.php. The Delhi page of a website for gay men in India.

International Gay and Lesbian Human Rights Commission Ⓦ www.iglhrc.org. Latest news on the human rights situation for gay people worldwide, including regular bulletins on India.

Purple Dragon Lobby of the Tarntawan Place Hotel, 119/5-10 Suriwong Rd, Bangkok 10500, Thailand Ⓣ +662/238-3227, Ⓦ www.purpledrag .com. Thai-based gay-friendly tour operator covering India with tours of Delhi and the "Golden Triangle", and add-ons including Ranthambore and Udaipur.

Sangini PO Box 7532, Vasant Kunj, New Delhi 110070, Ⓦ www.sanginii.org. Lesbian information, support and contacts. Helpline Tuesday noon–3pm and Friday 6–8pm on Ⓣ 011/5567 6450.

Timeless India 215–217 Somdutt Chamber-II, 9 Bhikaji Cama Place, New Delhi 110066 Ⓣ 011/2617 4205 or 6, Ⓦ www.timelessexcursions .com. Tour operator offering a gay-oriented tour of Rajasthan, staying in gay-friendly heritage hotels.

Insurance

In the light of the potential health risks involved in a trip to Rajasthan, Delhi or Agra – see pp.34–40 – travel insurance is too important to ignore.

In addition to covering medical expenses and emergency flights, travel insurance also insures your money and belongings against **loss** or **theft**. Before paying for a new policy, however, it's worth checking whether you are already covered: some all-risks home insurance policies may cover your possessions when overseas, and many private medical schemes include cover when abroad. In Canada, provincial health plans usually provide partial **medical cover** for mishaps overseas, while holders of official student/teacher/youth cards in Canada and the US are entitled to meagre accident coverage and hospital in-patient benefits. Students will often find that their student health coverage extends during the vacations and for one term beyond the date of last enrolment.

Internet

You'll find plenty of **internet** offices in Delhi, Agra, and all major towns in Rajasthan. Charges range from Rs20 to Rs50 per hour for checking mail and browsing, and extra for printing. ISDN broadband connections are increasingly common. A few hotels have

Rough Guides travel insurance

Rough Guides has teamed up with WorldNomads.com to offer great **travel insurance** deals. Policies are available to residents of over 150 countries, with cover for a wide range of **adventure sports**, 24hr emergency assistance, high levels of medical and evacuation cover and a stream of **travel safety information**. Roughguides.com users can take advantage of their policies online 24/7, from anywhere in the world – even if you're already travelling. And since plans often change when you're on the road, you can extend your policy and even claim online. Roughguides.com users who buy travel insurance with WorldNomads.com can also leave a positive footprint and donate to a community development project. For more information go to Ⓦ**www.roughguides.com/shop**.

wi-fi – more expensive places tend to charge for it, but in the few budget hotels that have it, it is usually free.

Laundry

In Rajasthan, Delhi and Agra, no one goes to the laundry: if they don't do their own, they send it out to a dhobi. Wherever you are staying, there will either be an in-house person, or one very close by to call on. The dhobi will take your dirty washing to a dhobi ghat, a public clothes-washing area (the bank of a river, for example), where it is shown some old-fashioned discipline: separated, soaped and given a damn good thrashing to beat the dirt out of it. Then it is hung out to dry in the sun and, once dried, taken to the ironing sheds where every garment is endowed with razor-sharp creases and then matched to its rightful owner by hidden cryptic markings. Your clothes will come back from the dhobi absolutely spotless, though this kind of violent treatment does take it out of them: buttons get lost and eventually the cloth starts to fray. If you'd rather not entrust your Savile Row made-to-measure to their tender mercies, there are dry-cleaners in most main towns.

Living in Delhi, Agra or Rajasthan

It is illegal for a foreign tourist to work in India, and there's no shortage of English teachers, but you may consider doing some voluntary charitable work. Several charities welcome volunteers on a medium-term commitment, say over two months. People visiting India on business or with employment arranged in advance may apply for a business visa, and non-resident Indians are entitled to stay for up to five years.

If you want to spend your time working as a volunteer for an **NGO (Non-Governmental Organization)**, you should make arrangements well before you arrive by contacting the body in question, rather than on spec. Special visas are generally not required unless you intend to work for longer than six months. For information about which NGOs are operating in Rajasthan, Delhi and Agra, log on to Ⓦwww.indianngos.com and select locations from the drop-down list.

It is also possible to study in Delhi as part of an exchange programme.

Charities and NGOs

Animal Aid 6900 37th Ave SW, Seattle, WA 98126, USA; Badi Village, Across from T.B. Hospital. Main Road, Udaipur 313004, Rajasthan ℡0294 251 3359; Ⓦwww.animalaidunlimited.com. Animal welfare group working to alleviate animal suffering in Udaipur (see p.327). No special skills are required, though volunteers with veterinary knowledge are especially welcome.

Concern India Foundation A-52, 1st Floor, Amar Colony, Lajpat Nagar-IV, New Delhi 110024 ℡011/2622 4482 or 3, Ⓦwww.concernindia .org. Charitable trust supporting grassroots NGOs working with disadvantaged people.

DISHA Foundation Disha Path, Near JDA Park, Nirman Nagar-C, Jaipur 302019, Rajasthan ℡0141/239 3319, Ⓦwww.dishafoundation.org. Resource centre for children with cerebral palsy. Needs donations, sponsors, and volunteers with time or specific skills.

Friends of Shekhawati c/o Apani Dhani, Nawalgarh 333042, Rajasthan ℡01594/222239, Ⓦwww.apanidhani.com/friend. Conservation group aiming to save Shekhawati's art heritage; needs writers, photographers, architects and architecture students to volunteer their services.

Mandore Medical and Relief Society 10-D Near Government Bus Stand, Paota, Jodhpur 342006, Rajasthan ☏ 0291/254 5210, ⓦ www.mandore .com. Takes on volunteers for periods as short as a week to work in health awareness and education projects in rural areas around Jodhpur.

Salaam Baalak Trust 2nd Floor, DDA Community Centre, Gali Chandiwali, Paharganj, Delhi 110055 ☏ 011/2358 4164, ⓦ www.salaambaalaktrust .com. Charity working to help street children in Delhi's Paharganj (see p.104). Their website has an application form for volunteers.

Sambhali Trust *Durg Niwas Guesthouse*, 1 Old Public Park, Raika Bagh, Jodhpur 342001, Rajasthan ☏ 0291/251 2385, ⓦ www.sambhali -trust.org. Locally based NGO dedicated to providing education, training and empowerment to girls and women from underprivileged backgrounds in rural Rajasthan.

Seva Mandir Old Fatehpura, Udaipur 313004, Rajasthan ☏ 0294/245 1041, ⓦ www.sevamandir .org. NGO working in "tribal" villages in the Udaipur district; takes interns to help with development projects.

SOS Children's Villages of India A-7 Nizamuddin (West), New Delhi 110013 ☏ 011/2435 7299, ⓦ www.soscvindia.org. SOS has projects in different parts of India, including Delhi and Rajasthan, giving shelter to distressed children by providing a healthy environment and education including vocational training.

Mail

Mail can take anything from three days to four weeks to get to or from India, and will be faster from Delhi, Jaipur and Agra than from rural Rajasthan. Stamps are not expensive: sending a postcard to anywhere in the world costs Rs8; an aerogramme is Rs8.50. Ideally, you should have mail franked in front of you.

Poste restante (general delivery) services are pretty reliable, though exactly how long individual offices hang on to letters is more or less at their own discretion. Letters are filed alphabetically. To avoid misfiling, your name should be printed clearly, with the surname in large capitals and underlined, but it is still a good idea to check under your first name too, just in case. Have letters addressed to you c/o Poste Restante, GPO (if it's the main post office you want), and the

name of the town and state. Don't forget to take ID with you to claim your mail.

Having **parcels** sent out to you in India is not such a good idea – chances are they'll go astray. If you do have a parcel sent, have it registered.

Sending a parcel abroad can be quite a performance. First you have to get it cleared by customs at the post office (they often don't bother, but check), then you take it to a tailor and have it wrapped in cloth, stitched up and sealed with wax. In big city GPOs, people offering this service will be at hand. Next, take it to the post office, fill in and attach the relevant customs forms (it's best to tick the box marked "gift" and give its value as less than Rs1000 or "no commercial value", to avoid bureaucratic entanglements), buy your stamps, see them franked, and dispatch it. Parcels should not be more than 1m long, nor weigh more than 20kg. Surface mail is incredibly cheap, and takes an average of six months to arrive – it may take half, or four times that however, and sometimes it goes astray, or may arrive damaged. It's a good way to dump excess baggage and souvenirs, but don't send anything fragile. Books and magazines can be sent more cheaply, unsealed or wrapped around the middle, as **printed papers** ("book post").

For further information about Indian mail services, visit ⓦ www.indiapost.gov.in.

Alternatively, there are numerous **courier** services. These are not as reliable as they should be and there have been complaints of packages going astray; it's safest to stick to known international companies such as DHL, FedEx or UPS. Note that packages from India may be considered suspect at home, and can be searched or X-rayed.

Maps

The maps in this book should be sufficient for tourist needs, but you may well need a good road map if you're driving. Road maps of Rajasthan are easy to find at bookshops and newsstands in any town in the state, or in Delhi. The best is published by TTK, on a scale of 1:1,200,000. The same firm also produces reasonably detailed street maps of Jaipur and Agra. In Delhi, the best maps are published annually by Eicher (see p.87 for more on Delhi city maps).

You can find a few interesting maps, including some quite quirky ones (a mineral map of Rajasthan, for example, or a map of the shopping complexes of New Delhi) on the Maps of India website at Ⓦwww.mapsofindia .com/maps/rajasthan for Rajasthan, Ⓦwww .mapsofindia.com/maps/delhi for Delhi, or Ⓦwww.mapsofindia.com/maps/agra for Agra.

Money

India's unit of currency is the **rupee**, usually abbreviated "Rs" and divided into a hundred **paise**. Almost all money is paper, with notes of 10, 20, 50, 100, 500 and 1000 rupees: notes of 5 rupees are still in circulation. Coins come in denominations of 1, 2 and 5 rupees; 10, 20, 25 and 50 paise coins exist but are rarely used.

Banknotes, especially lower denominations, can get into a terrible state, but don't accept **torn banknotes**; no one else will be prepared to take them, so you will be left saddled with the things, though you can change them at the Reserve Bank of India and large branches of other big banks. Don't pass them on to beggars; they can't use them either, so it amounts to an insult.

Outside of big cities, large denominations can also be a problem, as change is usually in short supply. Many Indian people cannot afford to keep much lying around, and you shouldn't necessarily expect shopkeepers or rickshaw-wallahs to have it (and they may – as may you – try to hold onto it if they do). Paying for your groceries with a Rs100 note will probably entail waiting for the grocer's errand boy to go off on a quest to try and change it. Larger notes – like the Rs500 note – are good for travelling with and can be changed for smaller denominations at hotels and other suitable establishments. A word of warning – the Rs500 note looks remarkably similar to the Rs100 note.

At the time of writing, the **exchange rate** was approximately Rs76 to £1 sterling, Rs47 to US$1, Rs68 to €1, Rs44 to Can$1, Rs42 to Aus$1, Rs34 to NZ$1.

Carrying your money

The easiest way to access your money is with **plastic**, though it's a good idea to also have some backup in the form of cash or travellers' cheques. You will find ATMs to withdraw cash at main banks in all major towns and tourist resorts, though your card issuer may well add a foreign transaction fee, and the Indian bank will also charge a small fee, generally around Rs25. The daily limit on ATM cash withdrawals is usually Rs10,000–20,000.

Credit cards are accepted for payment at major hotels, top restaurants, some shops and airline offices, but virtually nowhere else. American Express, MasterCard and Visa are the likeliest to be accepted. Beware of people making extra copies of the receipt, in order to bill you fraudulently later; insist that the transaction is done before your eyes.

One big downside of relying on plastic as your main access to cash, of course, is that cards can easily get lost or stolen, so take along a couple of alternative ones if you can, keep an emergency stash of cash just in case, and make a note of your home bank's telephone number and website addresses for emergencies.

US dollars are the easiest **currency** to convert, with euros and pounds sterling not far behind. Major hard currencies can be changed easily in tourist areas and big cities, less so elsewhere. If you enter the country with more than US$10,000 or the equivalent, you are supposed to fill in a currency declaration form.

In addition to cash and plastic (or as a generally less convenient alternative to the latter), consider carrying some **travellers' cheques**. You pay a small commission (usually one percent) to buy these with cash in the same currency, a little more to convert from a different currency, but they have the advantage over cash that, if lost or stolen, they can be replaced. Not all banks, however, accept them. Well-known brands such as Thomas Cook and American Express are your best bet, but in some places even American Express is only accepted in US dollars and not as pounds sterling. Visa and

Big numbers

A hundred thousand is a lakh, written 1,00,000; ten million is a crore, written 1,00,00,000. Millions, billions and the like are not in common use.

American Express offer pre-paid cards that you can load up with credit before you leave home and use in ATMs like a debit card – effectively travellers' cheques in plastic form.

It is illegal to carry rupees into India, and you won't get them at a particularly good rate in the West anyhow (though you might in Thailand, Malaysia or Singapore). It is also illegal to take them out of the country.

Banks and forex bureaux

Changing money in regular **banks**, especially government-run banks such as the State Bank of India (SBI), can be a time-consuming business, involving lots of form-filling and queuing at different counters, so change substantial amounts at any one time. Banks in Delhi, Jaipur and Agra are likely to be most efficient, though not all change foreign currency, and some won't take **travellers' cheques** or currencies other than dollars or sterling.

Also in the main cities and the tourist centres, there are usually **forex bureaux**, which are a lot less hassle than banks, though their rates may not be as good. In small towns, the State Bank of India or the State Bank of Jaipur and Bikaner are your best bets but you may want to ask around for an alternative. Rates of commission vary – most banks charge a percentage, many forex bureaux charge none, and some charge a flat rate, so it's always worth asking before you change.

Outside **banking hours** (Mon–Fri 10am–2/4pm, Sat 10am–noon), large hotels may change money, usually at a lower rate, and exchange bureaux have longer opening hours.

Hold on to **exchange receipts** ("encashment certificates") or ATM slips; they will be required if you want to change back any excess rupees when you leave the country, and occasionally to buy air tickets and reserve train berths with rupees.

If you are having **money wired**, many larger post offices act as agencies for Western Union (ⓦwww.westernunion.com), while Moneygram's agents (ⓦwww.moneygram.com) include branches of Trade Wings and the Central Bank of India – the websites of both list their agents. **American Express** (ⓦwww.americanexpress.com/india)

has an office in Delhi and an agent in Jaipur, and **Thomas Cook** (ⓦwww.thomascook.co.in) has representatives in Delhi, Agra, Jaipur and major Rajasthani cities.

Card issuers

Emergency numbers for lost or stolen credit cards.
American Express ☎1800/419 1249 or 0124/280 1111
Diners Club ☎1800/112 484
MasterCard ☎000-800/100 1087
Visa ☎000-117/866 670 0955

Opening hours and public holidays

Standard **shop opening hours** in Rajasthan, Delhi and Agra are Monday to Saturday 9.30am to 6pm. Most big stores, at any rate, keep those hours, while smaller shops vary, but usually keep longer hours. **Post office** hours are surprisingly variable, and small branch offices may open longer than a town's head post office or GPO. Typically, expect the GPO to open Monday to Saturday 10am to 4pm for services like parcel dispatch or poste restante, with branch offices open 10am to 5pm for sale of stamps. **Banks** are typically open Monday to Friday 10am to 2/4pm, Saturday 10am to noon.

India has only four national **public holidays** as such: Republic Day (Jan 26), Independence Day (Aug 15), Gandhi's birthday (Oct 2) and Christmas Day (Dec 25). In addition, each state sets its own calendar of official holidays, so those in Rajasthan may differ from those in Delhi or Agra. In fact, however, most major Hindu and Muslim holidays, plus the most important Sikh and Christian ones, are public holidays in Rajasthan, Delhi and Uttar Pradesh (which includes Agra) alike, so you won't find shops or offices in any of those places open on Holi, Dussehra, Diwali, Ashura, Id ul-Fitr, Id ul-Zuha, Christmas Day or Guru Nanak's birthday. For a complete list of festivals, including all those that are public holidays in Rajasthan, Delhi and Agra, see pp.53–55.

Phones

Privately run **phone services** with international **direct dialling** facilities are very

International dialling codes

	From India	To India
UK	☏00 44	☏00 91
Ireland	☏00 353	☏00 91
US and Canada	☏001	☏011 91
Australia	☏00 61	☏0011 91
New Zealand	☏00 64	☏00 91
South Africa	☏00 27	☏09 91

widespread. Advertising themselves with the acronyms **STD/ISD** (subscriber trunk dialling/international subscriber dialling), they are extremely quick and easy to use; some even stay open 24 hours. To call abroad, dial the international access code (00), followed by the code for the country you want – 44 for the UK, for example – the appropriate area code (leaving out any initial zero) and the number you want; then you speak, pay your bill, which is calculated in seconds, and leave. Prices vary from office to office, and are usually cheaper in Delhi than in Agra or Rajasthan. Foreign calls usually cost Rs25 a minute in Delhi, Rs15 in Agra and Rajasthan, but one or two places have a VoIP facility, which brings the price down to Rs7 for Britain, North America and Australasia, slightly more for Ireland and South Africa. Calling from hotels will be much more expensive. Collect calls ("back call") are possible at most phone booths and hotels, but you still have to pay around Rs5 per minute.

Home country direct services are now available from any phone to the UK, the US, Canada, Ireland, Australia, New Zealand and a growing number of other countries. These allow you to make a collect or telephone credit card call to that country via an operator there. To use it, you normally dial 000, followed by the country code, and 17; the exception is Canada, for which you dial 000-127.

Emergency numbers

Police ☏100
Fire ☏101
Ambulance ☏102

To **call India** from abroad, dial the international access code (00 in most countries, but generally 011 from North America, 0011 from Australia) followed by 91 for India, the local code minus the initial zero (11 for Delhi, for example), and then the number.

Mobile phones

Call charges to and from **mobile phones** are far lower in India than Western countries, and many foreign tourists sign up to a local network while in the country. To do this you'll need to buy an Indian SIM card from a mobile phone shop; these cost around Rs150, plus the price of a pay-as-you-go card, and you will need your passport and a passport-size photo of yourself. Your retailer will help you get connected and will advise you on which company to use. Airtel and Hutch should cover Rajasthan, Delhi and Agra, but check when buying your card that it will cover all the areas you intend to visit. Also get your card supplier (Shivam internet in Delhi, for example; see p.143) to turn on the "do not disturb" option, or you'll be plagued with spam calls and spam texts from the phone company.

Indian mobile numbers are ten-digit, starting with a 9. However, if you are calling from outside the state where the mobile is based (but not from abroad), you need to add a zero in front of that.

Photography

Getting **digital** shots burned onto CD is very easy – a lot of internet cafés will do it. Camera **film**, sold at average Western prices, is widely available (but check the date on the box, and note that false boxes containing outdated film are often sold – some firms print holograms on their boxes to prevent this). It's fairly easy to get films developed, though the pictures don't always come out as well as they might at home; Konica and Kodak film laboratories are usually of a good standard. If you're after slide film, slow film or fast film, buy it in the big cities, and don't expect to find specialist brands such as Velvia; it is rare to find a dealer who keeps film refrigerated.

When taking photographs, beware of pointing your camera at anything that might be considered "strategic", including airports and anything military, but even at bridges, railway stations and main roads. Remember too that some people prefer not to be photographed, so it is always wise (and only polite, after all) to ask before taking a snapshot of them. Quite often, you'll get people, especially kids, volunteering to pose. Also, remember to guard your equipment from dust – reliable repair is extremely hard to come by in India.

Time

India is on GMT+5 hour 30 minutes, which means it is 5 hour 30 minutes ahead of Britain and Ireland (4hr 30min when those places are on summer time), 10 hour 30 minutes ahead of the US east coast, Ontario and Quebec (9hr 30min when those places are on daylight saving time), 13 hour 30 minutes ahead of the US and Canadian Pacific coast (12hr 30min when those places are on daylight saving time), 2 hour 30 minutes behind Western Australia, 4 hour 30 minutes behind eastern Australia (5hr 30min when daylight saving time is in force there), 6 hour 30 minutes behind New Zealand (7hr 30min when daylight saving time is in force there), and 3 hour 30 minutes ahead of South Africa. Indian time is referred to as IST (Indian Standard Time, which cynics refer to as "Indian stretchable time").

Tobacco

Indian cigarettes, such as Wills, Gold Flake, Four Square and Charms, are rough but hardly break the bank (Rs20–50/pack), Alternatively, stock up on imported brands, or rolling tobacco, which is available in the bigger towns and cities. One of the great smells of India is the *bidi*, the cheapest smoke, made of a single low-grade tobacco leaf. If you smoke roll-ups, avoid Indian Capstan cigarette papers which are thick and don't stick very well; Rizlas are quite widely available, especially in places with a lot of tourists.

Tourist information

The main tourist website for India is ⓦ www .incredibleindia.org. Delhi and the states of Rajasthan and Uttar Pradesh (which includes Agra) have their own tourism departments, all of which publish an array of printed material, from city maps to glossy leaflets on specific destinations, and can generally answer any specific queries you might have about accommodation and visiting tourist sights.

The Indian government's tourist department has offices in Delhi, Agra and Jaipur, and in major cities and tourist destinations across India, including Mumbai, Kolkata (Calcutta), Chennai (Madras) and Bengaluru (Bangalore), plus offices in several foreign countries (see below). Uttar Pradesh's tourist information department, UP Tourism, maintains an office in Delhi, and one in Agra, with others elsewhere in Uttar Pradesh, while Rajasthan's Tourism Development Corporation (RTDC) has offices in Delhi, Mumbai, Kolkata and Chennai, as well as throughout Rajasthan. Locations of tourist offices in each town are given in the text.

All of these state and federal tourism organizations, aside from giving out advice and information, sell a wide range of travel facilities, including guided tours, car rental and their own hotels. The federal tourism department's corporate wing, the Indian Tourism Development Corporation (ITDC), for example, runs the Ashok chain of hotels, and operates tour and travel services, frequently competing with its state counterparts.

Indian government tourist offices abroad

Australia Level 5, Glasshouse Shopping Complex, 135 King St, Sydney NSW 2000 ☏ 02/9221 9555, ⓔ info@indiatourism.com.au.
Canada 60 Bloor St (West), Suite 1003, Toronto, ON M4W 3B8 ☏ 1-416/ 962-3787 or 8, ⓔ info @indiatourismcanada.ca.
The Netherlands Rokin 9–15, 1022 KK, Amsterdam ☏ 020/620 8991, ⓦ www .indiatourismamsterdam.com.
Singapore 20 Karamat Lane, 01–01A United House, Singapore 228773 ☏ 6235 3800, ⓔ indtour .sing@pacific.net.sg.
South Africa PO Box 412542, Craighall 2024, Hyde Lane, Lancaster Gate, Johannesburg 2000 ☏ 011/325 0880, ⓔ goito@global.co.za.
UK 7 Cork St, London W1S 3LH ☏ 020/7437 3677, ⓔ london5@indiatouristoffice.org.
US 1270 Ave of Americas, Suite 1808 (18th floor), New York, NY 10020 ☏ 1-212/586-4901 to 3,

Eny@itonyc.com; 3550 Wilshire Blvd, Suite 204, Los Angeles, CA 90010-2485 ☎1-213/380-8855, Eindiatourismla@aol.com.

State tourist office websites

Delhi Tourism and Transport Development Corporation (DTTDC) ⓦdelhitourism.nic.in
Rajasthan Tourism Development Corporation (RTDC) ⓦwww.rajasthantourism.gov.in
Uttar Pradesh Tourism ⓦwww.up-tourism.com

Travel advice

Australian Department of Foreign Affairs
ⓦwww.smartraveller.gov.au
British Foreign & Commonwealth Office
ⓦwww.fco.gov.uk
Canadian Department of Foreign Affairs
ⓦwww.voyage.gc.ca
Irish Department of Foreign Affairs ⓦwww
.foreignaffairs.gov.ie
US State Department ⓦwww.travel.state.gov

Guide

Guide

Delhi

The International boundaries on this map are neither purported to be correct nor authentic by Survey of India directives. Publisher.

N

PAKISTAN

HARYANA

UTTAR PRADESH

GUJARAT

MADHYA PRADESH

0   100 km

CHAPTER 1   # Highlights

* **Rajpath** From the Presidential Palace through the India Gate, this wide ceremonial boulevard was the centrepiece of Lutyens's New Delhi, expressing the might and power of the imperial British Raj. See p.98

* **Red Fort** Delhi's most famous monument, a huge palace-cum-fortress that formed the heart of the Mughal Empire under Shah Jahan. See p.111

* **Jama Masjid** Shah Jahan's pompous congregational mosque, with huge minarets offering bird's-eye views over the old city. See p.114

* **Humayun's Tomb** An elegant forerunner of the Taj Mahal in red sandstone and white marble, whose lovely gardens offer an escape from the heat. See p.121

* **Safdarjang's Tomb** A decadent Rococo successor to the Taj, built at the tail end of the Mughal era. See p.123

* **Qutb Minar Complex** The ruins of Delhi's first incarnation, a thirteenth-century city dominated by an impressive Victory Tower. See p.125

* **Baha'i Temple** A stupendous piece of iconic modern architecture in the form of a 27-petalled lotus. See p.128

▲ Jama Masjid

Delhi

S ite of no fewer than eight successive cities, India's capital **DELHI** is the hub of the Indian Subcontinent, a buzzing international metropolis which draws people from across India and the globe, utterly dwarfing Agra, Jaipur and the cities of Rajasthan, not only in size and density, but also in culture and sophistication. Home to 1.5 crore (fifteen million) people, it's big and it's growing. The National Capital Territory, which marks the city's limits, encompasses 1,483 square kilometres, but burgeoning suburbs like Faridabad, Gurgaon and Noida are expanding beyond its perimeter into the neighbouring states of Haryana and Uttar Pradesh (UP). Yet tucked away inside Delhi's modern suburbs and developments are tombs, temples and ruins that date back centuries; in some areas, the remains of whole cities from the dim and distant past nestle among homes and highways built in just the last decade or two. You'll even find a touch of rural India, in the form of villages where life appears to carry on in its sleepy way, as if they were still out in the countryside rather than slap-bang in the middle of one of the world's most dynamic metropolises. The result is a city full of fascinating nooks and crannies that you could happily spend weeks or even months exploring if you've a mind – or the time – to. You certainly won't run out of things to do. Quite apart from its historical buildings, Delhi has a host of **museums** and art treasures, while cultural performances and crafts provide a showcase for the entire country's diverse heritage. **Shops** trade in goods from every corner of India, and with a little legwork you can find anything from Tibetan carpets, antiques and jewellery to modern art and designer clothes.

Although Rajasthan has three commercial airports, Delhi is where you'll probably land if flying into the region from abroad, and for someone new to India, it isn't a bad place to start. Of all the cities in the region, Delhi is the most cosmo-politan and is quite used to outsiders; you'll find a wide range of hotels at all levels that cater specifically for tourists, and an endless stream of fellow travellers who can give you tips and pointers on anything you're unsure of. Meanwhile, there's no shortage of things to see and do while you acclimatize to Indian ways.

From a tourist's point of view Delhi divides into two main parts. **Old Delhi** is the city of the Mughals, created by Shah Jahan and dating back to the seventeenth century. It's the capital's most frenetic quarter, and its most Islamic, a reminder that for over seven hundred years, Delhi was a Muslim city, ruled by sultans. To its south, encompassing the modern city centre, is **New Delhi**, built by the British to be the capital of their empire's key possession. A spacious city of tree-lined boulevards, New Delhi is impressive in its own way; the Rajpath, stretching from India Gate to the Presidential Palace, is at least as mighty a statement of imperial power as Old Delhi's Red Fort. But today, Delhi is spreading southward, and as the city expands – which it is doing at quite a pace – the centre of New Delhi is

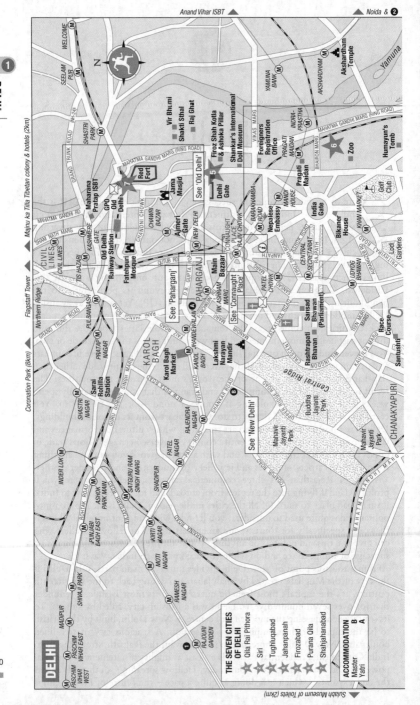

DELHI

THE SEVEN CITIES OF DELHI
★ Qila Rai Pithora
★★ Siri
★★★ Tughluqabad
★★★★ Jahanpanah
★★★★★ Firozabad
★★★★★★ Purana Qila
★★★★★★★ Shahjahanabad

ACCOMMODATION
Master   B
Yatri   A

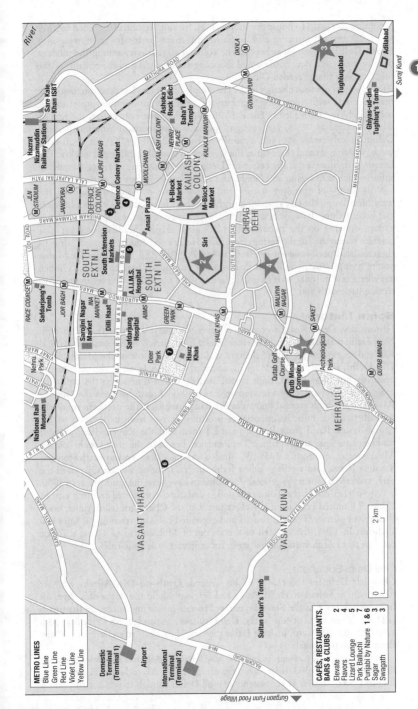

1

81

METRO LINES

Blue Line
Green Line
Red Line
Violet Line
Yellow Line

CAFÉS, RESTAURANTS, BARS & CLUBS

Elevate 2
Flavors 4
Lizard Lounge 5
Park Balluchi 7
Punjabi by Nature 1 & 6
Sagar 3
Swagath 3

0   2 km

Domestic Terminal (Terminal 1)
Airport
International Terminal (Terminal 2)

▲ Gurgaon Funn Food Village

Sultan Ghari's Tomb

National Rail Museum

Nehru Park

Safdarjang's Tomb

Sarojini Nagar Market
Dilli Haat
INA MARKET

South Extension Markets

SOUTH EXTN I
SOUTH EXTN II

Defence Colony Market

Ansal Plaza

Siri

Lajpat Nagar

JLN STADIUM

Hazrat Nizamuddin Railway Station

Sare Kale Khan ISBT

River

Ashoka's Rock Edict
Baha'i Temple

KAILASH COLONY
N-Block Market
M-Block Market

CHIRAG DELHI

Tughluqabad

Ghiyas-ud-din Tughluq's Tomb

□ Adilabad

▶ Suraj Kund

GOVINDPURI

GURU RAVIDAS MARG

MEHRAULI–BADARPUR ROAD

OKHLA

KALKAJI MANDIR
NEHRU PLACE
KAILASH COLONY
MOOLCHAND

MATHURA ROAD

BHISHAM PITAMAH MARG

LALA LAJPAT RAI PATH

RING ROAD

LODI ROAD

RACE COURSE

Safdarjang's Tomb

JOR BAGH

A.I.I.M.S. Hospital
Safdarjung Hospital
AIIMS

GREEN PARK

HAUZ KHAS

Hauz Khas

Deer Park

AFRICA AVENUE

MAHATMA GANDHI MARG

AURBINDO MARG

SRI AUROBINDO MARG

KHEL GAON MARG

OUTER RING ROAD

MALVIYA NAGAR

SAKET

QUTAB MINAR

Qutab Golf Course
Qutab Minar Complex
Archeological Park

MEHRAULI

ARUNA ASAF ALI MARG

NELSON MANDELA MARG

SAFDAR KHAN MARG

ABDUL GAFFAR KHAN MARG

VASANT KUNJ

VASANT VIHAR

OUTER RING ROAD

SARDAR PATEL MARG

VINAY MARG

SHANTIPATH

NH-8

RAJOKRI ROAD

2
3
4
5
6
7

becoming too small to house the shops, clubs, bars and restaurants needed to cater to its affluent and growing middle class. Thus many businesses are moving into **South Delhi**, the vast area beyond the colonial city, where, among the modern developments and new business and shopping areas, you'll find the remains of the medieval city that preceded Old Delhi.

Delhi's most obvious **change** in the last couple of decades has been the rise of the middle class, with increasing numbers of relatively prosperous professionals, particularly in South Delhi. The explosion of telephone call centres, the first of which opened in 1998, has brought lucrative jobs to many English-speaking Delhiites; call-centre workers typically earn Rs12,000–14,000 for a 50-hour week, which is around three times the wage of an unskilled industrial worker. The latest trend, however, is for better-off Delhiites to move out of town, to satellite suburbs such as Gurgaon and Noida, and often now even further afield.

With plenty of spending money and a new sense of confidence among the wealthier classes, the city's growing **nightlife** scene boasts designer bars, chic cafés and decent clubs. Its auditoriums host a wide range of national music and dance events, drawing on the richness of India's great classical traditions. Smart new cinemas screen the latest offerings from both Hollywood and Bollywood, while its theatres hold performances in Hindi and in English. And if it's from Delhi that you're flying home, you'll find that you can buy goods here from pretty much anywhere else in India, so it's a good place to stock up with souvenirs and presents to take back with you.

Some history

Historically, Delhi is said to consist of seven successive cities, with British-built New Delhi making an eighth. In truth, Delhi has centred on three main areas: **Lal Kot** and its extensions, where the city was located for most of the Middle Ages; **Old Delhi**, the city of the Mughals, founded by Shah Jahan in the seventeenth century; and **New Delhi**, built by the British just in time to be the capital of independent India. Delhi is located on a rich alluvial plain between the Yamuna River and the high ground known as the Ridge, which is the northern tip of the Aravalli range of hills; its importance probably derives from its location on the Grand Trunk Road from Bengal to the Punjab and the Khyber Pass, a major trading route since ancient times. The Pandavas, heroes of the great Hindu epic the *Mahabharata*, set around 1450 BC, had a capital called **Indraprastha** on the Yamuna River, and a village called Indrapat that stood at Purana Qila until the early twentieth century is generally assumed to have been the same place. In 1060, a Rajput clan called the **Tomars** founded **Lal Kot**, considered the first city of Delhi. A hundred years later, a rival Rajput clan, the **Chauhans** from Ajmer, made themselves overlords of the Tomars and expanded Lal Kot, renaming it **Qila Rai Pithora**. In 1191, the city fell to the armies of Muhammad of Ghor, a Turkic Muslim from Afghanistan, ushering in six centuries of Islamic rule.

The Delhi Sultanate

Ghur left Delhi in the charge of his general, **Qutb-ud-Din Aibak**, who set himself up as Sultan of Delhi. As he had originally held the status of a slave, his heirs were known as the **Slave Dynasty**. His son-in-law and successor **Iltutmish** (1211–36), greatest of the early Delhi sultans, expanded his territory both eastward and westward, making Delhi the capital of lands stretching all the way from Punjab to Bengal.

Another group of Central Asian Turks, the **Khaljis**, took over the Delhi Sultanate in 1290, and in 1303 their most illustrious king, **Ala-ud-Din** (1296–1316), founded **Siri**, known as the second city of Delhi, though it was actually just a citadel to give the unpopular king a base outside the city. Ala-ud-Din's successor was assassinated, giving Ala-ud-Din's lieutenant, **Ghiyas-ud-Din Tughluq**, the excuse to step in and became sultan himself, instituting the **Tughluq dynasty**, and building Delhi's third city at **Tughluqabad**, 8km east of Lal Kot, in 1321. His successor, **Muhammad Tughluq**, was responsible for Delhi's so-called fourth city, **Jahanpanah**, really just a northeastward extension of Lal Kot, filling in the area between that and Siri. The next sultan, **Firoz Shah**, left his mark by building a fortified palace at Firoz Shah Kotla in 1354, evidently meant to be the stronghold of a new city called **Firozabad**, considered Delhi's fifth incarnation.

In 1398, Delhi fell to the forces of Timur the Lame (Tamerlaine), a Central Asian warlord, who completely ransacked it, leaving a deserted city and a power vacuum, eventually filled by Timur's follower **Khizr Khan**, whose dynasty, the **Sayyids** (1414–44), ruled little more than Delhi and its hinterland. They were plagued by internal power struggles, which ended when **Buhlul Lodi**, a Punjabi ruler called in to support one of the Sayyid factions, took over, enlarging Delhi's territory and establishing the **Lodi dynasty**. His son Sikandar moved his capital to Agra, thus ending the Delhi Sultanate, but Sikandar's son, Ibrahim, laid the foundations for its successor by being such a tyrant that one of his nobles asked for help from the founder of the Mughals, **Babur**.

The Mughals

Babur's 1526 victory at Panipat (see p.360) made him master of Delhi and Agra, but his son, **Humayun**, lost them, along with most of his father's conquests, to the Afghan king **Sher Khan Sur**, who is credited with building the "sixth city of Delhi" at **Purana Qila**. Again, this was just a citadel, though it's likely a new city was intended to be built around it. Humayun retook Delhi in 1555, but died the following year and was succeeded by his son **Akbar**, who, like Sikandar Lodi, moved his capital to Agra. Akbar's grandson, **Shah Jahan**, shifted it back, creating Delhi's "seventh city", **Shahjahanabad**, now known as **Old Delhi**. In 1681 Shah Jahan's son **Aurangzeb** moved the capital to Aurangabad on the Deccan plateau, though his son and successor Bahadur Shah I moved it back in 1712.

After Aurangzeb's death in 1707, the Mughal empire started to disintegrate and Delhi fell victim to successive invasions. In 1739, **Nadir Shah** of Persia sacked the city and slaughtered an estimated 20,000 of its inhabitants. A decade later, Nadir Shah's ally, the Afghan ruler Ahmad Shah Durrani, threatened Delhi, and the Mughal governor of Avadh (eastern Uttar Pradesh), **Safdarjang**, took over as vizier and saved the day. When he was ousted for being a Shi'ite, his son led Avadh to independence, reducing Delhi's hinterland still further, so that the empire's tax base was not even sufficient to finance its army. In 1757, Ahmad Shah Durrani took Delhi just to plunder it, and of the next emperor, Shah Alam II (1761–1805), it was said, "The kingdom of Shah Alam/Runs from Delhi to Palam", Palam being a village near Dwarka, just northwest of Delhi airport. Urdu poets even developed a new genre of verse called *shahr ashob* ("ruined city") to lament the city's decline. In 1784, the **Marathas** (see p.362) subdued Delhi and made the emperor their vassal. They bit off more than they could chew, however, when they took on the **British**, who in 1803 beat them in battle at Patparganj (near Akshardham Temple) and brought Delhi into the North-Western Provinces of the East India Company's Bengal-based empire. The Brits allowed the emperor to stay on under their control, but his position was now purely ceremonial.

British rule

The Mughals' final undoing was the **1857 uprising** against the British – the Mutiny or First Independence War (see p.365). Most Delhiwallahs, particularly the poor, supported the uprising, though the rich were more ambivalent, especially when mobs started looting the city's havelis as gangs of sepoys robbed and extorted its inhabitants. With little discipline, strategy, or intelligence about the enemy, the insurgents failed to destroy the British position while they could. Meanwhile, bandits took control of the surrounding countryside, and the British called in reinforcements from the Punjab. When they finally recaptured the city, they went on a rampage of destruction and murder, killing some three thousand people in bloody and indiscriminate **reprisals**. Bahadur Shah was packed off to exile in Burma, and virtually the entire population of Delhi was turfed out, its Muslims not allowed to return for two years.

After the uprising, the British abolished both the East India Company and the Mughal empire, and the British crown assumed direct control of the country, and in 1911 decided to make Delhi India's new capital. Fervent construction of bungalows, parliamentary buildings and public offices followed, and in 1931, **New Delhi** – the city's eighth incarnation – was officially inaugurated as the capital, the same year the British agreed in principle to India's eventual independence. When **Independence** finally came, in 1947, the British handed over power to India's first democratically elected government under Jawaharlal Nehru. In the wake of **Partition**, however, Hindu mobs turned on Delhi's Muslim population, nearly half of whom fled to Pakistan, ending centuries of Muslim dominance in the city. They were replaced by Hindu and Sikh refugees from the Pakistani sectors of Punjab and Bengal.

In 1992, having previously been a Union Territory, administered directly by the federal government, Delhi gained a status similar to that of Washington DC or Canberra ACT, with its own government, but lesser powers than those of a state. The Hindu sectarian BJP won power that year in the first **Capital Territory** election, but lost in 1998 to Congress, who have controlled the administration since then.

Arrival

Delhi is India's main point of arrival for overseas visitors, and the major transport hub for north India, containing the country's main international airport as well as four long-distance railway stations and three intercity bus terminals.

The Seven Cities of Delhi (plus one)

1. **Lal Kot (Qila Rai Pithora)** The area around the Qutb Minar, at the heart of medieval Delhi, founded by the Tomars in 1060 (see p.125).
2. **Siri** Actually a fortress rather than a city, commissioned by Ala-ud-Din in 1303 (see p.124).
3. **Tughluqabad** A fortified city built for Ghiyas-ud-Din Tughluq in 1321 but deserted soon after (see p.129).
4. **Jahanpanah** Founded by Muhammad Tughluq in 1326 as an extension of Lal Kot, joining it to Siri (see p.124).
5. **Firozabad** A fortified palace, Firoz Shah Kotla, is the only part of this supposed city that we know of for sure, founded by Firoz Shah in 1354 (see p.118).
6. **Purana Qila** Built as a fortress for Sher Khan in 1533, possibly on the site of ancient Indraprastha (see p.106).
7. **Old Delhi (Shahjahanabad)** Founded by Shah Jahan in 1638 to be the capital of Mughal India (see p.107).
8. **New Delhi** Inaugurated by the British in 1931 as the capital of their prize colony, which gained independence just sixteen years later (see p.98).

By air

Indira Gandhi International (IGI) Airport, 20km southwest of the centre, has two separate terminals: international flights land at Terminal 2, domestic flights at Terminal 1. There are **no ATMs** at the airport (though this may change), but Punjab National Bank and Thomas Cook in the arrivals lounge offer 24-hour money-changing facilities; be sure to ask for some small change for taxis and rickshaws. For those seeking accommodation, 24-hour desks here, including Indian Tourism (ITDC) and Delhi Tourism (DTTDC), have a list of approved hotels and will secure reservations by phone. Although adjacent, the two terminals are 6km apart by road, but are connected by a free AAI **shuttle** bus running every twenty minutes.

From the international airport the easiest way to get into Delhi is by **taxi**, particularly advisable if you arrive late at night. There are several official pre-paid taxi kiosks in the restricted area outside the arrivals hall; the fare will be around Rs250 to the city centre, with a 25 percent surcharge between 11pm and 5am; prices vary from kiosk to kiosk, so you might check a few before plumping. It's worth noting, however, that even these pre-paid taxi drivers may try to take you to hotels not of your choice (see box, p.86).

Alternatively, there's a **bus** (Rs50; 40min), leaving every half-hour for Connaught Place, New Delhi Station (Ajmeri Gate side) and Maharana Pratap ISBT in Old Delhi; tickets are available from the DTC counter in the arrivals hall, and the bus travels via the domestic terminal too.

The **auto-rickshaws** that wait in line at the departure gate constitute the most precarious and least reliable form of transport from the airport, especially at night, though they're cheaper than a taxi; fares are around Rs150–180. Many hotels, including some of the Paharganj budget options, now offer **pick-up services** from the airport, where you will be met with a driver bearing your name on a placard. This presents the smoothest and most reliable method of getting to your hotel from the airport, though prices vary considerably, starting from around Rs250, but often twice as much or more.

An **Airport Express Link** metro line is now under construction, scheduled for completion in 2010. When finished, it should speed travellers into central New Delhi in as little as sixteen minutes.

By train

Delhi has two major **railway stations**. **New Delhi Station** is at the eastern end of Paharganj Main Bazaar, within easy walking distance of many of the area's budget hotels. The station has two exits: take the Paharganj exit for Connaught Place and most points south, and the Ajmeri Gate exit for Old Delhi. Cycle rickshaws ply the congested main bazaar toward Connaught Place – which is just 800m down the road – but cannot enter Connaught Place itself. Auto-rickshaws start at Rs20 for Connaught Place, or Rs40 to Old Delhi's Chandni Chowk – agree a price before getting in. **Old Delhi Station**, west of the Red Fort, is also well connected to the city by taxis, auto-rickshaws and cycle rickshaws; for autos there's a booth selling fixed-price pre-paid tickets – Connaught Place is Rs50, plus Rs5 per piece of baggage. Both rail stations are notorious for **theft**: don't take your eyes off your luggage for a moment. These stations are also served by stops on the city's metro system (see p.88), but travelling with heavy baggage is prohibited. The other long-distance stations are **Hazrat Nizamuddin**, southeast of the centre, for trains from Agra (except the Shatabdi Express); and **Sarai Rohilla**, west of Old Delhi station, for some services from Rajasthan. Hazrat Nizamuddin has a pre-paid auto-rickshaw booth; Connaught Place is Rs60 (plus Rs5 per piece of baggage), slightly less from Sarai Rohilla, but you may find that autos will not

Delhi scams

Delhi can be a headache for the first-time visitor because of **scams** to entrap the unwary – one dodge is to dump dung onto visitors' shoes, then charge to clean it off. The most common wheeze, though, is for taxi drivers or touts to convince you that the hotel you've chosen is full, closed or has just burned to the ground, so that they can take you to a hotel that pays them commission. More sophisticated scammers will pretend to phone your hotel to check for yourself, or will take you to a travel agent (often claiming to be a "tourist office") who will claim to dial the hotel for you. In fact, they call a different number, where the "receptionist" on the line will corroborate the story, or deny all knowledge of your reservation. The driver or tout will then take you to a "very good hotel" – usually in Karol Bagh – where you'll be charged well over the odds for a night's accommodation. To **reduce the risk of being caught out**, write down your taxi's registration number (make sure the driver sees you doing it), and insist on going to your hotel with no stops en route.

To avoid taxi drivers taking you to a hotel of their choice rather than yours, if heading to Paharganj, where most of the backpacker hotels are located, you could ask to be dropped at New Delhi railway station and walk from there. If someone outside your hotel claims that it's full, check at reception, and even if the claim is true, never follow a tout to anywhere they recommend. Better still, **reserve in advance**; many hotels will arrange for a car and driver to meet you at your point of arrival.

New Delhi railway station is the worst place for touts; assume that anyone who approaches you here – even in uniform – with offers of help, or to direct you to the foreigners' booking hall, is up to no good. Most are trying to lure travellers to the fake "official" tourist offices opposite the Paharganj entrance, where you'll end up paying way over the odds, often for unconfirmed tickets. And don't believe stories that the foreigners' booking hall has closed. On **Connaught Place** and along **Janpath**, steer clear of more phoney "tourist information offices" (which touts may try to divert you to), and never do business with any travel agent that tries to disguise itself as a tourist information office. For the record, India Tourism is at 88 Janpath and the DTTDC is at N-36, Middle Circle (in a street swarming with touts and lookalike agencies). Finally, be aware that taxi, auto and rental-car drivers get a hefty commission for taking you to certain **shops**, and that commission will be added to your bill should you buy anything. You can assume that auto-wallahs who accost you on the street do so with the intention of overcharging you, or of taking you to shops that pay them commission rather than straight to where you want to go. Always hail a taxi or auto-rickshaw yourself, rather than taking one whose driver approaches you, and don't let them take you to places where you haven't asked to go.

accept the slip from the pre-paid booth at Hazrat Nizamuddin unless you pay Rs20–30 extra. There are occasionally local trains to New Delhi, but they tend to be sardine-can packed, and buying a ticket can be a real scrum.

By bus

State buses pull in at the **Maharana Pratap Inter-state Bus Terminal (ISBT)**, north of Old Delhi railway station. Auto-rickshaws to New Delhi or Paharganj take about fifteen minutes (R60, plus Rs5 per piece of baggage), cycle rickshaws take twice that (and cost around Rs40). There's a pre-paid auto-rickshaw booth at the terminal, and also a metro station (Kashmere Gate). **Private buses** from all over India pull up in the street outside New Delhi railway station; some also drop passengers in Connaught Place. Some services from UP and Uttarakhand leave you at **Anand Vihar ISBT**, across the Yamuna towards Ghaziabad in east Delhi, which also has a pre-paid auto-rickshaw booth (Rs75 to Connaught Place, plus

Rs5 per piece of baggage), and is served by bus #73 or #85 to Connaught Place, and by the metro (though heavy baggage is not officially allowed). Buses from Agra and some from Rajasthan may leave you at **Sarai Kale Khan ISBT** by Hazrat Nizamuddin train station (cross over by the footbridge for pre-paid autos). Buses from Jaipur, Ajmer, Jodhpur and Udaipur may drop you at **Bikaner House** near India Gate, Rs40 from Connaught Place by auto.

Information

There are reasonably helpful tourist offices at the international and domestic airport terminals, railway stations and bus terminals, while **India Tourism** at 88 Janpath, just south of Connaught Place (Mon–Fri 9am–6pm, Sat 9am–2pm; ☏011/2332 0005 or 8), is a good place to pick up information on historical sites, city tours, shopping and cultural events, as well as free city maps. **DTTDC** (Delhi Tourism and Transport Development Corporation) have an office at *Coffee House*, 1 Annexe, Emporium Complex, Baba Kharak Singh Marg, opposite Hanuman Mandir (daily 7am–9pm; ☏011/2336 5358, ⓦwww.delhitourism.nic.in), another at N-36 Connaught Place (daily 10am–5pm; ☏011/4152 3073), and others in the two airport terminals. Beware of any other firms that look like or claim to be tourist offices (see box opposite) – DTTDC's office in Connaught Place is besieged by touts trying to divert you into dishonest lookalike travel agents, of which the street is full.

Exhibitions and cultural events are listed in local **magazines** such as the weekly *Delhi Diary*, fortnightly *Delhi City* and *Time Out Delhi*, and monthly *First City*, all available from bookshops and street stalls; *Delhi Diary* can sometimes be found for free at big hotels or at the GOI tourist office. **Online**, apart from the DTTDC's website, it's worth checking the Delhi pages of India for You at ⓦwww.indfy .com/delhi.html for sightseeing information (click on "Places to see in Delhi"). Other useful sources are the Delhi city government's tourism pages at ⓦdelhigovt .nic.in/page.asp for general information, and for current listings, ⓦdelhi .clickindia.com or www.delhilive.com.

Should you need a more detailed **map**, Eicher's *Delhi Road Map* (Rs75 from bookshops or newsstands) is one of the best; the same firm produces the even more comprehensive *Delhi City Map* in book form, with street index, for Rs290. If you're going to spend some time in Delhi and want an in-depth **guide** to its ancient monuments, *Delhi: a Thousand Years of Building* by Lucy Peck (INTACH/ Roli, 2005) covers just about every building or ruin of historical or architectural interest in the city, with exhaustive descriptions of each, and detailed maps showing their locations.

City transport

Even with the addition of a metro system, **public transport** in Delhi is inadequate for the city's population and size, and increased car ownership is adding to the general chaos. **Cows** have been banned from much of central Delhi, but not the city's more traditional districts. In an effort to reduce pollution, the city's buses, taxis and auto-rickshaws have all now been converted from petrol and diesel to run on **Compressed Natural Gas** (CNG), but most inner-city thoroughfares are still choked with exhaust fumes and congested.

The metro

Delhi's **metro system** opened in December 2002, with the capacity to carry 200,000 passengers daily. It's being built in several phases, with work projected to continue until at least 2021. There are three lines: red, yellow and blue, all due to be extended in the near future, with a green line and a violet line also due to open shortly (see map, opposite). For progress updates, ask at the tourist offices (see p.87) or visit Ⓦwww.delhimetrorail.com. The minimum fare is currently Rs8, while the highest fare from the centre is Rs23. The metro is wheelchair-accessible, and each station should have an ATM. Children under 90cm (3ft) tall travel free if accompanied by an adult. Photography is prohibited, as in principle is baggage weighing more than 15kg, or measuring more than 60cm x 45cm x 25cm.

Buses

With auto- and cycle rickshaws so cheap and plentiful, only hardened shoestring travellers generally use Delhi's confusing and overcrowded **buses**, but they do come in useful from time to time, and it's possible to check bus routes **online** at Ⓦdelhigovt.nic.in/dtcbusroute/dtc/Find_Route/getroute.asp, though the lists of bus stops do not always use location names that will be familiar to tourists (stops in Connaught Place, for example, are listed individually as "Regal Cinema", "Super Bazaar" and so on).

Auto-rickshaws and cycle rickshaws

There are pre-paid booths in Connaught Place (on the innermost circle between the two halves of Palika Bazaar, and on Janpath outside the Government of India tourist office) and some transport terminals (Old Delhi and Hazrat Nizamuddin stations, and Maharana Pratap and Anand Vihar ISBTs), but in general you'll need to negotiate a price before getting in; prices for foreigners vary according to your haggling skills, but as a sample fare, it should cost about Rs50 from Connaught Place to Old Delhi. In Connaught Place itself, there's a pre-paid auto-rickshaw kiosk, charging certified official fares.

Cycle rickshaws are not allowed in Connaught Place and parts of New Delhi, but are handy for short journeys to outlying areas and around Paharganj. They're also nippier than motorized traffic in Old Delhi. Rates should be roughly half that demanded by autos.

While auto- and rickshaw-wallahs may well try to overcharge you, do bear in mind that cycle rickshaw-wallahs in particular are among the city's poorest residents, and it really isn't worth haggling them down to the absolute minimum fare or arguing with them over what will amount in the end to a trifling sum. Most tourists accept that they are going to pay a bit more than local residents, and when you see how hard your rickshaw-wallah has to work, you may well feel he deserves a hefty tip on top of that.

Taxis

Delhi's **taxis** (white, or black and yellow) cost around fifty percent more than auto-rickshaws. Drivers belong to local taxi stands, where you can make bookings and fix prices; if you flag a taxi down on the street you're letting yourself in for some hectic haggling. A surcharge of around 25 percent operates between 11pm and 5am. Alternatively, radiocab firms such as Mega Cabs (☎011/4141 4141, Ⓦwww.megacabs.com) and Quick Cabs (☎011/4533 3333, Ⓦquickcabs.in) offer a 24-hour call-a-cab service with meters, though expect to pay a bit more than usual.

DELHI METRO

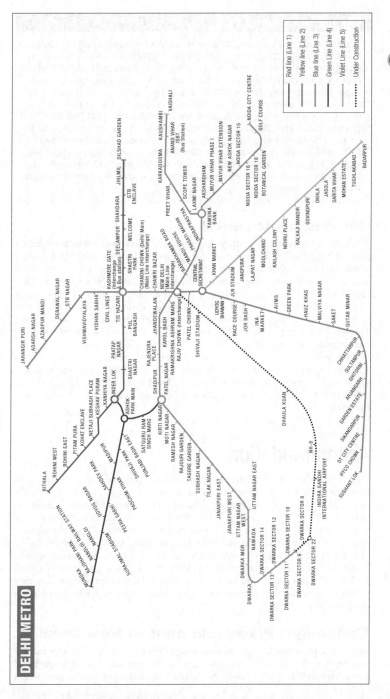

Legend:
- Red line (Line 1)
- Yellow line (Line 2)
- Blue line (Line 3)
- Green Line (Line 4)
- Violet Line (Line 5)
- Under Construction

Car and cycle rental

For local sightseeing and journeys beyond the city confines, **chauffeur-driven cars** are very good value, especially for groups of three to four. Many budget hotels offer cars and drivers, as does the DTTDC (for enquiries round the clock contact their transport office on Aurobindo Marg at Kidwai Nagar West, by Dilli Haat ☎011/2467 4153), and the booths at the southern end of the Tibetan Market on Janpath. DTTDC rates are Rs1495 for an eight-hour day within Delhi (more in an a/c vehicle), which includes 120km mileage. Alternatively, there's Kumar Tourist Taxi Service, K-14 Connaught Place (☎011/2341 5390, ⓦwww .kumarindiatours.com). Driving yourself in Delhi can be dangerous.

Cycling in the large avenues of New Delhi also takes some getting used to and can be hazardous for those not used to chaotic traffic. **Bicycle rental** is surprisingly difficult to come by; try Mehta Cycles (☎011/2358 9239) at 5109–10 Main Bazaar, Paharganj, a few doors from *Kholsa Cafe*, who rent bikes for Rs60 a day.

Accommodation

Delhi has a vast range of **accommodation**, from dirt-cheap lodges to extravagant international hotels. Its luxury hotels are as good as you'll get anywhere in the world, and in terms of service in particular, often far superior to their counterparts in the West, while the mid-range hotels offer unbeatable value for money, though you do have to pick and choose. Bookings for upmarket hotels can be made at airport and railway station tourist desks, but even budget hotels can be booked by phone or email, though it's often touch and go whether such bookings will be honoured if you turn up late in the day. Don't believe touts, taxi drivers or auto-wallahs telling you there are no rooms at your hotel, and avoid the places they recommend in Karol Bagh (see box, p.86). Most hotels in Delhi have a noon checkout time.

Connaught Place and central New Delhi

You pay a premium to stay on **Connaught Place**, so if you want value for money, stay elsewhere. To its south, grander hotels on and around **Janpath** and along **Sansad Marg** cater mainly for business travellers and tourist groups, but there are some very good ones among them. Most upmarket hotels have plush restaurants and swimming pools, and some require non-Indian residents to pay in foreign currency. Of the budget travellers' lodges that used to dot the lanes off the northern end of Janpath, only a couple remain, and they're often full, so book ahead.

Unless otherwise stated, the hotels listed below are marked on the Connaught Place **map** on p.92.

Alka P-16/90, Connaught Place ℡011/2334 4000, Ⓦwww.hotelalka.com. "The best alternative to luxury", they reckon, but the rooms, though a/c and carpeted, are pretty poky – the cheaper ones don't even have a window, though they do try to make up for it with mirrors to create an illusion of space. The staff, however, don't seem to believe in giving out smiles to create an illusion of friendliness. On the plus side, there's a reasonable veg restaurant, and an annexe on M-block for when the main hotel is full. ❼

Bright M-85, Connaught Place ℡011/4151 7766, Ⓔhotelbright@hotmail.com. A mixed bag of rooms, some attached, at this city-centre hotel, which was under refurbishment when we last visited, but due to reopen in 2010. The best room is no.11, spacious with big windows, but others are a bit on the dingy side, so try before you buy. Upstairs, *Blue* (℡011/2341 6666, Ⓔhotelbluedelhi@hotmail.com) has the benefit of a terrace and is a decent fallback option. ❸

Imperial Janpath, Connaught Place end ℡011/2334 1234, Ⓦwww.theimperialindia .com. See also New Delhi map, p.99. Delhi's classiest hotel, in a beautiful 1933 Art Deco building set amid large, palm-shaded gardens. The rooms are stylish, as is the cool lobby done out in cream and gold, while corridors double up as galleries depicting rather fascinating eighteenth- and nineteenth-century prints of India. Staff maintain just the right degree of courteousness, and there are a number of excellent restaurants including the renowned *Spice Route* (see p.132). Doubles from Rs24,750. ❾

The Lalit Off Barakhamba Rd and Tolstoy Marg, southeast of Connaught Place ℡011/4444 7777, Ⓦwww.thelalit.com. See also New Delhi map, p.99. Formerly the Intercontinental, now revamped into a stylish, modern hotel, with cool, elegant rooms and a spacious lobby decorated with some quite impressive works of art. When the hotel's at its busiest, doubles start from around Rs12,000, but prices are lower when business is slack. ❾

Le Meridien Windsor Place, Raisina Rd ℡011/2371 0101, Ⓦwww.lemeridien.com /newdelhi. See New Delhi map, p.99. Busy five-star with glass-walled elevators that take you up to bedrooms set around a massive atrium. The whole ensemble looks like a housing scheme in a sci-fi movie, though the rooms are spacious and comfortable, and service is excellent. Facilities include a swimming pool, health club, choice of restaurants and bars, wheelchair access throughout, including a room adapted for wheelchair users. Rack rates start from Rs17,600 per double. ❾

Master R-500 New Rajendra Nagar ℡011/2874 1089, Ⓦwww.master -guesthouse.com. See Delhi map, p.80. A lovely little *pension*-style guesthouse, comfortable, secure and family-run, with only four a/c double rooms of different sizes (a bathroom between each pair), free wi-fi and a secluded roof terrace. Located on the edge of the green belt only 10min by auto-rickshaw from Connaught Place (or bus #910 from Shivaji Terminal behind Block P) and not far from Karol Bagh metro. Veg meals are available, and rates include breakfast. Book ahead. ❻

The Park 15 Sansad Marg ℡011/2374 3000 or 1800/117 275, Ⓦwww.thepark hotels.com. See also New Delhi map, p.99. They don't come much snazzier than this place – from the super-cool lobby to the ultramodern rooms, the decor is state-of-the-art, down to the LCD TV in each room and the frosted glass walls that screen off the en-suite bathrooms. Service is snappy, the atmosphere is relaxed, and all the facilities you'd expect are here, including a bar, a good restaurant and a pool. A cut above your run-of-the-mill five-star. Doubles from Rs13,283. ❾

Ringo 17 Scindia House, Connaught Lane ℡011/2331 0605, Ⓔringo_guest_house@yahoo .co.in. An old backpacker favourite that's traded in its dorms for single and double rooms, which are plain but decent, some attached, and arranged around a central terrace that makes a pretty congenial little hangout. ❷

Sunny 152 Scindia House, Connaught Lane ℡011/2331 2909, Ⓔsunnyguesthouse1234 @hotmail.com. Another former backpacker dorm hotel that now offers cheap but rather box-like single and double rooms, some attached, with hot water at 20 minutes' notice. ❷

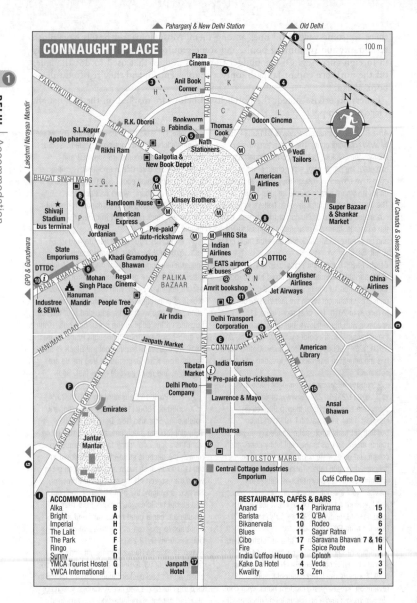

CONNAUGHT PLACE

DELHI | Accommodation

Paharganj & New Delhi Station

Old Delhi

0   100 m

N

Lakshmi Narayan Mandir

PANCHKUIN MARG

RADIAL ROAD

Plaza Cinema

Anil Book Corner

H

K

RADIAL RD 4

RADIAL RD 5

RADIAL RD 6

R.K. Oboroi

Bookworm
Fabindia

C

Odeon Cinema

L

D

S.L. Kapur
Apollo pharmacy

Thomas Cook

B

Rikhi Ram

Nath Stationers

M

Vedi Tailors

BHAGAT SINGH MARG

Galgotia &
New Book Depot

G

A

American Airlines

E

M

Shivaji Stadium
bus terminal

Handloom House

Kinsey Brothers

M

Super Bazaar
& Shankar Market

P

American Express

M

M

Royal Jordanian

Pre-paid
auto-rickshaws

M

RADIAL RD 7

BARAKHAMBA ROAD

State Emporiums

Khadi Gramodyog
Bhawan

HRG Sita

Indian Airlines

F

RADIAL RD 8

RADIAL RD 1

DTTDC

Mohan Singh Place

EATS airport
buses

DTTDC

Kingfisher Airlines

China Airlines

Industree
& SEWA

Hanuman Mandir

Regal Cinema

People Tree

PALIKA BAZAAR

Amrit bookshop

N

Jet Airways

Air India

Delhi Transport
Corporation

Janpath Market

KASTURBA GANDHI MARG

CONNAUGHT LANE

American Library

HANUMAN ROAD

Tibetan Market

India Tourism

Pre-paid auto-rickshaws

Delhi Photo
Company

Lawrence & Mayo

Ansal Bhawan

PARLIAMENT STREET

SANSAD MARG

Emirates

Jantar Mantar

Lufthansa

TOLSTOY MARG

Central Cottage Industries
Emporium

Café Coffee Day

JANPATH

ACCOMMODATION	
Alka	B
Bright	A
Imperial	H
The Lalit	C
The Park	F
Ringo	E
Sunny	D
YMCA Tourist Hostel	G
YWCA International	I

RESTAURANTS, CAFÉS & BARS			
Anand	14	Parikrama	15
Barista	12	Q'BA	8
Bikanervala	10	Rodeo	6
Blues	11	Sagar Ratna	2
Cibo	17	Saravana Bhavan	7 & 16
Fire	F	Spice Route	H
India Coffee House	0	Splash	1
Kake Da Hotel	4	Veda	3
Kwality	13	Zen	5

Janpath Hotel

YMCA Tourist Hostel Jai Singh Marg, southwest of Connaught Place ☎011/2336 1915, ⓦwww.newdelhiymca.org. See also New Delhi map, p.99. A rather staid establishment popular with American budgeteers (though it isn't all that cheap), the institutional corridors belie the spacious if simple rooms, and there are good restaurants, a large swimming pool (open April–Oct only) and attractive gardens. Wheelchair friendly. Half-board only. **G**

YWCA Blue Triangle Ashok Rd, southwest of Connaught Place ☎011/2336 0133, ⓦwww.ywcaofdelhi.org. See New Delhi map, p.99. Open to men and women, rooms here are nice and big, with large attached bathrooms. The whole place is clean, quiet and respectable, with lawns outside to relax on, and rates include breakfast. ❺

YWCA International 10 Sansad Marg, southwest of Connaught Place ☎011/2336 1561, ⓦwww .ywcaindia.org. See also New Delhi map, p.99. Clean and airy a/c rooms with private bathrooms,

though not as nice as at the *Blue Triangle* (but cheaper); set meals are available in the restaurant. Women are given priority but men can also stay. Rates include breakfast, and you even get a free copy of *The Times of India* every morning. ❻–❼

Paharganj

Running west from New Delhi railway station, the **Paharganj** area is prime backpacker territory, with innumerable lodges offering inexpensive and mid-range accommodation. Some are extremely good value; others offer very little for very little, and most can suffer from slamming-door syndrome and people shouting till dawn (especially if windows face inwards onto the communal stairwell), so choose carefully if you value quiet. Some hotels here run a 24-hour checkout system, which means you check out at the same time you checked in – good if you arrived late, but bad if you arrived early.

Unless otherwise stated, the hotels listed below are marked on the Paharganj **map** on p.94.

Ajay 5084-A Main Bazaar ☎011/2358 3125. Tucked away down an alley off the Main Bazaar, this well-run place with marble decor has clean rooms, some a/c, most with baths and TV, but not all with windows. There's a pool table, internet access, and a 24hr bakery downstairs, next to a big café area for breakfast or snacks. 24hr checkout. ❷

Camran 1116 Main Bazaar ☎011/3297 4474, ⓔsubhashthakur@yahoo.com. A small, somewhat run-down lodge in part of a late-Mughal period mosque, with some character and a panoramic rooftop terrace. As well as doubles, there are very cheap box-like single rooms, and some rooms have attached bathrooms, though only shared bathrooms have hot water showers (otherwise it comes in a bucket). Dorm beds also available (Rs100). ❶–❷

Downtown 4583 Main Bazaar ☎011/4154 1529, ⓔltctravel@rediffmail.com. This friendly lodging, just off the Main Bazaar, is bright and breezy, and not bad value, but it's worth asking for a room with an outside window. There's also a dorm (Rs100). 11am checkout. ❷

Hare Krishna 1572-3 Main Bazaar ☎011/4154 1341. Rooms here are clean, the best are spacious, and most are attached. There's hot running water and a pleasant rooftop café-restaurant, but the lower floors can be pretty noisy. 24hr checkout. ❷

Hare Rama T-298 off Main Bazaar ☎011/3536 1301 or 2, ⓦwww.hareramaguesthouse.com. Attached rooms, reasonable cleanliness and low prices, but hard beds and iffy hot water at this busy hotel down an alley off the Main Bazaar. 24hr checkout. ❷

Metropolis 1634 Main Bazaar ☎011/2358 5766, ⓦwww.metropolistravels.com. Main Bazaar's most upmarket and comfortable hotel, though somewhat overpriced for what you get. A few double rooms have large windows and bathtubs; others don't have a window. All are a/c with a TV, fridge and balcony, and there's a good restaurant and bar, with seating downstairs or on the roof terrace. ❹–❺

Namaskar 917 Chandiwalan, Main Bazaar ☎011/2358 2233, ⓔnamaskarhotel@yahoo.com. Popular family-run budget hotel off the Main Bazaar with a variety of attached rooms, some with a/c, but not all the cheaper ones have hot showers or outside windows. The staff are very attentive and helpful, but they also run tours which they can be pushy about selling. ❷

Navrang Tooti Chowk, 820 Main Bazaar ☎09818 243027. More like a down-at-heel lodge in a remote small town than a city hotel in the middle of Delhi, but it's very friendly, if somewhat basic. On the other hand, you get what you pay for, and at these rates it isn't bad value. Some rooms have bathrooms, but there's no hot running water (they'll bring you a bucket for Rs20). ❶

Rak International Tooti Chowk, 820 Main Bazaar ☎011/2356 2478, ⓦwww.hotelrakinternational .com. One of the most consistently popular Paharganj choices, in a small square off the Main Bazaar, good value with large, cool rooms, a/c, TV, fridge and hot water, and a nice rooftop too, but it could do with a lick of paint. ❶

Vishal 1575-80 Main Bazaar ☎011/2356 2123, ⓔvishalhotel@hotmail.com. There's a choice here between rather bare, cheap rooms with outside bathroom, and much nicer large attached ones,

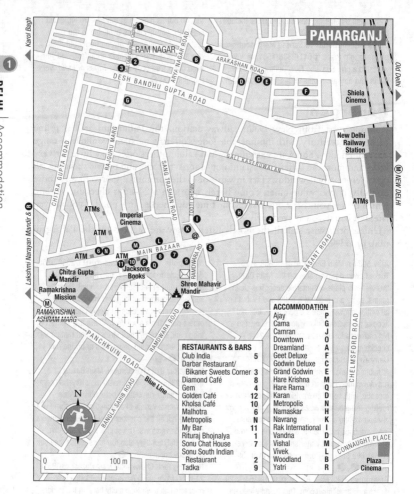

and there's a good restaurant too, but check the
sheets before you take a room. ❷
Vivek 1534-50 Main Bazaar ☎011/4154 1436,
ⓦwww.vivekhotol.com. A longstanding travellers'
favourite, with a 24hr rooftop restaurant, and
decent if unremarkable rooms, most with attached
baths and hot water, some a/c; the best have
windows facing the street. There's even room
service. ❷

Yatri 3/4 Jhansi Rd, off Punchkuin Rd, by Delhi
Heart and Lung Institute ☎011/2362 5563, ⓦwww
.yatrihouse.com. See map, p.80. This guoothouoc,
tucked away up a small residential street ten
minutes' walk from Paharganj, is like staying in a
private home, with clean and quiet attached rooms,
hot water, TV and a small enclosed garden for
breakfast or just for relaxing, though it's a bit pricey
for what you get. Book well in advance. ❼

Ram Nagar

Directly north of Paharganj, five minutes' walk from New Delhi railway
station and just beyond the flyover section of Desh Bandhu Gupta Road, **Ram
Nagar** is lined with hotels and a few restaurants. Accommodation tends to

be slightly more expensive than in Paharganj, but the rooms are generally better.

The hotels listed below are marked on the Paharganj **map** opposite.

Cama 3037 Chowk Chuna Mandi, Rajguru Marg ☏011/2358 0245, ✉hotelcama@yahoo.com. The best-value hotel on this street between Paharganj and Ram Nagar. All rooms are attached with hot water. ❷

Geet Deluxe 8570 Arakashan Rd ☏011/2361 6140 to 43. A cut above the other mid-range options in this area, well kept with nice touches, a certain charm, and clean, decent-sized rooms, all with TV, and either a/c or air-cooled. ❹

Grand Godwin 8502/41 Arakashan Rd ☏011/2354 6891 to 8, ⊛www.godwinhotels.com. Rooms start at merely "semi-deluxe" (on the ground floor and slightly smaller than the rest), but they're all well appointed and well kept, and there are super deluxe rooms and even suites, as well as a multi-cuisine restaurant. Rates include a buffet breakfast. The *Godwin Deluxe*, next door, has just been refurbished and offers even more deluxe rooms. ❺–❻

Vandna and **Karan** 47 Arakashan Rd ☏011/2362 8821 and 3. Two hotels next to each other and jointly run. The *Karan* has smaller and simpler rooms, while the *Vandna* – with mosaics of Krishna and the Qutb Minar flanking the doorway – has slightly larger rooms, though currently the same price; all the rooms in both hotels are attached with hot water and TVs, but mattresses are rather hard. ❷

Woodland 8235/6 Multani Danda, Arakashan Rd ☏011/4154 1304 to 7, ⊛www.hotelwoodland .com. Popular hotel with a choice of big a/c, or less expensive smaller, non-a/c rooms. If you want a cheaper room still, they'll send you to their sister establishment, the *Dreamland*, just across the street. ❸–❹

Old Delhi

Few tourists stay in **Old Delhi**: it's less central than Connaught Place and Paharganj, and it's dirtier, noisier and more crowded, with hotels geared mostly to Indian visitors rather than foreigners. The hotels around Old Delhi station in particular are bad value. On the other hand, there are a couple of good upmarket options on the area's fringes, and some reasonable budget hotels around the Jama Masjid, and of all the areas in town to stay in, this is the most colourful, with lots of character.

The hotels listed below appear on the Old Delhi **map** on p.108.

Broadway 4/15A Asaf Ali Rd ☏011/4366 3600, ✉broadway@oldworldhospitality.com. On the southern edge of Old Delhi, close to Delhi Gate, this mid-range hotel has a lot of old-fashioned charm, two bars, and an excellent restaurant specializing in Kashmiri cuisine (see p.134). Tours through Old Delhi are available. Rooms are a little bit sombre, but they're clean and well equipped, and some look out to the Jama Masjid. ❼

Duke 8 Netaji Suhaj Marg ☏011/2327 1501, ✉dukehotel08@gmail.com. A range of reasonably cosy rooms above the hubbub of Netaji Subhaj Marg on the east side of Old Delhi, handy for the Red Fort and Jama Masjid. ❸

Maidens 7 Sham Nath Marg, Civil Lines; metro Civil Lines ☏011/2397 5464, ⊛www .maidenshotel.com. A nice bit of understated luxury in a lovely old colonial mansion dating back to Company days; quiet and relaxing with comfortable period rooms, big bathrooms and leafy gardens as well as a swimming pool and a good restaurant. Doubles from Rs12,650. ❾

New City Palace 726 Jama Masjid Motor Market ☏011/2327 9548, ✉newcitypalace @hotmail.com. Though it doesn't quite live up to its billing of "a home for palatial comfort", this budget hotel is clean and well situated, directly behind the Jama Masjid (reserve ahead if you want a room with a view). Showers are hot and the best rooms have a/c, though not all the cheaper ones have outside windows. 24hr checkout. ❷–❸

New India 172 Katra Bariyan ☏011/2395 5117, ✉subhashkathuria@hotmail.com. Friendly and quite pleasingly rustic hotel with rooms around a bright upper-floor courtyard, mostly non-attached, though one or two have their own bathrooms, and the ones at the front share a veranda overlooking the street. 24hr checkout. ❷

South Delhi

Most of the accommodation **south of Connaught Place** lies firmly in the luxury category, although there are a few guesthouses in Sunder Nagar, the odd mid-range hotel tucked away in a residential area and a modern youth hostel near the exclusive diplomatic enclave in Chanakyapuri.

The hotels listed below appear on the New Delhi **map** on p.99.

Ambassador Sujan Singh Park, off Subramaniam Bharti Marg ☎011/2463 2600, ⓦwww.tajhotels .com. Low-key but well run and classy, this is a friendly place with comfortable-sized rooms and huge bathrooms, plus a couple of good restaurants and free use of the pool and health club at the other Taj Group hotel, *Taj Mahal*. Doubles start from Rs14,300. ❾

The Claridges 12 Aurangzeb Rd ☎011/3955 5000, ⓦwww.claridges.com. One of Delhi's oldest and finest establishments, oozing elegant 1930s style from its facade to its rooms and even its bathrooms. Facilities include four restaurants, a vodka bar and a swimming pool. Doubles start at Rs21,450. ❾

La Sagrita 14 Sunder Nagar ☎011/2435 9541, ⓦwww.lasagrita.com. Tucked away down a quiet side street in an exclusive colony, opposite a small park and next door to the Grenadian high commission, this small guesthouse might just suit if you want to escape the din of central Delhi. The rooms are cosy, carpeted, attached and tastefully done out, and there's a little garden out front to relax in. ❼

Maurya Sardar Patel Marg, Chanakyapuri ☎011/2611 2233, ⓦwww.itcwelcomgroup.in. An extremely plush hotel on the edge of Chanakyapuri, opposite the Ridge forest, with an imposing range of luxury rooms, and some of the best dining in Delhi (see p.134). It regularly hosts visiting heads of state, with Bill Clinton among those who have stayed here. Full-price room rates start at Rs19,311, but promotional rates are often available. ❾

Youth Hostel 5 Nyaya Marg, off Kautilya Marg, Chanakyapuri ☎011/2611 6285, ⓦwww.yhaindia .org. Away from the bustling city centre, this ultra-modern and eco-friendly grey concrete building, with dorms (a/c Rs350; non-a/c Rs150) and a/c or non-a/c singles and doubles, is the showpiece-cum-administration centre of the Indian YHA. You need to be an HI member to stay here (maximum stay seven days) but you can join on the spot (Rs250). Rates include breakfast. ❷–❸

Majnu Ka Tilla

If you want to avoid Delhi's hustle and bustle, or to have a change from Indian culture and cuisine, the Tibetan colony at **Majnu Ka Tilla** offers excellent-value budget hotels with immaculately kept rooms, much nicer than what you'd get for the same price in Paharganj, in a relatively quiet district with Tibetan food, internet facilities and money changers close at hand. It isn't, however, very convenient for central Delhi (Connaught Place is Rs80 away by auto, Vidhan Sabha metro Rs20 by rickshaw). Book ahead if you intend to stay here as hotels are often full. There's only one main drag in Majnu Ka Tilla, so everything's pretty easy to find.

Lhasa House 16 New Camp, just east of the main street ☎011/2393 9777 or 9008, ⓔlhasahouse @rediffmail.com. The rooms are a little bit smaller and simpler than at *Wongdhen House* next door, but all are attached, with TV and fan. Cheapest rooms are on the top floor. ❶–❷

White House 44 New Camp ☎011/2381 3644, ⓔwhitehouse02@yahoo.com. On the Tibetan colony's main street (such as it is), 100m north of the other two hotels mentioned here; the rooms are quite large, attached, with TV, and certainly well kept, but the mattresses are a bit hard. ❷

Wongdhen House 15-A New Camp, just east of the main drag, next to *Lhasa House* ☎011/6415 5330, ⓔwongdhenhouse@hotmail .com. Friendly guesthouse with a choice of rooms, some attached and some overlooking the Yamuna River. There's also a good restaurant (Tibetan food, or breakfast items) and a terrace with a great river view. ❷–❹

The City

Delhi is both daunting and alluring, a sprawling metropolis with a stunning backdrop of ancient architecture. Once you've found your feet and got over the initial impact of the commotion, noise, pollution and sheer scale of the place, the city's geography slowly slips into focus. Monuments in assorted states of repair are dotted around the city, especially in **Old Delhi** and in southern enclaves such as Hauz Khas. The British-built modern city centres on Connaught Place, the heart of **New Delhi** (though actually on its northern edge), from

▲ India Gate, Rajpath

which it's easy – by taxi, bus, auto-rickshaw or metro – to visit pretty much anywhere else in town.

New Delhi

At the 1911 durbar (ceremonial gathering), Britain's King George V, in his role as emperor of India, announced that Delhi would replace Calcutta as India's capital. The real reason for this was that opposition to British rule in Bengal had grown so strong that the colonialists wanted to move their administration to somewhere less militant. Architect **Edwin Lutyens**, thus far known mainly for building country houses in England, was commissioned to design the administrative centre, and decided to place **New Delhi** on a rise between Old Delhi and the city's more ancient incarnations at Lal Kot and Firozabad. Tombs, temples and buildings of historical importance were incorporated into the new area, but homes and a handful of villages were simply knocked down to make way for it. The new city was spacious, with wide tree-lined avenues, fine residential bungalows and solid colonial architecture. Its low density in the centre of such a populated city is rather peculiar, but Delhiites (or, more correctly, Delhiwallahs) are justifiably proud of its grand scale, and it does make for a splendid centre of government.

The axis of Lutyens' city is the arrow-straight royal mall, **Rajpath**, running from the presidential palace, **Rashtrapati Bhavan**, in the west, to **India Gate** in the east. In the spacious avenues to the south, the residences of Jawaharlal Nehru and Indira Gandhi have been preserved as memorials, as has **Gandhi Smriti**, where the Father of the Nation, Mahatma Gandhi, met his death. At the north edge of the new capital lies the thriving business centre, **Connaught Place** ("CP"), where neon advertisements for restaurants, bars and banks adorn the roofs and verandas of the buildings that circle its central park. On the fringes of New Delhi lie older areas: **Purana Qila**, Delhi's sixth incarnation, with its nearby **Crafts Museum**; and **Paharganj**, once a village, now the city's favourite backpacker hangout.

Rajpath and around

Running across the middle of New Delhi is the majestic mall, **Rajpath**, formerly known as Kingsway, flanked by gardens and fountains that are floodlit at night. The wide grassy margins are a popular meeting place for families, picnickers and courting couples, and the location of a huge parade held every year on January 26 to mark **Republic Day**, which features military marching bands, floats from all of India's states, folk dancing, elephants, even the Bikaner Camel Corps on camelback. Tickets (grandstand seats Rs150–300, standing room Rs10–50; no cameras, bags, food or drink) can be obtained from Government of India tourist offices, Dilli Haat market (see p.139) and outlets across town. Information is posted on the Press Information Bureau website (Ⓦpib.nic.in) in January. On January 29, a ceremony called **Beating the Retreat** is held at Janpath's western end on Raisina Hill, with military bands and fireworks, and Rashtrapati Bhavan gloriously floodlit for the occasion, but tickets are scarce; there is, however, a full dress rehearsal one or two days before, for which tickets (Rs20–150) are available from the same outlets as Republic Day tickets.

At the eastern end of Rajpath is **India Gate**, which was designed by Lutyens in 1921. The 42m-high arch commemorates ninety thousand Indian soldiers killed fighting for the British in World War I, and bears the names of more than three thousand British and Indian soldiers who died on the Northwest frontier and in the Afghan War of 1919. The memorial beneath the arch honours those who lost their lives in the Indo-Pakistan War of 1971. Despite its solemn commemoration, India Gate has something of a carnival atmosphere at times, with sellers of

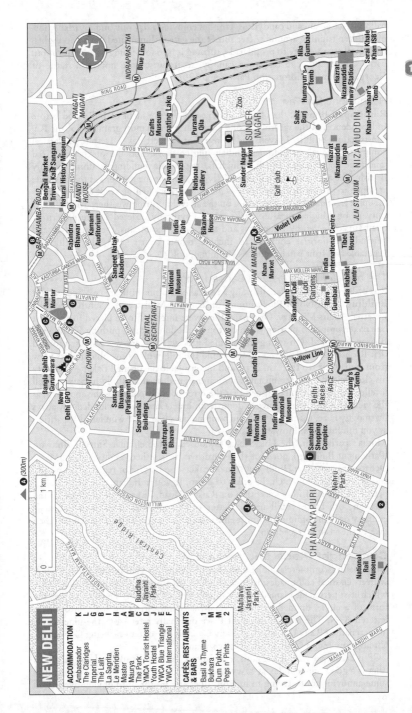

NEW DELHI

ACCOMMODATION
Ambassador	K
The Claridges	L
Imperial	G
The Lalit	B
La Sagrita	I
Le Meridien	A
Master	M
Maurya	C
The Park	D
YMCA Tourist Hostel	J
Youth Hostel	E
YWCA Blue Triangle	H
YWCA International	F

CAFÉS, RESTAURANTS & BARS
Basil & Thyme	1
Bukhara	M
Dum Pukht	M
Pegs n' Pints	2

DELHI

99

balloons, ice cream and candyfloss, families enjoying a day out, and invariably lots of children running around. After sunset the gate is illuminated with floodlights, and couples come here to promenade, turning it into something of an impromptu party. The empty chhatri (stone canopy) to its west once housed a statue of George V, now in Coronation Park (see p.120).

Rashtrapati Bhavan

Rashtrapati Bhavan, the official residence of the president of India (and before Independence, of the viceroy), is one of the largest and most grandiose of the Raj constructions built by Lutyens and his assistant Herbert Baker. Despite its classical columns, Mughal-style domes, Indian filigree work, and use of the same red sandstone so favoured by the Mughals, the whole building is unmistakeably British. The apartments inside are strictly private, but the **gardens** at the west side are open to the public for two weeks in late February (daily except Mon 9.30am–2.30pm; free; dates vary depending on the arrival of spring weather). Modelled by Lutyens on Mughal pleasure parks, with a typically ordered square pattern of quadrants dissected by waterways and refreshed by fountains, the gardens extend beyond the normal confines to include tennis courts, butterfly enclosures, vegetable and fruit patches and a swimming pool.

The ministry buildings and Sansad Bhawan

East of Rashtrapati Bhavan, flanking a rise called Raisina Hill, are two **Secretariat Buildings**. The North Block houses the Finance Ministry, the South Block the External Affairs Ministry. Originally they were intended to be placed further east but Baker proposed putting them on top of the hill instead, pushing Rashtrapati Bhavan westward. On seeing the finished product, Lutyens was horrified to find that Rashtrapati Bhavan was down behind the hill, which now obscured its view from India Gate, to the east. Livid and inconsolable, he blamed Baker – formerly his close friend – for the mistake, and campaigned unsuccessfully to have the hill levelled. In fact, it can be argued that the error actually enhances the approach, as the view of Rashtrapati Bhavan's dome from India Gate is often clouded nowadays by smoggy haze, through which the building rises like some wonderful apparition as you mount the hill towards it.

India's parliament, the Lok Sabha, is housed in the circular **Sansad Bhawan** (Parliament Building), north of the Rajpath at the southern end of Sansad Marg. Debates are mostly in Hindi, but some speakers use English or regional languages, and it is possible to watch. In order to do so, if you're Indian, you can obtain a permit from the visitors' reception on Raisina Road, just southeast of the Sansad Bhawan; otherwise you'll need a letter of introduction from your country's embassy or high commission (most embassies will charge for this), which you then take to the visitors' reception.

Connaught Place and around

New Delhi's commercial hub, **Connaught Place** (inevitably known as "CP"), with its classical colonnades, is radically different from the bazaars of Old Delhi, which it superseded. Named after a minor British royal of the day, it takes the form of a circle, divided by seven radial roads and three ring roads into blocks lettered A–N. The term Connaught Place originally referred to the inner circle (now renamed Rajiv Chowk after Rajiv Gandhi), the outer one being Connaught Circus (now Indira Chowk, after Rajiv's mum).

CP is crammed with restaurants, bars, shops, cinemas, banks and airline offices (there's a good online index at Ⓦ www.connaughtplacemall.com), not to mention some annoying touts (trying to lure unsuspecting visitors into buying overpriced tours – their opening line is usually to inform you, quite superfluously, which block you're on) and lots of street traders. It gets especially animated in the evenings, and even on Sunday, when most of the shops are closed, there's enough going on to make it worth a stroll. On the outer circle, one of the liveliest areas is by **Super Bazaar** and **Shankar Market**, just across from Block M; it's especially buzzing in the evening when people come down to dine at the many low-priced restaurants. The block opposite Palika Bazaar on the south side of the outer circle also gets very busy around nightfall, with street traders setting out their stalls, and customers jostling for position. The pavement in front of the **Regal Building**, named after a cinema in the middle of the block, is patrolled by itinerant vendors flogging sunglasses, socks and handkerchiefs. The **central park** in the middle of the circus, now beautifully landscaped, offers a quiet retreat from the hurly-burly. If you don't fancy getting run down on the busy road above, you are advised to use the pedestrian underpasses, also favoured by beggars, who strategically place themselves at each entrance.

The street life extends onto the roads radiating off from CP too. On Baba Kharak Singh Marg, beyond **Mohan Singh Place Shopping Complex** (a hive of shops selling mostly fabric and clothing), the **Hanuman Mandir** is an old-established and a very popular place of worship among Delhiwallahs, though not of any special interest to tourists. Around its entrance traders sell religious items, old coins and small knick-knacks to devotees and passers-by, directly across the street from where the various state emporiums (see p.139) showcase their respective crafts. On the other side of the Regal Building, **Janpath Market**, a line of stalls doing brisk business in cheap clothes, is always lively. At its western end, it meets the more touristy **Tibetan Market**, a row of shops originally established by refugees from Tibet, and a favourite stretch for souvenir shopping (see p.140).

Jantar Mantar

South of Connaught Place on Sansad Marg, the **Jantar Mantar** (daily sunrise–sunset; foreigners Rs100, Indian residents Rs5) was built in 1725, the first of five open-air observatories designed by the ruler of Jaipur, Jai Singh II, and precursor

▲ Jantar Mantar

to his larger one in Jaipur (see p.195). Huge red and white slanting stone structures looming over palm trees and neat flowerbeds were used to calculate time, solar and lunar calendars and astrological movements with an admirable degree of accuracy. Sadly, a lot of the instruments were damaged in the late eighteenth century when most of the original marble with its precisely carved gradations was stolen. Plaques explain how the instruments worked, but their explanations may not be too easy to follow if your trigonometry's a bit rusty. The most prominent instrument is the Samrat Yantra, which looks like a giant stairway to nowhere, but is actually a huge sundial: the position of its shadow tells the time of day, its length the sun's elevation; unfortunately, the marble scales on which these could be read off has long gone. To its south, the Ram Yantras, which resemble two mini coliseums, are for calculating the elevation of heavenly bodies such as the sun, moon and planets. The heart-shaped Misra Yantra, near the entrance, is a later addition and performed several functions, one of which was to track the progress of these objects across the sky. In recent years the Jantar Mantar has become the hub of political demonstrations in Delhi; people regularly gather here with placards and banners, or even camp out on hunger strikes, to protest about local, national or international issues.

Bangla Sahib Gurudwara

Southwest of Connaught Place, on Ashok Road by the GPO, the vast white marble structure of **Bangla Sahib Gurudwara** is Delhi's biggest Sikh temple, topped by a huge, golden, onion-shaped dome that is visible from some distance. The temple commemorates a 1664 visit to Delhi by the eighth Sikh guru, Hare Krishan, as a guest of Amber's ruler Jai Singh I, who had a haveli where the temple is now. At the time, Delhi was stricken with cholera and smallpox, and Krishan went around ministering to those stricken with illness. He also blessed a small pond at Jai Singh's haveli so that its waters would cure sufferers of their disease. Today, devotees still drink water from the same pond, which is located to the left of the main entrance and continually replenished from the mains. The temple welcomes visitors; deposit shoes at the information centre, where you can also enlist the services of a free guide. Remember to cover your head and dress conservatively. Live devotional music (vocals, harmonium and tabla) is relayed throughout the complex, and everybody is invited to share a simple meal of dhal and chapatis, served three times daily.

Lakshmi Narayan Mandir

Lakshmi Narayan Mandir (daily 4am–1.30pm & 2.30–9pm; deposit cameras, shoes and mobile phones at the entrance), northwest of the GPO and directly west of Connaught Place on Mandir Marg, is a modern Hindu temple that welcomes tourists. With its white, cream and red brick domes, it was commissioned by a wealthy merchant family, the Birlas (hence its alternative name, Birla Mandir), and was inaugurated in 1939 by Mahatma Gandhi. Its architect, Chandra Chatterjee, was founder of the Modern Indian Architectural Movement, which aimed to revive indigenous building styles in contrast to the grandiose foreign constructions of colonialists such as Lutyens. The main shrine is dedicated to Lakshmi, goddess of wealth (on the right), and her consort Narayana, aka Vishnu, the preserver of life (on the left, holding a conch). Shrines on either side are to Durga (in the left-hand shrine, riding a tiger), and her consort Shiva (in the right-hand shrine, meditating with a cobra round his neck). At the back is a tiny ornate chamber decorated with coloured stones and mirrors and dedicated to Krishna, one of Vishnu's earthly incarnations. Devotional music is played throughout, and quotes from Hindu scriptures adorn the walls, many translated into English. Behind the temple is a pleasant garden full of fountains and kitsch statues, including dragons and other mythical beasts; if you're really brave, you can even stand inside a dragon's mouth.

Paharganj

North of Connaught Place and directly west of New Delhi railway station, **Paharganj**, centred around Main Bazaar, provides the first experience of the Subcontinent for many budget travellers. Packed with cheap hotels, restaurants, cafés and *dhabas*, and with a busy fruit and vegetable market halfway along, it's also a paradise for shoestring shoppers seeking psychedelic clothing, joss sticks, bags, and oils of patchouli or sandalwood. A constant stream of auto- and cycle

▲ Cow in the streets of Paharganj

rickshaws, cars, handcarts and cows (this is the most cow-friendly part of central Delhi) squeezes through seemingly impossible gaps without the flow ever quite coming to a complete standstill, and the winding back-alleys seem worlds away from the commercial city centre just around the corner. Beware of opportunist thieves here, and the attentions of touts (see p.86). Formerly a village, Paharganj only survived the construction of New Delhi because its population density made it difficult for the British to get away with demolishing it, and its backstreets still harbour some fine old houses.

There is also a less-visible underside to life in Paharganj, in the shape of the **street children**. Most are runaways who've left difficult homes, often hundreds of kilometres away, and the majority sleep on the streets and inhale solvents to numb their pain. The Salaam Baalak Trust (ⓦwww.salaambaalaktrust.com), a local NGO working to help them, organizes **walking tours** of Paharganj conducted by former street children. Tours last for two hours and usually start at 10am, and cost Rs200. For bookings, contact ⓣ09873 130383 or ⓔsbttour@yahoo.com. Proceeds go towards providing shelter, education and healthcare for the area's street children.

National Museum

The **National Museum** (Tues–Sun 10am–5pm; foreigners Rs300, Indian residents Rs10; cameras Rs300 for foreigners, Rs20 for Indian residents; ⓦwww.national museumindia.gov.in), just south of Rajpath at 11 Janpath, provides a good overview of Indian culture and history. The foreigners' entry fee includes a free audio tour (Rs150 in English for Indian citizens), but you need to leave a passport, driving licence, credit card or Rs2000 (or US$40/£40/€40) as a deposit, and the exhibits it covers are rather random. At a trot, you can see the museum in a couple of hours, but to get the best out of your visit you should set aside at least half a day.

The most important exhibits are on the ground floor, kicking off in **room 4** with the Harappan civilization, which originated in the Indus Valley during the third millennium BC (contemporary with early ancient Egypt). The most impressive exhibits here are a diminutive dancing girl from Mohenjodaro in what is now Pakistan, and a bronze casting of a chariot pulled by oxen from Diamabad in Maharashtra. **Room 5** has a wonderful elephant relief from a Buddhist temple of the Shunga dynasty (second century BC) at Bharhut in Madhya Pradesh state. The Gandhara sculptures in **room 6** betray a very obvious Greek influence, a result of Alexander the Great's conquest of what is now Afghanistan and Pakistan. On your left as you enter **room 7**, two lintels of the Gupta period (sixth or seventh century AD) with friezes of cows and other animals, plus a fifth-century AD railing pillar, were all found embedded in the concrete roof of Sultan Ghari's tomb near Lal Kot (see p.128). They must have come from an earlier temple in the area, showing that it was inhabited by the fifth century.

Room 9 has some very fine bronzes, most especially those of the Chola period (from South India in the ninth to the thirteenth century), and a fifteenth-century statue of Devi from Vijayanagar (Hampi), in Karnataka, South India, by the left-hand wall. Among the late medieval sculptures in **room 10**, look out for a fearsome, vampire-like, late Chola *dvarapala* (a guardian figure built to flank the doorway to a shrine), also from South India, and a couple of performing musicians from Mysore.

Room 12 is devoted to the Mughals, and in particular their miniature paintings. Outstanding in the first section of the room is the wedding of Shah Jahan's son Dara Shikoh, later killed by his pious brother Aurangzeb during wranglings for the succession while the old emperor was still alive. The second section has a wonderful painting of the great Mughal emperor Akbar on a hunt in 1595, charging on horseback at a miscellany of animals including a lion devouring a deer. In a more sexually suggestive painting, a shy young virgin is brought into the harem of a Mughal noble, who waits expectantly on a bed to receive her. And look out also for two paintings depicting a subject you wouldn't expect – the Nativity of Jesus. The third section of room 12 has a portrait of Guru Nanak, first of the ten Sikh gurus, dating from the 1730s, while in the next section are representations of Udaipur's Jag Mandir (see p.319) and the legendary lovers Dhola and Maru (see p.305), as well as an action-packed painting from Kota of an elephant, ridden by two hunters, fighting a tiger.

Some of the remaining galleries, including the manuscripts collection, are currently closed, but it's worth popping upstairs to see the **jewellery**, the **textiles** and the **musical instruments**. The **Central Asian antiquities** collection includes a large number of paintings, documents, ceramics and textiles from Eastern Turkestan (Xinjiang) and the Silk Route, dating from between the third and twelfth centuries. Finally, on your way out, take a look at the massive twelve-tiered temple chariot from Tamil Nadu, an extremely impressive piece of woodwork in a glass shelter just by the southern entrance gate.

Nehru Memorial Museum

The **Nehru Memorial Museum** (Tues–Sun 9am–5.30pm; free; Ⓦwww .nehrumemorial.com) on Teen Murti Marg was built in 1930 as the grand and sombre residence of the British commander-in-chief. After Independence it became home to India's first prime minister, Jawaharlal Nehru, and is now preserved in his memory. The rooms are full of photographs recording Nehru's life, from his childhood and student years at Harrow and Cambridge to his appointment as prime minister. One of Nehru's passions was astronomy, and the **planetarium** (Rs2; 40min astronomy shows in English Tues–Sun 11.30am & 3pm, Rs15; Ⓦnehruplanetarium.org) in the grounds of the house has a few exhibits including the descent module used by the first Indian cosmonaut in 1984, its heat-shield charred by re-entry into the atmosphere. Next to the planetarium is an old hunting lodge dating back to the time of Ghiyas-ud-Din Tughluq (early fourteenth century), which you can also explore.

Indira Gandhi Memorial Museum

Nehru's daughter, Indira Gandhi, despite her excesses during the 1975–77 Emergency (see p.368), is still remembered by many with respect and affection. The **Indira Gandhi Memorial Museum** (Tues–Sun 9.30am–4.45pm; free), 1 Safdarjang Rd, occupies the house where she was assassinated by her Sikh bodyguards in 1984; her bloodstained sari is on display, along with letters, press cuttings, photos (many taken by her son Rajiv) and possessions. A section devoted to Rajiv includes the clothes he was wearing when he was in turn assassinated by Sri Lankan Tamil separatists in 1991. The study, drawing room and dining room conjure up images of how the family must have lived, in great style but not overt opulence. At weekends especially, arrive early to avoid the crowds.

Gandhi Smriti

Still more tragic than the deaths of Rajiv and Indira was the 1948 assassination of the nation's founder, Mahatma Gandhi, who shared their surname but was not related. The **Gandhi Smriti** (Tues–Sun 10am–5pm; free), 5 Tees January Marg, is the house where it happened, and where the Mahatma lived his last days. He had come to Delhi to quell the sectarian rioting that accompanied Partition, following his amazing success at ending it in Bengal, but Hindu sectarian extremists hated him for protecting Muslims, and on January 30, 1948, one of them shot him dead.

His assassination so shocked the nation that sectarian murders all but ended, for which Gandhi would no doubt have considered his death a worthy sacrifice. Today, you can follow in his last footsteps and even see the spot where he died. Exhibits in the house and grounds tell more about the life and death of the man regarded by many as the twentieth century's greatest statesman.

National Gallery of Modern Art

Once the residence of the Maharaja of Jaipur, the extensive **National Gallery** (Tues–Sun 10am–5pm; foreigners Rs150, Indian residents Rs10; Ⓦngmaindia .gov.in), housed in Jaipur House near India Gate, is a rich showcase of Indian contemporary art. The permanent displays, focusing on post-1930s work, exhibit many of India's most important works of modern art, including pieces by the "Bengali Renaissance" artists Abanindranath Tagore and Nandalal Bose, the great poet and artist, Rabindranath Tagore, and Jamini Roy, whose work, reminiscent of Modigliani, reflects the influence of Indian folk art. Also on show are the romantic paintings and etchings of Thomas Daniell and his nephew William, British artists of the Bombay or Company School, which combined Indian delicacy with Western realism. The ground-floor galleries are used for temporary exhibitions.

Purana Qila and around

The majestic fortress of **Purana Qila** (daily sunrise–sunset; foreigners Rs100, Indian residents Rs5), whose crumbling ramparts dominate busy Mathura Road, east of India Gate, is thought to stand on the site of Indraprastha, the Pandava city of Mahabharata fame. Considered the sixth city of Delhi, though actually – like Siri – it was just a citadel, it was begun by Humayun, the second Mughal emperor, as Din-Panah, and renamed Shergarh by Sher Khan, who displaced him in 1540 and oversaw most of the construction. In 1947, during Partition, Muslim refugees gathered in the fort to await transportation to Pakistan; tens of thousands of them were slaughtered en route. Purana Qila is served by **buses** #453, #454, #457 and #458 from New Delhi station gate 2 (Ajmeri Gate side) – ask for the zoo, which is the same stop.

Entry is through the **western gateway**, less impressive than the north and south entries, which can be seen from opposite the Crafts Museum and from the zoo respectively. Just inside the gate, a small **Archeological Museum** (daily except Fri, 10am–5pm; Rs5) houses some interesting finds, not all from the area.

Most of the inside of the fortress is taken up by pleasant lawns and gardens, but two important buildings survive. Of them, the **Qila-i-Kuhna Masjid** is one of Sher Khan's finest monuments. Constructed in 1541 in the Afghan style, it has five elegant arches, embellished with white and black marble to complement the red sandstone. The geometric patterns and carved Arabic calligraphy around the main doorway all represent a more sophisticated degree of decorative artwork than on anything seen before in Delhi. Previous decorative carving on buildings was in plaster, but here it's in stone, a more serious affair as it's obviously much harder to work.

The Purana Qila's other main building, the **Sher Mandal**, is a red sandstone octagonal observatory and library built for Sher Khan. It was here in 1556 that the emperor Humayun died. He stumbled down its treacherously steep steps while hurrying to answer the *muezzin*'s call to prayer, just a year after he had defeated one of Sher Khan's successors, Sikander Suri, and regained power.

The zoo and boating lake

Next door to Purana Qila, the **zoo** (Sat–Thurs April to mid-Oct 9am–4.30pm; mid-Oct to March 9.30am–4pm; foreigners Rs50, Indian residents Rs10) is highly popular with Delhiites, especially young ones, and particularly at weekends.

Spread over 212 acres of land, with some two thousand animal species and lots of greenery, it is the biggest zoo in India, and one of the biggest in Asia. As well as Indian rhinos and elephants, the top attraction is the white Bengal tigers, a rarity in the wild, but bred in captivity by the zoo, which has gifted some of their siblings to zoos elsewhere in India. Neither albino nor a separate species from ordinary Bengal tigers, white tigers are rare in nature because they are the result of a recessive gene that only surfaces if both parents carry it.

The **boating lake** in front of Purana Qila (daily: April–Sept noon–7pm; Oct–March 11am–6pm; Rs50 per half hour for a four-person boat) is not massively exciting, but it can be a laugh, especially if you have small people in tow, and it also allows you a good view of Purana Qila's northern gateway.

The Khairul Manazil

Across the street are more ruins worth checking out. The **Khairul Manazil** (daily sunrise–sunset; free) was a mosque built in 1562 on the orders of Maham Angah, Akbar's faithful nurse, and an important figure in his still shaky regime when he inherited the throne from Humayun at the age of fourteen. You can climb up the eastern gateway for a view down into the courtyard with its octagonal ablutions pool. North of the Khairul Manazil, the **Lal Darwaza** gateway stands at the end of what was once an avenue of shops. You can't walk up the avenue to the gate, but you can look up it from the road. The now rather ruined but still impressive gateway is known as the **bloody gate** after a British officer, William Hodson, shot dead three Mughal princes here. He'd arrested them at Humayun's Tomb, where they'd taken refuge following the fall of Delhi in 1857, having played a particularly active part in the uprising. Hodson then had their naked bodies put on public display in Chandni Chowk. They say that during the rainy season, the gateway drips blood in their memory, though it's more likely to be rust from iron parts of the gate structure colouring the rainwater red.

Crafts Museum

Immediately north of Purana Qila on Bhairon Marg, the **Crafts Museum** (Tues–Sun 10am–5pm; foreigners Rs150, Indian residents Rs10) is a dynamic exhibition of the rural arts and crafts of India, divided into three sections. The **exhibition galleries** show a range of textiles, carvings, ceramics, painting and metalwork from across India, while the **village complex** displays an assortment of traditional homes from different parts of the country. The **craft demonstrations** do feature a few artisans actually at work, but mostly they are more like shops selling crafts typical of different Indian regions. There's also a library and a fixed-price museum **shop**.

Old Delhi (Shahjahanabad)

Though it's not in fact the oldest part of Delhi, the seventeenth-century city of **Shahjahanabad**, built for the Mughal emperor Shah Jahan, is known as **Old Delhi**. Construction began on the city in 1638, and within eleven years it was substantially complete, surrounded by over 8km of ramparts pierced by fourteen main gates. It boasted a beautiful main thoroughfare, **Chandni Chowk**, an imposing citadel, the **Red Fort** (Lal Qila), and an impressive congregational mosque, the **Jama Masjid**. Today much of the wall has crumbled, and of the fourteen gates only four remain, but it's still a fascinating area, crammed with interesting nooks and crannies. More than anywhere else in town, Old Delhi teems with life. Its bazaars are always chock-a-block, a warren of cupboard-sized shops lining thoroughfares packed to the gunwales with rickshaws, barrows and hand-carts, all jostling for position as shoppers, hawkers, porters and pedestrians do their best to weave their way

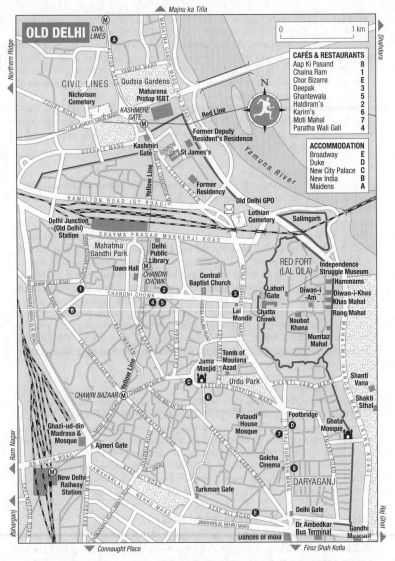

OLD DELHI

▲ Majnu ka Tilla

0   1 km

CAFÉS & RESTAURANTS	
Aap Ki Pasand	8
Chaina Ram	1
Chor Bizarre	E
Deepak	3
Ghantewala	5
Haldiram's	2
Karim's	6
Moti Mahal	7
Paratha Wali Gali	4

ACCOMMODATION	
Broadway	E
Duke	D
New City Palace	C
New India	B
Maidens	A

CIVIL LINES

Northern Ridge

Nicholson Cemetery

Qudsia Gardens

Maharana Pratap ISBT

KASHMERE GATE

Red Line

Kashmiri Gate

St James's

Former Deputy Resident's Residence

Yellow Line

Former Residency

HAMILTON ROAD (GT ROAD)

Old Delhi GPO

Lothian Cemetery

Salimgarh

Delhi Junction (Old Delhi) Station

SHAYMA PRASAD MUKHERJI ROAD

Mahatma Gandhi Park

Delhi Public Library

Town Hall

CHANDNI CHOWK

Central Baptist Church

RED FORT (LAL QILA)

Independence Struggle Museum

Khari Baoli Road

CHANDNI CHOWK

Lahori Gate

Diwan-i-Am

Hammams

Diwan-i-Khas

Khas Mahal

Lal Mandir

Chatta Chowk

Rang Mahal

Naubat Khana

Mumtaz Mahal

Darba Kalan Road

Jama Masjid

Tomb of Maulana Azad

Urdu Park

KASTURBA HOSPITAL MARG

SHANTI VANA MARG

Shanti Vana

Shakti Sthal

CHAWRI BAZAAR

Pataudi House Mosque

Footbridge

Ghata Mosque

Ghazi-ud-din Madrasa & Mosque

Ajmeri Gate

Golcha Cinema

Ram Nagar

DR GUPTA ROAD

New Delhi Railway Station

JAWAHARLAL NEHRU MARG

Turkman Gate

DARYAGANJ

Raj Ghat

Paharganj

ASAF ALI ROAD

JAWAHARLAL NEHRU MARG

Dances of India

Delhi Gate

Dr Ambedkar Bus Terminal

Gandhi Museum

▼ Connaught Place   ▼ Firoz Shah Kotla

between them. At one time, each residential quarter had just one entrance that could be closed off at night for security, and though this ended when the British drove wide streets such as Nai Sarak through the old city after the 1857 uprising, the back-alleys where most of its residents live still tend to end in cul-de-sacs. If you're short of time or hate dense throngs, then you'll probably want to stick to the two main sights – the Red Fort and Jama Masjid – but there's much more to Old Delhi than that, and it really does repay further exploration. Old Delhi is served by metro stations at Chandni Chowk (actually nearer Old Delhi train station), Chawri Bazaar, and the Ajmeri Gate side of New Delhi train station (the metro stop's name of "New Delhi" is in this instance misleading).

An excellent book, *Old Delhi: Ten Easy Walks* by Gaynor Barton and Lurraine Malone (available at Delhi bookstores), details ten short **walks** covering different aspects of Old Delhi. Alternatively, the *Broadway Hotel* (see p.95) offers walks around Old Delhi with a local guide; tours require a minimum of five people, and cost Rs1500 per person, including lunch at the Chor Bizarre restaurant (see p.134).

Chandni Chowk and around

Old Delhi's main thoroughfare, **Chandni Chowk**, was once a sublime canal lined with trees and some of the most opulent bazaars in the whole of Asia. "That marvellous artery of Delhi," an English visitor called it in 1903, "which epitomizes the magic and mystery of an Eastern city." To some extent, with its thronging crowds, its markets, temples, mosques and havelis, it still does today, though the British paved over the canal in 1857. In 2007, the courts ordered a daytime (8am–8pm) ban on cycle rickshaws along the street, and they were replaced by a fleet of green minibuses (fare Rs5), but the ban has been challenged and may not last. In any event, the best way to see the street is on foot. Along it, look out for numbered "heritage buildings" signposted at intervals, with placards outside explaining their historical importance, especially during the 1857 uprising.

At the western end of Chandni Chowk is **Fatehpuri Mosque**, commissioned in 1650 by Nawab Fatehpuri Begum, one of Shah Jahan's wives. During the 1857 uprising its religious scholars played a part in encouraging the insurgents, so when the British retook Delhi they sacked the mosque and sold it to a local businessman, though they bought it back twenty years later (for three times the price) and returned it to the Muslim community. The large courtyard contains graves of – alongside Sufi saints – some of those killed by the British in 1857. As Mughal mosques go, it isn't that impressive, but then it's up against some stiff competition in Old Delhi. To its west is **Khari Baoli** spice market (see p.115).

Though the 1857 British recapture of Delhi was a disaster for most of its residents, one or two people did well out of it. One such person was the man who bought Fatehpuri Mosque from the British, Lal Chunnamal, a Hindu merchant who had remained loyal to the East India Company, and was richly rewarded. Just how richly can be gauged from the size of his home, **Chunnamal Haveli**, a 126-room mansion just east of the mosque on Chandni Chowk. With the plunge in land prices, and his own wealth augmented and protected by the now victorious British, he was able to buy up half the north side of the street and construct this huge palace. The downstairs area has now largely been converted into shops, but Lal Chunnamal's family still lives in parts of the haveli.

Almost opposite, **Ballimaran**, the shoe bazaar, leads south towards Chawri Bazaar and its metro station. Three hundred metres down on the right, opposite no. 5134, is a turning called Qasimjan Street, in which **Mirza Ghalib Haveli** (Tues–Sun 10am–5pm; free) was home from 1860 until his death nine years later of the great Urdu poet, Mirza Ghalib, who's buried in Nizamuddin (see p.123). A pioneer in Urdu literature – of which Delhi was a major centre, with its own distinct Urdu dialect – Ghalib was most famous for his *ghazals*, a poetic form consisting of rhyming couplets with a repeated refrain, nowadays very popular in songs. Part of the haveli has been bought up by the government and restored to its original form, with a little display about Ghalib. Though he's considered Delhi's (and the Urdu language's) greatest poet, many during his lifetime regarded his verse as pretentious and overblown. Despite being the obvious candidate, he was passed over as poet laureate by the emperor Bahadur Shah II, who instead appointed Ghalib's rival Zauq ("the Salieri to Ghalib's

Mozart", as historian William Dalrymple calls him); Ghalib only inherited the post when Zauq died.

Gurudwara Sisganj and Fountain Chowk

Further east along Chandni Chowk, on the south side, is **Gurudwara Sisganj**, a Sikh temple founded in 1784, though almost all of the current building dates from the 1930s. It marks the spot where in 1675 the Mughal emperor Aurangzeb had the ninth Sikh guru, Tegh Bahadur, beheaded. The temple welcomes visitors, and has an information office to the left of the entrance, where you can leave shoes and borrow a scarf to cover your head before entering. Before he was killed, the guru was forced to see three of his followers executed in most unpleasant ways: one was sawn in half from head to foot, another wrapped in cotton and slowly burned to death, a third boiled alive in a cauldron of water. This happened across the street in what is now **Fountain Chowk** (the eponymous fountain is Victorian), where a **Sikh Museum** (daily 7am–7pm; free) contains paintings of incidents from the lives of the Sikh gurus, finishing with gory representations of the three martyrdoms. In 1857, the same spot saw further cruel deaths when the British (who had recaptured the city using a largely Sikh army) set up gallows here to hang suspected insurgents; the formality of a trial was barely followed, and sadistic British soldiers paid the hangman to let victims die slowly in order to watch them "dance".

A hundred metres east of Fountain Chowk, the **Central Baptist Church** was Delhi's first Christian mission when it was established in 1814, though the present building was constructed in 1858, after the bloody events of the previous year. Just to its east, between McDonald's and the State Bank of India, an electrical market leads up to a little Hindu temple. If you bear left at this and continue ahead past the Chitra Electric Company, and down the next turning to your right, you'll see what was once the classical facade of **Begum Samru's Palace**, now sadly crumbling away. Built in 1823 for the Indian widow of a soldier-of-fortune from Luxembourg, this is one of Delhi's oldest colonial buildings, and was once the grandest mansion in town; its front garden stretched all the way to Chandni Chowk. In 1843 it became the Delhi Bank, whose British manager was butchered by a mob when insurgents took over the city in 1857. It was subsequently taken over by Lloyds Bank, whose name can still be read above the portico. Today it's a mess of offices and workshops but some of the original interior is still visible in the Central Bank of India, which has a branch at the front of the building.

Lal Mandir and Gauri Shankar Temple

At Chandni Chowk's eastern end, opposite the Red Fort, the **Lal Mandir**, a Jain temple (daily 5.30–11.30am & 6–9.30pm) is not as ornate as the Jain temples in Rajasthan (see p.331 & p.337), but it does boast detailed carvings, and gilded paintwork in the antechambers surrounding the main shrine. Remove your shoes, and leave any leather articles at the kiosk before entering. The attached **bird hospital** (daily 7am–9pm; no charge but donations appreciated) puts into practice the Jain principle that all life is sacred by rescuing injured birds, with each species having its own ward. The sparrow ward is largely occupied by victims of ceiling fans, with which these poor critters apparently collide quite often. Next door, the eighteenth-century Hindu **Gauri Shankar Temple** (leave shoes in a room to the left of the entrance) is quite a warren of shrines, the biggest of which, right at the back, contains a thoroughly awesome statue of Shiva, the god of creation and destruction. The temple also boasts an 800-year-old lingam, a phallic symbol representing Shiva and the primeval energy of creation.

The Red Fort (Lal Qila)

The largest of Old Delhi's monuments is Lal Qila, known in English as the **Red Fort** because of the red sandstone from which it was built (Tues–Sun sunrise–sunset, museums 10am–5pm; foreigners Rs250, Indian residents Rs10). It was commissioned by Shah Jahan to be his residence, and modelled on the fort at Agra. Work started in 1638, and the emperor moved in ten years later. The fort contains all the trappings you'd expect at the centre of Mughal government: halls of public and private audience, domed and arched marble palaces, plush private apartments, a mosque, and elaborately designed gardens. The ramparts, which stretch for over 2km, are interrupted at ninety degrees by two gates – **Lahori Gate** to the west, through which you

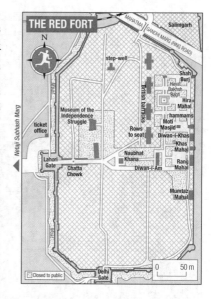

enter, and Delhi Gate to the south. Shah Jahan's son, Aurangzeb, who kept his father captive in Agra after usurping him, added barbicans to both gates, much to the old man's disgust. In those days, the Yamuna River ran along the eastern wall, feeding both the moat and a "stream of paradise" which ran through every pavilion. Inevitably, though, as the Mughal empire declined, the fort fell into disrepair. It was attacked and plundered by the Persian emperor Nadir Shah in 1739, and then again by the British in 1857. Nevertheless, it remains an impressive testimony to Mughal grandeur. Remember to keep your ticket stub as you will have to show it several times (for example, to enter the museums).

The main entrance to the fort from Lahori Gate opens onto **Chatta Chowk**, a covered street flanked with arched cells that used to house Delhi's most talented jewellers, carpet-makers, goldsmiths and silk-weavers, but is now given over to souvenir sellers. At the end, a path to the left leads to the **Museum of the Struggle for Independence**, depicting resistance to British rule. At this point, a street ran from the northern end of the fort down to the Delhi Gate, with the soldiers, palace workers' quarters and bazaars all kept strictly to its west. Ahead, the **Naubhat Khana** (Drum House, or Musicians' Gallery) marked the entrance into the royal quarters. Today, it houses a **Military Museum**, with swords, weapons and uniforms, but nothing worth stopping for unless you're an enthusiast.

Sound and light shows

Each night except Monday, a **sound and light show** takes place in the **Red Fort**: the palaces are dramatically lit, and a historical commentary blares from crackly loudspeakers. The show starts after sunset and lasts an hour (in English Feb–April & Sept–Oct 8.30pm; May–Aug 9pm; Nov–Jan 7.30pm; weekdays Rs60, weekends and public holidays Rs80; ☎011/2327 4580). The mosquitoes are ferocious, so bring repellent. Heavy monsoon rains may affect summer shows.

▲ Red Fort

From the Naubhat Khana, a path leads ahead through wide lawns to the **Diwan-i-Am**, or Hall of Public Audience, where the emperor used to meet commoners and hold court. In those days it was strewn with silk carpets and partitioned with hanging tapestries. Its centrepiece is a marble dais on which sat the emperor's throne, surrounded by twelve panels inlaid with precious stones, mostly depicting birds and flowers. The most famous of them, in the middle at the top (and not easy to see), shows the Greek god Orpheus with his lute. The panels were made by a

Florentine jeweller and imported from Italy, but the surrounding inlay work was done locally. When British troops occupied the fort, they looted many of its treasures, including the Orpheus panel, which a British captain had made into a table-top and sent home; it wasn't put back until the early twentieth century when viceroy Lord Curzon ordered its return.

The pavilions along the fort's east wall face spacious gardens and overlook the banks of the Yamuna. Unfortunately, you can't actually go inside most of them, but you can peer into them. Immediately east of the Diwan-i-Am, **Rang Mahal**, the "Palace of Colour", housed the emperor's wives and mistresses. It once had gilded turrets, delicately painted and decorated with intricate mosaics of mirrors, and its ceiling was overlaid with gold and silver and reflected onto a central pool in the marble floor. Unfortunately, it suffered a lot of vandalism when the British used it as an Officers' Mess after the 1857 uprising, and it's now a shadow of its former self. The similar **Mumtaz Mahal**, south of the main *zenana*, or women's quarters, and probably used by princesses, now houses an **Archeological Museum**, displaying manuscripts, paintings, ceramics and textiles, with a section devoted to the last Mughal emperor, Bahadur Shah II, whose exhibits include his silk robes and silver hookah pipe.

On the northern side of Rang Mahal, the marble **Khas Mahal** was the personal palace of the emperor, split into separate apartments for worship, sleeping and sitting. The southern chamber, **Tosh Khana** ("robe room"), has a stunning marble filigree screen on its north wall, surmounted by a panel carved with the scales of justice. The octagonal tower projecting over the east wall of the Khas Mahal was used by the emperor to appear daily before throngs gathered on the riverbanks below.

North of Khas Mahal, in the large **Diwan-i-Khas** ("Hall of Private Audience"), the emperor would address the highest nobles of his court. Today it's the finest building in the fort, a marble pavilion shaded by a roof raised on stolid pillars meeting in ornate scalloped arches and embellished with exquisitely delicate inlays of flowers made from semiprecious stones. On the north and south walls you can still make out the inscription of a couplet in Persian attributed to Shah Jahan's prime minister, which roughly translates as: "If there be paradise upon this earthly sphere, / It is here, oh it is here, oh it is here". More than just a paean, the verse refers to the deliberate modelling of the fort's gardens on the Koranic description of heaven. A marble and gold Peacock Throne inlaid with rubies, sapphires and diamonds once stood on the central pedestal of the Diwan, but Nadir Shah took it back to Iran as booty in 1739.

A little further north are the **hammams**, or baths, sunk into the marble floor inlaid with patterns of precious stones, and dappled in jewel-coloured light that filters through stained-glass windows. The western chamber contained hot baths while the eastern apartment, with fountains of rosewater, was used as a dressing room. Next to the hammams, the sweetly fashioned **Moti Masjid**, or Pearl Mosque, triple-domed in white marble, was added by Aurangzeb in 1659, but unfortunately it's currently closed to the public. The northernmost pavilion in the east wall, called **Shah Burj**, was used to pump water from the river to feed the "stream of paradise". To its west, the **Hayat Bakhsh Bagh** is the only one of the formal gardens – each divided into four by water channels – that still survives. The barrack-like buildings beyond it are just that: barracks, put up by the British to house their troops after the uprising.

To the northeast of the complex is an older fort, called **Salimgarh**, commissioned by Sher Khan's son Salim Shah around 1550. It is joined to the Red Fort by a bridge, but closed to the public, though you'll pass right through it if heading east out of Old Delhi by train.

The Jama Masjid and around

A wonderful piece of Mughal pomp, the red-and-white **Jama Masjid** (8am till half an hour before sunset; closed for half an hour in the afternoon for prayers; in summer opens earlier at 7am; free; Rs200 for cameras; no shorts, short skirts or sleeveless tops) is India's largest mosque. Soaring above the rooftops of the old city, it looks huge from a distance, and feels nothing short of immense once you've climbed the wide staircases to the arched gateways and entered the open courtyard, which is large enough to accommodate the prostrating bodies of twenty-five thousand worshippers. It was designed by Shah Jahan and built by a workforce of five thousand people between 1644 and 1656. Originally called Masjid-i-Jahanuma ("mosque commanding a view of the world"), this grand structure stands on Bho Jhala, one of Shahjahanabad's two hills, and looks east to the

Old Delhi's bazaars

Almost the whole of Old Delhi is divided into **bazaars** specializing in one type of product or another, from watches and cameras to spices and vegetables. This list of the more interesting bazaars barely scratches the surface.

Phool Mandi west of Netaji Subhash Marg. Once the flower market (which is what its name means), this is now Old Delhi's wholesale vegetable market, at its most animated late at night, when goods are arriving, and early in the morning as retailers come to purchase. By about 10am, most of the selling's been done for the day.

Meena Bazaar east of the Jama Masjid. This is the area from which slum dwellers and ramshackle market stalls were cleared during the Emergency (see p.368). Today, many of the stallholders are former residents selling Muslim religious paraphernalia, including wall hangings featuring Koranic quotations or pictures of the Kaaba in Mecca, but there are some stalls selling clothes and fabrics too.

Car Parts Bazaar southwest of the Jama Masjid. Claiming to be the biggest market for spare car parts in the world, this market sells used car parts great or small, from springs or bearings to wing mirrors, tyres, doors and even engines.

Guliyan Bazaar north of the Jama Masjid. Shops here have been selling fireworks for at least a hundred and fifty years, and possibly twice that long.

Dariba Kalan leading from Guliyan Bazaar to Chandni Chowk. Old Delhi's silver bazaar, lined with jewellers' shops, mostly selling silver, though some have gold and gemstones too.

Kinari Bazaar west off Dariba Kalan. If you're planning a wedding, this is the place to buy gold turbans (to be worn by the groom), garlands of banknotes (to bedeck the happy couple), tinsel, bridal veils and wedding paraphernalia in general. Wedding clothes can be rented too. At certain times of the year, and particularly around Holi and Dussehra, the bazaar also sells festive accessories.

Nai Sarak leading south from Chandni Chowk. This wide street was driven willy-nilly through the neighbourhood by the British after 1857 to make for easier access, and has become, especially at its southern end, Delhi's wholesale book market, each shop specializing in a different genre, though school and college textbooks predominate. At its northern end, books give way to clothes, particularly saris.

Chawri Bazaar southwest of Nai Sarak. In the nineteenth century, this street was known for its "dancing girls" (sometimes, but not always, sex workers as well). Nowadays, the northern end is a wholesale paper market selling writing paper, greetings cards and even wallpaper, while the southern end specializes in brass goods including oil lamps, pots, vases, ashtrays and statuettes of Hindu gods.

Khari Baoli west of Chandni Chowk. Delhi's wholesale spice market (see opposite), encompassing not only dry spices, but also dried and crystallized fruit, pickles and chutneys, and, at its western end, tea.

sprawling Red Fort, and down on the seething streets of Old Delhi. Broad red sandstone staircases lead to gateways on the east, north and southern sides, where worshippers and visitors alike must remove their shoes (the custodian will guard them for you for a small tip).

Once inside the courtyard, your eyes will be drawn to the three bulbous marble domes crowning the **main prayer hall** on the west side (facing Mecca), fronted by a series of high cusped arches, and sheltering the mihrab, the central niche in the west wall indicating the direction of prayer. The pool in the centre is used for ritual ablutions. At each corner of the square yard a slender minaret crowned with a marble dome rises to the sky, and it's well worth climbing the **tower** (Rs100; women must be accompanied by a man) south of the main sanctuary for an unrivalled view over Delhi. In the northeast corner a white shrine protects a collection of Muhammad's relics, shrouded in rose petals and watched over by keepers who will, in exchange for a tip, reveal the contents: two sections of the Koran written on deerskin by relatives of the prophet, a red beard-hair of Muhammad's, his sandals, and his "footprint" miraculously embedded in a marble slab.

The Jama Masjid is surrounded by a number of bazaars (see box opposite). Just to its east is the **tomb of Maulana Azad**, one of pre-Independence India's most important politicians. The youngest ever president of Congress, he was a prominent supporter of Gandhi (imprisoned by the British, of course), and the most outspoken Muslim opponent of Partition. When Partition nonetheless came, he worked hard to curtail sectarian bloodshed. His tomb is surmounted by a simple white chhatra (canopy); visitors should remove their shoes before approaching it.

Khari Baoli

The spice bazaar of **Khari Baoli**, west of the Fatehpuri Mosque in Old Delhi's northwestern corner, is even more congested than Chandni Chowk. The biggest spice market in Asia, it teems from dawn till dusk with shoppers, spice dealers, rickshaws trying to make progress through the crowds, and porters wielding barrowloads of roots, barks and seeds. Its shops are packed full of spices, teas, lentils, chutneys, pickles, and dried or crystallized fruit. **Gadodia Market**, immediately behind the Fatehpuri Mosque, is the epicentre of the whole affair, a veritable hive of spicy commerce, where untold quantities of pepper, cardamom, chutney and even the silver leaf used to cover Indian sweets are bought, sold, loaded, unloaded and haggled over all day long.

At Khari Baoli's western end, where once the Lahori Gate stood astride the road to Lahore, the **Sarhindi Masjid**, commissioned at the same time as the Fatehpuri Mosque by another of Shah Jahan's wives, Sarhindi Begum, is too hidden behind shops for you to get a decent view, but if you feel like exploring the backstreets you could seek out a more interesting if somewhat more modest mosque. Head south along Naya Bans Road and take a left after 100m (opposite no. 218). After 30m (opposite no. 6067), turn right into a narrow street full of stalls selling namkeens (the assorted constituents and permutations of what Westerners call "Bombay mix"). Continue for 100m or so, until you reach a blue doorway on the left with a small Urdu sign above it, which leads into a little courtyard in front of the simple **Hauzwali Mosque**. Situated next to the original *baoli* (step-well) – now long gone – from which the spice market takes its name, this little blue-washed mosque, with its three small, domed chambers, was built in the 1540s, a century before the rest of Old Delhi. Outside of Purana Qila it's one of very few buildings in Delhi dating from the Suri period (the time of Sher Khan and his family). And with its low domes, and unadorned doorways, decorated only by the simple flanging of one arch inside another, it really is quite strikingly different from all of Old Delhi's other mosques.

The street leading south from Khari Baoli road, alongside the railway line, **Shraddhanand Marg**, formerly GB Road, is Delhi's main red-light district; for much of the way down, particularly between nos. 53–72, the dark stairways on its east side lead mostly up to brothels.

Ajmeri Gate and around

Of Shahjahanabad's four surviving city gates, three are along Old Delhi's southern edge, on what is now Asaf Ali Road. **Ajmeri Gate**, so called because it stood astride the main road to Ajmer, was described by a British traveller in 1906 as "broad and tall and studded with sharp spikes of no friendly intent", though it looks tamer today, hived off from the street in a well-kept little garden (daily 5–8am), its spikes long gone.

Just west of the gate stand the red sandstone **Madrasa and Mosque of Ghazi-ud-Din**, designed in the classic Mughal style. Built in 1692, the *madrasa* was commissioned by Ghazi-ud-Din Bahadur Firoz Jang, a distinguished general in Aurangzeb's army. Though illness left him completely blind, Ghazi-ud-Din remained one of the emperor's most important military advisors, and went on to become nawab (governor) of Gujarat. When he died in 1727, he was buried by his *madrasa*, and the mosque was built to honour his memory. In 1825, the *madrasa*, originally a Koranic school, was renamed Delhi College and became a centre for perpetuating Urdu culture, though this role was deliberately curtailed by the British after the 1857 uprising. Today, the mosque is still in use, while the *madrasa*, which has become rather run-down, is now the Anglo-Arabic Secondary School. In principle, it's only open to the public Tuesdays and Thursdays 2 to 3pm, or by appointment (☎011/2321 0863), but they may let you in to look round at other times if you ask.

Another interesting little mosque, the **Masjid Mubarak Begum**, is on Lalkuan Bazaar Road, at Hauz Razi no. 4959, very near Chawri Bazaar metro station. The Indian wife of a British official had it built in 1823 as part of their estate, and it stands in its own terrace above the shops, accessible up a narrow staircase from the street (take off your shoes at the top).

Turkman Gate and around

Turkman Gate is named after a Sufi saint, Hazrat Shah Turkman, who died in 1240 and is buried nearby. His tomb, **Shah Turkman Durgah** – the oldest building in Old Delhi – can be found by heading north up what eventually becomes Sitaram Bazaar Road, though at these lower reaches it's called Turkman Main Bazaar. After some 300m, turn right through a courtyard (usually full of people cooking) between nos. 1900 and 2038. On the other side of the courtyard, straight ahead of you, is a little alley. Head down it, following it round to the right, and on your left you'll see the red and green door to the saint's tomb. The drop in floor level shows how much older it is than the surrounding streets. You may need to locate the caretaker if you want to look inside, as it's often locked, but the tomb still attracts devotees, who leave flowers and burn incense. As with all tombs and mosques, you must take off your shoes before entering.

Some 50m further up Mohammed Deen Ilaichi Marg, down an alley on the left (opposite no. 2053), and atop a steep staircase, is a mosque called the **Kalan Masjid**, resplendent in green and blue. Like Shah Turkman's tomb, the Kalan Masjid is older than the surrounding city. It was built in 1387 on the orders of Khan-i-Jahan Junan Shah, Firoz Shah's chief minister, and is noticeably Tughluq rather than Mughal in style, with its low domes and tapering shape. Khan-i-Jahan had seven mosques built across the Delhi area, but only this one remains in use today.

Thirty metres further, Mohammed Deen Ilaichi Marg bends to the left to become Sitaram Bazaar Road. But if you take a right instead (between nos. 2045 & 2451), then turn left, opposite a little mosque, and follow the increasingly tortuous alleyway all the way to the end (bear right where it forks), you come to a little enclosure containing two graves. The one on the left is the **tomb of Razia Sultan**, who was, until Queen Victoria, Delhi's only ever female ruler, reigning from 1236 to 1240; the other tomb belongs to her sister. The daughter of the great Delhi sultan Iltutmish, and his nominee to succeed him, Razia was blocked from the throne by sexist religious and military leaders, who put her brother there instead, but he proved utterly incompetent, and seven months later she ousted him. As sultan, she threw off the veil and appeared in public dressed in a tunic and conical hat, riding into battle on horseback armed with a bow and arrows. The people of Delhi strongly supported her, but the aristocracy never accepted the rule of a woman and her reign was plagued by rebellion. Forced to flee Delhi, she was murdered by bandits at a place called Kaithal, but although she has a grave there, Delhiwallahs reckon this is where she really lies, moved by her brother and successor Behram Shah to be near Hazrat Shah Turkman, of whom she was a follower.

Delhi Gate and Daryaganj

Delhi Gate faced what had previously been the city of Delhi (Lal Kot, Jahanpanah, Firozabad and Purana Qila). Today, it marks the southern end of the district known as **Daryaganj**. To its east and south are Raj Ghat and Firoz Shah Kotla (see p.118), but if you head north up Netaji Subhash Marg, you come to the Golcha Cinema, one of Delhi's oldest movie theatres. From the car park, follow the turning round to the left and then take a right after 20m, and you come to a singularly unimpressive domestic courtyard called **Naherwali Haveli**. Underwhelming though it may be, this was the birthplace of former Pakistani president Pervez Musharraf ("Mush" to the Indian press), whose family fled Delhi during Partition when Musharraf was four years old. Before 1857, the same compound was home to the chief minister of Bahdur Shah II, the last Mughal emperor.

Daryaganj also has one or two interesting mosques. On its eastern edge, almost at the city wall, the 1707 **Ghata Mosque**, or Zinat al-Masjid, commissioned by Aurangzeb's daughter, is like a smaller version of the Jama Masjid. Historian William Dalrymple describes it as "the most beautiful of all the Delhi mosques", but there are other contenders. One of them can be found further north, just beyond the footbridge over Netaji Subhash Marg, where two roads lead west; the first leads to the **Pataudi House Mosque**. White with three blue-washed domes and frilly doorways (best photographed in the morning), this pretty little mosque dates from the eighteenth century, when it was part of a haveli called Kalan Mahal, a name still given to the area behind it. The mosque's own name comes from its proximity to a nearby haveli that belonged to the Nawab of Pataudi.

Raj Ghat

When Shah Jahan established his city in 1638, its eastern edges bordered the River Yamuna, and a line of *ghats*, or steps leading to the water, was installed along the riverbanks. *Ghats* have been used in India for centuries, for mundane things like washing clothes and bathing, but also for worship and funeral cremation. **Raj Ghat** (daily: April–Sept 5am–7.30pm; Oct–March 5.30am–7pm; free), east of Delhi Gate – really more a park than a *ghat* – is the place where Mahatma Gandhi was cremated, on the day after his assassination in 1948. The Mahatma's *samadhi* (cremation memorial), a low black plinth inscribed with his reputed last words, "Hai Ram" ("Oh God"), receives a steady stream of visitors, and he is remembered through prayers here every Friday evening at 5pm, and on the anniversaries of his birth and death (Oct 2 & Jan 30). Opposite Raj Ghat's southwest corner, the small **Gandhi Memorial Museum** (daily except Mon 9.30am–5.30pm; free) houses some of Gandhi's photographs and writings, and at weekends you can watch a one-hour film on his political and personal life (English Sat 4pm; Hindi Sun 4pm).

North of Raj Ghat, memorials also mark the places where Jawaharlal Nehru (at Shanti Vana), his daughter Indira Gandhi (at Shakti Sthal), and his grandson Rajiv Gandhi (at Vir Bhumi) were cremated.

Firoz Shah Kotla

Supposedly, Firoz Shah, sultan of Delhi from 1351 to 1358, had a whole fifth city of Delhi built – Firozabad, founded in 1354. Today few traces survive of what was in any case probably never more than a suburb of the main city, still then centred on Lal Kot (around the Qutb Minar, see p.125) and Jahanpanah (its exension to the northeast, see p.124), but what does remain is the fortified palace of Firoz Shah Kotla (Tues–Sun sunrise–sunset; foreigners Rs100, Indian residents Rs5), now a crumbling ruin with ornamental gardens, 500m east of Delhi Gate. Its most incongruous and yet distinctive element is the third-century BC polished sandstone Ashokan pillar, carried down the Yamuna by raft from Ambala. The 14m-high column, one of two brought by Firoz to Delhi (the other is on the Northern Ridge – see p.120), is surrounded by a building full of tiny rooms, evidently built to house it. For a reasonable view of the column, you'll need to climb to the top of the building, entering the compound through a gate on the west side, then mounting a stairway in the northeast corner. From the top you also get a view of the neighbouring mosque and baoli (step-well), as well as the lawns that make the site such a pleasant place to visit. On Thursday evenings, after sunset, local residents come down to burn candles and joss sticks in the building around the Ashokan pillar to placate the djinn (spirits) that are believed to reside here.

Small children and doll lovers may well appreciate **Shankar's International Doll Museum** (Tues–Sun 10am–6pm; Rs15), south of Firoz Shah Kotla in Nehru House, 4 Bahadur Shah Zafar Marg (500m north of Pragati Maidan metro station). Over six thousand dolls from around the world include mannequins of John Wayne, Louis Armstrong, Henry VIII and Elizabeth I, and though none is antique, it's a prodigious collection.

North of the Red Fort

Heading north up Netaji Subhash Marg from the Red Fort, you pass under a railway bridge on the way to Old Delhi GPO. Just before the post office, on the east side of the road, **Lothian Cemetery** was the burial ground for officers of the East India Company from 1808 until just after the 1857 uprising. Today it's in a state of some disrepair, and occupied by squatters, though they don't mind curious tourists popping in for a look about. In the middle of the road in front of the post office, and still topped by an old cannon, the remains of the East India Company's **Magazine** or arsenal is now used mainly as an unofficial public toilet, so watch your step if you cross the street to explore it. Another chunk of the Magazine, on another traffic island just to the north, bears a plaque honouring the "nine resolute Englishmen" who defended it against "rebels and mutineers" for over four hours on May 11, 1857, blowing it up when all was lost to prevent it falling into enemy hands. A post-Independence plaque just below the Raj-era original points out that "The persons described as 'rebels and mutineers' in the above inscription were Indian members of the army in the service of the East India Company trying to overthrow the foreign government." Just north of the Magazine, a grey obelisk recalls the bravery of two of the Company's telegraph operators during the same episode who stayed on till the last moment to keep the army base at Ambala up to speed on the day's events.

Continuing north along Lothian Road, you'll pass another remnant of Company days on your right in the form of the old **Residency**, now the Archeology Department of Guru Gobind Singh Indraprastha University. A couple of hundred metres further is the rather fine cream and white Baroque facade of **St James's Church** (daily 8.30am–1pm & 2–5pm, or whenever you can find the caretaker), commissioned in 1836 by **James Skinner**, the son of a Scottish Company-wallah and a Rajput princess. Because of his mixed ancestry, and the increasing racism of the British regime, Skinner was refused a commission in the Company's army, but set up his own irregular cavalry unit (Skinner's Horse, also called the Yellow Boys after their uniform) and made himself pretty much indispensable to the Company in northern India. Though he was continually snubbed over pay and rank, his astounding victories over the forces of the Maharaja of Jaipur and the great Sikh leader Maharaja Ranjit Singh eventually forced the Company to begrudgingly grant him the rank of Lieutenant-Colonel and absorb his cavalrymen into its ranks. Skinner died in 1842 and is buried just in front of the altar.

Immediately north of the church, Church Road leads to the offices of the Northern Railway, where the East India Company's **Deputy Resident's Residence** is now the office of the railway's chief engineer. If you ask at the gate, you'll probably be allowed in to admire the bow-fronted veranda and balustrades, but you probably won't be allowed to take photos or to venture inside. A plaque to the left of its front door explains the building's history.

The double-arched **Kashmiri Gate**, on the west side of Lothian Road just 300m north of the church, was where the Mughal court would leave Delhi every summer bound for the cool valley of Kashmir. It was also here in September 1857 that the British made their assault on the city to recapture it from the insurgents.

The Civil Lines

North of the Kashmiri Gate is Maharana Pratap Inter-state Bus Terminal, beyond which, across the busy Lala Hardev Sahai Marg, is the district known as the **Civil Lines**. This area was created after the events of 1857, when the British no longer felt safe living among the Indian residents of Old Delhi and moved up here for a more secluded location.

Immediately north of Lala Hardev Sahai Marg, the peaceful **Qudsia Gardens** are a fading remnant of the magnificent pleasure parks commissioned in the mid-eighteenth century by Queen Qudsia, wife of the Mughal emperor Muhammad Shah, and mother of Ahmed Shah. Part of it was taken over by the British Freemasons, who built a hall and banned Indians from entering the park in the afternoons. A gate in the centre and a mosque in the southeast corner still remain from Queen Qudsia's original garden.

Nearby on Lala Hardev Sarai Marg is the nineteenth-century **Nicholson Cemetery**. A number of British casualties from 1857 are buried here, most prominently Brigadier-General John Nicholson, whose tomb is a little beyond the entrance, to the right, surrounded by railings. An uncompromisingly violent racist responsible for ordering numerous summary killings, but also fearless, charismatic and extremely popular with the troops, Nicholson was just the person the British needed to lead their assault on Delhi. Shot by a sniper as his men fought their way in through the Kashmiri Gate, he took ten days to die, and when he heard that the more cautious General who had replaced him was thinking of retreating back to the gate, he bellowed: "Thank God that I still have the strength yet to shoot him if necessary." The marble stone on his grave was looted from the gardens of the Red Fort. In 2006, a British company sponsored the cemetery's restoration, and it was reopened by the British High Commissioner, to raised eyebrows from people who felt that it glorified – or at the very least ignored – the horrific British war crimes of 1857, but the cemetery, once overgrown and vandalized, is now pristine and immaculate, and most would agree that this is a piece of history well preserved rather than an endorsement of imperialism or murder.

The Northern Ridge and Majnu Ka Tilla

West of the Civil Lines is the **Northern Ridge**, a forested area that was previously just scrub and gave views over the city. It was here that the British army holed up in 1857 prior to their final assault on Delhi. The ridge is strewn with a miscellany of monuments, among them a very Gothic Victorian **Mutiny Monument** originally dedicated to British soldiers killed in the uprising, now rededicated to the "immortal martyrs for Indian freedom" who died fighting against them. Just to the north is an **Ashokan pillar**, the second of two brought to Delhi by Firoz Shah (the other is at Firoz Shah Kotla – see p.118); this one originally came from Meerut, which is coincidentally where the 1857 uprising began. Firoz Shah brought the pillar here to adjoin his hunting lodge, of which a ruined section, called **Pir Ghaib**, survives, in the grounds just north of the Hindu Rao Hospital. Five hundred metres north of that, the 1354 **Chauburji Mosque** is thought by some to have originally been a tomb, but the mihrab in the west wall seems to suggest that it was always used for prayer. If you still fancy a long stroll or a rickshaw ride up Ridge Road – and the woods do make it pleasant, with birds and monkeys all along the way – you'll eventually come after 1.5km to its highest point, where the **Flagstaff Tower** was built in 1828 to relay signals and fly the flag (the Union Jack), unobscured by trees back then. It's also where British refugees gathered to flee the city when the 1857 insurgents first took it over. The tower is not far from Vidhan Sabha metro station.

A very different group of refugees, arriving in the 1950s following China's invasion of Tibet, set up what's now a veritable little Lhasa at **Majnu Ka Tilla**, with Tibetan shops and restaurants, saffron-clad monks, and pictures of the Dalai Lama in almost every establishment. The area also has a number of good budget hotels (see p.96), but it's a bit out of the way, on the east side of Dr K.B. Hedgewar Marg, 1km northeast of Vidhan Sabha metro.

Coronation Park

Now just a windblown piece of waste ground on the city's northern fringes, 10km north of Connaught Place, **Coronation Park** once showcased the pomp and might of the British Raj. The British held three **durbars** (huge imperial pageants) here: in 1887 on Queen Victoria's assumption of the title "Empress of India"; in 1903 to mark the coronation of her successor Edward VII; and in 1911 when George V came to be crowned in person as emperor. The high point of the durbar was a procession of elephants bearing all the princes of India, headed by the Nizam of Hyderabad, to pay homage to the British ruler, in the same way that they had previously to the Mughals. All but forgotten nowadays (your auto-wallah or taxi driver won't have heard of the place, and will need instructions on how to get here), the park is centred around a **granite obelisk** commemorating the 1911 coronation. In an enclosure close by, a grandiose statue of the king-emperor George, which once graced what is now the Rajpath, stands Ozymandias-like among other nameless and forgotten rulers from an empire fast receding into history. The park is located on Nirankari Marg, just south of the Outer Ring Road NH-1 bypass (Dr K.B. Hedgewar Marg) near Sant Nagar. It costs Rs100 by pre-paid auto from Connaught Place, or around Rs150 from town if you don't pre-pay.

South Delhi

Most of the early settlements of Delhi, including its first cities, are to be found not in "Old Delhi" but in **South Delhi**, the area south of Lutyens' carefully planned boulevards, where the rapid expansion of suburban Delhi has swallowed up what was previously countryside. Whole villages have been embedded within it, and the area is littered with monuments from the past. Meanwhile, as the centre becomes more and more congested, South Delhi's housing enclaves and colonies are increasingly home to the newest shopping centres and the most happening locales. There's lots to see in South Delhi if you've time to explore it, but if you need to stick with the bare minimum, don't miss the two great Mughal garden tombs – **Humayun's Tomb** and **Safdarjang's Tomb** – at either end of Lodi Road, and the **Qutb Minar complex** at Lal Kot, Delhi's first incarnation; if you can, also try to fit in the amazing lotus-shaped **Baha'i Temple**.

Humayun's Tomb and around

Close to the medieval Muslim centre of Nizamuddin and 2km from Purana Qila, Humayun's Tomb (daily sunrise–sunset; foreigners Rs250, Indian residents Rs10) stands at the crossroads of the Lodi and Mathura roads, 500m from Nizamuddin railway station (one stop from New Delhi station on the suburban line), and easily accessible by bus (#181 and #414 from Chelmsford Road by New Delhi station; #893, #894 and #966 from Kasturba Gandhi Marg by Connaught Place), or by pre-paid auto from Connaught Place (Rs60). Late afternoon is the best time to photograph it. Delhi's first Mughal mausoleum, it was constructed to house the remains of the second Mughal emperor, Humayun, who at the start of his reign lost Delhi and most of his father Babur's empire to the Afghan warlord Sher Khan Suri, but managed to regain it all from Sher Khan's son Sikander in 1555. Sher Khan had posthumous revenge, however, when Humayun died less than a year later after falling down the stairs of Sher Khan's Sher Mandal (see p.106). Humayun's tomb was built under the watchful eye of Haji Begum, his senior widow and mother of Akbar, who camped here for the duration, and is now buried here alongside her husband. The grounds were later used to inter several prominent Mughals, and served as a refuge for the last emperor, Bahadur Shah II, before his capture by the British in 1857.

From the ticket office you proceed to the West Gate of the *charbagh*, or quartered garden, in which the tomb stands. The tomb's sombre, Persian-style elegance marks this as one of Delhi's finest historic sites. It is constructed of red sandstone, inlaid with black and white marble, on a commanding podium in the centre of the *charbagh*, looking towards the Yamuna. The octagonal structure is crowned with a double dome that soars to a height of 38m. Though it was the very first Mughal garden tomb – to be followed by Akbar's at Sikander and of course the Taj Mahal at Agra, for which it can be seen as a prototype – Humayun's mausoleum has antecedents in Delhi in the form of Ghiyas-ud-Din Tughluq's tomb at Tughluqabad, and that of Sikandar Lodi in Lodi Gardens. From the second of those it adopted its octagonal shape and the high central arch that was to be such a typical feature of Mughal architecture – you'll see it at the Taj, and in Delhi's Jama Masjid, for example.

Other structures within the complex

Within the *charbagh*, southeast of the main mausoleum, a small but impressive square mausoleum, with a double dome and two graves bearing Koranic inscriptions, is the **Tomb of Humayun's Barber**, a man considered important because he was trusted with holding a razor to the emperor's throat.

Other interesting nooks lie off the path from the ticket office to the *charbagh*'s West Gate. The path itself leads through **Bu Halima's Garden**, beautifully kept and actually older than Humayun's Tomb. Little is known of the garden's origins, but within it is a low, rectangular tomb said to belong to the eponymous Bu Halima, whoever he may have been.

In an octagonal enclosure to the south of Bu Halima's garden, **Isa Khan's Tomb** and its attendant mosque are actually older than Humayan's tomb. Built in 1547 for one of Sher Khan's generals, they are typical of the architecture of his reign, with low pointed domes and lots of chhatris. The tomb, octagonal and set in a walled garden, in many ways presages that of Humayun.

A gateway on the south side of the path from the ticket office to the West Gate leads to the **Arab Sarai**, originally built as accommodation for the artisans brought in by Haji Begum to work on Humayun's Tomb. Within the same enclosure are the remains of the **Afsarwala Mosque**, commissioned by one of Akbar's generals in 1566, though it has lost much of its original sandstone facing. It is not known to whom the adjoining tomb belongs.

Outside the complex

To the east of Humayun's Barber's tomb, but outside the compound (so you'll have to walk right round for a closer look) stands the **Nila Gumbad** ("blue dome"), an octagonal tomb with a dome of blue tiles, supposedly built by one of Akbar's nobles to honour a faithful servant, and which may possibly predate Humayun's Tomb. The blue-domed structure in the middle of the road junction in front of the entrance to Humayun's tomb is a seventeenth-century tomb called Sabz Burj – the tiles on its dome are not original, but the result of a recent restoration. On your way round to the Nila Gumbad (depending on your route), you pass the **tomb of Khan-i-Khanan**, a Mughal general who died in 1626 (daily sunrise–sunset; foreigners Rs100, Indian residents Rs5). Though originally in the same tradition of Mughal garden tombs as Humayun's and the Taj, it looks rather ragged today as the facing was all stripped for use in Safdarjang's tomb, and the garden that surrounded it has mostly gone.

Nizamuddin

Just across the busy Mathura Road from Humayun's Tomb, and now engulfed by a busy road network and plush suburbs, the village of **Nizamuddin**, with its lack of traffic, its ancient mosques and tombs, and its slow pace of life, is so different from the surrounding city that to enter it is like passing through a time warp. At its heart, surrounded by a tangle of narrow alleyways lined with shops and market stalls, one of Sufism's greatest shrines, the **Hazrat Nizamuddin Dargah**, draws a constant stream of devotees.

The marble *dargah* is the tomb of Sheikh Nizam-ud-Din Aulia (1236–1325), fourth saint of the Chishtiya Sufi order, Sufism being the mystical branch of Islam, whose followers aim to bring themselves personally nearer to God, and the Chishtiya being the branch of Sufism founded by Khwaja Muin-ud-Din Chishti of Ajmer (see p.253). The *dargah* was built the year the sheikh died, but has been through several renovations, and the present mausoleum dates from 1562. In the inner sanctum (closed to women), the saint's tomb is surrounded by a marble rail and a canopy of mother-of-pearl. His disciple, the poet and chronicler **Amir Khusrau** – considered to be the first Urdu poet and the founder of *khyal*, the most common form of north Indian classical music – lies in a contrasting red sandstone tomb in front of his master's mausoleum.

Religious song and music play an important role among the Chishtiyas, as among several Sufi orders, and *qawwals* (bards) gather to sing in the evenings (especially on Thursdays and feast days). Comprising a chorus led by solo singing accompanied by clapping and usually a harmonium combined with a *dholak* (double-membraned barrel drum) and tabla (paired hand-drums), the hypnotic rhythm of their **qawwali music** is designed to lull its audience into a state of *mast* (spiritual intoxication), which is believed to bring the devotee closer to God.

The oldest building in the area, the red sandstone mosque of **Jamat Khana Masjid**, looms over the main *dargah* on its western side. It was commissioned in 1325 by Khizr Khan, the son of the Khalji sultan Ala-ud-Din. Enclosed by marble lattice screens next to Amir Khusrau's mausoleum, the tomb of **Princess Jahanara**, Shah Jahan's favourite daughter, is topped by a hollow filled with grass in compliance with her wish to have nothing but grass covering her grave. By the compound's north gate is a holy *baoli*.

Like Amir Khusrau and Princess Jahanara, other people also wanted to be buried in the saint's vicinity. Just east of the *dargah* compound, the elegant 64-pillared white marble **Chausath Khamba** was built as a mausoleum for the family of a Mughal politician who had been governor of Gujarat, and the building, with its low, wide form and elegant marble screens, bears the unmistakeable evidence of a Gujarati influence. The compound containing the Chuasath is usually locked, but the caretaker should be on hand somewhere nearby to open it up if you want to take a closer look. Just outside is the tomb of the poet Mirza Ghalib (see p.109), likewise buried here to benefit from the saint's blessing.

Lodi Gardens

Two kilometres west of Nizamuddin along Lodi Road, the leafy, pleasant **Lodi Gardens** (daily 5am–8pm; free) form part of a belt of fifteenth- and sixteenth-century monuments that now stand incongruously amid golf greens, large bungalows and elite estates. The park is especially full in the early mornings and early evenings, when fitness enthusiasts come for brisk walks or to jog through the manicured gardens against a backdrop of much-graffitied medieval monuments; it's also a popular lovers' hangout. The gardens, a Rs40 auto ride from Connaught Place, also contain the **National Bonsai Park**, which has a fine selection of diminutive trees. The best time to come is at sunset, when the light is soft and the tombs are all lit up.

Near the centre of the gardens, the imposing **Bara Gumbad** ("large dome") is a square late fifteenth-century tomb capped by the eponymous dome, its monotonous exterior relieved by grey and black stones and its interior adorned with painted stuccowork. **Shish Gumbad** ("glazed dome"), a similar tomb 50m north, still bears a few traces of the blue tiles liberally used to form friezes below the cornice and above the entrance. Inside, plasterwork is inscribed with ornate Koranic inscriptions.

The octagonal **tomb of Muhammad Shah** (ruled 1434–45) of the Sayyid dynasty stands 300m southwest of Bara Gumbad, surrounded by verandas and pierced by arches and sloping buttresses. Enclosed within high walls and a square garden, 300m north of Bara Gumbad, the **tomb of Sikandar Lodi** (ruled 1489–1517) repeats the octagonal theme, with a central chamber encircled by a veranda. **Athpula** ("eight piers"), a sixteenth-century ornamental bridge, lies east, in the northwest corner of the park.

Safdarjang's Tomb

At the western end of Lodi Road, **Safdarjang's Tomb** (daily sunrise–sunset; foreigners Rs100, Indian residents Rs5) is served by bus #505 from Ajmeri Gate or Connaught Place (Kasturba Gandhi Marg), or from Connaught Place by pre-paid auto-rickshaw (Rs70), and is at its most photogenic in the morning. Safdarjang was the Mughal nawab (governor) of Avadh who briefly became vizier before being overthrown for his Shi'ite beliefs. He died in 1753, by which time the empire was reduced to a fraction of its former size and most of the capital's grander buildings lay in ruins, and his tomb represents the last in a line of Mughal garden tombs that started with Humayun's and reached its apogee with the Taj Mahal. Compared with those two, Safdarjang's Tomb invariably gets a bad press. Where Humayun's Tomb is vigorous and solid, and the Taj is perfectly proportioned and delicately decorated, Safdarjang's Tomb is regarded as decadent and over-embellished. William Dalrymple, in *City of Djinns*, describes it as "blowzy Mughal rococo" typifying an age "not so much decaying into impoverished anonymity as one whoring and drinking itself into extinction". Certainly, its elongated proportions make it seem slender in comparison with earlier Mughal constructions, and its frills and fancies can be regarded as overdone, but for all that it has a certain feminine elegance that Humayun's Tomb lacks, and it's definitely worth the trip down Lodi Road to see it. The frills around the arches, the fussy decoration on the corner turrets, and the chhatris that surmount them may rouse the ire of Mughal architecture's more purist fans, but there's no denying they're pretty, and the tomb's ornate interior is filled with wonderful swirling plasterwork.

Hauz Khas

Set amid parks and woodland 4km south of Safdarjang's Tomb, the wealthy suburban development of **Hauz Khas** is typical of South Delhi in being a thoroughly modern area dotted with remnants of antiquity. The modern part takes the form of Hauz Khas village, a shopping area packed with chic boutiques and smart restaurants. There's also a very pleasant deer park and a rose garden. If you get off the #505 bus at Hauz Khas, the village is an 800m stroll to the west, on which you'll pass a whole slew of ancient tombs, but of most interest to visitors, apart from the upmarket shopping possibilities (see p.138), are the ruins of a fourteenth-century reservoir at the western end of the village.

Sultan Ala-ud-Din Khalji had the reservoir (or "tank") built in 1304 to supply water to his citadel at Siri, Delhi's "second city", and it was known after him as **Hauz-i-Alai**. Half a century later, it was expanded by Firoz Shah, who added a two-storey *madrasa* (seminary), and a mosque at its northern end. Among the anonymous tombs scattered throughout the area is that of Firoz Shah himself, directly overlooking the southern corner of the tank. Its high walls, lofty dome, and doorway spanned by a lintel with a stone railing outside are fine examples of Hindu Indian traditions effectively blended with Islamic architecture. At dawn every day, the surrounding woodlands and the paths around the immense tank, once the site of Timur's camp, come alive with people out walking, practising yoga and jogging, while later in the day, the tank itself springs to life with fountains.

Siri, Jahanpanah and Chiragh Delhi

Ala-ud-Din's citadel at **Siri** (see p.82) is a couple of kilometres east of Hauz Khas, and the remains of its ramparts can be seen from Khel Gaon Marg. Much of it has been given over to parkland, which makes it pleasant enough to visit, but short of a few very diminutive ruins and a Jat village, there isn't a lot to see.

Delhi's "fourth city", **Jahanpanah**, was built during the reign of Muhammad Tughluq to fill the space between Siri and Lal Kot (see opposite), of which it was really just a northeastward extension. All that remains of it today are some scattered mosques and tombs, mostly located south of Siri between Gamal Abdel Nasser Marg (the Outer Ring Road) and Press Enclave Road, which continues west to the Qutb Minar at Lal Kot. It isn't one of Delhi's top attractions, but it's certainly worth exploring. Starting at its junction with Gamal Abdel Nasser

Marg, head south for 300m along Khel Gaon Marg, until you come to a set of traffic lights where a right turn down Geetanjali Marg brings you eventually to a turning on the right by a "Guide Map of Begampur Park". That road leads into Begampur village, where you'll find the imposing edifice of the **Begampuri Mosque** (sunrise–sunset; free), an impressive piece of Tughluq architecture with a huge courtyard and a massive gateway into the main prayer area directly opposite the entrance. To its north (follow the street round the north side of the mosque and take a right just beyond it), the **Bijay Mandal** was almost certainly part of Muhammad Tughluq's palace. A sturdy if very ruined construction, it can be climbed for views over the area from the octagonal pavilion on its roof. Head back to the traffic lights at the start of Geetanjali Marg, and take a right turn (continuing along Khel Gaon Marg) which after 200m takes you past **Lal Gumbad** (sunrise–sunset; free), the 1397 tomb of a local Sufi saint, and reminiscent of Ghiyas-ud-din Tughluq's tomb at Tughluqabad (see p.129). If you continue for another 300m, you reach Khirki Main Road. This leads south to Khirki Village and the **Khirki Masjid** (sunrise–sunset; free), a solidly imposing mosque with typically Tughluq tapering turrets – one of seven commissioned by Firoz Shah's chief minister Khan-i-Jahan Junan Shah. Its interior, almost completely covered, with only four small areas open to the sky, is wierdly atmospheric and partly colonized by bats. From its eastern gateway, stairs lead up to the roof, where you can check out its mass of domes.

One of Delhi's least-known attractions is the almost perfectly square village of **Chiragh Delhi**, which lies just south of Gamal Abdel Nasser Marg to the east of Jahanpanah. Like Nizamuddin, this is a village that has been swallowed whole by Delhi, but even more than Nizammudin, it retains its village atmosphere and it's a great place for a wander. Once walled, it still has the remains of gateways in the middle of each of its four sides, and at its western side a *dargah*, the tomb of Hazrat Nizam-ud-Din's pupil and successor, the Chishti saint, Chiragh Delhi. Within the enclosure (take off shoes to enter) are several subsidiary tombs as well as that of the saint himself, who died in 1356. Just to its west, and worth the walk all the way round the north side of the compound to reach it, the **tomb of Bahlal Lodi**, sultan of Delhi from 1451 to 1489, is a curious castellated building, quite unlike any other royal tomb in the city.

Qutb Minar Complex

Above the foundations of **Lal Kot**, the "first city of Delhi" founded in the eleventh century by the Tomar Rajputs, stand the first monuments of Muslim India, known as the **Qutb Minar Complex** (daily sunrise–sunset; foreigners Rs250, Indian residents Rs10). You'll find it 13km south of Connaught Place off Aurobindo Marg, easy to reach by bus #505 from Ajmeri Gate, Connaught Place (Super Bazaar) or Kasturba Gandhi Marg, or by pre-paid auto from Connaught Place (Rs85). Qutab Minar metro station is 500m south of the site; Saket station is actually nearer. One of Delhi's most famous landmarks, the fluted red sandstone tower of the **Qutb Minar** tapers upwards from the ruins, covered with intricate carvings and deeply inscribed verses from the Koran, to a height of just over 72m. In times past it was considered one of the "Wonders of the East", second only to the Taj Mahal – in the words of the Victorian historian, James Ferguson, "the most beautiful example of its class known anywhere"; but historian John Keay was perhaps more representative of the modern eye when he claimed that the tower had "an unfortunate hint of the factory chimney and the brick kiln; a wisp of white smoke trailing from its summit would not seem out of place".

Work on the Qutb Minar started in 1202; it was Qutb-ud-Din Aibak's victory tower, celebrating the advent of the Muslim dominance of Delhi (and much of the

▲ Qutb Minar

Subcontinent) that was to endure until 1857. For Qutb-ud-Din, who died four years after gaining power, it marked the eastern extremity of the Islamic faith, casting the shadow of God over East and West. It was also a minaret, from which the *muezzin* called the faithful to prayer. Only the first storey has been ascribed to Qutb-ud-Din's own short reign; the other four were built under his successor Iltutmish, and the top was restored in 1369 under Firoz Shah, using marble to face the red sandstone.

Quwwat-ul-Islam Mosque
Adjacent to the tower lie the ruins of India's first mosque, **Quwwat-ul-Islam** ("the Might of Islam"), commissioned by Qutb-ud-Din and built using the remains of 27 Hindu and Jain temples with the help of Hindu artisans whose influence can be seen in the detail of the masonry and the indigenous corbelled arches. Steps lead to an impressive courtyard flanked by cloisters and supported by

pillars unmistakeably taken from a Hindu temple and adapted to accord with strict Islamic law forbidding iconic worship – all the faces of the decorative figures carved into the columns have been removed. Especially fine ornamental arches, rising as high as 16m, remain of what was once the prayer hall. Beautifully carved sandstone screens, combining Koranic calligraphy with the Indian lotus, form a facade immediately to the west of the mosque, facing Mecca. The thirteenth-century Delhi sultan Iltutmish and his successors had the building extended, enlarging the prayer hall and the cloisters and introducing geometric designs, calligraphy, glazed tiles set in brick, and squinches (arches set diagonally to a square to support a dome). In Iltutmish's tomb, on a plinth to the west of the Quwwat-ul-Islam, a relatively plain exterior with three ornate arches blending Indian and Muslim styles hides a 9m-square interior decorated with geometric arabesque patterns, calligraphy, and lotus and wheel motifs.

The Khalji sultan Ala-ud-Din had the mosque extended to the north, and aimed to build a tower even taller than the Qutb Minar, but his **Alai Minar** never made it beyond the first storey, which still stands, and is regarded as a monument to the folly of vain ambition. Ala-ud-Din also commissioned the **Alai Darwaza**, an elegant mausoleum-like gateway with stone lattice screens, just to the south of the Qutb Minar. Its inlaid marble embellishments are ascribed to an influx of Pathan artisans from Byzantine Turkey, and the import of Seljuk influences.

The Iron Pillar

In contrast to the mainly Islamic surroundings, an **Iron Pillar** (7.2m) in the precincts of Qutb-ud-Din's original mosque bears a fourth-century Sanskrit inscription attributing it to the memory of King Chandragupta II (375–415 AD). Once topped with an image of the Hindu bird god, Garuda, the extraordinarily rust-free pillar, made of 98 percent pure iron (a purity that could not be replicated until at least the end of the nineteenth century), has puzzled metallurgists. Its rust resistance is apparently due to it containing as much as one percent phosphorus, which has acted as a chemical catalyst to create a protective layer of an unusual compound called misawite ($FeOOH$) around the metal. The pillar's origins remain hazy; it was evidently transplanted here by the Tomars, but we do not know where from. Tradition has it that anyone who can encircle the column with their hands behind their back will have their wishes granted, but as you are not allowed to go right up to the pillar, you'll never know.

Around the Qutb Minar Complex

The area to the north, south and west of the Qutb Minar Complex was the original site of Lal Kot. To the east, encompassing the village of Lado Sarai, is the area in which the Chauhans built their extension, **Qila Rai Pithora**, though little of it survives today (part of the wall can be seen along the edge of Qutab Golf Course, on Press Enclave Road), and the tombs you can see across Anuvrat Marg (the Mehrauli Bypass) from the Qutb Minar Complex all date from the fourteenth and fifteenth centuries.

The Archeological Park

The area south of the Qutb Minar Complex, rich with remains from all sorts of historical periods, has been turned into an **Archeological Park** (daily sunrise–sunset; free). Here, within a very pleasant stroll of each other, and of Qutab Minar metro station, you'll find: the tomb of Ghiyas-ud-Din Balban, one of the Slave Dynasty sultans (reigned 1265–87), believed to be the first building in India constructed with true arches; the beautiful 1528 mosque and tomb of the poet Jamali Kamali (you may need to find the caretaker to open up the tomb for you);

and the octagonal Mughal tomb of Muhammad Quli Khan, one of Akbar's courtiers, which was occupied in the early nineteenth century by Sir Thomas Metcalfe, the East India Company's resident at the Mughal court, who rather bizarrely converted it into a country house. Metcalfe made his mark on the area in other ways too, restoring a Lodi-period dovecote and constructing "follies" – mock-ancient pavilions, a typical feature of English country estates of the time, except that Metcalfe's were Indian in style. The park extends over 250 acres and contains over eighty monuments, including tombs, mosques, gateways and *baolis*, dating from every century between the thirteenth and the twentieth.

Mehrauli

West of the park, the village of **Mehrauli** was built around the *dargah* of Qutb Sahib, a disciple of Khwaja Muin-ud-Din Chishti (see p.254), who died in 1235 and is considered the second great Chishti saint, after Khwaja Muin-ud-Din himself. Next door is a summer palace commissioned by Akbar II early in the nineteenth century, by which time Khwaja Muin-ud-Din's *dargah* at Ajmer was outside the Mughals' domains and it was easier and more politic to pay homage to his disciple instead, the palace being a handy place to stay on such occasions. At the northern edge of the village, built on the remains of Lal Kot's walls, **Adham Khan's tomb** is the last resting place of a general in Akbar's army (Mohammed Quli Khan's brother) who was hurled from the ramparts of Agra Fort on the orders of the emperor after some murderous court feuding. You can get good views of both the tomb and the Qutb complex from the roof of the **Church of St John**, an incongruous little chapel with an Anglican nave, monastic cloisters and a Hindu *chhapra* (tower), tucked down a lane opposite the tomb entrance.

Tomb of Sultan Ghari

Five kilometres west of the Qutb Minar, just south of the Mahipalpur–Mehrauli Road at Vasant Kunj, Sultan Ghari's tomb (daily sunrise–sunset; foreigners Rs100, Indian residents Rs5) was commissioned by Sultan Iltutmish in 1231 for his son and heir-apparent, Prince Nasir-ud-Din Mahmud, who died before he could reach the throne. The oldest Islamic mausoleum in India, with its sturdy walls and domed bastions, it looks from the outside more like a fort than a tomb. Entering through the main gate, with its fine Arabic calligraphy, you come into a courtyard built around an octagonal raised platform. The tomb itself is in a crypt-like burial chamber underneath the octagonal platform – hence its nickname, "Sultan Ghari", which means "royal cave". The subterranean chamber, the octagonal platform and the mosque-like compound surrounding it are all pretty unusual for early Islamic tombs. The construction technique, using lintels rather than arches, is indigenous rather than Islamic, and the fact that pieces of earlier temples were used in the tomb's construction (see p.104) is evidence that there were settlements in this area going back to at least the fifth century. Several pieces are clearly visible embedded in the walls, and there's a yoni base from a Shiva lingam in the floor by the western wall's central mihrab. Today, people from neighbouring villages, mostly Hindu, regard the tomb as a holy site and leave offerings every Thursday; local brides come to pray here before their wedding, and it is possible that the tomb may stand on what was originally a Hindu holy site.

Baha'i Temple

Often compared visually to the Sydney Opera House, Delhi's 1986 **Baha'i Temple** (Mon–Sat: April–Sept 9am–7pm; Oct–March 9.30am–5.30pm; you may be asked to wait briefly outside during services, which are on the hour 9am–noon & 3–5pm), on open ground atop Kalkaji Hill, 12km southeast of Connaught Place, is an iconic piece of modern architecture that dominates the surrounding suburban sprawl. Twenty-seven spectacular giant white petals of marble in the shape of an unfolding lotus spring from nine pools and walkways, to symbolize the nine unifying spiritual paths of the Baha'i faith; each petal alcove contains an extract from the Baha'i holy scriptures. You're welcome to meditate in silence inside the central hall, which rises to a height of 34m. Set amid well-maintained gardens, the temple is at its most impressive at sunset. It'll cost you Rs80 to get here by pre-paid auto from Connaught Place, or you can take bus #440 from New Delhi station (gate 1) or Connaught Place (the stop in Kasturba Gandhi Marg) to the Outer Ring Road by Kalkaji bus depot, a short walk from the temple. Kalkaji Mandir metro (violet line) will also be within walking distance when it opens (at the end of 2010 or shortly thereafter). The University of Georgia's Baha'i Association has further information about the temple online at ⓦ www.uga.edu/bahai/india.html.

Ashoka's Rock Edict

Northwest of the Baha'i Temple, just off Raja Dhirsain Marg, **Ashoka's Rock Edict** is a ten-line epigraph inscribed in ancient Brahmi script on a smooth, sloping rock. The rock, now protected by a shelter in its own little park, was used as a slide by neighbourhood kids until 1966, when local residents noticed the ancient inscription, promulgated by the Mauryan emperor Ashoka the Great, who ruled most of the Indian Subcontinent bar the far south in the third century BC. In the eighth year of his reign (262 BC), Ashoka became a devout Buddhist and started having edicts inscribed on prominent rocks across his empire. This one was among the earliest, and it shows there must have been an important settlement nearby. It states that the emperor's exertions in the cause of dharma (righteousness) had brought the people closer to the gods, and that through their efforts, irrespective of their station, this attainment could be increased even further. Later, Ashoka had his edicts inscribed on columns, of which ten survive today, including the Ashokan pillars on the Northern Ridge (see p.118) and at Firoz Shah Kotla (see p.120). Unlike those, though, this earlier rock edict still stands at its original site.

Tughluqabad

Fifteen kilometres southeast of Connaught Place on the Mehrauli–Badarpur Road (the entrance is 1km east of the junction with Guru Ravidas Marg), a rocky escarpment holds the crumbling 6.5km-long battlements of the third city of Delhi, Tughluqabad (daily sunrise–sunset; foreigners Rs100, Indian residents Rs5), built during the short reign of Ghiyas-ud-Din Tughluq (1320–24). After the king's death the city was deserted, probably due to the lack of a clean water source nearby, and the cyclopean ruins were almost entirely abandoned, overgrown with scrubland and occupied by rhesus monkeys and nomadic Gujar herders; according to legend, this fulfils a curse put on it by the Sufi saint, Sheikh Nizam-ud-Din Aulia (see p.122), because Ghiyas-ud-Din's labourers had been moonlighting, building a *baoli* for the saint, until Ghiyas-ud-Din forbade them to do so while under his employ. The most interesting area is the high-walled citadel in the south-western part of the site, though only a long underground passage, the ruins of several halls and a tower now remain. The grid pattern of some of the city streets to the north is still traceable. The palace area is to the west of the entrance, and the former bazaar to the east.

The southernmost of Tughluqabad's thirteen gates still looks down on a causeway, breached by the modern road, which rises above the flood plain, to link the fortress with **Ghiyas-ud-Din Tughluq's tomb** (same hours and ticket as Tughluqabad). The tomb is entered through a massive red sandstone gateway leading into a courtyard surrounded by cloisters in the defensive walls. In the middle, surrounded by a well-kept lawn, stands the distinctive mausoleum, its sloping sandstone walls topped by a marble dome, and in its small way a precursor to the fine series of garden tombs built by the Mughals, which began here in Delhi with that of Humayun (see p.121). Inside the mausoleum are the graves of Ghiyas-ud-Din, his wife and their son Muhammad Shah II. Ghiyas-ud-din's chief minister Jafar Khan is buried in the eastern bastion, and interred in the cloister nearby is the sultan's favourite dog.

The later fortress of **Adilabad** (free entry), built by Muhammad Shah II in much the same style as his father's citadel, and now in ruins, stands on a hillock to the southeast.

Tughluqabad is served by buses #34, #525 and #717 along the Mehrauli–Badarpur Road from Lado Sarai near the Qutb Minar, and by #430 from Kalkaji near the Baha'i Temple. From Connaught Place, the easiest way to get here is by pre-paid auto-rickshaw (Rs115). The violet line's Tughluqabad metro station (violet line), scheduled to open at the end of 2010, will be around 1km east of the site.

Akshardham Temple

Across Nizamuddin Bridge on the east side of the Yamuna River (metro blue line or Rs70 by pre-paid auto from Connaught Place), the opulent **Akshardham Temple** (Tues–Sun: April–Sept 10am–7pm, Oct–Mar 9am–6pm; free; Ⓦwww.akshardham.com) was put up in 2005 by the Gujarat-based Shri Swaminarayan, sect. A stunning piece of work, the temple is an eloquent reminder of the sect's wealth, embellished with wonderful carvings made using the same tools and techniques as in ancient times, without rivets or screws. Cameras, mobile phones, mirrors and any electronic equipment, including USB keys, are prohibited and should be deposited at the cloakroom outside, and visitors may not enter wearing shorts or skirts above the knee. The sect's founder, Bhagwan Shri Swaminarayan was born in 1781 and set up an ashram in Gujarat preaching non-violence and unity. He died in 1830, but his followers believe he is "eternally present on earth". His original devotees were poor Gujarati peasants, but the growth of a wealthy Gujarati diaspora has brought the sect money and influence, though it remains much respected for its spiritual values. The **main shrine** is surrounded by a pink sandstone relief (you must walk round it clockwise) whose theme is elephants: wild, domesticated or in legend. Inside (closed for renovation at the time of writing), the centrepiece and main object of devotion is a 3m-high gold statue of Shri Swaminarayan, attended by four disciples. Behind it are paintings depicting scenes from his life, and also some personal objects such as his sandals and even some of his hair and nail clippings. The four subsidiary shrines are devoted to Hindu gods.

National Rail Museum

The cream of India's royal coaches and oldest engines is on permanent display at the **National Rail Museum** (Tues–Sun: April–Sept 9.30am–1pm & 1.30–7.30pm; Oct–March 9.30am–1pm & 1.30–5.30pm; Rs10, video Rs100) in the Embassy enclave of Chanakyapuri, southwest of Connaught Place; take bus #620 from Shivaji Stadium terminal by Connaught Place, or a pre-paid auto (Rs60). Some 27 locomotives and 17 carriages – including the ornate 1886 gold-painted saloon car of the Maharaja of Baroda (Rs50 to go inside), the teak carriage of the Maharaja of Mysore, trimmed in gold and ivory, and the cabin used by the Prince of Wales in 1876 – are kept in the grounds. A steam-hauled miniature "Joy Train" does a circuit of the grounds (Rs10) whenever it has enough passengers.

The covered section of the museum houses models of famous engines and coaches, displays of old tickets, and even the skull of an elephant hit by a train near Calcutta in 1894. The pride of the collection, however, is a model of India's very first train, a steam engine that made its inaugural journey of 21 miles from Mumbai to Thane in 1853.

Sulabh International Museum of Toilets

The light-hearted nature of the **Sulabh International Museum of Toilets** (Mon–Sat 10am–5pm; free; ⓦ www.sulabhtoiletmuseum.org; Rs40 by auto from Uttam Nagar East metro station), on Palam Dabri Marg in Mahavir Enclave I, in Delhi's western suburbs, belies the importance of the organization that runs it. Basing itself soundly on Gandhian principles, the Sulabh Movement aims to free members of the lowest rank of outcastes from the demeaning job of cleaning out non-flush latrines and carrying away the excrement, and to end the insanitary practice of open-air defecation by promoting hygienic, eco-friendly toilets in towns, cities and villages across India – you'll no doubt see some of their "toilet complexes" around Delhi.

The museum illustrates lavatorial history from Harappan times through to the modern day, and its grounds house examples of easy-to-build hygienic flush latrines for use in communities without sewerage or running water. Pride of place goes to the movement's machine for converting human excrement into fertilizer and fuel, an average poo yielding a cubic metre of methane gas that can be used for cooking, heating or lighting. The movement's toilet technology is self-financing, making brass from muck, while promoting caste equality and public health awareness at the same time.

Eating

Delhi has quite an eating culture, and enough prosperous foodies to sustain a large variety of **restaurants** and worldwide cuisines, while less rarified establishments cater for office workers in need of somewhere to fill up cheaply at lunchtime or after work. The result is something for every budget, with excellent food on offer at humble roadside *dhabas* and unassuming diners, and truly magnificent Indian and foreign cuisine in Delhi's more renowned restaurants. The Western junk food franchise chains are all here too, if you need them (though their hamburgers are actually lamb burgers), and there are vast buffets and superlative à la carte menus at many of the luxury hotels.

Most restaurants close around 11pm, but those with bars usually stay open until midnight. If you're looking for a **late-night** meal, you have a number of choices: eat in one of the restaurants in a top hotel, or at the 24-hour coffee shops in *Le Meridien*, the *Park* or *The Claridges*; try a snack in Paharganj's round-the-clock rooftop cafés; or head to Pandara Road market (open till 1.30am). Old Delhi railway station also has a couple of 24-hour places, and the refreshment hall just down the corridor from the foreigners' booking office in New Delhi station is also open 24/7.

If you want to explore Delhi's eating places beyond those listed here, you might want to pick up a copy of the annual *Hindustan Times Eating Out Guide* (Rs150 at newsstands and bookshops), which covers just about every restaurant in the city and its suburbs, cross-referenced by district and cuisine, with reviews ranging from glowing to witheringly scathing.

Connaught Place

Connaught Place ("CP") is dominated by upmarket restaurants and Western-style fast-food places, with a few cheap and cheerful eateries hidden away if you know where to look. The **Bengali Market**, on Tansen Marg, off Barakhamba Road, is a good place for sweets and snacks.

The restaurants and cafés listed below are marked on the Connaught Place **map** on p.92.

Anand Connaught Lane, three doors from *Sunny Guest House*. Good, cheap veg and non-veg eats including great biriyanis and thalis (non-veg dishes at around Rs93 (thali Rs94 veg, Rs114 non-veg).

Barista N-16 Connaught Place. Popular coffee bar, the first of what is now a nationwide chain that claims to do the best espresso in India (100 percent Arabica), plus cakes and muffins to accompany. Rival chain *Café Coffee Day* has numerous CP outlets (almost one on every block).

Bikanervala 1st floor, Rajiv Gandhi Bhawan, between the two state emporium buildings, Baba Kharak Singh Marg. Sparkling canteen-style restaurant serving snacks, meals (thalis Rs125–140), sweets and namkeens.

Fire *Park Hotel*, 15 Sansad Marg ☎ 011/2374 3000 ext 1827. Scintillating if expensive modern restaurant whose contemporary Indian cuisine bears a strong hint of European influence. Menu depends on the season, with lighter dishes in summer, fierier ones in winter. Main non-veg dinner dishes are Rs775–1150, but at lunchtime there's a set meal (Rs1200 veg, Rs1500 non-veg). Booking advisable.

India Coffee House 2nd floor, Mohan Singh Place Shopping Complex, Baba Kharak Singh Marg. Down-at-heel canteen with a large roof terrace, part of a mainly south Indian co-op chain, serving filter and espresso coffee, snacks and basic meals (thalis Rs40) to an eclectic cross-section of downtown New Delhi's daytime population.

Kake Da Hotel 74 Municipal Market, Outer Ring, Connaught Place. A small, cramped diner (the term "hotel" does not imply accommodation) that's been here so long it's become a Delhi institution, known for unpretentious but reliably good Punjabi curries, mostly non-veg, such as butter chicken or sag meat (palak mutton), at around Rs100 a plate. Takeaway available.

Kwality 7 Regal Building, Sansad Marg. Originally set up to serve American GIs during World War II, this is one of CP's better mid-market choices (non-veg mains Rs225–325), quite elegantly decorated with lots of mirrors and chandeliers (though the odd mouse has been spotted scurrying across the floor). Good choices include chicken tikka with green peas, and mutton *shahi kurma*.

Parikrama Kasturba Gandhi Marg ☎ 011/2372 1616. Novel and expensive Indian (mainly tandoori) and Chinese cuisine in a revolving restaurant affording superb views over Delhi; a single rotation takes ninety minutes. Main dishes cost Rs220–650. Specialities include *murg pasandey parikrama* (chicken breast stuffed with minced chicken and nuts in a cashew-nut sauce) and *murg tikka parikrama* (chicken tikka in a spicy cashew-nut marinade). Booking advisable.

Q'BA E-42/3 Connaught Place. Cool and stylish upmarket bar-restaurant on two floors and two terraces, with views over CP, though its "world cuisine" actually boils down to Indian, Italian and Thai, with pizza, pasta, green and red curry, and specialities such as *Q'BA raan* (char-grilled leg of lamb with herbs) and *sarsun wali machi tikka* (tandoori fish pieces in a mustard marinade). Main courses go for Rs350–700.

Sagar Ratna K-15 Connaught Place. The CP branch of the renowned Defence Colony restaurant (see p.135), great for *vadas*, *dosas* or a south Indian veg thali (Rs130). Main dishes Rs80–120.

Saravana Bhavan P-15 Connaught Place and 46 Janpath. Excellent low-priced south Indian snacks and meals, including thalis (Rs117) and quick lunches (Rs80), as well as the usual *dosas*, *iddlis* and *uttapams*. The mini tiffin (Rs80) has a taste of everything.

Spice Route *Hotel Imperial*, Janpath. This beautifully decorated restaurant, exclusive and expensive, if perhaps a little overpriced (non-veg main dishes Rs650–775, seafood Rs1150–1850), specializes in spicy Southeast Asian and Keralan cuisine. If you want to eat well in the CP vicinity, this is one of your best bets.

Veda H-27 Connaught Place ☎ 011/4151 3535. CP's swankiest restaurant, charging a premium for its "ambience" (all smoochy red and black decor with low lights), though the food isn't at all bad (main dishes such as Peshawari kebabs and malai fish tikka at Rs400–800; a tandoori platter for Rs355 veg, Rs755 non-veg).

Zen B-25 Connaught Place. Excellent Chinese meals (as well as a few Thai and Japanese dishes) served in a relaxed and traditional style, plus Western snacks (3–7pm), and a broad selection of wines, spirits and beers. Most non-veg main dishes are Rs285–300 (prawns Rs400–600).

Paharganj and Ram Nagar

With so much good food on offer in Delhi, it's a shame to dine in **Paharganj**, even if that's where your hotel is. Most of the restaurants on the Main Bazaar are geared to unadventurous foreign tastebuds, offering poor imitations of Western, Israeli, Japanese and even Thai dishes, or sloppy, insipid versions of Indian curries for foreigners who can't handle chilli. Most serve breakfasts of toast, porridge, muesli and omelettes, though they'll do you a *paratha* as well. Eating options in **Ram Nagar** are more indigenous. If you decide to eat in any of the *dhabas* opposite New Delhi Station, especially those with waiters outside trying to hustle you in, always ask the price of a dish before ordering, because unless you can read the price list in Hindi, you're likely to be overcharged.

The restaurants listed below are marked on the Paharganj **map** on p.94.

Club India 4797 Main Bazaar. First-floor and rooftop restaurant with the best views over central Paharganj, lively music, and the usual travellers' breakfast options plus reasonable stabs at Israeli, Japanese, Tibetan and even tandoori dishes. Non-veg main courses go for Rs60–150, thalis and meal combos Rs100–175.

Darbar Restaurant and **Bikaner Sweets Corner** 9002 Multani Dhanda Chowk, just off D B Gupta Rd ☎011/2351 6666. Upstairs, it's a no-nonsense moderately priced veg restaurant, serving tasty thalis (Rs50–106) and Punjabi veg curries (Rs70–105); it also has a takeaway service, and delivers orders over Rs100 within a kilometre radius. Downstairs, it's a wonderful sweets emporium, with all sorts of multicoloured Bengali and Rajasthani confections, plus namkeens and savouries.

Diamond Café 5069 Main Bazaar. Backpacker restaurant with a good, if typical, menu (main dishes Rs70–150 non-veg), including a choice of set breakfasts (Continental, Indian, American, Israeli; Rs60–80), fruit salads, pancakes and also some Indian dishes. *Kholsa Cafe*, down the street at no. 5024, is very similar, but slightly cheaper.

Golden Café 1 Nehru Bazaar, Ramdwara Rd, opposite Sri Mahavir Mandir. Cheap and cheerful café popular with Korean and Japanese travellers, serving Chinese, Korean and European food with main dishes at Rs60–135.

Malhotra Laksmi Narain Rd. One of the better restaurants in Paharganj, offering passable tandoori and Mughlai dishes at reasonable prices

(Rs130–225 for non-veg dishes). There's a basement, and an a/c upstairs section, plus a veg south Indian branch two doors down.

Metropolis 1634 Main Bazaar. Cosy a/c ground-floor restaurant in the hotel of the same name (downstairs, or on the roof terrace). Paharganj's priciest venue serves full breakfasts, reasonable curries and tandoori specials, plus Western dishes, beer, spirits, cocktails and non-alcoholic "mocktails". Main dishes are Rs125–200 veg, Rs250–350 non-veg.

Ritu Raj Bhojnalya Arakashan Rd, below *Delhi Continental Hotel*. Cheap, popular *dhaba* serving excellent Indian breakfasts, simple veg curries and south Indian snacks (Rs20–50). A great place for *chana* rice or *iddli sambar*.

Sonu Chat House 5046 Main Bazaar. Popular cheap diner serving noodles, soup, samosas, curries and even masala dosa to the backpacker crowd. Set breakfasts Rs60–80, non-veg main dishes Rs65–120.

Sonu South Indian Restaurant 8849/2 Multani Dhanda Chowk, off D B Gupta Rd, Ram Nagar. Basic south Indian grub (masala dosa, *iddlis, vadas* and the like) at low prices (Rs35–65 a go, or Rs60–80 for a thali).

Tadka 4986 Ramdwara Rd (Nehru Bazaar) ☎011/3291 5216. The best dining in Paharganj: a clean, bright, modern little restaurant serving low-priced Indian veg dishes (main dishes Rs65–75, thalis Rs85–100). They'll deliver to any address within 2km.

Old Delhi

Old Delhi's crowded streets contain numerous simple food-halls that serve surprisingly good, and invariably fiery, Indian dishes for as little as Rs20. Upmarket eating is thin on the ground, but some of the mid-range restaurants serve food every bit as good as the posh eateries of South Delhi, and the sweets and snacks in Old Delhi are the best in town.

The restaurants listed below are marked on the Old Delhi **map** on p.108.

Aap ki Pasand 15 Netaji Subhash Marg ⓦwww .aapkipasandtea.com. Of course you can get a chai on any street corner, but for a superior cuppa, head to this refined tea room, where Rs50 will buy you a bone china cup of first- or second-flush Darjeeling, Assam or Nilgiri, and you can buy it by the packet too.

Chaina Ram 6499 Fatehpuri Chowk, next to Fatehpuri Mosque. Established in Karachi in 1901, and forced to relocate in 1947, this little shop is well known for its Sindhi-style sweets; their delicately aromatic Karachi halwa, with almonds and pistachios, is the best in town.

Chor Bizarre *Hotel Broadway*, 4/15 Asaf Ali Rd. A wide selection of excellent Indian dishes from around the country, but above all from Kashmir. Eccentric, delightful decor featuring a four-poster bed, sewing table and a servery made from a 1927 vintage Fiat. Non-veg main dishes go for Rs325–495. The speciality is a Kashmiri sampler (*tarami*).

Deepak Chandni Chowk. A *dhaba* in the bazaar opposite the Jain temple, serving inexpensive south Indian snacks (*iddli sambar*, *dosas*, *uttapams*, at Rs22–65) and thalis (Rs38–40).

Ghantewala 1862-A Chandni Chowk. Established in 1790, this famous confectioner supplied sweets to the last Mughal emperors; its *ladoo* was already renowned in the nineteenth century, and the cashew fancies are out of this world, but their speciality is a nutty, butterscotch-like sweet called *sohan halwa*.

Haldiram's 1454 Chandni Chowk. Super-hygienic low-priced snack-bar and takeaway with sweets and samosas downstairs, drinks and snacks (Rs36–50) upstairs, including excellent *puris*, lassis, lime sodas, kulfis and thalis (Rs140). If you've never tried one, check the *raj kachori* (Rs46), a crunchy pastry shell enclosing a tangy chickpea curry with yoghurt.

Karim's Gali Kababian. A perennial Delhiite favourite, located in a passage down a side street, opposite the south gate of the Jama Masjid, consisting of four eating halls (same kitchen) offering the best meat dishes in the old city, at moderate prices, with delicious fresh kebabs, hot breads and great Mughlai curries. Full dishes cost Rs110–385, but half dishes are also available.

Moti Mahal 3704 Netaji Subhash Marg. Renowned for its tandoori chicken, this medium-priced restaurant is another local favourite – one of the first Punjabi restaurants in town – with both indoor seating and a large open-air courtyard. Main dishes go for Rs160–265, or Rs270 for the speciality, *murg musallam* (chicken with kidney, egg and mincemeat).

Paratha Wali Gali Off Chandni Chowk, opposite the Central Bank. Head down this alleyway by Kanwarji Raj Kumar Sweet Shop (itself pretty good), and you'll be rewarded with *parathas* filled with anything from *paneer* and *gobi* to *muttar* and *mooli*, all cooked to order and served with a small selection of curries for Rs30–45. There are three *paratha*-wallahs in the alley, all good, but the most renowned is the first one, *Pandit Babu Ram*.

South Delhi

The enclaves and villages spread across the vast area of **South Delhi** offer countless eating options, and most of its upmarket shopping zones (Hauz Khas, Defence Colony, Ansal Plaza and the like) contain several good restaurants. **Dilli Haat**, the tourist market in Safdarjang, has 25 food stalls offering dishes from nearly every state in India. **Pandara Road Market**'s restaurants and snack bars, just south of India Gate, stay open until 1.30am.

Unless otherwise stated, the restaurants listed here are marked on the **Delhi map** on pp.80–81.

Basil & Thyme Santushti Shopping Complex. See New Delhi map, p.99. Bistro-style Mediterranean eating with dishes like shitake crepes, asparagus and arugula risotto, and desserts including seasonal fruit cheesecake or tiramisu. Mains Rs355–525. The 6pm closing time, however, means it's lunch not supper, unless you want to make that tea. Closed Sun.

Bukhara *Maurya Hotel*, Sardar Patel Marg, Chanakyapuri ☎011/2611 2233. See New Delhi map, p.99. Delhi's top restaurant, specializing in succulently tender tandoori kebabs (Rs1550), with

a menu that's short but very sweet, and a kitchen separated from the eating area by a glass partition, so you can watch the chefs at work. Bill Clinton is among the many celebs who have eaten here. The *Maurya* also has another fine restaurant, *Dum Pukht* (evenings only), which specializes in the *dum* (slow-cooked casserole) cuisine of Avadh (central Uttar Pradesh), with à la carte dining or a choice of set menus (Rs2400–3000).

Flavors C-52 Defence Colony. Run by a Mizo–Italian couple, this is one of Delhi's best Italian eateries, where you'll find excellent risotto, great pasta and pizzas, and wonderful tiramisu. Main dishes cost Rs335–500.

Park Balluchi Deer Park, Hauz Khas ☏011/2685 9369, ⊛www.parkballuchi.com. Kebabs and Baluchi dishes (veg Rs205–295, non-veg Rs360–450) amid sylvan surroundings. The speciality is a Murg Potli kebab, served on a flaming sword.

Punjabi by Nature Priya Cinema Complex, Basant Lok, Vasant Vihar ☏011/4151 6666. It's quite a haul from the centre (Rs120 by pre-paid auto from CP), but this restaurant has made a big name for itself among Delhiite foodies with its fabulous Punjabi and north Indian cuisine – expensive, but worth it (most main dishes Rs425–575). The Amritsari fish tikka is succulent, the tandoori prawns wonderful, but for something really special, try the *raan-e-Punjab* (leg of lamb, Rs725). There's now a more easily accessible

branch on the third floor of City Square Mall, Raja Garden (☏011/4222 5656 or 5757), by Rajaouri Garden metro.

Sagar 18 Defence Colony Market. Delicious, inexpensive south Indian vegetarian food, with *vadas, iddlis, ravas* and *dosas* (Rs60–85), plus great thalis (Rs130). They've also opened a north Indian restaurant a few doors down at no. 24, and they have branches all over town, but the original is still the best.

Swagath 14 Defence Colony Market. A non-veg offshoot of *Sagar*, a few doors away. There are Indian and Chinese meat dishes on the menu, but ignore them and go for the Mangalore-style seafood – the *Swagath* special (chilli and tamarind), *gassi* (coconut sauce) and *sawantwadi* (green masala) dishes are all great, at Rs295–305 a throw with pomfret, Rs335–605 for versions made with prawns.

Bars and nightclubs

With an ever-increasing number of pubs and clubs, Delhi's **nightlife** scene is in full swing. During the week, lounge and dance bars are your best bet, but come the weekend the **discos** really take off. Most, if not all, of the discos popular with Delhi's young jet-set are in the luxury hotels, and many don't allow "stag entry" (men unaccompanied by women), which makes them a whole lot more comfortable for women, but is tough luck if you're male and alone; the big exception is *Elevate* – Delhi's venue for serious clubbers. Cover charges are Rs500–2000 per couple depending on the club and the night. India Gate and Rajpath attract nightly **"people's parties"** where large crowds mill about, snacking and eating ice cream; these are not advisable for women on their own, as you're likely to get hassled.

For **drinking**, the five-star hotels all have plush and expensive bars, and many of the better ones have dancefloors. Lounge bars with laidback music have become very popular of late, and there are some good ones scattered about the southern suburbs. Note that the drinking age in Delhi is 25, though there are proposals to lower it to 21.

Bars

Blues N-17 Connaught Place. See map, p.92. Snazzy bar and restaurant, offering an eclectic range of loud music (Thurs is rock night). The bar staff are pros at mixing extravagant cocktails. Happy hour (buy 1, get 1 free) is 4–8pm, after which there's a Rs300 minimum food order, and lone males aren't allowed in.

Cibo Janpath Hotel, Janpath. See map, p.92. An Indian version of a Mediterranean ambience, including an outside dining area decorated with gilded statues where you can eat Italian food, and, through the tiled doorway, a bar surrounded by gilt fireplaces, almost managing to be chic rather than kitsch.

Gem 1050 Main Bazaar, Paharganj. See map, p.94. Not a place to seek out from elsewhere in town, but handy if you're in Paharganj and don't want to venture too far afield for a beer, though women won't be comfortable drinking here without a male escort; for a classier drink in Paharganj, try the *Metropolis Hotel* (see p.93).

Lizard Lounge E-5, 1st Floor, South Extension II. See Delhi map, p.81. Lounge music (what else?) and hookah pipes (21 flavours) at this well-established, but still trendy lounge bar, with Mediterranean and Middle Eastern food.

My Bar 5136 Main Bazaar, Paharganj. See map, p.94. A decent bar that also serves food, but it's the cheap beer (Rs84) that you come for. It's a bit dead during the day, but livens up in the evening.

Pegs n' Pints Forte Grand Complex, Chanakya Lane (behind Akbar Bhawan), Chanakyapuri ℡011/2687 8320. See map, p.99. Scruffy, inexpensive bar with music (mainly hip-hop) and an impressive wine list, but mostly of note for its Tuesday gay nights.

Rodeo A-12 Connaught Place. See map, p.92. Saloon-style bar with Wild West waiters, swinging-saddle bar stools, pitchers of beer, tequila slammers, and Mexican-style bar snacks (tacos, enchiladas, fajitas, quesadillas).

Splash Minto Rd (Viveknand Marg), just north of the rail bridge. See Connaught Place map, p.92. Quite a civilized bar with food and reasonably priced beer, a stone's throw from Connaught Place.

Nightclubs

Capitol *Ashoka Hotel*, 50-B Chanakyapuri ℡011/2687 9802. See map, p.99. Upmarket disco playing unashamedly commercial filmi and pop music. Open Wed & Thurs till 2am, Fri & Sat till 4am.

Elevate 6th floor, Center Stage Mall, Sector 18, Noida ℡0120/436 4611, ⊛www.elevateindia.com. Delhi map, p.80. Across the river, and indeed just across the state line in UP, this is the biggest and most kicking club in town, modelled on London's Fabric, with three floors (dancefloor, chill-out and VIP), a roof terrace, and Indian and international DJs playing bhangra, filmi, hip-hop, trance or techno, depending on the night (techno and trance is Fri). Wed–Sat till 3.30am (check the website for what's on).

Cultural pursuits

A range of indoor and outdoor venues hosts performances of **dance**, such as Bhawai (a folk dance from Rajasthan and, typically of that state, very colourful), Bharatnatyam (the best-known classical Indian dance form, from the southern states of Karnataka, Andhra Pradesh and Tamil Nadu) and Kathakali (also from the south, but this time from the state of Kerala), as well as regular **classical music** concerts – check the listings magazines detailed on p.87 to see what's on.

Dance and drama

Dances of India Parsi Anjuman Hall, Bahadur Shah Zafar Marg, near Delhi Gate ℡011/2623 4689. See map, p.108. Excellent classical, folk and tribal dance featuring six to seven items every night from different parts of India, usually including Bharatnatyam, Kathakali, Bhawai and the graceful dance of the northeastern state of Manipur. Daily 6.45pm.

India Habitat Centre Lodi Rd ℡011/2468 2001 to 5, ⊛www.indiahabitat.org. See map, p.99. Popular venue for dance, music and theatre as well as talks and exhibitions. Forthcoming events are listed on the website.

Kamani Auditorium 1 Coporniouo Marg ℡011/4350 3351 or 2, ⊛www.kamaniauditorium .org. See map, p.99. Bharatnatyam and other dance performances.

Sangeet Natak Akademi Rabindra Bhavan, 35 Firoz Shah Rd ℡011/2338 7246 to 8, ⊛www .sangeetnatak.com. See map, p.99. Delhi's premier performing arts institution.

Triveni Kala Sangam 205 Tansen Marg, just south of the Bengali Market ℡011/2371 8833. See map, p.99. Bharatnatyam dance shows, also art exhibitions.

Cultural centres and libraries

American Information Resource Center (USIS) 24 Kasturba Gandhi Marg, southeast of Connaught Place ℡011/2331 4251, ⊛newdelhi.usembassy .gov. American newspapers and periodicals, plus books on current affairs, trade, politics and economics.

Delhi Public Library SP Mukherjee Marg, opposite Old Delhi station, with branches around town ℡011/2396 2682, ⊛www.dpl.gov.in. See map, p.108. Reading rooms open to all. Daily 8.30am–8pm.

India International Centre 40 Max Müller Marg, near Lodi Gardens ℡011/2461 9431, ⊛www .iicdelhi.nic.in. See map, p.99. Exhibitions, lectures, films, dance and music performances and a library.

Lalit Kala Galleries Rabindra Bhawan, 35 Firoz Shah Rd, by Mandi House Chowk ℡011/2338 7241 to 3. See map, p.99. Delhi's premier art academy, with an extensive collection of paintings, sculpture, frescoes and drawings. Also shows films and stages seminars and photographic exhibitions.

Sahitya Akademi Rabindra Bhawan, 32 Firoz Shah Rd, by Mandi House Chowk

011/2338 6626 to 8, www.sahitya-akademi
.gov.in. See New Delhi map, p.99. An excellent
library devoted to Indian literature through
the ages, with some books and periodicals in
English.

Tibet House 1 Institutional Area, Lodi Rd
011/2461 1515, www.tibethousenewdelhi.org.
See map, p.99. A library on all aspects of Tibetan
culture, plus a small museum of Tibetan artefacts
(Rs10). Mon–Fri 9.30am–5.30pm.

Cinemas

Bollywood movies are shown at **cinemas** such as the Regal (011/2336 1583) in Connaught Place, the Imperial in Rajguru Marg, Paharganj (011/2252 8253), or the Shiela (011/2367 2100) on D B Gupta Road, near New Delhi railway station. Tickets cost Rs25–80. CP's Odeon (011/4151 7899) and Plaza (011/4151 3787) cinemas, and suburban multiplexes such as those run by PVR (www.pvrcinemas.com, click on "NCR"), are plusher and nowadays more popular. In addition, some of the cultural centres listed opposite and above occasionally run international film festivals. If you want to see Hindi films with English subtitles, your best bet is to buy them on DVD.

Sports and outdoor activities

The recreational activity most likely to appeal to visitors in the pre-monsoon months has to be a dip in one of Delhi's **swimming pools**. Unfortunately most public pools require you to take out membership; aside from Siri Sports Complex (listed below), try Talkatora Pool, Park Road (011/2309 4832; see New Delhi map, p.99). Luxury hotels usually restrict their pools to residents, but may allow outsiders to join their health clubs; the *Ashoka Hotel*, 50-B Chanakyapuri (011/2611 0101; same location as Capitol on the New Delhi map, p.99), usually allows non-guests to use its pool (Rs400).

Other local diversions include **tennis**, **golf** (there are fifteen courses in the Delhi area), **horseriding** and even **rock climbing**, on crags on the outskirts of the city during the cooler months. Spectator sports are mainly equestrian, in the form of **horse racing** and **polo**.

Army Polo & Riding Club B Squadron 61 Cavalry, Cariappa Marg 011/2569 9444 or 9555 or 9666, www.armypoloclub.com. Polo tournaments in winter (Nov–Feb). To watch, contact the club for an invitation.

Delhi Golf Club Dr Zakir Hussein Marg 011/2436 2235, www.delhigolfclub.org. Busy and beautiful 220-acre golf course on the fifteenth-century estate of the Lodi dynasty. With more than two hundred varieties of trees, it also acts as a bird sanctuary. Monuments and mausoleums, such as the ruined *barakhamba* on a hillock next to the seventh green, dot the grounds. Temporary membership is available to foreigners and NRIs who can demonstrate that they are genuine golfers.

Delhi Lawn Tennis Association R K Khanna Tennis Stadium, 1 Africa Ave 011/2619 3955. There are 21 courts and a pool at this complex near Hauz Khas village. Courts should be booked a day in advance.

Delhi Races Kamal Ataturk Rd 011/2379 2869. Regular horse racing Tues from 1.30pm, sometimes other days too. Men usually Rs50, women Rs20. Mobile phones not allowed in (you can deposit them at the entrance).

Delhi Riding Club Safdarjang Rd, behind Safdarjang's Tomb 011/2301 1891. Rides for adults at 7.30am, 8.30am and 9.30am, and for children at 2.45pm, 3.45pm and 4.45pm; open to the public by prior arrangement through the Club Secretary.

Indian Mountaineering Foundation 6 Benito Juárez Marg 011/2411 1211, www.indmount .org. Official organization governing mountaineering throughout India, with a library and an outdoor climbing wall. Some equipment can be rented here, and you can get information on local crags and climbing groups.

Qutab Golf Course Press Enclave Rd, Lado Sarai 011/2696 9127, www.dda.org.in. Run by the

Delhi Development Authority, this club with an 18-hole course is open to non-members with green fees of Rs1250/$20 (Indian residents Rs250) on weekdays, or Rs1500/$30 (Rs400) at weekends.
Siri Fort Sports Complex Siri Fort ☎011/2649 7482, ⓦ www.dda.org.in. An Olympic-size swimming pool, a toddlers' pool, plus tennis, squash and badminton courts are among the facilities here, at the most central of the DDA's 14 sports complexes. Out-of-towners may use it for Rs100 (Indian residents Rs40) a day, or join on a temporary basis for up to three months for Rs3000 (Rs1500) plus Rs150 a month.

Children's Delhi

In addition to the sporting facilities mentioned above, children may appreciate a visit to the **Planetarium** (see p.105) or **Shankar's International Doll Museum** (see p.118). The **National Rail Museum** (see p.130), and in particular the "Joy Train" ride, can also be a good diversion. At Purana Qila (see p.106), there's the **zoo** and a **boating lake**, and in Old Delhi, a visit to the Jain Temple's **bird hospital** (see p.110) is usually a winner. The **Natural History Museum** (Tues–Sat 10am–5pm; free; ⓦ www.nmnh.nic.in), on Barakhamba Road by Mandi House Chowk, has a rather uninspiring collection of fossils and stuffed animals, and some educational exhibitions aimed mainly at schoolchildren.

On the southern edge of town, **Fun 'n' Food Village** (daily: March–April 9.30am–7pm; May–June 9am–7pm; July–Oct 9.30am–8pm; Nov–Feb 9.30am–6pm; Rs450, children Rs400; ☎011/4326 0000, ⓦ www.funnfood.com) on Old Gurgaon Road at Kapashera has a water park, a snow park and lots of rides, including a Ferris wheel.

Shopping

Although the traditional places to **shop** in Delhi are around **Connaught Place** (particularly the underground Palika Bazaar) and **Chandni Chowk**, a number of suburbs created by the rapid growth of the city are emerging as fashionable shopping districts. **Hauz Khas Village**, in South Delhi, has numerous boutiques, jewellery shops and galleries, while artists and artisans from all over India sell their products at the pleasant open-air **Dilli Haat** craft centre, also in South Delhi. **Old Delhi** is divided into traditional bazaars, each with its own specific trade (see p.114 for the main ones). For more hippyish wares, there's **Paharganj** and the **Tibetan Market** near Connaught Place. To check prices and quality, you can't do better than the **state emporiums** on Baba Kharak Singh Marg.

Unlike the markets of Old Delhi, most shops in New Delhi take credit cards, but wherever you end up, beware of touts trying to sweet-talk you into visiting supposed "government shops" which pay them a commission. In all bazaars and street markets, the rule is to **haggle** – it's even worth asking for a discount at shops that display "fixed price" notices.

Shopping precincts

Ansal Plaza Khel Gaon Marg. See map, p.81. If you want to shop in a mall, you can't get better than this, Delhi's modern and most popular plaza, geared towards middle-class Delhiites rather than tourists, with lots of department stores, plus a pub (*Geoffrey's*), cafés (*Barista*, for example) and various junk food outlets.

Defence Colony Market Varum Marg, off Bhisham Pitamah Marg, Defence Colony. See map, p.81. There are shops here, but mostly you'd come to eat, at restaurants such as *Sagar* and *Swagath* (see p.135). *Moti Mahal* (see p.134) also has a branch here.
Hauz Khas Village Hauz Khas, west of Aurobindo Marg. See map, p.81. An upmarket shopping "village" with some interesting art and antiques

shops and galleries, including Cottage of Arts and Jewels, Plutus, and Indian Art Collection (see p.141). There are also stylish cafés and restaurants for a bite to eat. Most places are closed on Tuesdays.

Khan Market Subramaniam Bharti Marg. See map, p.99. Upmarket open-air shopping precinct, popular with foreign expats and well-heeled Delhiites. There are good bookshops (including Bahrisons at no. 21, opposite the main gate, Faqir Chand at no. 15-A and Full Circle at no. 5-B), and lovely fabric shops (Anokhi, see p.140), as well as Neemrana (see p.141), plus cafés and snack bars. Closed Sundays.

M-Block Market and **N-Block Market** Greater Kailash Part I. See map, p.81. Two generally upmarket shopping precincts within walking distance of each other, N-Block's being the more interesting, with great clothes shops such as Fabindia (see p.141) as well as bars and cafés including a branch of *Barista* (see p.132).

Palika Bazaar Connaught Place. See map, p.92. A generally downmarket subterranean shopping mall, and a good place to buy CDs, DVDs and video games, though it also has clothes shops, a bookshop (see p.140) and some interesting odd shops including Jain Super Store (see p.141) and a branch of Shaw Brothers (see p.141).

Santushti Shopping Complex Panchsheel Marg. See map, p.99. A fave with diplomats from nearby Chanakyapuri, this rather twee little precinct was set up by the Air Force Wives Welfare Association. Shops are upmarket and pretty classy, selling high-quality clothing, textiles and jewellery. Among them is Anokhi (see p.140), and if you're hungry you could stop for some food at *Basil & Thyme* (see p.134). Mon–Sat 10am–6pm.

South Extension I and II Mahatma Gandhi Marg (Ring Rd). See map, p.81. Two upmarket shopping areas, facing each other across the busy Ring Rd (there's a pedestrian underpass). Good shopping includes a number of clothes stores, lots of designer shops, and the *Lizard Lounge* bar (see p.135). Closed Mondays.

State government emporiums Along Baba Kharak Singh Marg near Connaught Place. Each of India's 28 state governments has its own showroom here. Prices are fixed but fair, and browsing is hassle-free. Goods are high quality, if not very excitingly displayed, and include wooden and stone carvings, brassware, textiles, clothing and jewellery. The West Bengal emporium has high-grade Darjeeling teas, and Himachal Pradesh's sells some lesser-known tea varieties, but for Assam, you're better off going to Khari Baoli. Delhi's own emporium stocks good sandalwood

carvings, as does that of Karnataka, which also has some excellent *bidri* ware. The Kashmir emporium sells carpets, of course, while those of Punjab and Nagaland have lovely shawls, in rather different styles, and Orissa's has some quite jolly textiles. Between the two rows of state emporiums is Rajiv Gandhi Bhawan, whose more modern-looking shops are run mostly by NGOs. All are closed on Sundays.

Sunder Nagar Market Off Mathura Rd, south of Purana Qila. See map, p.99. A row of shops, rather than a market as such, but a good if pricey place to shop for art, antiques and jewellery; try shops 5, 9, 14, 20, 26 and 30 for the best variety. Most are closed on Sundays, but for fine Darjeeling teas, Regalia at no. 12 is open seven days a week (though shorter hours on Sunday).

Markets

Bengali Market Tansen Marg, off Barakhamba Rd. See map, p.99. This is really a food market, known for its sweet shops, snack stalls and large bustling cafés.

Daryaganj Book Market North of Delhi Gate. See map, p.108. Delhi's bibliophiles flock to this weekly gathering of 200 stallholders selling secondhand and remaindered books at very low prices. Sundays 10am–5pm.

Dilli Haat Aurobindo Marg, Safdarjang Ⓦ www .dillihaat.org. See map, p.81. You have to pay to visit this market, but it's only Rs15, and it keeps out the beggars and the touts. Other excluded undesirables are smokers, even though it's open-air. It's full of stalls selling crafts from across the country, and the range and quality are excellent. It can be a bit touristy, but it's a great place to buy souvenirs, and have a bite to eat, with food stalls from almost every Indian state, as well as Tibet (those from the northeastern states such as Assam and Meghalaya, with their delicately spiced curries, are the most popular). Open daily 10.30am–10pm.

Janpath Market Janpath Lane. See map, p.92. Adjoining the Tibetan Market (see p.140), this one sells mainly clothes, and is a lot less interesting.

Karol Bagh Market Around Ajmal Khan Rd. See map, p.80. Mainly sells clothes and fabrics, though it has food and household goods too; this open-air market is quite busy, and handy for the metro, but not as interesting as Paharganj. The motorbike section, a few blocks west along Arya Samaj Rd, is useful if you want a bike or some spare parts.

Khari Baoli Old Delhi. See p.115. This is Delhi's wholesale spice market, but most shops will be happy to sell you retail quantities; the quality here is the best in town, and must be close to the best in the world. Unless you live where they grow, you won't find cardamoms as big, fat and fresh as the ones you'll get here; cinnamon, cloves, black peppercorns and Assam tea are all good buys too (for the latter, look in particular around the junction of Khari Baoli Rd and Naya Bans Rd; try for example Jain Traders at 6050 Naya Bans).

Paharganj Main Bazaar Paharganj. See p.103. The place for joss sticks, patchouli oil and Ganesh T-shirts. It's certainly bustling, if a bit seedy (ignore the touts and their boot-polish charas), and it does have a great range of goods, including wall-hangings, chillums, even fruit and veg. At the junction of Rajguru Marg in particular, you'll also find itinerant vendors selling things like peacock feather fans and even leather whips.

Sarojini Nagar (SN) Market Lane E and Cross rds 1 & 2, Sarojini Nagar. See map, p.81. A clothes market specializing in export surplus, especially seconds, at bargain-basement prices

(watch out also for "Kevin Clein" and "Ralphe Lawren" labels), but give them a good look-over for flaws before you buy. The market has been a popular stomping ground for Hindu sectarian extremists, who used to hold regular meetings here, and it was among three Delhi targets in October 2005 for their Muslim counterparts, who bombed it, killing 43 people, but did little to dent the market's popularity. It's especially crowded on Sundays, and closed on Mondays.

Tibetan Market Northern end of Janpath near Connaught Place. See map, p.92. Only a few stalls are still run by the Tibetan refugees who originally set this market up, and all the shops promote their goods squarely at tourists, but there's more than just the usual tat here and it is worth a browse. You can find statues, incense, shawls, T-shirts, paintings, and Tibetan artefacts including jewellery and semiprecious stones. Haggle like mad.

Books

Delhi has a wide selection of places to buy **books**. Connaught Place has many good general bookshops, including Amrit (N-21), Galgotia & Sons (B-17), New Book Depot (B-18) and Rajiv Book House (30 Palika Bazaar). **Secondhand bookstalls** include Jacksons at 5106 Paharganj Main Bazaar, opposite *Vishal* hotel, as well as an unnamed stall around the corner by Imperial cinema on Rajguru Marg, and Anil Book Corner by the Plaza Cinema on Connaught Place; on Sundays there's also Daryaganj Market by Delhi Gate in Old Delhi.

Musical instruments, cassettes and CDs

Lahore Music House Netaji Subhash Marg, Old Delhi (next door to *Moti Mahal* restaurant) ☎011/ 2327 1305, ⊛www.lmhindia.com. Long-established north Indian musical instrument makers with a reputation for quality.

Rikhi Ram G-8, Outer Circle, Connaught Place ☎011/2332 7685, ⊛www.rikhiram.com. Once sitar makers to the likes of renowned

musician Ravi Shankar, and still maintaining an exclusive air, with prices to match. Check out the display of their own unique instrumental inventions.

Shielma 11 & 27 Palika Bazaar, Connaught Place ☎011/2332 2900. CDs of classical, folk and film music, plus DVDs of Hindi (and English) movies.

Fabrics and clothes

Delhi's **fabric** and **clothes** shops sell everything: from high-quality silks to homespun cottons; and from saris, Kashmiri shawls and traditional kurta pyjamas to multicoloured tie-dyed T-shirts and other hippy gear. For T-shirts and tie-dye clothing (not to mention joss sticks and chillums), try **Paharganj** or the **Tibetan Market**. For bargain Western-style trousers, skirts and shirts the export-surplus market at **Sarojini Nagar** (see above) is very good. Roadside stalls behind the Tibetan Market off Janpath sell lavishly embroidered and mirrored spreads from Rajasthan and Gujarat, but silks and fine cotton are best bought in **government emporiums** on Baba Kharak Singh Marg.

Anokhi 5 & 6 Santushti Shopping Complex ☎011/2688 3076, ⊛www.anokhi.com. Soft cotton and raw silk clothes and soft furnishings; particularly

renowned for hand-block printed cottons combining traditional and contemporary designs. Also at 32 Khan Market and 16 N-Block Market.

Fabindia 5, 7 & 14, N-Block Market, Greater Kailash ☎011/4669 3724, ⓦwww.fabindia.com. Spread over several shops in the market, with a range from furnishings and interiors to chic cotton clothing for men, women and children and wearable block-printed cottons, sourced from villages across India; also sells organic spices, jams and pickles, and has branches around town including Khan Market (central hall, above nos. 20 & 21) and B-28 & N-5 Connaught Place.

Handloom House 3rd floor, Rajiv Gandhi Bhawan, between the two state emporium buildings, Baba Kharak Singh Marg ☎011/2334 1984. Government outlet with roll after roll of fine hand-woven cotton and silk textiles, plus cotton and linen shirts and silk saris.

Harsiba 5 Rajiv Gandhi Bhawan, between the two state emporium buildings, Baba Kharak Singh Marg ☎011/3948 9374. Lovely clothes, accessories and furnishings made by self-employed women, mostly working at home, and sold through their own cooperatively run outlet.

Khadi Gramodyog Bhawan 24 Regal Building, corner of Sansad Marg and Connaught Place ☎011/2336 0902, ⓦwww.kvic.org.in.

Government-run and a great place to pick up hardy, lightweight travelling clothes. Reasonably priced, ready-made traditional Indian garments include *salwar kameez*, woollen waistcoats, pyjamas, shawls and caps, plus rugs, cloth by the metre, tea, incense, cards and tablecloths.

People Tree 8 Regal Building, Sansad Marg, Connaught Place ☎011/2334 0699, ⓦwww .peopletreeonline.com. An interesting selection of alternative designs, with an emphasis on T-shirts, ethnic chic and jewellery.

Shaw Brothers D-47 Ground Floor, Defence Colony ☎011/2469 0364, ⓦwww.shaw-brothers .com. Upmarket purveyors of shawls, rugs, pashminas and silks. Also at 8 Palika Bazaar, Connaught Place ☎011/2332 9080.

Vedi Tailors M-60 Connaught Place ☎011/2341 6901. Originally established in Rangoon in 1926, this gents' tailor can run you up a made-to-measure suit for anything from Rs8000 to Rs30,000, depending on fabric and cut. They usually take a week, but for a little extra they can do it in 24 hours. S.L. Kapur at G-7 is an equally reputable firm offering a similar service.

Art, antiques, crafts and jewellery

For crafts and jewellery, the **government emporiums** on Baba Kharak Singh Marg should be your first stop, especially if you want to check prices. **Paharganj** and Janpath's **Tibetan market** are good for trinkets such as cheap jewellery, decorated boxes and sandalwood carvings. For upmarket art, antiques (remember that export of anything over a hundred years old requires a permit) and jewellery, there's **Sunder Nagar Market** (see p.139).

Central Cottage Industries Emporium Jawahar Vyapar Bhawan, Janpath, opposite *Imperial Hotel* ☎011/2332 0439, ⓦwww.cottageemporium.in. Popular and convenient multistorey government-run complex, with handicrafts, carpets, leather and reproduction miniatures at fixed (if fractionally high) rates. Jewellery ranges from tribal silver anklets to costume pieces and precious stones.

Cottage of Arts and Jewels 50 Hauz Khas Village ☎011/2696 7418. Interesting, eccentric mix of jewellery, curios and papier-mâché crafts. The best of the collection, including miniatures and precious stones, is not on display: you have to ask to see it.

Neemrana Shop 22-B Khan Market ☎011/2462 0262. Run by the hotel group of the same name, the shop has a chic clientele and offers a range of clothes and a small collection of antiques and objets d'art.

Plutus 10 Hauz Khas Village ☎011/2653 6898, ⓦwww.plutusexports.com. An attractively

presented shop selling replica antiques, bronze statues and an assorted collection of silver and gold jewellery. Ethnic Silver, two doors down at 9A, has a nice selection of jewellery and silverware.

Miscellaneous

Indian Art Collection 1 Hauz Khas Village. Old Bollywood film posters are the speciality here, mostly in the Rs1000–5000 range. You can buy them framed, but it's generally easier, if you're transporting them, to have them rolled up and slipped into a protective tube. Indian Popular Art, a few doors away at no. 5, also sells film posters.

Jain Super Store 172 Palika Bazaar, Connaught Place ☎011/2332 1031, ⓦwww.jainperfumers .com. Essential oils, natural perfumes and their own in-house fragrances, as well as joss sticks, scented candles and aroma diffusers.

Mother Earth (Industree) 8 Rajiv Gandhi Bhawan, between the two state emporium buildings, Baba Kharak Singh Marg ⓦwww.industreecrafts.com.

A light, bright shop with equally light, bright designs, including mats, blinds, boxes and bags made of natural fibres such as jute, reeds and rattan, crafted by small producers mostly working from home and sold by a fair-trade NGO.

Nath Stationers (The Card Shop) B-38 Connaught Place. A small shop with a big selection of greetings cards featuring Indian artwork and designs.

Listings

Airlines Aeroflot, N-1 Tolstoy House, 15-17 Tolstoy Marg ☏011/2331 0426; Air Canada, 803, 8th floor, Ansal Bhawan, 16 Kasturba Gandhi Marg ☏011/4152 8181; Air France, c/o KLM; Air India, 2nd floor, Tower 1, Jeevan Bharati Building, 124 Connaught Circus at Sansad Marg ☏011/2373 1225; Asiana Airlines, 2 Ansal Bhawan, ground floor, 16 Kasturba Gandhi Marg ☏011/2331 5631; British Airways, DLF Plaza Tower, DLF Qutab Enclave, Gurgaon, Haryana ☏95124/412 0747 from Delhi, or 0124/412 0747 from outside Delhi, or toll-free 1800/102 3592; Cathay Pacific, 413 Ashoka Estate Building, Barakhamba Rd ☏011/4354 4777 or 1800/209 1616; China Airlines, c/o Ascent Air, upper ground floor, Kanchenchunga Building, 18 Barakhamba Rd ☏011/2332 7131; Continental, 2nd floor, Tower C, Cyber Green, DLF Phase 3, Gurgaon, Haryana ☏95124/431 5500 from Delhi, or 0124/431 5500 from outside Delhi; Delta, c/o Interglobe Enterprises, Thapar House, 124 Janpath ☏011/4351 3140 or 41; Emirates, 7th floor, DLF Centre, Sansad Marg ☏011/6631 4444; Gulf Air, 201 Ansal Bhawan, 16 Kasturba Gandhi Marg ☏011/4352 1482; Indian Airlines, c/o Air India; IndiGo, Level 1, Tower C, Global Business Park, Mehrauli–Guragon Rd, Gurgaon ☏1800/180 3838 or 0124/435 2500; Jet Airways, N-40 Connaught Place ☏011/4132 3247; JetLite, IGI Airport ☏011/2567 5879 (domestic) or 2565 3609 (international); Kenya Airways, Ground Floor, Ambadeep Building, 14 Kasturba Gandhi Marg ☏011/2376 6248; Kingfisher, N-42 Connaught Place ☏1800/180 0101; KLM, airport terminal 2 ☏011/2335 7747; Kuwait Airways, 4 Ansal Bhawan, ground floor, 16 Kasturba Gandhi Marg ☏011/2335 4373; Lufthansa, 56 Janpath ☏011/2372 4200; Malaysia Airlines, 16th floor, Dr Gopaldas Bhawan, 28 Barakhamba Rd ☏011/4151 2121; Nepal Airlines, 44 Janpath ☏011/2332 1164; Qatar Airways, ground floor, Dr Gopaldas Bhawan, 28 Barakhamba Rd ☏011/4363 6000; Royal Jordanian, G-56 Connaught Place ☏011/2332 7418; SAA, Thapar House, 124 Janpath ☏011/4351 3131; Singapore Airlines, Unit 514 A & B, Time Tower, MG Rd, Gurgaon, Haryana ☏0124/431 0999; SpiceJet, 319 Udyog Vihar, Phase IV, Gurgaon

☏1800/180 3333; Thai, *Hotel Intercontinental Eros*, American Plaza, Nehru Place ☏011/4149 7777; United, Corporate Park, Block 2B, DLF City, DLF Phase III, Gurgaon, Haryana ☏95124/235 8201 from Delhi, or 0124/235 8201 from outside Delhi; Virgin Atlantic, 8th floor, DLF Centre, Sansad Marg ☏011/4130 3030 or 1800/102 3000.

Banks and exchange Almost every block on Connaught Place has ATMs that take Visa or MasterCard, as do metro stations, and there are several along Chandni Chowk and Asaf Ali Rd in Old Delhi. There's an HDFC ATM opposite the *Metropolis Hotel* on Paharganj Main Bazaar, and a couple more just up Rajguru Marg beneath the *Roxy Hotel*. You can also change money at the DTTDC office, N-36 Connaught Place, and at numerous other authorized exchange offices in Connaught Place and Paharganj (but if you're changing travellers' cheques, make sure before signing that they're not going to mess you around demanding receipts and such like, or sting you with unmentioned commissions). All major hotels have exchange facilities; the *Ajanta*, near the *Grand Godwin* on Arakashan Rd in Ram Nagar, has a 24hr bureau. Thomas Cook is upstairs at C-033 Connaught Place (☏011/6627 1971; Mon–Fri 9.30am–6pm, Sat 10am–5.30pm), with branches at CP post office and the *Hotel Janpath*, among other places. American Express is represented for financial transactions by Standard Chartered Bank at A-1 Connaught Place (☏011/4365 4027; Mon–Fri 9am–6pm, Sat 9am–4pm).

Car rental Avis, D-4 Shubam Gardens, near Hari Bhawan, Ram Mandir Marg, Vasant Kunj ☏011/6568 0664 or 0627, ✉crsdelhi@avis.co.in; Budget, Lemon Tree Hotel, East Delhi Mall, Kaushambi, Ghaziabad ☏0120/442 3202; Europcar, Suite 105, 1st floor, Indra Prakash Building, 21 Barakhamba Rd ☏011/4166 7760, ✉reservation.del@europcar.co.in; Hertz, c/o Carzonrent, Khasra no. 78, Dagar Farm House (opposite BP petrol pump), Bijwasan ☏011/4184 1212, ✉reserve@carzonrent.com (also in Dwarka, near airport & Dwarka Sector 12 metro station, at F-3 Building 1, Malik Plaza, Plot no. 2, pocket 6, Sector 12, Dwarka ☏011/4553 5501/2, ✉dwarka@carzonrent.com).

Courier services DHL, 71/3 Najafgarh Industrial Estate, Rama Rd ☎1800/111 345; FedEx, R-12 Ground Floor, behind Regal Cinema ☎1800/209 6161; UPS, c/o Jetair Express, D-12/1, Okhla Industrial Area Phase II ☎011/2638 9323.

Dental treatment Delhi Dental Centre, C-56 South Extension II ☎011/2625-5918; Swedish Dental Clinic, C-118 Defence Colony ☎011/2433 6853.

Embassies, consulates & high commissions Call ahead for opening hours before you visit. Afghanistan, 5/50-F Shanti Path, Chanakyapuri ☎011/2688 3601; Australia, 1/50-G Shanti Path, Chanakyapuri ☎011/4139 9900; Bangladesh, EP-39, D Radha Krishan Marg, Chanakyapuri ☎011/2412 1389; Bhutan, Chandragupta Marg, Chanakyapuri ☎011/2688 9230; Burma, 3/50-F Nyaya Marg, Chanakyapuri ☎011/2467 8822; Canada, 7/8 Shanti Path, Chanakyapuri ☎011/4178 2000; China, 50-D Shanti Path, Chanakyapuri (entrance for visa applications in Nyaya Marg) ☎011/2611 2345; Denmark, 11 Aurangzeb Rd ☎011/4209 0700; European Commission, 65 Golf Links ☎011/2462 9237 or 8; Indonesia, 50-A Kautilya Marg, Chanakyapuri ☎011/2611 8642 to 5; Iran, 5 Barakhamba Rd ☎011/2332 9600 to 02; Ireland, 230 Jor Bagh-3 (near Safdarjang's Tomb) ☎011/2462 6733; Malaysia, 50-M Satya Marg, Chanakyapuri ☎011/2611 1291 to 3; Maldives, B-2 Anand Niketan ☎011/4143 5701; Nepal, Barakhamba Rd by Mandi House Chowk, southeast of Connaught Place ☎011/2332 7361; Netherlands, 6/50-F Shanti Path, Chanakyapuri ☎011/2419 7600; New Zealand, 50-N Nyaya Marg, Chanakyapuri ☎011/2688 3170; Norway, 50-C Shanti Path, Chanakyapuri ☎011/4177 9200; Pakistan, 2/50-G Shanti Path, Chanakyapuri ☎011/2467 6004; Singapore, E-6 Chandragupta Marg, Chanakyapuri ☎011/4600 0800; South Africa, B-18 Vasant Marg, Vasant Vihar ☎011/2614 9411; Sri Lanka, 27 Kautilya Marg, Chanakyapuri ☎011/2301 0201 to 3; Sweden, 4–5 Nyaya Marg, Chanakyapuri ☎011/2419 7100; Thailand, 56-N Nyaya Marg, Chanakyapuri ☎011/2611 8103 or 4; UK, Shanti Path, Chanakyapuri ☎011/2687 2161; USA, Shanti Path, Chanakyapuri ☎011/2419 8000.

Festivals Republic Day (Jan 26) is celebrated by a huge parade along Rajpath (see p.98), with tickets for seats to watch the parade available at travel agents, hotels and tourist offices. Beating the Retreat on Jan 29 sees military bands perform on Vijay Chowk (see p.98). In the first two weeks of February, the state government of Haryana holds a two-week crafts fair, Suraj Kund Mela, at Suraj Kund, which is just across the state line south of Tughluqabad Fort, with transport laid on from central Delhi.

Hospitals All India Institute of Medical Sciences (AIIMS), Ansari Nagar, Aurobindo Marg (☎011/2658 8500), has a 24hr emergency service and good treatment, as does Lok Nayak Jai Prakash Hospital, Jawaharlal Nehru Marg, Old Delhi (☎011/2323 6000), near Delhi Gate. Dr Ram Manohar Lohia Hospital, Baba Kharak Singh Marg (☎011/2334 8200, ⓦrmlh.nic.in), is another government hospital. Private clinics include East West Medical Centre, B-28 Greater Kailash Part I (☎011/2924 3701 to 3, ⓦwww.eastwestrescue.com), and Indraprastha Apollo Hospital, Sarita Vihar, Delhi–Mathura Rd (☎011/2692 5801, ⓦwww.apollohospdelhi.com). The US embassy maintains a list of hospitals and doctors on its website at ⓦnewdelhi.usembassy .gov/medical_information2.html.

Internet access Internet cafés are surprisingly thin on the ground in Delhi; those in Paharganj are usually cheaper than the ones around Connaught Place. Sunrise, N-9/II Connaught Place (Rs35/hr); Shivam, 651 Tooti Chowk, just off Main Bazaar, Paharganj (Rs20/hr); Kesri, 5111 Main Bazaar, Paharganj (near *Kholsa Café*, Rs20/hr).

Left luggage Rs10–15/day at the railway stations. In addition, most hotels in Paharganj offer a left-luggage service for their guests.

Money transfers Western Union agents include several post offices, most conveniently Old Delhi and New Delhi GPOs, but if having money sent to a post office, be sure to specify the name correctly, as with poste restante (see p.144). WU agents also include the Punjab and Sind Bank, M-14 Connaught Place, and Bank of Baroda at B-3 and M-9. Money-Gram's agents can be found in branches of Thomas Cook (such as at C-33 Connaught Place), and branches of the Central Bank of India including 1763 Chuna Mandi near Paharganj, and 70 Janpath near Connaught Place.

Motorcycles The Karol Bagh area has many good bike shops selling new or secondhand Enfields. Reliable dealers include Inder Motors, 1744-A/55 basement, Hardhyan Singh Nalwala St, Abdul Aziz Rd (☎011/2875 0869, ⓦwww.lallisingh.com), two blocks east of Ajmal Khan Rd, turning right at the *chowki*, then the third alley on the left; closed Mon. Also worth trying is Ess Aar Motors, 1-E/13 Jhandewalan Extension, between Karol Bagh and Paharganj (☎011/2367 8836).

Opticians Lawrence & Mayo, 76 Janpath; R.K. Oberoi, H-14 Connaught Place.

Pharmacies Nearly every market has at least one pharmacy. Apollo, G-8 Connaught Place and at New Delhi Station (*Ginger Hotel*), is open 24hr.

Photographic services Kinsey Brothers, 2-A Connaught Place (under *India Today*); Delhi Photo Company, 78 Janpath.

Police ☎100 (national number). Delhi now has a dedicated squad of tourist police based at the airport, main stations and major tourist sights and hotel areas, whose aim is specifically to help tourists in trouble. If you have a problem that needs to involve the police, your hotel reception or the Government of India tourist office will direct you to the appropriate station.

Post offices Poste restante (Mon–Sat 9am–5pm) is available at the GPO (Gole PO) on the roundabout at the intersection of Baba Kharak Singh Marg and Ashoka Rd (sale of stamps Mon–Sat 9am–8pm). You must show your passport to claim mail or check the register for parcels. Have mail for this post office addressed to "Poste Restante, New Delhi GPO, Gole Dakhana, Delhi 110001", as letters sent to "Poste Restante, Delhi" will go to Old Delhi GPO, north of the railway line on Lothian Rd (but if you want mail to be held at there, specify "Old Delhi GPO, Lothian Rd, Delhi 110006" just to be sure). There is a useful branch office at A-6 Connaught Place (Mon–Sat 10am–5.45pm).

Telephones Way2Talk, 1126 Main Bazaar, Paharganj, has low-cost international VoIP calls (Rs7/min to the UK, North America, Australia and New Zealand), and the first ten seconds are free, which is handy if you get an answering machine and hang up immediately.

Visa extensions and exit formalities The first place to go if you need to extend your visa is the Ministry of Home Affairs, Foreigners' Division, Jaisalmer House, 26 Man Singh Rd (Mon–Fri 10am–noon). If your total stay will exceed six months, you will also need to go to the Foreigners' Regional Registration Office (FRRO), East Block 8, Level 2, Sector 1, Ramakrishna Puram (Mon–Fri 9.30am–1.30pm & 2–4pm; ☎011/2671 1443). Forms can be downloaded from ⓦwww.immigrationindia.nic .in. If you've been in India more than 120 days, before leaving you'll need to fill in a tax clearance certificate, obtainable from the Foreign Section, Income Tax Office, Central Revenue Building, Indraprastha Estate (Mon–Fri 10am–1pm & 2–5pm; ☎011/2337 9171 ext 1650); have foreign exchange certificates and ATM receipts to hand.

Moving on from Delhi

Delhi has very good international and domestic **travel connections**. Scores of **travel agents** (see box opposite) sell bus and air tickets, while many hotels will book private buses for you; **touts**, concentrated at the top of Janpath, waylay tourists with promises of cheap fares, but rarely give a good deal. Buses leave Delhi frequently, and tourists can usually find places on trains in a reserved **tourist quota**. There's an ever-expanding network of internal flights, but it's still best to book as far ahead as possible; bear in mind that at peak times such as Diwali, demand is very high.

By air

Indira Gandhi International Airport (ⓦwww.newdelhiairport.in; automated information line for international flights ☎011/2560 2999, domestic flights ☎011/2566 2275) is 20km southwest of the city centre. Most tourists on night-flights book a **taxi** to the airport in advance (around Rs250; 30–60min) through their hotel. By **auto-rickshaw** it's around Rs150 (Rs115 pre-paid from CP) Otherwise, there's a half-hourly bus service from Maharana Pratap ISBT via New Delhi station gate 2 (Ajmer Gate side) and Connaught Place (Scindia House), costing Rs50.

Domestic flights leave from Terminal 1. Tickets can be bought through travel agents or direct from the airlines. Flights from Delhi are currently operated by Air India (AI), Air India Express (IX), Indian Airlines (IC), Kingfisher (IT), Paramount Airways (I7), SpiceJet (SG), JetLite (S2), IndiGo (6E) and Jet Airways (9W).

Generally speaking, only Indian Airlines, Jet and Kingfisher fly to Rajasthan, though Air India Express serves Jaipur. At present, services from Delhi to Rajasthan are as follows: Jaipur (8–9 daily; 40–45min; IC, IT, 9W, IX); Jodhpur (2–3 daily; 1hr 20min–3hr 10min; IT, IC, 9W; IC's is the fastest); Udaipur (4–5 daily; 1hr 10min–2hr 30min; IC, IT 9W; 9W's midday flight is the fastest).

Travel agents and tour operators

The Rajasthan Tourism Development Corporation, Bikaner House, Pandara Road (☎011/2338 3837 or 6069), organizes **package tours** including wildlife tours and trips on the *Palace on Wheels* and *Heritage on Wheels* trains. The Delhi Tourism and Transport Development Corporation (DTTDC), N-36, Bombay Life Building, Middle Circle, Connaught Place (☎011/5152 3073), offers day-trips to Agra (Rs950) and three-day "Golden Triangle" excursions to Agra, Ajmer, Bharatpur and Jaipur (Rs4200). For competitively priced car tours around Rajasthan try *Hotel Namaskar*, Paharganj (☎011/2358 2233, ⓔnamaskarhotel@yahoo.com). The India Tourism Development Corporation's commercial arm, Ashok Travels, *Janpath Hotel*, Janpath (☎011/2334 9062, ⓔtravel@attindiatourism.com), sells excursions and air tickets.

For **ticketing**, recommended operators specializing in international and domestic flights include: HRG Sita, F-12 Connaught Place (☎011/2462 2152), and Travel Corporation of India, 5th floor, New Delhi House, 27 Barakhamba Rd (☎011/2341 6082 to 5, ⓦwww.tcindia.com). Aa Bee Travel, in the lobby of *Hare Rama Guest House* (☎011/2356 2171 or 2117, ⓔaabee@mail.com) at T-298 off Main Bazaar, Paharganj, are a reliable firm for competitively priced air and private bus tickets. The Student Travel Information Centre, STIC Travels, G-55 Connaught Place (☎011/4620 6600, ⓦwww.statravel.co.in), can issue or renew ISIC cards.

It's a very bad idea to book flights or excursions through any agency that you're directed to by a street tout, and that goes double for any agency spuriously trying to pass itself off as a tourist information office.

There are direct flights from Delhi to most other Indian airports, including Bengaluru (32 daily; 2hr 30min–4hr; IC, IT, SG, S2, 6E, 9W); Chennai (21 daily; 2hr 35min–4hr 30 min; IC, IT, I7, SG, S2, 6E, 9W); Kolkata (20–21 daily; 2hr 10min–6hr 45min; AI, IC, IT, SG, S2, 9W) and of course Mumbai (65 daily; 1hr 50min–2hr 55min; AI, G8, IC, IT, IX, SG, S2, 6E, 9W).

International flights leave from Terminal 2. If you don't already have a ticket for a **flight** out of India, you'll have little trouble finding one, except between December and March when it may be difficult at short notice. While you can buy tickets directly from the airlines (addresses are given on p.142), it saves time and legwork to book through an **agency** (see box above). Remember that many airlines require you to reconfirm your flight between a week and 72 hours before leaving.

By train

You can check train services online at ⓦwww.indianrail.gov.in (click on "Trains between Important Stations"). The most convenient trains are listed in the box on p.147.

New Delhi station (entry from Chelmsford Road or Ajmeri Gate) has a very efficient **booking office** (Mon–Sat 8am–8pm, Sun 8am–2pm; ☎011/2334 6804) for foreign and NRI tourists, on the first floor (above ground) of the main departure building. Foreigners must bring passports, and in theory pay in foreign currency or show exchange certificates, though these are often not demanded.

The best trains tend to leave from New Delhi, but many trains to Rajasthan (except those to Bharatpur, Kota and Sawai Madhopur) leave from **Old Delhi station** (officially Delhi Junction), which is on Shayma Prasad Mukerji Marg, north of Chandni Chowk, and some trains leave from **Sarai Rohilla**, which is inconveniently situated 6km northwest of the centre (Rs60 by pre-paid auto from

CP), or from **Hazrat Nizamuddin** (6km southeast of the centre near Humayun's Tomb, Rs60 by pre-paid auto from CP), so check when you buy your ticket. Bookings for all trains can be made in New Delhi station.

For **Agra** (24–29 daily; 2hr–4hr 25min), the most comfortable and convenient service, if you can get up in time to catch it, is the 6.15am Bhopal-bound Shatabdi Express #2002 out of New Delhi, which pulls in to Agra Cantonment shortly after 8am, well in time for a day's sightseeing; if you want to make it a day-trip, you can catch the same train back to New Delhi at 8.30pm, arriving at 10.30pm, but note that it does not run on Fridays. It is also possible to do a day's excursion on the cheaper Taj Express #2280 from Hazrat Nizamuddin at 7.10am, arriving at Agra Cantonment at 10.07am, which gives you time to see the Taj and the main sights in town – even Fatehpur Sikri if you run around like a mad thing – and still get back to Delhi that evening (it leaves Agra at 6.55pm, arriving in Hazrat Nizamuddin at 10pm). UP tourism even lay on a coach tour of Agra and Fatehpur Sikri especially for day-trippers using the Taj Express; see p.154. In January, fog can disrupt all these timetables. Note also that trains on the Delhi–Agra route, and particularly the Taj Express, being popular with tourists, are also popular with thieves, so keep hold of your baggage at all times, especially just before departure.

For **Bikaner**, there's the overnight Sampark Kranti Express #2463 (3 weekly), or you could travel from Old Delhi to Jaipur on the Jaisalmer Express #4059 (departs 5.40pm, arrives 11.42pm) to connect with the Howrah-Jammu Express #2307 (leaves Jaipur 12.15am, arrives Bikaner 8.15am), but it's a tight connection if the Jaisalmer Express is late, though the Howrah–Jammu is coming through from Kolkata (Calcutta), so it may well be late too.

Other **frequencies and journey times** to destinations in Rajasthan are: Abu Road (3–6 daily; 11hr 23min–12hr 32min); Ajmer (4–9 daily; 6hr 55min–8hr 22min); Alwar (5–9 daily; 2hr 02min–2hr 42min); Bharatpur (8–9 daily; 2hr 21min–4hr 28min); Bikaner (3 weekly; 12hr); Chittaurgarh (2–3 daily; 9hr 15min–14hr 10min); Jaipur (6–10 daily; 4hr 40min–5hr 27min); Jaisalmer (1 daily; 17hr 15min); Jodhpur (2–3 daily; 10hr 17min–10hr 45min); Kota (10–14 daily; 4hr 25min–9hr 10min); Sawai Madhopur (10–11 daily; 3hr 40min–7hr 45min); Udaipur (1 daily; 12hr 15min). Recommended trains are listed in the box opposite.

If you're heading out of the region, there are plenty of trains to **Mumbai** (9–13 daily; 12hr 05min–31hr 10min), the best being the overnight #2952 Rajdhani Express from New Delhi. For **the South**, the best trains are: to Chennai (2–4 trains daily; 28hr 15min–43hr 45min), the #2434 Rajdhani Express from Hazrat Nizamuddin or the #2622 Tamil Nadu Express from New Delhi; to Bengaluru (1–2 daily; 40hr 25min–47hr 30min), the #2628 Karnataka Express from New Delhi; and to Hyderabad (2–4 daily; 21hr 45min–30hr 10min), the daily #2724 AP Express and the four-times-weekly Bangalore Rajdhani #2430, both from New Delhi. To Thiruvananthapuram (Trivandrum), the only direct train is the #2626 Kerala Express from New Delhi (50hr 50min). For **Kolkata** (Calcutta; 4–7 daily; 16hr 55min–35hr 35min), the most convenient trains are the #2314 Rajdhani service to Sealdah and the #2302/2306 Rajdhani to Howrah. Best services for **the Northeast** are the #2424/2436 Rajdhani Express, or the #2506 Northeast Express, both from New Delhi to Guwahati (3–5 trains daily; 27hr 20min–44hr 10min).

The twice-weekly train from Old Delhi to Lahore in Pakistan currently carries only Indian and Pakistani citizens, but this may change if the political situation eases up.

Recommended trains from Delhi to Agra and Rajasthan

The trains below are the fastest and/or most convenient. There may be others which are slower, or arrive at inconvenient times. Train timetables change frequently; check latest schedules either at your nearest station or online at Ⓦ www.indianrail.gov.in before travel.

Destination	Name	No.	From	Departs	Arrives
Abu Road	Rajdhani Express*	2958	ND	7.55pm (daily)	6.20am
	Ahmedabad Mail	9116	OD	10.35pm (daily)	12.37pm
Agra	Shatabdi Express*	2002	ND	6.15am (exc Fri)	8.12am
	Taj Express	2280	HN	7.10am (daily)	10.07am
	Mangala Express	2618	HN	9.20am (daily)	12.20pm
	Kerala Express	2626	HN	11.30am (daily)	2.25pm
	Nanded Express	2716	ND	1.25pm (daily)	4.40pm
	Gondwana Express	2412	HD	3.25pm (daily)	6.47pm
	AP Express	2724	ND	5.35pm (daily)	8.37pm
	GT Express	2616	ND	6.40pm (daily)	9.47pm
Ajmer	Shatabdi Express*	2015	ND	6.05am (exc Wed)	1pm
	Ahmedabad Mail	9106	OD	10.35pm (daily)	7.28am
Alwar	Shatabdi Express*	2015	ND	6.05am	8.42am
	Hazrat Express	4311	OD	11.45am (Tues, Thurs, Fri, Sat)	2.47pm
	Ashram Express	2916	OD	3.05pm (daily)	5.38pm
	Jaisalmer Express	4059	OD	5.40pm (daily)	8.57pm
Bharatpur	Golden Temple Mail	2904	ND	7.45am (daily)	10.39am
	Jan Shatabdi Express	2060	HN	1.20pm (daily)	3.41pm
	Paschim Express	2926	ND	4.55pm (daily)	7.39pm
Bikaner	Sampark Kranti Express	2463	SR	10.35pm (Wed, Fri, Sun)	10.35am
Chittaurgarh	Dheradun Express	9020A	HN	9.55pm (daily)	12.05pm
Jaipur	Shatabdi Express*	2015	ND	6.05am (daily)	10.45am
	Rajdhani Express	2958	ND	7.55pm (daily)	12.40am
	Garib Nawaj Express	5715	OD	1.35pm (Mon, Wed, Sat)	7.15pm
	Ashram Express	2916	OD	3.05pm (daily)	8.25pm
Jaisalmer	Jaisalmer Express	4059	OD	5.40pm (daily)	11.30am
Jodhpur	Kranti Express	2463	SR	10.35pm (Wed, Fri, Sun)	9.10am
	Jaisalmer Express	4059	OD	5.40pm (daily)	5am
	Mandor Express	2461	OD	8.55pm (daily)	8am
Kota	Golden Temple Mail	2904	ND	7.45am (daily)	2.25pm
	Rajdhani Express*	2432	HN	11am (Tues, Wed, Sun)	3.30pm
	Rajdhani Express*	2952	ND	4.30pm (daily)	8.55pm
	Dheradun Express	9020	HN	9.55pm (daily)	7.05am
Sawai Madhopur	Golden Temple Mail	2904	ND	7.45am (daily)	1.05pm
	Jan Shatabdi Express	2060	HN	1.20pm (daily)	6pm
Udaipur	Mewar Express	2963	HN	7.05pm (daily)	7.20am

OD Old Delhi   ND New Delhi   HN Hazrat Nizamuddin   SR Sarai Rohilla   *a/c only.

By bus

Generally speaking, trains are more comfortable than buses, and most people prefer to use the train if possible. The main exception to this rule is to Pushkar, where privately run overnight sleeper buses will take you straight there, whereas a train journey would only take you as far as Ajmer, from where you'd need to get a local bus. Some people prefer the option of a luxury state-run bus from Delhi to Jaipur too, especially as these are much more frequent than trains.

The **Rajasthan Roadways terminal** at Bikaner House, India Gate (T011/2338 3469), has the best services to major destinations in Rajasthan, with comfortable deluxe Silver and Gold Line buses: to Jaipur (33 daily; 6hr); to Ajmer (3 daily; 9hr); to Jodhpur (2 daily; 12hr); Udaipur (1 daily; 14hr). Otherwise, a lot of **state-run buses** depart from the **Maharana Pratap ISBT** (T011/2386 5181; Rajasthan Roadways T011/2386 4470; UP Roadways T011/2386 8709) by Kashmere Gate metro (Rs60 from CP by auto). There are services from Maharana Pratap to Ajmer (8 daily; 9hr), Jaipur (hourly; 6hr 30min), Jodhpur (1 daily; 12hr) and Udaipur (1 daily; 15hr). Be sure to arrive well before departure to allow time to find the correct counter (there are thirty or so) and book your ticket. Ask for the numbers of both platform and licence plate to ensure that you board the right bus. Buses to Agra (every 30min; 4hr), and some buses to Jaipur (approx every 20min; 7hr), Ajmer (approx every 20min; 9hr) and Jodhpur (1 daily; 12hr), leave from the **Sarai Kale Khan ISBT** (T011/2435 8343) east of Hazrat Nizamuddin.

Private buses usually depart from near the Ramakrishna Mission at the end of Main Bazaar, Paharganj, but some pick up passengers at hotels; you can book tickets a day or two in advance at agencies in Paharganj or Connaught Place such as Aa Bee Travel (see p.145). Private buses tend to be better than the ordinary state buses, but not as deluxe as the RSTDC Silver Line or Gold Line services. However, some overnight private buses have the option of a sleeper berth. Of most interest are the buses to Pushkar (2 daily; 10hr).

The only **international service** is to Lahore in Pakistan, leaving from Dr Ambedkar Terminal on Jahwaharlal Nehru Marg near Delhi Gate daily except Sunday at 6am (T011/2331 8180, Wwww.dtc.nic.in/lahorebus.htm).

2

Agra

The International boundaries on this map are neither purported to be correct nor authentic by Survey of India directives. Publisher.

N

PAKISTAN

HARYANA

UTTAR PRADESH

4

3

2

5

GUJARAT

MADHYA PRADESH

0   100 km

CHAPTER 2 # Highlights

Taj Mahal The most beautiful building in the world: iconic, mysterious and completely unforgettable, whether you're seeing it for the first time or the fiftieth. See p.158

Agra Fort Former residence of the Mughal emperors, its high walls concealing a fascinating complex of elaborate royal apartments, pearl-white mosques and spacious courtyards. See p.162

Itimad-ud-Daulah Small but exquisitely decorated tomb, its marble walls covered in intricately patterned and coloured inlay work. See p.167

* **Akbar's mausoleum, Sikandra** Tucked away on the edge of Agra, the huge sandstone tomb of India's greatest Mughal emperor offers a tranquil and atmospheric contrast to the city's more touristy sights. See p.169

* **Fatehpur Sikri** The enigmatic abandoned city of Akbar, straddling an arid ridge near the Rajasthan border. See p.174

▲ Akbar's Mausoleum, Sikandra

2

Agra

T he splendour of **AGRA** – capital of all India under the Mughals – remains undiminished, from the massive fort to the magnificent Taj Mahal. Along with Delhi and Jaipur, Agra forms the third apex of the "Golden Triangle", India's most popular tourist itinerary. It fully merits that status; the **Taj** effortlessly transcends all the frippery and commercialism that surrounds it, while the city's other sights – most notably **Agra Fort**, the **Itimad-ud-Daulah**, Akbar's Mausoleum at **Sikandra** and the abandoned city of **Fatehpur Sikri** – together comprise one of India's greatest architectural legacies, offering a unique insight into the opulent and cultured lives (and deaths) of the great Mughal emperors.

Mughal architecture aside, Agra can be quite intense, even for seasoned India hands. The traffic pollution is appalling (some mornings you can barely see the sun through the fog of fumes), and as a tourist you'll have to contend with crowds at the major monuments, high admission fees, and some of Asia's most persistent touts, commission merchants and rickshaw-wallahs. Don't, however, let this put you off. Although it's possible to see Agra on a day-trip from Delhi, the Taj alone deserves so much more – a fleeting visit would miss the subtleties of its many moods, as the light changes from sunrise to sunset – while the city's other sights and Fatehpur Sikri can easily fill several days.

Some history

Little is known of the pre-Muslim history of Agra, but a 1080 AD account describes a robust fort here, with a flourishing city strategically placed at the crossroads between the north and the centre of India. Agra remained a minor administrative centre until 1504, when the Delhi Sultan, **Sikandar Lodi**, moved his capital here to keep a check on the warring factions of his empire. The ruins of his city can still be seen on the River Yamuna's east bank. After defeating the last Lodi sultan, Ibrahim Lodi, at Panipat in 1526, **Babur**, the founder of the Mughal empire, sent ahead his son **Humayun** to capture Agra. In gratitude for their benevolent treatment at his hands, the family of the Raja of Gwalior rewarded the Mughal with jewellery and precious stones – among them the legendary **Koh-i-noor Diamond**, now among Britain's crown jewels.

Agra saw its heyday under Humayun's son, **Akbar the Great** (1556–1605), when Agra Fort was built, and it remained the empire's capital for over a century. Even when Akbar's grandson **Shah Jahan** built a new capital at Shahjahanabad (Old Delhi) in 1639, his heart remained in Agra. He pulled down many of the earlier red-sandstone structures in the fort, replacing them with his trademark – exquisite marble buildings. The empire flourished under his successor Aurangzeb (1658–1707), although his intolerance towards non-Muslims stirred up a hornets' nest. Agra was occupied successively by the Jats, the Marathas, and eventually the British.

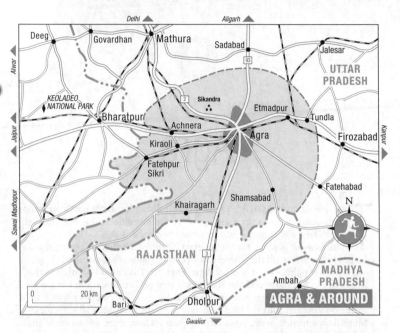

After the 1857 uprising, the city lost the headquarters of the government of the Northwestern Provinces and the High Court to Allahabad and went into a period of decline. Its Mughal treasures have ensured its survival, and today the city is once again prospering, as an industrial and commercial centre as well as a tourist destination.

Arrival and information

Agra has six **railway stations**, but visitors generally use only two of them. The busiest is **Agra Cantonment** ("Cantt"), in the southwest, which serves Delhi, Gwalior, Jhansi and most points south. Trains from Rajasthan pull in close to the Jama Masjid at **Agra Fort station** (a few also stop at Agra Cantt – see box, p.174). Agra Cantt is more convenient for the hotels around Sadar Bazaar, while Agra Fort Station is slightly closer to the Taj Ganj, the tangle of streets to the immediate south of the Taj Mahal; both are a fair way from the hotels along Fatehabad Road.

There's a pre-paid auto-rickshaw/taxi booth at Agra Cantonment Station (Rs52/85 to anywhere in town); drivers may collar you on your way out, trying to grab you before you reach the pre-paid booth so as to overcharge you or work some commission scam. Cycle rickshaws wait in the forecourt outside, but are slow if you're going to Fatehabad Road or Taj Ganj. As ever, cycle rickshaw and auto drivers may try to earn commission by taking you to a hotel of their choosing, and may therefore claim (falsely) that the hotel of your choice is closed.

Buses from Rajasthan and some services from Delhi terminate at **Idgah Bus Stand** close to Agra Cantonment Station, and a few local services from other destinations arrive at **Agra Fort Bus Stand**, just west of the fort. In addition, several buses from Delhi stop outside the fort gate, where you'll have no trouble finding a rickshaw. Other bus services, however, arrive at the new Inter-state Bus

Terminal (ISBT), 12km north of town at Transport Nagar, just off the Delhi–Agra highway. From there, an auto into town will cost some Rs70, but if you're really determined to get into town on the cheap, you can walk down to the highway and pick up a shared auto (Rs5–7) to Baghwan Cinema, and another one from there to Gwalior Road or Agra Fort bus station (Rs10). One **scam** to be aware of on buses to Idgah is that they sometimes make a stop in the suburbs, about 6km out, where rickshaw drivers (sometimes in collusion with the bus drivers) may claim that your vehicle has reached the end of the line, and that you need to disembark; if there are still Indian passengers on the bus, sit tight till you get to Idgah.

In the unlikely event that you arrive at Kheria **airport**, expect to spend about Rs100 for the 7km taxi ride into town.

Information

Agra has two **tourist offices**, one in Sadar Bazaar run by the Government of India at 191 The Mall (Mon–Fri 9am–5pm, Sat 9am–2pm; ☎0562/222 6378), and another run by UP Tourism at 64 Taj Rd (Mon–Sat 10am–5pm; ☎0562/222 6431, ⓦwww.up-tourism.com); there's also a UP Tourism information booth (open 24hr; ☎0562/242 1204) at Agra Cantonment Station. All have information on hotels and local sights, but the Government of India office also has information about other destinations in India, and can also set you up with a registered guide

▲ An elderly man waits for a train at Agra Fort Station

(half day Rs600, full day Rs750 for up to 5 people) who can take you around all the city sights as well as Fatehpur Sikri.

UP Tourism runs a whistlestop **tour** (daily except Friday) of Agra aimed mainly at day-trippers from Delhi. The tour leaves the India Tourism office at around 9.45am, and Agra Cantt Railway Station at around 10.20am, coinciding with the Taj Express from Delhi, which arrives at 10.07am. The full-day tour (Rs1700 including all entrance and guide fees) whisks you at breakneck speed around the Taj, Agra Fort and Fatehpur Sikri, ending at around 6pm in time for the Taj Express back to Delhi at 6.55pm; you can also join the tour just for the afternoon visit to Fatehpur Sikri (Rs550). Tours can be booked either through the UP Tourism or India Tourism offices.

City transport

Agra is very spread out and its sights too widely separated to explore on foot, so wherever you're staying you'll end up spending a fair amount of time in rickshaws or taxis. Getting from one part of the city to another can prove surprisingly time-consuming, and crossing from one side of the Yamuna River to the other is particularly tedious, given the condition of the city centre's two over-used and under-maintained bridges.

Cycle rickshaws are good for short trips and provide a livelihood for some of the city's poorest inhabitants, as well as being cleaner and greener than autos, but are slow for long journeys, and rickshaw drivers are the biggest source of hassle in Agra – attempt to walk anywhere, and they will be constantly on your case, though walking on the right-hand side of the street makes it harder for them to follow you.

Auto-rickshaws are faster and fares, including waiting time, are very reasonable if you haggle: sample fares from Taj Ganj are Rs40–50 to Sadar Bazaar, Rs50–70 to Agra Cantonment Station, and Rs30–40 to the fort. **Taxis** are handy for longer trips to Sikandra or Fatehpur Sikri; agree a fare before you set off. There are taxi ranks at the stations, or your hotel should be able to arrange a vehicle. There's also a cheap and environmentally friendly **electric bus** (Rs5) which shuttles back and forth between the fort and the west gate of the Taj Mahal, though you could easily spend twenty or thirty minutes waiting for it to arrive.

On rickshaws and taxis, haggle hard. Agra sees so many "fresh" tourists that drivers almost always quote significantly inflated prices to start with (the best policy, if a rickshaw driver names a silly price, is simply to walk away – they'll usually chase after you and offer a more realistic fare). Also, note that the main agenda for many rickshaw- and taxi-drivers is to get you into the city's jewellers, marble shops and other such places where they can earn **commission**, often a more important source of income for them than what they earn in actual fares. Some will even quote you a lower fare if you agree to visit a couple of emporiums en route – though if you agree to this and then decide to buy anything, remember that the rickshaw driver's commission will be added to your bill.

Many locals get around by **bicycle**, but for foreigners unused to the anarchic traffic and treacherous road surfaces, travel on two wheels can be stressful and potentially dangerous. You're better off hiring a cycle rickshaw and getting someone else to do the pedalling for you.

Motorized vehicles are excluded from a small area around the Taj, supposedly to protect it from pollution. This makes the roads beside the Taj quite peaceful, but a taxi or auto will have to drop you short of your hotel if it's within the exclusion zone.

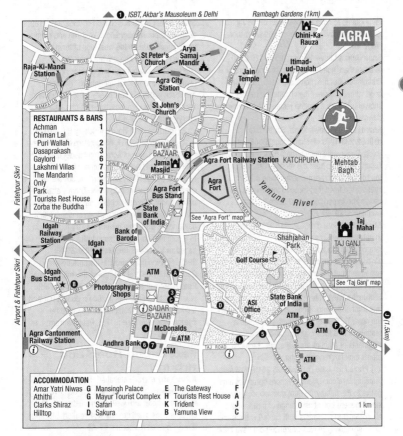

RESTAURANTS & BARS
Achman	1
Chiman Lal	
Puri Wallah	2
Dasaprakash	3
Gaylord	6
Lakshmi Villas	7
The Mandarin	C
Only	5
Park	7
Tourists Rest House	A
Zorba the Buddha	4

ACCOMMODATION
Amar Yatri Niwas	G	Mansingh Palace	E	The Gateway	F
Athithi	G	Mayur Tourist Complex	H	Tourists Rest House	A
Clarks Shiraz	I	Safari	K	Trident	J
Hilltop	D	Sakura	B	Yamuna View	C

Accommodation

Taj Ganj, the jumble of narrow lanes immediately south of the Taj, is where most budget travellers end up in Agra. With their unrivalled rooftop views, laidback cafés and low room rates, the little guesthouses here can be great places to stay, though some are quite basic. There are more modern and upmarket lodgings along Fatehabad Road, southwest of Taj Ganj, while the leafier **Cantonment** area and the adjacent Sadar Bazaar have places to suit every budget, as well as offering a convenient location more or less at the centre of the city.

Taj Ganj

Amarvilas East Gate ☏0562/223 1515, ⓦwww.oberoihotels.com. Easily the loveliest (and most expensive) hotel in Agra, virtually a work of art in its own right, constructed in a serene blend of Mughal and Moorish styles around a gorgeous *charbagh*-style courtyard water garden – particularly magical by night. Most rooms have Taj views (prices start at Rs32,025). Facilities include a large pool, idyllic terraced gardens, two smart restaurants and a very chichi bar. ⓭

Kamal Chowk Kagzi, South Gate ☏0562/233 0126, ⓔhotelkamal@hotmail.com. Right in the thick of the Taj Ganj action, with well-maintained rooms (but no hot showers in the cheapest ones) and a great view from the rooftop restaurant. ❷–❹

Raj 2/26 South Gate ☏09999 450107. The cheap rooftop rooms lack hot running water, but are the best deal in this paan-stained establishment, which fairly claims to have the best view of the Taj from its rooftop restaurant. Pricier rooms are rather dingy. ❷

Shah Jahan Chowk Kazgi ℡0562/320 0240, Ⓔshahjahan_hotel@hotmail.com. Looks grotty at first glance, but the rooms are fresh, clean and good value, and even the cheapest have hot showers. There's a rooftop restaurant, and internet downstairs. ❷–❹

Shanti Lodge Chowk Kazgi, South Gate ℡0562/233 1973, Ⓔshantilodge2000@yahoo .co.in. Deservedly popular backpacker lodge with superb Taj views from the rooftop restaurant, a mixed bag of rooms, including some of the cheapest in town (but those in the annexe are newer and larger), and good deals for single occupancy. ❶–❸

Sheela East Gate ℡0562/233 1973, Ⓦwww .hotelsheelaagra.com. Clean and spacious rooms ranged around a lovely little garden, with fan, air-cooled and a/c options, friendly staff and a good restaurant, but the cheapest rooms aren't such great value, with hot water in buckets only. ❷–❹

Sidhartha West Gate ℡0562/233 0901, Ⓦwww .hotelsidhartha.com. Bigger and better rooms than the other Taj Ganj budget joints, set around a restaurant in a leafy courtyard that includes fragments of Mughal-era walls, but cheapest rooms lack hot running water. ❷–❸

Taj Plaza East Gate ℡0562/233 2515, Ⓦwww .hoteltajplaza.com. A slightly more upmarket alternative to the nearby Taj Ganj guesthouses, this small modern hotel has a range of clean, bright air-cooled and a/c rooms with cable TV; the more expensive ones are well overpriced but have good Taj views. ❸–❼

Cantonment and Sadar Bazaar

Clarks Shiraz 54 Taj Rd ℡0562/222 6121, Ⓦwww.hotelclarksshiraz.com. Sprawling five-star in a pleasant cantonment setting with small but cosy rooms; the more expensive ones with distant Taj views. Facilities include three restaurants, two bars, a swimming pool and a health club. Rooms start at Rs6300. ❾

Hilltop 21 The Mall ℡0562/222 6836, Ⓔhotelhilltopagra@yahoo.com. Set in pleasant grounds with peacocks and parrots, this place is a little bit ramshackle, and the cheaper rooms are on the small side, but the smarter ones are better value. If you're utterly strapped for cash, there are also some ultra-basic cell-like singles with shared bath for just Rs120, and you can camp for Rs150. Rough Guide readers are promised a discount. ❸–❹

Sakura Near Idgah Bus Station ℡0562/242 0169, Ⓦwww.hotelsakuraagra.com. Well-run and good-value guesthouse on the west side of town. Rooms (all with air-coolers) are large, bright, spacious and nicely furnished, and the helpful owner is a mine of local information. The only drawback is the location: handy for Idgah bus and Cantonment train stations, but a bit of a hike from everywhere else. ❷–❸

Tourists Rest House Kutchery Rd, Baluganj ℡0562/246 3961, Ⓔdontworrychickencurry @hotmail.com. One of Agra's top budget options, with a range of bright, competitively priced rooms around a tranquil leafy courtyard; all but the very cheapest with hot running water. There's also a phone booth, internet facilities, back-up generator and free pick-up from bus or train stations with a day's notice (rickshaw drivers may try to take you to a commission-paying "soundalike"). ❷–❸

Yamuna View 6-B The Mall ℡0562/246 2989, Ⓦwww.hotelyamunaviewagra.com. Conveniently central but run-of-the-mill five-star. Rooms are rather plush, though showing a little wear and tear. Facilities include a pool, a bar and a couple of smart restaurants, including the snazzy *Mandarin* (see p.171). Doubles from Rs4725. ❼–❽

Fatehabad Road and around

Amar Yatri Niwas Fatehabad Rd ℡0562/223 3030, Ⓦwww.amaryatriniwas.com. Good-value mid-range hotel with well-maintained rooms (the cheaper ones small but still very comfortable) and a multi-cuisine restaurant. ❺–❻

Atithi Fatehabad Rd ℡0562/233 0880, Ⓦwww .hotelatithiagra.com. Good-sized rooms, not plush but well turned-out, and there's a pool in a yard round the back. A bit impersonal, but the staff try hard to please. ❺–❻

Mansingh Palace Fatehabad Rd ℡0562/233 1771, Ⓦwww.mansinghhotels.com. There's quite an old-fashioned feel to the slightly sombre rooms (doubles from Rs8925, or Rs13,050 for a distant Taj view) at this understated five-star. Facilities include a small pool, health club, multi-cuisine restaurants and a surprisingly chic little Tequila Bar. ❽

Mayur Tourist Complex Fatehabad Rd ℡0562/233 2302, Ⓔmayur268@rediffmail.com. Dinky pagoda-like cottages with attached bathrooms around a large garden (generally peaceful, but often used for weddings Nov–Jan). Facilities include a multi-cuisine restaurant, dingy bar and swimming pool. Camping is also possible (Rs600/head). ❺

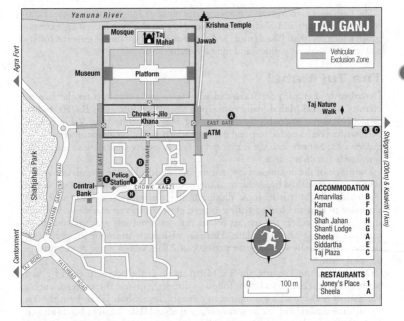

Safari Shaheed Nagar, Shamsabad Rd ☎0562/248 0106, ⓔ hotelsafari@hotmail.com. Friendly and relaxed hotel on the southern side of town. Rooms (fan, air-cooled and a/c) are rather old, but clean and very well looked after, and there are views of the distant Taj from the rooftop café. Good value, though the location is a bit out of the way. ❷

The Gateway Fatehabad Rd ☎0562/660 2000, ⓦ www.tajhotels.com/gateway. This boxy little place doesn't look like much from the outside, but has lots of style within. Rooms (some with distant Taj views) are among the most attractive in Agra,

cheerfully decorated in orange and white, while public areas are pleasantly plush and there's the usual range of five-star amenities including a pool. Doubles from Rs9450 at the rack rate, but usually less. ❽

Trident Tajnagri, Fatehabad Rd ☎0562/233 2400, ⓦ www.tridenthotels.com. A peaceful five-star, whose cheerful rooms (including two adapted for wheelchair users) are in low-lying buildings around a spacious garden with a large pool and multi-cuisine restaurant. The rack rate for doubles starts at Rs9975. ❽

The City

Agra is huge and disorienting. There's no real "centre", but rather a series of self-contained bazaar districts embedded within the formless urban sprawl, which stretches over an area of well over twenty square kilometres. Most of the city's major Mughal monuments are lined up along the banks of the **Yamuna River**, which bounds the city's eastern edge, including the Taj Mahal. Clustered around the Taj, the tangled little streets of **Taj Ganj** are home to most of the city's cheap accommodation and backpacker cafés. A couple of kilometres to the west, on the far side of the leafy **Cantonment** area, lies **Sadar Bazaar**, linked to Taj Ganj by **Fatehabad Road**, where you'll find many of the city's smarter places to stay, as well as numerous restaurants and crafts emporia. Northwest of Taj Ganj lies **Agra Fort** and, beyond, the third of the city's main commercial districts, **Kinari Bazaar**, centred on the massive Jama Masjid.

The monuments in Agra date from the later phase of Mughal rule and the reigns of Akbar, Jahangir and Shah Jahan – exemplifying the ever-increasing extravagance which, by Shah Jahan's time, had already begun to strain the imperial coffers and sow the seeds of political and military decline.

The Taj Mahal

Described by Bengali poet Rabindranath Tagore as "a teardrop on the face of eternity", the **Taj Mahal** (daily 6am–7pm, closed Fri; foreigners Rs750, Indian residents Rs20) is undoubtedly the zenith of Mughal architecture. Volumes have been written on its perfection, and its image adorns countless glossy brochures and guidebooks; nonetheless, the reality never fails to overwhelm all who see it, and few words can do it justice.

The magic of the monument is strangely undiminished by the crowds of tourists who visit, as small and insignificant as ants in the face of the immense mausoleum. That said, the Taj is at its most alluring in the relative quiet of early morning, shrouded in mist and bathed with a soft red glow. As its vast marble surfaces fall into shadow or reflect the sun, its colour changes, from soft grey and yellow to pearly cream and dazzling white. This play of light is an important decorative device, symbolically implying the presence of Allah, who is never represented in physical form.

Overlooking the Yamuna, the Taj Mahal stands at the northern end of a vast walled garden. Though its layout follows a distinctly Islamic theme, representing Paradise, it is above all a monument to romantic love. **Shah Jahan** built the Taj to enshrine the body of his favourite wife, Arjumand Bann Begum, better known by her official palace title, **Mumtaz Mahal** ("Chosen One of the Palace"), who died shortly after giving birth to her fourteenth child in 1631 – the number of children she bore the emperor is itself a tribute to her hold on him, given the number of other wives and concubines upon whom the emperor would have been able to call. The emperor was devastated by her death, and set out to create an unsurpassed monument to her memory – its name, "Taj Mahal", is simply a shortened, informal version of Mumtaz Mahal's palace title. Construction by a workforce of some 20,000 men from all over Asia commenced in 1632 and took over twenty years, and it was not completed until 1653. Marble was brought from Makrana (see p.259), and semiprecious stones for decoration – onyx, amethyst, lapis lazuli, turquoise, jade, crystal, coral and mother-of-pearl – were carried to Agra from Persia, Russia, Afghanistan, Tibet, China and the Indian Ocean. Eventually, Shah Jahan's pious and intolerant son Aurangzeb seized power, and the former emperor was interned in Agra Fort, where as legend would have it, he lived out his final years gazing wistfully at the Taj Mahal. When he died in January 1666, his body was carried across the river to lie alongside his beloved wife in his peerless tomb.

The Chowk-i-Jilo Khana and charbagh

The south, east and west **entrances** all lead into the **Chowk-i-Jilo Khana** forecourt. The main entrance into the complex, an arched gateway topped with delicate domes and adorned with Koranic verses and inlaid floral designs, stands at the northern edge of Chowk-i-Jilo Khana, directly aligned with the Taj, but shielding it from the view of those who wait outside.

Once through the gateway, you'll see the Taj itself at the end of the huge **charbagh** (literally "four gardens"), an expansive, park-like garden divided into four quadrants by raised marbled walkways – a style introduced by the first Mughal emperor Babur from central Asia which remained enduringly fashionable

▲ Taj Mahal

throughout the Mughal era. Dissected into four quadrants by waterways (usually dry), the gardens evoke the Islamic image of the Gardens of Paradise, where rivers flow with water, milk, wine and honey. Unlike other mausoleums in Agra such as the Itimad-ud-Daulah and Akbar's Mausoleum, the Taj doesn't stand at the centre of the *charbagh*, but at the far northern end, presumably to exploit its riverside setting; the central intersection of the four "rivers" is instead marked by a large marble tank corresponding to *al-Kawthar*, the celestial pool of abundance mentioned in the Koran.

The Taj's **museum**, in the enclosure's western wall (in theory daily except Fri 8am–5pm, although it sometimes shuts for no apparent reason; Rs5), features exquisite miniature paintings, two marble pillars believed to have come from the fort, and portraits of Mughal rulers including Shah Jahan and Mumtaz Mahal, as well as architectural drawings of the Taj and examples of *pietra dura* stone inlay work.

The mausoleum

Steps lead from the far end of the gardens up to the high square marble platform on which the **mausoleum** itself sits, each corner marked by a tall, tapering minaret. To the west of the tomb is a domed red-sandstone **mosque** and to the east a replica **jawab**, put there to complete the architectural symmetry of the complex – it cannot be used as a mosque as it faces away from Mecca.

The Taj itself is essentially square in shape, with pointed arches cut into its sides and topped with a huge central dome which rises for over 55m, its height accentuated by a crowning brass spire almost 17m high. On approach, the tomb looms ever larger and grander, but not until you are close do you appreciate both its sheer size and the extraordinarily fine detail of relief carving, highlighted by floral patterns of precious stones. Arabic verses praising the glory of Paradise fringe the archways, proportioned exactly so that each letter appears to be the same size when viewed from the ground.

The south face of the tomb is the main entrance to the **interior**: a high octagonal chamber whose weirdly echoing interior is flushed with pale light. A marble screen, decorated with precious stones and cut so finely that it seems almost translucent, protects the cenotaph of Mumtaz Mahal in the centre, perfectly aligned with the doorway and the distant gateway into the Chowk-i-Jilo Khana, and that of Shah Jahan crammed in next to it – the only object which breaks the perfect symmetry of the entire complex. The inlay work on the marble tombs is the finest in Agra, and no pains were spared in perfecting the inlay work – some of the petals and leaves are made of up to sixty separate stone fragments. Ninety-nine names of Allah adorn the top of Mumtaz's tomb, and set into Shah Jahan's is a pen box, the hallmark of a male ruler. These cenotaphs, in accordance with Mughal tradition, are only representations of the real coffins, which lie in the same positions in a crypt below.

Taj Mahal viewing practicalities

India's most famous monument became the centre of heated controversy in December 2000, when the Agra Municipality and Archeological Survey of India (ASI) jointly imposed a hike in **admission charges** for foreign visitors from Rs15 to a whopping Rs960 for a day ticket; it's since been reduced to its present level of Rs750 for foreign visitors (Rs250 for the ASI, Rs500 in local tax). Galling though the price increase is, few regard the expense as money wasted once they are inside, but foreign tourists now rarely visit the Taj on several consecutive days. To appreciate the famous play of light on the building, you'd have to stick around from dawn until dusk (ticket valid all day, but only for one entrance). Ticket queues are longest at the west gate, shortest at the south gate, and at the east gate the ticket office has been shifted half a kilometre down the road to the Shilpgram crafts village. You are not allowed to enter with food (and none is available inside), nor with a mobile phone or a travel guidebook (not even this one) – those can be deposited at lockers near the entrances. Foreigners are given a free bottle of water

The Taj Mahal: a monument under threat

Despite the seemingly impregnable sense of serenity and other-worldliness which clings to the Taj, in reality, India's most famous building faces serious threats from traffic and industrial pollution, and from the millions of tourists who visit it each year. Marble is all but impervious to the onslaught of wind and rain that erodes softer sandstone, but it has no natural defence against the sulphur dioxide that lingers in a dusty haze and shrouds the monument; sometimes the smog is so dense that the tomb cannot be seen from the fort. Sulphur dioxide mixes with atmospheric moisture and settles as sulphuric acid on the surface of the tomb, making the smooth white marble yellow and flaky, and forming a subtle fungus that experts have named "marble cancer".

The main sources of pollution are the continuous flow of vehicles along the national highways that skirt the city, and the 1700 factories in and around Agra – chemical effluents belched out from their chimneys are well beyond recommended safety limits. Despite laws demanding the installation of pollution-control devices, the imposition of a ban on all petrol- and diesel-fuelled traffic within 500m of the Taj Mahal, and an exclusion zone banning new industrial plants from an area of 10,400 square kilometres around the complex, pollutants in the atmosphere have continued to rise (many blame the diesel generators of nearby hotels), and new factories have been set up illegally.

Cleaning work on the Taj Mahal rectifies the problem to some extent, but the chemicals used will themselves eventually affect the marble – attendants already shine their torches on "repaired" sections of marble to demonstrate how they've lost their translucency. The government has responded by setting up a pollution monitoring station to check on levels of N_2O and SO_2 in the atmosphere, but in 2007 a parliamentary committee reported that, aside from the threat from these acidic gases, particulate matter in the air was slowly turning the Taj yellow; the recommended treatment was a non-corrosive clay pack to remove particle deposits on the marble.

From time to time scare reports surface to the effect that the Taj's four minarets are listing and in danger of keeling over. Luckily, this proves to be a false alarm: the minarets were deliberately constructed leaning slightly outwards, in order to counteract an optical illusion which would have made them appear to lean inwards when seen from ground level if they were actually exactly vertical.

and a pair of shoe covers on entry. The Taj entrance ticket also entitles you to tax-free entry at a few other sites if used on the same day, giving you Rs50 off the admission fee at Agra Fort, and Rs10 off at Sikandra, Itimad-ud-Daulah and Fatehpur Sikri.

It's possible to see the Taj by moonlight on the night of the full moon itself and on the two days before and after. Only four hundred visitors are admitted per night (in batches of fifty between 8pm and midnight, but not Fridays or during Ramadan). Tickets (foreigners Rs750, Indian residents Rs510) have to be purchased a day in advance from the Archeological Survey of India office, 22 Mall Rd (Mon–Sat 10am–6pm; ☎0562/222 7261). If a viewing is cancelled, you'll get a refund.

You can **see the Taj for free** by climbing onto a Taj Ganj hotel rooftop, or heading down the eastern side of the compound to a small Krishna temple by the river, where you can see the Taj, and also take a little boat ride (Rs100 to Rs1000, depending on the size of your camera) to see it from the river.

From across the river at **Mehtab Bagh** (daily sunrise to sunset; foreigners Rs100, Indian residents Rs5), the view is breathtaking, especially at dawn; to get to it, cross the river on the road bridge north of Agra Fort, and turn right when you reach the far bank, following the metalled road until it enters the village of Katchpura; here, it becomes a rough track that eventually emerges at a small Dalit shrine on the riverside, which is directly opposite the Taj, and next to the entrance of Mehtab Bagh. The gardens were laid out by Shah Jahan, probably to serve as a place from which to admire his masterpiece, though, views apart, they're now eminently forgettable, planted with tedious lines of prim ornamental shrubs, enlivened only by a few ornate scalloped tanks in various stages of disrepair and a fine riverside cupola. You can enjoy the Taj views without paying the steep admission fee simply by walking down the path to the river by the entrance to the gardens, but you'll then be pestered by opportunistic nuisance-wallahs who hang out on the riverbank waiting to pounce on tourists. Unfortunately, you can no longer access the gardens by boat from across the river by the Taj itself.

The Taj Nature Walk

A few hundred metres up East Gate Road from the Taj, the **Taj Nature Walk** (daily 9am–6.30pm; foreigners Rs50, Indian residents Rs10) offers a pleasant retreat from the touts and another welcome chance to stretch one's legs in peace and quiet. A paved path loops and twists for 500m through light woodland full of birds and butterflies, with lawns for a picnic and fine Taj views from the little wooden tower at the far end of the gardens (where you'll also find drinks for sale).

Agra Fort

The high red-sandstone ramparts of **Agra Fort** (sunrise to sunset; foreigners Rs300, Indian residents Rs20, Rs50 discount for foreigners on production of a Taj ticket for the same day) dominate a bend in the Yamuna River 2km northwest of the Taj Mahal. Founded by Akbar on the remains of earlier Rajput fortifications, this major citadel developed as the seat and stronghold of the Mughal empire for several generations. Akbar laid the foundations, in the form of a half moon, between 1565 and 1573, and commissioned the walls and gates; his grandson, Shah Jahan, had most of the principal buildings erected; and Aurangzeb, the last great emperor, was responsible for the ramparts.

The curved sandstone bastions reach a height of over 20m and stretch for around 2.5km, punctuated by a sequence of massive gates, (although only the **Amar Singh Pol** is currently open to visitors). The original and grandest entrance, however, was through the western side, via the outer **Delhi Gate**, which leads to the more impressive inner gate, called **Hathi Pol** ("Elephant Gate"), now flanked by two red-sandstone towers faced in marble, but once guarded by colossal stone elephants with riders which were destroyed by Aurangzeb in 1668. Access to much of the fort is restricted, and only those parts open to the public are described here.

Note that there's nowhere to buy drinks inside the fort, and exploring the complex can be thirsty work, so unless you're happy to take your chances at the public drinking taps, it's a good idea to take water in with you.

Diwan-i-Am and the great courtyard

Entrance to the fort is through the **Amar Singh Pol**, actually three separate gates placed close together and at right angles to one another to disorientate any potential attackers and to deprive them of the space in which to use battering weapons against the fortifications. From here a ramp climbs gently uphill flanked by high walls (another defensive measure), through a second gate to the spacious courtyard, with tree-studded lawns, which surrounds the graceful **Diwan-i-Am**

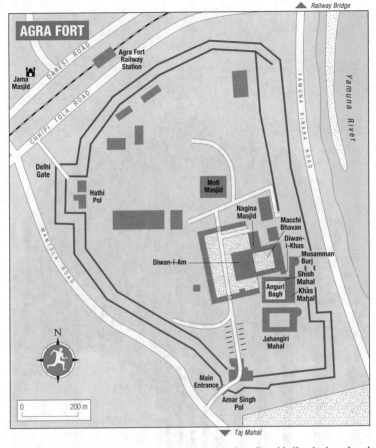

("Hall of Public Audience"). Open on three sides, the pillared hall, which replaced an earlier wooden structure, was commissioned by Shah Jahan in 1628. The elegance of the setting would have been enhanced by the addition of brocade, carpets and satin canopies for audiences with the emperor.

The ornate throne alcove was built to house a gem-encrusted Peacock Throne that was eventually moved to Delhi, only to be looted from there by Nadir Shah and finishing up in Tehran. It is inlaid in marble decorated with flowers and foliage in bas-relief, and connects to the royal chambers within. In front of the alcove, the **Baithak**, a small marble table, is where ministers would have sat to deliver petitions and receive commands. This is also where trials would have been conducted, and justice speedily implemented.

The area to the north of the Diwan-i-Am courtyard is closed to visitors, though you can make out the delicate white marble domes and chhatris of the striking, if rather clumsily proportioned, **Moti Masjid** ("Pearl Mosque") rising beyond the courtyard walls, best seen from the Diwan-i-Am itself. Directly in front of the Diwan-i-Am an incongruously Gothic Christian tomb marks the **grave of John Russell Colvin**, lieutenant governor of the Northwestern Provinces, who died here during the 1857 uprising, when Agra's British population barricaded themselves inside the fort.

▲ Agra Fort

The Macchi Bhavan and Diwan-i-Khas

Heading through the small door to the left of the throne alcove in the Diwan-i-Am and climbing the stairs beyond brings you out onto the upper level of the **Macchi Bhavan** (Fish Palace), a large but relatively plain two-storey structure overlooking a spacious, grassy courtyard. This was once strewn with fountains and flowerbeds, interspersed with tanks and water channels stocked with fish on which the emperor and his courtiers would practise their angling skills, though the Maharaja of Bharatpur subsequently removed some of its marble fixtures to his palace in Deeg, and William Bentinck (governor general from 1828 to 1835) auctioned off much of the palace's original mosaics and fretwork.

On the north side of the courtyard (to the left as you enter) a small door leads to the exquisite little **Nagina Masjid** (Gem Mosque), made entirely of marble. Capped with three domes and approached from a marble-paved courtyard, it was commissioned by Shah Jahan for the ladies of the *zenana* (harem). At the rear on the right, a small balcony with beautifully carved lattice screens offers a discreet viewpoint from where ladies of the harem were able to inspect luxury goods – silks, jewellery and brocade – laid out for sale by merchants in the courtyard below, without themselves being seen.

The raised terrace on the far side of the Macchi Bhavan is adorned by two **thrones**, one black slate, the other white marble. The white one was used by Shah Jahan, the black one by his father Jahangir, as a young man, to watch elephant fights in the eastern enclosure. It now serves, somewhat less gloriously, as a favoured perch for couples posing for photos against the backdrop of the Taj.

To your right (as you face the river), a high terrace overlooking the Yamuna is topped with a sequence of lavish royal apartments designed to catch the cool breezes blowing across the waters below. The first is the delicate **Diwan-i-Khas** (Hall of Private Audience), erected in 1635, where the emperor would have received kings, dignitaries and ambassadors, and is one of the most finely decorated buildings in the fort, with paired marble pillars and peacock arches inlaid with lapis lazuli and jasper.

The Mina Masjid to the Anguri Bagh

A passageway behind it leads to the tiny **Mina Masjid**, a plain white marble mosque built for Shah Jahan and traditionally said to have been used by him during his imprisonment here. Beyond, the passageway leads to a two-storey pavilion known as the **Musamman Burj**, the most elaborately decorated structure in the fort, famous as the spot where he is said to have caught his last glimpse of the Taj Mahal before he died. Its lattice-screen balustrade is dotted with ornamental niches and with exquisite *pietra dura* inlay covering almost every surface. In front of the tower a courtyard, paved with marble octagons, centres on a **pachisi board** where the emperor, following his father's example at Fatehpur Sikri (see p.178), played *pachisi* (a form of ludo) using dancing girls as pieces.

Past the Musamman Burj, another large courtyard, the **Anguri Bagh** (Grape Garden), is a miniature *charbagh*, its east side flanked by the marble building known as **Khas Mahal** (Private Palace), possibly a drawing room or the emperor's sleeping chamber. Designed essentially for comfort, it incorporates cavities in its flat roofs to insulate against the searing heat of an Agra summer, and affords soothing riverside and garden views. The palace is flanked by two so-called **Golden Pavilions**, their curved roofs (a form that would later become a staple of Rajput architecture) covered with gilded copper tiles in a style inspired by the thatched roofs of Bengali village huts, their arches framing further photogenic Taj vistas. In front of the Khas Mahal, steps descend into the northeast corner of the Anguri Bagh and the **Shish Mahal** (Glass Palace), where royal women bathed in the soft lamplight reflected from the mirror-work mosaics that covered the walls and ceiling; unfortunately the building is currently locked, so you can only peek in through the windows.

South of the Khas Mahal lies the **Shah Jahani Mahal** (Shah Jahan's Palace), a heavily graffitoed cluster of four rather sorry-looking rooms (originally painted in bright colours and embossed in gold), plus another delicate octagonal open-sided two-storey chhatri with further Taj views.

The Jahangiri Mahal

Immediately beyond the Shah Jahani Mahal lies the huge **Jahangiri Mahal** (Jahangir's Palace), although the name is misleading since it was actually built for Jahangir's father, Akbar, and probably served not as a royal palace, but as a harem – parts of the complex are thought to have been the living quarters of Akbar's Rajput wife Jodhbai, after whom one of the major palaces at Fatehpur Sikri is named (see p.180). Compared to the classic Mughal designs of the surrounding buildings, this robust sandstone structure has quite a few Hindu elements mixed up with traditional Mughal and Islamic motifs.

The first courtyard shows a rather haphazard mix of both elements, but the remarkable **central courtyard** is almost entirely Hindu in design, with characteristically Indian corbelled arches and lavishly carved columns and capitals supporting heavy overhanging eaves, above which rises a second storey of even more fantastically embellished balconies and roof brackets. The courtyard is flanked by large halls; the ceiling of that to the north is supported on enormous stone beams carved with fantastic mythological animals, including a serpentine form being emitted from a dragon's mouth. This whole section of the palace marks a decisive, if temporary, shift in Mughal architecture. Whereas the design of previous Mughal buildings was essentially Islamic, gently modified by the inclusion of a few Hindu motifs, here the few Islamic motifs (such as the pointed arches on the upper storeys) are more or less buried beneath a surfeit of Hindu design elements – a mix-and-match style which can also be seen throughout Akbar's palace complex at Fatehpur Sikri. The whole concept appears to be the logical architectural result of the tolerant embracing of rival faiths and cultures which Akbar achieved during his enlightened rule, although the rather random mingling of Hindu and Islamic elements exemplified by this palace would soon be eclipsed by the classic synthesis of Persian and Subcontinental styles achieved by Shah Jahan in works such as the Taj Mahal.

From the central courtyard, a gateway leads out through the main gateway into the palace, whose impressive facade shows a characteristic mix of Mughal and Indian motifs, with Islamic pointed arches and inlaid mosaics combined with Hindu-style overhanging eaves supported by heavily carved brackets. Immediately in front of the palace sits **Jahangir's Hauz** (Jahangir's Cistern), a giant bowl with steps inside and out, made in 1611 from a single block of porphyry and inscribed in Persian. Filled with rosewater, it would have been used by the emperor as a bathtub, while it's also believed that the emperor took it with him on his travels around the empire – though it seems difficult to credit this, given the bath's size and weight.

Kalakriti

Every night at 6.30pm, the story of the Taj is performed as an eighty-minute **stage musical** at the Kalakriti Centre, on the road from Fatehabad Road (near Trident hotel) to the Taj's east gate (☎0562/404 5370, ⓦwww.kalakritionline.com). It's a kitsch extravaganza, with singing, dancing, and a marble model of the Taj bathed in coloured lights, all performed in Hindi, with headphone translations into English and other languages for those in the gold (Rs700) and platinum (Rs1000) seats, but not in the silver (Rs300) seats furthest from the stage.

Jama Masjid and Kinari Bazaar

Opposite the fort, and overlooking Agra Fort train station, is the city's principal mosque, the soaring red-sandstone **Jama Masjid** (Friday Mosque). Built in 1648, it was originally connected directly to the fort's principal entrance, the Delhi Gate, by a large courtyard, but after the 1857 uprising, the British ran a railway line between the two, leaving the mosque stranded in no-man's-land on the far side of the tracks.

Standing on a high plinth above the chaotic streets of the surrounding bazaar (of which it affords fine views), the mosque is crowned by three large sandstone domes covered in distinctive zigzagging bands of marble. Five huge arches lead into the main prayer hall, topped by a prettily inlaid band of sandstone decorated in abstract floral patterns while, inside, the mihrab is surrounded by delicate flourishes of Koranic script, inlaid in black, a design mirrored in the principal archway. Despite the grandeur of its design and the fineness of some of its details, however, much of the mosque is now showing the ravages of time and the depredations of the resident swarms of bats, pigeons and parakeets which nest among its eaves, while clusters of huge beehives dangle ominously from the summits of several of the larger arches.

The space around the base of the mosque is now filled with the crowded – but refreshingly hassle-free – streets of **Kinari Bazaar**, a fascinating warren of streets crammed full with shops and stalls, though the numbers of people, scooters, cycle rickshaws and cows pushing their way through the streets make exploring it a slow and tiring business. Opposite the northeast corner of the complex, look out for the **petha-wallahs**, purveyors of Agra's most famous sweet (see p.171).

Itimad-ud-Daulah

On the east bank of the Yamuna some 3km north of Agra Fort, the beautiful **Itimad-ud-Daulah** (pronounced "Atma Dolla"; daily sunrise to sunset; foreigners Rs110, Indian residents Rs15) is the tomb of Mirza Ghiyas Beg, *wazir* (chief minister) and father-in-law of Emperor Jahangir, who gave him the title of Itimad-ud-Daulah, or "Pillar of the State". The tomb is popularly known among Agra's rickshaw-wallahs as the "**Baby Taj**", and though it's much smaller and less successfully proportioned than its more famous relative, it does foreshadow the Taj in being the first building in Mughal Agra to be faced entirely in marble, with lavish use of *pietra dura* inlay to decorate its translucent exterior walls.

As usual, the tomb sits at the centre of a *charbagh* garden, though here entered from the eastern (rather than the usual southern) side, presumably to highlight its setting against the backdrop of the Yamuna River – another element of its design which anticipates that of the Taj. The building's undersized rooftop pavilion replaces the usual dome, and has four stocky minarets stuck onto each corner. However, these imperfections seem unimportant given the superbly intricate **inlay work** which covers virtually the entire tomb – an incredible profusion of floral and geometrical patterning in muted reds, oranges, browns and greys that give it the appearance of an enormous, slightly hallucinogenic experiment in medieval op art. Elegant inlaid designs showing characteristic Persian motifs, including wine vases, trees and honeysuckles, adorn the arches of the four entrances, and the walls inside are covered in rather eroded and clumsily restored paintings of further vases, flowers and cypresses. The replica tombs of Ghiyas Beg and his wife (the real tombs, as usual, are buried underground) stand behind an intricately carved wall, surrounded by subsidiary family tombs.

Chini-ka-Rauza

Around 1km north of Itimad-ud-Daulah is the **Chini-ka-Rauza** (daily 24hr; free), built between 1628 and 1639 to serve as the mausoleum of Afzal Khan, a Persian poet from Shiraz who served as one of Shah Jahan's ministers until his death in 1639. As befits his origins, Afzal Khan's tomb is of purely Persian design, the only such building in Agra. Although now rather neglected and decaying, the exterior, topped with a bulbous dome, still retains substantial quantities of the delicate tiles that once enhanced the whole of the exterior – predominantly blue, with discreet highlights in orange, yellow, green and turquoise. Inside, the large dome is decorated with rich *muqarna* vaulting covered in fading paintwork and Koranic script.

Rambagh

A kilometre or so north of the Chini-ka-Rauza, amid the dusty sprawl of northern Agra, the **Rambagh** gardens (daily sunrise–sunset; foreigners Rs100, Indian residents Rs5) are of considerable historical interest, being one of the very few surviving physical remains in India of the reign of Babur, the founder of the Mughal dynasty – although there's little left to see here now, and the site is unlikely to excite anyone but serious students of Mughal history or the unnaturally curious.

Nur Jahan, Light of the World

Despite the detailed records of contemporary Mughal court historians and the efforts of modern scholars, relatively little is known about the myriad wives and concubines of the great Mughal emperors, whose personalities, ambitions and intrigues have been largely lost to history within the shadows of the imperial harem in which they spent the majority of their lives (Akbar alone had some three hundred wives, and perhaps five thousand concubines). A few emblematic figures do stand out – Akbar's formidable mother Hamida Banu Begum, for instance, and Shah Jahan's beloved wife Mumtaz Mahal – but of the very few Mughal matriarchs who suceeded in breaking through the veils of purdah and leaving their mark on the history of the empire, none had a career as dramatic or influential as **Nur Jahan**, favourite wife of Jahangir and – at least during the latter part of his reign – the de facto power behind the Mughal throne.

Nur Jahan's origins were relatively humble. She was born in 1577 in Kandahar, in present-day Afghanistan, while her family were travelling from their ancestral home in Persia to India, where her father, **Ghiyas Beg**, hoped to revive their declining fortunes. Having arrived at Akbar's court, Ghiyas Beg quickly established himself as a valued member of Mughal society, serving first Akbar and then Jahangir, who conferred the official title of Itimad-ud-Daulah, "Pillar of the State", upon him. Mehrunissa (as Nur Jahan was originally named) was married to her first husband, another Persian, Sher Afkun, at the age of 17. Sher Afkun died in 1607, however, and the 30-year-old Mehrunissa was brought to court, where Jahangir met the attractive young widow, fell in love, and married her (in 1611), making her his twentieth wife and giving her the official title first of Nur Mahal ("Light of the Palace") and subsequently Nur Jahan ("Light of the World").

Following Nur Jahan's marriage, her father's already considerable influence grew even stronger, while her brother Asaf Khan was also promoted to a senior position at court, making the family the most powerful in Mughal India, their influence significantly increased thanks to Jahangir's own frequent incapacitation due to alcohol and opium. Neither father nor brother, however, could rival the influence of Nur Jahan. As Thomas Roe, the English ambassador to the Mughal court, wrote of the empress: "[she] governs him, and wynds him up at her pleasure…all justice or care of any thing

The extensive gardens were originally laid out by Babur in 1526 following the Persian *charbagh* plan, which the new ruler of northern India had first seen at Samarkand, and which would subsequently prove the prototype for all later Mughal gardens in the Subcontinent. Their original name was Aram Bagh (Garden of Rest), subsequently corrupted to "Ram", after the Hindu god Rama. Babur himself was apparently buried here for a time before his body was exhumed and taken to its final resting place in Kabul.

The gardens originally consisted of three descending terraces, with water drawn from the Yamuna by a system of watermills, although later additions and alterations make it difficult to get much sense of how the gardens would have looked. The walkways and watercourses have been heavy-handedly restored (though, ironically, are now completely lacking in any water), leading up to a terrace high above the Yamuna, from where the crumbling remains of a trio of riverside chattris can be seen to the north, perched in melancholy isolation amidst the ugly industrial suburbs of the northern city.

Akbar's mausoleum: Sikandra

Given the Mughal tradition of building magnificent tombs, it is no surprise that the mausoleum of the most distinguished Mughal ruler was one of the most ambitious structures of its time. **Akbar's mausoleum** (daily dawn–dusk;

or publique affayrs either sleepes or depends on her, who is more unaccesable than any goddesse or mystery of heathen impietye."

During the following sixteen years, Nur Jahan became the major power behind the throne of perhaps the greatest empire in the world of its time without ever breaking the strict rules of purdah which enclosed her on every side. She issued orders and edicts, while Jahangir even had coins struck bearing her image, the first queen of India to be so honoured since the reign of Chandragupta some 1300 years earlier. By 1622, Jahangir's failing health had made her effective ruler of the empire in all but name. Nor were her energies confined to administrative dealings. When not managing affairs of state, Nur Jahan would go hunting on elephants, shooting from a closed *howdah* which simultaneously allowed her to enjoy the thrill of the chase while remaining inviolate to male eyes (and obviously developing considerable skills in marksmanship in the process, on one occasion dispatching four tigers with only six bullets). At one point she even rode into battle in a litter slung between two elephants – hardly the behaviour one would expect of a traditional seventeenth-century Indo-Islamic wife.

Ultimately, Nur Jahan's passion for intrigue and love of power was to prove her undoing. An early champion of Prince Khurram, later to become the emperor Shah Jahan, she subsequently changed her allegiances to his rival, Prince Shahriyar, although she rapidly found herself in conflict not only with Khurram, but with her own brother, Asaf Khan, who had sided with the rival prince. Following Jahangir's death in 1627 and Shah Jahan's seizure of the Mughal throne, Nur Jahan was forced finally to retire from court life. She lived for a further 18 years, during which she built the superb memorial for her father in Agra, the **Itimad-ud-Daulah**, by which she is now best remembered, as well as a fine tomb for Jahangir in Lahore, next to which she was herself interred upon her death in 1645.

The special relationship between the Mughals and the family of Ghiyas Beg did not end with Nur Jahan's fall from power, however. Shortly afterwards, her niece, Asaf Khan's daughter Arjumand Banu, married the new emperor Shah Jahan, becoming in her turn the favoured Mughal consort of the age, and ultimately receiving the compliment of an even finer mausoleum: the Taj Mahal.

foreigners Rs110, Indian residents Rs10) borders the side of the main highway to Mathura at **SIKANDRA**, 10km northwest of Agra. Rickshaws charge at least Rs120 to make the round trip, although it's a long ride, and you might want to take a taxi; alternatively, hop on a Mathura-bound bus from Agra Fort bus stand.

The complex is entered via its huge **Buland Darwaza** (Great Gate), surmounted by four tapering marble minarets, and overlaid with marble and coloured tiles in repetitive geometrical patterns, bearing the Koranic inscription "These are the gardens of Eden, enter them and live forever". Through the gateway, extensive, park-like **gardens** are divided by fine raised sandstone walkways into the four equal quadrants of the typical Mughal *charbagh* design. Langur monkeys may be seen along the path, while deer roam through the tall grasses, just as they do in the Mughal miniature paintings dating from the era when the tomb was constructed, lending the whole place a magically peaceful and rural atmosphere.

The **mausoleum** itself sits in the middle of the gardens, at the centre of the *charbagh* and directly in front of Buland Darwaza. The entire structure is one of the strangest in Mughal Agra, its huge square base topped not by the usual dome but by a three-storey open-sided sandstone construction crowned with a solid-looking marble pavilion. The mishmash design may be attributable to Jahangir, who ordered changes in the mausoleum's design halfway through its construction, Akbar himself having neglected to leave finished plans for his mausoleum. By the standards of India's other Mughal buildings, it's architecturally a failure, but not without a certain whimsical charm, and much of the inlay work around the lower storey is exquisite.

A high marble gateway in the mausoleum's southern facade frames an elaborate lattice screen shielding a small vestibule painted with rich sea-blue frescoes and Koranic verses. From here a ramp leads down into a large, echoing and absolutely plain subterranean **crypt**, lit by a single skylight, in the centre of which stands Akbar's grave, decorated with the pen-box motif, the symbol of a male ruler, which can also be seen on Shah Jahan's tomb in the Taj Mahal.

Mariam's Tomb

Off the road on the opposite side, 1km north of Sikandra (take an auto, hop on a passing bus, or just walk), lies the altogether more modest **Mariam's Tomb** (daily sunrise–sunset; foreigners Rs100, Indian residents Rs5), the mausoleum of Mariam Zamani, a wife of Akbar and mother of Salim, the future emperor Jahangir, who ordered the construction of this large mausoleum for his mother following her death in 1623. The sandstone tomb is looking rather dilapidated nowadays, but remains impressive and also rather atmospheric, given the almost complete lack of visitors. Architecturally, the mausoleum belongs to the style embodied by Jahangir's own palace in Agra Fort, a weighty sandstone structure, with fine (though very eroded) carvings covering most of its exterior walls. The lack of the usual Mughal dome is compensated for by the large chhatris placed at each corner and the four rectangular kiosks surmounting the centre of each facade, the whole roof enclosed by a large overhanging eave supported by heavy stepped capitals – all showing the increasingly strong Hindu influence which had begun to creep into the Mughal style during the reigns of Akbar and Jahangir. The plain interior is subdivided by a tight grid of intersecting corridors, while Mariam's own tomb sits in lonely isolation in the crypt below.

Eating

In culinary terms, Agra is famous as the home of **Mughlai cooking**. Imitated in Indian curry houses throughout the world, the city's traditional Persian-influenced cuisine is renowned for its rich cream- and curd-based sauces, accompanied by naan and tandoori breads roasted in earthen ovens, pilao rice dishes and milky sweets such as *kheer*. Mughlai specialities can be sampled in many of the town's better restaurants, the majority of which can be found in **Sadar Bazaar** and along **Fatehabad Road**. There are also innumerable scruffy little travellers' cafés around **Taj Ganj**, though standards of hygiene are often suspect, and the food is generally uninspiring, with slow service the norm. Taj Ganj's saving grace is the **rooftop cafés**, many with fine Taj views, which cap most of its buildings – the best views are from the *Kamal* and *Shanti Lodge* guesthouses – though of course you can't see anything after dark, except on or around full-moon days.

Local **specialities** of Agra are *petha* (crystallized pumpkin) – the best is the Panchi brand, available at various outlets all over Agra, particularly in the row of *petha* shops in Kinari Bazaar along the northeast side of the Jami Masjid (past *Chimman Lal Puri Wale*). Look out too for *ghazak*, a rock-hard candy with nuts, and *dalmoth*, a crunchy mix made with black lentils.

There's not much to get excited about when it comes to **drinking** in Agra. Easily the nicest place in town is the gorgeous bar at *Amarvilas* (see p.155), which has a good international selection of tipples at slightly less stratospheric prices than you might fear, given the sublime setting. Apart from this you're limited to surreptitious beers in the unlicensed Taj Ganj guesthouses, or the licensed but characterless bars in the various hotels along Fatehabad Road – the *Gaylord* bar and restaurant, opposite the *Park* restaurant in Sadar Bazaar, is as nice as any.

Agra's restaurants – including even apparently reputable establishments – are not immune to the epidemic of **credit-card fraud** (see p.172). It's best not to pay with credit card except in the city's five-star establishments, or, if you do, to supervise the operation carefully.

Other than *Sheela* and *Joney's Place*, which are shown on the Taj Ganj map (p.157), all the places listed below are marked on the Agra map, p.155.

Achman Agra–Delhi Highway (NH–2), Dayal Bagh, 5km out of town near Baghwan Cinema. Highly rated among Agra-wallahs in the know, famous for its navratan korma (a mildly spiced mix of nuts, dried fruit and *paneer*), malai kofta and chickpea masala, as well as wonderful stuffed naans. Well off the tourist trail in the north of the city, but ideally placed for dinner on your way home from Sikandra (to which it's about halfway), and reachable by shared auto from Agra Fort bus station or Gwalior Rd. Mains Rs95–145.

Chiman Lal Puri Wallah Opposite northeast wall of Jami Masjid. An Agra institution for five generations, this much-loved little café-restaurant looks a touch grubby from the outside, but serves delicious *puri*-thalis, with two veg dishes and a sweet – all for Rs30. Ideal pit stop after visiting the Jami Masjid.

Dasaprakash Meher Theatre Complex, 1 Gwalior Rd, close to the *Tourists Rest House*. The Agra branch of a famous Chennai restaurant, serving a limited menu of top-notch South Indian food and an extensive ice-cream menu – the "hot fudge bonanza split" wins by a nose. Most mains Rs80–150, thalis Rs100–210.

Joney's Place Chowk Kagzi, Taj Ganj. Oldest and best of the Taj Ganj travellers' cafés, going since 1978, and open from 5am in case you need breakfast ahead of a dawn visit to the Taj. The Indian breakfast (*puris*, chickpea curry, *jalebi* and chai) is pretty good, or there's spaghetti, macaroni, veg or non-veg curries, even (on occasion) hummus and a version of falafel. Main dishes Rs30–70.

Lakshmi Villas 50-A Sadar Bazaar. Unpretentious but deservedly popular South Indian café in the middle of Sadar Bazaar offering the usual *iddli-dosa-uttapam* menu, plus a couple of thalis – a good, and much cheaper, alternative to *Dasaprakash*, with most dishes at a bargain Rs55–80, thali Rs88.

The Mandarin Yamuna View Hotel. One of the best non-Indian restaurants in town, this rather snazzy

Chinese offers a possibly welcome change from Mughlai curries and masala dosas. The large (though rather expensive) menu features a good selection of delicately prepared dishes like stir-fried vegetables in almond sauce and chicken in honey chilli, with the emphasis on light ingredients and subtle flavours. Non-veg mains Rs330–400 (seafood Rs400–575).

Only Corner of The Mall and Taj Rd. One of Agra's most popular North Indian restaurants, usually packed with local families and tourist groups and known for its well-prepared tandoori and Mughlai creations, though there's also a wide selection of more mainstream North Indian meat and veg standards, plus a few Chinese and Continental offerings. There's seating in an indoor a/c dining room or in the pleasant courtyard. Non-veg mains Rs140–295.

Park Restaurant Taj Rd, Sadar Bazaar. A long-established favourite with both locals and tourists, this simple a/c restaurant dishes up an excellent range of classic Mughlai chicken dishes, along with more mainstream tandooris and meat and veg curries accompanied by superb naan breads, plus a modest selection of Continental and Chinese

favourites. Most mains Rs90–185; the house speciality is a banno kebab, made of chicken pieces in spicy cashew paste (Rs200).

Sheela East Gate, Taj Ganj. The most dependable and pleasant place to eat near the Taj, with outside seating in the shady garden or inside the narrow café. The menu features a good choice of simple Indian dishes, as well as drinks and snacks, and the fruit lassis are more of a yoghurty dessert than a drink. Non-veg mains Rs90–250.

Tourist Rest House Baluganj. Atmospheric, candle-lit garden restaurant serving a modest selection of breakfasts and Indian veg dishes to a clientele of foreign backpackers. Try the tasty vegetable kofta, rounded off with banana custard. Mains Rs35–80.

Zorba the Buddha E-19 Shopping Arcade, Sadar Bazaar. Aimed unashamedly at foreign tourists, though you'll find Indian people eating here too, this prettily decorated little place promises no chilli unless you ask for it, and offers, along with Indian veg dishes, odd specialities such as a Hawaiian spree (vegetables and pineapple in pineapple sauce) or a fiesta (vegetables in tomato and cashew sauce), but generally tasty and well presented, at Rs90–150 a throw, with a Rs350 (plus VAT) set meal. Closed June.

Shopping

Agra is renowned for its **marble** tabletops, vases and trays, inlaid with semi-precious stones in ornate floral designs, in imitation of those found in the Taj Mahal. It is also an excellent place to buy **leather**: Agra's shoe industry supplies all India, and its tanneries export bags, briefcases and jackets. **Carpets** and **dhurries** are manufactured here too, and traditional embroidery continues to thrive. *Zari* and *zardozi* are brightly coloured, the latter building up three-dimensional patterns with fantastic motifs; *chikan* uses more delicate overlay techniques.

There are several large emporiums such as the official-sounding **Cottage Industries Exposition** on the Fatehabad Road, which is well presented but outrageously expensive; it is one of the places you're likely to be taken to by a commission-seeking driver. Shops in the big hotels may be pricey, but their quality and service are usually more reliable. State emporiums round the Taj include UP's Gangotri, which has fixed prices. Close to the East Gate, **Shilpgram** is an extensive crafts village with arts and handicrafts from all over India, and occasional live music and dance performances.

Shopping or browsing around The Mall, MG Road, Munro Road, Kinari Bazaar, Sadar Bazaar and the Taj Complex is fun, but you need to know what you're buying and be prepared to haggle; you should also be wary of ordering anything to be sent overseas. It's advisable never to let your credit card out of your sight, even for the transaction to be authorized, and you should make sure that all documentation is filled in correctly and fully so as not to allow unauthorized later additions. A large number of serious cases of **credit-card fraud** have been reported in Agra, even in some of the most popular tourist restaurants. A list of stores against whom complaints have been lodged is maintained by the local police department. Remember that if you arrive at any shop in a **rickshaw** or **taxi**, the prices of anything you buy will be inflated to cover the driver's commission. If you're planning on buying, ask to be dropped off nearby, and then walk to the shop.

Listings

Airlines Indian Airlines, *Hotel Clarks Shiraz* ☏0562/222 6821; Jet, *Hotel Clarks Shiraz* ☏0562/222 6527.

Banks and exchange There are two ATMs at Cantonment railway station, and a few dotted around the city (marked on the maps on p.155 & p.157). The State Bank of India is just south of Taj Rd in the Cantonment (Amex travellers' cheques not accepted); Allahabad Bank is in the *Hotel Clarks Shiraz*. There are several private exchange offices in Taj Ganj, and in the Tourist Complex Area around *Amar Yatri Niwas* and *Mansingh Palace* hotels, including Varun Forex, opposite *Amar Yatri Niwas* on Fatehabad Rd.

Hospitals Clean and dependable private hospitals with English-speaking doctors: SR Hospital, Namner Cross Roads ☏0562/242 1362; GG Nursing Home, 106/2 Sanjay Place ☏0562/285 3952; Pushpanjali, Delhi Gate ☏0562/252 7566 to 8. The District Hospital, MG Rd, Chipitola ☏0562/236 3043 gives free treatment, and may be preferable for minor injuries. Avoid backstreet clinics, even if recommended by your hotel manager, and in particular, if you fall ill with what appears to be food poisoning, do not go to a clinic or doctor suggested by someone in the restaurant concerned.

Internet access There's plenty of internet access available around town, particularly in Taj Ganj; rates virtually everywhere are Rs30/hr. Many hotels and guesthouses have their own internet connections too (*Tourists Rest House* and *Shah Jahan* for example; *Tourists Rest House* has wi-fi).

Photography A number of places around Taj Ganj can download and burn digital images to disc or make prints – try Moonlight Studio on the corner of West Gate and Chowk Kagzi.

Police There are police stations on Chowk Kagzi in Taj Ganj (☏0562/233 1015) and on Mahatma Gandhi Rd in Sadar Bazaar, slightly south of the intersection with Fatehpur Sikri Rd (☏0562/222 6561). Agra now has a dedicated tourist police force, specifically to protect tourists from crime; they can be contacted through UP Tourism or on ☏09454 402764.

Post The Head Post Office is on The Mall, near India Tourism.

Swimming The pools at most of Agra's hotels are usually reserved for the use of hotel guests only, though a few places admit outsiders on payment of a fee. These currently include the *Yamuna View* (Rs350) and *Clarks Shiraz* (Rs500), and (both near *Amar Yatri Niwas*) the *Amar* (Rs300) and *Mansingh Palace* (Rs400).

Moving on from Agra

Kheria airport, 7km out of town (☏0562/240 0569), has seasonal Kingfisher flights to Delhi, but given the time needed to check in and travel between airports and city centres, it's just as fast, and a lot cheaper and easier, to go by train. There have in the past been flights to Jaipur too, but none was operating at time of writing.

By train

Train tickets should be booked in advance at either Agra Cantonment or Agra Fort stations, both of which have fully computerized booking offices with dedicated tourist counters. Some services leave from Fort station, and some from Cantonment (and some call at both) – see box, p.174, for details. There are numerous services (over 25 daily; 2–5hr) from Agra Cantt to **Delhi**, but most are pretty slow; the #2189 is the fastest morning service but comes overnight from central India, so it is quite likely to be late (check on ☏133 or 0562/242 1039 if possible before you head down to the station); the same is true of the #2625, which comes all the way from South India. The early-morning #4211 is slower but may prove more convenient. Services into **Rajasthan** are surprisingly sparse – you might find it

173

Recommended trains from Agra

The following services are the fastest and/or most convenient in terms of departure/arrival times. Train timetables change frequently; check latest schedules either at your nearest station or online at ⓦ www.indianrail.gov.in before travel.

Destination	Name	No.	From	Departs	Arrives
Bharatpur	Udaipur Super Express	2965	AC	5.40pm (daily)	6.50pm
Bikaner	Howrah–Jodhpur Express	2307	AF	7.35pm (daily)	8.15am
Bundi/ Chittaurgarh	Haldighati Passenger	282	AF	7.05pm (daily)	7.13am/ 10.35am
Delhi	Intercity Express	4211	AC	6am (daily)	10.15am (ND)
	Mahakaushal Express	2189	AC	8.23am (daily)	11.35am (HN)
	Kerala Express	2625	AC	10.28am (daily)	1.40pm (ND)
	Taj Express	2279	AC	6.55pm (daily)	10pm (HN)
	Shatabdi Express	2001	AC	8.30pm (exc Fri)	10.30pm (ND)
Fatehpur Sikri	Haldighati Passenger	1772	AF	7.05pm	8.03pm
Jaipur	Marudhar Express	4863	AF	6.15am (daily)	11.30am
	Udaipur Super Express	2965	AC	5.40pm (daily)	10.13pm
Jodhpur	Marudhar Express	4863	AF	6.15am (daily)	6.20pm
	Howrah–Jodhpur Express	2307	AF	7.35pm (daily)	6.30am
Udaipur	Udaipur Super Express	2965	AC	5.40pm (daily)	6.10am

AC = Agra Cantonment, AF = Agra Fort, HN = Hazrat Nizamuddin, ND = New Delhi

easier to catch a bus to Jaipur and pick up onward connections there. Aside from those listed in the box, there are a couple of inconveniently timed services to **Sawai Madhopur** (for Ranthambore National Park) and **Kota**. There are also two or three daily services to **Bharatpur** (but no direct connections to Alwar).

By bus

Services to Rajasthan and frequent buses to Delhi (every ten minutes or so) leave from **Idgah bus stand**, on the western side of town. Private buses generally leave from **Ajmer Road**, nearby. Delhi buses leave you at Sarai Kale Khan, near Hazrat Nizamuddin station. Heading into **Rajasthan**, it's simplest to take a bus to **Jaipur** (half-hourly; 5–6hr) and pick up an onward connection there, though there are four direct buses a day to Ajmer (10hr), and half-hourly buses to Bharatpur (2hr). Buses for Fatehpur Sikri leave every half-hour from Idgah, and take a little over an hour. Agra has two more bus stands: Agra Fort, serving some local destinations, and the ISBT in Transport Nagar (see p.153), which mostly serves destinations to the north and west of Agra, though it also has half-hourly buses to Delhi.

Fatehpur Sikri

The ghost city of **FATEHPUR SIKRI**, former imperial capital of the great Mughal emperor **Akbar**, straddles the crest of a rocky ridge 40km southwest of Agra. It occupies the site of the formerly obscure village of Sikri (the "Fatehpur", meaning

"City of Victory", was added in 1573 following Akbar's brilliant military campaign in Gujarat). The city was built here between 1569 and 1585 as a result of the emperor's enthusiasm for the local Muslim divine **Sheikh Salim Chishti** (see p.181), though the move away from Agra may also have had something to do with Akbar's weariness with the crowds of Agra and his desire to create a new capital that was both an appropriate symbol of imperial power, and a sympathetic backdrop for the philosophical debates and artistic pursuits that were his passion. The buildings of the new palace would become the very embodiment of his unorthodox court, fusing Hindu and Muslim architectural traditions in a unique Indo–Islamic synthesis whose mixed styles say much about the religious and cultural tolerance of Akbar's reign.

Fatehpur Sikri's period of pre-eminence among the cities of the Mughal empire was brief, however, and after 1585 it would never again serve as the seat of the Mughal emperor. The reasons for the **city's abandonment** remain enigmatic. The most popular theory is that the city's water supply proved incapable of sustaining its population, though this hypothesis is no longer widely accepted – even after the city had been deserted, the nearby lake to its northwest still measured over 20km in circumference and yielded good water. A more likely explanation is that the city was simply the victim of the vagaries of the empire's day-to-day military contingencies. Shortly after the new capital was established, the empire was threatened by troubles in the Punjab, and Akbar moved to the more strategically situated Lahore to deal with them. These military preoccupations kept Akbar at Lahore for over a decade, and at the end of this period he decided, apparently for no particular reason, to return to Agra rather than Fatehpur Sikri. The demise of Fatehpur Sikri, therefore, may have been an almost accidental by-product of the emperor's transitory mood, rather than a meaningful strategic decision. If this suggests a certain wastefulness, in building a city and then abandoning it, then it's one that is wholly consistent with the Mughal character, which was never noted for its sense of economy.

Fatehpur Sikri is an enjoyably atmospheric place to stay, with a friendly village and scattering of simple but comfortable guesthouses. Most visitors visit on a day-trip from Agra, but if you're continuing on to Bharatpur, Alwar or even Jaipur, it can make sense to **stay overnight here**, and avoid the rather tedious hour-plus return bus journey from Agra – a plan which also gives you the chance

▲ Fatehpur Sikri

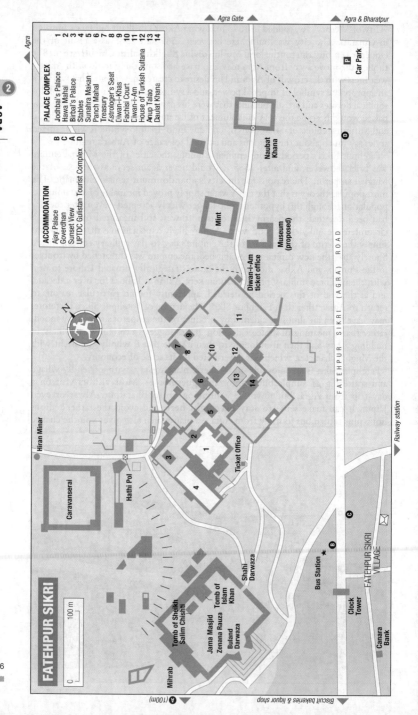

FATEHPUR SIKRI

100 m

PALACE COMPLEX

Jodhbai's Palace	1
Hawa Mahal	2
Birbal's Palace	3
Stables	4
Sunahra Makan	5
Panch Mahal	6
Treasury	7
Astrologer's Seat	8
Diwan-i-Khas	9
Pachisi Court	10
Diwan-i-Am	11
House of Turkish Sultana	12
Anup Talao	13
Daulat Khana	14

ACCOMMODATION

Ajay Palace	B
Goverdhan	C
Sunset View	A
UPTDC Gulistan Tourist Complex	D

Agra Gate

Agra & Bharatpur

Agra

Car Park

Naubat Khana

Mint

Museum (proposed)

Diwan-i-Am ticket office

FATEHPUR SIKRI (AGRA) ROAD

Railway station

Hiran Minar

Caravanserai

Hathi Pol

Ticket Office

Mihrab

Tomb of Sheikh Salim Chishti

Jama Masjid

Zenana Rauza

Tomb of Islam Khan

Buland Darwaza

Shahi Darwaza

Bus Station

FATEHPUR SIKRI VILLAGE

Clock Tower

Canara Bank

Biscuit bakeries & liquor shop

A (100m)

to give the palace remains the time they deserve, and to explore some of the little-visited outlying remains as well.

The Royal Palace

Shunning the Hindu tradition of aligning towns with the cardinal compass points, Akbar chose to construct his new capital following the natural features of the terrain, which is why the principal thoroughfare, town walls, and many of the most important buildings face southwest or northeast. The mosque and most private apartments do not follow the main axis, but face west towards Mecca, according to Muslim tradition, with the palace crowning the highest point on the ridge.

There are two **entrances** to the **Royal Palace** and court complex (daily sunrise–sunset; foreigners Rs260, Indian residents Rs20, video Rs25). Independent travellers mostly use the one on the west side, by Jodhbai's Palace; organized tours tend to use that on the east, by the Diwan-i-Am. Official **guides** offer their services at the booking office for Rs50–100. Note that there's nowhere to buy drinks in the palace, so take water in with you; you're not allowed to eat inside.

The palace complex's myriad buildings can be rather disorienting on first acquaintance. Despite the apparent disorder, however (not helped by the various spurious and confusing names applied to buildings throughout the palace), the complex actually divides neatly into two: the **mardana** (or men's quarters) on the east side, and the **zenana** (women's quarters) to the west. The only exception is the Diwan-i-Am (see below), on the far eastern side of the palace, which was open to the public at large, with its own entrance to avoid having the hoi polloi traipse through the main palace itself.

The Diwan-i-Am

A logical place to begin a tour of the palace complex is the **Diwan-i-Am**, where important festivals were held, and where citizens could exercise their right to petition the emperor. Unlike the ornate pillared Diwan-i-Am buildings at the forts in Agra and Delhi, it is basically just a large courtyard, surrounded by a continuous colonnaded walkway with Hindu-style square columns and capitals, broken only by the small pavilion, flanked by elaborately carved jali screens, in which the emperor himself would have sat – the position of the royal platform forced the emperor's subjects to approach him from the side in an attitude of humility.

The Diwan-i-Khas

A doorway in the northwest corner of the Diwan-i-Am leads to the centre of the *mardana* (men's quarters), a large, irregularly shaped enclosure dotted with a strikingly eclectic range of buildings. At the far (northern) end of the enclosure stands the tall **Diwan-i-Khas** (*Hall of Private Audience*), topped with four chhatris and embellished with the heavily carved Hindu-style brackets, large overhanging eaves and corbelled arches which are typical of the architecture of Fatehpur Sikri.

The interior of the building consists of a single high hall (despite the appearance outside of a two-storey building) centred on an elaborately corbelled column known as the **Throne Pillar**, supporting a large circular platform from which four balustraded bridges radiate outwards. Seated upon this throne, the emperor held discussions with representatives of diverse religions, aiming to synthesize India's religions into one. The pillar symbolizes this project by incorporating motifs drawn from Hinduism, Buddhism, Islam and Christianity. Eventually, the *ulemas* (Islamic jurists), reacting against all this, instigated an uprising, which Akbar ruthlessly crushed in 1581. He then evolved a concept of divine kingship, which the overall architecture of the Diwan-i-Khas, with its axial pillars radiating from a central point, serves to underline.

Next to the Diwan-i-Khas lies the three-roomed **Treasury**, its brackets embellished by mythical sea creatures, guardians of the treasures of the deep; it's also known as Ankh Michauli, meaning hide and seek, which it's said was played here – in fact both names are probably just fanciful inventions, and the building most likely served as a multipurpose pavilion which could be used for a variety of functions, as could most buildings in Mughal palaces. Attached to it is the so-called **Astrologer's Seat**, a small pavilion embellished with elaborate Jain carvings.

The Pachisi Court
In the middle of the courtyard, separating the Diwan-i-Khas from the buildings on the opposite (south) side of the complex, is the **Pachisi Court**, a giant board used to play *pachisi* (similar to ludo). Akbar is said to have been a fanatical player, using slave girls dressed in colourful costumes as live pieces. Abu'l Fazl, the court chronicler, related that at times "more than two hundred persons participated, and no one was allowed to go home until he had played sixteen rounds. This could take up to three months. If one of the players lost his patience and became restless, he was made to drink a cupful of wine. Seen superficially, this appears to be just a game. But His Majesty pursues higher objectives. He weighs up the talents of his people and teaches them to be affable."

House of the Turkish Sultana
Diagonally opposite the *pachisi* board, the **House of the Turkish Sultana** (or Anup Talao Pavilion) gained its name from the popular belief that it was the residence of one of Akbar's favourite wives, the Sultana Ruqayya Begum – though this seems unlikely given its location in the centre of the men's quarters. The name was probably made up by nineteenth-century guides to titillate early tourists, and the building is more likely to have served as a simple pleasure pavilion. Its superbly carved stone walls are covered with a profusion of floral and geometrical designs, plus some partially vandalized animal carvings. Legend has it that the great musician Mian Tansen once sang *Deepak*, the raga of fire, here. So effective was his performance that he grew hotter and hotter, until his daughter had to come to the rescue by performing the rain raga, *Malhar*. Understandably nervous at this great responsibility, she faltered on the seventh note of the scale, thereby creating one of North India's most stirring ragas – the *Mian ki Malhar* – with its famously expressive emphasis on this ultimate note of the raga, on which Tansen's daughter had inadvertently lingered. Happily, the raga had the desired effect; rain fell, and Tansen was saved.

South of here is the **Anup Talao** (Peerless Pool), a pretty little ornamental pond divided by four walkways connected to a small "island" in the middle – a layout strangely reminiscent of the raised walkways inside the Diwan-i-Khas.

The Daulat Khana
Facing the Turkish Sultana's house from the other side of the Anup Talao are Akbar's former private sleeping and living quarters, the **Daulat Khana** (Abode of Fortune). The room on the ground floor with alcoves in its walls was the emperor's library, where he would be read to (he himself was illiterate) from a collection of 50,000 manuscripts he allegedly took everywhere with him. Behind the library is the imperial sleeping chamber, the **Khwabgah** (House of Dreams), with an enormous raised bed in its centre.

The Panch Mahal
One of Fatehpur Sikri's most famous structures, the **Panch Mahal** or "Five-Storeyed Palace", looms northwest of here, marking the beginning of the **zenana** (women's quarters) which make up the entire western side of the palace complex.

Akbar's harem

Although remembered primarily for his liberal approach to religion, Akbar was typically Mughal in his attitude to women, whom he collected in much the same way as a philatelist amasses stamps. At its height of splendour, the **royal harem** at Fatehpur Sikri held around five thousand women, guarded by a legion of eunuchs. Its doors were closed to outsiders, but rumours permeated the sandstone walls and several notable travellers were smuggled inside the Great Mughals' seraglios, leaving for posterity often lurid accounts of the emperors' private lives.

The size of Akbar's harem grew in direct proportion to his empire. With each new conquest, the defeated rulers and nobles would make gifts of their most beautiful daughters, who, together with their maidservants, would be installed in the luxurious royal **zenana**. In all, the emperor is thought to have kept three hundred wives; their ranks were swollen by a constant flow of concubines (*kaniz*), dancing girls (*kanchni*) and female slaves (*bandis*), or "silver bodied damsels with musky tresses" as one chronicler described them, purchased from markets across Asia. Screened from public view by ornately pierced stone *jali* windows were women from the four corners of the Mughal empire, as well as Afghanis, Turks, Iranians, Arabs, Tibetans, Russians and Abyssinians, and even one Portuguese, sent as presents or tribute.

The **eunuchs** who presided over them came from similarly diverse backgrounds. While some were hermaphrodites, others had been forcibly castrated, either as punishment following defeat on the battlefield, or after having been donated by their fathers as payment of backdated revenue – an all too common custom at the time.

Akbar is said to have consumed prodigious quantities of Persian wine, *araq* (a spirit distilled from sugar cane), bhang and opium. The lavish dance recitals held in the harem, as well as sexual liaisons conducted on the top pavilion of the Panch Mahal and in the *zenana* itself, were doubtless fuelled by these substances. Over time, Akbar's hedonistic ways incurred the disapproval of his highest clerics – the *Ulema*. The Koran expressly limits the number of wives a man may take to four, but one verse also admits a lower form of marriage, known as *muta*, which was more like an informal pact, and could be entered into with non-Muslims. Akbar's abuse of this long-lapsed law was heavily criticized by his Sunni head priest during their religious disquisitions.

What life must actually have been like for the women who lived in Akbar's harem one can only imagine, but it is known that alcoholism and drug addiction were widespread, and that some also risked their lives to conduct illicit affairs with male lovers, smuggled in disguised as physicians or under heavy Muslim veils. If the reports of a couple of foreign adventurers who secretly gained access to Jahangir's seraglio are to be believed, the eunuchs were also required to intercept anything (other than the emperor) that might excite the women's passion.

In fact, the notion that the harem was a gilded prison whose inmates whiled their lifetimes away in idle vanity and dalliance is something of a myth. Many of the women in the *zenana* were immensely rich in their own right, and wielded enormous influence on the court. Jahangir's wife, Nur Jahan, virtually ran the empire from behind the screen of purdah during the last five years of her husband's ailing reign, while her mother-in-law owned a ship that traded between Surat and the Red Sea, a tradition continued by Shah Jahan's daughter, who grew immensely wealthy through her business enterprises.

Partly as a result of the money and power at the women's disposal, jealousies in the harem were also rife, and the work of maintaining order and calm among the thousands of foster mothers, aunties, the emperor's relatives and all his wives, minor wives, paramours, musicians, dancers, amazons and slaves, was a major preoccupation. As Akbar's court chronicler wryly observed, "The government of the kingdom is but an amusement compared with such a task, for it is within the (harem) that intrigue is enthroned."

The palace tapers to a final single kiosk and is supported by 176 columns of varying designs; the ground floor contains 84 pillars – an auspicious number in Hindu astrology. The open spaces between the pillars were originally covered with latticed screens, so that ladies of the *zenana* could observe goings-on in the courtyard of the *mardana* below without themselves being seen.

The Sunahra Makan

Directly behind the Panch Mahal, a courtyard garden was reserved for the *zenana* (harem). The adjoining **Sunahra Makan** (Golden House), also known as Mariam's House, is variously thought to have been the home of the emperor's mother or of Akbar's wife Mariam. It is enlivened by the faded remains of paintings on its walls (whose now vanished golden paint gave the pavilion its name); by the lines of verse penned by Abu'l Fazl, inscribed around the ceiling in blue bands; and by the quaint little carvings tucked into the brackets supporting the roof, including several elephants and a tiny carving of Rama attended by Hanuman (on the north side of the building, facing the *zenana* courtyard garden).

Jodhbai's Palace

Solemnly presiding over the whole complex is the main harem, known as **Jodhbai's Palace**. The residence of several of the emperor's senior wives, this striking building is the grandest and largest in the entire city, and looks decidedly Hindu even in the eclectic context of Fatehpur Sikri, having been modelled after Rajput palaces such as those at Gwalior and Orchha. Surrounding the central courtyard are four self-contained raised terraces; those on the north and south sides are surmounted by unusual roofs, thought to imitate the shape of bamboo and thatch, with traces of blue-glazed tile that forms an eye-catching, distinctly Persian, counterpoint to the building's rich red sandstone.

On the north side of the palace, the **Hawa Mahal** (Palace of the Winds), a small screened tower with a delicately carved chamber, was designed to catch the evening breeze, while a raised covered walkway, lined with five large chhatris, leads from here to a (now vanished) lake.

Birbal's Palace

Northwest of Jodhbai's Palace lies a third women's palace, known as **Birbal's Palace** – though this is another misnomer, as Birbal, Akbar's favourite courtier, was a man and would have been most unwelcome in the middle of the *zenana*. It's more likely to have been the residence of two of Akbar's senior wives. The palace is even more lavishly carved than Jodhbai's, covered in a profusion of decoration including a ceiling crafted to resemble a canopy of blossoms. The whole thing looks more like a South Indian temple than a Mughal palace – not that surprising, really, given that many of the sculptural features used here have been lifted straight out of Hindu temple-building traditions – though Islamic touches can be seen too in the geometrical patterns which cover parts of the facade, the two styles muddled up together in an extraordinarily lavish, if decidedly haphazard, way.

South of Birbal's Palace stretches the large rectangular enclosure, surrounded by small rooms popularly referred to as the palace **stables**, though it's unlikely that so many horses would have been quartered so close to the ladies' palaces – it's more probable that the building was used to accommodate some kind of market, or perhaps the female servants of the ladies of the *zenana*.

Outlying remains

Further significant remains of the palace complex lie scattered among the surrounding rocky hills. These can be visited for free and make for a pleasant ramble, especially towards sunset or early in the morning. From the main Agra road, just west of the *Gulistan* hotel, a track heads north, emerging on the side-road up to the palace close to the **Naubat Khana**, a caravanserai-type structure flanked by an impressive pair of gateways. Heading west from here, the road passes a small **mint** and the Diwan-i-Am ticket office, where a rocky little path downhill to your right brings you to the small road that runs along the northern edge of the city. Turn left and walk along the road for fine views of its myriad chhatris and domes before reaching the impressive **Hathi Pol** (Elephant Gate), decorated with the vandalized remains of large sculptured elephants. Through the gate and down past the large **Caravanserai**, you reach the strange **Hiran Minar**, a slender tower studded with dozens of stone protuberances, said to be modelled after elephant tusks.

Jama Masjid

At the southwestern corner of the palace complex, with the village of Fatehpur Sikri nestling at its base, stands the **Jama Masjid** (daily dawn to dusk) or Dargah Mosque, one of the finest in the whole of India. Unfortunately, the mosque is rife with self-appointed "guides" (around Rs20 for a tour) who make it all but impossible to enjoy the place in peace.

The alignment of the entire palace complex, which faces west instead of following the ridge, was determined by the orientation of the mosque's mihrab (prayer niche) towards Mecca. The building of the mosque was apparently completed in 1571, before work on the palace itself commenced, showing the religious significance which Akbar accorded the entire site thanks to its connections with Sheikh Salim Chishti (see box below).

The neck-cricking **Buland Darwaza** (Great Gate), a spectacular entrance scaled by an impressive flight of steps, was added around 1576 to commemorate a military campaign in Gujarat. Flanked by domed kiosks, the archway of the simple sandstone memorial is inscribed with a message from the Koran: "Said Jesus Son of Mary (peace be on him): The world is but a bridge – pass over without building houses on it. He who hopes for an hour hopes for eternity; the world is an hour – spend it in prayer for the rest is unseen." The numerous horseshoes nailed to the

Sheikh Salim Chishti

During the early years of Akbar's reign, the young emperor was much troubled by the fact that none of his numerous wives had succeeded in producing a male heir who survived beyond infancy. The disconsolate monarch consulted a certain elderly Muslim holy man, **Sheikh Salim**, a member of the Chishti order, who lived a reclusive life atop a hill at Sikri, west of Agra. The Sheikh Salim obligingly predicted the birth of three sons to the emperor. Soon after, one of Akbar's wives fell pregnant. She was moved to Sikri and subsequently gave birth, on August 30, 1569, to a son, the future Jahangir (though he was originally named Salim, in honour of the divine). The second and third sons were subsequently born, as predicted, and the grateful Akbar chose to show his respect by constructing a huge new mosque and palace at Sikri (significantly, the mosque preceded the palace) in the saint's honour. Sheikh Salim himself, who was already almost 90 years old, died soon after; all three sons survived to adulthood, however, though their constant rebellions against their father (and one another) were to blight Akbar's later years.

The *dargah* still attracts women who come here to pray for offspring, tying string onto the marble screen; when entering the main chamber, visitors cover their heads with cloth as a mark of respect. During Ramadan, an *urs* is held here, attracting *qawwals* (singers of Sufi songs) from all over the country.

doors here date from the beginning of the twentieth century – an odd instance of British folk superstition in this very Islamic place.

The gate leads into a vast cloistered courtyard, far larger than any previous mosque in India. The **prayer hall**, on the west (left) side, is the focus of the mosque, punctuated by an enormous gateway. The pointed exterior arches are impeccably Islamic in design, but the inside shows the architectural miscegenation typical of Fatehpur Sikri, with the dome supported by decidedly Hindu-looking columns and pot-shaped corbels, perhaps the work of Gujarati craftsmen who were brought to work on the new mosque following Akbar's dramatic conquest of the region.

More eye-catching is the exquisite **Tomb of Sheikh Salim Chishti** (see p.181), directly ahead as one enters the courtyard. Much of this was originally crafted in red sandstone and only later faced in marble: the beautiful lattice screens – another design feature probably imported from Gujarat, though it would later become a staple of Mughal architecture – are unusually intricate, with striking serpentine exterior brackets supporting the eaves. To the right stands the lattice-screen **Tomb of Islam Khan**, housing the remains of the grandson of Sheikh Salim Chishti, who later became the Mughal governor of Bengal, along with other related nobles, while behind lies the **Zenana Rauza** (Tomb of the Royal Ladies), housing numerous tightly packed graves of various ladies of the *zenana*.

Practicalities

Buses leave either from the crowded bus stand in the centre of the village or from the bus stop on the bypass near Agra Gate, about 1.5km from town (about Rs10 by tonga from the village) – it's usually quickest to pick up a bus from Agra Gate, especially if you're heading to Jaipur (every 30min; 4hr). Services from the bus stand itself go to Agra's Idgah bus stand (every 30min; 1hr–1hr 30min) and to Bharatpur (hourly; 30–45min). There are shared Jeeps from the village to Agra (Rs25), but they go very full, the driving isn't marvellous, and they frequently have accidents. Transport around the village takes the form of tongas (horse-drawn carriages) and auto-rickshaws, but for most people it's just as easy to walk. There are four daily **trains** from Fatehpur Sikri to Agra, and an overnight service to Kota, Bundi and Chittaurgarh; the station also has a computer reservation office.

Accommodation and eating

You'll probably **eat** where you stay. If you want to go out, try the *Goverdhan* or the *Ajay Palace* hotel. Fatehpur Sikri's delicious biscuits are not to be missed – you can savour them hot out of the oven each evening at the bakeries on the lane leading up from the bazaar to the Jami Masjid.

Ajay Palace Agra Rd ☎05613/282950. Simple hotel in the village, with small, plain, but very clean rooms (though hot water comes in buckets), and a nice little rooftop terrace. ❶

Goverdhan Buland Gate Rd, just east of the bus stand ☎05613/282643, ⓦwww .hotelfatehpursikriviews.com. A wide range of well-kept rooms arranged around a neat lawn, as well as good food (made with filtered or mineral water) and a friendly and helpful proprietor. ❷–❹

Sunset View 100m west of the Jama Masjid ☎05613/283129. Backpacker guesthouse offering neat, clean if basic rooms, and superb views over the Jama Masjid and the countryside beyond. ❶

UPDTC Gulistan Tourist Complex Agra Rd, 1km east of the village ☎05613/282490. A low-rise, modern building in red sandstone, which looks rather like an academic institution, and has decent if functional rooms, plus a restaurant, a pool room and a small bar. ❸

Jaipur and eastern Rajasthan

The International boundaries on this map are neither purported to be correct nor authentic by Survey of India directives. Publisher.

N

PAKISTAN

HARYANA

UTTAR PRADESH

GUJARAT

MADHYA PRADESH

0   100 km

CHAPTER 3 # Highlights

Jaipur City Palace The historic home of the maharajas of Jaipur, with sumptuously decorated courtyards and pavilions, and an absorbing collection of royal mementoes. See p.139

* **Shopping in Jaipur** Shop till you drop in Rajasthan's crafts capital, with endless bazaars crammed full of traditional handmade local artefacts. See p.202

Amber Fort Eastern Rajasthan's most dramatic fort, perched on a rugged hilltop on the edge of Jaipur. See p.205

* **Nawalgarh** One of the most atmospheric towns in the fascinating Shekhawati region, its dusty streets crammed full of ornate, crumbling havelis decorated with quirky murals. See p.213

* **Keoladeo National Park, Bharatpur** Flocks of rare birds – and birdwatchers – travel from across Asia and Europe each winter to visit this remarkable wetland sanctuary. See p.238

* **Ranthambore National Park** India's most popular wildlife park, and one of the easiest places in the world to see tigers in the wild, thanks to its large and exhibitionist population of big cats. See p.240

▲ Jaipur City Palace

Jaipur and eastern Rajasthan

A short journey by road or rail from either Delhi or Agra, the dynamic city of **Jaipur** is the capital of Rajasthan and easily its largest and busiest city, with a population of well over three million and an upwardly mobile skyline which seems to sprout smart modern high-rises on an almost weekly basis. Jaipur is also one of Rajasthan's most touristed destinations and home to a rich clutch of sights, most of them built by the ruling maharajas, whose considerable military power and seemingly bottomless personal coffers are encapsulated in the flamboyant sequence of forts, palaces and other creations which dot the city – a highlight of any visit to Rajasthan, if you can cope with the city's dense crowds and gridlocked traffic.

North of Jaipur, and in complete contrast to it, the fascinating region of **Shekhawati** remains one of Rajasthan's most absorbing – and least visited – regions. Dozens of dusty little towns lie scattered around the desert here, their streets lined with magnificent, decaying havelis constructed by wealthy local merchants during the nineteenth and early twentieth centuries, many of them painted with superb murals showing everything from traditional religious scenes to fancifully inaccurate pictures of newfangled European inventions – trains, telephones and flying machines.

The area east and south of Jaipur is of exceptional wildlife interest, being home to a pair of world-famous national parks: the celebrated ornithological wonderland of the **Keoladeo National Park**, just outside the engrossing little town of **Bharatpur**; and the even more popular **Ranthambore National Park** further south, which offers as good a chance of spotting tigers in the wild as anywhere on the planet. Despite the name, you're unlikely to see any tigers at the region's third major national park, the **Sariska Tiger Reserve**, although the reserve has plenty of other wildlife and offers a peaceful alternative to the area's more touristed parks. Close by, the absorbing little city of **Alwar** is a rewarding destination in its own right, with a fine old city palace and a craggy hilltop fort surrounded by many kilometres of dramatic switchback walls.

Jaipur and around

A flamboyant showcase of Rajasthani architecture, **JAIPUR**, 260km southwest of Delhi and 230km west of Agra, has long been established on tourist itineraries as the third corner of India's "Golden Triangle". At the heart of Jaipur lies the **Pink City**, the old walled quarter whose **bazaars** rank among the most vibrant in Asia, renowned for their hand-dyed and embroidered textiles, jewellery, and the best selection of precious stones and metals in India. For all its colour, however, Jaipur's traffic, crowds and pushy traders can make it a taxing place to explore, and many visitors stay just long enough to catch a train to more laidback destinations further west or south – though if you can put up with the urban stress, the city's forward-looking residents and commercial hustle and bustle offer a stimulating contrast to most other places in the state.

If you're anywhere near Jaipur in March, don't miss the **Elephant Festival**, one of India's most flamboyant parades, celebrated with full Rajput pomp during Holi (March; see p.53).

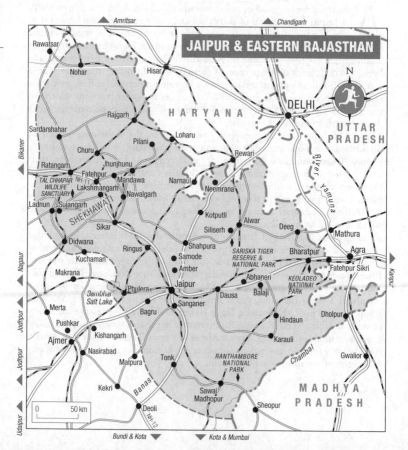

Some history

Established in 1727, Jaipur is one of Rajasthan's youngest cities, founded by (and named after) **Jai Singh II**, ruler of the **Kachchwaha** royal family, one of the most powerful Rajput dynasties, who controlled a sizeable portion of northern Rajasthan from their venerable palace-fort at nearby Amber. Jai Singh's decision to move the Kachchwaha capital from Amber to Jaipur represented a landmark in Rajput political thinking. The region's major cities had hitherto been located in positions of maximum military strength, usually occupying easily defensible positions atop craggy hilltops overlooking the surrounding plains. Jaipur was the Rajput's first city to place mercantile above military considerations, occupying a commercially strategic location on the plains next to the main Ajmer to Agra highway – one that quickly attracted traders from across the region.

Jai Singh's fruitful 43-year reign was followed by an inevitable battle for succession, and the state was thrown into turmoil. Much of its territory was lost to the Marathas and Jats, and the British quickly moved in to take advantage of Rajput infighting. In 1818 a **treaty** was signed whereby the British agreed to provide military protection to the Kachchwaha dynasty in return for an annual tribute and the maharajas' continuing loyalty. This alliance survived the 1857 uprising and lasted through until Independence, after which Jaipur merged with the states of Mewar, Bikaner, Jodhpur and Jaisalmer, becoming **state capital** of Rajasthan in 1956.

Today, with a population of over three million, Jaipur is far and away Rajasthan's largest and most economically developed city – some estimates put it among the world's 25 fastest-growing urban centres, with an annual population growth of over 3.5 percent. Smart modern high-rises and shopping malls are mushrooming all around the city, and the slightly frantic pace of development is in striking contrast to the traditional, rural rhythms of life elsewhere in the state. Problems remain, however. Plans for a new metro within the next decade may do something to ease the city's creaking infrastructure and appalling traffic, although no one has yet come up with a convincing way of securing the city's long-term water needs in the face of Rajasthan's chronic ongoing drought.

Arrival, information and city transport

Jaipur's **railway station** lies 1.5km west of the Pink City, close to many of the city's hotels; state buses from all over Rajasthan and further afield pull in at the **Inter-state Bus Terminal** on Station Road. Arriving from Delhi or Agra, you skirt the southern side of the city, stopping briefly first at Narain Singh Circle, where rickshaw-wallahs frequently board the bus and, with the connivance of the bus driver, announce that it's the end of the line ("bus going to yard"); this is a ploy to get you onto their rickshaws and into a hotel that pays commission. The city's modern Sanganer **airport** is Rajasthan's only international airport and has flights to and from major cities across the rest of the state and India-wide, as well as Sharjah, Dubai and Muscat in the Gulf. The airport is 15km south of the centre; if flying out of Jaipur, make sure you know which of the two **terminals** you're going to: the sparkling new Terminal 1 handles international and Air India flights; Terminal 2 handles other domestic carriers. There are no buses from the airport into town at present; a rickshaw will cost around Rs200, a taxi Rs350–400.

Information

The **RTDC** has tourist information offices on Platform 1 of the railway station (daily 7am–10pm; ☏0141/231 5714); on MI Road opposite the GPO (daily

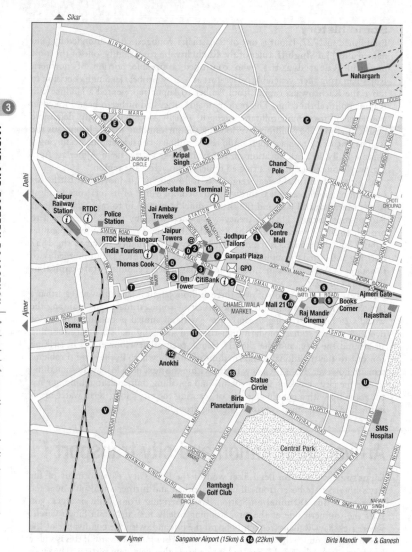

8am–8pm; ☎0141/237 5466); and on platform 3 at the state bus terminal (daily 9.30am–5pm). **RTDC tours** (see p.190) can be booked through any of these offices. There's an **India Tourism** office at the *Khasa Kothi* hotel (Mon–Fri 9am–6pm, Sat 9am–1.30pm; ☎0141/237 2200), with a good range of leaflets and countrywide information. The monthly *Jaipur City Guide* (Rs40), available at some hotels, bookshops and newspaper stalls, has **listings** of all the latest events in the city.

City transport and tours

Jaipur is very spread out, and although it's possible to explore the Pink City on foot (despite the crowds), you may need some form of transport to get you there

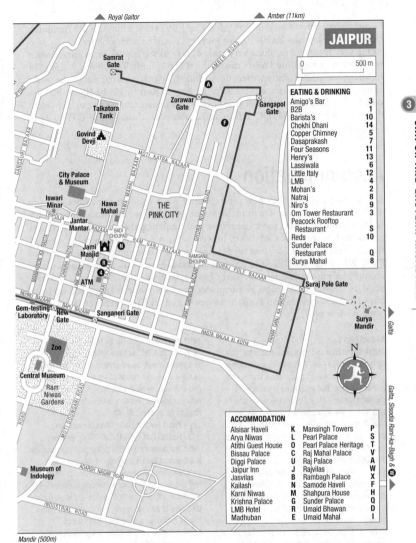

 Royal Gaitor   Amber (11km)

JAIPUR

3

JAIPUR AND EASTERN RAJASTHAN | Arrival, information and city transport

0   500 m

Samrat Gate

Zorawar Gate

Gangapol Gate

EATING & DRINKING

Amigo's Bar	3
B2B	1
Barista's	10
Chokhi Dhani	14
Copper Chimney	5
Dasaprakash	7
Four Seasons	11
Henry's	13
Lassiwala	6
Little Italy	12
LMB	4
Mohan's	2
Natraj	8
Niro's	9
Om Tower Restaurant	3
Peacock Rooftop Restaurant	S
Reds	10
Sunder Palace Restaurant	Q
Surya Mahal	8

Talkatora Tank

Govind Devji

City Palace & Museum

Iswari Minar

Hawa Mahal

Jantar Mantar

THE PINK CITY

Jami Masjid

ATM

Gem-testing Laboratory

New Gate

Sanganeri Gate

Suraj Pole Gate

Surya Mandir

Zoo

Central Museum

Ram Niwas Gardens

Museum of Indology

N

Galta

Galta, Sisodia Rani-ka-Bagh &

ACCOMMODATION

Alsisar Haveli	K	Mansingh Towers	P
Arya Niwas	L	Pearl Palace	S
Atithi Guest House	O	Pearl Palace Heritage	T
Bissau Palace	C	Raj Mahal Palace	V
Diggi Palace	U	Raj Palace	A
Jaipur Inn	J	Rajvilas	W
Jasvilas	B	Rajmahal Palace	X
Kailash	N	Samode Haveli	F
Karni Niwas	M	Shahpura House	H
Krishna Palace	G	Sunder Palace	Q
LMB Hotel	R	Umaid Bhawan	D
Madhuban	E	Umaid Mahal	I

Mandir (500m)

from your hotel. It's best to avoid the morning and evening rush hours, especially within the Pink City. **Auto-rickshaws** are available all over the city, as are **cycle rickshaws**, though these can take forever to get anywhere in the heavy traffic. **Prepaid auto-rickshaws** can be booked at the kiosks (open 24hr) in front of the railway station (turn left as you exit the station and look for a small pink hut) and in front of the bus station (on Station Road next to the easternmost of the two entrances). Rates for these are much cheaper than you're likely to get on the street (Rs380/Rs212 for a full/half day's hire, for example, or just Rs84 for a one-way ride to Amber). **Cars with driver** can be rented through most hotels or through any RTDC office, usually costing around Rs900–1000 per day. Alternatively, **radio taxis** offer the convenience of fixed, metered rates and rarely take more than twenty minutes for a pick-up; try Meri Car (☎0141/418 8888; Rs25 minimum charge, Rs10/km plus Rs50–100 for journeys outside the city centre).

One very inexpensive, albeit very rushed, way to see Jaipur's main attractions is on one of the two **guided tours** run by the RTDC (5hr half-day tour, Rs150; 9hr full-day tour, Rs200; entrance fees not included), which cram in most of the major city sights. They also run a "Pink City by Night" tour (6.30–10.30pm; Rs250), which includes dinner at Nahargarh Fort. Tours depart from (and can be booked through) any of the RTDC offices listed above or through the RTDC *Hotel Gangaur* on MI Road.

Accommodation

As a major tourist and business centre, Jaipur has a wide range of **hotels**, many of them excellent value. There are plenty of good budget options, while the city also has some of India's most impressive and opulent **palace hotels**. Few places are located in the Pink City itself, however; most accommodation lies west of the city centre, along (or close to) MI Road and in the upmarket suburb of Bani Park. Wherever you choose to stay, it's a good idea to **book ahead**, particularly around the Pushkar camel *mela* (early Nov) and the Elephant Festival (first half of March). Note that almost all the places listed below offer **free pick-up** from bus or train station if you book in advance, and all have **internet access** (and often wi-fi as well).

Budget

Atithi Guest House 1 Park House Scheme, just off MI Rd ☎0141/237 8679, ℮atithijaipur@hotmail.com. Long-established guesthouse that is still one of the nicer budget places in town, with pleasant modern tiled rooms (air-cooled and a/c) and an attractive rooftop terrace. A smart new in-house Indian veg restaurant and coffee shop should have opened by the time you read this. ❸–❹

Jaipur Inn Shiv Marg, Bani Park ☎0141/220 1121, ⓦwww.jaipurinn.com. Reliable, pleasantly old-fashioned budget option, with comfortable and well-equipped rooms with TV and (optional) a/c, plus nightly buffets on the breezy rooftop. ❸–❹

Kailash Johari Bazaar ☎0141/257 7372. One of the few budget hotels in the Pink City itself. Rooms are a bit shabby and pokey, but perfectly comfortable (although avoid the noisy ones directly overlooking Johari Bazaar), while the brilliantly central location can't be beaten. ❸

Karni Niwas C-5 Motilal Atal Rd (behind *Hotel Neelam*) ☎0141/236 5433, ⓦwww.hotelkarniniwas.com. Long-running budget stalwart, with comfortable air-cooled and a/c rooms (either in the old-fashioned main building or the more modern extension) and pleasant communal seating on outside balconies overlooking a small garden. ❸–❹

Krishna Palace E-26 Durga Marg, Bani Park ☎0141/220 1395, ⓦwww.krishnapalace.com. Set in a rather grand, haveli-style building, this friendly, family-run budget option offers a range of bright and comfortable air-cooled and a/c rooms, all newly renovated and decorated with traditional Rajasthani touches. ❷–❹

Pearl Palace Hari Kishan Somani Marg, Hathroi Fort ☎0141/237 3700, ⓦwww.hotelpearlpalace.com. One of the best guesthouses in Rajasthan, with a selection of spotless and excellent-value modern air-cooled and a/c rooms (a few with shared bathroom) attractively decorated with local arts and crafts. The well-drilled staff can take care of all your needs, and there's also 24hr money exchange and an excellent rooftop restaurant (see p.200). Advance bookings strongly recommended. ❷–❸

Pearl Palace Heritage 54 Gopal Bari, Lane no. 2, Ajmer Rd ☎0141/237 5242, ⓦwww.pearlpalaceheritage.com. Attractive new sister-hotel to the excellent *Pearl Palace*, with a slightly more upmarket heritage theme – each of the spacious a/c rooms is individually themed (Jaisalmer, Colonial, Shekhawati, etc), complete with traditional wooden doors, assorted artworks and artefacts, and a superb sequence of stone carvings adorning the first-floor corridors – a miniature museum in itself. Given the quality, room rates are a steal. ❸–❺

Sunder Palace Sanjay Marg, Hathroi Fort, Ajmer Rd ☏0141/236 0878, ⓦwww .sunderpalace.com. One of the city's standout budget options, with spotless, attractively decorated modern rooms (air-cooled or a/c) at very competitive prices. There's a choice of garden and rooftop restaurants (see p.201), while the two friendly brothers who run the place can also take care of money exchange, travel arrangements and anything else you're likely to think of. Advance bookings strongly recommended. ❷–❹

Mid-range

Arya Niwas Sansar Chandra Rd ☏0141/237 2456, ⓦwww.aryaniwas.com. Dependable old hotel, arranged around a couple of intimate court-yards, with a lovely expanse of lawn and spacious veranda out front. Rooms (most of which have been recently renovated) are comfy and nicely furnished; all come with a/c, apart from a few air-cooled singles. Popular with tour groups. ❹–❺

Bissau Palace Khetri House Rd ☏0141/230 4371, ⓦwww.bissaupalace.com. Tucked away in a down-at-heel part of town, this attractive heritage hotel is less flash than others in Jaipur but has bags of old-world atmosphere, especially the time-warped antique library and *sheesh mahal*; also has a decent-sized pool and Ayurveda room. Discounts of 20–30 percent in summer. ❺

Diggi Palace SMS Hospital Rd ☏0141/237 3091, ⓦwww.hoteldiggipalace.com. One of the city's most appealing heritage hotels, occupying a characterful old haveli set amid huge gardens in a conveniently central location. Rooms are a mixed bunch, and the air-cooled budget rooms are rather drab. It's worth splashing out on one of the more expensive traditional-style rooms in the main building, or (nicer still) one of the stylish modern "Premium" rooms in the new annexe. ❹–❼

LMB Hotel Johari Bazaar ☏0141/256 5844, ⓦwww.hotellmb.com. Passable mid-range hotel next door to the well-known *LMB* restaurant and right in the thick of the Pink City action. The cheaper "Executive" rooms are neat and comfort-able; the more expensive "Royal Deluxe" rooms have nothing to recommend them apart from some spectacularly ugly furniture. Avoid the noisy rooms overlooking Johari Bazaar. ❻

Madhuban D-237 Behari Marg, Bani Park ☏0141/220 0033, ⓦwww.madhuban.net. Less imposing than the city's other heritage hotels – it's more of an overgrown suburban villa than a genuine palace – though also better value than most, with attractively furnished rooms (though some of the cheaper ones are a bit small) and plenty of quaint

Rajasthani decorative touches, plus a pleasant garden and small pool round the back. ❺

Umaid Bhawan D1-2A Off Bank Rd, Bani Park ☏0141/220 6426, ⓦwww.umaidbhawan.com. Flamboyantly decorated heritage hotel, full of delicately painted murals, old wooden furnishings and other Rajasthani artefacts. Rooms (all a/c) are spacious and cool, and there's also a pool. Discounts in summer. ❺

Umaid Mahal C-20/B-2 Bihari Marg, Bani Park ☏0141/220 1952, ⓦwww.umaidmahal.com. Extravagantly decorated heritage-style modern hotel, with virtually every surface covered in colourful traditional murals. The spacious a/c rooms are attractively furnished with antique-style wooden furniture, and there's also a nice basement pool and bar. Check the website for discounts. ❺

Expensive

Alsisar Haveli Sansar Chandra Rd ☏0141/236 8290, ⓦwww.alsisar.com. An unexpectedly upmarket haven in a ramshackle part of town, occupying a large and immaculately modernized century-old haveli. It's not the most atmospheric heritage hotel in Jaipur, though it's comfy and well run, and the pool is one of the prettiest in town. ❼

Jasvilas C-9, Sawai Jai Singh Highway, Bani Park ☏0141/220 4638, ⓦwww.jasvilas.com. Welcoming family-run guesthouse in a gracious old suburban mansion, with spacious and comfortable a/c rooms, a neat little pool and attractive enclosed gardens. The adjacent *Meghniwas*, occupying the other half of the same building, is similar, but not quite as nice. ❻

Mansingh Towers Sansar Chandra Rd ☏0141/237 8771, ⓦwww.mansinghhotels.com. Modern hotel occupying an attractive red-sandstone building with graceful Rajput decorative touches, offering cosy (if characterless) rooms and a conveniently central location. Guests can use the pool, health club and spa at the *Hotel Mansingh* next door. ❽

Raj Mahal Palace Sardar Patel Marg ☏0141/510 5666, ⓦwww.royalfamilyjaipur.com. This former palace of Jai Singh's favourite maharani has plenty of rather dog-eared period charm, with a grand old banqueting hall, wood-panelled library and spacious lawns, plus a medium-size pool, although the large, old-fashioned rooms (all a/c) are rather gloomy and somewhat past their best. ❼

Raj Palace Zorawar Gate, Amer Rd ☏0141/263 4077, ⓦwww.rajpalace.com. One of the smartest addresses in Jaipur, regularly patronized by

Bollywood film stars and Arab sheikhs. The central location on the edge of the Pink City can't be beaten, while the setting – in a wonderful old haveli of 1727 arranged around a pair of idyllic courtyards – is pure romance. Rooms (including one decorated entirely in gold) are all individually styled and stuffed full of historical artefacts and curios, while facilities include a beautiful little pool and sumptuous spa. Rooms from around $500. ⑨

Rajvilas Goner Rd, 7km from the city centre ☎0141/268 0101, ⓦ www.oberoihotels.com. This dreamy resort occupies a superb fake Rajasthani fort-style complex beautifully landscaped with pools and pavilions. Accommodation is either in delectable rooms or luxury a/c tents, and there are all the mod cons and facilities you'd expect at this price, including a beautiful spa. Rack rates from around $800, but check the website for discounts. ⑨

Rambagh Palace Bhawani Singh Marg ☎0141/221 1919, ⓦ www.tajhotels.com. This opulent palace complex, set amid 47 acres of beautiful gardens, is indisputably the grandest hotel in Jaipur, and one of the most romantic places to stay in India. Rooms are superbly equipped, with Rajasthani artworks, reproduction antique furniture

and all mod cons. Facilities include a clutch of fine restaurants and bars (see p.201), indoor and outdoor pools (guests only) and a Jiva spa. Even if you can't afford to stay, call in for afternoon tea (Rs1200 for two). Check the website for discounts, especially in summer. Doubles from $950. ⑨

🏃 **Samode Haveli** Gangapole ☎0141/263 2370, ⓦ www.samode.com. In an unbeatably central location on the northeastern edge of the Pink City, this superb old haveli is brimful of atmosphere, centred on an idyllic central courtyard and with the prettiest pool in town (guests only). Rooms are a mishmash: some are functional, modern and fairly characterless; others are pure museum pieces; and others are a bit of both – ask to see several before you make a choice. Rooms from around $320. A good deal in summer (May–Sept), when rates can fall by forty percent. ⑨

🏃 **Shahpura House** Devi Marg, Bani Park ☎0141/220 3392, ⓦ www.shahpurahouse .com. The most characterful of the heritage hotels in this part of town, superbly decorated throughout with lavish murals and Rajasthani architectural touches. Rooms all come with a/c, minibar and bathtub, and are attractively furnished with old wooden furniture; there's also a small pool. ❻

The City

Jaipur's attractions fall into three distinct areas. At the heart of the urban sprawl, the historic **Pink City** is where you'll find the fine City Palace, along with the Jantar Mantar observatory and Hawa Mahal, plus myriad teeming bazaars stuffed with enticing Rajasthani handicrafts. The much leafier and less hectic area **south of the Pink City** is home to the Ram Niwas Gardens, Central Museum, Birla Mandir and a handful of other low-key sights. Finally, the city's **outskirts** are dotted with a string of intriguing relics of royal rule, most notably the fort of Nahargarh, the cenotaphs at Royal Gaitor, and the temples (and monkeys) of Galta.

The Pink City

At the heart of Jaipur lies Jai Singh's original capital, popularly known as the **Pink City**, enclosed by the remains of lofty walls and imposing gateways which were designed to offer it some measure of protection against hostile forces, and which still serve to demarcate it from the sprawling modern suburbs around. One of the Pink City's most striking features is its regular **grid-plan**, with wide, dead-straight streets, laid out at right angles and broadening to spacious plazas (*choupads*) at major intersections. The design was created in accordance with the *Vastu Shastras*, a series of ancient Hindu architectural treatises, whereby the entire layout can be read as a kind of *mandala*, or sacred diagram, in which the city becomes a divinely ordained part of the cosmic design – and also offers a notable contrast to the wildly irregular street plans of most north Indian cities (although similar divinely inspired urban grids are relatively common in the South Indian temple towns of Tamil Nadu).

The city's other striking feature is its uniform **pink colour**, intended to camouflage the poor-quality materials from which its buildings were originally constructed and to lend the whole place a roseate hue reminiscent of the great imperial marble monuments of the Mughals. The colour was briefly changed to a sickly yellow during the 1860s before being restored to the original regal pink, an event which led to the widely held but erroneous belief that the uniform colour scheme was a nineteenth-century innovation dating from a visit by England's Prince Albert in 1876.

The neatly rectilinear streets are home to Jaipur's three most famous monuments – the **Hawa Mahal**, **City Palace** and **Jantar Mantar** observatory – as well as an extraordinary collection of **bazaars**, with different trades and crafts allotted their own streets within the grid. Johari Bazaar, for example, is full of shops selling silver, jewellery and textiles, while Chaura Rasta is the place to go for Hindi books, textbooks and stationery, and Kishanpole is devoted to bicycle shops and other types of hardware. An audioguided **heritage walk** (2.5km; around 2hr; Rs110) covering some of the most interesting sights in the Pink City is available from the Hawa Mahal.

Hawa Mahal

East of the City Palace stands Jaipur's most instantly recognizable landmark, the extravagant **Hawa Mahal**, or "Palace of Winds" (daily 9am–5pm, last entrance 4.30pm; foreigners Rs50, Indian residents Rs10; audioguide Rs110; guided tours around Rs100); the spectacular exterior is at its best during the early morning, when it exudes an orangey-pink glow in the rays of the rising sun. The palace was built in 1799 to enable the women of the court to watch street processions while remaining in strict purdah. It's really nothing but an enormous facade, just one room deep in most parts, though its five-storey exterior, decked out with no fewer than 593 finely screened windows and balconies, makes it seem far larger than it really is. You can go inside the palace itself – the entrance is on the lane which runs north from Tripolia Bazaar around the back of the building, a five-minute walk from the front. There's actually not much to see, though the screened niches from which the ladies of the court would once have looked down still offer unparalleled views over the multitudinous mayhem of Jaipur far below.

City Palace

Enclosed by a high wall in the centre of the city stands Jaipur's magnificent **City Palace**, open to the public as the **Sawai Man Singh Museum** (daily 9.30am–5.45pm, last entry 5pm; foreigners Rs300 including audioguide; Indian residents Rs40; video Rs200; same ticket also valid for Jaigarh Fort at Amber if used within two days). To reach the palace entrance, go through the small archway on the north side of Tripolia Bazaar, just west of the junction with Chaura Rasta, and follow the road as it veers round to the right, past the Jantar Mantar (see p.195). The entrance is past here, on your left.

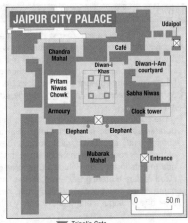

The palace was originally built by Jai Singh on the site of the Jai Niwas pleasure gardens and hunting lodge that occupied the area before the foundation of Jaipur. Many of the apartments and halls were added by his successors, but the exhibits and interior design have lost none of the pomp and splendour of their glory days. The royal family still occupies part of the palace, advancing in procession on formal occasions through the grand **Tripolia Gate** on the south side of the palace. Less exalted visitors must enter through a small gate on the eastern side of the palace leading into the first of the palace's two main courtyards, centred on the elegant **Mubarak Mahal**. Built as a reception hall in 1899, the building now holds the museum's **textile collection**, housing some of the elaborately woven and brocaded fabrics which formerly graced the royal wardrobe, including a very fine "billiard dress" created for Ram Singh II (1835–80), complete with fancifully decorated cue; the voluminous red-and-gold wedding costume (*jama*) worn by Sawai Pratap Singh for his wedding (the skirt alone boasts no less than 320 pleats); and the huge *atam sukha* (a type of quilted jacket designed for the cold winter months) created for the famously large Maharaja Sawai Madho Singh I, which looks more like a tent than an item of clothing. On the north side of the courtyard the **Armoury** is probably the finest such collection in Rajasthan, with a vast array of blood-curdling but often beautifully decorated weapons of mass destruction including a particularly nasty looking spiked *gurj* (mace), superb crystal- and jade-handled daggers and an unusual crocodile-skin shield.

Past the Mubarak Mahal an ornate gateway, flanked by a pair of fine stone elephants, leads into the palace's second main courtyard, painted a deep salmon pink and centred on the raised **Diwan-i-Khas** (Hall of Private Audience). Open-sided, with its roof raised on marble pillars, this was the place in which all important decisions of state were taken by the maharaja and his advisors. The hall contains two silver urns, or *gangajalis*, listed in the *Guinness Book of World Records* as the largest crafted silver objects in the world, each more than 1.5m high with a capacity of 8182 litres. When Madho Singh II went to London to attend the coronation of King Edward VII in 1901, he was so reluctant to trust the water in the West that he had these urns filled with Ganges water and took them along with him.

On the left (west) side of the courtyard, a small corridor leads through to the **Pritam Niwas Chowk**, or "Peacock Courtyard", adorned with four superbly painted doorways representing the four seasons – the "Peacock Gate" (autumn) through which you enter and the verdantly painted "Green Gate" (spring)

One-and-a-quarter maharajas

Prior to his accession to the throne, the young Jai Singh (see p.187) – the Kachchwaha heir apparent and future founder of Jaipur – was sent for a period to the Mughal court to demonstrate his fealty to the imperial overlords. The young Rajput's wit and sharpness so impressed the then emperor, Aurangzeb, that the crusty old Muslim potentate described him as *sawai*, or "one-and-a-quarter", implying that even as a young teenager, Jai Singh already added up to considerably more than the average man.

The soubriquet stuck. Upon attaining the throne of Amber, the new ruler incorporated *sawai* into his official title – Sawai Jai Singh II – and the honorific was subsequently adopted by all following rulers of Jaipur, becoming an integral part of the city's royal traditions; look up at the flag of Jaipur flying over the maharaja's apartments in the City Palace's Chandra Mahal and you'll see a miniature, *sawai*-sized replica fluttering next to it on the flagpole. It also accounts for the unusual name of the town of Sawai Madhopur, near Ranthambore National Park, named after one of Jaipur's eighteenth-century rulers, Sawai Madho Singh I.

opposite are particularly striking. This courtyard gives the best view of the soaring yellow **Chandra Mahal**, the residence of the royal family (and closed to the public), its heavily balconied seven-storey facade rising to a slope-shouldered summit, with the maharaja's flag (and its miniature companion – see box opposite) flying from the topmost pavilion when he's in residence.

On the opposite (east) side of the Diwan-i-Khas courtyard, beneath a large clocktower, sits the ornate **Sabha Niwas**, the Hall of Public Audience (or **Diwan-i-Am**, as it's also known), bare except for a pair of thrones in the middle and portraits of various former maharajas ranged around the walls. Beyond here lies the small **Diwan-i-Am courtyard**, with a collection of old carriages tucked into one end.

Jantar Mantar

Immediately south of the City Palace lies the remarkable **Jantar Mantar** (daily 9am–4.30pm; Rs10, camera Rs50, video Rs100), a large grassy enclosure containing eighteen huge stone astronomical measuring devices constructed between 1728 and 1734 at the behest of Jai Singh, many of them his own invention, their strange, abstract shapes lending the whole place the look of a weird futuristic sculpture park. The Jantar Mantar is one of five identically named observatories created by the star-crazed Jai Singh across north India (including the well-known example in Delhi; see p.101), though his motivation was astrological rather than astronomical. Astrology has always played a key practical role in Indian culture, and it was in order to more accurately map events in the heavens – and thus more precisely predict their effects on earth – that the observatory was constructed, rather than from any abstract love of science.

It's a good idea to pay (Rs150) for the services of a **guide** to explain how the observatory's complex sequence of instruments works. Using Greek and Arabic brass astronomical devices as a model, the instruments were designed so that shadows fall onto marked surfaces, thereby allowing the resident astronomers to tell the time, calculate the Hindu lunar calendar, identify the positions of stars and planets, and even predict the intensity of the monsoon. Probably the most impressive of the observatory's constructions is the 27m-high sundial, the **Samrat Yantra**, which can calculate the time to within two seconds (the time calculated is unique to Jaipur, between 10 and 41 minutes behind Indian standard time, depending on the time of year). A more original device, the **Jaiprakash Yantra**, consists of two hemispheres laid in the ground, each composed of six curving marble slabs with a suspended ring in the centre, whose shadow marks the day, time and zodiac symbol – vital for the calculation of auspicious days for marriage. It's from the word *yantra* (instrument), incidentally, that the observatory gets its quirky name, "Jantar" being a slang version of *yantra*, and "mantar" from *mantra* (formula), altered to rhyme – a typical example of Hindi wordplay.

Govind Devji

North of the city palace is the **Govind Devji** (or Deoji), the family temple of the maharajas of Jaipur, although it also remains enduringly popular with the hoi polloi of Jaipur, who flock here in droves for the evening puja around 6pm. The temple is dedicated to Krishna in his character of Govinda, the amorous cowherd whose dalliances with Radha and the *gopis* form one of the main subjects of Rajasthani art. The principal shrine houses an image of Govinda, brought here from Vrindavan (near Agra) in 1735, which is considered the guardian deity of the rulers of Jaipur.

The temple building itself occupies an unusual open-sided pavilion, more like a Mughal audience hall than a traditional Hindu temple. Local tradition states that it was originally a palace pavilion, but that Krishna appeared to Jai Singh in a dream and expressed a fondness for the building, after which the dutiful maharaja had it converted into a temple. Whatever the building's origins, the open-sided structure had the notable advantage in that Govinda's shrine could be seen by the maharaja from his rooms in the lofty Chandra Mahal in the City Palace, thus allowing him to commune with his tutelary god without the inconvenience of having to leave his private apartments.

A large shallow pool lies around the back – until quite recently home to a healthy population of crocodiles – along with further temples and a pleasant stretch of garden.

Iswari Minar Swarg Suli

Rising from the centre of the Pink City is the slender **Iswari Minar Swarg Suli**, or **Isar Lat** (Heaven-piercing Minaret; daily 9am–4.30pm; Rs10, Indian residents Rs5), whose summit offers the definitive view of old Jaipur, with fascinating vistas down into the tangled labyrinth of alleyways and courtyards which honeycomb the city in the spaces between the major roads, and which remain largely invisible at street level. The minaret is the only significant remaining physical evidence of the reign of Jai Singh II's dithering son and successor, Iswari Singh, who erected this excessively grandiose monument to celebrate his army's minor victory over a combined Maratha–Rajput force in 1747 (although bazaar gossip later claimed that the tower was built so that the maharaja could spy on local girls making their ablutions in the houses below). The triumph was short-lived, however, and a rather more accurate assessment of Iswari Singh's modest military abilities is provided by the fact that he poisoned himself in 1750 rather than face the returning Marathas in battle. To reach the minaret, go through the archway off Tripolia Bazaar which leads to the City Palace, but then head round to the left, away from the palace, and you'll see the minaret ahead of you.

South of the Pink City

Dotted with a handful of quirky museums and temples, the leafy, low-key suburbs south of the Pink City offer a complete change of pace from the traffic and crowds of the centre. Attractions include the rewarding **Central Museum**, housed in the fanciful Albert Hall, one of Rajasthan's most imposing – and most kitsch – colonial buildings, and the bizarre little **Museum of Indology**. Further south, the sumptuously marbled **Birla Mandir** provides a fittingly lavish memorial to one of India's wealthiest industrial dynasties.

Central Museum

Immediately south of the Pink City, the road leading out from New Gate is flanked by the lush **Ram Niwas Gardens**, named after their creator, Ram Singh, who ruled Jaipur from 1835 to 1880. The gardens' centrepiece is the florid **Albert Hall** of 1867, designed by British architect Sir Samuel Jacob in a whimsical mix of Venetian and Mughal styles (Italian below, Indian on top). This eye-catching structure houses the city's recently renovated **Central Museum** (daily except Mon 9am–5.30pm (last entrance 5pm); foreigners Rs100, Indian residents Rs15; audioguide Rs110, Indian residents Rs80), whose formerly motley and moth-eaten galleries have been given a thorough spring-clean and upgrading. The bulk of the collection focuses on regional and Indian themes, including fine displays of Jaipur pottery, Hindu statuary and one of the state's best collections of Mughal and Rajasthani miniature paintings, supported by an interestingly eclectic array of other artefacts from around the globe – everything from Egyptian antiquities to decorative tiles from Stoke-on-Trent, with forays into Japan, Burma and Persia en route.

Next to the museum, the city's **zoo** (daily except Tues: mid-March to mid-Oct 9am–5pm; mid-Oct to mid-March 9am–5pm; foreigners Rs100, Indian residents Rs10) is a fairly depressing affair, with animals kept in grim conditions, while the hiked-up entry price for foreigners is a further turn-off.

Museum of Indology

Further south, off Jawaharlal Nehru Road, the **Museum of Indology** (daily 8am–6pm; Rs20 including guided tour, plus tip) holds assorted curiosities collected by the late writer and painter Acharya Vyakul stuffed into what is – despite the grandiose name – basically just a rambling suburban house. Exhibits include oddities such as a map of India painted on a grain of rice, letters written on a hair and a glass bed, along with enormous quantities of hopeless junk, all heaped up together in great mouldering piles – it's all fairly unedifying, and whatever one might get out of the strange little collection is largely negated by the resident caretaker, whose whistle-stop tour and largely incomprehensible "explanations" are followed by inevitable demands for further cash.

Birla Mandir and around

Flanking the roadside 1km south of the Museum of Indology stands the **Birla Mandir** (summer 6am–noon & 3–9pm; winter 6.30am–noon & 3–8.30pm), or Laxmi Narayan Temple, a flashy modern marble edifice built in 1988 by the fabulously wealthy Birla family, the creators of one of India's largest industrial corporations, who originally hailed from the town of Pilani in Shekhawati. The dazzlingly white exterior is embellished with fine carvings and statues featuring an eclectic array of religious figures including Jesus, Sts Anthony and Peter, Confucius, Zarathustra and Socrates. The spacious, bare interior and large stained-glass windows give the place a slightly churchy feel. Images of Lakshmi (the goddess of wealth, with whom the billionaire Birlas clearly feel a close affinity) and Narayan (a form of Vishnu) stand in the shrine at the far end, with a finely carved dome overhead; also note the Ganesh over the entrance door, whose marble has been so finely carved that it has become almost transparent. A very modest little **museum** (same hours; free) occupies one side of the temple building, housing photos of the Birla family, plus a few family mementoes. Overlooking the temple is the diminutive **Moti Dungri** fort, perched atop a steep-sided hillock and surrounded by thick walls – an eye-catching little stronghold, though sadly it's closed to visitors.

Just north of the Birla Mandir is the altogether livelier and more down-at-heel **Ganesh Mandir**. A string of little shops outside sell various offerings, including the little round sweets (*ladoos*) that are popularly offered to the rotund orange Ganesh figure inside the temple – although judging by the size of his capacious pot belly it looks as if he's had quite enough to eat already.

Outlying sights

The rocky hills which overlook Jaipur to the north and east are home to a string of spectacularly situated forts and temples, all reachable via steep paths climbing up from the city (or, for the less energetic, via longer roads around the back of the hills). Closest to the city centre, the old royal fort and palace at **Nahargarh** offers superlative views, as does the path up past the Surya Mandir to the atmospheric temples at **Galta** – popularly known as the "Monkey Palace" thanks to its large population of engaging macaques. The grandiose marble chhatris at **Royal Gaitor**, last resting place of Jaipur's royal family, are also worth a visit, most easily combined with a trip to Amber.

Nahargarh

Teetering on the edge of the hills north of Jaipur, **Nahargarh**, or "Tiger Fort" (open 24hr; free), was built by Jai Singh II in 1734. The imposing walls of the fort sprawl for the best part of a kilometre along the ridgetop, although the only significant surviving structures within are the **palace apartments** (daily 9.30–5.30pm; foreigners Rs30, Indians Rs10), built inside the old fort by Madho Singh II between 1883 and 1892 as a love nest in which he installed a selection of his most treasured concubines away from the disapproving eyes of his courtiers and four official wives. The large and rather plain pale pink structure is filled with dozens of virtually identical rooms with simple floral decorations and a disorienting labyrinth of corridors and stairwells arranged around a large central courtyard; the perplexing layout was allegedly designed to allow the canny Madho Singh to come and go at will without anyone being aware of his movements.

The main reason for coming up here, however, is to sample the superb views of Jaipur, best enjoyed towards dusk over a beer at the *Padao* café, located at the far end of the complex, a five-minute walk past the palace at the highest point of the fortifications, from where there are fine vistas over the labyrinth of battlemented walls which encircle the fort, and the city below. Refreshments without views can also be found at the *Durg Cafeteria* right next to the palace.

Vehicles of any kind can only get to the fort along a road that branches off Amber Road, a 15km journey from Jaipur. It's simpler to **walk** to the fort along the steep path that climbs up from the north side of the city centre, a stiff fifteen- to twenty-minute walk, although the beginning of the path is a bit tricky to find, so you might want to take a rickshaw to the bottom. At the top of the path, go through the first gate and then head left, up the steps opposite a large bathing pool and through a second gate into the palace area, then head around to the left to reach the palace itself. It's best to avoid going up too late in the day or returning after dark – the fort is popular with delinquent teenagers and assorted lowlife, and the atmosphere can be a tad seedy at the best of times.

Royal Gaitor

On the northern edge of the city centre, the walled funerary complex of **Royal Gaitor** (daily 9am–4.30pm; free, camera Rs10, video Rs20) contains the stately marble chhatris commemorating the expired members of Jaipur's ruling family. The compound consists of two main courtyards, each crammed full of imposing memorials to various maharajas both ancient and modern. The first (and more recent) courtyard is dominated by the grandiose though slightly shoddy-looking twentieth-century cenotaph of **Madho Singh II** (d. 1922), a ruler of famously gargantuan appetites, whose four wives and fifty-odd concubines bore him a grand total of "around 125" children (two of the wives and fourteen children are entombed in smaller chhatris directly behind). To the left of Madho Singh II's cenotaph lies that of **Man Singh II** (d. 1970), the most recent arrival.

The second, original, courtyard is dominated by the elaborate tomb of **Jai Singh II** (d. 1743), the founder of Jaipur and the first ruler to be interred at Gaitor. This is the finest of the chhatris, its base decorated with delicately carved elephant- and lion-hunting scenes, while the inside of the dome is covered in images from Hindu mythology. Immediately behind is the cenotaph of Jaipur's outstanding nineteenth-century ruler **Ram Singh II** (d. 1880), smaller but strikingly similar in design and fashioned out of finely carved white marble. To the right of Jai Singh's memorial lies that of **Madho Singh I** (d. 1768), a ruler of prodigious personal stature who (as the resident guide will fondly relate) reputedly stood seven feet tall and four feet broad – perhaps the result of a daily breakfast comprising a hundred chapatis and five litres of milk – although the poor man probably needed all the sustenance he could get, given his entourage of nine wives and 350 concubines. Further memorials to Pratap Singh (d. 1803) and Jagat Singh (d. 1819) fill out the rest of the enclosure.

On the ridgetop above Gaitor (and reachable from it via a steep path) lies the **Ganesh Mandir**, the second of the city's two major Ganesh temples – a huge and eye-catching building instantly recognizable from the huge swastika painted on its side.

Galta "Monkey Palace"

Nestling in a steep-sided valley 3km east of Jaipur, **Galta** (daily sunrise–sunset; free, camera Rs50, video Rs150) comprises a picturesque collection of 250-year-old temples squeezed into a narrow rocky ravine. Galta owes its sacred status in large part to a freshwater spring that seeps constantly through the rocks in the otherwise dry valley, keeping two **tanks** full. Traditionally humans bathe in the upper water tank, but except during the holy month of Kartika (usually Nov), the putrid-smelling ponds are the domain of over five thousand macaque monkeys which call Galta home and which have earned the place its nickname of the "Monkey Palace". For many tourists the sight of the splashing monkeys outstrips the attraction of the temples themselves, though the assorted shrines, dedicated variously to Krishna, Rama and Hanuman, are attractively atmospheric – a tiny shrine in the secondary courtyard of the Hanuman temple (it's the one closest to the main entrance on the north side of the path) is lit by a candle whose flame is claimed to have been kept burning continuously since a visit by Akbar more than four centuries ago. It's also worth walking up to the spectacularly situated **Surya Mandir**, perched above the tanks on the ridgetop overlooking Jaipur, for dramatic views of the city below.

The only way to reach Galta **by vehicle** is to drive the 10km or so along the road past Sisodia Rani-ka-Bagh (see below) around the hills behind Jaipur, passing through beautiful countryside en route – remarkably quiet and unspoilt given its proximity to the city. You can also **walk** to Galta, following the path beyond Suraj Pole gate on the eastern edge of the Pink City and climbing steeply up to the Surya Mandir on the crest of the hill above the main temple complex – a stiff twenty-minute walk.

Sisodia Rani-ka-Bagh

The road to Galta runs past a sequence of pleasure gardens, most of them now sadly dilapidated, established by the ruling nobility to serve as retreats from the city. The best preserved of these is the former royal palace and gardens of **Sisodia Rani-ka-Bagh** (Garden of the Sisodia Queen; daily 8am–8pm; 8am–5pm Rs10; 5–8pm Rs20). The palace itself, built in the eighteenth century by Jai Singh II for the Udaipur princess he married to secure relations with his neighbouring Sisodia Rajputs, is a small but florid building covered in painted floral decorations and with a fine array of murals on its outer wall (facing the road to Galta) depicting scenes from the life of Krishna. Below the palace a sequence of walled and terraced gardens falls away down the hillside, dotted with small kiosks, marble fountains and (usually dry) water channels – a pleasant enough spot, though of no particular architectural or horticultural distinction. About 250m back up the main road to Jaipur is a second and similar palace and garden complex, the **Vidhyadhar-ka-Bagh**, whose crumbling walls loom over the southern side of the road. The gardens are sometimes used for weddings, but aren't currently open to visitors.

Eating, drinking and entertainment

Jaipur has Rajasthan's best selection of quality **restaurants**, both veg and non-veg, albeit at higher-than-average prices. Alternatively, if you're watching the pennies, most of the city's budget guesthouses serve up decent food.

Barista's Bhagwan Das Rd, opposite the Raj Mandir cinema. Smart coffee house serving up excellent freshly ground coffee – as popular with Jaipur's affluent twenty-somethings as it is among caffeine-crazed foreigners.

Chokhi Dhani 22km south of Jaipur on the Tonk Rd ☎0141/277 0554. This Rajasthani theme-park-cum-restaurant attracts droves of well-heeled Jaipuris, especially at weekends, when the whole place gets wildly busy. The Rs300 entrance fee includes an evening meal plus access to a wide range of attractions (though tips are expected at many) – elephant, camel and bullock-cart rides, folk dances, drumming, puppet shows, archery, chapati-making demonstrations and a superb magician, to name just a few. When you've done with the entertainment, head off to the mud-walled restaurant where you'll be seated on the floor and served an authentically genuine (albeit very salty) Rajasthani village thali quite unlike anything you'll find in the restaurants of Jaipur, with lots of rustic rural delicacies like cornflour chapatis, Rajasthani *gatta* (gram flour balls cooked in yoghurt) and unusual curried vegetables. It's all a bit hokey, but fun, in a real kitsch way. An auto-rickshaw charges Rs300–350 for the round trip. Open Mon–Sat 6–11pm & Sun from 11am.

Copper Chimney MI Rd. Plush glass-fronted restaurant with a good range of north Indian standards (albeit sometimes a bit heavy on the oil and spices), plus local specialities like *laal maans* (special Rajasthani desert-style mutton) and *gatta*, and a few Chinese and continental dishes. Mains Rs85–205. Licensed.

Dasaprakash MI Rd. This unpretentious a/c restaurant serves up a tasty range of classic south Indian veg fare – *iddlis*, *vadas*, *uttapams*, *upuma*, thalis, and no less than seventeen types of *dosa* – plus a selection of sweet-toothed ice-cream sundaes in various colourful combinations. Mains Rs90–150.

🏃 **Four Seasons** Bhagat Singh Marg. Generally reckoned the best Indian veg restaurant in town, with top-notch *dosas* and *uttapams* along with a big choice of more-ish north Indian curries, plus some Chinese. You may have to queue, especially later on in the evening when the place fills with locals.

Lassiwala 312 MI Rd. A Jaipur institution for its sublime lassis, served in old-style terracotta mugs.

Its popularity has sparked a small lassi-wallah-war, with two impostors setting up shop to the right (as you face it) of the original – check for the correct street number. Closes early afternoon.

Little Italy KK Square Mall, Prithviraj Rd. Svelte modern restaurant serving up passable – if not particularly authentic – pizza, pasta, risottos and a few Italian-style meat dishes, plus (for culinary reasons which remain unclear) assorted Mexican snacks. Also has a decent selection of Indian wines. Mains from around Rs300.

LMB Johari Bazaar. The only real restaurant in the Pink City, although the food (mains from around Rs120) is disappointingly pedestrian, compensating for a lack of flavour with incendiary amounts of chilli. Alternatively, stick to the sweet counter outside, which dishes up snacks including a famous *paneer ghewar* (honeycomb cake soaked in treacle) and piping-hot *tikkis* (a kind of small, deep-fried potato-cake) in spicy mango sauce.

Mohan's Motilal Atal Rd opposite *Hotel Neelam*. Cosy and unpretentious little veg restaurant, popular with locals thanks to its well-prepared and excellent-value food, with virtually everything under Rs50. There's not much room, so you might end up sharing a table.

Natraj MI Rd. Long-established pure veg restaurant offering a big range of North Indian standards, plus thalis, *dosas* and superb sweets – *rasmalai* (small balls of *paneer* in a creamy milk sauce), *barfi*, *halwa* and *ladoo* – piled up at the counter by the door. Mains Rs70–175.

Niro's MI Rd. Some of the best non-veg food in Jaipur, with Rajasthani specialities such as *sula* (a distinctively tangy-tasting lamb, marinated in yoghurt and spices and grilled), *lal maans* (mutton) and *gatta* along with a big choice of tandoori dishes and other meat and veg curries, plus Western and Chinese. Mains Rs155–300. Licensed.

Om Tower Restaurant Om Tower, MI Rd. Rajasthan's first revolving restaurant, on the 14th floor of the landmark Om Tower. The head-spinning views are the main attraction; the north Indian food (veg only) is acceptable but rather expensive (mains Rs150–350), and there's no alcohol.

🏃 **Peacock Rooftop Restaurant** *Pearl Palace* hotel, Hari Kishan Somani Marg, Hathroi Fort. The city's most appealing rooftop restaurant, with quirky original decor featuring cute metal chairs and a striking peacock canopy – particularly pretty after dark. There's a big menu of veg and non-veg Indian options, all well prepared, with flavoursome sauces, crisp breads and cold beers, plus Chinese, pizzas and the usual Western snacks. Mains Rs60–260.

Rambagh Palace Bhawani Singh Marg ☎0141/221 1919, ⊛www.tajhotels.com. Jaipur's most opulent hotel serves up a pair of memorable dining options. Choose between *Swarna Mahal*, offering Indian fine-dining in a superbly over-the-top Neoclassical-style dining room, or the slightly less ostentatious *Rajput Room* multi-cuisine restaurant (Indian, Continental and Chinese). Mains at both start at around Rs850. Reservations strongly recommended.

Reds 5th floor, Mall 21. Stylish modern bar-cum-restaurant, with red and black sofas and fine views

of the Raj Mandir cinema opposite. There's a good range of mainly North Indian food (veg and non-veg), or just come for a drink. Mains Rs225–595.

Sunder Palace *Sunder Palace* hotel, Sanjay Marg, Hathroi Fort, Ajmer Rd. Breezy, flower-filled rooftop restaurant at this popular guesthouse specializing in tasty, pure-veg Indian cooking at bargain prices. Mains Rs50–85. Licensed.

Surya Mahal MI Rd. Neat little modern veg restaurant specializing in South Indian food, with tasty *dosas*, *uttapam*, *iddli*, *vadas* and thalis. There's also a good range of North Indian veg curries and a few Rajasthani specialities like *kadi pakora* (gram-flour pakoras in a spicy yoghurt-based sauce) and *gatta masala*; plus pasta, pizza and Chinese. Mains Rs70–175.

Drinking and entertainment

For **drinks**, *Amigo's Bar*, on the ninth floor of the Om Tower (see opposite) on MI Road, offers fine city views, a reasonable drinks list (including a few cocktails) and passable Tex-Mex snacks, while the nearby *Reds* bar-restaurant (see above) offers more upmarket decor and food, plus fine views of the adjacent Raj Mandir cinema. *Henry's* in the *Hotel Park Prime* on Prithviraj Road is the city's most appealing English-style pub, complete with oak bar and sporting memorabilia; alternatively, the same hotel also boasts a fine rooftop bar with a small pool and city views – particularly attractive after dark. For a truly memorable tipple, head to the *Rambagh Palace* (see p.192), where you can choose between the swanky, colonial-style *Polo* bar or the more laidback *Steam lounge-bar* (evenings only; closed Tues), built inside the carriages of an old steam train.

B2B (Fri & Sat only 8.30pm–2am; couples only), at the *Country Inn* on MI Road, is Jaipur's best stab at a Western-style **club** and attracts a mix of locals and

▲ Shop, Jaipur

foreigners with its good live DJs and big drinks list. Entrance is Rs1000 (all of which is redeemable in food and drink).

If you go to the **cinema** just once while you're in India, it should be at the Raj Mandir on Bhagwan Das Road just off MI Road, which boasts a stunning Art Deco lobby and 1500-seat auditorium. Most movies have four daily showings (usually at 12.30pm, 3.30pm, 6.30pm and 9.30pm), and there's always a long queue, so get your tickets (Rs60/80) an hour or so before the show starts. The city also hosts the **Jaipur Literature Festival** (Ⓦ www.jaipurliteraturefestival.org), one of Asia's biggest bookfests, held over five days in late January at the *Diggi Palace* hotel (see p.191) – previous festivals have attracted luminaries such as William Dalrymple, Hari Kunzru, Colin Thubron and Simon Schama.

Shopping

Foreign buyers and wholesalers flock to the Pink City to shop for textiles, clothes, jewellery and pottery, and if you come across Indian **handicrafts** or garments abroad, chances are they will have been bought in Jaipur. As a regular tourist, you'll find it harder to hunt out the best merchandise, but as a source of souvenirs, perhaps only Delhi can surpass it. The large, government-run Rajasthali emporium (see opposite), just south of Ajmer Gate, is a good place to get a sense of the range of handicrafts available and to gauge approximate costs – although you'll probably find similar items at cheaper prices in the Pink City bazaars. The upmarket stores along MI Road also tend to be pricier than those in the Pink City.

In keeping with Maharaja Jai Singh's original city divisions, different streets are reserved for the purveyors of different goods. **Bapu Bazaar**, on the south side of the Pink City, is the best place for clothes and textiles, including Jaipur's famous **block-print** work and *bandhani* **tie-dye**. On the opposite side of town, along Amber Road just beyond Zorawar Gate, rows of emporiums are stacked with gorgeous patchwork wall-hangings and **embroidery**; these places do a steady

---

Jewellery and gemstones in Jaipur

The two best places for silver jewellery are **Johari Bazaar**, the broad street running north of Sanganeri Gate in the Pink City, and **Chameliwala Market**, just off MI Road in the tangle of alleyways behind the *Copper Chimney* restaurant. The latter also has the city's best selection of gems, though it's also one of the hardest places to shop in peace, thanks to a particularly slippery breed of scam merchant, known locally as *lapkars*. These young men – usually smartly dressed and speaking excellent English – will regale you with beguiling tales about how you can buy gems in Jaipur and re-sell them back home for a massive profit. This is nonsense, of course, but by the time you realize this you'll be thousands of kilometres away with a handful of worthless cut-glass "gems" wondering where all the mysterious entries on your credit-card bill came from. If you're paying for gemstones or jewellery with a credit card in Jaipur, don't let it out of your sight, and certainly don't agree to leave a docket as security.

There's a government-sponsored **gem-testing laboratory** (Mon–Fri & every first and third Sat of month 10am–4pm) at the Gem and Jewellery Export Promotion Council, 2nd floor, Rajasthan Chamber Bhavan, MI Rd near Ajmeri Gate, where you can have gemstones tested for authenticity. The cost is Rs605 per stone, with reports delivered the following working day (or Rs935 per stone for a same-day report; deliver stone before 2pm). Obviously it's best to get a gem tested before you buy it, assuming you can get the seller to release it to the laboratory for examination.

trade with bus parties of wealthy tourists, so be prepared to haggle hard. south off Tripolia Bazaar (just west of the Iswari Minar), the small Maniharon ka Rasta is home to dozens of **lac bangle** shops, while a short to the west, Khajane Walon ka Rasta is lined with the dozens of s workshops selling **religious statues** in marble and other types of stone.

For old-style Persian-influenced vases, plus tiles, plates and candleholders, visit the outlets of the city's renowned **blue potteries** along Amber Road or the workshop of the late Kripal Singh (see below). Bear in mind though that Jaipur's blue pottery is essentially decorative. The pottery's shiny appearance is achieved through the application of lead-based glazes that become unstable and poisonous if exposed to heat meaning that they're unsuitable for hot food (though see Kripal Kumbh below for an exception).

Anokhi 2nd Floor, KK Square Mall, Prithviraj Rd ⓦ www.anokhi.com. Started by a British designer, this is the place to buy high-quality "ethnic" Indian evening wear, *salwar kameez* and shirts. They also do lovely bedspreads, quilts, tablecloths and cushion covers. Daily 9.30am–8pm.

Jodhpur Tailors Motilal Atal Rd (behind *Hotel Neelam*). One of the best tailors in town, patronized by the maharaja himself. Hand-stitched suits run from around Rs7500 and up, or you could just pick up a shirt (from Rs700) or a pair of trousers (Rs1200) or jodhpurs (Rs1400). Mon–Sat 10.30am–9.30pm, Sun 2–6pm.

Kripal Kumbh Shiv Marg, near the *Jaipur Inn*. The former workshop-cum-home of Jaipur's most famous ceramist, the late Kripal Singh, full of attractive and affordable examples of the city's

traditional blue-and-white pottery. They also claim to be the only workshop in Jaipur producing entirely lead-free pottery that can safely be used with hot food (as well as featuring colours such as red and orange which are impossible to achieve with lead glazes). Daily 10am–7pm.

Rajasthali MI Rd, just south of Ajmer Gate. This large, government-run emporium (Mon–Sat 11am–7.30pm) is a good place to get a sense of the range of handicrafts available and to gauge approximate costs – although you'll probably find similar items at cheaper prices in the Pink City bazaars.

Soma 5 Jacob Rd ⓦ www.somashop.com. Similar range of clothes (ladies' wear only) and fabrics to Anokhi, though at slightly cheaper prices. Mon–Sat 10am–8pm, Sun 10am–6pm.

Listings

Airlines Jaipur Towers on MI Rd is home to dozens of airline agents, not all of them particularly reliable. The best place to head for is Travel-Care (open 24hr; ☎0141/237 1832, ⓦ www.travelcareindia.com), on the ground floor around the right-hand side of the building, who act as agents for virtually every domestic airline and most major international operators, including Air India, BA, Air France, KLM, Lufthansa, Thai Airways, Singapore Air and Gulf Air.

Astrologer Dr Vinod Shastri (☎0141/261 3338), based at Chandni Chowk, behind Tripolia Gate near the City Palace, is one of Rajasthan's leading astrologers. Computer-aided astrological predictions and palm-readings can be arranged; a short consultation will cost from around Rs1000.

Banks and exchange There are plentiful ATMs around town, especially along MI Rd, and lots of private exchange places offering more or less the same rates as the banks; these include two branches of Thomas Cook on MI Rd (both Mon–Sat 9.30am–5.30pm), one on the ground floor of Jaipur

Towers, the other opposite Ganpati Plaza, where you can also get cash advances on Visa and MasterCard. Many of the guesthouses and hotels listed on pp.190–192 can change money (though rates can be poor); the *Pearl Palace Hotel* has 24hr money-changing facilities.

Hospitals For emergencies, the government-run SMS Hospital (☎0141/256 0291), on Sawai Ram Singh Rd, is best; treatment is usually free for foreigners. The best private hospital is the Santokba Durlabhji Memorial Hospital (SDMH), Bhawani Singh Marg ☎0141/256 6251.

Internet access All the guesthouses and hotels listed on pp.190–192 have internet access (and an increasing number also have wi-fi). If you can't get online where you're staying (or at another guest-house), the iWay Internet café (daily 9am–11pm; Rs30/hr), opposite the *Atithi* guesthouse, is one of the few reliable alternatives.

Meditation The Dhamma Thali Vipassana Centre (☎0141/268 0220, ⓦ www.dhamma.org) is one of y centres across the world set up to promote the practice of Vipassana meditation, a technique first practised by the Buddha, which aims to make practitioners more aware of physical sensations and mental processes. The centre is located in beautiful countryside a couple of kilometres beyond Sisodia Rani-ka-Bagh on the road to Galta. Courses last for three to 45 days (see website for details) and involve a strict regime, with 4am starts, no solid food after noon, segregation of the sexes and around ten hours of meditation a day. Courses are free, but a donation is expected.

Photography Sentosa Colour Lab (Mon–Sat 10am–8pm), Ganpati Plaza (on the side facing MI Rd), and Goyal Colour Lab, next to *Lassiwalla* on MI Rd, both offer good digital and print services.

Police stations The main police post is on Station Rd opposite the railway station ☏0141/220 6324.

Post and couriers For poste restante, go to the GPO on MI Rd (Mon–Sat 10am–6pm). Parcels and registered mail are kept at the sorting office behind the main desks; packages are cotton-wrapped and sewn at the concession (Mon–Sat 10am–4pm) by the main entrance. It's preferable to bring your own box. If you're sending a parcel, take it to the customs office on the first floor to have it checked before wrapping and posting; this will speed up delivery by about ten days. The city's DHL office is

at G-8, C Scheme, Vinobha Marg ☏0141/236 1159; they also have a desk inside Standard Chartered Bank on the south side of MI Rd just west of Panch Batti, while the owner of the *Pearl Palace Hotel* is also a registered DHL agent.

Swimming pools The nicest hotel pool currently open to non-guests is at the *Alsisar Haveli* (a pricey Rs200/hr); cheaper options include the pools at the following hotels: *Shahpura House* (free if you take a meal at the hotel), *Umaid Bhawan* (Rs150/3hr), *Madhuban* (Rs100) and *Raj Mahal* (Rs170).

Travel agents It's usually easiest to arrange something through your hotel or guesthouse. Alternatively, the reputable Rajasthan Travel Service, on the ground floor of Ganpati Plaza on MI Rd (☏0141/238 9408, ⊛www.rajasthantravelservice .com), can arrange airline ticketing and organize local and all-India tours.

Visas For renewals go at least a week before your visa expires to the Foreigners' Registration Office (☏0141/261 8508), at the Rajasthan Police Head Office behind the Hawa Mahal.

Yoga Jaipur has several reputable yoga schools, including the Rajasthan Swasth Yog Parishad, New Police Academy Rd (☏0141/239 7330); the Rajasthan Yoga Centre, 2km north of Bani Park in Shastri Nagar; and Madhavanand Ashram (☏0141/220 0317), also in Bani Park.

Moving on from Jaipur

Jaipur is Rajasthan's main **transport hub**, with frequent bus and train services to all major destinations around the state, as well as excellent air connections with major cities in Rajasthan and elsewhere around India. Short journeys to destinations like Bharatpur, Ajmer (for Pushkar) and towns in Shekhawati are usually best made by road; the main exception is Sawai Madhopur, the jumping-off place for Ranthambore National Park, which is most easily reached by train.

By bus

RSRTC buses leave from the Inter-state Bus Station (also known as "Sindhi Camp") on Station Road, with frequent, direct services to pretty much every major town in Rajasthan. For longer journeys, faster but less frequent deluxe Gold Line ("Volvo") and Silver Line government services guarantee seats (enquiries on ☏0141/220 4445, bookings up to 24hr in advance on ☏0141/220 5790); for other services it's easier to just turn up at the bus stand and head for the relevant booking office; destinations are listed outside each cabin. The deluxe services have their own separate booking hatch on platform 3 (open 24hr).

There's an RTDC bus for Pushkar daily at 1pm; otherwise catch one of the regular buses for Ajmer and change there, or take a private bus (see opposite). Other services include: Agra (every 1–2hr; 5hr); Ahmedabad (1 daily; 16hr); Ajmer (8 daily; 2hr–2hr 30min); Alwar (hourly; 4hr); Bharatpur (every 30min; 4hr 30min); Bikaner (11 daily; 7hr 30min); Chittaurgarh (2 daily; 7hr); Delhi (every 30min; 6hr);

Jaisalmer (1 daily; 13–15hr); Jhunjhunu (every 30min; 5hr); Jodhpur (7 daily; 7–8hr); Kota (4 daily; 6hr); Mount Abu (1 daily; 11hr); Nawalgarh (every 30min; 3hr); Pushkar (1 daily; 3hr 30min–4hr); Sawai Madhopur (2 daily; 4hr 30min); Udaipur (1 daily; 10hr).

Private bus services also serve a wide range of destinations, often in comfortable modern coaches, although they may cram too many passengers on board and make unscheduled stops during the journey to tout for custom. You can book tickets for these at the string of agents on Station Road. A reliable company for direct buses to **Pushkar** is Jai Ambay Travels (℡0141/220 5177), on Station Rd near the junction with MI Rd, whose comfortable deluxe coaches leave at 9.30am, taking 3hr 30min; it's a good idea to get tickets in advance (you can also book by phone). They also sell tickets for private buses to Agra (hourly; 5hr 30min), Ajmer (6 daily; 2hr 30min), Bharatpur (hourly; 4hr 30min), Bikaner (5 daily; 6hr), Bundi (2 daily; 4hr), Chittaurgarh (1 daily; 6hr), Jaisalmer (1 nightly; 12hr), Jodhpur (3 daily, including 10.30pm sleeper; 6–7hr), Kota (2 daily; 5hr), Nawalgarh (hourly; 3hr) and Udaipur (2 nightly; 9hr).

By train

Bookings should be made at least a day in advance at the computerized reservations hall just outside the main station (Mon–Sat 8am–8pm, Sun 8am–2pm; ℡0141/220 1401); there's a special "Foreign Tourist and Freedom Fighter" counter.

By plane

Flights are currently operated out of Jaipur's **Sanganer Airport** by Air-India Express (IX), Air India Regional (CD), GoAir (G8), Indian Airlines (IC), IndiGo (6E), Jet Airways (9W), Kingfisher (IT) and SpiceJet (SG). The following is a list of services and schedules available at the time of writing, though carriers and schedules change regularly. ⓦwww.expedia.co.in and www.travelocity.co.in are useful for checking latest timetables. A **rickshaw** to the airport should cost around Rs200; a taxi, Rs350–400.

Jaipur to: Ahmedabad (SG; 1 daily; 1hr 15min); Bengaluru (IT, SG, 6E; 3 daily; 3hr 20min–4hr30min); Chandigarh (IT; 1 daily; 2hr 35min); Chennai (SG; 1 daily; 3hr 20min); Delhi (IC, IT, 9W; 35min–1hr); Goa (SG; 1 daily; 3hr 45min); Guwahati (6E; 1 daily; 3hr 55min); Jammu (IT; 1 daily; 4hr 20min); Jodhpur (IT; 1 daily; 1hr); Kolkata (SG, 6E; 2 daily; 1hr 55min–2hr 25min); Mumbai (IC, IT, SG, 6E, 9W; 8 daily; 1hr 35min–2hr 35min); Srinagar (IT; 1 daily; 5hr 35min); Udaipur (IC, IT, 9W; 3 daily; 45min–2hr 30min).

Around Jaipur

The superb fort at **Amber** provides the most obvious destination for a day-trip, easily combined with a visit to the impressive **Jaigarh** fort that crowns the hills above. Many tourists also travel south to search out the traditional potters, block printers and dyers of **Sanganer**, while the romantic palace-hotel at **Samode** is another major draw.

Amber

On the crest of a rocky hill 11km north of Jaipur, the Rajput stronghold of **AMBER** (or Amer) was the capital of the leading **Kachchwaha** clan (see p.187) from 1037 until 1728, when Jai Singh established his new city at Jaipur. Amber's

Recommended trains from Jaipur

The following daily trains are **recommended** as the fastest and/or most convenient from Jaipur. Bear in mind that timetables change – check online at ⓦ www.indianrail.gov.in before travel.

Destination	Name	No.	Departs	Arrives
Abu Road	Aravali Express	9708	(daily) 8.45am	5.10pm
Agra	Gwalior Express	2987	(daily) 6.10am	10.55am
	Sealdah Express	2988	(daily except Thurs) 2.50pm	7.30pm
	Marudhar Express	4864/4854/4866	(daily) 3.40/3.50pm	9pm
Ajmer	Shatabdi Express	2015	(daily except Wed)10.55pm	1am
	Aravali Express	9708	(daily) 8.45am	11am
Alwar	Jammu Tawi Express	2413	(daily) 4.35pm	6.56pm
	Shatabdi Express	2016	(daily except Wed) 5.45pm	7.26pm
Bikaner	Bikaner Intercity	2468	(daily) 3.50pm	10.45pm
	Hanumangarh Special	0234	(daily) 9.05pm	4.55am
Chittaurgarh	Udaipur Express	2965	(daily) 10.28pm	3.50am
Delhi	Jaisalmer Express	4060	(daily) 5am	11.05am
	Shatabdi Express	2016	(daily except Wed) 5.50pm	10.40pm
Jaisalmer	Jaisalmer Express	4059	(daily) 11.57pm	11.30am
Jodhpur	Marudhar Express	4853/4863/4865	(daily) 11.50am	5.30pm
	Ranthambore Express	2465	(daily) 5.05pm	10.30pm
	Jaisalmer Express	4059	(daily) 11.57pm	5am
Kota	Intercity Express	2466	(daily) 10.55am	2.45pm
	Mumbai Superfast	2956	(daily) 2.10pm	5.25pm
Sawai Madhopur (for Ranthambore National Park)	Intercity Express	2466	(daily) 10.55am	1.15pm
	Mumbai Superfast	2956	(daily) 2.10pm	4pm
Udaipur	Udaipur Express	2965	(daily) 10.28pm	6.10am
Varanasi	Marudhar Express	4854/4864/4866	(daily) 3.40pm	8.35/9.30/10.30am

palace buildings are less impressive than those at Jaipur (or many other places in the state), but the natural setting, perched high on a narrow rocky ridge above the surrounding countryside and fortified by natural hills, high ramparts and a succession of gates along a cobbled road, is unforgettably dramatic – a suitably imposing stronghold for one of Rajasthan's most eminent families.

The path from the village leads up to Suraj Pole (Sun Gate) and the large **Jaleb Chowk** courtyard at the entrance to the main **palace complex** (daily 8am–6pm; foreigners Rs150, Indians Rs25, audioguide Rs150); this is where you'll find the ticket office and assorted official guides, who offer tours of the palace for around Rs200. On the left-hand side of the courtyard is the **Shri Sila Devi temple** (closed noon–4pm), dedicated to the goddess of war, Sila, an aspect of Kali. The revered statue of Sila Devi within ranks, along with the image at the Govind Devji (see p.195), as one of the two most important in Jaipur state. The statue was created in 1604 at the behest of the great Rajput general Man Singh, then serving the Mughals in Bengal. The goddess (legend runs) had appeared in a dream to Man Singh, announcing that she was trapped in a slab of stone and demanding to be released. The relevant stone was located, carved into Sila Devi's likeness, and installed at Amber within a shrine framed by an unusual arch formed from stylized carvings of banana leaves. The goddess quickly became one of most revered of the idols under the royal family's protection, its presence at the entrance to their palace offering an important symbolic seal of divine approval to Kachchwaha rule.

Next to the Shri Sila Devi temple, a steep flight of steps leads up to **Singh Pole** (Lion Gate), the entrance to the main palace. The architectural style is distinctly

▲ Amber Fort

Rajput, though it's clear that Mughal ideas also crept into the design – the practice of covering walls with mirrored mosaics, for example, is pure Mughal, first introduced to India at Agra and Fatehpur Sikri. Passing through Singh Pole leads one into the first of the palace's three main courtyards, on the far side of which stands the **Diwan-i-Am** (Hall of Public Audience), used by Jai Singh I and his successors from 1639. This open-sided pavilion is notably similar in its overall conception to contemporary Mughal audience halls in Delhi and Agra, even if the architectural details are essentially Rajput – the Mughal emperor Jahangir was so jealous of the building that he reputedly once declared, in a fit of artistic jealously, that he wished to have it destroyed. The decidedly Islamic-looking cusped arches of the adjacent terrace offer further architectural homage to the era's Muslim rulers.

Diagonally opposite, the exquisitely painted **Ganesh Pole** leads into a second courtyard, its right-hand side filled with a miniature fountain-studded garden, behind which lie the rooms of the **Sukh Mahal**, set into the side of the courtyard. The marble rooms here, decorated with delicate carving of blue, yellow and red vases, were cooled by water channelled through small conduits carved into the walls, an early and ingenious system of air conditioning. The central room has a particularly finely carved example, from which water was fed through the room and back into the fountains in the gardens outside.

On the opposite side of the courtyard, the dazzling **Sheesh Mahal** houses what were the private chambers of the maharaja and his queen, its walls and ceilings decorated with intricate mosaics fashioned out of shards of mirror and coloured glass. On the far side of the courtyard beyond the Sheesh Mahal, a narrow stairwell leads up to the small **Jas Mandir**, decorated with similar mosaics and guarded from the sun by delicate marble screens.

From the rear of the Sheesh Mahal courtyard, a narrow corridor leads into a further expansive courtyard at the heart of the **Palace of Man Singh I**, the oldest part of the palace complex. The buildings here are notably plain and austere compared to later structures, though they would originally have been richly decorated and furnished. The pillared *baradari* in the centre of the courtyard was once a meeting area for the maharanis, shrouded from men's eyes by flowing curtains. This section of the palace can also be reached via various labyrinthine passages that run around the top of the **Sheesh Mahal** courtyard beyond the Jas Mandir. The impressionable Rudyard Kipling was particularly taken with this section of the complex, describing the "cramped and darkened rooms, the narrow smooth-walled passages with recesses where a man might wait for his enemy unseen, the maze of ascending and descending stairs leading no-whither, the ever-present screens of marble tracery that may hide or reveal so much – all these things breathe of plot and counter-plot, league and intrigue" – though present-day visitors are likely to suffer nothing worse than the occasional stubbed toe.

Practicalities

It's worth visiting Amber independently, since tour groups are rarely given enough time to explore the entire complex properly. Arrive early in the day if you want to avoid the big coach parties. Regular **public buses** to Amber leave from outside Jaipur's Hawa Mahal every five to ten minutes, stopping on the main road below the palace; the journey takes around 20–30 minutes, depending on traffic; alternatively, an auto will cost around Rs250 return, including a couple of hours' waiting time. There's a small **tourist office** (daily 8am–4pm) at the bottom of the path to the palace. It's a pleasant fifteen-minute uphill walk from here to the palace. Alternatively you could hire a Jeep (Rs200 for the return trip, including 2hr waiting time) or waddle up on the back of an elephant (Rs900 for up to two

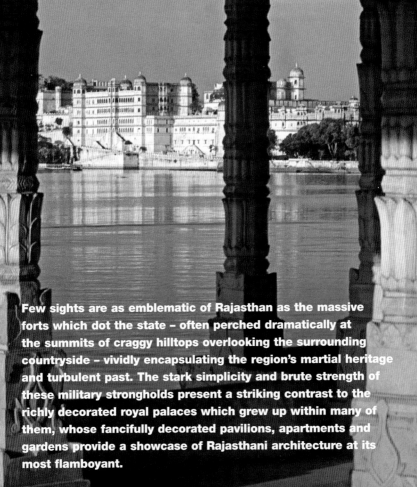

Forts and palaces of Rajasthan

Few sights are as emblematic of Rajasthan as the massive forts which dot the state – often perched dramatically at the summits of craggy hilltops overlooking the surrounding countryside – vividly encapsulating the region's martial heritage and turbulent past. The stark simplicity and brute strength of these military strongholds present a striking contrast to the richly decorated royal palaces which grew up within many of them, whose fancifully decorated pavilions, apartments and gardens provide a showcase of Rajasthani architecture at its most flamboyant.

Mural painting, Bundi ▲

Hawa Mahal, Jaipur ▼

Rajput retreats

The possession of a serviccable fort (denoted in Hindi by the suffix *-garh*) underpinned the power and influence of all Rajput rulers – the great Mewar leader Rana Kumbha, for instance, built or restored no less than 32, bringing his kingdom's tally to a staggering 84. Rajputana's mightiest dynasties generally boasted strategically situated and impregnable citadels, the most famous at Meherangarh (Jodhpur), Chittaurgarh and Amber.

Some forts remained no more than military outposts from which to command the surrounding area. Others (such as Chittaurgarh and Jaisalmer) grew into self-contained fortified settlements housing sizeable towns. Still others (such as Amber and Bundi) developed into lavish palace complexes, their huge, simple exterior walls giving no hint of the extravagance of the buildings and artworks within.

The history of Rajasthan can be read in the evolution of its forts and palaces. The earliest – such as Chittaurgarh, Amber, Kumbalgarh and the Bala Qila at Alwar – place the emphasis firmly on security over aesthetics, generally located in positions of maximum military strength (usually meaning the top of a hill) with numerous strategically positioned gateways and enormous defensive ramparts and bastions (those at Kumbalgarh snake around the surrounding hills for an astonishing 36km). Later structures show a diminishing attention to military concerns. The City Palace at Udaipur, for example, is more palace than fort, while the region's city palaces, such as those at Jaipur and Alwar, demonstrate little concern with self-defence, reflecting the more settled times in which they were built.

Pieces of a palace

The layout of the typical Rajput **palace** (in Hindi, *mahal*, pronounced "mahel") has much in common with those of their great Mughal adversaries, an indication of shared views of the nature of kingship, courtly life and the status of women. The region's forts and palaces are typically entered through one or more **gateways** (*pole* or *pol*), often flanked by triumphal statues of regal elephants. Inside, palaces are divided into male and female quarters, the **mardana** and **zenana** respectively, each usually set around their own courtyard, or **chowk** (pronounced "chalk"). Typically these include a **khas mahal**, the ruler's private apartment, plus a range of other chambers usually adorned with fanciful names such as *phool mahal* (flower palace), *moti mahal* (pearl palace) and *sukh mahal* (palace of bliss). The zenana sections of many palaces also include a small room covered in mirrorwork mosaics (a Mughal innovation) known

▲ Meherangarh Fort

▼ Jaipur City Palace

▼ Jaigarh Fort, Amber

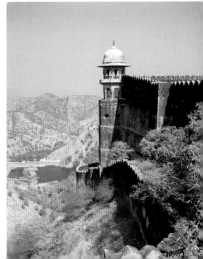

Living like royalty

In the years since Independence, many maharajas and other Rajput royals have had problems making ends meet and in maintaining their vast ancestral homes. The obvious solution for many has been to convert their family palaces into hotels, meaning that foreign hoi polloi can now stay in many of the region's finest palaces and enjoy the sumptuous accommodation that was formerly the preserve of a privileged royal few. The ultimate palace stays are to be had at the *Lake Palace* and *Fateh Prakash Palace* hotels in Udaipur, at the *Rambagh Palace* in Jaipur, and at the *Umaid Bhawan Palace* in Jodhpur, but there are now dozens of heritage hotels across the region offering more intimate (and much more affordable) options.

Meherangarh Fort interior ▲

City Palace, Udaipur ▼

Five top Rajput forts and palaces

▶▶ **Amber Palace** Elegant blend of Rajasthani and Mughal design, crowning a rugged ridge-top just north of Jaipur.

▶▶ **Chittaurgarh Fort** The archetypal Rajput fortress, as famous for its blood-soaked history as for its superb collection of monuments.

▶▶ **Jaisalmer Fort** Stunning desert citadel, its huge bastions enclosing a fascinating tangle of alleyways, havelis and intricately carved Jain temples.

▶▶ **Meherangarh Fort** Rajasthan's most spectacular citadel, overlooking the city of Jodhpur in massive, impregnable splendour.

▶▶ **Udaipur City Palace** Rajasthan's ultimate royal palace, with a labyrinthine assortment of opulent apartments and courtyards in a spectacular lakeside location.

generically as the sheesh (or shish) mahal. Imagining exactly how these apartments would originally have looked, however, requires some imagination. Private rooms and pavilions in Rajput palaces rarely had a fixed function or large pieces of heavy furniture, but were filled with easily movable soft furnishings such as carpets, draperies and bolsters, enabling them to be adapted to various uses. Later Rajput palaces also followed Mughal tradition in having two audience chambers, the diwan-i-am (hall of public audience), usually a large open-sided pavilion in which all classes of local society could come to lay their problems before the ruler; and the diwan-i-khas (hall of private audience), a much smaller pavilion in which the maharaja would discuss matters of state with his ministers and advisors.

people) – though some tourists have complained that the *mahouts* are unnecessarily cruel to their animals.

Jaigarh

Perched high on the hills behind Amber Palace, the rugged **Jaigarh** fort (daily 9am–5pm; foreigners Rs75, Indians Rs25) offers incredible vistas over the hills and plains below. The fort was built in 1600, although as the Kachchwahas were on friendly terms with the Mughals, it saw few battles. Jaigarh is also renowned as the most likely hiding place of the Kachchwahas' famous **lost treasure**. A huge hoard of gemstones and jewellery disappeared after Independence, probably to prevent its confiscation by the government. Income tax officials scoured the building with metal detectors in 1977 but found nothing.

At the centre of the fort, a small **museum** has a rather dusty display of the usual old maps and photographs, plus a good little selection of cannons dating back to 1588. Jaigarh was an important centre for the manufacture of these highly prized weapons (the buildings which once housed the fort's cannon foundry can be seen near the Awani Gate); the respect with which they were treated can be judged from the fact that all the cannons on display – even the smallest – were individually named. None of them, however, can hold a candle to the immense **Jaivana** cannon, the largest in Asia, which sits in solitary splendour at the highest point of the fort, five minutes' walk beyond the museum, commanding superlative views of the countryside below. Needing 100kg of gunpowder for a single shot, the Jaivana could purportedly shoot a cannonball 35km – though its true military value was never accurately gauged since it was never fired in anger.

Most people walk to Jaigarh from Amber Palace, a steep fifteen- to twenty-minute climb. The path to the fort goes from just below the entrance to the palace, branching off from near the top of the zigzagging road (the one used by elephants; not the pedestrian path). The alternative is to descend to the valley and follow the much longer road that leads to both Jaigarh and Nahargarh by vehicle; Jeeps can be hired in Amber village for the return trip to the fort (Rs400, including 2hr waiting time). If you've walked up you'll arrive at the Awani Gate – go through the gate and head left to reach the museum; if you've driven, you'll arrive on the opposite side of the fort, near the Jaivana cannon, where you'll also find several **cafés**.

Amber town

Below the palace, the atmospheric but little-visited **Amber town** is full of remnants of Kachchwaha rule including crumbling havelis, chhatris, and almost four hundred temples. The most striking local landmark is the **Jagat Shiromani Temple**, built by Man Singh after the death in battle of his son and would-have-been successor, a large and florid structure, its shrine topped by an enormous *shikhara* and fronted by an unusually large, two-storey *mandapa* with a curved roof inspired by those on Mughal pavilions. The image of Krishna within is said to have been rescued by Man Singh from the fort at Chittaurgarh after it had been sacked by Akbar. Just beyond the Jagat Shiromani Temple stand the ruins of the much smaller Narsinghji Temple, alongside the remains of the small **palace** which was the original home of the Kachchwaha rulers before the construction of Amber palace proper.

To reach the **Jagat Shiromani Temple**, walk from Amber Fort down the main road away from Jaipur into the centre of Amber Town, then turn left down the road in front of the Government Higher Secondary School – the temple is around 250m ahead on the left. En route you'll pass (also on your left) the fine sixteenth-century **Gyara Mahadev Temple**, approached via a steep flight of steps topped by

a pair of fine elephant statues. The temple was originally built as a Jain shrine but subsequently converted to Hindu use, with an unusual garden courtyard and three *shikhara*-topped shrines fronted by a *mandapa* with a group of pillars at its centre arranged in an octagon – a typical Jain motif.

Walk back towards the main road then turn right to reach the excellent **Anokhi Museum of Hand Printing** (Tues–Sat 10.30am–5pm, Sun 11am–4.30pm; closed May to mid-July; Ⓦwww.anokhimuseum.com; Rs30, camera Rs50, video Rs510) at Kheri Gate, a five-minute walk, passing a superb step-well en route. Housed in an attractive old haveli, the museum has an interesting collection of hand block-printed textiles and garments, along with live demonstrations of printing and carving by resident craftsmen.

Samode

Hidden among the scrubby Aravalli Hills, **SAMODE**, on the edge of Shekhawati, is notable for its impeccably restored eighteenth-century **palace**. This became famous in the 1980s as the setting for the hit Raj-romance movie *The Far Pavilions*, and has now been converted into one of the state's most captivating heritage **hotels**, the ⚜ *Samode Palace* (Ⓣ01423/240014, Ⓦwww.samode.com; from around US$400; discounts during summer; ⓪). It's possible to come here on a day-trip from Jaipur, 42km to the southeast, but if your budget can stretch to it, spend a night in one of the palace's uncompromisingly romantic rooms, plastered with murals and filled with antiques and ornate stonework. Non-guests have to shell out a hefty Rs100 to visit, but it's worth it just to see the beautiful **Sheesh Mahal** on the south side of the building. Three hundred steps lead up from the palace to a hilltop **fort**, the rawal's ruined former residence, with impressive views over the surrounding countryside. Samode village itself is a centre for block printing and lacquered bangle making.

The owners of the Samode Palace also have fifty richly appointed air-conditioned tents, 3km southeast of Samode at *Samode Bagh* (⑥), with their own swimming pool, croquet lawns and tennis courts.

Sanganer and Bagru

SANGANER, 16km south of Jaipur, is the busiest centre for handmade **textiles** in the region, and the best place to watch traditional block printers in action (much of what's on offer can be bought in Jaipur). There are a couple of large factories here, but most of the printing is done in family homes as a cottage industry. Sanganeri craftsmen and women also decorate pottery in Rajasthan's distinctive style – floral designs in white or deep sea-green on a traditional inky-blue glaze. Within the town itself, there are ruined palaces and a handful of elegant Jain temples, most notably the Shri Digamber temple near the Tripolia Gate. Government **buses** and minibuses to Sanganer from Jaipur run from Chand Pol via Ajmer Road (every 15min), or you can catch government bus #201 from Ajmeri Gate.

Serious students of local art might want to continue to **BAGRU**, about 20km further west of Sanganer (and 30km from Jaipur). This small village is well known for its characteristic style of block printing using traditional vegetable dyes. Local artisans can be seen at work in the Chippa Mohalla (printers' quarter). Regular government **buses** #102 run from Jaipur to Bagru (every 15–20min; 45min), passing through the Pink City via Badi Choupad, Choti Choupad and Chand Pol and down Ajmer Road to Bagru.

Sambhar Salt Lake

Around 60km west of Jaipur, the vast **Sambhar Salt Lake** covers almost 200 square kilometres of arid countryside. The lake's water levels and precise extent

vary considerably depending on recent rainfall, though prolonged drought has taken its toll, and the lake has completely dried up in places. About a third of the lake is still used for salt farming, which has been going on here for at least a thousand years, while the lake also attracts migratory birds from across Asia, including large flocks of flamingoes during years when there's been a good monsoon. The railway line from Jaipur to Jodhpur runs around the northern edge of the lake; there are one or two trains each morning from Jaipur to Sambhar Lake station.

On the far side of the lake (around 140km from Jaipur), the bustling little town of **Kuchaman** is home to the attractive *Kuchaman Fort* hotel (☎0/921 404 0882, Ⓦ www.thekuchamanfort.com; ❼), occupying the town's superb old fort – splendidly rugged on the outside, with delicately restored, white-painted rooms within.

Abhaneri step well and Mehandipur Balaji Temple

Some 80km east of Jaipur just north of the main Agra highway, the small village of **ABHANERI** is the unlikely home of the extraordinary **Chand Baori** step well. Built in the ninth century, the well is one of the largest and deepest in India, looking rather like one of Escher's brain-twisting geometrical conceits, with 3500 zigzagging steps descending through thirteen levels to a depth of around 30m (you can climb down, but watch your step). Next to the well stands the interesting **Harshat Mata Temple**, dating back to around the ninth century and decorated with some fine religious panels carved in low relief and with an image of the four-armed Harshat Mata, goddess of mirth and merriment, at its centre. Abhaneri is very difficult to reach by **public transport**, but an easy detour if you have your own vehicle and are travelling between Jaipur and Bharatpur or Agra.

Around 20km east of Abhaneri (and 100km from Jaipur), just south of the Jaipur–Agra highway, lies the remarkable **Mehandipur Balaji Temple**, one of Rajasthan's more outlandish sights. The temple's resident deity is believed to have the power to cure those possessed by evil spirits, attracting a steady string of the afflicted (Tuesdays and Sundays are particularly busy, with long queues to enter the temple). Exorcisms are effected by a range of therapies – anything from reading holy texts or adopting a vegetarian diet to being weighed down beneath heavy stones or chained up to the wall.

North of Jaipur: Shekhawati

North of Jaipur, the land becomes increasingly arid and inhospitable, with farms and fields gradually giving way to wind-blown expanses of undulating semi-desert dotted with endless *khejri* trees and isolated houses enclosed in stockades of thorn. Although now something of a backwater, this region, known as **Shekhawati**, lay on an important caravan route connecting Delhi and Sind (now in Pakistan) with the Gujarati coast, until the rise of Bombay and Calcutta diverted the trans-Thar trade south and eastwards. Having grown rich on trade and taxes from the through traffic, Shekhawati's Marwari merchants and landowning thakurs spent their fortunes competing with one another to build the grand, ostentatiously decorated

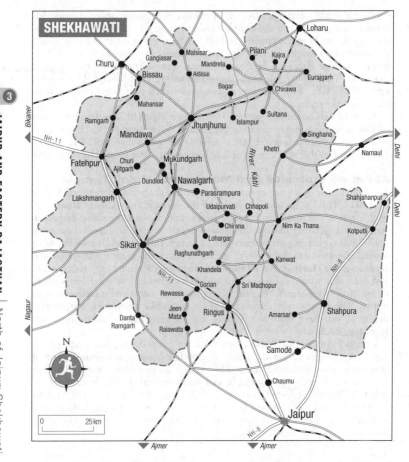

SHEKHAWATI

havelis (see box, p.218) that still line the streets of the region's dusty little towns – an incredible concentration of mansions, palaces and cenotaphs decorated inside and out with elaborate and colourful **murals**.

Considering the wealth of traditional art here, and the region's proximity to Jaipur, most of Shekhawati still feels surprisingly far off the tourist trail, making it one of the most rewarding parts of Rajasthan to explore. **Nawalgarh** and **Mandawa** are the best bases, with a surprisingly good range of accommodation and within easy striking distance of the area's other leading attractions, including the bustling town of **Jhunjhunu**, with its fine collection of crumbling havelis and Indo-Islamic monuments, as well as smaller and sleepier destinations like **Ramgarh**, **Mahansar** and **Fatehpur**. **Getting around** is best done by road. Regular local buses, always overcrowded, connect Shekhawati's main towns, while Jeeps also shuttle between towns and villages, picking up as many passengers as they can cram in. Railway services are hopelessly slow, unreliable and inconvenient. Ilay Cooper's excellent *The Painted Towns of Shekhawati* makes an ideal **guide** to the region, though copies of its last printing are hard to find.

Some history

Shekhawati's history is an intriguing blend of Muslim and Rajput influences. The district's major town, **Jhunjhunu**, was ruled by the Rajput Chauhans of Ajmer until 1450, when it was taken over by Muslim nawabs of the Khaimkani clan, who also gained control of nearby **Fatehpur**. The Khaimkanis ruled for almost three centuries, and parts of Jhunjhunu, in particular, still retain a distinctly Islamic flavour. At about the same time that the Khaimkanis were taking possession of Jhunjhunu, **Rao Shekhaji** (1433–88), a grandson of the Kachchwaha maharaja of Amber, was carving out his own small kingdom in the region, named **Shekhawati**. After centuries of largely peaceful coexistence, Muslim Jhunjhunu was incorporated into Rajput Shekhawati in 1730 when **Sardul Singh** of the **Shekhawat** clan took over Jhunjhunu following the death of the last nawab, Rohilla Khan. Two years later he consolidated Shekhawat rule by helping his brother (already ruler of the nearby town of Sikar) to seize Fatehpur from its Muslim ruler.

Shekhawati is best known, however, not for its Rajput rulers but for its **Marwari merchants** (see p.367). Attacks by brigands against the Marwaris led to their forming an alliance with the British, and in 1835 the latter, eager to gain a foothold in the region, despatched a small force of cavalry called the Shekhawati Brigade to control the robbers. This gave the Marwaris the security they needed to trade, using the profits to build the magnificent havelis that adorn every town in the region. Even though many of the Marwaris subsequently moved to Bombay, Madras and, especially, Calcutta, they continued to send their earnings back to Shekhawati, erecting elaborate buildings either to prove their worth as prospective bridegrooms or simply as work-creation schemes during times of famine.

Following Independence, a number of Marwaris bought British industries, and Marwari families such as Birla and Poddar remain prominent in business today. Many merchant families now live outside the region, with the result that their old mansions have been allowed to fall into a state of disrepair, though renewed tourist interest in the region's heritage has encouraged some owners to embark on much-needed restoration work.

Nawalgarh and around

More or less at the dead centre of Shekhawati, **NAWALGARH** came into its own in 1737, when the Shekhawat Nawal Singh claimed what was then a small village as the site for a fort. Now a lively little market town surrounded by desert and *khejri* scrub, Nawalgarh – along with nearby Mandawa – makes the most convenient and congenial base for exploring Shekhawati, with a bumper crop of painted havelis and a picturesque bazaar, along with a good range of accommodation.

Arrival and information

Nawalgarh's **bus** and **Jeep** stand is 1.5km west of town, around Rs50–70 by auto-rickshaw to the town's various hotels and guesthouses. For trips around the region, you can either jump on and off cheap, cramped village-to-village **Jeeps** (which leave when they're full), or rent a vehicle for the day through Ramesh Jangid at *Apani Dhani* or his son Rajesh at the *Ramesh Jangid Tourist Pension* (see p.214 & p.215). Ramesh and Rajesh also run socially responsible **tours** of Shekhawati. These include Jeep tours of nearby towns and other places of interest (Rs1500–2000), walking tours of Nawalgarh (Rs350/person) and tours by camel cart (Rs1200/day). Babloo Sharma at the Moraka Haveli (☎09828 191232; beware of imitators in the streets outside) can also arrange car and walking tours at similar prices, plus horseriding

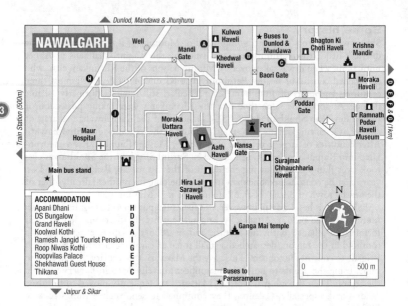

Train Station (500m)

excursions (Rs600/hr). The *Roop Niwas Kothi* hotel also offers horseriding jaunts (Rs600/hr) on its stable of Marwari steeds, a celebrated thoroughbred from the Jodhpur region, originally bred by the crossing Indian ponies with Arabian horses, as well as short camel rides (Rs500/hr) and more extended horse and camel safaris – see ⓦwww.royalridingholidays.com for full details. **Cycles** can be rented at *Apani Dhani* and the *Ramesh Jangid Tourist Pension* (Rs50/day).

Accommodation

Apani Dhani ☎01594/222239, ⓦwww .apanidhani.com. Occupying a fetching cluster of mud-walled Rajasthani village-style huts, this pretty little eco-resort offers an exemplary example of sustainable local tourism – a proportion of profits goes to support environmental and

educational projects, and local artisans earn some income through involvement in the resort's stimulating programme of craft and cultural activities. Rooms (especially those in the slightly more expensive superior category) have plenty of rustic charm, and there's excellent organic food, served

Moving on from Nawalgarh

RSRTC buses leave the main bus stand for **Jaipur** every 15min (3hr 30min), and there's also a deluxe service at 8am; some private buses also serve Jaipur, though these drop passengers 5km outside the centre of Jaipur and are best avoided. Other services include **Jhunjhunu** (every 15–30min; 1hr), **Fatehpur** (1–2 hourly; 1hr 15min) and **Bikaner** (hourly; 3hr 30min). There are a few direct morning buses to **Delhi** (8hr); otherwise change at Jhunjhunu, from where there are hourly services. Buses to **Dundlod** and **Mandawa** (every 30min; 20min & 45min respectively) leave from the bus stand just past Baori Gate on the north edge of town.

The **train station** is a further kilometre beyond the bus station. The line between Nawalgarh and **Delhi** is currently being converted from metre gauge to broad gauge and there are no through trains; it's much easier to take the bus. There are several trains to **Jaipur**, including the #9737 (departs 9am/arrives 1.15pm), #466 (11.25am/3.20pm), and the #474 (3.26pm/7.30pm), but again the bus is faster and more reliable.

up in the bougainvillea-strewn garden, as well as activities including tie-dye and cookery classes, plus tours (see p.213). Book ahead. ❸–❹

DS Bungalow Next to the *Shekhawati Guest House* ☎01594/222703. Cheap and cheerful family guesthouse, with small, cosy air-cooled rooms decorated with quirky ornaments and knick-knacks, plus food fresh from the family farm. ❷

The Grand Haveli and Resort Baori Gate ☎01594/225301, ⓦwww.grandhaveli.com. Occupying the beautifully restored, century-old Patna walo ki Haveli, with attractive heritage-style rooms arranged around a pair of richly painted courtyards. ❼

Koolwal Kothi ☎01594/225817, ⓦwww .welcomheritagehotels.com. Atmospheric heritage hotel in a superbly ornate (if incongruous) Italianate mansion of 1934. Rooms (all a/c) are spacious and comfortable, with bags of period character; ten more replica heritage-style rooms (plus a pool) are planned in the new annexe next door. ❼

Ramesh Jangid Tourist Pension Near Maur Hospital ☎01594/224060, ⓦwww.touristpension .com. Homely guesthouse offering simple but spotless and good-value rooms in a sociable Brahmin family home; the more expensive rooms have solar-heated water and beautiful murals. There's also excellent pure-veg food, internet access, Jeep tours, plus tie-dye, cooking and Hindi classes. ❷–❸

Roop Niwas Kothi 1km east of the town centre ☎01594/222008, ⓦwww.roopniwaskothi.com.

Popular with passing coach parties, this rambling Raj-era mansion has a certain faded elegance, old-fashioned rooms and plenty of period charm at a fairly modest price. ❻

Roopvilas Palace 1km east of the town centre, next to *Roop Niwas Kothi* hotel ☎01594/224321, ⓦwww.roopvilas.com. Gracious heritage hotel, occupying a nineteenth-century royal palace and modern outbuildings scattered around spacious and beautifully maintained grounds. Facilities include a swimming pool and Ayurvedic massage centre. ❻, tents ❼

Shekhawati Guest House 1km east of the town centre, 200m south of the *Roop Niwas Kothi* ☎01594/224658, ⓦwww.shekhawatiguesthouse .com. Run by charming owner Kalpana Singh, this friendly family guesthouse offers accommodation in neat and clean, though rather dark, air-cooled rooms in the main house, or in slightly more expensive garden cottages (with fan). Fresh organic produce is used in the excellent food (veg and non-veg), and guests also get free cookery lessons, while tours can be arranged. ❷, cottages ❸

Thikana (also known locally as *Vishnu Basotia's*) 100m west of the Bhagton ki Haveli ☎09414 082 791, ⓦwww.heritagethikana.com. Friendly family-run hotel in an unbeatably central location, with nicely furnished rooms and lovely views from the upstairs terrace – even if the slightly chintzy pink modern building doesn't really live up to its billing as a "heritage" hotel. ❹

The Town

The logical place to start a tour of Nawalgarh is on the east side of town at the magnificent Anandi Lal Podar Haveli, now housing the **Dr Ramnath A. Podar Haveli Museum** (daily 8am–7pm; foreigners Rs100, Indian residents Rs75, camera Rs30, video Rs50; ⓦwww.podarhavelimuseum.org). Built in 1920 and now doubling up as a school, this is one of the few havelis in Shekhawati to have been restored to its original glory, and has the most vivid murals in town (although purists point out that restoration has involved repainting rather than simple cleaning and restoration). These include the usual scenes from the life of Krishna which appear on virtually every haveli throughout Shekhawati, along with more modern subjects including steam trains, soldiers with rifles and well-dressed local worthies flying kites, as well as false windows with painted people staring out into the courtyard below and a clever 3D-like trompe l'oeil picture of a bull's head which transforms into an elephant's as you move from left to right. The haveli also houses a mildly diverting series of **exhibits** showcasing various aspects of Rajasthani life, including musical instruments, miniature paintings and assorted dolls in traditional wedding costumes.

A short walk to the north lies the fine **Moraka Haveli** (daily 8am–7pm; foreigners Rs50, Indian residents free), whose principal courtyard boasts murals of Shiva, Parvati and Krishna and a *baithak* complete with a fine old hand-pulled *punkah* (fan). The beautiful second courtyard is decorated with friezes showing scenes out of the Ramayana and other episodes from Hindu mythology around the top of its arches, while a small portrait of Jesus can be seen on the topmost storey in the courtyard's

The havelis of Shekhawati

The **havelis** (after the Persian word for "enclosed space") of Shekhawati typically follow a fairly standard pattern. The **entrance** from the street is usually through a grandly decorated gateway or porch with carved brass or wooden doors; this is sometimes placed at the top of a large ramp, designed to be broad enough to be ridden up on an elephant when the occasion required. Inside, most havelis consist of two main court-yards. Entering the haveli, you step into the first courtyard, the **mardana**, or men's, courtyard; visitors were normally received here in the **baithak**, an open-sided meeting room, usually to the left of the main entrance, often finely embellished with ornate pillars and sometimes equipped with a huge, manually operated fan, or *punkah*.

From the *mardana* courtyard, a second doorway (often the most richly decorated in the entire haveli, and usually surmounted by a figure of Ganesh, the Hindu god of prosperity and good fortune) leads into the second principal courtyard, the **zenana**, or women's courtyard. This is where the ladies of the house lived in purdah, shielded from the public eyes, although a latticed window next to the *zenana* entrance allowed them to spy on proceedings in the *mardana*, while in some havelis there is also an upper storey above the *mardana* courtyard reserved for the use of women to observe proceedings in the *baithak* below. The *zenana* was also home to the haveli's kitchen, often recognizable by the areas of smoke-blackened plaster surrounding it.

Although the majority of havelis consist of just these two main courtyards, some of the grander examples boast four or even six separate courtyards, while there are also occasional examples of so-called "**double havelis**", basically two separate havelis joined together, each of which would have been used by related families, typically those belonging to a pair of brothers. In addition, many also have a subsidiary courtyard to one side which was used for stabling horses, camels or even elephants.

Murals

The flamboyant murals that often cover both the interior and exterior walls of Shekha-wati's havelis were painted by craftsmen from outside the region. Religious themes, especially episodes from the life of Krishna, were often depicted along the lintels above the main exterior doors to cultivate faith among the uneducated masses, as well as on walls inside the havelis.

What sets the murals of Shekhawati apart from those elsewhere in India, however, is not their religious paintings but the incongruous and often charmingly naive depic-tions of contemporary machines, outlandish foreigners and the latest European fashions, from pictures of early aeroplanes, steam trains and boats to Edwardian memsahibs in big hats. Quaintly old-fashioned now, at the time when they were painted these exotic images represented everything that was most modern and exotic in the outside world, one which the women and poor townsfolk of Shekhawati had no hope of ever seeing with their own eyes (nor, for that matter, the artists themselves, most of whom had probably never seen the newfangled European novelties they were asked to depict). Nowadays, most of the murals are faded, defaced, covered with posters or even just whitewashed over. In some ways this simply adds to their haunting appeal, and there are so many – and the towns are so small – that you cannot fail to see a work of art virtually everywhere you look.

Visiting Shekhawati's havelis

An increasing number of havelis have now been restored and opened as museums. Most, however, remain in a state of picturesque dilapidation and are still occupied by local families, while others have been abandoned, and are now empty apart from a solitary *chowkidar* (caretaker-cum-guard). Visitors are welcome to look around inside some havelis in return for a small tip (Rs20–30 is sufficient), while others remain closed to outsiders. If in doubt, just stick your head in the front door and ask, but remember that you're effectively entering someone's private home, and never go inside without permission.

southeast corner (on the far left-hand side as you enter). Directly opposite the Moraka Haveli lies the eye-catching **Krishna Mandir**, dating from the mid-eighteenth century, a florid mass of delicate chhatris housing no less than eleven lingas.

About 200m east of the Moraka Haveli, the unrestored, 150-year-old **Bhagton ki Choti Haveli** (no set hours, though the resident *chowkidar* can usually be found sitting on the doorstep waiting for visitors; Rs40) has an unusually varied selection of murals including a European-style angel and Queen Victoria (over the arches by the right of the main door) along with Krishna and Radha on a swing. On the left, a trompe-l'oeil picture shows seven women arranged into the shape of an elephant, plus a painting of a festive stick dance, while other pictures show Europeans riding bicycles along with a steamboat and a train. A fine brass door leads into the *zenana* courtyard, from where a latticed window allowed the ladies of the house to keep an eye on events in the men's courtyard. A room overlooking the entrance to the *zenana* boasts a quirky mural showing a mournful European man smoking a pipe, while a woman plays an accordion.

A further fine pair of havelis lies west of here, side by side, due north of the Nansa Gate. The first, the **Khedwal Haveli**, is still inhabited and can usually only be viewed from the outside; look through the main entrance and you can catch a glimpse of the lovely mirrorwork (and a train) on the upper storey of the main courtyard. A few metres north, the **Kulwal Haveli** is also inhabited, though open for visitors on payment of a small baksheesh. Pictures of Gandhi and Nehru adorn the entrance porch, while a European woman sits above the main door applying her lipstick; the bizarrely ornate Italianate building opposite formerly served as the haveli's guesthouse and now houses the *Koolwal Kothi* hotel. Inside the haveli, a fine door, studded with miniature peacocks, leads through to the *zenana* courtyard, with pretty red and blue floral motifs covering every surface, along with the usual religious pictures, although the murals in the vicinity of the kitchen have been more or less completely obliterated by smoke from cooking fires – a common occurrence in havelis throughout Shekhawati.

The fort

Central Nawalgarh has plenty of old-fashioned, small-town charm, with dozens of tiny shops and lots of street vendors hawking piles of merchandise by the side of the road. At the heart of the town, the **fort** (Bala Qila) has more or less vanished under a cluster of modern buildings huddled around a central courtyard that now hosts the town's colourful vegetable market. The dilapidated building on the far left-hand side of the courtyard (by the Bank of Baroda) has a magnificent, eerily echoing **Sheesh Mahal**, covered in mirrorwork, which once served as the dressing room of the maharani of Nawalgarh, its ceiling decorated with pictorial maps of Nawalgarh and Jaipur. You'll have to pay the usual Rs20–30 baksheesh to see the room; if no one's around, ask at the sweet factory on the opposite side of the courtyard.

East of Nansa Gate

The havelis on the eastern side of Nawalgarh are less striking than those on the west, though this part of town is generally more peaceful, with fewer roving teenage touts. Heading west through the Nansa Gate (signed, confusingly, as the "Rambilas Podar Memorial Gate") and following the road around brings you to the so-called **Aath Haveli** (Eight Havelis, built by eight brothers, although only six were actually completed), a complex of heavily decorated mansions featuring murals in a range of styles depicting the usual mishmash of subjects both ancient and modern. The haveli in the southwest corner of the compound is the most interesting, sporting pictures of European ladies going for a ride in a very early motorcar, and a rather odd-looking steam train whose carriages look like little houses on wheels, along with the usual horses, elephants and camels. The newly restored **Moraka Uattara Haveli**, opposite (daily 8am–6pm; Rs50), also has a richly painted exterior and *mardana* courtyard, with elephants and horses framed in a mass of florid decoration. Close by stands the **Hira Lal Sarawgi Haveli**, its facade adorned with three large cars, plus an elaborate bridge.

Further havelis dot the streets south and southeast of the Nansa Gate, one of the quietest and most atmospheric parts of town. These include the **Surajmal Chhauchharia Haveli**, whose murals include two small pictures of Europeans floating past in hot-air balloons. The painter took some playful licence as to the mechanics involved, with the passengers keeping their balloons aloft by blowing into them through small pipes.

Around Nawalgarh

The most obvious target for a day-trip from Nawalgarh is **DUNDLOD**, 7km north and the site of an old fort and some large havelis. It's possible to get there by bus, but most people walk across the fields – a leisurely two-hour amble that's enjoyable save for the last couple of kilometres, which you have to cover via a rough sandy track linking the village with the main road. The musty old **fort** (Rs20) is worth a quick visit for its atmospheric Diwan-i-Khana, a fine old drawing room painted a vivid orange and filled with antique European furniture and books. Entry to the *diwan* was restricted to men; women were confined to the *duchatta*, on the storey above, whose blue-columned rooms are filled with further old bric-a-brac. The fort also houses the *Dundlod Fort hotel* (℡01594/252519 or 0141/211275, ⓦwww.dundlod.com; ❻); rooms are a bit shabby and overpriced, though it's a good place to organize local horseriding tours (3–12 days) on one of the castle's thoroughbred Marwari mounts.

Radiating from the southeastern walls of the fort, the **village** harbours several interesting havelis, most notably the meticulously restored Seth Arjun Das Goenka Haveli of 1870 (daily 8am–7pm; Rs40; ⓦwww.goenkahaveli.com), its interior covered in a profusion of finely detailed frescoes on assorted religious themes. Close by lies the delicate chhatri of Ram Dutt Goenka (1888), with vibrant friezes lining its dome.

A few kilometres north of Dundlod on the road to Mandawa lies the flyblown little town of **MUKUNDGARH**. The atmospheric old fort here hosts an atmospheric if rather moth-eaten heritage hotel, though the whole place was closed for renovations and upgrading at the time of writing. A five-minute walk from the fort, straddling either side of a quiet back road, lie the two large **Saraf Havelis** (Rs50, if you can find the *chowkidar*), built by a pair of brothers around 1900 in quasi-European style, with Italianate arcaded courtyards and a rather sombre pea-soup colour scheme. The haveli closest to the fort is one of the largest in Shekhawati, with no less than eight courtyards (although only the first two are open to visitors); the second haveli is smaller but more finely decorated.

There are more painted buildings dotted around the serene hamlet of **PARAS-RAMPURA**, 20km southeast of Nawalgarh, set amid rolling hills dotted with *janti* trees that makes for some of the most attractive desert scenery in Rajasthan. Buses run every thirty minutes or so, or you could cycle (although be warned that several stretches of the track degenerate into soft sand). Monuments include the **Gopinath temple**, built in 1742, whose murals depict the torments of hell (a common theme in the eighteenth century) alongside images of the local Rajput ruler, Sardul Singh, with his five sons. Some of the paintings are unfinished, as the artists were diverted to decorate the **chhatri of Rajul Singh**, who died that same year. The large dome of this exquisite memorial contains a flourish of lively murals, once again including images of hell, and of Sardul Singh with his sons. Parasrampura's modest **fort**, in reasonable repair, is on the west bank of the dry river bed.

Jhunjhunu

Spreading in a mass of brick and concrete from the base of a rocky hill, **JHUNJHUNU** is a busy and largely unprepossessing town, though it preserves an interesting old central bazaar and a fine collection of havelis decorated with vigorous murals – less technically accomplished than those in many other parts of Shekhawati, but possessing a distinct, naive charm all of their own. Jhunjhunu is usually visited as a day-trip from nearby Nawalgarh or Mandawa, though it has a couple of good accommodation options if you want to stay overnight.

Arrival

The government bus stand is just south of the town centre; the private bus stand is east of the main bazaar, though you're unlikely to need to use it. The **Tourist Reception Centre** is at the *RTDC Tourist Bungalow* on Mandawa Circle at the western edge of town, though it was closed at the time of writing. Jhunjhunu is quite spread out, and walking around can be tiring, but many of the streets of the old town are too narrow for cars; **rickshaws** operate as taxis, picking up as many passengers as they can. Laxmi Jangid at the Jamuna Resort

Moving on from Jhunjhunu

Buses run from the government stand in the south of town to Nawalgarh (every 30min; 1hr) and towns throughout Shekhawati, as well as to Bikaner (hourly; 5hr 30min), Jaipur (every 30min; 4hr–4hr 30min) and Delhi (hourly; 7hr 30min). Buses to Mandawa (every 30min; 45min–1hr) also stop by Mandawa Circle near the *RTDC Tourist Bungalow*. **Train** services are currently in a state of flux due to the conversion of the line to Delhi from metre gauge to broad gauge, meaning that there are no direct services to the capital at present – it's much easier to catch a bus. There are a number of services to Jaipur, though again the bus is faster and more reliable.

(see below) offers full-day **tours** around Shekhawati by car or Jeep for Rs2000, as well as shorter camel tours (2hr; Rs600/person).

Accommodation and eating

The following are the best of the **accommodation** options in and around Jhunjhunu. There are no good restaurants in town, and you'll almost certainly end up **eating** where you're staying, unless you fancy braving one of the *dhabas* around the government bus stand.

Jhunjhunu

Fresco Palace Paramveer Path, off Station Rd ☎01592/395233, ⓦwww.frescopalace.com. Pleasant modern hotel (although there aren't many frescoes in evidence), with comfortable, slightly chintzy rooms (all a/c) and a relaxing garden restaurant. ❺

Jamuna Resort Delhi–Sikar Rd ☎01592/232871, ⓦwww.shivshekhawati.com. This attractive village-style resort on the eastern edge of town comprises a cluster of thatch-roofed cottages (all a/c) set amid extensive grounds complete with pool (non-guests Rs50) and garden restaurant. The more expensive rooms are exquisitely decorated with mirrorwork and traditional murals. They also run courses in Indian cooking and art, plus free yoga classes. Also a good place to arrange tours. ❹–❺

Sangam Paramveer Path, opposite the government bus stand ☎01592/232544. Basic cheapie with large but bare and slightly shabby rooms – make sure you get one away from the noisy main road. ❷

Shekhawati Heritage ☎01592/237134. A cheaper, if significantly less appealing, alternative to the *Fresco Palace* next door, with

plain but comfortable a/c rooms. Not much English spoken. ❹

Shiv Shekhawati Khemi Shakti Rd, near Muni Ashram ☎01592/232651 or 32651, ⓦwww .shivshekhawati.com. Well-maintained modern hotel with large, clean rooms (all a/c), restaurant and internet access. ❷–❹

Around Jhunjhunu

Alsisar Mahal Alsisar Village, 15km north of Jhunjhunu ☎01595/275271, ⓦwww.alsisar.com. The ancestral home of the thakurs of Alsisar, this grand old fort has now been spruced up and reopened as a luxurious hotel, complete with spotless traditional-style rooms, lofty courtyards and an attractive swimming pool. Good value. ❼

Piramal Haveli Bagar Village, 15km northeast of Jhunjhunu ☎01592/221220, ⓦwww.neemrana hotels.com. Intimate, self-styled "non-hotel" with just eight rooms in an unusual 1920s Rajasthani-cum-Italianate villa set in a peaceful rural location. Rooms are simple but comfortable, and there's a lovely garden. ❹, with 20–40 percent discounts from May to Aug.

The Town

Hidden away in the alleyways behind the main bazaar is Jhunjhunu's most striking building, the magnificent **Khetri Mahal** of 1760 (no set hours; Rs20), a superb, open-sided sandstone palace with cusped Islamic-style arches which wouldn't look out of place amid the great Indo-Islamic monuments of Fatehpur Sikri. The whole edifice seems incongruously grand amid the modest streets of central Jhunjhunu and now stands empty and largely abandoned, apart from the upper terraces, which serve as impromptu open-air classrooms for local schoolchildren. A covered ramp, wide enough for horses, winds up to the roof, from where there are sweeping views over the town and across to the massive ramparts of the sturdy **Badalgarh Fort** (currently closed to the public, although there are plans to renovate it as a hotel) on a nearby hilltop. The Khetri Mahal is surprisingly tricky to find for such a grand building – you'll probably need to ask for directions; entrance to the building is via the school around the back.

Stretching east of the Khetri Mahal is Jhunjhunu's main bazaar, centred around **Futala Market**, a fascinating (and hopelessly confusing) tangle of narrow streets crammed with dozens of tiny, charmingly old-fashioned shops painted in pastel greens and blues, many of them owned by the town's sizeable Muslim population. On the northern edge of the bazaar, facing each other across the small square of Chabutra Chowk, lie the two so-called **Modi Havelis**. The one on the eastern side is most impressive, entered via a grand, 3m-high ramp (a common feature of havelis in Jhunjhunu). The facade boasts symmetrical murals on either side featuring a pair of rabbits, while soldiers on horseback race a train above; the right-hand side also sports a small plane and a lady listening to a gramophone. The western haveli is less well preserved, with sections of the interior arches now blocked up with concrete and large chunks of missing plaster. Despite the encroaching dereliction, a few touchingly naive pictures remain, including various moustachioed Indian bigwigs around the door into the zenana courtyard, though the comic effect is perhaps the result of a lack of painterly skill rather than deliberate satirical intent.

Along Nehru Bazaar

Jhunjhunu's finest havelis are spread out along **Nehru bazaar**, immediately east of the main bazaar. Heading east, you'll first reach the striking **Kaniram Narsinghdas Tibrewala Haveli** of 1883, perched on a platform above the surrounding vegetable stalls; the entrance is around the back, on the north side of the haveli. On the west wall of the *mardana* courtyard two quaint trains chunter towards each another, one filled with livestock and the other with stylized little people – a lot more orderly than your average Indian railway carriage. On the north wall of the same courtyard a man combs his luxuriant beard in a mirror, while in adjacent panels a man and woman manipulate a puppet and another gentleman smokes a pipe while stroking a small and rather bizarre-looking dog.

Further east down Nehru Bazaar, entered via an impressive ramp up from street level, the **Mohanlal Ishwardas Modi Haveli** has a good selection of entertainingly naive portraits. Unusual oval miniatures of various Indian grandees frame the entrance to the *zenana* courtyard, while in the zenana itself a long frieze of miniature portraits runs around the top of the arches showing assorted European and Indian personages sporting a range of flouncy costumes, silly hats and magnificent moustaches. Immediately north of here, the striking little **Bihari temple** features some of the oldest murals in Shekhawati, painted in 1776 in black and brown vegetable pigments, including a dramatic depiction inside the central dome of the scene from the Ramayana in which the Hanuman's monkey army takes on the forces of the many-headed demon king Ravana; the five sons of Sardul Singh (each of whom built a fort in the town) regard the scene impassively from across the dome.

Outlying sights

West of the Khetri Mahal at the foot of the craggy Nehara Pahar lies the **Dargah of Kamaruddin Shah**, an atmospheric complex comprising a mosque and *madrasa* arranged around a pretty courtyard (still retaining some of its original murals), with the ornate *dargah* (tomb) of the Sufi saint Kamaruddin Shah in the centre. Next to the roadside immediately to the south, and now almost buried in the scrub, stands a touching monument to the infant son of Henry Forster, commander of the British-run Shekhawati Brigade (see p.213), who died in 1841 aged 1 year and 5 months.

North of the town centre lies the **Mertani Baori**, one of the region's most impressive step-wells, while further east is the huge **Rani Sati Mandir**. Few foreigners visit this shrine, the centre of the phenomenally popular Sati Mata cult and reputedly the richest temple in the country after Tirupati (in Andhra Pradesh), receiving hundreds of thousands of pilgrims each year and millions of rupees in donations. Its immense popularity bears witness to the enduring awe with which *satis* – women who commit ritual suicide by climbing onto the funeral pyre of their husband – are regarded in the state. Although banned by the British in 1829 in areas under their rule, the practice has survived in parts of rural Rajasthan; forty cases are known to have occurred since Independence, the most infamous being that of **Roop Kanwar**, an 18-year-old Rajput girl who committed self-immolation in 1987 in the village of Deorala, near Jaipur, sparking off nationwide outrage and controversy. The *sati* commemorated here was performed by a merchant's wife in 1595. Her image, rendered in tiles and mirrorwork, adorns the ceiling of the main prayer hall, while a sequence of panels on the north wall relates the legend surrounding the events of her death.

Mandawa

Roughly halfway between Jhunjhunu and Fatehpur, the much younger town of **MANDAWA** was founded in 1755 by the Shekhawats, who constructed the town's imposing **fort**, now home to the upmarket *Castle Mandawa* hotel. This is the most touristy place in Shekhawati, although the handicraft shops, touts and guides detract very little from the town's profusion of beautifully dilapidated mansions.

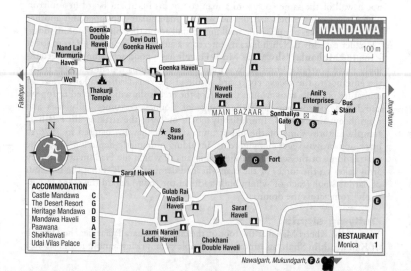

MANDAWA

0   100 m

Fatehpur

Jhunjhunu

Goenka Double Haveli
Devi Dutt Goenka Haveli
Nand Lal Murmuria Haveli
Well
Goenka Haveli
Thakurji Temple
Naveti Haveli
Anil's Enterprises
Bus Stand
MAIN BAZAAR
Sonthaliya Gate Ⓐ Ⓑ
Bus Stand
N
Fort Ⓒ
Saraf Haveli
Gulab Rai Wadia Haveli
Saraf Haveli
Laxmi Narain Ladia Haveli
Chokhani Double Haveli

ACCOMMODATION
Castle Mandawa   C
The Desert Resort   G
Heritage Mandawa   D
Mandawa Haveli   B
Paawana   A
Shekhawati   E
Udai Vilas Palace   F

RESTAURANT
Monica   1

Nawalgarh, Mukundgarh, Ⓕ &

Moving on from Mandawa

Regular **buses** run from Sonthaliya Gate to Jhunjhunu (every 30min; 1hr) and Nawalgarh (every 30min; 45min). Services to Fatehpur (every 30min; 1hr) leave from the stand in the centre of town, just off the main bazaar. There are also a number of services (mostly in the morning) from Sonthaliya Gate to Jaipur (4hr) and Bikaner (3hr 30min).

Arrival and information

Buses from Jhunjhunu, Nawalgarh, Jaipur and Bikaner arrive at Sonthaliya Gate in the east of town. From Fatehpur, most buses pull in at a stand in the centre, just off the main bazaar. **Jeeps** also run to Jhunjhunu, Nawalgarh and other nearby towns. The town is so small that both bus stands are within walking distance of most hotels. **Internet** access is generally available at all hotels; if not, there are various places along the main bazaar – try Anil's Enterprises (Rs50/hr; open 24hr), opposite the *Mandawa Haveli* hotel; they also **change cash and travellers' cheques**.

Taking a **walking tour** to see Mandawa's scattered havelis is recommended; guides can be arranged through your hotel, or at Classic Shekhawati Tours (℡01592/223144, ⓔclassicshekhamnd@yahoo.co.in), by the entrance to the fort. Count on around Rs250–350 for a two- to three-hour walk. Most guesthouses and hotels can also arrange Jeep tours and trips out into the surrounding desert either on horseback, camelback or in camel-drawn carts. Prices for all these activities vary wildly, but are usually cheapest if booked through the *Hotel Shekhawati*, who also run overnight **camel safaris** camping out in the desert. Classic Shekhawati Tours arranges more upmarket day and overnight camel safaris, though you'll need to book five days in advance.

Accommodation and eating

Mandawa has a good spread of **hotels** in all price ranges. You'll probably **eat** at your hotel; evening meals at *Castle Mandawa*, *Heritage Mandawa* and *Mandawa Haveli* are usually accompanied by live music and folk dancing, if you like that sort of thing. If you want to venture out, head for the *Monica* rooftop restaurant (follow the signs from the entrance road to the fort), which dishes up probably the best food in town, with well-prepared veg and non-veg North Indian standards (mains Rs90–250) backed up with cold beer and friendly service.

Castle Mandawa ℡01592/223124, ⓦwww
.castlemandawa.com. Set in the old town fort, with an atmospheric mishmash of buildings around a sand-filled courtyard. All rooms are different, so look at several before you decide, since standards of comfort and decor vary considerably – and prices are relatively high for what you get. Amenities include a spa, gym, pool (guests only) and spacious gardens. ❼

▊▊▊▊▊▊▊▊ Mukandgarh Rd, 1.5km from Mandawa ℡01592/223151, ⓦwww.mandawa hotels.com. Just outside Mandawa, this attractively rustic little resort occupies a tangle of mud-walled traditional village-style Rajasthani cottages in a soothingly peaceful rural setting,

with a mixture of comfy rooms and nicely decorated (though rather dark) a/c cottages, plus a pool. Rooms ❻, cottages ❼

Heritage Mandawa Off Mukandgarh Rd south of the bus stand ℡01592/223742, ⓦwww.hotel heritagemandawa.com. Brightly painted, late nineteenth-century mansion with a mixed bag of rooms (all a/c), some cosily furnished in period style (although the standard rooms are rather poky), others boasting vibrant Shekhawati-style murals. ❹–❺

Mandawa Haveli Near Sonthaliya Gate ℡01592/223088, ⓦhttp://hotelmandawa.free.fr. Far and away Mandawa's most atmospheric heritage hotel, occupying a superb old haveli plastered with original murals. Rooms (all a/c) and, especially, suites, have bags of period character, and there's also a nice rooftop restaurant. Rates discounted in summer by 20–40 percent. ⑤–⑥

Paawana Main bazaar ☎01592/223663, ⓦwww .hotelpaawana.com. Recently opened hotel in a neat modern building, done up with the obligatory murals and offering attractively furnished a/c rooms at surprisingly affordable prices. ③

Shekhawati Off Mukandgarh Rd south of the bus stand ☎09314 698079, ⓦwww.hotelshekhawati .com. Excellent budget option in an eye-catchingly decorated house (although the paintings are all

modern). Rooms are spacious and clean (the more expensive ones come with a/c and pretty murals), and there's also good food and cheap tours. Local drivers in search of commission may try to take you to the nearby (but considerably more expensive) *Heritage Mandawa*. ①–④

Udai Vilas Palace Mukandgarh Rd ☎09414 023378, ⓦwww.uvpmandawa.com. Upmarket resort hotel in a peaceful rural location five minutes' drive south from Mandawa, set amid three acres of landscaped grounds with fine desert views and accommodation in smart modern rooms. Facilities include a Keralan Ayurvedic spa, gym and pool. ⑥

The Town

Tours usually begin with the **Naveti Haveli** (now the State Bank of Bikaner & Jaipur), on the main bazaar in the centre of town. Duck through the metal gate to the right of the bank (no charge) for a look at Mandawa's most entertaining wall of murals, including well-preserved images of a bird-man attempting to take flight, the Wright brothers' aeroplane, a man using a telephone and a strongman pulling a car.

A ten-minute walk west from here brings you to an interesting cluster of buildings centred around the **Nand Lal Murmuria Haveli**. The murals here are relatively modern, dating from the 1930s and executed in a decidedly flowery and sentimental style, perhaps influenced by contemporary European magazines, with various Venetian scenes (the Grand Canal, Rialto and San Marco), along with George V, Nehru riding a horse and the legendary Maratha warrior Shivaji. Next door, the sun-faded **Goenka Double Haveli** (comprising the Vishwanath Goenka Haveli and Tarkeshwar Goenka Haveli – and not to be confused with either of the town's other Goenka havelis nearby) is one of the largest and grandest in Mandawa, with two separate entrances and striking elephants and horses on the facade. The **Thakurji temple** opposite has a rather odd mural (on the right-hand side of the facade) showing soldiers being fired from the mouths of cannon, a favoured British method of executing mutinous sepoys during the 1857 uprising. Further west are a couple of chhatris, and a step-well, still used today and bearing paintings inside its decorative corner domes.

South of the main bazaar, the **Gulab Rai Wadia Haveli** is one of the finest in town. The south-facing exterior wall is particularly interesting, with unusually racy (albeit modestly small) murals depicting, among other things, a Kama Sutra like scene in a railway carriage and (up in the eaves) a woman giving birth and a pair of copulating horses. Erotic carvings elsewhere on the building have been whitewashed over. The interior of the haveli is entered via a grand ramp, with Belgian glass mirrorwork over the finely carved door (topped by the usual Ganesh figure) leading into the *zenana* courtyard.

Immediately south of here lies the almost equally fine **Laxmi Narain Ladia Haveli**. The *zenana* courtyard boasts naive paintings of a plane and a steamship, along with a cannon being pulled by horses and a tiger attacking a centaur. Some 100m further south, the unusually large **Chokhani Double Haveli** (Rs20) consists of two separate wings built for two brothers; look for the miserable British soldiers and chillum-smoking sadhu facing one another in the recess at the centre of the facade.

Fatehpur and around

Lying just off NH-11, **FATEHPUR** is the closest town in Shekhawati to Bikaner, 116km west, and a convenient place to stop if you're taking the northern route across the Thar to or from Jaisalmer. The town itself is run-down and drab, but it does boast several elaborately painted mansions, temples, wells and chhatris.

The most celebrated of Fatehpur's havelis is the **Nadine Le Prince Haveli** (daily 8am–7pm; Rs100), an 1802 mansion restored to its original splendour by its current owner and namesake, a French artist, who purchased the haveli in 1998. Some local aficionados complain about the manner in which the haveli has been restored – with large-scale repainting of murals, rather than the simple cleaning and preservation of existing art – but the overall effect is undeniably impressive, and the haveli as a whole is one of the few in Shekhawati where you get a real sense of how these lavish mansions would originally have looked, complete with superbly carved wooden doors and beams and a dense spread of murals, including pictures showing Lakshmi

Lakshmangarh & RTDC Hotel Haveli (2km)

being showered by elephants. An impressively large and deep (albeit seriously dilapidated) **well**, flanked by chhatris, stands immediately south of the haveli.

Several further fine havelis lie clustered immediately around the Nadine Le Prince Haveli. Next door on the west side, the **Saraf Haveli** has fine exterior murals (albeit missing large chunks of plaster – a common sight in Fatehpur), while opposite lies the expansive **Devra Lal Haveli**, fronted by an unusually elaborate sequence of arched porches, their undersides covered with well-preserved medallion portraits.

Close to the Nadine Le Prince Haveli, the imposing **Jagannath Singania Haveli** (also closed to visitors) towers over the main road north. Most of the exterior paintings have faded; the best are on the western facade of the small building around the back, including Krishna and Radha framed by elephants and some heavily bewhiskered Europeans toting guns. South from here, the **Geori Shankar Haveli** (next to an unusually fine bangle stall) is the polar opposite of the Nadine Le Prince Haveli, dilapidated but hugely atmospheric, and still inhabited by a number of impoverished local families. There's fine mirrorwork in the ceiling of the main entrance arch and around the doorway into the *zenana* courtyard, while the predominantly religious paintings of the *mardana* courtyard include a fine Narashima (Vishnu in his lion incarnation) and a panel showing legendary local folk heroes Dhola and Maru (see p.305) on a camel. It's also worth climbing up to the rooftop terrace, decorated with unusual elephant statues, for the fine views over town.

Further havelis lie dotted around town. These include the two well-preserved Barthia Havelis, next to the main road at the northern end of town, built in an unusual but rather elegant Neoclassical style; and the more traditional (though very dilapidated) **Keria** and **Das Saraogi Havelis**, just south of the private bus stand.

Practicalities

Fatehpur has two **bus stands**, near each other in the centre of town on the main Sikar–Churu (north–south) road. Buses from the government Roadways stand, furthest south, serve Jaipur (every 30min; 3hr 30min), Ramgarh (hourly; 30min), Bikaner (14 daily; 3hr 30min–4hr) and Delhi (5 daily; 6hr). Private buses run from the stand further north along the bazaar to Mandawa (every 30min; 45min), Jhunjhunu (every 30min; 1hr), Mahansar (4 daily; 45min) and Ramgarh (hourly; 30min). Arriving in Fatehpur, note that many buses drop passengers off at the NH-11 intersection, about 1km south of town. The **railway station** lies east of town, though the line north of Fatehpur is currently being converted from metre gauge to broad gauge, meaning that there are no through services to Bikaner. For Jaipur, there are a couple of services daily, though the bus is quicker and more reliable.

Just off NH-11, the modern RTDC *Hotel Haveli* (℡01571/230293; ❹) is the town's only plausible **hotel**, though its large and light rooms, some with air contioning, don't quite compensate for the dodgy plumbing and general air of neglect. It's also a fair walk from the bazaar and bus stand. For **food**, you've a less than inspiring choice between the RTDC *Hotel Haveli*'s hit-and-miss overpriced menu, or the row of basic *dhabas* near the bus stand.

Around Fatehpur

Some of Shekhawati's finest monuments and murals are scattered across three small towns in the far north and west of the region: **Mahansar**, **Ramgarh** and **Lakshmangarh**. Of these, only Mahansar has any accommodation, though the other two are easily visitable on day-trips from Mandawa or Nawalgarh. Slightly further afield, outside Shekhawati proper, the **Tal Chhapar Wildlife Sanctuary** is home to one of India's most important populations of blackbuck.

Mahansar

The relative inaccessibility of **MAHANSAR**, marooned amid a sea of scrub and drifting sand north of Mandawa, has ensured that its monuments remain among the least visited in the region, making the village a peaceful place to hole up for a day or two. There are two main reasons to come here. The first is to **stay** at the quirky *Narayan Niwas Castle* (℡01595/264322, ⊛www.mehansarcastle.com; ❹). Managed by Mahansar's royal family in their crumbling 1768 abode, it contains fourteen rooms of varying standards, including two memorably appointed heritage rooms (#1 and #5) and some cheaper, but still deeply atmospheric, standard doubles (albeit stronger on period charm than creature comforts).

The second reason is to visit the stunning **Sona ki Dukan Haveli** ("Gold Shop Haveli"; Rs100; no set hours; ask around the shops for the key) in the middle of the village. The paintings in the entrance hall are the finest in Shekhawati, with three sequences of murals depicting the exploits of Rama, the various incarnations of Vishnu, and the life of Krishna, all painted in superb detail and picked out in lavish gold leaf (hence the haveli's name).

While you're here, it's also worth having a look at the nearby **Raghunath Mandir**. Like many temples in Shekhawati, this looks more like a haveli than a traditional Hindu shrine, built on a square ground plan around a single interior courtyard and covered inside and out in a flourish of colourful murals. Upstairs, there are good views over town from the eye-catching rooftop, lined with a long line of small chhatris alternating with pavilions topped with the distinctively curved bangaldar ("Bengal") roofs which are such a characteristic feature of Rajasthani and Mughal architecture.

Ramgarh

RAMGARH, 20km north of Fatehpur, was founded in 1791 and developed as something of a status symbol by disaffected members of the wealthy Poddar merchant family, who made every effort to outshine nearby Churu, which they left following a dispute with the local thakur over the wool tax. They succeeded in their aim: Ramgarh is one of the most beautiful – but also one of the least-visited – towns in Shekhawati, with the usual fine havelis along with an exceptional array of religious architecture as well.

Starting from the bus stand on the west side of town, follow either of the two roads east into the town centre. After about five minutes' walk you'll reach the **Poddar family havelis**, a superb cluster of ornate mansions that cover the entire area immediately west of the main town square. The streets here form one of the most architecturally perfect ensembles in Shekhawati, the havelis' patrician ochre facades decorated with scenes from local folk stories and a frequently repeated motif, comprising three fishes joined at the mouth, which is unique to Ramgarh.

Just beyond here lies the town's main square, surrounded by the disintegrating remains of further lavishly painted havelis. Turn left here and head through the Churu Gate, beyond which the road is lined with a dense cluster of extraordinarily ornate **temples and memorial chhatris** erected by various members of the Poddar clan, their rooftops capped with a fantastical array of domes and arcades. Walking along the road you'll pass (on your right) the Ganga Temple, its entrance steps flanked by a fine elephant mural (the companion painting which stood on the opposite side of the steps has recently disintegrated – a fairly typical example of the parlous condition of many of Shekhawati's finest murals) and (on your left) the Ganesh temple, boasting a richly painted forecourt. These are followed by a number of elaborate chhatris erected to commemorate assorted Poddar notables. If you have a guide (it's virtually impossible to find otherwise) it's also worth searching out the nearby **Shanicharji Mandir**, a diminutive temple dedicated to Saturnand decorated with sparkling mirrorwork.

If you want to stay in Ramgarh, the newly opened *Ramgarh Fresco* hotel (℡09971 133230, ⓦwww.ramgarhfresco.com; ❺–❻) offers characterful lodgings in the lovingly restored Khemka Haveli of 1910, decorated with a fine series of murals. The hotel has a varied selection of attractively furnished rooms (all attached with fan), plus two air-conditioned suites, and there's also internet access, a massage centre and café.

Lakshmangarh

The small town of **LAKSHMANGARH**, 20km south of Fatehpur, is another archetypal, but seldom visited, Shekhawati destination, its neat grid of streets (a layout inspired by that of Jaipur's Pink City) dotted with dozens of ornate havelis in various stages of picturesque decay. The town is dominated by its dramatic nineteenth-century **fort**, which crowns a rocky outcrop on the west side of town. The fort is currently closed to the public, though you can walk up the steep track to the entrance to enjoy the fine views over town and its

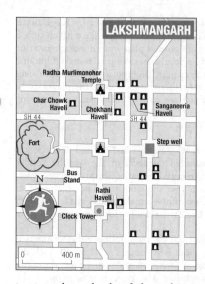

various crumbling mansions, including the extensive **Char Chowk Haveli** (Four-Courtyard Haveli), off to the left, the finest in town and one of the largest in Shekhawati. Most of the haveli's exterior paintings have faded (some impressive but now rather faint elephants, horses and camels survive on the northern and eastern exterior walls) and large sections of plaster have fallen off, although the paintings under the eaves remain well preserved. The haveli remains inhabited, and the interior is generally off limits to visitors.

Walk east from here past the attractive Radha Murlimanohar Temple to reach the **Sanganeeria Haveli**. The whole building is in a rather sorry state, and the west wall is missing large chunks of plaster, but you can still make out some entertaining details, including a Ferris wheel, a man ploughing with a buffalo and another two sawing a plank, a pair of wrestlers, women spinning cotton and a lady on a swing, as well as a curious picture showing a large number of people in a huge cart being pulled by an elephant (they look as if they're sitting in boxes in a theatre). There are several other fine havelis along the street here. Just south of here, opposite the Oriental Bank of Commerce, the **Chokhani Haveli** sports a particularly fine and colourful crop of animals, as well as rifle-wielding soldiers on horseback and a picture of Dhola and Maru (see p.305) shooting a bow and arrow from the back of a camel.

Head south to reach the town's clock tower, the centre of a lively little vegetable market; the **Rathi Haveli**, on the northeast corner of the clock tower square, has some relatively modern twentieth-century murals in kitsch Western style, with floral flourishes, classical columns and a European lady working away at a sewing machine. There's a further crop of interesting havelis in the sandy backstreets southeast of here, including a particularly fine (though apparently nameless) haveli two blocks east and one block south of the clock tower, with well-preserved murals showing Krishna being driven to his wedding in a bullock cart by Hanuman next to a fine European carriage with two musket-carrying soldiers guarding a diminutive lady and gentlemen, while a pair of bewhiskered Indian nobles follow in a camel-drawn carriage behind.

Tal Chhapar Wildlife Sanctuary

Some 70km southwest of Fatehpur, the little-visited **Tal Chhapar Wildlife Sanctuary** (daily sunrise to sunset; foreigners Rs80, Indian residents Rs10, plus Rs100 camera, Rs200 video and Rs65/vehicle) is Rajasthan's most important refuge for the elegant blackbuck, a type of Indian antelope instantly recognizable thanks to its distinctive spiral horns. About two thousand blackbuck can be found here, alongside nilgai, *chinkaras* (Indian gazelle), desert foxes and plentiful birdlife ranging from eagles and vultures through to demoiselle cranes. There are no Jeeps for hire, although you can hire a bike at the entrance, go inside in your own vehicle, or just walk.

East of Jaipur

The fertile area **east of Jaipur**, interspersed with the forested slopes of the Aravalli Hills, holds an inviting mixture of historic towns and wildlife sanctuaries. To the northeast is the fortified town of **Alwar**, jumping-off point for the **Sariska Tiger Reserve**. Further east are the former princely capitals of **Deeg** and **Bharatpur**, and India's finest bird sanctuary, the **Keoladeo National Park**. The wildlife sanctuary at **Ranthambore**, in idyllic scenery southeast of Jaipur, offers the best chance in India of spotting wild tigers.

Alwar

Roughly 140km northeast from Jaipur towards Delhi, the large, bustling town of **ALWAR** sprawls across a valley beneath one of eastern Rajasthan's larger and more impressive **forts**, whose massive ramparts straggle impressively along craggy ridges above. Traditionally the northern gateway to Rajasthan, Alwar's strategic position on the Rajput border resulted in incessant warfare from the tenth century to the seventeenth century between the Jats of Bharatpur and the Kachchwahas of Amber. An independent Alwar state was established under the leadership of Pratap Singh Prabhakar (r.1775–91); in 1803, his adopted son and successor Bakhtawar Singh (r.1791–1815) became one of the first Rajput rulers

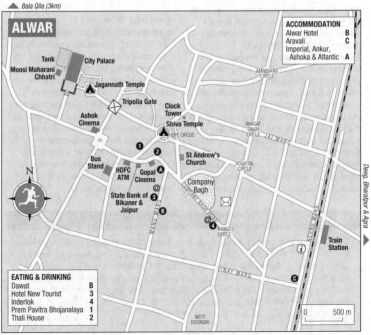

▲ Bala Qila (3km)

ALWAR

ACCOMMODATION
Alwar Hotel	B
Aravali	C
Imperial, Ankur,	
Ashoka & Atlantic	A

Tank
Moosi Maharani Chhatri
City Palace
AMBEDKAR CIRCLE
Jagannath Temple
Tripolia Gate
Clock Tower
Ashok Cinema
Shiva Temple
BHAGAT SINGH CIRCLE
JAL MARG
HOPE CIRCUS
Bus Stand
HDFC ATM
Gopal Cinema
St Andrew's Church
HOSPITAL CIRCLE
Company Bagh
State Bank of Bikaner & Jaipur
N
NANGLI CIRCLE
Train Station
VINAY MARG

Deeg, Bharatpur & Agra

EATING & DRINKING
Dawat	B
Hotel New Tourist	3
Inderlok	4
Prem Pavitra Bhojanalaya	1
Thali House	2

MOTI DOONGRI

0   500 m

▼ Sariska Tiger Reserve & Siliserh Palace

to sign a treaty with the British, an alliance which survived until Independence despite the notorious excesses of Jai Singh, the flamboyant great-grandfather of the present maharaja. Official British reports from the 1930s describe various instances of maharajal madness, including Jai Singh's habit of burying his luxury Hispano-Suiza cars once he had tired of them, and the occasion on which he doused his favourite polo pony in petrol and set fire to it; rumours also circulated suggesting a predilection for young boys.

Arrival and information

The **bus stand** is in the centre of town; the **railway station** is about 2km east of the centre; you'll find plenty of cycle rickshaws for getting around, but surprisingly few autos (try the train station). The **tourist office** (Mon–Fri 10am–5pm; T0144/234 7348) is just south of the station. You can **change currency** and travellers' cheques at the State Bank of Bikaner & Jaipur, in the centre of town, which also has an **ATM** that accepts foreign Visa and MasterCards; if this isn't working, there's an HDFC ATM nearby. For **internet** access, try the well-equipped Cyberlink (daily 8am–8pm; Rs20/min) on the south side of Company Bagh, or Manish Cyber on Manu Marg (daily 8.30am–10pm; Rs20/hr).

Accommodation

There's a small selection of accommodation in Alwar itself, plus a couple of seductive upmarket options in the surrounding countryside.

Alwar

Alwar Hotel 26 Manu Marg T0144/270 0012, W www.alwarhotel.com. This trim little mid-range hotel is easily the nicest place to stay in Alwar itself, with smart and spacious a/c rooms set around a neat garden. The in-house *Dawat* restaurant (see opposite) is another major bonus. ❺

Ankur, Ashoka, Atlantic and **Imperial** hotels. Clustered together on the corner of Manu Marg, a 5min walk from the bus station, this group of four adjacent and more or less indistinguishable hotels offers a range of simple but cheap, tolerably clean and reasonably comfortable fan and a/c rooms, and there are always plenty of vacancies. ❷–❸

Aravali Just south of the railway station on Nehru Marg T0144/233 2883. The town's only plausible budget alternative to the *Ankur* group of hotels. It's definitely seen better days, and the wide variety of rooms (fan, air-cooled and a/c) are all rather run-down, though reasonably clean. There's also a bar, internet access, and a pool (guests only) in summer. ❷–❺

Around Alwar

Amanbagh Ajabgarh, around 50km from Alwar T01465/223333, W www.amanresorts.com. Part of the prestigious Aman group of hotels, this is one of the most alluring bolt holes in Rajasthan, set in a verdant oasis amid a remote corner of the Aravalli hills. The resort has all the style you'd expect at the price, set in a lavish contemporary re-creation of a Mughal-style palace occupying a walled compound once used for hunting camps by the maharaja of Alwar. Accommodation io in sumptuous two-storey "haveli" suites (around $700) or in even more stunning "pool pavilions" (around $1400) with private swimming pool. There's also a gorgeous spa. ❾

Moving on from Alwar

There are **bus** services to Bharatpur via Deeg (every 15min; 4hr), Sariska (every 30min; 1hr–1hr 30min), Delhi (every 30min; 5hr) and Jaipur (hourly; 4hr). **Trains** run to Delhi, Jaipur, Jodhpur, Ajmer and Ahmedabad (but not Bharatpur). For Jaipur, the best service is the Ajmer Shatabdi (#2015; daily except Wed; dep. 8.44am, arr. 10.45am); for Delhi, the Jaisalmer–Delhi Express (#4060; daily; dep. 07.19am, arr. 11.05am) and the Ajmer Shatabdi (#2016; daily except Wed; dep. 7.33pm, arr. 10.40pm) are two of the faster services.

Hill Fort Kesroli 12km east of Alwar ☎01468/289352, ⓦwww.neemranahotels.com. India's oldest heritage hotel, occupying a rugged old fifteenth-century fort impeccably restored and centred on a lush inner courtyard filled with plants and birds. Rooms are pleasantly rustic and have great views over Kesroli village and the surrounding countryside. ❻

Neemrana Fort-Palace Neemrana (just north of the Delhi–Jaipur NH8 Highway, close to the state border, around 75km from Alwar, 120km from Delhi and 140km from Jaipur) ☎01494/246006, ⓦwww.neemranahotels.com. One of Rajasthan's longest-running heritage hotels, offering a wide range of rooms in Rajasthani and colonial style inside the vast and wonderfully crusty old Neemrana Fort (1464) – a labyrinthine maze of courtyards and corridors spread over ten levels up a steep hillside. Facilities include a pool, yoga and meditation classes, Ayurvedic treatments and India's only flying-fox aerial zipwire. ❻–❽

Eating and drinking

Alwar is famous for its cavity-causing **milk cakes**, which you can buy at the stalls around Hope Circus. Note that none of the following places serves alcohol. If you want a **drink**, the gloomy and mosquito-plagued garden at the *Hotel New Tourist* on Manu Marg is about as good as it gets – which isn't very.

Dawat Hotel Alwar, Manu Marg. Reliable little a/c restaurant serving up a good range of veg and non-veg North and South Indian food, plus better-than-average Chinese. Mains Rs40–140.

Inderlok Company Bagh Rd, near Nangli Circle. Comfortable a/c veg restaurant, popular with locals, offering good North and South Indian standards along with a few Chinese dishes. Mains Rs80–125.

Prem Pavitra Bhojanalya Near Hope Circus. This cosy little restaurant dishes up the best food in town, with a very short, very cheap menu of basic North Indian standards (all mains under Rs50). The entrance is easily missed: go up the road roughly opposite the State Bank of Jaipur & Bikaner, past the Bharat Petroleum petrol station. It's on the left about 50m up.

Thali House Simple little a/c café serving up a short but passable range of South Indian dishes (plus a few Chinese offerings). Mains Rs35–65.

The Town

Alwar's principal attraction is its rambling and atmospheric **City Palace**, or Vinai Vilas Mahal, built during the reign of Bhaktawar Singh – a sprawling complex of ornate but now slightly dilapidated buildings, covered in crumbling ochre plaster and studded with endless canopied balconies. Most of the palace's innumerable rooms are now put to more mundane use as government offices – their dimly lit interiors piled high with musty mounds of official documents – while the courtyard in front provides open-air office space for dozens of typists, lined up behind clanking old antique metal machines, and lawyers, who prosecute their business under the trees. The whole place is marvellously atmospheric – the crumbling palace, the poky little offices and the crowds of ambling clerks lending it a genuine charm which is sometimes lacking from the region's more polished tourist attractions.

On the top floor of the palace, an atmospherically time-warped **museum** (Tues–Sun 10am–5pm; foreigners Rs10, Indian residents Rs5) showcases a haphazard collection of royal bric-a-brac. The first room houses a medley of objects belonging to former maharajas including ornately embroidered costumes, musical instruments, stuffed animals (notably a tiger and a large bear), plus an equally fearsome-looking bust of Queen Victoria, Empress of India. The second room is taken up by an excellent collection of seventeenth- to nineteenth-century Mughal and Rajput miniature paintings, while the third room is filled with an impressive array of scary swords and knives (and some slightly silly helmets).

Go up the steps at the left-hand end of the main facade to reach the large **tank** which bounds this end of the palace, a beautiful spot, overlooked on one side by the palace's delicate balconies, and flanked by symmetrical ghats and pavilions. On the terrace overlooking the tank stands the **Moosi Maharani Chhatri**, built in memory of Bhaktawar Singh's mistress, who immolated herself on his funeral pyre. Steps lead up (take off your shoes) from the sandstone base to the ornate marble monument, with finely decorated arches and dome, decorated with a battle scene featuring elephants and horses. At the centre of the floor, the former maharaja and his mistress are represented by two pairs of marble feet, strewn with flower petals.

An interesting walk leads east from the City Palace to the centre of town. Work your way round to the northeast side of the palace, then head east, past the Jagannath Temple to the large **Tripolia Gate**, which shelters a busy crossroads at the eastern edge of Alwar's main commercial area. From here, a road arrows straight ahead to **Hope Circus** at the heart of the town's frantically busy – and wildly disorienting – central bazaar, a fascinating labyrinth of narrow alleyways packed with tiny shops selling every imaginable type of merchandise. You'll probably get lost at least a couple of times, but that's half the fun – if in doubt, the large **Shiva Temple** at the very centre of Hope Circus provides a useful landmark, rising high above the surrounding melee on a plinth crisscrossed by symmetrical staircases.

Bala Qila

Perched high above Alwar is **Bala Qila** fort, whose well-preserved walls stretch for over 10km, climbing dramatically up and down the thickly wooded hillsides that rise above town. Much of the area inside the walls has now reverted to scrub and jungle and there's not much to see besides a temple and a few old cannons, while the elegant but dilapidated eighteenth-century building which crowns the highest part of the fort is off limits without a permit from the local superintendant of police (whose office is in the courtyard facing the City Palace back down in town). Nevertheless, it's a pleasant walk up from town, with fine views and fresh hill breezes. It takes about ninety minutes on foot to make the return trip up to the first gate, or about twice that to reach the topmost point of the fortifications. If you don't want to walk, you'll have to arrange for a taxi through your hotel or hunt down an auto-rickshaw – the road up is far too steep for a cycle rickshaw to tackle.

Sariska Tiger Reserve and around

Alwar is the access point for **Sariska Tiger Reserve and National Park**, a former maharaja's hunting ground managed since 1979 by Project Tiger. Accustomed to being overshadowed by the more famous Ranthambore, Sariska was suddenly thrust into the headlines in 2005 when it was discovered that its tiger population, estimated at around 28 in 2003, had all but vanished – one of India's biggest ever conservation scandals. Prime Minister Manmohan Singh ordered a high-profile police investigation after rumours surfaced that a famed taxidermist had orchestrated a mass poisoning in collusion with corrupt wardens – the investigation, and subsequent arrests, continue. Tigers were reintroduced to Sariska in 2008, with the arrival of one male and two females from Ranthambore, with two more planned to follow in the near future. Unfortunately, in their rush to reintroduce big cats to Sariska the authorities neglected the important fact that all three new tigers were apparently sired by the same father (and that the two tigresses also share the same mother), raising serious concerns that any future offspring may well be inbred and incapable of surviving in the wild.

One silver lining from the whole affair is that the number of visitors to the sanctuary has dwindled significantly, and for birders and wildlife enthusiasts put off by the crowds and hassle of Ranthambore, Sariska's relative serenity comes as a welcome relief. The 881-square-kilometre sanctuary encompasses acres of woodland that are home to abundant **wildlife** including sambar, *chital*, wild boar, nilgai and other antelopes, jackals, mongooses, monkeys, peacocks, porcupines, and numerous birds, as well as around fifty (extremely elusive) leopards. The park is also dotted with a number of evocative ruins and other man-made structures, including the ruined **Kankwari Fort**, deep in the heart of the park, where the Mughal emperor Aurangzeb imprisoned his brother and rival for the throne, Dara Shikoh, before having him executed; and a **Hanuman temple** which gets surprisingly lively on Saturdays and Tuesdays, when locals are allowed into the park for free.

Practicalities

Sariska is **open** daily from October to June (Oct–Feb 7am–3.30pm; March–June 6am–4pm); note that the **park is closed** from July to September. The park lies 35km southwest of Alwar on the main Alwar–Jaipur road; **buses** between the two (every 30min; 1hr journey from Alwar) will stop, on request, at the *Sariska Palace* hotel, a five-minute walk from the park. Alternatively, you may be able to arrange a **taxi through a hotel at Alwar** (around Rs1000), which also gives you time to visit Siliserh (see p.234) on the way back.

Entrance to the park costs Rs200 per person (Indians Rs25) plus Rs125 per vehicle, Rs200 for a compulsory guide, and Rs200 for a video camera. **Jeeps** can be hired at the entrance and cost Rs900 for a three-hour drive around the park; Rs1400 for the longer (4–5hr) ride to Kankwari Fort; or Rs2700 for a full day. You can also take your own vehicle into the park, but you'll be restricted to metalled roads. There's nowhere **to eat** in the park, so you'll need to bring a picnic if coming for the day.

Accommodation

There are several **places to stay** close to the reserve, although all are seriously overpriced.

Alwar Bagh 20km from Sariska (and 16km from Alwar) on the Sariska–Alwar highway ℡0294/241 2081, ⓦwww.alwarbagh.com. Large and comfortable a/c rooms in a sequence of attractive lemon-yellow buildings arranged around spacious gardens, plus a fine pool. Much better value than the various places closer to the park. ⑥

RTDC Hotel Tiger Den ℡0144/284 1342. Attractive, if rather overpriced, option conveniently situated right next to the park entrance, with spacious, old-fashioned fan and a/c rooms, plus a nice garden, though service can be lackadaisical. ⑤–⑥

Sariska Palace A couple of minutes' drive down the main road from the park entrance ℡011/4651 5651, ⓦwww.thesariskapalace.in.

This former maharaja's residence has plenty of atmosphere, though rooms in the main building are surprisingly shabby given the price, while those in the various modern annexes scattered around the grounds are poky and boring. There's also a pool, and large swathes of manicured lawns to loll around on. ⑧

Sariska Tiger Heaven Off the main road 5km before the park entrance on the Jaipur side (signposted as "Sariska Tiger Haven") ℡0911465 224815, ⓦwww.nivalink.com/sariskatigerhaven. In a very peaceful rural setting, arranged around attractive gardens with pool, although the cottages are surprisingly shabby given the hefty price tag, and the restaurant is nothing but a concrete bunker. ⑦

Siliserh Palace

Fifteen kilometres south of Alwar, **Siliserh Palace** is easily visited en route to or from Sariska if you've got your own vehicle (there's no public transport here). Maharaja Vijay Singh had the palace built in 1845 to win over a beautiful commoner, a certain Sheela, who agreed to marriage on the condition that she live within sight of her family's modest home. The whitewashed palace itself is fairly humdrum, but the Shangri-La setting, on the edge of a ten-square-kilometre lake ringed by uninhabited, jungle-clad hills, is idyllic. The lake is Alwar's water source – look out for the crumbling, sandstone aqueducts built more than a century ago. The palace now houses the *RTDC Lake Palace Hotel* (☎0144/288 6322; ❹–❺; Fri–Sun half-board rates only ❺–❻), though rooms are disappointingly shabby, and service is haphazard, so you probably wouldn't want to stay. It's a nice spot to while away an afternoon, even so, and you can also rent out paddle-boats and motorboats if you want to get out onto the water – which also offers the best views of the palace itself, rising high above the lake.

Deeg

Some 30km northwest of Bharatpur, the dusty little market town of **DEEG** is the unlikely home of one of eastern Rajasthan's most lavish **palaces** (daily except Fri 9.30am–5.30pm; foreigners Rs100, Indian residents Rs5), a fascinating blend of Mughal and Hindu architectural styles constructed by the local Jat overlords in the mid-eighteenth century. Badan Singh, the first Jat ruler of Bharatpur state (see p.236), began work on the palace in 1730, though most of the buildings were completed by his son and successor Suraj Mal in 1756.

The palace consists of a sequence of imposing *bhawans* surrounding a large *charbagh*-style garden, divided into four by raised walkways, with a water tank at the centre, dotted with thirty-odd water jets – sadly, the water channels are dry, and the fountains are only switched on during local festivals. Entering the complex, the first and largest of the various *bhawans* lies immediately ahead. This is the **Gopal Bhawan** (closed Fri), Suraj Mal's summer residence, a spacious hall with sculpted pillars, majestic archways and six huge *punkahs* (fans) overhead, the whole thing filled – slightly incongruously – with elegant colonial-era European furniture. Behind the *bhawan* is one of the palace's two extensive tanks, the **Gopal Sagar** – the lowest floor of the Gopal Bhawan actually stands below the waterline of the lake, an innovation designed to keep the building cool in the hot summer months; two pavilions stand to either side of the *bhawan*, also with their feet in the water and named *Saawan* and *Bhaadon* after the lunar months during which Suraj Mal and his courtiers would have retired to the palace here.

In front of the Gopal Bhawan stands a marble arch that formerly supported a **swing** – popularly known as Nur Jahan's Swing – said to have been looted from Delhi. Continue past this to reach the ornate **Kesav Bhawan**, or "Monsoon Palace", an open-sided and richly carved pavilion surrounded by a deep water channel dotted with hundreds of tiny fountains. This unusual structure was designed to re-create the cool ambience of the rainy season, with water released from rooftop pipes to imitate a shower of monsoon rain, while metal balls were agitated by further streams of pressurized water to simulate the sound of thunder – an extravagant entertainment, since the reservoir for the cascades took a week to fill and only a matter of hours to empty. Immediately behind here is another large **tank** (its stepped *ghats* usually covered in washing laid out by local housewives), while beyond rise the enormous walls of the town's huge fort, erected by Suraj Mal in 1730.

The rear of the main gardens is bounded by the **Kishan Bhawan**, which served as the maharaja's Hall of Private Audience, or Diwan-i-Khas. Past here lies the **Suraj Bhawan**, named after Suraj Mal and centred on its own small *charbagh* courtyard, bounded at one end by the Hardev Bhawan and at the other by a fine white marble pavilion – perhaps Suraj Mal's own private apartment – in pure Mughal style, embellished with delicate inlay work and intricate carving.

Deeg is served by **bus** from Alwar (every 15min; 3hr) and Bharatpur (every 15min; 1hr). The town is easily visited as a day-trip from Bharatpur, or en route between Bharatpur and Alwar. There's nowhere to stay, and eating possibilities are limited to the usual row of basic *dhabas* along the main road.

Bharatpur and the Keoladeo National Park

Just a stone's throw from the border with Uttar Pradesh and a mere 18km from Fatehpur Sikri, the walled town of **BHARATPUR** has an interesting mix of traditional bazaars, temples, mosques, palaces and a massive fort, although the main attraction is the famous **Keoladeo National Park**, one of India's – if not the world's – top birdwatching destinations.

Some history

The Bharatpur area was ruled by the Tomara Rajputs of Delhi, and the Jadon Rajputs of Bayana, before falling under Mughal control. Following the death of the Mughal emperor Aurangzeb in 1707, the local **Jats** (a warlike agricultural

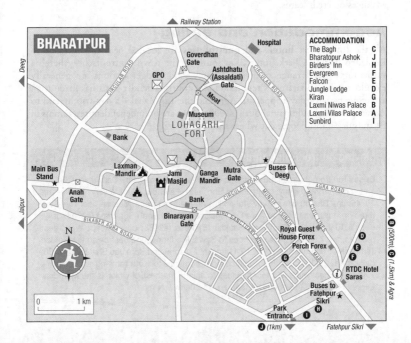

caste who had been present in Rajasthan for at least as long as the Rajputs, or perhaps much longer) began to seize control of the area, and in 1722 Bharatpur state was recognized by the Mughals as autonomous under the leadership of **Badan Singh**, with its capital at Deeg (see p.234). His son and successor, **Suraj Mal**, commonly recognized as the greatest of all Jat leaders, moved his capital from Deeg to Bharatpur in 1733, and subsequently took advantage of the chaotic political situation following the collapse of Mughal power to expand Jat authority over a considerable area, plundering Delhi in 1753 and briefly taking control of Agra and Alwar a few years later. His death in 1763, however, led to an immediate decline in Jat fortunes. Even so, Bharatpur successfully withstood a four-month siege by British forces in 1805, and it wasn't until a second campaign was launched against it by the British in 1826 that the town was finally subdued.

Arrival and information

Bharatpur's **bus stand** is in the west of town near Anah Gate. If you're arriving from Fatehpur Sikri, you'll save yourself time (and a rickshaw fare) by getting off the bus at the crossroads on the southeast side of town near the park gates and guesthouses – look out for the prominent Rajasthan government tourist office right on the crossroads, or the large *RTDC Hotel Saras* opposite. The **railway station** is a couple of kilometres northwest of the town centre, a Rs40–50 ride from Keoladeo National Park and the nearby guesthouses.

The town's **tourist office** (Mon–Sat 9.30am–6pm; ☏05644/222542, ⓦwww .bharatpur.nic.in) is at the crossroads near the park entrance where Fatehpur Sikri buses pull in. Nearby, on New Civil Lines, The Perch and the Royal Guest House Forex (both open till around 10/11pm) offer **internet** access (Rs30/hr) and also change cash and travellers' cheques and can arrange taxis; The Perch also gives cash advances on credit cards.

Accommodation and eating

All the town's best **hotels** and **guesthouses** are located near the entrance to Keoladeo National Park, some 3km south of the town centre itself – there's a surprisingly good range of places to stay, and budget options are generally excellent value. Bharatpur's reputation as a tourist-friendly oasis has made it an attractive base for day-trippers to Agra and the Taj Mahal – a day-trip by taxi to Agra and back should cost about Rs1000. There are no independent restaurants in Bharatpur – most people **eat** where they're staying.

Moving on from Bharatpur

Buses run from the main bus stand to Jaipur (every 30min; 4hr), Delhi (every 30min–1hr; 5hr), Agra (hourly; 1hr 30min–2hr) and Fatehpur Sikri (every 30min–1hr; 30–45min). Bharatpur's railway station lies on the main Delhi–Mumbai line. There are three or four **trains** daily to Agra Fort, including the Howrah Superfast (#2308; daily; dep. 5.10am, arr. 6.35am) and Sealdah Express (#2988; daily except Wed; dep. 5.35pm, arr. 7.30pm); seven services to Sawai Madhopur, the best being the Golden Temple Mail (#2904; daily; dep. 10.41am, arr. 1.14pm) and Kota Jan Shatabdi (#2060; daily; dep. 3.43pm, arr. 6pm), which both continue to Kota (arriving at 2.25pm & 7.40pm respectively); and four services to Jaipur, the best of which is the Marudhar Express (#4853/63/65; dep. 7.13am, arr. 11.30am).

Budget

Evergreen ☎05644/225917. One of the cheapest options in Bharatpur, with simple but clean rooms with fan and private bathroom (though hot water comes in a bucket in some rooms). ❶

Falcon ☎05644/225306, ✉falconguesthouse @hotmail.com. Attractive modern guesthouse with a selection of comfortable fan, air-cooled and a/c rooms, plus a small garden restaurant with good food. Internet access available. ❷–❸

Jungle Lodge ☎05644/225622, ⓦwww .junglelodge.dk. Run by a knowledgeable naturalist, this friendly place has a range of clean and spacious modern rooms (fan, air-cooled and a/c) overlooking a tranquil flower-filled garden. The pleasant little terrace restaurant and evening fires (in winter) give the place a pleasantly sociable feel, and there are bikes and binoculars for rent, as well as internet access. ❶–❷

Kiran ☎05644/223845. Run by an extremely friendly and helpful pair of brothers, this place offers a range of clean and comfortable fan, air-cooled and a/c rooms at rock-bottom prices. There's free pick-up and drop-off from bus and train stations, plus binoculars for rent (Rs50). ❶–❸

Mid-range to expensive

The Bagh Agra Rd, 1km past *Laxmi Vilas Palace* ☎05644/228333, ⓦwww.thebagh.com. This idyllic upmarket hotel occupies a cluster of pink, low-rise buildings scattered around *charbagh*-style gardens that are home to over fifty species of bird. Rooms are cool, spacious and attractively furnished, and there's also a spa and large pool. Prices from US$180. ❽

Bahratpur Ashok 1km inside park ☎05644/222760, ⓦwww.bharatpurashok.com. In a pleasantly sylvan setting inside the park (note that you'll have to pay one day's park entrance fee for every night you stay here), this very sleepy hotel has spacious and comfortable old-fashioned rooms with balconies overlooking the sanctuary, a pleasant garden out the back and a passable restaurant. Relatively expensive, but the setting is pretty much unbeatable. ❻, with 20 percent discounts in summer.

Birders' Inn ☎05644/227346, ⓦwww .birdersinn.com. The most inviting place in town, usually full of serious birdwatchers who gather nightly to compare checklists in the inviting thatch-roofed restaurant. Rooms (all a/c) are large, smart and excellent value. Internet access available. ❺

Laxmi Niwas Palace Agra Rd ☎05644/223522, ⓦwww.laxminiwas.com. Swanky new hotel in traditional Rajasthani style right next to the *Laxmi Vilas Palace* – a bit more comfortable than its older neighbour, though not nearly as atmospheric. ❼

Laxmi Vilas Palace Agra Rd ☎05644/223523, ⓦwww.laxmivilas.com. Former royal palace, set amid extensive grounds east of town. It's all a trifle kitsch, but undeniably romantic, with charmingly OTT and reasonably priced a/c rooms complete with four-poster beds and other regal decorative touches. The old-fashioned restaurant (complete with stuffed tiger head) and big pool (open to outsiders if you take lunch or dinner) are further bonuses. ❼

Sunbird ☎05644/225701, ⓦwww.hotelsunbird .com. Attractive mid-range hotel, and a decent alternative if you can't get into the adjacent *Birders' Inn*, with a range of modern and very comfortably furnished fan and a/c rooms, plus a few traditional Rajasthani-style cottages in the spacious garden. ❹–❺

The Town

Bharatpur was founded by the Jat king Suraj Mal, and quickly developed into a busy market centre, popularly known as the eastern gateway to Rajasthan. The virtually impregnable **Lohagarh** (Iron Fort) was built by Suraj Mal at the heart of town in 1732; the original moat, 45m wide and up to 15m deep, still encircles the fort, and time and modern development have had little effect on its magnificent 11km-long bastions – the British spent four months in 1805 trying in vain to breach them, before suffering their heaviest defeat in Rajasthan. You're most likely to enter the fort from the south, though it's worth continuing across the fort to the impressive **Ashtdhatu** (or Eight-Metal) **Gate**, named on account of the number of different types of metal that apparently went into the making of its extremely solid-looking doors.

The fort is home to no less than three large royal palaces in various stages of dereliction, all built by the Jats between 1730 and 1850. The best preserved is the large orange **Kamra Khas Mahal**, on the west side of the fort, an atmospherically ramshackle structure, ranged around a lush garden, which now serves as the town's mildly diverting **museum** (daily except Fri 10am–4.30pm; Rs10, video Rs20). Entering the palace, the first building on your right houses a large collection of finely carved sculptures, including some exquisitely detailed Jain statues, while tucked away to the rear of this section of the palace (and easily missed) is a superb little *hamman* (baths), its interior fashioned from beautifully carved marble, with ornate tiles and painted floral decorations. Head up the grand staircase on the opposite side of the courtyard to reach a further trio of rooms housing a medley of moth-eaten artefacts, including pictures of various maharajas, assorted nineteenth-century miniatures, some very unpleasant stuffed animals and lots of guns and swords. From here, a further broad flight of stairs leads up to the rooftop, offering fine views over the rest of the fort.

There are wonderful views from the lofty **Jawahar Burj** next door – turn left as you exit the museum, and follow the narrow road up around the edge of the palace. This small, elevated platform is topped with four delicately carved pavilions and an unusual iron pole embellished with the family tree of the maharajas of Bharatpur, though its principal attraction is the superb panorama over the fort and modern town, with bird's-eye views of the other two crumbling palaces – the **Kishori Mahal** and **Purana Mahal** – which dominate the old fort (though neither is now open to the public).

Immediately south of the fort lies the bizarre **Ganga Mandir**, a large Hindu temple dedicated to the proprietary goddess of India's most sacred river, though the elaborately carved sandstone building itself looks more like a Neoclassical French chateau than a Subcontinental temple, perhaps an expression of the westernized sensibilities and patriarchal largesse of the maharajas of Bharatpur, who built the temple – very slowly and at enormous expense – between 1845 and 1937.

Beyond here, narrow roads snake southwest through Bharatpur's characterful bazaar district to reach the imposing **Jama Masjid**, fronted by a fine arched portal and set high on a raised platform above the densely populated surrounding streets. Work on the construction of the mosque is said to have been started on the same day in 1845 that the Ganga Mandir was begun – evidence of the ruling family's commendable even-handedness in dealing with their subjects' competing religious sympathies. A short distance further east lies the finely embellished **Laxman Mandir**, dedicated to the family deity of the maharajas of Bharatpur, Laxman, one of the brothers of Lord Rama, after whose other brother, Bharat, the town itself was named.

Keoladeo National Park

Keoladeo National Park (daily April–Sept 6am–6pm; Oct–March 6.30am–5pm; foreigners Rs200, Indian residents Rs25, video Rs200) is India's premier bird-watching sanctuary – an avian wonderland that attracts vast numbers of feathered creatures thanks to its strategic location, protected status and extensive wetlands (although ongoing drought has taken its toll on the last – see p.240). Dedicated ornithologists also flock to the park in droves, though it's a richly rewarding place to visit even for novices who don't know the difference between an egret and an elephant.

Keoladeo (also known as Keoladeo-Ghana – *ghana* meaning "thick forest") was for sixty years a royal hunting reserve, a past memorialized inside the park by a plaque recounting the murderous exploits of former "illustrious" visitors. (On one particularly gruesome day, in 1938, the party of viceroy Lord Linlithgow bagged a staggering 4273 birds.) Despite the depredations of such trigger-happy hunters, the reserve's avian population continued to thrive. The area became a

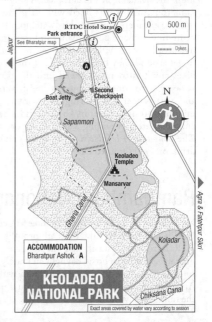

Keoladeo through the seasons

The physical appearance and avian population of Keoladeo change dramatically during the course of the year. The **monsoon** arrives (all being well) in July/August, continuing until September, filling the park's lakes and wetlands and turning the entire sanctuary a lush green. Many of the **migratory species** arrive just before the monsoon breaks, competing furiously for the best perches and nesting frantically in preparation for the coming deluge. A further wave of migratory birds from colder northern climes arrives at the onset of **winter**, during which the park's bird population reaches its height. As winter draws on and temperatures begin to rise, the park's waters start drying up, and migratory visitors return to their summer homes. By May the park's wetlands have begun to evaporate, leaving turtles and fishes stranded among muddy puddles for those birds still in residence to feast upon. By the beginning of July the park has become dry, brown and parched, before the rains return, and the entire cycle begins again.

sanctuary in 1956 and a national park in 1982, and was declared a UNESCO World Heritage Site in 1985.

Today, Keoladeo's 29 square kilometres, including extensive areas of swamp and lake, constitute one of the world's most important ornithological breeding and migratory areas, with a staggering number of birds packed into a comparatively small area. Some 375 species have been recorded here, including around two hundred year-round residents plus 150-odd migratory species from as far afield as Tibet, China, Siberia and even Europe, who fly south to escape the northern winter. Keoladeo is probably best known for its stupendous array of **aquatic birds**, which descend en masse on the park's wetlands following the dramatic arrival of the monsoon in July. These include the majestic saras crane and a staggering two thousand painted storks, whose nesting cries create a constant background din, as well as snake-necked darters, spoonbills, pink flamingos, white ibis and grey pelicans (although sadly the extremely endangered Siberian cranes which were formerly one of the park's most prized visitors have not been seen in significant numbers since the early 1990s, other than a single pair who last visited in 2002). There are also around thirty species of **birds of prey**, among them vultures, marsh harriers, peregrine falcons and ospreys, as well as smaller and more colourful exotics including hoopoes, bulbuls, bee-eaters and numerous dazzlingly coloured kingfishers. An added bonus is the number of large **mammals** who frequent the park, and you stand a good chance of glimpsing wild boar, mongoose, *chital*, nilgai and sambar along the paths, as well as hyenas, jackals and otters, and perhaps even elusive jungle cats. Rock pythons sun themselves at Python Point, just past Keoladeo temple, and in the bush land off the main road close to the entrance barrier.

Sadly, the **drought** suffered by Rajasthan in the past decade has taken its inevitable toll on Keoladeo, leading to a significant reduction in the size of the park's lakes and wetlands, with a consequent steep fall in the number of visiting aquatic birds (the healthy 2008 monsoon briefly restored the park to its former watery splendour, though drought returned in 2009). A scheme to provide the park with reliable water by connecting it via a canal to the Yamuna River at Agra has been proposed, though whether this scheme ever actually materializes is anyone's guess. For the time being, even a waterless Keoladeo is still a richly rewarding place to visit, albeit not quite the world-class bird sanctuary of rainier seasons.

Park practicalities

Planning **when to visit** Keoladeo (see box, p.239) has an important bearing on what you're likely to see. The **best time to visit** is usually following the monsoon, from around October through to March, when the weather is dry but the lakes are still full (monsoon permitting) and the migratory birds in residence (although mists in December and January can hinder serious birdwatching). At any time of year it's best to visit at **dawn or dusk**, when the weather is coolest and the birds most active. It's well worth visiting the sanctuary a couple of times, perhaps going in with a guide on the first visit for a couple of hours (you should get down to the Keoladeo temple in the centre of the park – and after which it's named), and then returning on your own later in the day to explore the wilder southern reaches of the park – although you'll have to buy a new ticket for each visit.

The park entrance is around 4km south of Bharatpur railway station. Free **maps** are available at the entrance. A single road passes through the park, while numerous small paths lined with *babul* trees cut across lakes and marshes and provide excellent cover for birdwatching. If you need help identifying the birds, or finding vantage points, you can hire a **guide** at the gate (Rs100/hr for up to five people), who will probably have binoculars for you to borrow. The best way to get around is by **bike**, available at the main entrance (Rs25; note that outside bikes aren't currently allowed into the park), or by cycle rickshaw (Rs70/hr; same price for one or two people) – drivers are trained by the park authorities and very clued up. During the winter, gondola-style **boats** (Rs25/person, minimum four people) make short rides across the wetlands, assuming there's enough water, providing a superb opportunity to get really close to the birds. The *Bahratpur Ashok Hotel* at the north end of the park is a reliable place to get a drink or something **to eat**.

Ranthambore National Park

No Indian nature reserve can guarantee a tiger sighting, but at **RANTHAMBORE NATIONAL PARK** the odds are probably better than anywhere else: the park itself is relatively small, and the resident tigers are famously unperturbed by humans, hunting in broad daylight and rarely shying from cameras or Jeep-loads of tourists. Combine the big cats' bravado with the park's proximity to the Delhi–Agra–Jaipur "Golden Triangle", and you'll understand why Ranthambore attracts the number of visitors it does.

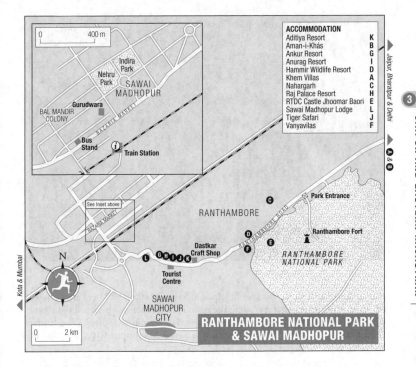

Arrival and information

Ranthambore National Park is reached via the small and rather grubby town of **Sawai Madhopur**, which is served by **trains** on the main Mumbai–Delhi line, and thus easily accessible from Bharatpur, Agra, Jaipur and Delhi, as well as destinations further south, such as Kota. The **station** is right in the middle of town, close to the **bus stand** and bustling Bazriya market area. The helpful **tourist office** (Mon–Sat 10am–5pm; ☏07462/220808) in the station hands out free **maps** of town and is a good place to check transport timings. There are **exchange** facilities at many hotels

Dastkar Crafts Centre

Three kilometres beyond the turning for the park, near the village of Kutalpura, it's worth popping into the excellent **Dastkar Crafts Centre**, which trains local low-caste women to make patchwork quilting and appliqué. Most of the pieces they produce are sold in Delhi, but a small shop on site showcases their exceptional work, and prices are very fair. The scheme is a laudable attempt to combat poverty in the villages bordering the park, lessening the hardships that, in the past, have pushed villagers into illegal poaching. While you're in the area, have a wander around the houses on the opposite side of the road, whose walls are decorated with some wonderful traditional murals. If you can't make it to the crafts centre, it also has an outlet in town, the Dastkar Crafts Shop, immediately north of *Ranthambore Regency Hotel*. The success of the Dastkar Centre has prompted a slew of imitators to set up shop, and the main road through Ranthambore is now lined with places selling local handicrafts and paintings, most of them purporting to have some social and/or environmental higher purpose.

▲ Monkey at Ranthambore

and in the State Bank of Bikaner & Jaipur in Sawai Madhopur. There are a couple of places with **internet** access along the main road just before you reach the *Ankur Hotel* including the reasonably reliable Tiger Track shop (Rs50/hr). The town's industrial zone, rather confusingly known as **Sawai Madhopur City**, lies south of the main town, though is of no interest to visitors.

Accommodation and eating

Most of the area's numerous **hotels and guesthouses** are strung out along the 14km road between Sawai Madhopur and the national park; many are featured on Ⓦ www.hotelsranthambhore.com. Accommodation **prices** are significantly higher than average, despite the fierce competition and number of places in business (hotel owners claim that they only really see six months' business every year – and that they therefore have to charge double prices). Genuine budget accommodation is almost nonexistent except for a few dingy options around the train station in Sawai Madhopur itself, although there's plenty of choice of lower mid-range places. Try bargaining hard wherever you go – you may be able to score a discount if business is slow, especially during the hot summer months. Many places in town have pretty little gardens around the back surrounded by what the local hoteliers like to describe as "cottages", though in fact they're simply garden rooms; most places also have swimming pools.

Food in Ranthambore is very average, unless you want to push the boat out and go for a meal at one of the area's top-end places, like the lovely *Vanyavilas* or the *Sawai Madhopur Lodge* (which does lunch and dinner buffets for Rs550/650 respectively). For budget food, the garden restaurant at the *Tiger Safari* hotel is cheap and reasonably tasty, and usually as lively as anywhere in town.

Budget to mid-range

Aditiya Resort Ranthambore Rd, 3km north of town ℡ 09414 728468. The cheapest option in Ranthambore, with just six simple but clean modern rooms (including a couple of very cheap ones with shared bath, plus a couple with a/c) in a small family house. ❶–❸

Ankur Resort Ranthambore Rd, 2km from town ℡ 07462/220792, Ⓦ www.hotelankurresort.com. A wide array of accommodation, ranging from uninspiring budget rooms with fan in the bare and institutional main building, up to smarter and much more cheerful a/c "cottages" in the gardens behind (though some are decidedly overpriced). There's also a small pool (non-guests Rs150) and a passable restaurant. ❷–❻

Anurag Resort Ranthambore Rd, 2.5km from town ☏07462/220751, ⓦwww.anuragresort.com. Sprawling pink resort set around expansive, rambling gardens. Rooms (all air-cooled) are uninspiring but modern and spacious, and there are also some slightly more expensive a/c cottages set around the gardens at the back, plus the biggest pool in town (non-guests Rs200/hr) and a Kerala Ayurvedic massage centre and gym. Fifty percent discounts April–Sept. ❹–❺

Hammir Wildlife Resort Ranthambore Rd, 7km from town ☏09414 446566, ⓦwww.nivalink .com/hammir. Popular with Indian tourists, this is one of the more sensibly priced places in town (though the rooms are much better value than the garden cottages). Facilities include a pool (non-guests Rs100) and money exchange. ❺–❻

Raj Palace Resort Ranthambore Rd, 2km from town ☏07462/224793, ⓦwww.rajpalace ranthambhore.com. One of the best-value places in Ranthambore, with spacious and clean modern a/c rooms in the main building and some slightly more homely a/c "cottages" around the gardens at the back, plus a pool (non-guests Rs200/hr). ❸

Tiger Safari Ranthambore Rd, 2.5km from town ☏07462/221137, ⓦwww.tigersafariresort.com. The best of Ranthambore's cheaper hotels, with helpful service and comfortably furnished rooms

(almost all with a/c) plus spacious cottages around the rear garden. There's also internet access, a pool (free to non-guests), free pick-up/ drop-off from the station, and a pleasant garden restaurant. ❸–❺

Expensive

Aman-i-Khás ☏07462/252052, ⓦwww .amanresorts.com. Situated in a very quiet rural setting, this small outpost of the ultra-exclusive Aman chain rivals *Vanyavilas* (see p.244) for tasteful opulence (and even outdoes it for wallet-crunching expense, with rates at around $950/day). Accommodation is in just ten superb, cavernous luxury tents, and there's also a traditional step-well for swimming, fresh produce from the on-site organic farm, and a spa tent. Closed May to Sept. ❾

Khem Villas ☏07462/252099, ⓦwww .khemvillas.com. Delightful little eco-resort on the far side of the park entrance, set amid ten acres of carefully nurtured wilderness which is home to abundant birdlife and other fauna. Accommodation is in a mix of rooms, luxury tents and stylish little cottages with private plunge-pools, and there's also home-grown organic vegetarian food and an interesting range of excursions. ❽–❾ full board.

Nahargarh 2km south of park entrance, Khilchipur Village, Ranthambore Rd ☏07462/252281, ⓦwww.alsisar.com. Superbly theatrical-looking hotel, built in the style of an old-fashioned Rajput palace and looking every inch the regal retreat. Rooms are sumptuously decorated in traditional style and there's also a large pool. Rooms from around $140. ❼

Moving on from Ranthambore

There are virtually no **rickshaws** in Ranthambore, so you'll have to arrange transport to the bus or train station through your hotel when you come to leave. Many places offer free transport into town; even if not, the trip shouldn't cost more than Rs30–40.

Sawai Madhopur straddles the main Delhi–Mumbai railway line and is well served by **trains**. There are daily services for Jaipur (6.45am, 10.10am, 10.45am & 2.40pm; 2hr 10min–2hr 45min), Bharatpur (7.10am & 12.35pm; 2hr 10min–2hr 30min), Jodhpur (2.40pm; 8hr), Kota (1.08pm, 1.30pm, 4.10pm, 6.05pm & 7.40pm; 1hr 20min–1hr 30min), Delhi (6.33am, 7.10am, 12.35am & 1.08am; 4hr 30min–6hr) and Mumbai (1.08pm, 4.10pm, 8.37pm & 10.05pm; 16–17hr). For Bundi, it's easiest to take a train to Kota and then catch a bus, or catch a direct bus all the way (see below).

Ongoing improvements to the previously awful roads around Ranthambore are gradually making **bus** travel a quicker and more comfortable option, although taking the train is still preferable for most destinations. Services run to Jaipur (6 daily; 4–5hr), Bundi (3 daily; 4–5hr) and Ajmer (1 daily; 8hr). Buses depart from one of the two bus stands close to one another in the middle of Sawai Madhopur; check with the person who's taking you that you're at the right stand.

RTDC Castle Jhoomar Baori On a hillside 7km out of town ☎07462/220495, ⓦwww.hotels ranthambhore.com. Former royal hunting lodge on a lofty hilltop site inside the park, with superb views from the roof terrace and large, and atmospheric – albeit slightly shabby – a/c rooms. ❻

Sawai Madhopur Lodge Ranthambore Rd, 1.5km from town ☎07462/220541, ⓦwww.tajhotels.com. Occupying an atmospheric 1930s hunting lodge, this luxury heritage hotel has bags of charm, with pleasantly leafy grounds and accommodation in beautifully appointed colonial-style rooms (from around $350 – it's worth paying a little extra for one of the more stylish luxury

rooms), plus a pool (non-guests Rs400) and attractive restaurant. ❾ including obligatory full board.

Vanyavilas Ranthambore Rd, about 7km from town ☎07462/223999, ⓦwww.oberoihotels.com. Part of the upmarket Oberoi chain, this superbly stylish (and expensive) jungle resort is centred around a lavishly decorated building in the style of a royal hunting palace, with accommodation scattered around the rustic grounds in beautifully equipped wooden-floored a/c tents. Facilities include a fine spa, resident yoga teacher and a large heated pool. Non-guests can visit for a romantic terrace dinner (around Rs1000). Rooms from around US$850. ❾

The park

Ranthambore National Park (ⓦwww.ranthamborenationalpark.com) covers one of the last sizeable swathes of verdant bush in Rajasthan, fed by several rivers that have been dammed to form lakes, dotted with delicate pavilions, while the ruined tenth-century Ranthambore Fort (see opposite), towering above the forest canopy from atop a dramatic crag, is straight out of Kipling's *Jungle Book*. The area has been controlled by the Rajputs for most of its existence, and was set aside by the rulers of Jaipur for royal hunting jaunts. Soon after Independence the area was declared a sanctuary, becoming a full-fledged national park under **Project Tiger** in 1972. Over time, Ranthambore became world-renowned for its "friendly tigers", unperturbed by humans. Its reputation as Project Tiger's flagship operation, however, took a severe dent a decade later when it transpired that some of Ranthambore's own wardens were involved in **poaching**, and that, as a result, the tiger population here had plummeted to single figures (to this day, park staff deny the allegations). Since then, more rigorous policing is said to have brought the problem under control, and numbers have recovered. There are currently around 35 adult tigers in the park, plus healthy populations of *chital*, nilgai, jackals, leopards, jungle cats and a wide array of birds.

In comparison to the tranquil tiger sanctuaries in the neighbouring state of Madhya Pradesh, the crowds can be off-putting, to say the least – the park is one of India's most popular, with more than eighty thousand visitors a year, and can get ridiculously busy throughout the cool winter months, especially around holiday periods such as Diwali and New Year. The summer months from April to June are a lot quieter, but obviously very hot.

The original core section of the national park has recently been extended with the addition of three new **buffer zones**, designed to provide space for the park's ever-expanding number of tigers (although five have also been sent off to Sariska – see p.232). You're also allowed to get out of your vehicle and walk in these areas (which you're not allowed to do in the main park), although in general they're not so good for tigerspotting.

Note that **Ranthambore is closed** annually from July 1 to September 30; the **best time to visit** is during the dry season (Oct–March), when the lack of water entices the larger animals out to the lakeside. During and immediately after the monsoons, they are more likely to remain in the forest. More information can be gleaned from Project Tiger's excellent booklet, *The Ultimate Ranthambore Guide* (Rs250), on sale in local souvenir shops.

Visiting the park

Rules about **visiting Ranthambore** seem to change every couple of years, so don't be surprised if the following information has become obsolete by the time you arrive. At present, the number of vehicles allowed into the park is strictly controlled, with a maximum of around fifteen six-seater **Jeeps** (also known as "Gypsys") and 25 **Canters** (open-top buses seating twenty people) being allowed in during each morning and afternoon session. Obviously, most visitors prefer the much smaller and quieter Jeeps, although demand usually outstrips supply, and a lot of people find themselves having to make do with a place on a Canter instead. It's worth emphasizing that your chances of seeing a tiger are the same whether you're in a Canter or a Jeep – travelling by Jeep may make it feel more like a real safari, but doesn't actually make any difference to your chances of spotting a big cat. **Safaris** run daily every morning and afternoon, and last around three hours. Departure times vary slightly depending on sunrise, leaving between 6.30am and 7am and between 2.30pm and 3pm. Dress in layers: early mornings can be surprisingly cold.

Booking seats

Seats officially cost Rs555 in a Canter and Rs600 in a Jeep (or Rs370/430 for Indian residents; all prices include the park entrance fee). There's also a charge for video cameras of Rs200. You shouldn't have any problems getting a seat in a Canter if you book the day before via your hotel (except possibly on Fridays and Sundays between October 1 and April 15, when five to eight Canters are block-booked for visitors arriving on the Palace on Wheels and Royal Rajasthan on Wheels heritage trains – see Basics p.29). If you want to go in a Jeep it's best to book ahead, although you might get lucky, especially from around April through to June, when visitor numbers fall significantly. Your chances drop considerably closer to Diwali, New Year and around any other public holiday.

The easiest option is to book a seat in a Jeep or Canter **through your hotel** – in fact it's a good idea to book your safari at the same time you book your room (or even before). You'll pay a surcharge for this, which can be anything from Rs50/100 for a seat in a Canter/Jeep booked through a budget hotel up to Rs2000 for a place in a Jeep booked through a top-end establishment.

If you want **to book your own seat**, the best option is to **reserve online** at Ⓦ www.rajasthanwildlife.in – as always, the further ahead you book, the better your chances of getting the trip you want. The only other alternative is to battle the chaotic, feral and occasionally violent crowds of local touts at the **Ranthambore Tiger Reserve Tourist Centre** (daily 5.30–6.30am & 12.30–1.30pm) near the *Tiger Safari* hotel, about 7km along Ranthambore Road, where you can buy tickets for tours on the day, though you'll be lucky to bag a seat in a Jeep, and the whole experience can be deeply unpleasant.

Ranthambore Fort

It's well worth setting aside some time from the tigers to visit the dramatic **Ranthambore Fort** (daily 6am–6pm; free), set atop a rocky crag near the entrance to the national park. The fort was founded as early as 944 by the Chauhan Rajputs and, following the decisive defeat of Prithviraj III by Muhammad of Ghor in 1192, became a key strategic focus in Rajput resistance to the expanding power of the Delhi Sultanate. The fort changed hands on several occasions, being conquered by Ala-ud-Din Khalji's army in 1301, and by Akbar in 1559, before finally passing into the hands of the Kachchwahas of Amber in the seventeenth century.

A few kilometres along the road into the park, a twisting flight of around two hundred eroded stone steps leads up through a sequence of impressively large gateways and crumbling fortifications to reach the fort, enclosed by some 7km of walls and bastions which snake around the ridgetop, offering fine views over the surrounding countryside. The numerous remains within the fort include a mosque, a large tank, assorted chhatris and several temples – the one dedicated to Ganesh is particularly revered, and people from all over the country write to the elephant-headed god's shrine here to invite him to their weddings.

The easiest way to **visit the fort** is to go on a tour; these can be arranged through the *Tiger Safari* hotel (Rs600/Jeep), or just ask at your hotel to see if they can arrange transport. Alternatively, you could book an early-morning safari and ask to be dropped at the fort on the way out. Unfortunately, once you've explored the fort, you'll be stuck without transport and probably a considerable distance from your hotel, unless you're lucky enough to hitch a lift.

Note that you don't have to pay the park entry fee if you're just going to the fort.

Western Rajasthan

The International boundaries on this map are neither purported to be correct nor authentic by Survey of India directives. Publisher.

N

PAKISTAN

HARYANA

UTTAR PRADESH

GUJARAT

MADHYA PRADESH

0   100 km

CHAPTER 4 # Highlights

* **Dargah Khwaja Sahib, Ajmer** The holiest Muslim shrine in India, attracting thousands of pilgrims every day. See p.253

* **Savitri Temple, Pushkar** For optimum views of the famous lake and whitewashed holy town, climb to the hilltop Savitri temple at sunrise. See p.263

* **Meherangarh Fort, Jodhpur** Spectacular hilltop citadel, offering maximum-impact views of the blue city below. See p.272

* **Jaisalmer Fort** One of India's most beautiful forts, with massive, honey-coloured bastions enclosing a labyrinth of narrow streets dotted with sandstone havelis and temples. See p.285

* **Camel trekking** There's no better way to experience the Thar desert than by riding through it on camel. See p.289

* **Bikaner** Explore the beautiful Junagarh Fort and the labyrinthine old city, dotted with some of Rajasthan's most unusual havelis. See p.297

▲ Meherangarh Fort

Western Rajasthan

Western Rajasthan, the region north and west of the Aravalli Hills, is a desert land rich in history, whose warrior kings built huge forts that still rise majestically out of the arid landscape. These were the strongholds of kingdoms that grew rich from taxing the caravans carrying silk, spices and precious stones across the mighty **Thar Desert**, which begins at the Aravallis and stretches west into Pakistan. Though this may conjure up images of sweeping sand dunes, most of the desert is actually scrub, inhabited by animals such as blackbuck, chinkara and desert fox. Dunes do exist, however, deep in the desert – to see them, you'll generally need to go out on a **camel trek**, which is one of the region's most popular tourist activities.

Not surprisingly, western Rajasthan is a major draw for tourists and home to some of Rajasthan's most memorable sights and iconic landscapes. The Sufi shrine at **Ajmer** has long attracted pilgrims from across the Subcontinent and beyond, as has the holy lake at nearby **Pushkar**, sacred to the Hindu god Brahma, the site of Rajasthan's biggest camel fair, and a major stop on the hippy trail since the first overlanders hit the road to Kathmandu back in the 1960s. **Jodhpur**, the region's largest city, boasts the state's most imposing fort, dominating a walled old town of blue-painted houses, while further out in the Thar, the golden city of **Jaisalmer** is the epitome of a Rajasthani desert town, with its still-inhabited fort and intricately carved havelis. **Bikaner**, to the north, is less visited, but no less rewarding, its old city a maze of temples and early twentieth-century havelis built in a medley of architectural styles.

Legend of the Thar

Legend ascribes the **creation of the Thar** to Rama, hero of the Ramayana. In it, Rama, an earthly incarnation of the god Vishnu, has to rescue his wife Sita from the clutches of the demon Ravana, who is holding her on the island of Sri Lanka. To cross to the island, Rama loads his bow with a magical arrow that will dry up the ocean, but the sea god Sagara begs him not to shoot, offering him free passage instead. Well, says Rama, my bow is now drawn and must be shot, where shall I aim it? There is a sea to the north, replies Sagara, where evil-doers drink my water and hurt me; shoot your arrow there, and you'll be doing me a favour. So Rama takes aim and shoots, drying up the sea that Sagara has described, and creating the desert of Marwar ("Land of the Dead"). By Rama's special boon, this new land, though desert, is blessed, full of sweet herbs and fit for grazing cattle.

In fact, the legend would seem to be based on some degree of truth, for the fossil record shows that back in the Jurassic period (206–144 million years ago), the Thar was covered by sea. Indeed, you may notice that slabs of sandstone often bear tell-tale ripple marks showing that they once formed part of the sea bed.

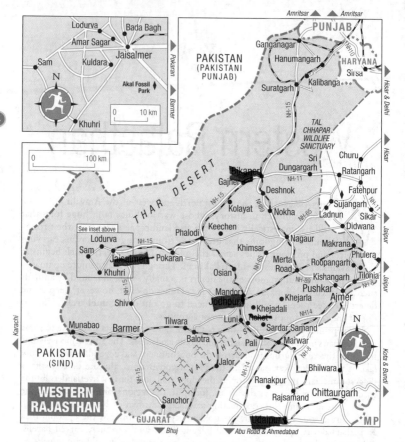

Ajmer

The Nag Pahar ("Snake Mountain"), a steeply shelving spur of the Aravallis west of Jaipur, forms an appropriately epic backdrop for **AJMER**, home of the **Dargah Khwaja Sahib**, the tomb of the great Sufi saint **Khwaja Muin-ud-Din Chishti**, founder of the Chishtiya Sufi order. The tomb is the most important place of Muslim pilgrimage in India, attracting thousands of pilgrims and dervishes daily (it is believed that seven visits here are the equivalent of one to Mecca). Things get especially busy during Muharram (Muslim New Year) and Id, and for the saint's anniversary day, or **Urs Mela** (see box opposite). For Hindu pilgrims and foreign travellers, Ajmer is important primarily as the jumping-off point for **Pushkar**, a thirty-minute bus ride away across the Nag Pahar, and most stay only for as long as it takes to catch a bus out. As a day-trip from Pushkar, however, it's extremely worthwhile, and as a stronghold of Islam, Ajmer is quite unique in Hindu-dominated Rajasthan.

History

Ajmer was founded in the tenth century by local Rajput chieftain Ajay Pal Chauhan, a ruler of the **Chauhan** clan, the dominant power in eastern Rajasthan until defeated by Muhammad of Ghor 1193 (see p.358). The Delhi sultans allowed the Chauhans to carry on ruling as their tributaries, but in 1365, with Delhi on the wane as a regional power, Ajmer fell to the kingdom of Mewar (Udaipur).

During the sixteenth century, the city became the object of rivalry between Mewar and the neighbouring kingdom of Marwar (Jodhpur). The Marwaris took it in 1532, but the presence of Khwaja Muin-ud-Din Chishti's *dargah* made Ajmer an important prize for the Muslim Mughals, and Akbar's forces marched in only 27 years later. Akbar himself came on pilgrimage to the *dargah* every year, and his successor Jahangir frequently used the city as his base. It was here that Jahangir finally agreed to see England's ambassador Thomas Roe, and to give English (and subsequently British) merchants the right to trade.

The Mughals held onto Ajmer for over two centuries, but as their empire began to fragment, rival powers once again started casting covetous eyes on the city. It was eventually taken in 1770 by the Marathas, Hindu rebels from Maharashtra (the hinterland of Mumbai), who had broken away from the Mughal empire to form their own kingdom. In 1818, the Marathas sold the city to the East India Company for fifty thousand rupees. Thus, while most of Hindu-dominated Rajasthan retained internal independence during the Raj, Ajmer was a little Muslim enclave of directly-ruled British territory, only reunited with Jodhpur and Udaipur, its former overlords, when it became part of Rajasthan in 1956.

Arrival and information

Ajmer's **railway station** is slap-bang in the centre of town. The **State Bus Stand** lies some 2km to the northeast on the Jaipur Road – an auto-rickshaw from here into town will cost around Rs40. If you're heading straight on to **Pushkar**, buses depart from the bus stand every fifteen minutes or so until around 9pm. The majority of travellers visit Ajmer on a **day-trip from Pushkar**, but note that buses to and from Pushkar do not travel through the centre of Ajmer en route to the bus stand, so you'll have to traipse into town from the bus stand, and then back out again at the end of your visit.

There are two RTDC **tourist offices**: the main office (Mon–Sat 10am–5pm; ☏0145/262 7426) adjoins the RTDC *Hotel Khadim* near the state bus stand. There's a second office at the railway station (daily 10am–5pm; no phone).

Accommodation

Ajmer's **hotels** aren't great value and you're better off staying in Pushkar and visiting from there. Accommodation also tends to get chock-full during the Urs Mela (see box below). Note that many cheaper hotels tend to operate a 24-hour checkout system.

The Urs Mela

The **Urs Mela**, or Urs Ajmer Sharif, held on the sixth day of the Islamic month of Rajab, is predominantly a religious celebration in honour of the city's Sufi saint, Khwaja Muin-ud-Din Chishti (see box, p.254), on the anniversary of his death. Pilgrims flock to the town to honour the saint with *qawwali* (Sufi devotional) chanting. *Kheer* (rice pudding) is cooked in huge vats at the *dargah* and distributed to visitors, while at night religious gatherings called *mehfils* are held. It isn't really an affair for non-religious tourists, but the city does take on a festive air, with devotees from across the Subcontinent and beyond converging on Ajmer for the week leading up to it. The festival is due to fall on approximately June 7, 2011; May 27, 2012 and May 16, 2013 – dates are fixed according to the lunar calendar and recede against the Western calendar by about eleven days a year.

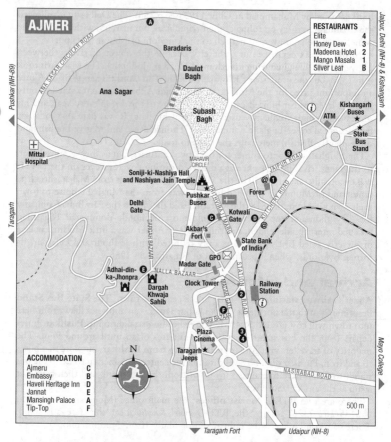

AJMER

RESTAURANTS

Elite	4
Honey Dew	3
Madeena Hotel	2
Mango Masala	1
Silver Leaf	B

Baradaris

Daulat Bagh

Ana Sagar

Subash Bagh

Pushkar (NH-89)

Ana Sagar Circular Road

Jaipur, Delhi (NH-8) & Kishangarh

ATM

Kishangarh Buses

State Bus Stand

Mittal Hospital

Taragarh

Mahavir Circle

Soniji-ki-Nashiya Hall and Nashiyan Jain Temple

Pushkar Buses

Delhi Gate

Dargah Bazaar

Prithviraj Marg

Jaipur Road

Forex

Kotwali Gate

Kutchery Road

Akbar's Fort

State Bank of India

GPO

Madar Gate

Nalla Bazaar

Adhai-din-ka-Jhonpra

Dargah Khwaja Sahib

Clock Tower

Madar Gate

Station Road

Railway Station

Diggi Bazaar

Plaza Cinema

Taragarh Jeeps

Nasirabad Road

Mayo College

N

0   500 m

ACCOMMODATION

Ajmeru	C
Embassy	B
Haveli Heritage Inn	D
Jannat	E
Mansingh Palace	A
Tip-Top	F

Taragarh Fort   Udaipur (NH-8)

Ajmeru Off Prithviraj Marg, just inside Kotwali Gate ☎0145/243 1103, ⊛www.hotelajmeru.com. This comfortable modern hotel is one of the best-value places to stay in town, with bright, clean and well-kept fan, air-cooled and a/c rooms. 24hr checkout. ③–④

Embassy Jaipur Rd ☎0145/242 5519, ⊛www .hotelembassyajmer.com. Comfortable modern three-star. All rooms come with a/c, TV and minibar, and there's also the good in-house *Silver Leaf* restaurant (see p.257). ④–⑤

Haveli Heritage Inn Kutchery Rd ☎0145/262 1607, ⊛www.haveliheritageinn .com. In an old house from the 1870s that was once used as the state HQ of the Congress Party – Nehru and Gandhi both stayed here. It actually sounds grander than it is, but if you think of this as a *pension* rather than a haveli, you'll get the right idea – the big attractions are the peaceful atmosphere and the delightful family who run it. Rooms

(air-cooled and a/c) are bright, spacious and attractively furnished, and there's great home-cooking too. ③–⑤

Jannat Dargah Bazaar, near Nizam Gate ☎0145/243 2494, ⊛www.ajmerhoteljannat.com. A stone's throw from the Dargah Khwaja Sahib, and the best hotel in the area, this fills up quickly on Thurs and Fri, but usually has space the rest of the week. There's a range of rooms, all modern and clean, some a/c, plus a good restaurant and friendly service. 24hr checkout. ③–⑤

Mansingh Palace Vaishali Nagar (Ana Sagar Circular Rd) ☎0145/242 5702, ⊛www .mansinghhotels.com. Three kilometres northwest of town on the main road to Pushkar, this is Ajmer's poshest option, though inconveniently situated, and unless you absolutely have to take the top hotel, it isn't worth the price, though it has a go at being deluxe, with quite stately rooms and a decent restaurant, but no pool. ⑦

comfortable a/c or non-a/c attached rooms. 24hr checkout. ❷–❹

The Town

Although Ajmer's dusty main streets are choked with traffic, the narrow lanes of the bazaars and residential quarters around the **Dargah Khwaja Sahib** retain an almost medieval character, with lines of rose-petal stalls and shops selling prayer mats, beads and lengths of gold-edged green silk offerings. Finely arched Mughal gateways still stand at the main entrances to the **old city**, whose skyscape of mosque minarets and domes is overlooked from on high by the crumbling **Taragarh** – for centuries India's most strategically important fortress.

Dargah Khwaja Sahib

Housing the tomb of the revered Sufi saint, Khwaja Muin-ud-Din Chishti, the **Dargah Khwaja Sahib**, or Dargah Sharif (daily 5am–midnight; Ⓦwww.dargah ajmer.com), is the most important Muslim shrine in India, attracting thousands of pilgrims daily. Founded in the thirteenth century, the *dargah* contains structures financed by many Muslim rulers, particularly the three great Mughals – Shah Jahan, Jahangir and, especially, Akbar, who came to the *dargah* to pray for a male heir and rewarded it with a new mosque when his wish was granted. The shrine remains massively popular, and the continual murmur of prayer, the heady scent of rose attar and hypnotic *qawwali* music (performed in front of the shrine from an hour or so before sunset until 9pm) still create an unforgettable atmosphere, unchanged for seven hundred years.

You enter the complex through the lofty **Nizam Gate**, donated by the Nizam of Hyderabad in 1911. Once inside, you may be accosted by stern-looking young men claiming they are "official guides". In fact, they are *khadims*, hereditary priests operating in much the same way as Hindu *pujaris*, leading pilgrims through rituals in the sacred precinct in exchange for donations. Their services are not compulsory, whatever they may say, although you may wish to employ one to point out the features of religious and historical significance inside.

▲ Dargah Khwaja Sahib, Ajmer

Beyond the Nizam Gate lies the smaller **Shajahani Gate**, commissioned by Shah Jahan. Carry on through this to reach a courtyard, from where steps lead up on the right to the **Akbari Masjid (Akbar's Mosque)**, built by a grateful Akbar following the birth of his son Salim (the future emperor Jahangir).

The next gateway is the imposing, white **Buland Darwaza**, commissioned in the fifteenth century by Mahmoud Khalji, the ruler of Malwa (now part of Gujarat). On the far side, resting on raised platforms, are two immense cauldrons, known as **degs**. The one on the right, the larger of the two, was donated by Akbar after the battle of Chittaurgarh in 1567; the other was a gift from Jahangir upon his accession in 1605. Continuing the saint's tradition of giving succour to the needy, pilgrims throw money into them to be shared among the poor. The *degs* can hold 98 maunds (3658kg) of rice between them, and are the focus of an extraordinary ritual during Urs Mela, in which both are used to cook up the creamy Indian pudding *kheer*, paid for by wealthy patrons. When the *kheer* is ready, a mad scramble begins as the devout, dressed in protective plastic bags, dive head first into the bubbling *degs* to fill their buckets with the pudding, which is regarded by the faithful as *tabarruk* (or "consecrated" – the equivalent of Hindu *prasad*). The best place from which to view this spectacle is the platform above the main entrance archway, on which you can usually gain a place by slipping a tip to one of the *khadims*.

Khwaja Muin-ud-Din Chishti

In 1992–93, following the demolition by Hindu fundamentalists of the mosque at Ayodha (see p.369), sectarian riots swept across India as Hindus turned on their Muslim neighbours nationwide, but Ajmer – a Muslim city in a Hindu fundamentalist state, and an obvious flashpoint – escaped unscathed. No one had any doubt that peace prevailed because of the enduring influence of the Sufi saint enshrined at the heart of the city, **Khwaja Muin-ud-Din Chishti**.

Born in 1156, in Afghanistan, Muslim India's most revered saint, also known as Khwaja Sahib or Garib Nawaz, began his religious career at the age of thirteen, when he distributed his inheritance among the poor and adopted the simple, pious life of an itinerant Sufi *fakir* (the equivalent of the Hindu sadhu). On his travels, he soaked up the teachings of the great Central Asian Sufis, whose emphasis on mysticism, ecstatic states and pure devotion as a path to God were revolutionizing Islam during this period. By the time he came to India with the invading Afghan armies, Khwaja Sahib had already established a following, but his reputation as a saint and a sage only really snowballed after he and his disciples settled in Ajmer at the beginning of the thirteenth century.

Withdrawing into a life of meditation and fasting, he preached a message of renunciation, affirming that personal experience of God was attainable to anyone who relinquished their ties to the world. More radically, he also insisted on the fundamental **unity of all religions**: mosques and temples, he asserted, were merely material manifestations of a single divinity, with which all men and women could commune. In this way, Khwaja Sahib became one of the first religious figures to bridge the gap between India's two great faiths. With its wandering holy men, emphasis on mysticism and miracles, and devotional worship involving music, dance and states of trance, Sufism would have been intelligible to many Hindus. Moreover, it readily absorbed and integrated aspects of Hindu worship into its own beliefs and rituals. After Khwaja Sahib died at the age of 97, his followers lauded the Bhagavad Gita as a sacred text, and even encouraged Hindu devotees to pray using names of God familiar to them, equating Ram with "Rahman", the Merciful Aspect of Allah. The spirit of acceptance and unity central to the founder of the Chishti order's teachings explains why his shrine in Ajmer continues to be loved by adherents of all faiths.

Past the *degs*, over to the left, is the **Langer Khana**, where five maunds (some 186kg) of barley meal are cooked up every day for distribution to the poor. Shops here and in the inner courtyard sell rose petals to scatter over the saint's tomb. Opposite is the **Mehfil Khana**, which is used during the Urs Mela for the nightly recitation of *qawwali* music, accompanied by drums, harmonium and hand-claps, whose hypnotic rhythm lulls the participants into a trance-like state called *mast* which is believed to bring them closer to God.

Beyond the *khanas* is an inner courtyard where the tomb of Khwaja Sahib itself lies inside the **Mazar Sharif**, a domed mausoleum made of marble, its door painted with gold leaf, green and red. The **tomb** inside (closed daily 3–4pm, except Thurs when it's shut 2.30–3.30pm) is surrounded by silver railings and surmounted by a large gilt dome. Devotees file past carrying brilliant *chadars*, gilt-brocaded silk covers for the saint's grave, on beds of rose petals in flat, round head-baskets. Visitors are asked by the *khadims* for donations, and are offered blessings, lightly brushed with peacock feathers and given the chance to touch the cloth covering the tomb.

Subsidiary shrines in the inner courtyard include one belonging to a daughter of Shah Jahan plus a handful of generals and governors, and some Afghani companions of the saint. The delicately carved marble mosque behind the saint's tomb, the **Jama Masjid** or Shahjahani Masjid, was commissioned by Shah Jahan in 1628 and took nine years to build. Despite its grand scale, the emperor deliberately had it built without a dome so as not to upstage the saint's mausoleum next door.

Other Islamic monuments

Often overlooked by visitors, the **Adhai-din-ka-Jhonpra**, 400m west of the Dargah Khwaja Sahib, is the oldest surviving monument in the city and unquestionably one of the finest examples of medieval architecture in Rajasthan. Originally built in 660 AD as a Jain temple, it was converted into a Hindu college on the orders of the Chauhan ruler Visan Dev in 1153 and then destroyed forty years later by the invading Afghan chieftain Muhammad of Ghor, who later had it renovated as a mosque. Tradition holds that its name, meaning "two-and-a-half-day hut", derived from the speed with which it was converted into a mosque, but in fact the reconstruction took fifteen years, using bricks and finely sculpted panels plundered from the original Hindu and Jain temples; the name actually refers to a *fakirs'* festival which used to be held here in the eighteenth century, a *jhonpra* (hut) being the abode of a *fakir* (Sufi mendicant). The mosque's most beautiful feature is its graceful seven-arched facade, decorated with bands of Koranic calligraphy; the interior looks more like a Jain temple than a mosque, with floridly carved pillars and domes – an example of architectural recycling even more incongruous than that at the Quwaat-ul-Islam mosque in Delhi (see p.126), which was built at around the same time using a similar combination of reused temple columns combined with a new Islamic screen.

Back in the centre of town there's a more recent Islamic relic in the form of **Akbar's Fort**, a massive rectangular palace made of golden sandstone – this is actually only the innermost part of a much larger fort which was used by Akbar and his son Jahangir during their visits to the Dargah. It was here in 1616 that Jahangir received Sir Thomas Roe, the first British ambassador to be granted an official audience, after four years of trailing between the emperor's encampments. In 1818 the palace came under British control, and after being used as an arsenal during the 1857 uprising, earned the nickname **Magazine**. Today, the old palace houses a small **museum** (daily except Fri 10am–4.30pm; Rs3, free on Mon; Rs10 for camera, Rs20 video), displaying mainly Rajasthani Hindu statues including an impressive twelfth-century sculpture of Varaha (Vishnu in his incarnation as a boar) and a fourteenth- or fifteenth-century white marble Vishnu.

Further relics of Mughal rule can be found on the northwestern side of Ajmer, around the artificial lake of **Ana Sagar**, laid out in the twelfth century. The long embankment, or bund, on its southwest shore was originally built to moderate the flow of the river through the city and now serves as a popular lakeside promenade – a scenic and mercifully traffic-free venue for a pleasant morning or evening stroll. On top of the bund, and exposed to the cooling breezes off the water, stands a line of exquisite white marble pavilions, or **baradaris**, built by Shah Jahan to serve as summer shelters. Four of the five pavilions remain, all beautifully preserved, standing in the shade of trees and ornamental gardens – the former **Daulat Bagh** – planted by Jahangir.

Taragarh Fort

Three kilometres to the south, and just visible on the ridge high above the city, sits the imposing **Taragarh** (Star Fort), its crumbling walls rising from a ring of forbidding escarpments – even the indomitable Mahmud of Ghazni failed in his attempt to capture the fort during a siege of 1024. The fort was one of the most strategically significant in northwest India from the time of the early Chauhan dynasty through until the Mughal era, since whoever commanded it effectively controlled the region's trade. It's now badly ruined, but is still visited in large numbers by pilgrims, who come to pay their respects at what must be one of the few shrines in the world devoted to a tax inspector, the **Dargah of Miran Sayeed Hussein Khangsawar**. Muhammad of Ghor's chief revenue collector was one of many slain in the Rajput attack of 1202 when, following one of the fort's rare defeats, the entire Muslim population of the fort was put to the sword. Today, a vestigial Muslim community still survives in a tumbledown village inside the walls, clustered around his whitewashed *dargah*.

The best way of getting to Taragarh is to take a ninety-minute **hike** along the ancient paved pathway from Ajmer, which offers superb **views** across the plains and neighbouring hills. To pick up the trailhead, follow the lane behind the Khwaja Sahib Dargah, past the Adhai-din-ka-Jhonpra and on towards the saddle in the ridge visible to the south. Bring **food**, as the only places to eat inside the battlements are a handful of fly-infested non-veg cafés. Alternatively, you can take one of the **Jeeps** (Rs50) that leave from the Plaza Cinema on Diggi Chowk, west of the train station; ask for the "Ta-ra-garh Jeeps", pronouncing all the syllables clearly, or you may end up at the main Khwaja Sahib Dargah. To return to Ajmer, you can either follow the path back downhill, or catch a Jeep from the lot at the northeast side of the village, near the *dargah*.

Other attractions

While most of Rajasthan consisted of princely states, Ajmer was under British rule, and relics of the Raj lie scattered around the city, among them the **Jubilee clock tower** opposite the railway station and the **King Edward Memorial Hall** a little to the west. Some 2km west of the centre lies the famous **Mayo College**, an imposing Indo-Saracenic pile, popularly known as the "Eton of the East", which was established by the British in 1875 as a school for young Indian nobles (particularly those from the princely states of Rajputana).

Perhaps the most bizarre sight in Ajmer is the mirrored **Soniji-ki-Nashiya** hall adjoining the **Nashiyan Jain temple**, or "red temple" (daily 8.30am–5.30pm; Rs20). Commissioned in the 1820s by an Ajmeri diamond magnate, the hall contains a huge diorama-style display commemorating the life of Rishabha (or Adinath), the first Jain *tirthankara*, believed to have lived countless aeons in the past. From the uppermost of the two storeys that surround it, you can look down on a glowing sculptural tableau featuring musicians flying above the sacred Mount

Sumeru on swans, peacocks and elephants, and a huge procession of soldiers and elephants carrying the infant *tirthankara* to the mountain to be blessed. The display, sealed behind glass, contains a tonne of gold. Admission to the main temple alongside is restricted to Jains.

There's another striking monument to the Jain faith some 7km southeast of Ajmer on the Jaipur bypass, the angular modern **Nareli Temple**, a striking edifice mixing traditional and contemporary architectural styles to somewhat quirky effect, with 23 further miniature temples lined up on the hill above. The entire complex is still very much a work in progress: craftsmen have been labouring on it for the past fifteen years, and it's expected to be another decade before all the various structures are finally completed. A rickshaw there and back should cost around Rs200.

Eating

In addition to the snack and fruit-juice places around Dargah Bazaar and Delhi Gate, Ajmer has a handful of larger **restaurants**. None of the following serves alcohol; if you want a drink you'll either have to order it on room service at your hotel or find a liquor store.

Elite Station Rd. Reliable veg restaurant serving moderately priced curries and thalis (Rs50–90), plus a sprinkling of vegetarian Chinese, Continental and south Indian dishes. You can eat either inside in the white-tablecloth dining room or outside at a table in the garden. The *Honey Dew* restaurant, a few doors to the north, is very similar.

Madeena Hotel Station Rd. Muslim establishment serving very tasty non-veg Mughlai curries, mostly involving "mutton" (ie goat), in the form of korma, mughlai, *keema*,

masala or biriyani, in full or half portions (Rs40–80) with freshly baked tandoori breads. There are also chicken, egg and veg dishes.

Mango Masala Sardar Patel Marg. Popular studenty establishment serving pizzas, snacks, veg burgers, salads, shakes, mocktails and ice-cream sodas, as well as veg set-meals and thalis, and lots of *paneer* curries. Mains Rs60–145.

Silver Leaf *Embassy Hotel*, Jaipur Rd. Sedate veg restaurant, with a big selection of curries (most around Rs70–120), plus Chinese and Continental dishes, snacks and breakfasts.

Listings

Banks and exchange There are State Bank of India ATMs opposite the GPO on Prithviraj Marg and near the tourist office, a Bank of Baroda ATM between the *Elite* and *Honey Dew* restaurants, and ICICI and HDFC ATMs at either end of Sardar Patel Marg (the road which *Mango Masala* restaurant is on). If you need a forex bureau, UAE Money Exchange at 10 Sardar Patel Marg (Mon–Sat 9am–1.30pm & 2–7pm) changes cash and travellers' cheques, and also receives MoneyGram money transfers.

Bookshop Bookland, 75 Kutchery Rd, opposite *Haveli Heritage Inn*.

Hospital Mittal Hospital, Pushkar Rd ☎0145/260 3600 to 07 is well equipped and has a 24hr emergency department.

Internet access Satguru has branches at 61 Kutchery Rd (daily 9am–10pm; Rs20/hr) and near *Haveli Heritage Inn*, and at 10 Sardar Patel Marg (daily 11am–9pm; Rs20/hr).

Post office The main GPO is at the southern end of Prithviraj Marg, near Madar Gate (Mon–Sat 10am–8pm, Sun 10am–4pm).

Moving on from Ajmer

Ajmer station (☎0145/243 2535) is on the main Delhi–Ahmedabad **train line**, but there are considerable variations between the journey times of services passing through here (see the box on p.258 for recommendations). The computerized **reservations** hall is on the first floor of the railway station's south wing; get there early in the morning to avoid queues, which can sometimes be very long, or alternatively shell out a little extra for a travel agent.

Recommended trains from Ajmer

The following trains are recommended as the fastest or most convenient. Other services exist, but take longer, or arrive at inconvenient times, or don't run every day. Train timetables change frequently; check latest schedules either at your nearest station or online at ⓦwww.indianrail.gov.in before travel.

Destination	Name	No.	Departs	Arrives
Abu Road	Ahmedabad Mail	9106	7.40am (daily)	12.37pm
	Aravalli Express	9708	11.10am (daily)	5.10pm
Agra	Sealdah Express	2988	12.35am (daily)	7.30pm
Alwar	Ajmer Shatabdi	2016	3.50pm (except Wed)	7.31pm
	Jammu Tawi Express	2413	1.55pm (daily)	6.54pm
Chittaurgarh	Udaipur Express	2992	3.55pm (daily)	6.55pm
	Ratlam Express	9654	1.20pm (daily)	5.05pm
Jaipur	Ajmer Shatabdi	2016	3.50pm (except Wed)	5.45pm
	Jaipur Special	9655A	7am (daily)	9.30am
	Aravalli Express	9707	4.15pm (daily)	6.40pm
Jodhpur	Fast passenger train	2JA	2.25pm (daily)	7.45pm
New Delhi	Ajmer Shatabdi	2016	3.50pm (except Wed)	10.40pm
	Rajdhani Express	2957	12.42am (daily)	7.25am
Udaipur	Udaipur Express	2992	3.55pm (daily)	9.20pm

State buses depart from the **bus stand** on Jaipur Road, about 2km northeast of the centre (☎0145/242 9398). There are buses from here to **Pushkar**'s Ajmer Bus Stand roughly every fifteen minutes until around 9.30pm. There are also buses to Agra (hourly; 9hr), Bikaner (every 1–2hr; 7hr), Bundi (every 1–2hr; 5–6hr), Chittaurgarh (every 1–2hr; 5–6hr), Delhi (hourly; 10–11hr), Jaipur (every 30min; 2hr 30min), Jaisalmer (2 daily plus 1 nightly; 11hr), Jodhpur (hourly; 5hr), Kishangarh (every 15min; 30min), Kota (every 2hr; 6hr) and Udaipur (hourly; 7hr). Seats on private buses – many of which have connecting services from Pushkar – can be reserved at travel agents along Kutchery Road towards Prithviraj Marg.

Kishangarh and around

You won't see many other tourists at **KISHANGARH**, 30km northeast of Ajmer. The former capital of a small Rajput state, Kishangarh was founded in 1609 by Kishan Singh, a son of the maharaja of Jodhpur, and is now a medium-sized regional centre with an unspoilt walled old quarter and a functional modern town. Kishangarh is famous for its tradition of **miniature painting**, particularly the work of Nihal Chand (1710–82), whose paintings of the celebrated local courtesan-poetess Bani Thani posing as Radha – with huge, almond-shaped eyes and sinuously exaggerated features – are some of the most famous in Indian art. Latter-day Kishangarh-style miniatures can be bought at a shop inside the entrance to the *Phool Mahal* hotel (see opposite) and at RK Art's by Tanga Stand, just through the gateway by the fort.

Kishangarh's walled **old town** is a great place for an aimless wander among venerable old temples, crumbling havelis and pastel-coloured houses. As in Jodhpur, many houses are painted blue, made by mixing indigo in with the whitewash, which is thought to keep the interior cool and deter insects. One or two of the houses have murals, Shekhawati-style, but many of these have been whitewashed (or blue-washed) over. The **fort** that looms over the entrance to the town is generally closed to the public, although guests at the *Phool Mahal Palace* hotel can arrange visits (Rs150).

Arriving by bus or train, you'll find yourself in the nondescript **new town**, about 3km distant. This is a centre for working the locally quarried marble (used to make the Taj Mahal) from Makrana, 71km to the north – you'll find marble being cut up in workshops along Ajmer Road south of the bus stand.

TILONIA, 25km east of Kishangarh, is known for its leatherware, and is an excellent place to pick up things like wallets and slippers. It's also home to the Social Work and Research Centre (SWRC), commonly known as **Barefoot College** (W www.barefootcollege.org), established in 1972 to provide teaching to rural people who would otherwise have had no access to formal education. The college has also helped set up local projects to harness solar power, combat desertification and conserve drinking water, as well as helping to sustain traditional village craft industries – including hand-woven, tie-dyed, appliqué and embroidered textiles – which can be bought at the college's crafts showroom.

Practicalities

You can take in Kishangarh on a **day-trip** from Pushkar or Ajmer. If you want **to stay**, the best option is the fine *Phool Mahal Palace* (T 01463/247405, W www .royalkishangarh.com; ⊙), in a 175-year-old former palace of the maharaja of Kishangarh next to the entrance to the old city – a wonderfully tranquil spot, overlooking beautiful open countryside. It's a good stop for lunch (Rs370 buffet) even if you don't stay. The maharaja of Kishangarh maintains a second heritage hotel 25km north of Kishangarh in the fort at **Roopangarh** (T 01497/220217, W www.royalkishangarh.com; ⊙), originally built in 1648 for maharaja Roop Singh, who made it his capital. The rooms, which are spacious and elegantly furnished, are in the newer section of the fort, which stands in a quiet little village.

Kishangarh can be reached from Ajmer by **bus** (every 15min; 30min) or by **train** (seven daily). Both the bus stand on Ajmer Road, and the train station, just off Ajmer Road (and 1km north of the bus stand), are in the new part of town, 3km from the old city. A *tempo* or rickshaw to Tanga Stand at the entrance to the old town will cost Rs40.

Pushkar

According to legend, **PUSHKAR**, 15km northwest of Ajmer, came into existence when Lord Brahma, the Creator, dropped a lotus flower (*pushpa*) to earth from his hand (*kar*). At the three spots where the petals landed, water magically appeared in the midst of the desert to form three small blue lakes, and on the banks of the largest Brahma subsequently convened a gathering of some 900,000 celestial beings – the entire Hindu pantheon. Surrounded by whitewashed temples and bathing *ghats*, the lake is today revered as one of India's most sacred sites: *Pushkaraj Maharaj* literally "Pushkar King of Kings". During the auspicious full-moon phase of October/November (the anniversary of the gods' mass meeting, or *yagya*), its waters are believed to cleanse the soul of all impurities, drawing pilgrims from all over the country. Alongside this annual religious festival, Rajasthani villagers also buy and sell livestock at what has become the largest **camel market** (*unt mela*) in the world, when more than 150,000 dealers, tourists and traders fill the dunes to the west of the lake.

The *mela* is a hugely colourful affair, and this combined with the beautiful desert scenery and heady religious atmosphere of the temples and *ghats* has inevitably made Pushkar a prime destination for foreign tourists; over a million domestic

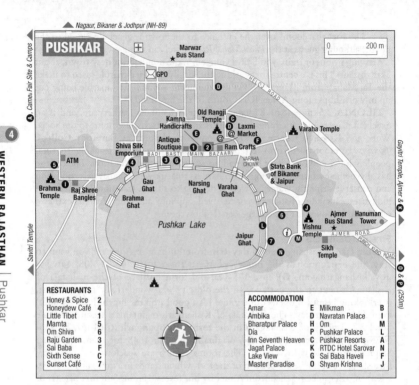

PUSHKAR

Nagaur, Bikaner & Jodhpur (NH-89)

Camel, Fair Site & Camps

Gayitri Temple, Ajmer & K

Savitri Temple

0 200 m

Marwar Bus Stand

GPO

Old Rangji Temple

Kamna Handicrafts

Laxmi @ Market

Varaha Temple

Antique Boutique

Ram Crafts

Shiva Silk Emporium

BADI BASTI (MAIN BAZAAR)

VARAHA CHOWK

ATM

State Bank of Bikaner & Jaipur

Brahma Temple

Raj Shree Bangles

Gau Ghat

Brahma Ghat

Narsing Ghat

Varaha Ghat

Pushkar Lake

Ajmer Bus Stand

Hanuman Tower

Vishnu Temple

AJMER ROAD

PUNG KUND ROAD

Jaipur Ghat

Sikh Temple

O & P (250m)

N

RESTAURANTS

Honey & Spice	2
Honeydew Café	4
Little Tibet	1
Mamta	5
Om Shiva	6
Raju Garden	3
Sai Baba	F
Sixth Sense	C
Sunset Café	7

ACCOMMODATION

Amar	E	Milkman	B
Ambika	D	Navratan Palace	I
Bharatpur Palace	H	Om	M
Día	P	Pushkar Palace	L
Inn Seventh Heaven	C	Pushkar Resorts	A
Jagat Palace	K	RTDC Hotel Sarovar	N
Lake View	G	Sai Baba Haveli	F
Master Paradise	O	Shyam Krishna	J

tourists come here every year too, but most are day-trippers. Pushkar's spiritual energy also attracted the hippy overlanders of the 1960s, and the budget hotels and cafés set up to cater for them have kept it firmly on the backpacker trail. The main bazaar, which just 25 years ago comprised a string of stalls selling traditional puja paraphernalia, is now a kilometre-long line of shops, many selling hippy trinkets, jewellery and CDs, others offering forex, internet, or international phone facilities, while the streetside cafés churn out banana pancakes, pizzas and the occasional bhang-laced "special lassi".

Arrival and information

Pushkar doesn't have a railway station, and most long-distance journeys to and from Pushkar, even by bus, have to be made via Ajmer. The **Ajmer bus stand** in the east of town is served by buses from Ajmer, while travellers from destinations further afield, such as Delhi, Jaipur, Jodhpur and Bikaner (some of which also travel via Ajmer), arrive in the north of town at **Marwar bus stand**. There are very few cycle rickshaws in Pushkar, and no auto-rickshaws, so you'll probably have to walk to your hotel. Pushkar's **tourist office** (daily 10am–5pm; 24hr during camel fair; ☎0145/277 2040) is conveniently located inside the main gate of the RTDC *Hotel Sarovar*, a short walk from the Ajmer bus stand.

Accommodation

Note that prices rise dramatically during the **camel fair**, with increases of anything from two to five times the normal rate.

Budget

Amar Holika Chowk (back entrance on Main Bazaar) ☏0145/277 2809, ✉amar-hotel@yahoo .co.in. Very central place set around a large and peaceful garden, though rooms (all attached with fan, air-cooler or a/c) are decidedly shabby. ❶–❸

Ambika Opposite Old Rangji Temple ☏0145/277 3154. Colourful, and at times, noisy place, right in the thick of the action, with simple but cheap and clean whitewashed rooms, all attached, some with views over the street below and temple opposite. Good value during the Camel Fair. ❶

Bharatpur Palace Main Bazaar ☏0145/277 2320, ✉bharatpurpalace_pushkar@yahoo.co.in. A bit basic and overpriced for what you get (especially during Camel Fair), but the location's wonderful, right on the lake, with views across the *ghats* from some rooms. A couple of rooms have a/c; cheaper ones have shared bathroom. ❶–❸

Lake View Main Bazaar ☏0145/277 2106, ⓦwww.lakeviewpushkar.com. Pretty basic rooms (even the ones with a/c and private bathroom), and well overpriced, but you do get great views over the lake from the terrace and the rooftop restaurant (which gets crowded at sunset). ❶–❸

Milkman Maili Mohalla ☏0145/277 3452. Intimate and sociable little family-run place hidden away in the backstreets with a range of cosy, well-kept rooms (fan, air-cooled or a/c; some with shared bath) and a nice rooftop café and terrace. Good value. ❶–❸

Navratan Palace near Brahma Temple ☏0145/277 2145, ⓦwww.pushkarhotel.com. Aimed at Indian rather than foreign visitors, this modern place has fresh, spotless rooms (some a/c), well-kept gardens and one of the best pools in town (non-guests Rs50). Great value. ❷–❸

Om Ajmer Rd ☏0145/277 2672, ⓦwww.hotelom pushkar.co.cc. Pleasantly tranquil hotel with a wide variety of very competitively priced fan, air-cooled and a/c rooms (all attached), a relaxing garden for lounging and a nice little pool. Good value during Camel fair. ❶–❸

Sai Baba Haveli Off Varaha Chowk ☏0145/510 5161, ✉lola_singh_modiano@hotmail.com. Run by a French–Indian couple, this place offers a range of fan rooms with attached bathroom in an attractive old house set around a pleasant garden patio. There's also a good restaurant (see p.264). ❷–❸

Shyam Krishna Guesthouse Main Bazaar near Vishnu temple ☏0145/277 2461. Attractively tranquil guesthouse with a variety of rooms (some with shared bathroom) set around a garden in a lovely old blue-washed former temple compound. Excellent value, especially during the camel fair. ❶–❷

Mid-range to expensive

Dia Next to *Masters Paradise*, Panch Kund Rd ☏0145/277 2585, ⓦwww.inn-seventh-heaven .com. Low-key new guesthouse recently opened by owner of *Inn Seventh Heaven*, with just four attractively furnished rooms in a very peaceful location on the edge of town, around 500m from the Ajmer Bus Stand. ❺

Inn Seventh Heaven Chhoti Basti ☏0145/510 5455, ⓦwww.inn-seventh -heaven.com. Beautiful hotel in a fine old haveli, mixing traditional and contemporary styles to memorable effect, with vine-draped balconies around a spacious interior courtyard and a range of beautifully furnished rooms. Excellent value. ❷–❺

Jagat Palace Ajmer Rd ☏0145/277 2953, ⓦwww.hotelpushkarpalace.com. Well-run luxury hotel in a slightly inconvenient location on the outskirts of town. The impressive buildings incorporate masonry plundered from an old fort, decorated with elaborate wall paintings and period fittings. Sweeping views, a huge pool, steam bath, Jacuzzi and walled garden add to the allure. ❻

Master Paradise Punch Kund Rd ☏0145/277 3933, ⓦwww.masterparadise.com. Spotless, well-kept three-star in a peaceful setting just outside town, with lovely gardens, a pool, steam bath and Jacuzzi. ❺

Pushkar Palace ☏0145/277 3001, ⓦwww .hotelpushkarpalace.com. Attractive hotel occupying a characterful old maharaja's palace in a plum position overlooking the lake. The whole place has lots of charm, with period-style rooms (most with lake views) and a pretty courtyard garden, though rates are a bit steep – and exorbitant during the Camel Fair. ❼

Pushkar Resorts Motisar Rd, Ganehara ☏011/2649 4531, ⓦwww.sewara.com. Modern resort, inconveniently situated 5km out of town in the desert, with 40 swish a/c cottages in pristine gardens and a kidney-shaped pool. Their restaurant is the only one hereabouts with a non-veg menu, and an alcohol licence. Booking recommended. ❻

RTDC Hotel Sarovar ☏0145/277 2040, ⓦhttp://rtdc.in/sarover.htm. State-run hotel, a bit institutional but boasting a nice lakeside setting, garden and pool, and spacious, pleasantly old-fashioned rooms (air-cooled or a/c; the cheapest ones have shared bath). Very expensive during the fair. ❸–❺

The Town

There are more than five hundred **temples** in and around Pushkar; many had to be rebuilt after pillaging during the merciless rule of Mughal emperor Aurangzeb (1656–1708), while others are recent additions. Some, like the splendid **Vishnu Temple**, on your right as you enter the village from Ajmer, are out of bounds to non-Hindus. Pushkar's most important temple, **Brahma Temple**, houses a four-headed image of Brahma in its main sanctuary, and is one of only a few temples in India devoted to him. Aurangzeb had the original structure demolished in 1679, but Jai Singh II of Jaipur ordered its reconstruction in 1727. Raised on a stepped platform in the centre of a courtyard, the inevitably crowded chamber is surrounded on three sides by smaller subsidiary shrines topped with flat roofs providing views across the desert to Savitri Temple (see opposite) on the summit of a nearby hill.

The lake and ghats

Everything in Pushkar revolves around the **lake**, although this was almost completely waterless at the time of writing, having been drained for cleaning in 2009; all being well, it will have refilled naturally during the 2010 monsoon, assuming there's sufficient rain. The lake is ringed by five hundred beautiful white-washed temples, connected to the water by 52 **ghats** – one for each of Rajasthan's maharajas, who built separate guesthouses and employed their own private *pujaris* (priests) to perform rituals during their stays here. Each is named after an event or person, and three in particular bear special significance. **Gau Ghat**, sometimes called Main Ghat, is where visiting ministers and politicians come to worship, and from which ashes of Mahatma Gandhi, Jawaharlal Nehru and Shri Lal Bahadur Shastri were sprinkled into the lake. **Brahma Ghat** marks the spot where Brahma himself is said to have worshipped, while at the large **Varaha Ghat**, just off the market square, Vishnu is believed to have appeared in the form of Varaha (a boar), the third of his nine earthly incarnations. At all the *ghats*, visitors should remove their shoes at a respectful distance from the lake and refrain from smoking and taking photos.

▲ Pushkar

Brahma, Savitri and Gayitri

Although **Brahma**, the Creator, is one of the trinity of top Hindu gods, along with Vishnu (the Preserver) and Shiva (the Destroyer), his importance has dwindled since Vedic times, and he has nothing like the following of the other two, featuring nowadays more in Hindu legend than in Hindu devotion. The story behind his temple here in Pushkar serves to explain why this is so, and also reveals the significance of the temples here named after Brahma's wives, **Savitri** and **Gayitri**.

The story goes that Lord Brahma was to marry Savitri, a river goddess, at a sacrificial ritual called a *yagna*, which had to be performed at a specific, astrologically auspicious, moment. But Savitri, busy dressing for the ceremony, failed to show up on time. Without a wife, the Creator could not perform the *yagna* at the right moment, so he had to find another consort quickly. The only unmarried woman available was a shepherdess of the untouchable Gujar caste named Gayitri, whom the gods hastily purified by passing her through the mouth of a cow (*gaya* means "cow", and *tri*, "passed through"). When Savitri finally arrived, she was furious that Brahma had married someone else and cursed him, saying that henceforth he would be worshipped only at Pushkar. She also proclaimed that the Gujar caste would gain liberation after death only if their ashes were scattered on Pushkar lake – a belief which has persisted to this day. After casting her curses, disgruntled Savitri flew off to the highest hill above the town. To placate her, it was agreed that she should have her temple on that hilltop, while Gayitri occupied the lower hill on the opposite, eastern, side of the lake, and that Savitri would always be worshipped before Gayitri, which is exactly how pilgrims do it, visiting Savitri's temple first, and Gayitri's temple afterwards.

Indian and Western tourists alike are urged by local Brahmin priests to worship at the lake; that is, to make **Pushkar Puja**. This involves the repetition of prayers while scattering rose petals into the lake, and then being asked for a donation, which usually goes to temple funds, or to the priest, who depends on such benefaction. On completion of the puja, a red thread taken from a temple is tied around your wrist. Labelled the "Pushkar passport" by locals, this simple token means that you'll no longer attract pushy Pushkar priests and can wander unhindered onto the *ghats*. Indians usually give a sum of Rs21 or Rs31; Rs51 or, at most, Rs101 should suffice for a foreign tourist. A favourite trick of (usually phoney) priests is to ask how much you want to pay, then say a blessing for assorted members of your family, and demand the amount you stated times the number of family members blessed, but you needn't be bullied by such cheap tricks into giving any more than you agreed. Indeed, you should really report anyone impersonating a priest to the RTDC office or the tourist police.

In years past, the lake used to be prowled by dozens of man-eating **crocodiles** that would often pick off unwary pilgrims. Elderly Brahmins can still recall the days when they regularly had to beat the rapacious reptiles on the head with long sticks before entering the water, but their strict vegetarian principles prevented them from doing anything about the problem. Eventually, the British intervened by fishing the crocodiles out with nets and transporting them to a nearby reservoir. Nart Singh Ghat, a few steps down from Varaha Ghat, still has on display one rather dusty stuffed crocodile, which didn't make it as far as the reservoir.

Savitri and Gayatri temples

Visible for many kilometres around, Pushkar's rustic little **Savitri Temple** sits atop a saw-tooth hill on the west side of town – a one-hour climb which is rewarded by matchless vistas over town, lake and desert. The ascent is best done at dawn, to reach the summit for sunrise, though it's also a great spot to watch the sun set. The temple itself is modern, but the image of Savitri is supposed to date back to the seventh century. On the opposite, eastern, side of town, the **Gayitri Temple** (Pap Mochini Mandir) also offers great views, especially at sunrise.

Eating

As Pushkar is sacred to Lord Brahma, all food within city limits is strictly veg: meat, eggs and alcohol are banned, as are drugs other than bhang (though *charas* is easy enough to find if you want it, and you should think twice before downing a bhang lassi, for reasons explained on p.57). Most **restaurants** tend to cater for foreign rather than Indian palates, offering bland curries alongside pizza, falafel and chow mein. Pushkar's sweet speciality is **malpua**, basically a fried chapati soaked in syrup, sold at sweetshops around town, and on Halwai Gali, the street directly opposite Gau Ghat.

Honey & Spice Laxmi Market, Main Bazaar. A bit more imaginative than your average Pushkar backpacker café, with a short but sweet menu of tasty vegetarian wholefood dishes (Rs40–75), plus juices, lassis and speciality teas. Good for breakfast. Closes 7pm.

Honeydew Café Main Bazaar near *Bharatpur Palace Hotel*. A hole-in-the-wall place that's been a hippy hangout since the days of the overland trail. It still knocks out a decent breakfast, especially if you like filter coffee, and its pasta dishes (Rs40–70) aren't bad either.

Little Tibet *Payal Guesthouse*, Main Bazaar. Attractive garden restaurant set beneath the overhanging boughs of an enormous tree, serving up decent Tibetan and Indian food alongside the usual medley of faux Italian, Israeli and Mexican tourist fodder accompanied by the inevitable chill-out soundtrack – and even sleepier service. Mains Rs50–170.

Mamta Near Brahma Temple. This is where a lot of Pushkar's Indian visitors come to eat, not surprisingly as it serves up the best veg curries (Rs60) in town. What's available depends on what vegetables are in season, but there's always a good selection.

Om Shiva On the lane heading down to *Pushkar Palace* from Main Bazaar. The best of Pushkar's various all-you-can-eat buffet deals – superb value considering the Rs70 price tag. Avoid copycats with similar names.

Raju Garden Main Bazaar. Above-average Indian, Chinese and Western food in a lovely lakeside setting, dishing up good veg shepherd's pie and baked potatoes, plus a decent range of veg curries. Mains Rs40–80.

Sai Baba Off Varaha Chowk. The usual Indian veg curries (Rs50–80) plus great pasta and the best pizzas (Rs60–110) in Pushkar (the tandoor doubles as a pizza oven). You can sit out front or, more atmospherically, in the garden. There's gypsy dancing on Saturdays at 8pm, when there's also a good Rs150 buffet.

The Sixth Sense *Inn Seventh Heaven*. On the top floor of the *Inn Seventh Heaven*, this stylish café-restaurant offers a welcome alternative to Pushkar's grungy backpacker cafés, with a small but carefully chosen range of Indian and Italian food using fresh seasonal ingredients, plus snacks, fresh juices and breakfasts. Mains Rs40–120.

Sunset Café East side of the lake near the *Pushkar Palace*. The perfect place to enjoy Pushkar's legendary lakeside sunsets, with great views (the outside seats fill up quickly towards dusk) and an impressive selection of juices, lassis, shakes, plus the usual range of Italian, Mexican, Tibetan and Chinese food. Mains Rs50–120.

Shopping

Though it isn't a craft centre as such, Pushkar is a good place to pick up **touristy souvenirs**, with its shops conveniently strung out along the Main Bazaar. As well as lots of hippy-type clothes, T-shirts and silver jewellery, not to mention ceramic chillums (Pushkar's rival those of Hampi and Pondicherry in the south), you'll find lac bangles, Rajasthani textiles, incense, essential oils and – always handy for a paint fight – Holi dyes. For new and used **books**, there's a slew of shops on the Main Bazaar just south of Varaha Chowk.

Kartika Purnima and Pushkar camel fair

Hindus visit Pushkar year-round to take a dip in the redemptory waters of the lake, but there is one particular day when bathing here is believed to relieve devotees of all their sins, and ultimately free them from the endless cycle of death and reincarnation. That day is the full moon (*purnima*) of the **Kartika** month (usually Nov). Over the five days leading up to and including the full moon, Pushkar hosts thousands of devotees, following prescribed rituals on the lakeside and in the Brahma Temple.

At the same time, a huge, week-long **camel fair** is held west of the town, with hordes of herders from all over Rajasthan gathering to parade, race and trade over forty thousand animals. With the harvest safely in the bag and the surplus livestock sold, the villagers, for this brief week or so, have a little money to spend enjoying themselves, which creates a light-hearted atmosphere that's generally absent from most other Rajasthani livestock fairs, backed up with entertainments including camel races, moustache competitions and a popular funfair, complete with an eye-catching sequence of enormous big wheels.

The popularity of Pushkar's fair has – inevitably – had an effect on the event. The number of foreign tourists crossed the ten thousand mark for the first time in 2004, and these days zoom lens-saddled package tourists now bump elbows with traditional pilgrims, camel traders and backpackers. But while the commercialism can be off-putting, the festive environment and coming together of cultures does produce some spontaneous mirth: in 2004 the second prize in the moustache contest was won by a bloke from Manchester.

Practicalities

It's best to get here for the **first two or three days** to see the *mela* in full swing; by the final few days of the festival most of the buying and selling has been done and the bulk of the herders have packed up and gone home. The **day before the festival** officially starts is also good – pretty much all the traders and livestock have arrived, but there are relatively few tourists around.

It's best to **book a room** as far ahead as possible, though if you arrive early in the day – and with a bit of hunting – securing accommodation shouldn't be a problem. If you get stuck, the RTDC runs several tented compounds close to the fairgrounds, offering a choice between dormitory beds (Rs400) and deluxe tents (⑨), or huts (⓪) complete with private bathrooms – ask at the tourist office or check RTDC's website at Ⓦ www.rajasthantourism.gov.in. Additional luxury camping, complete with carpets, furniture, running water and Western toilets, is offered by the maharaja of Jodhpur's *Royal Camp* (for reservations contact WelcomHeritage Ⓣ0291/257 2321, Ⓦ www.welcomheritagehotels.com; from around $400), or *Royal Desert Camp* (for reservations contact the *Pushkar Palace* or *Jagat Palace* hotels; Ⓦ www.hotelpushkarpalace.com; around $200). The **dates** of the next few camel fairs are: Nov 13–21, 2010; Nov 2–10, 2011; Nov 20–28, 2012 and Nov 9–17, 2013.

Antique Boutique Main Bazaar, opposite *Lake View Hotel*. Hassle-free little place with a good selection of modern village-style silver jewellery, plus some antique pieces in the same owner's second shop opposite.

Kamna Handicraft Main Bazaar (north side), a few doors west of Laxmi Market. Kitsch wooden toys, including quaint little fold-up miniature wooden temples from Bassi.

Raj Shree Bangles Brahma Temple Rd, two doors east of *Navratan Palace Hotel*. Colourful shop stocking the largest selection of lac bangles in town.

Ram Crafts Main Bazaar (north side), west of Varaha Ghat Ⓣ0145/277 2890. Good selection of miniature paintings at very affordable prices.

Shiva Silk Emporium Main Bazaar, just east of Gau Ghat Ⓣ0145/277 2150. Lovely silk and cotton garments, which they make themselves for export.

Moving on from Pushkar

Buses for **Ajmer** leave from the Ajmer bus stand (every 15min; 30min). State and private intercity **buses** leave from the **Marwar bus stand** (℡0145/242 9398) for **Bikaner** (9 daily, including overnight services; 6hr 30min), **Bundi** (2 daily; 5hr), **Delhi** (5 daily, including 3 overnight sleeper services; 10hr), **Jaipur** (8 daily; 3hr 30min), **Jodhpur** (1 daily plus 1 nightly; 5hr) and **Jaisalmer** (2 nightly; 9hr). For Udaipur, change at Ajmer. Many more destinations are served from Ajmer, and connecting services are available, but it is not unknown for people who have bought tickets at agencies in Pushkar to find their seats double-booked when they try boarding in Ajmer. To avoid mishaps, it's best to make bookings for bus journeys from Ajmer in Ajmer itself. Services to Delhi in particular are often reserved days ahead.

For recommended **trains from Ajmer**, see p.258. The efficient EKTA Travels acts as Indian Railways' agents in Pushkar and can arrange tickets for train journeys out of any station in India for a Rs40 charge, and also handles bus and plane tickets. They have offices at both the Marwar (℡0145/277 2131) and Ajmer bus stands (℡0145/277 2888).

Listings

Banks and exchange There's a useful State Bank of Bikaner & Jaipur ATM near the Brahma Temple. Alternatively, you can change cash or travellers' cheques quickly at any of the dozens of forex offices in the Main Bazaar. Two reliable places are the Thomas Cook office (Mon–Sat 9.30am–6.30pm) opposite the *Shyam Krishna* guesthouse, and Mantri Forex, on the main bazaar a few doors east of Laxmi Market, near the *Honey & Spice* café (daily 9am–8pm), which is also open Sun. Both also give cash advances on Visa and MasterCard.

Bicycle rental Malakar Bicycle Shop, by the Ajmer Bus Stand (the unsigned pink shop next to EKTA Travels), has basic bikes for Rs25/24hr.

Camel safaris A number of places arrange short camel rides and safaris (including overnight trips) in the desert around Pushkar – try EKTA Travels (see above), who run trips for around Rs130/hr.

Dance The Colleena Shakti Dance Center (℡www .colleenashakti.com) in the old Rangji Temple runs intensive courses in Odissi dance, plus drop-in sessions covering a range of styles.

Hospital Government Hospital, opposite the GPO near Marwar bus stand ℡0145/277 2029.

Internet access Numerous small places around town charge around Rs30/hr. Try the well-equipped New Cyber Space, along the road near the Old Rangji Temple, or KK Internet opposite.

Laundry Chhotu just off Varaha Chowk (daily 7am–8.30pm). Bring clothes early for same-day service.

Motorcycle rental There are a number of places just east of the Ajmer Bus Stand renting out scooters and motorbikes for around Rs100–200/day.

Police Next to the GPO ℡0145/277 2046.

Post office The GPO (Mon–Sat 9am–5pm), for parcels, poste restante and Western Union money transfers, is in the north of town near Marwar bus stand. There's a smaller branch (Mon–Sat 9.30am–5pm) in the middle of town, at Varaha Chowk on the Main Bazaar.

Swimming pools The *Navratan Palace Hotel* charges non-guests Rs50 to use theirs, or you can use the smaller pool at the *Om* hotel if you take a meal or drink.

Yoga and meditation Experienced teacher Yogesh Yogi runs intensive yoga and meditation courses (3–30 days) at the tranquil Pushkar Yoga Garden (℡09828 279835, ℡www.pushkaryoga.org), on Vamdev road opposite the Ajmer Bus Stand, behind the Sikh gurudwara.

Jodhpur and around

On the eastern fringe of the Thar Desert, **JODHPUR**, dubbed "the Blue City" after the colour-wash of its old town houses, huddles below the mighty **Meherangarh Fort**, the most spectacular citadel in Rajasthan. Jodhpur was once the most important town of Marwar, the largest princely state in Rajputana, and now has a population of around a million. Most people stay just long enough to visit the fort,

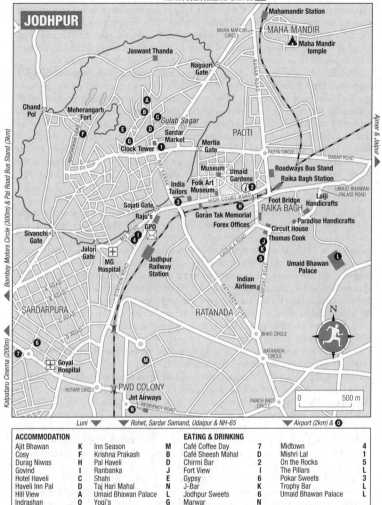

ACCOMMODATION				EATING & DRINKING				
Ajit Bhawan	K	Inn Season	M	Café Coffee Day	7	Midtown		4
Cosy	F	Krishna Prakash	B	Café Sheesh Mahal	D	Mishri Lal		1
Durag Niwas	H	Pal Haveli	D	Chirmi Bar	2	On the Rocks		5
Govind	I	Ranbanka	J	Fort View	I	The Pillars		L
Hotel Haveli	C	Shahi	E	Gypsy	6	Pokar Sweets		3
Haveli Inn Pal	D	Taj Hari Mahal	N	J-Bar	K	Trophy Bar		L
Hill View	A	Umaid Bhawan Palace	L	Jodhpur Sweets	6	Umaid Bhawan Palace		L
Indrashan	O	Yogi's	G	Marwar	N			

though there's plenty to justify a longer visit. Getting lost in the blue maze of the old city you'll stumble across Muslim tie-dyers, puppet-makers and traditional spice markets, while Jodhpur's famed cubic roofscape, best viewed at sunset, is a photographer's dream. In addition, the encroaching desert beyond the blue city is dotted with small settlements where you can escape the urban congestion for a taste of rural Rajasthan.

Some history

The **kingdom of Marwar** came into existence in 1381 when Rao Chanda, chief of the **Rathore** Rajput clan, seized the fort of Mandor (see p.278) from its former rulers, the Parihars. In 1459, the Rathore chief **Rao Jodha** moved from the exposed site at Mandor to a new fort atop a massive steep-sided escarpment, naming his new capital Jodhpur, after himself. His high barricaded fort proved virtually impregnable, and the city soon amassed great wealth from trade. The Mughal emperor **Akbar** captured the city in 1561, but allowed Marwar to retain its independence so long as the Rathore maharajas allied themselves to him.

This alliance was shaken in the mid-seventeenth century, when **Jaswant Singh I** supported Shah Jahan's elder son Dara Shikoh in an unsuccessful power struggle against his brother Aurangzeb. Furious, but unable to subdue Jodhpur, Aurangzeb eventually had to be content with sending Jaswant Singh to battle in Afghanistan, where he was killed, and procuring the death of his son, leaving him without an heir – or so he thought. But Jaswant Singh's wife was pregnant and, defying a summons to Delhi, went into hiding. Her son, **Ajit Singh**, was swapped by his wet-nurse, Goran Tak, with her own son to protect him (a 1711 monument on the south side of High Court Road commemorates Goran Tak's selfless deed). Ajit Singh lived to recapture his kingdom, which he ruled until murdered in 1724 by his own son, Bakhat Singh.

In the eighteenth century, Marwar, Mewar (Udaipur) and Jaipur sealed a triple alliance to retain their independence against the Mughals, and revived the tradition (dropped during Marwar's alliance with the Mughals) that every maharaja of Marwar would marry a Mewari princess, though this led to dynastic squabbles, and the three states were as often at each other's throats as allied together. At the end of the century, Jodhpur maharaja **Man Singh** found himself in conflict with Jaipur, first when his step-mother attempted (with Jaipuri support) to gain the throne for her own son, and then because he and the maharaja of Jaipur both wanted to marry the same Mewari princess. Man Singh also found himself under pressure from the Maratha empire to his south, to whom he was obliged to pay an annual tribute.

In 1818, Man Singh turned for help to a new power, the **British**. Under the terms of his deal with them – not unlike Marwar's old arrangement with the Mughals – the kingdom retained its internal independence, but had to pay the East India Company an annual tribute equivalent to the one previously enforced by the Marathas. The city went on to prosper under the Raj, becoming the largest princely state in Rajputana, while local Marwari merchants became some of the wealthiest in India. In 1880, under maharaja Jaswant Singh II, Marwar got its own train line, the Jodhpur Railway, the brainchild of **Sir Pratap Singh**, the maharaja's younger brother and prime minister, most famous abroad for his invention of Jodhpur britches (see p.275).

The last but one maharaja before Independence, **Umaid Singh**, is commemorated by his immense Umaid Bhawan Palace. In 1930 he agreed in principle with the British to incorporate Marwar into an independent India. When that eventually came, his son and successor, Hanuwant Singh, attended the Independence ceremony wearing a black turban. "Today," he explained, "the 500-year-old reign of my family has come to an end, so I am in mourning." Nonetheless, his descendants retain much of their wealth, and a great deal of influence and genuine respect in Jodhpur, of whose culture the present maharaja remains a great patron.

Arrival, orientation and information

The heart of Jodhpur is its walled **old city**, a maze of higgledy-piggledy streets hugging the base of **Meherangarh Fort** on three sides, and almost impossible to navigate on your first visit, but most easily approached up **Nai Sarak**, the broad, modern street that connects Jodhpur's modern centre with **Sardar Market**, the old city's commercial hub with its landmark **clock tower**. The modern city stretches south of here, centreing on the smart suburb of **Sardarpura** and the broad and pleasantly calm B and C roads, lined with shops and cafés.

Jodhpur's main **railway station** is pretty central, just south of the old city on Station Road. If you're heading for the old city, you can walk to the clock tower (turn right out of the station) in fifteen minutes, or take an auto-rickshaw for Rs30. **Government buses** use the Roadways (Raika Bagh) **bus stand**, east of the old city, a longish walk (1km) from the clock tower (or Rs40 by auto). Most **private buses** deposit passengers at the stand in Pal Road, 4km west of the centre (about Rs40 by auto). A few terminate at Kalpataru Cinema, 4km southwest of town (about Rs30 by auto), while private buses for Jaisalmer pull into Bombay Motors Circle, nearby. From the **airport**, 4km south, a pre-paid auto-rickshaw into town costs Rs10; taxis charge a fixed rate of Rs220.

The **tourist office** (Mon–Fri 9.30am–6pm; ☎0291/254 5083) is next to the RTDC *Goomar Hotel* on High Court Road. **Online**, ⓦjodhpur.nic.in and www .maharajajodhpur.com both have lots of interesting background information on the city.

Accommodation

Jodhpur has plenty of good accommodation in all price brackets, although **commission rackets** are a real problem, meaning that some auto-wallahs will do all they can to avoid taking you to any hotel that doesn't pay them commission. Most guesthouses offer **free pick-up** from bus or train stations; alternatively, take an auto to a point nearby and then walk.

Budget

Cosy Old City ☎0291/261 2066, ⓦwww .cosyguesthouse.com. Friendly little guesthouse in a pretty blue-washed building buried deep in the maze of lanes in the west of the old city (call for free pick-up; it's tricky to find otherwise). Rooms (fan, air-cooled and a/c; a few with shared bathroom) are simple but neat and cosy, and there are killer views of the fort from the rooftop terrace. ❶–❸

Durag Niwas 1 Old Public Park, Raika Bagh ☎0291/251 2385, ⓦwww.durag-niwas.com. Very friendly and well-run little place with cosy air-cooled and a/c rooms set around a peaceful courtyard. Also runs various programmes helping disadvantaged local women (half the guests are usually long-stay volunteers). Gay and lesbian friendly. ❷–❸

Govind Station Rd ☎0291/262 2758, ⓦwww.govind-hotel.com. A long-standing travellers' favourite, with bright, spotless rooms (some with a/c; all air-cooled in summer), a clean dorm (Rs110), excellent rooftop restaurant (see p.274) with wi-fi, and friendly, professional management. There's also an in-house cybercafé and travel agents (see p.276), and it's conveniently close to the station if you're arriving late or leaving early. ❷–❹

Hill View Old City, on the road up to the fort (about 200m beyond *Krishna Prakash* hotel – see p.270) ☎09829 153196, ⓔhill_view2004@yahoo.com.

Sociable guesthouse run by hotelier turned local Congress politician Zafran and family. Rooms (all attached) are basic but very cheap, and there are fine views over town. ❶–❷

Hotel Haveli Old City (exit the northern gateway of Sardar Market, turn left then first right, then right again past the *Ganpati* guesthouse) ☎0291/261 4615, ⓦwww.hotelhaveli.net. One of the oldest and tallest havelis in the Sardar Bazaar area, with accommodation ranging from simple, inexpensive fan rooms to much fancier a/c rooms with window seats and traditional decor. Great views from the obligatory rooftop restaurant. ❷–❺

Yogi's Old City (about 50m beyond *Krishna Prakash* hotel) ☎0291/264 3436, ⓔyogiguest house@hotmail.com. The best of the innumerable guesthouses just north of Sardar Bazaar, with lovely blue decor, clean, comfy rooms (most with a/c) and excellent fort views from the rooftop restaurant. ❶–❸

Mid-range

Haveli Inn Pal near Gulab Sagar Lake, 200m north of the clock tower (out of the north gate of Sardar Market, turn right and first left) ☎0291/261 2519, ⓦwww.haveliinnpal.com. Appealing mid-range option right in the heart of the old city, with large, well-appointed a/c rooms (some with fort or lake views) in an eighteenth-century haveli. ❺

Indrashan 593 High Court Colony, 3km south of town ☎0291/244 0665, ⓦwww.rajputana discovery.com. Eight comfortable rooms in an authentic homestay. The husband/wife team offer excellent food and cooking classes, and non-guests are welcome for dinner if they call ahead (Rs425). The owner also arranges homestays in other parts of the state, and in Delhi and Agra. ❺

Inn Season PWD Rd ☎0291/261 6400, ⓦwww .innseason.in. Unusual boutique hotel, with eye-catching Art Deco-style rooms and (especially) suites. One drawback: it's noisy during wedding season (approx Oct–March) due to the wedding ground next door. Book ahead. ❺–❻

Krishna Prakash Nayabas (exit the northern gateway of Sardar Market, turn left then first right and continue straight ahead; it's on your left after about 150m) ☎09829 241547, ⓦwww .kpheritage.com. Heritage hotel in an old haveli right below the fort walls. The building itself isn't that exciting, but rooms (all with a/c) are nicely furnished with antique bric-a-brac and rates are surprisingly inexpensive, although the minuscule pool, under a dirty corrugated plastic roof, is horrible. ❹

Shahi Gandhi St, City Police district, off Katla Bazaar opposite Narsingh Temple ☎0291/262 3802, ⓦwww.shahiguesthouse.com. Welcoming family guesthouse occupying a quirky 350-year-old haveli buried deep in the warren of lanes beneath the fort's southwest wall – and with superb views of it from the roof. The six rooms (with optional a/c) are brimful of character, decorated with a medley of quaint murals and assorted curios. Call for free pick-up (it's difficult to find otherwise). ❸–❺

Expensive

Ajit Bhawan Airport Rd ☎0291/251 1410, ⓦwww.ajitbhawan.com. This self-contained miniature resort – built to resemble a dhani village – is one of Jodhpur's quirkier and more appealing places to stay, with accommodation in cute little round thatched chalets or more conventional rooms. Facilities include a quaint waterfall-fed pool, thatch-roofed outdoor restaurant and spa. ❽

Pal Haveli Near Gulab Sagar Lake ☎0291/329 3328, ⓦwww.palhaveli.com. Atmospheric heritage hotel in the heart of the old city with attractively furnished rooms and plenty of period character. Standard ("Royal Heritage") rooms are reasonably affordable, though the "Historical" rooms are only slightly nicer, and twice the price. ❼–❽

Ranbanka Airport Rd ☎0291/251 2800, ⓦwww .ranbankahotels.com. In the other half of the palace occupied by the Ajit Bhawan (see above), this is more authentic in some ways (the rooms are actually inside the palace), but generally less appealing, with uninspiring rooms and flakey service – though the expansive gardens and good-sized pool (non-guests Rs700) are a major plus. ❼

Taj Hari Mahal 5 Residency Rd, 1km south of town ☎0291/243 9700, ⓦwww.tajhotels.com. All the luxury you'd expect from a five-star Taj hotel, with swanky traditional-style decor, two good restaurants (including Marwar, see p.274), a spa and good-sized pool, and spacious and attractively furnished rooms (from around US$310) are a major plus. ❾

Umaid Bhawan Palace ☎0291/251 0101, ⓦwww.tajhotels.com. The Maharaja of Jodhpur's princely pile (also see p.273) ranks among the world's grandest hotels, with celebrity guests and lashings of trendy Art Deco. But being king or queen for a day can be a solitary experience – some find the oversized suites, stately salons and dark, marbled passageways a bit foreboding. Rooms start at around US$950. ❾

The City

Jodhpur is dominated by the dramatic **Meherangarh Fort**, looming massively above the city from its huge sandstone plinth. Below it, the houses of the walled **old city** huddle like a Cubist painting, most of them decorated in the blue wash that gives the city its distinctive colour. Blue originally denoted a high-caste Brahmin residence, resulting from the addition of indigo to lime-based whitewash, which was thought to protect buildings from insects, and to keep them cool in summer. Over time the colour caught on – there's even a blue-wash mosque on the road from the Jalori Gate, west of the fort.

The bazaars of the old city, with different areas assigned to different trades, radiate out from the 1910 **Sardar Market** with its tall **clock tower**, a distinctive local landmark marking the centre of town. Most of the ramparts on the south side of the old city have been dismantled, leaving **Jalori Gate** and **Sojati Gate** looking rather forlorn as gates without a wall. South of the old city, the **train station** was constructed in 1880 as part of Marwar's own Jodhpur Railway.

There are quite a few very attractive **heritage hotels** in the region around Jodhpur. Often, they're in the middle of nowhere, but you can usually arrange a pick-up from Jodhpur.

Bal Samand Lake Palace Off Mandor Rd, 8km north of town ☏0291/257 2321, ⓦwww.welcomheritagehotels.com. Among the most attractive heritage hotels in the state, converted from the maharaja's lakeside summer palace, with ten beautiful "Palace Suites" in the main building – all huge, airy and exquisitely furnished. You also get the run of a lush, monkey-filled garden with a pool and croquet lawn. Rooms around $380. Rs16,000+10 percent.

Fort Chanwa Luni (36km south of Jodhpur) ☏02931/284216, ⓦwww.fortchanwa .com. Set in an old red-sandstone fort of 1895, though the standard rooms aren't all that old-fashioned and it's worth forking out an extra Rs1000 for one of the heritage rooms. Facilities include a pool, sauna, Jacuzzi and croquet lawn, while the endearingly named village of Luni, in which the fort stands, is also rather pretty, with some interesting old houses and temples. ❽

Fort Khejarla Khejarla (84km east of Jodhpur) ☏02930/258486, ⓦwww.jodhpur fortkhejarla.com. A mightily imposing fort with lots of carved red sandstone, tastefully furnished rooms and views over the surrounding countryside. Best rooms are in the turrets. ❼

Jhalamand Garh Jhalamand (7km south of Jodhpur) ☏0291/272 0481, ⓦwww .heritagehotelsindia.com. Occupying the elegant, late eighteenth-century palace belonging to the thakurs of the village of Jhalamand, the hotel is still close enough to Jodhpur to actually see the city. Meals feature traditional Rajput cuisine, while dance performances by a Kalbelia Gypsy troupe are held around an outdoor fire every night. ❼

Khimsar Fort Khimsar (91km northeast of Jodhpur) ☏01585/262345, ⓦwww .khimsar.com. Set in a sprawling sixteenth-century fort with a variety of rooms in different styles – some traditional, some Art Deco – plus a pool, spa and health centre. Antelope-spotting safaris are available, and the location is also handy for Nagaur (see p.309), just 40km away. They also run a tented desert camp, the *Khimsar Dunes Village*, 6km down the road. ❽

Mihir Garh Rohet (50km south of Jodhpur) ☏02936/268231, ⓦwww.mihirgarh.com. Ultra-luxurious heritage hotel in an old rural fort, with just nine huge suites with private plunge pools, Jacuzzis and other upmarket touches. Activities include village safaris, horse and camel rides, "royal picnics" and yoga. Rooms from around $350. ❾

Rohet Garh Rohet (39km south of Jodhpur) ☏02936/268231, ⓦwww.rohetgarh .com. This sleek hotel was a palace given in 1622 by the maharaja of Jodhpur to the thakur of Rohet, whose heirs still live in it. There are cool, spacious rooms, candle-lit poolside dinners, royal-style picnics with liveried attendants, plus culinary workshops, village safaris and birdwatching expeditions. ❼

Sardar Samand Palace Sardar Samand Lake (55km southeast of Jodhpur) ☏02960/245001, ⓦwww.welcomheritagehotels.com. Birdwatchers and fans of Art Deco will love this hunting lodge built in 1930 for the maharaja of Jodhpur. On the highest piece of land for many kilometres, with magnificent panoramic views over the neighbouring lake and surrounding countryside, the palace has retained many of its original features, fittings and furniture, including stuffed animal heads gazing down from the dining-room walls. Activities include birdwatching, nature walks, village safaris, or just lazing by the pool. ❼

Meherangarh Fort

For size, strength and sheer physical presence, few sights in India can rival Jodhpur's mighty **Meherangarh Fort** (daily 9am–5.30pm; foreigners Rs300 entry includes audio tour if you leave ID, credit card or deposit, students Rs250, Indian residents Rs30; video Rs200; elevator Rs20, guide Rs150; ⓦwww .meherangarh.org), a great mass of impregnable masonry whose soaring, windowless walls appear to have grown directly out of the enormous rock outcrop on which it stands. The walk up to the fort from the old city is pretty steep, but you can reach the entrance by taxi or auto along the road from Nagauri Gate. The excellent audio tour takes about two hours to complete.

You enter the fort through **Jai Pol** (or Jey Pol), the first of seven defensive gates on the way up to the fort's living quarters, constructed in 1806 to celebrate Meherangarh's successful holdout against a siege mounted by the Jaipuri and Mewari armies during a dispute over the hand of a Mewari princess (see p.268).

The sixth of the seven gates, **Loha Pol**, has a sharp right-angled turn and even sharper iron spikes to hinder the ascent of charging enemy elephants. On the wall just inside it you can see the handprints of Maharaja Man Singh's widows, placed there in 1843 as they left the palace to commit *sati* on his funeral pyre – the last mass *sati* by wives of a Marwari maharaja.

Beyond the final gate, the **Suraj Pol**, lies the **Coronation Courtyard** (Shangar Chowk), where maharajas are crowned on a special marble throne. Looking up from the courtyard, you can see the fantastic *jali* (lattice) work that almost entirely covers the surrounding sandstone walls. The adjoining apartments now serve as a **museum**, with exhibits including solid silver *howdahs* (elephant seats) and palanquins alongside assorted armaments including Akbar's own sword. One prize exhibit is a grand glass palanquin seized in battle from the Mughal governor of Gujarat. Upstairs (though sometimes moved during temporary exhibitions) are some fine **miniature paintings** of the Marwari school, mostly featuring maharaja Man Singh, who greatly encouraged miniature painting during his reign.

The most elaborate of the royal apartments, the magnificent 1724 **Phool Mahal** (Flower Palace), with its jewel-like stained-glass windows and gold filigree ceiling, was used as a venue for dancing, music and poetry recitals. The nearby **Takhat Vilas** was created by nineteenth-century Maharaja Takhat Singh, its ceiling hung with huge Christmas tree balls, while the walls are painted with murals reminiscent of those in Shekhawati (see p.216).

A colourful array of cradles used by former infant rulers fills the **Jhanki Mahal**, or Queen's Palace. The *jali* screens on either side of the room allowed the women of the palace to look out onto the courtyards on both sides without themselves being seen. This was important, for purdah, usually thought of as a Muslim custom, was strictly applied in the Hindu Rajput kingdoms.

The **Moti Mahal** (Pearl Palace – so called because crushed seashells were added to the lime plaster of the walls to give them a pearly sheen) was used for councils of state and holds the nine cushions reserved for the nine heads of the Marwari state, plus one central cushion for the maharaja himself. The five alcoves in the wall opposite the entrance are actually concealed balconies where the maharaja's wives could listen in secretly on the proceedings, perhaps overhearing and reporting private conversations between those attending which the maharaja wasn't meant to know about.

Beyond the Moti Mahal is the **Zenana**, or women's quarters, otherwise known as the harem, and formerly guarded by eunuchs. From here, you descend past the museum shop to the **Temple of Chamunda**, the city's oldest temple, dedicated to Jodhpur's patron goddess, an incarnation of Durga. In 1965, during one of India's frequent set-tos with its sibling state of Pakistan, three hundred Pakistani bombs fell on the city, but the only thing hit was a wall of the city jail, and nobody was hurt;

Jodhpuris ascribe this luck to the goddess's intervention, and she is even said to have appeared in the form of a huge kite-like bird to intercept a bomb destined for the fort.

Jaswant Thanda

Some 500m north of the fort, and connected to it by road, **Jaswant Thanda** (daily 9am–5pm; Rs20, camera Rs25, video Rs50) is a pillared marble memorial to the popular ruler Jaswant Singh II (1878–95), who purged Jodhpur of bandits, initiated irrigation systems and boosted the economy. The cenotaphs of members of the royal family who have died since Jaswant are close to his memorial; those who preceded him are commemorated by chhatris at Mandor (see p.278). In the morning, this southwest-facing spot is also a top place from which to photograph the fort.

Umaid Bhawan Palace

Dominating the city's southeast horizon is the **Umaid Bhawan Palace**, a colossal Indo-Saracenic heap commissioned by Maharaja Umaid Singh in 1929 as a famine relief project. It kept three thousand labourers gainfully employed for sixteen years, used a hundred wagon-loads of marble from the quarries at Makrana (see p.259), and its 26-acre garden needed half a million donkey-loads of soil. The project cost nearly 95 lakh (nine and a half million) rupees. When completed in 1944, it boasted 347 rooms, plus a cinema and indoor swimming pool. Its furniture and fittings, ordered from Maples in London at the height of World War II, were sunk by a U-boat en route to India, and the maharaja had to turn instead to a wartime Polish refugee, Stephen Norblin, who gave the palace its fabulous Art Deco interiors. Umaid Singh unfortunately had little time to enjoy his new home; only three years after it was finished he died.

The present incumbent, Maharaja Gaj Singh, occupies only one-third of the palace; the rest is given over to a luxury **hotel** (see p.270) and a rather dull **museum** (daily 9am–5.30pm; foreigners Rs50, Indian residents Rs15), containing various items from the maharaja's collection of luxuries and curiosities, including assorted European crockery and glassware, plus a mildly entertaining gallery of clocks and barometers, some in the form of railway locomotives, lighthouses and windmills. Far more interesting (and expensive) is the palace itself, its Art Deco furniture and fittings nearly all original, enlivened with lashings of typically Rajasthani gilt and sweeping staircases. Non-guests wanting to have a look will need to spend a minimum of Rs3000 to visit the hotel's bar or one of its restaurants (see p.275). A cheaper option is to take the **virtual tour** at Ⓦwww.photowebusa.com/taj/umaid-bhawan-palace.

Umaid Gardens

On High Court Road, the small **Umaid Gardens** are home to the city's depressing **zoo** (daily except Tues 8.30am–5.30pm; Rs50, camera Rs10, video Rs40), whose animals are housed in enclosures scattered around the park. It's also home to the **Sardar Government Museum** (Tues–Sun 10am–4.30pm; foreigners Rs10, Indian residents Rs5) with a few mildly interesting exhibits including (in the natural history gallery) a pickled scorpion with two stings, and (in the last gallery) some lovely miniature paintings, notably one featuring a rather inebriated-looking Rajput eating goat heads and trotters. Just outside the gardens, the Rajasthan Sangeet Natak Akademi runs a **Folk Art Museum** (Mon–Sat 11am–5pm; free) with a slightly moth-eaten collection of Rajasthani musical instruments.

Maha Mandir

In a bustling suburb northeast of town, the **Maha Mandir** temple was commissioned in 1804 by maharaja Man Singh. Before succeeding to the throne, Man Singh was forced into hiding by Bhim Singh, the previous maharaja, who wanted him killed. Man Singh was considering fleeing Jodhpur until a Nath yogi guru by the name of Aayas Deonath told him to hold out for five more days. At the end of this time, Bhim Singh died and Man Singh emerged to take the throne, subsequently commissioning the temple in gratitude to the yogi.

The temple is supported by 84 pillars, and the main shrine, dedicated to Aayas Deonath, is decorated with murals depicting the 84 positions of Nath yoga. Like many medieval churches in Europe, the temple was once a sanctuary for criminals. Today it's used as a school, but members of the public are allowed in. To reach it take an auto from town (Rs60) or a bus (#1, #5, #7 or #15) to Maha Mandir circle, walk over the level crossing and through the arch (one of four gates into the formerly walled Brahmin settlement around the temple), and turn left after 300m or so.

Eating and drinking

Jodhpur's **restaurants** cater for all tastes and all budgets, though most of them are outside the old city. Local **specialities** include *mirchi bada*, a chilli in wheatgerm and potato, which is deep-fried like a *pakora*. Jodhpuri sweets, often made with *mawa* (milk that's been boiled down until solid), include *makhan wada* (a sweet made of wheatflour, semolina and sugar, fried in ghee) and *mawa kachori* (a *kachori* filled with *mawa* and drizzled with syrup). In winter, there's *doodh feni*, consisting of wheat strands (sweet or plain) in hot milk.

The most memorable place for a **drink** is the *Trophy Bar* at the *Umaid Bhawan Palace* (see p.273) – if you can afford the Rs3000 minimum charge; alternatively, the beautiful *J-Bar* at the *Ajit Bhawan* hotel has comfy chairs, cool decor and assorted tipples at a fraction of the price. Other options include the uninspiring but quiet *Chirmi Bar* at the RTDC *Hotel Goomar*, next to the tourist office, which also has a pleasant garden, or the rather grungy, male-dominated bars around the *Midtown* restaurant on Station Road.

Cafés, sweets and snacks

Cafe Sheesh Mahal Sardar Bazaar (exit the northern gate of Sardar Bazaar and turn right; it's ahead of you on the corner just before the entrance to the *Pal Haveli* hotel). Surprisingly smart little a/c coffee shop offering a good range of real coffees and speciality teas, along with snacks, sandwiches and light meals, plus entertaining bird's-eye views of the street below.

Jodhpur Sweets C Rd, Sardarpura, next to *Gypsy*. The best sweet shop in town, and an excellent place to try *makhan wada*, *mawa kachori*, or any other Rajasthani or Bengali sweets.

Mishri Lal In the eastern arch of the south gate to Sardar Market. The most famous purveyor of *makhania lassi*, made with cream, saffron and cardamom, very rich and thick, but those with delicate stomachs should take note that they use crushed ice made from tap water. They also do good *doodh feni*.

Pokar Sweets Corner of Nai Sarak with High Court Rd. Not all their sweets are good, but they're known for their *makhan wada*, and their *mirchi bada*'s pretty hot too. This is also a good place to try *doodh feni*.

Restaurants

Fort View On the roof of the *Govind Hotel*, Station Rd. A cut above the usual tourist places, with good, reasonably priced veg curries and thalis (Rs45–120), local specialities such as *makhania* lassi and excellent *gulab jamun* (not the Bengali sweet, but a savoury Rajasthani dish made with *mawa*), plus good breakfast options, including real coffee. Also has wi-fi coverage, and you can hang out here while waiting for a bus or train (baggage storage facilities are available).

Gypsy C Rd, Sardarpura. Downstairs is a run-of-the-mill diner selling Indian snacks and ice cream. Upstairs is a comfortable restaurant serving one thing only: an unlimited and delicious veg thali (Rs125) that they keep refilling for as long as you carry on eating.

Marwar At the *Taj Hari Mahal* hotel ☎0291/243 9700. Pricey, but the best place in town to sample traditional Marwari cuisine, such as *Jodhpuri mas* (a spicy mutton dish) or *gatta di subzi* (its veg equivalent), rounded off with *kulfi*. Mains Rs230–400.

Midtown On side road off Station Rd opposite the station. Bright, clean and friendly pure-veg restaurant with a delicious range of curries, south Indian dishes, Gujarati and Rajasthani thalis and other Rajasthani specialities, as well as some pizza and Chinese. Mains Rs70–150. Licensed.

On the Rocks Next to *Ajit Bhawan* hotel, Airport Rd ☏ 0291/230 2701. A renowned upmarket non-veg garden restaurant specializing in kebabs and tandoori cuisine. Though service is slow, and the buffet no great shakes, it's fun and festive at night. The lunch crowd is mostly tour groups. Mains Rs70–120 veg, Rs120–300 non-veg.

Umaid Bhawan Palace ☏ 0291/251 0101, ⓦ www.tajhotels.com. The opulent *Umaid Bhawan Palace* has various eating and drinking possibilities, though whatever you do you'll have to stump up a Rs3000 minimum charge, payable on entry (and advance reservations for the restaurants are also strongly recommended) – although this at least gives you the chance to wander around the hotel's opulent Art Deco interior. *The Pillars* veranda café has sweeping views over the palace gardens and light snacks during the day, and is also a good place for a sundowner; alternatively, head to the sumptuous *Trophy Bar*. Full meals (with fixed menus for around Rs4000) are available at the *Risala* multi-cuisine restaurant, set in a lavish, olde-worlde European-style dining room, and at *The Pillars* during the evening.

Shopping

Jodhpur's first-rate **antique reproductions** – everything from chests of drawers to sculptures of Jain *tirthankaras* – attract dealers from around the world. There's a line of shops selling them along Umaid Bhawan Palace Road east of the Circuit House. Other good buys in town are **textiles**, including mirrorwork dresses, patchwork bedcovers, and *Bandhani* (tie-dye) fabric and saris, not to mention **Jodhpur riding britches** (see box below). For bookshops see p.276.

India Tailors High Court Rd, 200m east of the junction with Nai Sarak. Despite its small and unprepossessing appearance, this little shop can't be beaten for custom-made suits or Jodhpur riding britches, and counts the maharaja among its customers. They can run you up a pair of (expensive) jodhpurs within 8hr for around Rs6000.

Lalji Handicrafts Umaid Bhawan Palace Rd. Huge, warehouse-like shop stuffed with all sorts of bric-a-brac including unusual collectibles like old enamel signs and colonial-era prints, plus a considerable amount of junk. The much smaller Paradise Handicrafts a few doors along is also worth a look.

Mohanlal Verhomal's (MV) Spice Shop 209-B Kirana Merchant Vegetable Market, west of the clock tower, and also at the fort entrance, ⓦ www.mvspices.com. Lots of spices, whole and ground, including pukka saffron, masalas and teas. Has a reliable pay-on-receipt mail-order service, though in fact you can buy many of the same spices more cheaply at open stalls in the adjoining spice market.

Raju's MG Rd, almost opposite Sojati Gate, and also on C Rd, Sardarpura. Embroidered and *bandhani* saris and *salwar kameez* suits: very classy, very colourful, very Rajasthani. Lucky Silk Stores, a few doors away on MG Rd, is also worth a look.

Shriganesham Pal Haveli, north of Sardar Market, opposite the eastern arch of the north gate. Wonderful Rajasthani fabrics, old and new, including dhurries, mirrorwork dresses, patchwork bedspreads made from recycled garments, and some sumptuous embroidered coats and dresses.

Jodhpurs

The city of Jodhpur gives its name to a type of trouser – baggy around the thigh but narrow around the calf – designed for horseriding. They were invented for his own personal use by Sir Pratap Singh, brother of Maharaja Jaswant Singh II and effectively his prime minister. In 1887, Sir Pratap went to London as the maharaja's emissary to attend Queen Victoria's golden jubilee celebrations. En route, the ship carrying his clothes and jewellery sank. Divers managed to rescue his jewels, but his clothes, including his riding britches, were lost, so Sir Pratap went to a Savile Row tailor, who managed to replicate his design, and his custom-made riding trousers caught on big-time among Britain's aristocracy, who were soon flocking to Savile Row to get their own pairs made. So successful was the design that a new type of boot – the jodhpur boot – was invented specifically to go with them.

Listings

Airlines Indian Airlines, East Patel Nagar, Airport Rd ☎0291/251 0758; Jet Airways, Osho Apartments, Residency Rd ☎0291/510 3333.

Banks and exchange There are AIMs at 151 & 157 Nai Sarak; on MG Rd 100m east of Sojati Gate; on the little street off MG Rd opposite Sojati Gate; on Station Rd near *Govind Hotel*; and next to the tourist office. Forex offices can be found north of the clock tower in Sardar Market and on Hanwant Vihar just north of Circuit House (there's also a Thomas Cook on Airport Rd).

Bookshops Sarvodaya Bookstall, opposite Raj Ranchodji Temple on the same branch of Station Rd as *Midtown* restaurant, has a good selection of English-language books. Krishna Book Depot, upstairs at Krishna Art and Export in Sardar Market, just east of the north gate, has a wide selection of used books at reasonable (but unmarked) prices.

Festival Jodhpur's annual two-day Marwar Festival, held at the full moon of the Hindu month of Ashvina (Oct 21–22, 2010; Oct 10–11 2011; Oct 28–29, 2012; Oct 17–18, 2013), is a showcase of performing arts, mainly music and dance.

Hospital The best private hospital is the Goyal on Residency Rd in the Sindhi Colony, 2km south of town (☎0291/243 2144). The government infirmary is Mahatma Gandhi Hospital on MG Rd, near Jalori Gate (☎0291/263 9851).

Internet access Internet (usually around Rs30–40/hr) is widely available, even amid the medieval labyrinth of the old city. Handy internet stations include *Govind Hotel*'s Internet office on Station Rd (daily 24hr; Rs40/hr) and Sify I-Way (daily 9am–11pm; Rs40/hr), opposite the north gate from Sardar Market.

Motorcycle rental Jodhpur Travels, Station Rd (a few doors south of the *Govind Hotel*), has motorbikes and mopeds for rent for Rs300–1000/day.

Police ☎0291/265 0777. There's a police tourist assistance booth by the Clock Tower in Sardar Market.

Post office The GPO is opposite the *Govind Hotel* on Station Rd for sale of stamps (right-hand entrance; Mon–Sat 8am–4pm, Sun 10am–2pm) or for poste restante and parcel packing (left-hand entrance; Mon–Sat 10am–3pm).

Swimming pool Non-guests can use the lovely pool at the *Ajit Bhawan* hotel (see p.270) for Rs500.

Travel agents Staff at the *Govind Hotel* (see p.269) can book train, bus and plane tickets for a modest service charge (Rs40–50), and can also arrange car hire for Rs1200–1700/day.

Moving on from Jodhpur

Jodhpur stands at the nexus of Rajasthan's main **tourist routes**, with connections northeast to Jaipur, Pushkar and Delhi, south to Udaipur and Ahmedabad, and west to Jaisalmer. Buses for most destinations are faster than the train. The five-hour journey to **Jaisalmer** is certainly more rewarding by road, as it allows for stops at Osian, Keechen and Pokaran, though most travellers end up on the freezing-cold sleeper rail service across the Thar instead. If you do end up taking the train, take plenty of warm clothes and a blanket, and stay alert for thieves and con merchants – well-spoken *lapkars* from Jaisalmer routinely bribe the conductors to be allowed on board, where they attempt to lure customers to their "uncle's" dodgy hotels and desert safaris.

By train

The **railway station** (☎0291/243 2956) is on Station Road, 300m south of Sojati Gate. Recommended services are listed in the box opposite; there's also a once-weekly Thar Express train to Karachi in **Pakistan** (leaves at 11.30pm on Sat; 24hr). Train tickets should be booked at least a day in advance at the computerized **reservations office** (Mon–Sat 8am–8pm, Sun 8am–2pm), just north of the station behind the GPO. If you're a foreigner or NRI, you're entitled to use the musty International Tourist Waiting Room on the ground floor of the main station building. *Govind Hotel* will also allow customers at its *Fort View* restaurant (see p.274) to leave baggage free of charge and use toilet facilities while waiting for a train.

Recommended trains from Jodhpur

The following trains from Jodhpur are recommended as the fastest or most convenient. Other services exist, which take longer, arrive at inconvenient times, or do not run every day. Train timetables change frequently; check latest schedules either at your nearest station or online at ⊛www.indianrail.gov.in before travel. All the following depart daily. Note that there are no direct trains to **Udaipur** or **Chittaurgarh** – it's much easier to catch the bus.

Destination	Name	No.	Departs	Arrives
Abu Road	Ahmedabad Express	9224	5.50am	10.40am
	Ranakpur Express	4707	3pm	7.55pm
Agra	Howrah Superfast	2308	8pm	6.35am
Ajmer	Fast passenger train	1JA	7am	12.35pm
Alwar	Jaisalmer–Delhi Express	4060	10.30pm	7.50am
Bikaner	Ranakpur Express	4708	10.05am	4pm
	Barmer-Kalka Express	4888	10.45am	4.40pm
	Howrah Express	2307	midnight	8.15am
Delhi	Mandor Express	2462	7.30pm	6.25am
	Jaisalmer–Delhi Express	4060	10.30pm	11.05am
Jaipur	Jaipur Intercity Express	2466	5.55am	10.45am
	Marudhar Express	4854/ 4864/4866	9.30am	3.20pm
Jaisalmer	Delhi–Jaisalmer Express	4059	5.20am	11.30pm
	Jaisalmer Express	4810	11pm	5am
Sawai Madhopur	Intercity Express	2466	5.55am	1.15pm
	Bhopal passenger train	492	7.30am	8.25pm

By bus

Destinations served by bus include: Abu Road (12 daily; 6–7hr), Agra (3 daily; 15hr), Ahmedabad (2 daily; 10hr), Ajmer (every 30min; 5hr), Bharatpur (2 daily; 10hr), Bikaner (hourly; 6hr), Bundi (3 daily; 10hr), Chittaurgarh (3 daily; 9hr), Delhi (6 daily; 12hr), Jaipur (every 30min–1hr; 7–8hr), Jaisalmer (hourly; 5hr), Kota (5 daily; 11hr), Mount Abu (1 daily; 7–8hr 30min), Osian (every 30–45min; 2hr), Pushkar (6 daily; 4hr 30min–6hr 30min), Ranakpur (4 daily; 4–5hr) and Udaipur (hourly; 7–9hr).

Most **private buses** leave from the stand on Pal Road, 4km west of the centre (about Rs40 by auto); a few private buses leave from Kalpataru Cinema, 4km southwest of town (about Rs30 by auto). Private buses for Jaisalmer leave from Bombay Motors Circle, nearby. You can book **tickets** on private buses at most travel agents and a lot of hotels (for a Rs50 fee); *Govind Hotel* is a reliable option. **Government buses** leave from the Roadways (Raika Bagh) Bus Stand just east of town – turn up an hour or so before departure to buy a ticket. For timetable information, it's best to ask your hotel or guesthouse to ring on your behalf (☏0291/254 4686 or 0291/254 4989). There are Silver and Gold Line buses to Delhi, Agra, Ajmer, Jaipur and Udaipur.

By air

The **airport** (☏0291/251 2617) is 4km south of town (Rs60 by auto; Rs250–300 by taxi). Flights are currently operated by Indian Airlines (IC), Jet Airways (9W) and Kingfisher (IT), though carriers and schedules change regularly – ⊛www .expedia.co.in and ⊛www.travelocity.co.in are useful for checking latest timetables. At the time of writing, schedules were: Delhi (IC, IT, 9W; 2–3 daily; 1hr 10min–3hr 15min); Jaipur (IT; 1 daily; 1hr); Mumbai (IC, 9W; 1–2 daily; 2hr 5min–2hr 35min); Udaipur (IC, IT; 1–2 daily; 40min–1hr).

Mandor

Some 9km north of Jodhpur lies the sleepy village of **MANDOR**, former capital of the state of Marwar and home to a superb sequence of **royal cenotaphs** erected in memory of the kingdom's former rulers. Mandor served as the capital of the Parihar Rajputs from the sixth century until 1381, when they were ousted by Rathore Rao Chauhan, and although the capital was subsequently moved to Jodhpur in 1459, the Marwari rulers continued to have their memorial cenotaphs (*dewals*) erected here. Temple-like in their sombre dark red sandstone, the cenotaphs grew in size and grandeur as the Rathore kingdom prospered (the canopy-like chhatris next to them are for lesser royals). The largest is Ajit Singh's, built in 1724. His six queens, along with assorted mistresses, concubines, maids and entertainers – 84 women in all – committed *sati* on his funeral pyre.

At the end of the gardens, over to the left of the chhatris, you'll find the **Hall of Heroes**, a strange display of life-sized gods and Rajput fighters hewn out of the rock face early in the eighteenth century and covered with lime plaster and paint. Nearby is the octagonal **Ek Thamba Mahal** (Single Pillared Palace), a three-storey pagoda-like affair in red sandstone with filigree *jali* screens for windows. It was built at the beginning of the eighteenth century for royal ladies to watch public events without breaking their purdah. Behind it is a small **museum** (daily except Fri 10am–4pm; Rs5), whose main item of interest is a twelfth-century porno-graphic sculpture from Kiradu, alongside an amorous ninth-century couple (labelled "Erotic") from Mandor itself, and, also of local origin, a rather contorted thirteenth-century statue of Kichak (a character in the Mahabharata).

Steps behind the gardens lead up to the old **Mandor Fort**, citadel of the Parihar and Rathore Rajputs when Mandor was their capital. From here, a path leads over the hill to a set of **queens' cenotaphs** commemorating the ranis of Jodhpur. Though smaller than those of the men, they are more stately, with exquisitely detailed carving on the pillars and domed roofs.

Mandore can be reached on **minibuses** #1, #5 and #7 from Sojati Gate. If you'd like to **stay** in Mandor, you could try the *Mandore Guesthouse* on Dadawari Lane (①0291/254 5210, Ⓦwww.mandore.com; ④), which has clean and pleasant air-conditioned attached huts and cottages set around a garden full of trees.

The Bishnoi villages

Jodhpur's surroundings can be explored on organized "**village safaris**", which take small groups of tourists out into rural Rajasthan, usually stopping at four or five **Bishnoi villages** where you can taste traditional food, drink opium tea, and watch crafts such as spinning and carpet-making.

The Bishnois – a religious sect rather than an ethnic group in the usual sense – are among the world's earliest **tree huggers**. Their origins go back to a drought in the year 1485. Observing that this was caused largely by deforestation, a guru by the name of Jambeshwar Bhagavan formulated 29 rules for living in harmony with nature and the environment – his followers are called Bishnoi after the Marwari word for twenty-nine (*bish* = twenty, *noi* = nine). As well as enforcing strict vegetari-anism, Jambeshwar's rules forbid the killing of animals or felling of live trees. In particular, Bishnoi hold the *khejri* tree sacred. In 1730, at the village of **Khejadali**, workers sent by the maharaja of Marwar to make lime for the construction of a palace started felling *khejri* trees to burn the local limestone. A woman by the name

Tilwara Cattle Fair, also known as Mallinath Fair, is one of Rajasthan's biggest livestock markets, held annually over a fortnight in March or April at Tilwara near **Balotra**, 93km southwest of Jodhpur. The fair has been going since 1374 and was originally held in honour of a local holy man, Rawal Mallinath; offerings are still made at his shrine nearby. Today it attracts some eighty thousand head of livestock – goats, sheep, camels and horses as well as cattle – plus buyers and sellers from all over Rajasthan and the neighbouring states of Gujarat and Madhya Pradesh. So far it remains largely undiscovered by tourists, and there's no accommodation; visitors are advised to bring a tent. As well as livestock trading, attractions include animal races and a crafts market.

of Amrita Devi put her arms around a tree and declared that if they wanted to cut it down, they would have to cut her head off first. The leader of the working party ordered her decapitation, upon which her three daughters followed her example, and were similarly beheaded. Bishnoi people from the whole of the surrounding region then converged on the site to defend the trees – 363 of them gave their lives doing so. When news reached the maharaja, he ordered the felling to cease and banned cutting down trees and hunting animals in Bishnoi territory. Today, a small temple marks the place where all this happened, while in its grounds, 363 *khejri* trees commemorate the martyrs. Although it is possible to go to Khejadali by bus, you'll be hard-pressed to find a villager who speaks English, and it's a lot better to go with a tour group, which will also visit other villages. Most tours stop at Khejadali for lunch. This is usually followed by an **opium ceremony** in which opium is dissolved in water in a specially designed wooden vessel, and poured through a strainer into a second receptacle. The process is repeated twice more, and the resulting tea is drunk from the palm of a hand. Strictly speaking, it's illegal, but blind eyes are turned to this kind of traditional opium use, though in fact opium addiction is something of a social problem in rural Rajasthan.

On most village safaris you'll spot nilgai (bluebull) antelopes, gazelles and countless varieties of birds. Though the invasiveness of the tours can prove unsettling, they are almost always fascinating – a lot depends on the integrity of the operators and the relations they have with the villagers. Good and inexpensive **tours** of the Bishnoi villages are run by several guesthouses in Jodhpur, including *Govind Hotel*, *Durag Niwas* and *Yogi's Guesthouse*. Rates start at around Rs600–700 per person in a couple (cheaper in larger groups).

Osian

Rajasthan's largest group of early Jain and Hindu temples lies on the outskirts of the small town of **OSIAN (or Osiyan)**, 64km north of Jodhpur. RSTDC buses take a scenic route that drops you at a bus stand on the main road just south of town; the railway station (served by the Jodhpur–Jaisalmer train, 1hr 15min trip from Jodhpur) is 1km west. Alternatively, book a Jeep through Jodhpur's tourist office (Rs1200 for up to six people with a guide). The temples date from the eighth to the twelfth centuries when Osian was a regional trading centre. The town's ruler and population apparently converted to Jainism in the eleventh century, and Osian gives its name to the Oswal sect, which originated in the town. Today, though many Jain pilgrims come to visit, none actually lives in Osian.

The town centre is dominated by the imposing twelfth-century **Sachiya Mata Temple**, overlooking the whole of Osian from its elevated hilltop position. At the very top of the complex, the main shrine to Sachiya (an incarnation of Durga) is decorated with multicoloured mirrorwork and topped by a cluster of ved *shikharas*.

minute walk from the Sachiya Mata Temple lies Osian's most beautiful nt, the **Mahavira Jain Temple** (Rs5, Rs40 camera, Rs100 video; no tems permitted, and women should not enter during menstruation). Built in the eighth century, renovated in the tenth, and restored quite recently, the temple's beautifully carved central shrine is fronted by twenty elegant pillars and surrounded by shrines to further *tirthankaras*. A trio of smaller temples lies nearby, including a pair of Surya temples and the unusual **Peeplaj Temple**, surrounded by gargoyle-like projecting elephants, along with a massive Pratihara-period (eighth and ninth centuries) step-well.

Just south of the bus stop lies Osian's oldest collection of temples, centred on the **Vishnu and Harihara temples**, built in the Pratihara period. The nine temples in this group retain a considerable amount of decorative carving, particularly in the surrounding friezes.

Most people **stay** at the basic but welcoming *Priest Bhanu Sarma Guesthouse* (T09414 440479; ●) opposite the Mahavira temple, run by the (Hindu) priest who looks after the (Jain) temple, who can also provide information and arrange camel safaris and tours of local Bishnoi villages. More upmarket accommodation can be found at the luxury *Camel Camp Osian*, perched on a sand dune overlooking the railway line west of town (book in advance through the *India Safari Club* in Jodhpur on T0291/243 7023, Wwww.camelcamposian.com; ●), with carpeted tents and a pool. The daily rate of around $260 includes three meals and a camel safari. **Camel treks** around Osian can also be arranged through the *Govind* and *Cosy* guesthouses in Jodhpur starting from around Rs1000 per person per day in a couple. There are government **buses** from Jodhpur (every 30min–1hr; 1hr 30min) plus two trains daily, both at hopeless times.

Jaisalmer and around

In the remote westernmost corner of Rajasthan, **JAISALMER** is the quintessential desert town, its golden, sand-coloured ramparts rising out of the arid Thar like a scene from the *Arabian Nights*. Rampant commercialism may have dampened the romantic vision somewhat, but even with all the touts and tour buses, the town deservedly remains one of India's most popular destinations. Villagers dressed in voluminous red and orange turbans still outnumber foreigners in the bazaar, while the exquisite sandstone architecture of the "Golden City" is quite unlike anything else in India.

Some history

Rawal Jaisal of the Bhati clan founded Jaisalmer in 1156 as a replacement for his less easily defensible capital at Lodurva (see p.294). Constant wars with the neighbouring Rajput states of Jodhpur and Bikaner followed, as did conflict with the Muslim sultans of Delhi. In 1298 a seven-year siege of the fort by the forces of Ala-ud-Din Khalji (see p.358) came to an end, when the male survivors burned everything they could and then rode out to their deaths, while the women committed *johar* (voluntary death by sword and fire). The sole survivors were two infant princes who were smuggled out to continue the Bhati line. Rajput forces continued to harry the Muslims from the surrounding countryside, and with no local food supplies, Ala-ud-Din's forces were unable to continue their occupation. The Bhatis resumed their rule but were again besieged by Sultanate forces in 1326, resulting in another desperate act of *johar*, but Gharsi Bhati – one of the two

JAISALMER

▲ Bada Bagh

& Jodhpur (NH-15) ▲   ▲ Barmer (NH-15)

N

Railway Station

Government Bus Stand (NH-15)

BARMER ROAD (NH-15)

JODHPUR ROAD (NH-15)

Gadi Sagar Tank

GAJROOP SAGAR ROAD

Malka Pol

Desert Culture Museum

GADI SAGAR LAKE

FolkLore Museum

Tilon-ki-Pol

Gadi Sagar Pol

i

GADI SAGAR ROAD

Sunset Point

Patwa Haveli

Barmer Embroidery House

Salim Singh ki Haveli

6

Shiva Rent a Bike

Adventure Travels

Desert Bikes

Golden City Hotel

A

E

Nathmalji ki-Haveli

Desert Handicrafts Emporium

5

GOPA CHOWK

MAIN CHOWK

Fort

▲ N (100m)

▲ Khuhri

G

D

Bhatia News Agency

COURT

GANDHI CHOWK

B

H

1

Thar Heritage Museum

4

BHATIA BAZAAR

L

Palace

Jain Temples

See Jaisalmer Fort map

Private Buses

★ AIR FORCE CIRCLE

Amar Sagar Pol

Rajasthali

2

3

HANUMAN CIRCLE

Police Station

Laxminath Temple

K

ATM

M

SHIV MARG

ATM

Local Buses

★

Hospital

+

ATM

District Magistrate

Amar Sagar Road

AMAR SAGAR ROAD

Government Bus Stand

★

SAM ROAD

BADA BAGH ROAD (RAMGARH ROAD)

Government Museum

F

0   250 m

▲ Amar Sagar, Lodurva, Sam & 6

ACCOMMODATION

Artist Hotel	A
Fort Rajwada	J
Golden Haveli	N
Gorbandh Palace	G
Jawahar Niwas Palace	F
Mandir Palace	I
Nachana Haveli	H
Pol Haveli	B
Ratan Palace	C
Residency Centre Point	E
Roop Mahal	K
Shahi Palace	M
Shri Giriraj Palace	L
Swastika	D

EATING & DRINKING

Chandan Shree	3
Dhanraj Ranmal Bhatia	5
Natraj	6
RK Juice Center	4
Saffron	H
Shree Bikaner	1
Trio	2

Jaisalmer in jeopardy

Signboards, banners and electric wires may have horribly disfigured Jaisalmer, but the tourist boom has created a far more serious threat to the town's survival. Erected on a base of soft bantonite clay, sand and sandstone, the **foundations** of Rajasthan's most picturesque citadel are rapidly eroding because of huge increases in water consumption. At the height of the tourist season, around 120 litres per head are pumped into the area – twelve times the quantity used a couple of decades ago. Many believe the troubles started in the late 1980s when the city spent Rs9million on replacing the open sewers with covered drainage; unfortunately this backfired and large quantities of water ended up seeping into the soil, weakening the citadel's foundations. Compounding the problem has been the increased planting of trees, which keeps the ground moist. The result has been disastrous: houses have collapsed and significant damage has been done to the sixteenth-century Maharani's Palace. In 1998 six people died when an exterior wall gave way, and five more bastions fell in 2000 and 2001. Ironically, the subsequent drought in Rajasthan has dried the fort out, and no great damage has been reported, although a normal monsoon could change that quickly. Jaisalmer is now listed among the World Monument Fund's 100 Most Endangered Sites.

The Indian National Trust for Art and Cultural Heritage (INTACH; ⊛www.intach.org) has spent more than $100,000 restoring the Maharani's Palace, and an international campaign, **Jaisalmer in Jeopardy** (JiJ), has been set up to facilitate repairs throughout the fort. JiJ has already upgraded more than half of the 350 homes in the fort with underground sewerage, as well as restoring their facades and replacing grey cement with traditional material. Despite the repairs, city authorities still think the best way to save the fort is to evacuate its two thousand inhabitants and start the drainage repairs over from scratch, an expensive and time-consuming venture much opposed by the thirty-plus hotel owners inside whose earnings depend on tourism. The JiJ campaign relies substantially on donations. If you'd like to help, contact JiJ at 3 Brickbarn Close, London SW10 0UJ, UK (☎+44(0)20/7352 4336, ⊛www.jaisalmer-in-jeopardy.org).

Given all this, some people (and guidebooks) suggest that travellers **should avoid staying in the fort** in order to relieve pressure on its crumbling foundations. Unfortunately, this also has a serious side-effect in that it deprives many local hoteliers – some of whom have been in the fort for decades, and who are in no way responsible for Jaisalmer's current plight – of a living. We have therefore continued to list certain guesthouses within the fort. All are long-established, low-impact, and occupy original and largely unmodified buildings. On the other hand, we haven't listed any of the fort's modern, custom-built hotels. Remember, too, that if you do stay in the fort, you can do your bit by minimizing your water usage as much as possible.

princes who had been smuggled out – managed to negotiate the return of his kingdom as a vassal state of Delhi, and it remained in Bhati hands from then on.

In 1570 the ruler of Jaisalmer married one of his daughters to Akbar's son, cementing an alliance between Jaisalmer and the Mughal Empire, of which it nonetheless remained a vassal state. Its position on the overland route between Delhi and Central Asia – which led ultimately to the vast markets of the Middle East, North Africa and Europe – made it an important entrepôt for goods such as silk, opium and spices, and the city grew rich on the proceeds, as the magnificent havelis of its merchants bear witness. However, the emergence of Bombay and Surat as major ports meant that overland trade diminished, and with it Jaisalmer's wealth. The death-blow came with Partition, when Jaisalmer's life-line trade route was severed by the new, highly sensitive, Pakistani border. The city took on renewed strategic importance during the Indo-Pakistani wars of 1965 and 1971, and it is now a major **military outpost**, with jet aircraft regularly roaring past the ramparts.

Arrival and information

Jaisalmer's **railway station** is 2km east of the city; if you arrive without having booked accommodation, you can calmly enquire among the sandwich-board toting hoteliers lined up in the parking lot. The majority of hotels in town offer free rides; otherwise an auto-rickshaw into town will cost around Rs30. **Government buses** stop briefly at a stand near the railway station before continuing to the more convenient new **government bus stand** southwest of the fort. **Private buses** will drop you at Air Force Circle south of the fort.

RTDC's **tourist office**, southeast of town near Gadi Sagar Pol (Mon–Sat 10am–5pm; ☎02992/252406), is of little use, and its "recommended" operators pay for the privilege. **Online**, you'll find some travellers' tips and a rundown of the sights at ⓦwww.jaisalmer.org.uk, and more general information at ⓦjaisalmer.nic.in. If you need more detailed information about Jaisalmer, look out for two excellent **booklets**: *Jaisalmer: Folklore, History and Architecture*, by local historian L.N. Khatri, creator of the Thar Heritage Museum (see p.289); and *Jaisalmer: the Golden City*, by N.K. Sharma, the man behind the Folklore and Desert Culture museums (see p.288); both are available at the respective museums or at city bookshops such as the Bhatia News Agency (see p.291).

Accommodation

Jaisalmer has plenty of places to stay in all categories, and fierce competition keeps prices low. The basic choice is between staying in one of the old places within the wonderfully atmospheric fort itself (but read the "Jaisalmer in jeopardy" box opposite first) or in one of the newer places outside (many of which are built in traditional sandstone and come with superb fort views). Most places offer free pick-up from the bus or train stations, and the majority also have internet access. Almost all accommodation offers **camel treks**, which vary in standard and price, and some managers even at reputable hotels can be uncomfortably pushy if you don't arrange a safari through them.

In the fort

The hotels listed below are shown on the Jaisalmer Fort map on p.285.

Desert ☎02992/250602, ⓦwww.deserthotel.com. Friendly little budget place with cheaper rooms downstairs (including a couple of bargain singles with shared bathroom), and brighter rooms upstairs, some with fort views. ❶–❷

Desert Haveli ☎02992/251555, ⓔdesertguest house@hotmail.com. Simple guesthouse offering stone-walled rooms of various sizes with attached bathroom at rock-bottom prices. ❶–❷

Moti Palace ☎02992/254693, ⓔkailash _bissa@yahoo.co.uk. Friendly budget option, with a range of good-value rooms (all attached, and air-cooled in summer) and unbeatable views over the main gate. ❶–❸

Paradise ☎02992/252674, ⓦwww .paradiseonfort.com. Atmospheric old haveli with a leafy courtyard and a wide selection of rooms,

ranging from cheap downstairs rooms with common baths to prettily decorated upstairs rooms with a/c. ❶–❹

Suraj ☎02992/251623, ⓦwww.hotelsuraj jaisalmer.webs.com. This superbly atmospheric haveli of 1526 is one of the nicest places to stay in the fort (though rates are relatively pricey), with simple but characterful old fan rooms (including one with spectacular paintings) and a privileged rooftop view of the Jain temples. ❸–❺

Surja ☎09414 391149, 09414 761394, ⓦwww .surjahotel.com. A range of basic attached fan rooms (the more expensive ones with fine views) and a relaxing rooftop terrace with one of the best panoramas in town. ❶–❸

In town

Unless otherwise stated, the hotels listed below are shown on the Jaisalmer map, p.281.

Artist Hotel Manganyar colony ☏ 02992/252082, Ⓦ www.artisthotel.info. Run by an Austrian expat as a co-op for members of the Manganyar (minstrel musician) caste, who play here most evenings. The rather rustic stone-walled rooms (fan or air cooled) are comfortable enough, if a bit gloomy, and there's a nice rooftop restaurant with good food and a genuine pizza oven. ②–③

Golden Haveli Bera Rd ☏ 02992/250821, Ⓦ www .goldenhaveli.com. Stylish new hotel occupying a modern sandstone haveli in a peaceful location on the southern edge of town. Rooms (all a/c) are unusually spacious and attractively furnished, and there's also a pleasant rooftop restaurant overlooking the desert. Good value at current rates. ④

Mandir Palace Gandhi Chowk ☏ 02992/252788, Ⓦ www.mandirpalace.com. Occupying part of the exquisite Mandir Palace (see p.288), with pleasantly spacious rooms sporting discreet heritage touches, attractive public areas (including the fine old Durbar Hall, now housing a miniature museum) and a pool (non-guests Rs350). ⑦

Nachana Haveli Gandhi Chowk ☏ 02992/251910, Ⓦ www.nachanahaveli.com. This venerable old haveli is one of the best choices in its class. The atmospheric stone-walled ground-floor rooms (all a/c) are virtually windowless but attractively decorated with antique fittings; the suites upstairs are brighter. There's also the good *Saffron* rooftop restaurant (see p.290). ⑥

Pol Haveli Near Geeta Ashram, Dedansar Rd ☏ 02992/250131, Ⓦ www.hotelpolhaveli.com. Attractive new guesthouse in a stylish little sandstone building, offering mid-range quality at budget prices. Rooms (fan or a/c) are neat and comfortable (although larger ones are slightly lacking in furniture), and there's a lovely rooftop terrace for idle lounging and fort-gazing. ①–⑤

Ratan Palace Off Gandhi Chowk ☏ 02992/252757, Ⓔ hotelrenuka@rediffmail.com. One of the best cheapies in this part of town, with a friendly owner and hassle free accommodation in old-fashioned but spotless rooms (the cheapest with shared bathrooms; the more expensive with a/c). They run good camel treks (see p.289) and have further, slightly larger and more expensive rooms (②–③) in the *Renuka* guesthouse just down the street. ①–③

Residency Centre Point Khumbara Para ☏ 09414 760421, Ⓔ residency_guesthouse@yahoo.com. Small, family-run guesthouse in the backstreets near Patwa Haveli and Nathamal ki Haveli. Rooms (a couple with a/c) are comfortable and good value, and there are nice town views from the rooftop. Advance booking recommended. ②–③

Roop Mahal Off Shiv Marg ☏ 02992/251700, Ⓔ hotelroopmahal@yahoo.com. Comfortable new guesthouse in a good central location, with bright, inexpensive modern rooms (some with fort views and cheap a/c), helpful staff and a pleasant rooftop restaurant. There's also wi-fi, parking space and free use of an Enfield motorbike. ①–②

Shahi Palace Off Shiv Marg ☏ 02992/255920, Ⓦ www.shahipalacehotel .com. See also Fort map opposite. Outstanding little hotel tucked away just south of the fort in a stylish modern sandstone building with stunning views of the fort from the rooftop terrace restaurant and immaculate rooms. The only caveat is that the cheaper rooms are a bit small – it's well worth coughing up for one of the superb larger a/c rooms. The same family also run the slightly cheaper *Oasis Haveli* and *Star Haveli* next door. ②–⑤

Shri Giriraj Palace Near Gopa Chowk ☏ 02992/252268. Simple, friendly local hotel with some of the cheapest rooms in town, including ultra-cheap shared bath doubles, plus budget attached and a/c rooms – great value at current prices. ①–②

Swastika Off Gandhi Chowk ☏ 02992/252152, Ⓔ swastikahotel@yahoo.com. Old-fashioned guesthouse offering simple but comfy fan and a/c rooms (a couple with shared bathroom) at bargain prices, although planned renovations may bump rates up slightly. ①–③

Out of town

Fort Rajwada Off Jodhpur Rd, 3.5km east of town ☏ 02992/253233, Ⓦ www.fortrajwada.com. One of the best of the new resort hotels on the outskirts of town, with five-star facilities (pool, bar, good restaurant and grand coffee shop), and 25 percent discounts April–Sept. ⑦

Gorbandh Palace Sam Rd, 2km west of town ☏ 02992/253801, Ⓦ www.eternalmewar.in. Another upmarket, resort-style hotel just outside town. Not the most atmospheric lodgings in Jaisalmer, but well run and very comfortable, and with facilities including a smart restaurant and bar, pool and Ayurvedic spa. Fifty percent discounts in summer. ⑦

Jawahar Niwas Palace 1 Bada Bagh Rd ☏ 02992/252208, Ⓦ www.jawaharniwaspalace .co.in. Late nineteenth-century royal guesthouse with turreted sandstone exterior straight out of a Kipling novel. The rooms are large and graceful, and there's a good pool (Rs250 for non-guests). ⑦

The Town

Getting lost in the narrow winding streets of Jaisalmer is both easy and enjoyable, though the town is so small that it never takes long to find a familiar landmark. Main roads lead around the base of the fort from the central market square, **Gopa Chowk**, east to **Gadi Sagar Tank**, and west to **Gandhi Chowk**. Within the fort the streets are narrower still, but orientation is simple: head west from the main *chowk* and **Maharawal's Palace** to reach the **Jain temples**. For optimum **sunset views**, head for "Sunset Point" north of the main bazaar area, or the northwest corner of the fort.

Jaisalmer Fort

Every part of **Jaisalmer Fort**, from its outer walls to the palace, temples and houses within, is made of soft yellow Jurassic sandstone. The medieval fort, founded by Rawal Jaisal in 1156, so inspired Bengali film-maker Satyajit Ray that he wrote a story about it called *Shonar Kella* (The Golden Fortress), which he later made into a movie. Inside, the narrow winding streets are flanked with carved golden facades, and from the barrel-sided bastions, some of which still bear cannons, you can see the thick walls that drop almost 100m to the town below. Two thousand people live within the fort's walls; seventy percent of

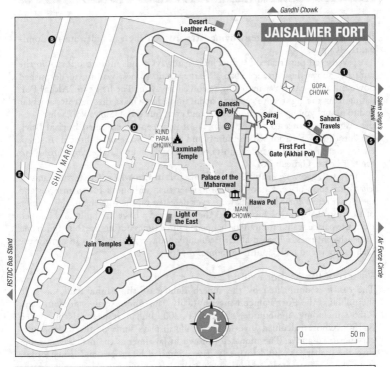

ACCOMMODATION			
Desert	D	Shahi Palace	E
Desert Haveli	H	Shri Giriraj Palace	A
Moti Palace	C	Suraj	I
Paradise	G	Surja	F
Roop Mahal	B		

EATING & DRINKING			
8 July	7	Krishna's Boulangerie	8
Bhang Shop	3	Little Italy	4
Dhanraj Ranmal Bhatia	1	Little Tibet	6
Joshi's German Bakery	2	Monica	5

▲ Jaisalmer Fort

them are Brahmins; the rest, living primarily on the east side, are predominantly Rajput.

A paved road punctuated by four huge gateways winds up to the fort. On the ramparts above the entrance road sit large round stones, waiting to be pushed down onto any enemy army trying to force its way in. The first gate, **Akhai Pol**, dating from the eighteenth century, opens into a large plaza that narrows at its far end to funnel you up through to the second gate, **Suraj Pol** (Surya Pol), which was the original entrance to the fort. Next to it is a deep trench called **Berisal Burj**, the "death tower" from which traitors and criminals were once thrown. A steep, enemy-deterring sharp bend, almost doubling back on itself, takes you through to the third gate, **Ganesh Pol**.

The fourth gateway, **Hawa Pol**, leads into **Main Chowk**, where terrible acts of *johar* once took place. Choosing death rather than dishonour for themselves and their children if their husbands were ever defeated on the battlefield, the women of the royal palace, which overlooks the *chowk*, had a huge fire built, and jumped from the palace walls into it. This happened three times during the fourteenth and fifteenth centuries, when Jaisalmer frequently had to fight bloody wars against the Delhi sultans and its Rajput neighbours.

Palace of the Maharawal

The *chowk* is dominated by the superb **Palace of the Maharawal**, open to the public as the **Fort Palace Museum** (daily 9am–6pm, April–Sept from 8am; Rs250 including audioguide, students Rs200, Indian residents Rs30, video Rs150), whose balconied, five-storey facade displays some of the finest stone-carving in Jaisalmer. The monarch (known in Jaisalmer as the maharawal rather than the maharaja) would formerly have addressed his troops and issued orders from the large ornate marble throne to the left of the palace entrance. In the **armoury**, a silver **coronation throne** surmounted with lions and peacocks is used only for crowning the maharawal on his accession. Beyond the armoury, the **Tripolia Mahal** features portraits of the maharawals and a family tree tracing their ancestry all the way back to Krishna.

Beyond here lies a sequence of (surprisingly small) rooms which once formed the living quarters of the various maharawals. The nineteenth-century **Gaj Vilas** includes an unusual room decorated with blue and white Delft tiles from the Netherlands, along with the ruler's bed and silver thali dish. **Akhey Vilas**, the apartment of Maharawal Akhai Singh (1722–61), houses an exhibition of **stamps and banknotes** issued by Rajputana's 22 princely states as a statement of their continuing independence while most of the rest of India was under British rule. The beautifully preserved **fifteenth-century sculptures** in the next gallery include an unusual one of Ramayana hero Rama depicted – most unconventionally – with a beard, and, flanking him, a belly-dancer and a courtesan looking into a hand-mirror.

The sculpture gallery leads into the **Rang Mahal**, private bedroom of Maharawal Mool Raj II (1761–1819), its walls lovingly painted with wonderful murals, including depictions of Jaisalmer, Jaipur and Udaipur. Strikingly incongruous among them, in an alcove over the second window, is a very European portrait of a western woman. Who she was and why the maharawal had her picture in his bedroom remain a mystery. Upstairs, in **Sarvottam Vilas**, more Delft tiles, and a ceiling painted to match, decorate Akhai Singh's bedroom, while the **rooftop terrace** gives unrivalled views over the city and the surrounding countryside. The tour ends with the *zenana* (women's quarters), known as **Rani ka Mahal**, which was little more than a pile of rubble a few years ago but has now been meticulously restored with the support of Jaisalmer in Jeopardy (see p.282).

Hindu and Jain temples

The Fort has a number of Hindu temples, the most venerable of which is the 1494 **Laxminath Temple**, dedicated to Laxmi, the goddess of wealth, and her consort Vishnu (Nath), the preserver of life. However, none is as impressive as the complex of **Jain temples** (daily 8am–noon; Rs30, camera Rs70, video Rs120, mobile-phone camera Rs30; usual entry restrictions apply). Built between the twelfth and fifteenth centuries in the familiar Jurassic sandstone, with yellow and white marble shrines and exquisite sculpted motifs covering the walls, ceilings and pillars, the temples are connected by small corridors and stairways. In a vault beneath the Sambhavnath temple, the **Gyan Bhandar** (daily 10–11am) contains Jain manuscripts, paintings and astrological charts dating back to the eleventh century, among them one of India's oldest surviving palm-leaf books, a 1060 copy of Dronacharya's *Oghaniryaktivritti*. Two of the seven temples are open between 8am and noon; the other five only open from 11am to noon, when the whole place gets very busy with coach parties, so it's best to visit before 11am to see the first two temples, then come back later to see the rest.

The havelis

The streets of Jaisalmer are flanked with numerous pale-honey facades, covered with latticework and floral designs, but the city's real showpieces are its extravagant **havelis**, commissioned by wealthy merchants during the eighteenth and nineteenth centuries. Their stonework was the art of *silavats*, a community of masons responsible for much of Jaisalmer's unique sculpture.

Just north of Bhatia Bazaar (take the small road between the Ajanta Photo Studio and Dev Handicrafts), the **Nathmalji-ki-Haveli** was built in 1885 for the prime minister of the state of Jaisalmer by two brother stonemasons, one of whom built the left half, the other the right, as a result of which the two sides are subtly different. It's guarded by two elephants, and if you look carefully at the intricate carvings around the first-floor bay window above the main doorway, you'll see that it's surmounted by a frieze of little figures including not only elephants and horses, but also a steam train and a horse-drawn carriage. It's free to pop in and see the patio, which has a gift shop, but it's the outside that impresses.

The larger and even more finely decorated **Patwa Haveli**, or Patwon-ki-Haveli (daily 8am–6.30pm; Rs20), lies a couple of blocks north of here down a street to the right, its exterior a positive riot of exuberantly carved *jharokhas* (protruding balconies). The haveli was constructed in the first half of the nineteenth century by the Patwa merchants – five brothers from a Jain family who were bankers and traders in brocade and opium. There are actually five separate suites within the haveli. Two are closed to visitors. Two, preserved in their original condition, are open as **government museums** (daily 10am–5pm; foreigners Rs50 combined ticket, Indian residents Rs10). One, the **Kothari Patwa Haveli Museum** (daily 10am–5pm; foreigners Rs120, Indian residents Rs40, camera Rs30), has been done up as a museum with various traditional artefacts on display plus replica mirrorwork on the walls, giving you some idea of how the haveli would originally have looked. As well as visiting the interior of the Patwa Haveli, it's worth taking a little stroll down the street whose entrance it bridges, to check out the stonework on four impressive neighbouring havelis.

The third of Jaisalmer's famous trio of havelis, the **Salim Singh ki Haveli** (daily summer 8am–7pm; winter 8am–6pm; Rs20, camera Rs20), lies on the east side of town and is immediately recognizable thanks to the lavishly carved overhanging rooftop balcony that gives the whole building a strangely top-heavy appearance. Its upper floor, enclosed by an overhanging balcony, is best seen from the roof of *Natraj Restaurant*.

In addition to these three famous havelis, parts of the **Mandir Palace**, still inhabited by the maharawal, but partly converted into a heritage hotel (see p.284), can be visited (daily 10am–5pm; Rs20), but its most striking feature, the elegant Badal Vilas tower, is best seen from the west, just outside Amar Sagar Pol.

Gadi Sagar Tank and museums

South of town through an imposing triple gateway, **Gadi Sagar Tank**, built in 1367 and flanked with sandstone *ghats* and temples, was once Jaisalmer's sole water supply; you can rent boats here (around Rs100 for 30min) for a spin on the water. This peaceful place staring out on the desert hosts the festival of **Gangaur** in March, when single women fling flowers into the lake and pray for a good husband, and the maharawal heads a procession amid pomp and splendour unchanged for generations. The gateway over the *ghat* leading down to the lake, **Tilon-ki-Pol**, was commissioned in 1909 by a rich courtesan named Tilon, who was famed for her beauty. While it was being built, a group of town prudes went to the maharawal to persuade him that it would be inauspicious to have to access the lake through a gate built with the earnings of a prostitute. The maharawal ordered it dismantled, but Tilon was smarter than him: she had incorporated into the top of the structure a shrine to Vishnu, so that its destruction would be an insult to the god. She won the day and her gate still stands.

The little **Folklore Museum** (daily 8am–6pm; Rs20, camera Rs20) near the tank's main gate has displays of folk art, textiles, and opium and betel nut paraphernalia from the personal collection of its proprietor, N.K. Sharma. You'll find a large selection of local curiosities, including musical instruments, fossils, manuscripts, tools and utensils, at the **Desert Culture Museum** (daily 10am–5pm; Rs20), another creation of N.K. Sharma, next to the tourist office on the main road. The main exhibit (though other museums seem to have identical ones), right at the back, is a cloth painting depicting the life of local folk hero Pabuji (see p.377), a legendary figure credited with introducing the camel to Rajasthan. The museum puts on a half-hour puppet show (Rs30) at 6.30pm and 7.30pm each evening, using traditional Rajasthani puppets.

Few visitors who make it as far as Jaisalmer pass up the opportunity to go on a **camel trek**, which provides an irresistibly romantic chance to cross the barren sands and sleep under one of the starriest skies in the world. Sandstorms, sore backsides and camel farts aside, the safaris are usually great fun.

Treks normally last from one to four days, with **prices** varying from Rs600 to Rs1500 per person per night. The highlight is spending a night under the desert stars, and most travellers find that an overnight trip, departing around 3pm and returning the next day at noon, is sufficient. Unfortunately, the price you pay is not an adequate gauge of the quality of services you get. Hotels are notorious for sizing up potential clients and charging prices on a whim, so it pays to shop around, ask other travellers for recommendations and bargain appropriately. We've listed a few dependable operators below, though the list is far from exhaustive. Make sure you'll be provided with your own camel, an adequate supply of blankets (it can get very cold at night), food cooked with mineral water, and a campfire. Ensure that you wear a broad-brimmed hat and take high-factor sun-protection lotion and plenty of water, especially in summer. You should also make sure that your operator is committed to either burning or removing all rubbish (including plastic bottles).

The traditional Jaisalmer camel safari formerly headed out west of town to Amar Sagar, Bada Bagh, Lodurva, Sam and Kuldera (see pp.293–295). Some operators still cover these areas, although encroaching development and crowds of other tourists (around Sam especially) mean that you'll get very little sense of the real desert hereabouts. The better operators are constantly seeking out new and unspoilt areas to trek through – this usually means an initial drive out of Jaisalmer of around 50–60km, though it's worth it to avoid the crowds. Longer seven- to ten-day treks to Pokaran, Barmer and Bikaner can also be arranged, though these shouldn't be attempted lightly.

Finally, don't book anything until you get to Jaisalmer. Touts trawl trains and buses from Jodhpur, but they usually represent dodgy outfits. Some offer absurdly cheap rooms if you agree to book a camel trek with them (sometimes claiming to represent a newly opened hotel offering heavily discounted prices in order to establish itself in business). Guesthouse notice boards are filled with sorry stories by tourists who accepted. As a rule of thumb, any firm that has to tout for business – and that includes hotels – is worth avoiding.

Recommended operators

Celebrating its 25th birthday in 2011, **Adventure Travel** (☏09414 149176, ⓦwww .adventurecamels.com), just south of the First Fort Gate, gets rave reviews for seeking out remote locations and providing fringe amenities, like real mattresses and sheets, at low prices. Slightly cheaper, but equally dependable, is **Sahara Travels** in Gopa Chowk (☏02992/252609, ⓦwww.mrdesertemeritus.com), run by the instantly identifiable "Mr. Desert", a former truck driver turned Rajasthani model and movie star. "Don't make a booking until you see the face," is his motto. Of the **hotels** that organize camel safaris, *Shahi Palace* has a deservedly good reputation and virtually guarantees you won't see another tourist, while the friendly *Renuka* offers reliable tours at some of the lowest rates in town.

Back in the centre of town, the modest little **Thar Heritage Museum** (daily 9am–9pm; Rs40) showcases the personal collection of local historian L.N. Khatri, who may be on hand to explain some of the stories and customs behind the quirky array of local artefacts on display, ranging from bits of fossilized tree and old chillums through to camel regalia and antique musical instruments. If you still haven't had your fill of little local museums, head for the **government museum** (daily 10am–4.30pm; Rs3) by the *RTDC Moomal Hotel* on the western edge of town. Among the assorted fossils, sculptures and folk artefacts is a twelfth-century statue of a Jain dancer from Kiradu, and next to her, from the same period and location, a bearded man in drag.

Eating and drinking

Jaisalmer's tourist **restaurants**, usually rooftop affairs with fort views, offer pizza, pancakes, apple pie and cakes on their menus alongside Indian dishes. Some of them are pretty good, although there are also a number of excellent restaurants, aimed more at locals than tourists, that are worth trying for authentic Rajasthani food and other regional specialities.

The only licensed **bars** in town are to be found in the bigger hotels, though most restaurants also serve beer. For posh tipples, head out to *Fort Rajwada* (see p.284). Right in the heart of town, *Nachana Haveli* on Gandhi Chowk is about to open a bar in its former stables, which should be a cut above Jaisalmer's other drinking spots.

Unless otherwise indicated, the restaurants and snack bars listed here are shown on the Jaisalmer map on p.281.

Restaurants

8 July Main Chowk, Fort. See Fort map, p.285. Recommended for its privileged terrace view of the fort's bustling main *chowk* and palace rather than for its food, though it has a good selection of smoothies, lassis, juices and snacks, along with Indian, Italian, Chinese and Mexican mains (Rs70–95). Good spot for breakfast to watch the fort wake up before it's invaded by tourists.

Chandan Shree Restaurant Just west of Amar Sagar Pol. Popular local diner for inexpensive veg curries (Rs25–90) and thalis (Rs60–140), as well as Rajasthani specialities such as *govind gatta* and *ker sangri*.

Little Italy just inside first fort gate. See Fort map, p.285. Italian restaurant with a superb terrace directly opposite the main ramparts – wonderful when they're floodlit at night. There are great pasta dishes (Rs120–180), served in heaped portions at reasonable prices, but though the pizzas make a stab at authenticity, they don't really cut it.

Little Tibet In the Fort. See Fort map, p.285. Run by a team of young Tibetans, this travellers' café serves up all the usual Indian and Chinese choices, plus pasta, Mexican, and a good range of Tibetan specialities. Also a good venue for breakfast. Mains Rs60–95.

Monica Near the first Fort gate. See Fort map, p.285. Moderately priced Rajasthani and tandoori dishes, plus delicious veg and non-veg Rajasthani thalis (Rs145/210). Mains Rs65–145.

Natraj Opposite the Salim Singh ki Haveli. Friendly rooftop non-veg restaurant, popular for its

excellent, gently spiced Mughlai chicken, *malai kofta* and other Indian dishes (mains Rs85–190).

Saffron Gandhi Chowk, in the entrance to *Nachana Haveli* ☎ 02992/251910. Slightly upmarket restaurant with fine tandoori and Mughlai food, plus Indian veg, Italian and Chinese options (mains Rs60–170) and live music in the evenings.

Shree Bikaner Restaurant North of Hanuman Circle. There are Punjabi veg curries (Rs45–100) and a choice of thalis (Rajasthani, Gujarati or Bengali, at Rs80–125), but what this pure-veg place is really known for is its wonderful *dal bati churma* (Rs125), which they'll keep refilling till you've had enough.

Trio Gandhi Chowk ☎ 02992/252733. Slightly upscale choice known for its sumptuous tandoori and Mughlai meat dishes (mains Rs145–280), while there are also some Rajasthani specialities and a reasonable veg selection. Book early for the best tables overlooking the Mandir Palace and fort. Licensed.

Drinks and snacks

Bhang shop Gopa Chowk. See Fort map, p.285. If you like bhang (and be warned that it doesn't agree with everybody – see p.57), this is one of the best places in the country to get it, with a whole menu of bhang-laced drinks and sweets, and a choice of different strengths.

Dhanraj Ranmal Bhatia Court Rd. Wonderful, moist milk-based sweets (*ladoo*, *barfi* and the like), plus great samosas and *mirchi badas*, and you can even watch them being made, as they do it all out front.

Hot milk stalls Hanuman Circle. From nightfall till around midnight, the chai- and paan-wallahs just east of Hanuman Circle sell glasses of hot sweet milk boiled with saffron and almonds, ladled from huge bubbling vats outside their shops.

Joshi's German Bakery Gopa Chowk. See Fort map, p.285. Scrumptious range of fresh cakes, croissants and cookies, especially in the morning. Too bad the coffee's instant.

Krishna's Boulangerie In the fort, near the Jain temples. See Fort map, p.285. A handy place to stop for a breather in the fort, with decent coffee and light snacks, plus pizza and pasta. A good breakfast option too.

RK Juice Center Bhatia Bazaar. Wonderful freshly pressed juices using whatever fruits are available on the day (usually including some or all of orange, pomegranate, pineapple, banana, carrot and ginger). They promise not to add ice or tap water (though they do use it to rinse out the juice extractor).

Shopping

Jaisalmer is one of the best places in India to **shop** for souvenirs. Prices are comparatively high and the salesmen push hard, but the choice of goods is excellent – virtually the whole fort has now been turned into an enormous souvenir bazaar, while there are dozens of further places along Bhatia Bazaar. It's a particularly good place to pick up traditional Rajasthani textiles and fabrics, as well as cheap hippy-style clothes, while leatherwork (both cow and camel, made into slippers, bags and belts) is another local speciality.

Barmer Embroidery House Near Patwa Haveli. The oldest textile shop in Jaisalmer, stocking a wide range of new work (block-printed, mirrorwork, appliqué) from Barmer alongside older and more unusual pieces from Rajasthan, Gujarat and beyond, such as door-hangings (*torans*), Lamani chillum pouches and silk-woven *mashru* skirts from remote Muslim villages of Kutch in Gujarat. The knowledgeable owner has an even bigger stock, including rare antique pieces, at his home close by.

Desert Handicrafts Emporium Bhatia Bazaar, a few doors along from the Thar Heritage Museum. Run by L.N. Khatri, proprietor of the nearby Thar Heritage Museum, this has an above-average selection of local textiles, including standard Rajasthani patchwork and embroidery alongside more unusual items from Gujarat, including distinctive mirrorwork designs from Kutch.

Desert Leather Arts Near Gopa Chowk, opposite *Shri Giriraj Palace* hotel ℡02992/254 495. See map, p.285. Inexpensive camel leather goods made on the spot – they claim to be able to make up anything in leather to order.

Light of the East Tewata Para, in the fort. See map, p.285. Rocks, minerals and crystals, including amethyst and rose quartz marbles, crystal balls, and all sorts of semiprecious stones. One item is not for sale – a football-sized apophyllite crystal, which the owner keeps under lock in a glass case.

Rajasthali Outside Amar Sagar Pol. The official Rajasthan state crafts emporium, rather dry and unattractively arranged, and not always the very best quality, but handy for checking prices as they're fixed and marked.

Listings

Banks and exchange There are ATMs just inside Amar Sagar Pol, one directly opposite the gate on the outside, one by the District Magistrate's office on Sam Rd, and a couple just outside the southern edge of the fort. There's a cluster of Forex bureaux in Gandhi Chowk, while the reliable Adventure Travels (see p.289) also change cash and travellers' cheques.

Bicycle rental Narayan Cycles, in the street directly opposite *Nachana Haveli* hotel (100m up on the left, just where the street starts to bend); Rs5/hr.

Bookshops Bhatia News Agency on Court Rd, just beyond Gandhi Chowk, has guidebooks and English-language novels. There are also a few shops in the fort selling new and used English books.

Doctor Dr S.K. Dube (℡02992/251560) speaks good English; Rs500 for a consultation at your hotel.

Festival Jaisalmer's Desert Festival is held over three days at the full moon in the lunar month of Magha (Feb 16–18, 2011; Feb 5–7, 2012; Feb 23–25, 2013). Unlike many of the region's other festivals, this is not a livestock fair, but a festival of performing arts, and generally a fun occasion, with folk dancing, turban-tying and moustache competitions, camel racing, camel-back polo matches, and craft bazaars. Main events are held at Dedansar Polo Ground. Hotels tend to get full at this time, but they don't generally increase their prices. There's usually a programme of events posted at Ⓦ jaisalmer.nic.in.

Hospital The government hospital is on Sam Rd, west of Hanuman Circle (☎ 02992/252495), but a better bet is the small, private Maheshwari Hospital off Sam Rd opposite the court and District Magistrate's Office (☎ 02992/250024).

Internet access Internet is widely available but mostly slow. The *Chai Bar*, inside the fort just beyond Ganesh Gate, has the best machines (Rs50/hr including a drink). Joshi Cyber Café (Rs30/hr), in *Joshi's German Bakery* nearby, is slower but cheaper.

Motorbike rental There are a couple of places south of Gopa Chowk including Desert Bikes (☎ 09414 150033) and Shiva Rent a Bike

(☎ 09462 094620) with bikes and scooters for Rs300–400/day.

Police There's a police station just south of Hanuman Circle on Amar Sagar Rd (☎ 02992/252233). A new Tourist Protection Police office on Sam Rd should have opened by the time you read this.

Post office The main post office, with poste restante, is on Amar Sagar Rd 200m south of Hanuman Circle (Mon–Sat 9am–3.30pm); there's a smaller office opposite the fort wall behind Gopa Chowk (Mon–Sat 10am–5pm).

Swimming pool Non-guests can use the pools at the *Mandir Palace* hotel (Rs350) and the small pool at the *Golden City* hotel (Rs100) on the south side of town. Alternatively, try the pools at *Fort Rajwada*, *Gorbandh Palace* and *Jawahar Niwas Palace* hotels, out of town; these usually cost around Rs250–300.

Travel agents Adventure Travel (see p.289) can arrange bus, train and plane tickets for a modest commission, and can also sort out hotel bookings.

Moving on from Jaisalmer

The **train station** (☎ 02992/252354) is east of town on the Jodhpur road; the journey there by auto from the centre shouldn't cost more than Rs40. The #4060 **Jaisalmer–Delhi** Express, which departs daily at 4.45pm, stops at, among other places, Pokaran (6.10pm), Phalodi (7.22pm), Osian (8.27pm), Jodhpur (9.50pm), Jaipur (4.50am), Alwar (7.17am) and Old Delhi (11.05am). The overnight #4809 **Jaisalmer-Jodhpur** Express departs daily at 11.15pm, arriving in Jodhpur at 5.10am. There are two daily services to **Bikaner**: the #4703 and #4701, departing at 11.20am and 10.45pm and arriving at 4.50pm and 3.55am respectively; note that the #4703 terminates at Lalgarh Junction, on the edge of Bikaner, rather than at the main Bikaner Junction station. If you do take a night train, make sure you have something to keep you warm as it can get very cold (close to freezing in winter).

Buses serve Abu Road (1 daily; 12hr); Ahmedabad (3–4 daily; 12hr); Ajmer (2 daily; 11hr); Bikaner (4 daily; 6–7hr); Jaipur (2 daily; 13hr); Jodhpur (hourly; 6hr); Pushkar (1 daily; 12hr); Udaipur (1 daily; 12–14hr). Most **government buses** (☎ 02992/251541) depart from the bus stand east of town on Barmer Road, although early morning departures leave from the more conveniently located stand at the southern end of Amar Sagar Road; check when you buy your ticket. Private buses leave from Air Force Circle, directly south of the fort. An auto to either from town shouldn't cost more than Rs40. **Tickets** for private buses can be purchased from agents such as Swagat Travels or Hanuman Travels, just north of Hanuman Circle, or from Adventure Travels (see p.289); for RSTDC services you'll have to buy your ticket at the government bus stand. **Local buses**, serving places like Lodurva, Khuhri and Sam, leave from a stand to the north of Hanuman Circle.

Jaisalmer's **airport** lies 14km west of town on Khuri Road. There are no flights at present, though a new passenger terminal is currently under construction, due for completion in 2010, after which it's expected that flights will resume – probably to Delhi via Jaipur, and possibly also to Mumbai via Udaipur, though exact details remain vague.

Around Jaisalmer

The desert around Jaisalmer harbours some unexpected monuments, dating from the era when the area lay on busy caravan routes. Infrequent buses negotiate the dusty roads, or you can rent a Jeep through your hotel. Being close to the Pakistani border, the area west of Highway NH-15 is **restricted**. In the (fairly unlikely) event that you want to enter a restricted area, you'll need a **permit** from the District Magistrate's Office, just west of Hanuman Circle in Jaisalmer (Ⓣ02992/252201; Mon–Fri 10am–5pm). On the few camel treks where permits are necessary, the organizers should obtain them for you.

Bada Bagh, Amar Sagar and Lodurva

Six kilometres north of Jaisalmer, in the fertile area of **Bada Bagh** (daily sunrise to sunset; foreigners Rs50, Indian residents Rs20, camera Rs20, video Rs50), a cluster

Moomal and Mahendra: a desert Romeo and Juliet

Though not as famous as the story of Dhola and Maru (see p.305), the tale of Moomal and Mahendra – Rajasthan's Romeo and Juliet – has inspired countless storytellers, poets and painters. Moomal was a princess of Lodurva, famed for her beauty, though none of her many suitors had succeeded in gaining her hand. Mahendra was a prince of Umerkot (now in Pakistan), Lodurva's deadly enemy, and already married with seven wives. Curious to see the celebrated princess, Mahendra arranged a hunting expedition incognito to the sacred River Kak, which ran alongside the palace at Lodurva. Moomal saw him from her chamber and, smitten with love, sent out a servant to invite the handsome stranger inside. Mahendra entered the palace and, setting eyes upon Moomal, fell instantly in love. The prince revealed his identity to Moomal, who immediately realized that their relationship would have to remain a secret.

So, every night, Mahendra rode hotfoot on his trusty camel to the river, and swam across to the palace, returning each morning at dawn. Suspicions, however, were gradually raised. Mahendra's blind father, the king of Umerkot, asked why none of the prince's seven wives had borne him an heir. The wives retorted that Mahendra never spent the night with them, but vanished every evening at dusk, returning each morning with his hair wet. Hearing this, the king asked the wives to comb some of the water out of Mahendra's hair and keep it for him, which the wives duly did. Taking the water, the king placed a few drops into his eyes, whereupon his sight was suddenly restored and the location of Mahendra's nightly excursions revealed, since only water from the River Kak boasted such miraculous powers.

Meanwhile, Moomal's sister, Soomal, had also got wind of her sister's secret lover and demanded to see him. Moomal arranged for Soomal to attend her in her room, disguised as a minstrel boy. They waited and waited, but Mahendra failed to appear, delayed by a lame camel which his father had ordered be given to him to impede his journey. Eventually the two princesses fell asleep in each other's arms, so that when Mahendra finally arrived he saw his love asleep in the embrace of – as he thought – a young rival. And so the prince departed sorrowfully, swearing never to see her again.

The distraught Moomal sent Mahendra message after message, to no avail. Finally, she disguised herself as a wandering merchant and managed to gain an audience with the prince. They sat down for a game of *chopar* (similar to backgammon) when suddenly the prince began to cry. "What is it?" asked Moomal. "The birthmark on your hand," replied Mahendra. "My lost love had one just the same. If only I could see her once more!"

Throwing aside her disguise, the princess cried, "Oh my love, it is me, your Moomal! Truly I have never loved anyone but you!" And so the couple were reunited, but already weak with pining, they expired in each other's arms – and at the very moment of their deaths the sacred River Kak ceased to flow, and has never done so since.

of **cenotaphs** built in memory of Jaisalmer's rulers stands on a hill, looking rather incongruous amid a very modern field of electricity-generating wind turbines, while the equally surreal green oasis below is where most of the region's fruit and vegetables were grown until sealed roads and modern transport allowed regular food supplies to be trucked in from less arid areas. The cenotaphs date from the sixteenth to eighteenth centuries, with domed roofs shading small marble or sandstone slabs bearing inscriptions and images of expired rulers on horseback – unfortunately the cenotaphs are badly neglected, and a number have already collapsed.

Seven kilometres northwest of Jaisalmer is **AMAR SAGAR**, a peaceful small town set around a large artificial lake (usually waterless during the dry season). On the edge of this are the neatly restored eighteenth-century Amar Singh Palace and a Jain temple complex (Rs10 entry, Rs50 camera). The biggest of the three Jain temples, the Adeshwar Nath Temple, was commissioned in 1928 by a member of the same family who put up the Patwa Haveli (see p.288) in Jaisalmer.

A further 10km northwest of Amar Sagar, **LODURVA** was the capital of the Bhati Rajputs from the eighth century until the twelfth, when it was sacked by Mohammed Ghori, after which the Bhatis moved their capital to Jaisalmer. Of the city's fine buildings, only a few **Jain temples**, rebuilt in the seventeenth century, remain. The main temple (daily 7am–8pm; foreigners Rs30, Indian residents free, camera Rs70, video Rs120) is dedicated to Parshvanath, the 23rd Jain *tirthankara*. The 8m *toran* (arch), just inside the entrance to the main temple compound, is one of the most exquisite in Rajasthan: unusually tall and narrow, and topped by a richly carved pediment which seems to balance precariously on the triangular arch below. The temple itself has detailed tracery work in the stone walls and a finely carved exterior. Inside are images of Parshvanath in black and white stone. To the right of the temple is a structure built in a series of diminishing square platforms, out of which springs a stylized Kalpataru (a mythological wish-granting tree), made from an alloy of eight metals, with copper leaves.

There are three or four daily **buses** to Lodurva, but taking a **rickshaw** or **taxi** is a more leisurely option (Rs250/400 respectively for the round-trip including stops at Amar Sagar and Bada Bagh) – or you could **cycle**.

Kuldara

South of the Sam road, around 25km west of Jaisalmer, the ghost village of **Kuldara** (daily sunrise–sunset; Rs10, vehicles Rs100) was one of 84 villages abandoned simultaneously one night in 1825 by the Paliwal Brahmin community, which had settled here in the thirteenth century. Stories vary as to why, but the consensus is that the onerous taxes imposed by Jaisalmer's rapacious prime minister Sallim Singh forced the Paliwals to complain to the maharawal. When he ignored them, they upped and left in protest, en masse.

Close-knit and industrious, the Paliwals were a prosperous community. Their sense of order is attested by their homes, each with its living quarters, guest room, kitchen and stables, plus a parking space for the camel, and you can take an atmospheric stroll through them to the temple at the heart of the village. A story that they buried their wealth before leaving – which probably stems from the fact that each house had an underground safe – led a group of foreigners in 1997 to scour the place with metal detectors in search of the alleged treasure. Following this, the village was made a protected area and some of its houses have been restored, along with its temple. It has also featured as a backdrop in a number of Hindi movies such as Milan Luthria's 1999 *Kachhe Dhaage*, with Ajay Devgan and Manisha Koirala, and John Matthan's *Sarfarosh*, released the same year, with Aamir Khan and Sonali Bendre.

Sam and the Desert National Park

The huge, rolling sand dunes 40km west of Jaisalmer are known as **SAM**, though strictly this is the name of a small village further west. Unfortunately, the once pristine desert here has vanished beneath endless tented camps, while around five thousand tourists (mainly domestic) descend daily to watch sunset and make merry in the desert. If you've come to the Thar in search of vast crowds, psychotic camel touts and endless piles of windblown plastic, then you'll be in seventh heaven. If not, the entire area is best given a wide berth. You can overnight here in one of the numerous tented camps, but we wouldn't recommend it.

Around 60km from Jaisalmer, south of Sam on the road to Khuhri, the huge **Desert National Park** (foreigners Rs80, Indian residents Rs10; Jeep Rs65; open 24hr) protects some 3000 square kilometres of desert, providing sanctuary for blackbuck, chinkara, bustards and many other rare desert species, although you're as likely to see similar wildlife on a good camel safari. Getting into the park is also a hassle. You'll need to get a permit form from the Deputy Director of the Desert National Park at Khuhri Circle on Khuhri Road in **Jaisalmer** (Mon–Fri 10am–5pm; ☎02992/252489), then take the completed form to the office of the District Magistrate, just west of Hanuman Circle (Mon–Fri 10am–5pm; ☎02992/252201). You can hire a Jeep or camel at the entrance to the park, as well as guides (Rs200).

Khuhri

A marginally nicer place to watch the sun set over the dunes is the village of **KHUHRI**, 42km south of Jaisalmer. Many camel safaris either start here or pass through – most time their arrival so that tourists can see local women, dressed in flamboyantly coloured dress, arriving with large jugs on their heads to fill up with water at caste-specific wells. The village also has a certain charm – many of its homes are still made of mud and thatch rather than concrete, their exterior surfaces beautifully decorated with ornate white murals. Unfortunately, tourist development has already eroded much of Khuhri's traditional character. Virtually every building now seems to have been converted into a guesthouse, while ugly new concrete buildings and endless signboards are beginning to mushroom on every available space, accompanied by the usual tide of discarded plastic and other rubbish.

Khuhri can be reached by four daily **buses** (10.30am, 1.30pm, 3pm & 5.30pm) from the local bus stand in Jaisalmer, or by Jeep (Rs500 for the round trip from Jaisalmer) or taxi (Rs250 round trip). Despite the profusion of guesthouses in the village (and upmarket tented camps around it), prices tend to be steep. If you want **to stay**, you probably can't do better than the very simple but extremely peaceful *Badal House* (☎09966 053 53 89; ❷ full board), which is much more like staying with a local family, and a good place to chill out for a few days and get a feel of village life. They can also arrange camel safaris.

Akal Wood Fossil Park

A 52-acre slice of desert off the Barmer road, 17km east of Jaisalmer, the **Akal Wood Fossil Park** (daily 8am–5pm; foreigners Rs20, Indian residents Rs5, vehicle Rs10) is less exciting than it sounds. There are some fossilized trees here from the Jurassic period, but don't expect to be meandering through a stone forest: the trees are just fallen trunks that lie on the ground, protected by mesh cages under metal shelters. That said, these petrified logs – 25 of them in all – are impressive in their own way. The largest measures 13m in length, and they all date from around 180 million years ago, when the whole region was rainforest, which is hard to imagine looking around at the barren landscape today. You'll pay around Rs200 to get here and back from town by auto, or around Rs300 by Jeep.

POKARAN, with its red-sandstone fort and superb havelis, is a quiet, seldom-visited desert pit stop 110km east of Jaisalmer, situated at the road and rail junctions between Jodhpur, Bikaner and the west. Once included in the territory of Jodhpur, it passed into the huge state of Jaisalmer after Independence. Pokaran became the unlikely object of world attention in May 1998, when five nuclear bombs were detonated at the army test range 20km northwest of town (see box, below). Despite this incongruous fifteen minutes of fame, Pokaran remains something of an outpost, but it does offer excellent **accommodation** at the sixteenth-century **fort** (☏02994/222274, ⓦwww.fortpokaran.com; ⓞ), a wonderful old sandstone building that feels all the more authentic for having only been partly restored. The fort now houses a **museum** (daily 8am–6pm; Rs50, Rs30 camera, Rs50 video) featuring a dusty collection of medieval weapons and clothing, plus a hand-cranked air-conditioning system. The only other accommodation is the RTDC *Motel* at the road junction on the edge of town (☏02994/222275; Rs800–1150). Should you need cash, the State Bank of Bikaner and Jaipur in the middle of town has an **ATM**.

Around 12km north of Pokaran, the dusty village of **RAMDEVRA** (served by regular buses between Phalodi and Pokaran) is home to the **Ramdev Mandir**, one of the holiest religious sites in Rajasthan and a favoured destination for local pilgrims, though it sees very few foreign tourists. The temple is devoted to **Ramdevji** (ⓦwww.ramapir.org), a local Tanwar Rajput and medieval proto-Gandhi, who spoke out against all forms of social inequality, oppression and untouchability. According to legend, five sceptical Muslim *pirs* from Mecca came to visit Ramdev in order to test his credentials and were duly persuaded of the saint's divinity, since when he has been worshipped both by Muslims (who call him Ramapir) and Hindus (who regard him as an incarnation of Krishna). Ramdev departed this life in around 1450 at the age of 33 – according to tradition, he didn't die, but simply passed into *samadhi*, making the conscious decision to leave his mortal body for ever. The temple was built by Bikaner's Maharaja Ganga Singh on

The Pokaran N-tests

On May 11, 1998, three massive explosions erupted 200m beneath the sands of the Thar Desert, 20km northwest of **Pokaran**, a stone's throw north of the main Bikaner–Jaisalmer highway. The bombs were small by modern standards – 20 kilotonnes, like the bomb that destroyed Hiroshima – but their political shockwaves resounded from western Rajasthan to Islamabad, Beijing and Washington. By May 13, after two more detonations, India's transition from so-called "threshold state" to fully fledged atomic power was complete.

In the Indian press, the tests were hailed as "A Moment of Pride", and celebratory fireworks lit the skies of the capital. The widespread euphoria, however, temporarily faltered when the scale of the international outcry became apparent. The US immediately announced that it was suspending all aid to India, and recommended a freeze in IMF and World Bank loans, while the country's barely disguised triumphalism took a further battering when, two weeks later, Pakistan detonated its own thermonuclear devices in reply. India suddenly found itself locked into a spiralling nuclear arms race in one of the most geopolitically sensitive parts of the world. The rupee took a severe tumble, plummeting to an all-time low, as did tourist bookings.

Meanwhile, in Pokaran itself, hundreds of poor farmers and their families fell ill soon after the explosions in the villages surrounding the test site. Although no fatalities have been directly attributed to the blast, scientists warn that the full public health and environmental consequences of the explosions may take years to materialize.

the site of the saint's *samadhi* in 1931 and is constantly busy with crowds of pilgrims, who come to leave toy wooden horses in the shrine in memory of an occasion when the young saint is said to have taken flight on a similar toy. The village is particularly busy during the **Ramdevra Fair**, held here over nine August or September.

Phalodi and Keechen

The main highway and broad-gauge train wind in tandem east from Jaisalmer across the desert, separating at the small junction settlement of **PHALODI**, almost exactly midway between Jaisalmer and Bikaner. This scruffy salt-extraction colony would be entirely forgettable were it not the jumping-off place for one of Rajasthan's most beautiful natural sights, one that shouldn't be missed if you're passing. Sheltered by a rise of soft yellow dunes, the village of **KEECHEN**, 4km east on the opposite side of the main road, hosts a four thousand-strong flock of **demoiselle cranes** (*Anthropoides virgo*) which migrate here each winter from their breeding grounds on the Central Asian steppes. Known locally as *kurja*, the birds are encouraged to return by the villagers, who scatter specially donated grain for them to feed on twice a day – a custom that has persisted for 150 years or more. At feeding times (6.30am & 3.30–4pm), the entire flock descends on a fenced-off area just outside the village, where you can watch and photograph them at close quarters. At other times, the birds usually congregate just outside the fenced-off area on the nearby dunes, or at a small reservoir about 2km from the feeding ground.

From Phalodi, the best way to **get to Keechen** is to rent a bicycle from one of the stalls near the bus stand – a pleasant, mostly flat 4km ride on well-surfaced roads. Alternatively, jump in an auto-rickshaw (Rs100) or taxi (Rs200); Ambassador taxis queue outside the railway station. For **accommodation**, *Hotel Chetnya Palace* (T02925/223945; ❷–❹), next to the bus stand serving Jaisalmer, is the best budget option, with a decent restaurant and a variety of rooms, though the cheaper ones look a bit moth-eaten. Your other option is the *Lal Niwas* (T02925/223813, W www.lalniwas.com; ❻), a three-hundred-year-old red-sandstone haveli converted into a top-notch heritage hotel, with a pool, thirteen prettily furnished rooms and two suites. The hotel also has a small **museum** (daily 10.30am–7pm; Rs50), with a well-presented collection of ivory carvings, coins, jewels, manuscripts and miniatures. The town's other attraction is the 1847 **Gori Pashnar Jain Temple** (daily 6.30am–noon & 6–8pm; free, camera Rs20, video Rs30, usual entry restrictions apply), with its fine mirrorwork and old Belgian glass, which attracts Jain pilgrims from across the state.

If you're only stopping for a couple of hours, **check bus times** before you head off to Keechen, as services can be sporadic, though theoretically there's a bus roughly every hour to Jaisalmer and Bikaner. For Jaisalmer, **trains** depart at 7.29am and 9.55am; to Jodhpur at 7.27pm; and to Bikaner (Lalgarh Junction) at 2.20pm.

Bikaner and around

The bustling commercial city of **BIKANER** has none of the aesthetic magic (or tourist crowds) of its more venerable neighbour, Jaisalmer, over 300km southwest, but travellers who make it here are usually surprised by the abundance of attractions. In addition to the spectacular **Junagarh fort**, Bikaner boasts an atmospheric old city dotted with colourful temples and some of Rajasthan's strangest havelis, not to mention the unique **rat temple** at nearby Deshnok – one of India's weirdest attractions. If you're around in January, Bikaner's lively **camel fair** is an added bonus.

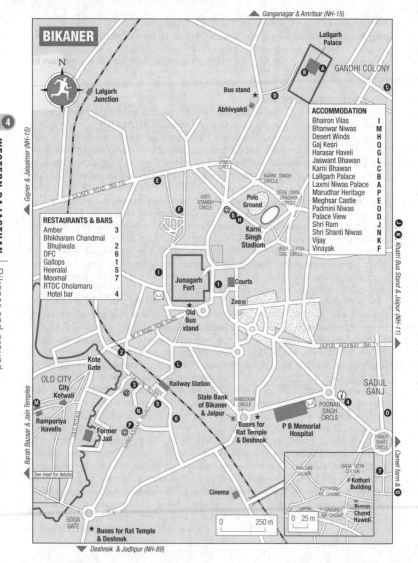

▲ Ganganagar & Amritsar (NH-15)

BIKANER

N

Lallgarh Palace

GANDHI COLONY

Bus stand ★

Abhivyakti

Lalgarh Junction

ACCOMMODATION

Bhairon Vilas	I
Bhanwar Niwas	M
Desert Winds	H
Gaj Kesri	Q
Harasar Haveli	G
Jaswant Bhawan	L
Karni Bhawan	C
Lallgarh Palace	B
Laxmi Niwas Palace	A
Marudhar Heritage	P
Meghsar Castle	E
Padmini Niwas	O
Palace View	D
Shri Ram	J
Shri Shanti Niwas	N
Vijay	K
Vinayak	F

URMUL CIRCLE

KARNI SINGH CIRCLE

KIRTI STAMBH CIRCLE

DEEN DAYAL UPADHYA CIRCLE

Polo Ground

Karni Singh Stadium

VEER DURGA DAS CIRCLE

RESTAURANTS & BARS

Amber	3
Bhikharam Chandmal Bhujiwala	2
DFC	6
Gallops	1
Heeralal	5
Moomal	7
RTDC Dholamaru Hotel bar	4

Junagarh Fort

Courts

Zoo

Old Bus stand

JAIPUR HIGHWAY (NH-11)

SADUL GANJ

Kote Gate

OLD CITY

City Kotwali

Rampuriya Havelis

Former Jail

Railway Station

State Bank of Bikaner & Jaipur

AMBEDKAR CIRCLE

Buses for Rat Temple & Deshnok

P B Memorial Hospital

POONAN SINGH CIRCLE

PANCH SHATI CIRCLE

See inset for details

Cinema

RANGARI CHOWK

DAGA SITYA CHOWK

Kothari Building

KOTHRIAN KA CHOWK

DABUHU KA CHOWK

Punan Chand Haweli

GOGA GATE

★ Buses for Rat Temple & Deshnok

0 — 250 m

0 — 25 m

▼ Deshnok & Jodhpur (NH-89)

◄ Gajner & Jaisalmer (NH-15)

◄ Barah Bazaar & Jain Temples

Khatri Bus Stand & Jaipur (NH-11)

Camel farm & ▶

Some history

The city was founded in 1486 by **Bika**, a disaffected son of Rao Jodha, the Rathore king who established Jodhpur, and gradually developed into an important link on the overland trading route across the Thar. The city's most important ruler, **Rai Singh**, came to the throne in 1573, ordering the construction of **Junagarh Fort** and forging closer ties with the Mughals, by giving his daughter in marriage to Akbar's son Salim, who later became the emperor Jahangir – one of the first Rajput rulers to ally themselves with the Mughals. Much of the seventeenth century was spent in periodic conflicts with the Marwars of Jodhpur, before both parties signed treaties with the British in 1818.

In the early 1900s, new agricultural schemes, irrigation work and the construction of a rail link with Delhi helped Bikaner to flourish, while in 1949, it became one of the first of the princely states to join independent India. The modern city has now long since outgrown the confines of the city walls, while the population has more than tripled in size since 1947 to around 700,000.

Arrival and information

Auto-wallahs working on commission are a nuisance in Bikaner, employing all the usual tricks to avoid taking you to any establishment that doesn't pay them – even if you ask to be dropped at a location nearby, they may try to second-guess you, hotfooting it to the hotel they reckon you're bound for in order to claim commission. A ride across town from the **state bus stand**, near Lallgarh Palace a few kilometres north of the centre, to the **railway station** should cost around Rs40. From the **old bus stand**, just south of the fort, used by some private firms, the fare is Rs20. Auto-wallahs frequently offer Rs10 rides to arriving passengers; the trick is to take the ride without having the commission added to your room rent.

The helpful **tourist office** (daily 10am–5pm; ☏0151/222 6701) is in the RTDC *Dholamaru Hotel* at Pooran Singh Circle. **Online**, check out the excellent ⓦwww .realbikaner.com. Jitu Solanki (see box, p.300) is a government-approved **guide** and can arrange Bikaner city tours (Rs200), while Vijay Singh Rathore at the *Vijay Guesthouse* runs an enjoyable one-day **tour** combining Gajner, Kolayat, Deshnok and the camel farm for Rs2000.

Accommodation

Bikaner has a surprisingly large selection of **hotels**, and because competition is cut-throat, some of the best-value accommodation in Rajasthan, though the shoestring-priced flophouses along Station Road are best avoided.

Budget and mid-range

Bhairon Vilas Next to Junagarh Fort ☏0151/254 4751, ⓦhotelbhaironvilas.tripod .com. Characterful heritage hotel in an old royal haveli, surrounded by an attractive garden and kitted out with quirky antiques and family curios. Rooms (all a/c) are a mixed bag: the cheaper ones are rather poky; it's worth spending a little extra to get

▲ Camel trekking

Camel safaris from Bikaner

Bikaner offers a good alternative to Jaisalmer as a starting point for **camel treks** into the Thar Desert. This eastern part of the desert, while just as scenic as the western Thar, is not nearly as congested with fellow trekkers, with the result that local people in the villages along the route don't wait around all day for the chance to sell Pepsi to tourists. Wildlife is also abundant, with plentiful blackbuck, nilgai and desert foxes.

Your choices of **operator** are somewhat limited, but the same advice applies as that outlined in the Jaisalmer camel safaris box, p.289. The city's leading and longest-established operator is the personable Vijay Singh Rathore (aka "Camel Man"), based at *Vijay Guesthouse* (see below). Full details of his various treks are posted at ⓦwww.camelman.com; rates start from Rs900 per person per day. Safaris are also offered by *Vino Guesthouse* (☎0151/227 0445, ⓦwww.vinodesertsafari.com) and promoted by various touts hanging around the old city (book directly by phone or email to avoid commission) and by Thar Camel Safari, c/o the *Meghsar Castle* hotel or direct on ☎09351 206093. The *Vinayak Guesthouse* (see opposite) also organizes safaris. These are led by Jitu Solanki, a trained zoologist, whose trips offer fascinating insights into the wildlife and environment of the desert, and also include visits to remote Bishnoi villages. Safaris can be customized to focus on particular areas of interest, including wildlife, birdwatching, snake-spotting and photography.

---

one of the more spacious and atmospheric heritage rooms; some also have good fort views. ④–⑤
Desert Winds 200m east of Kirti Stambh Circle ☎0151/254 2202, ⓦwww.hoteldesertwinds.in. Functional, medium-sized hotel with clean and comfy rooms (all a/c) and a decent veg restaurant. A slightly more low-key alternative to the very similar *Harasar Haveli* next door, minus the tour groups. ④
Harasar Haveli Next to *Desert Winds* ☎0151/220 9891, ⓦwww.harasar.com. Not a haveli, but a functional, medium-sized modern hotel, with a range of bright, comfortable and spotlessly clean rooms (the more expensive with a/c and TV), plus rooftop and terrace restaurants offering reasonable veg and non-veg food. Popular with tour groups. ②
fan, ④–⑤ a/c.
Jaswant Bhawan Alakhsagar Rd (go out of the rear exit of the train station) ☎0151/254 8848, ⓦwww.hoteljaswantbhawan.com. Relaxing hotel in a nice old house very close to the station. Surprisingly quiet given the location, with comfortable fan, air-cooled and a/c rooms. ③–④
Marudhar Heritage Gangashahar Rd ☎0151/252 2524, ⓔhmheritage2000@yahoo.co.in. Friendly, tranquil hotel near the station with a variety of neat and clean air-cooled and a/c rooms, all attached. Free pick-up. ②–③
Meghsar Castle 9 Gajner Rd, 300m west of Urmul Circle ☎0151/252 7315, ⓦwww .hotelmeghsarcastle.com. A standard-issue cheap hotel rather than a castle, offering comfortable, if slightly shabby, air-cooled and a/c rooms and a friendly owner who goes out of his way to assist

independent travellers. Try to get a room away from the main road. ②–④
Padmini Niwas 148 Sadul Ganj, off Jaipur Rd 1.5km east of the city centre ☎0151/252 2794, ⓔpadmini_hotel@rediffmail.com. A little bit out of the way, but quiet and good value, with spacious, clean rooms (some with a/c), and a neat little pool. ②–④
Palace View Lallgarh Palace Campus ☎0151/254 3625, ⓔhotelpalaceview@gmail.com. Welcoming guesthouse in a quiet location, with comfortable and pleasantly old-fashioned rooms (some a/c), a homely little dining room and views of Lallgarh Palace. ③–④
Shri Ram Sadul Ganj, 1.5km east of the city centre ☎0151/252 2651, ⓦwww.hotelshriram.com. Friendly suburban hotel. The more expensive rooms are spacious and very comfortably furnished; the cheaper ones a bit cramped. There are also five-bed dorms (Rs200). ③–⑤
Shri Shanti Niwas Gangashahar Rd ☎0151/252 4231. The cleanest of the ultra-cheapies near the station, although they might be reluctant to accept non-Indians. The various rooms include some very inexpensive singles (Rs80) with shared bath. Doubles are all attached. 24hr checkout. ①–④
Vijay Opposite Sophia School, 5km east of centre along the Jaipur Highway ☎0151/223 1244, ⓦwww.camelman.com. Sociable family guesthouse with spacious and very comfortable rooms (some with optional a/c) at bargain prices. There's also camping space, plus a nice garden and free bicycles. ②–③

Vinayak Old Ginani ☎09414 430948. Welcoming little family guesthouse offering simple but very cheap doubles (all with bathroom, though not all with hot water). Free cooking lessons are available and there are motorbikes for hire (Rs200/day). Also a good place to arrange camel safaris (see box, opposite). ❶–❷

Expensive

Bhanwar Niwas Old city ☎0151/220 1043, ⓦwww.bhanwarniwas.com. Bikaner's most ostentatious haveli, built for a textile tycoon in the late 1920s and crammed with kitsch fittings and furniture, complete with a 1927 Buick in the lobby, an atmospheric *fin de siècle* dining room and an array of memorably chintzy rooms. ❽

Gaj Kesri Bypass Rd ☎0151/240 0372, ⓦwww.gajkesri.com. Grandiose, heritage-style red-sandstone palace, a 15min drive from the city centre near the Camel Farm, with beautiful public areas and well-equipped rooms. ❼

Karni Bhawan Palace Gandhi Colony, 1km east of Lallgarh Palace ☎0151/252 4701, ⓦwww .hrhindia.com. On the outside it looks like an oversized English suburban house, but the interior is wonderful, with superb Art Deco suites in the main building, complete with original 1930s furniture (but don't bother with the standard rooms in the annexe). Rooms ❻, suites ❼; forty percent discounts in summer.

Laxmi Niwas Palace Lallgarh Palace ☎0151/220 2777, ⓦwww.laxminiwaspalace .com. The better of two palatial hotels in the Lallgarh Palace complex, offering large rooms (from around $140) with period English furniture – the best is #108, which has hosted British monarchs Queen Victoria, George V and Elizabeth II. Rooms at the neighbouring *Lallgarh Palace Hotel* are slightly cheaper and less impressive, though still boast plenty of old colonial character. ❼

The City

Many visitors see no more of Bikaner than the imposing **Junagarh fort**, although it's well worth making time to explore the city's less-heralded attractions, particularly the labyrinthine streets of the **old city**, dotted with eye-catching early twentieth-century havelis in a range of outlandish styles, plus a couple of **temples** with half a millennium more on the clock.

Junagarh Fort

Built at ground level and defended only by high walls and a wide moat, **Junagarh Fort** (daily 10am–5.30pm (last entry 4.30pm); foreigners Rs150, students Rs100, Indian residents Rs20; camera Rs30, video Rs100; or combined ticket including entrance, camera and audioguide Rs250) isn't as immediately imposing as the mighty hill forts elsewhere in Rajasthan, though its richly decorated interiors are as magnificent as any in the state. The entrance price includes a **compulsory guided tour**. You'll probably have to wait five or ten minutes until enough people have arrived to form a group, though it's easy enough to break away from the tour once inside and make your own way around.

The fort was built between 1587 and 1593 during the rule of Rai Singh, and embellished by later rulers, who added their own palatial suites, temples and plush courtyards. Although never conquered, the bastion was attacked – handprints set in stone near the second gate, **Daulat Pol**, bear witness to the *satis* of royal women whose menfolk had lost their lives in battle.

From the entrance, a passageway climbs up to the small Vikram Vilas courtyard, beyond which you'll find the main courtyard, surrounded by several finely decorated rooms. The first of these is the **Karan Mahal**, built in the seventeenth century to commemorate a victory over the Mughal emperor Aurangzeb. The room's pillars and walls are decorated with fine gold-leaf painting, while hanging from the ceiling is a huge *punkah* – a rope-pulled fan which would have been operated by a specially designated servant, or *punkah*-wallah, hidden behind the scenes. Next to here is the **Rai Niwas**, the oldest part of the palace, built for Rai Singh himself. Among the items on display are Maharaja Gai Singh's ivory slippers, one of Akbar's swords, and a set of regal insignia including a representation of the Pisces zodiac sign which looks remarkably like a dinosaur in a headscarf.

Past here is the **Anup Mahal** (Diwan-i-Khas), the grandest room in the palace, formerly used by the maharajas for public audiences, with stunning red and gold filigree *usta* (decorative painting). The red satin throne sits in a niche surmounted by an arc of glass and mirrors like a huge jewelled tiara. The carpet was made by inmates of Bikaner jail, who were famous for the craft – a manufacturing tradition that has only recently ceased. After such a hectic display of opulence, the **Badal Mahal** ("cloud palace"), built in the mid-nineteenth century for Maharaja Sardar Singh (1851–72) and painted with blue sky and clouds, is pleasantly understated. Upstairs, a room exhibits beds of nails, sword blades and spear heads used by sadhus to demonstrate their immunity to pain, while across the terrace in the finely painted **Gaj Mandar** is the maharaja's chaste single bed and the maharani's more accommodating double.

The next part of the palace, the twentieth-century **Ganga Niwas**, created by Maharaja Ganga Singh (1887–1943), can be reached either via a long and labyrinthine passageway from the Gaj Mandar or, more directly, from the Vikram Vilas courtyard (see p.301). This section of the palace is centred on the cavernous **Diwan-i-Am**, dominated by a World War I Haviland biplane, a present from the British to Bikaner's state forces. Next door is the early twentieth-century office of Ganga Singh, followed by several further rooms stuffed full of guns and swords, including several German machine guns which was among items seized during World War I, when Bikaner troops fought in Europe alongside the British.

Also in the fort complex, the **Prachina Museum** (daily 9am–6pm; foreigners Rs50, Indian residents Rs10, camera Rs20, video Rs70; ⓦwww.prachina -museum.com) houses a pretty collection of objects (glassware, crockery, cutlery and walking sticks) demonstrating the growing influence of Europe on Rajasthani style in the early twentieth century. A whole circa-1900 salon has been re-created, and there's also an interesting collection of Rajasthani textiles and clothing.

The old city

Bikaner's labyrinthine **old city** is notable for its profusion of unusual **havelis** whose idiosyncratic architecture demonstrates an unlikely fusion of indigenous sandstone carving with *fin-de-siècle* Art Nouveau and red-brick municipal Britain. The city is confusing to navigate, so accept getting lost as part of the experience.

Entering the old city through Kote Gate, bear left (south) down Jail Road. After 300m, turn right just past the florid pink gateway to a Hindu temple to reach the City Kotwali (the old city's central police station). More or less straight ahead, along the left-hand (south) wall of the Kotwali, Rampuriya Street leads after 300m to a small chowk with a little shrine, overlooked by two of the **Rampuriya Havelis**, three mansions commissioned by three brothers from a Jain trading family. The first, on the left, built in 1924, is faced with reliefs of Bikaner's Maharaja Ganga Singh, and Britain's King (India's Emperor) George V and Queen Mary. The second, directly ahead, on the right-hand side of the street, is bigger and generally more impressive, but no royalty graces its facade. The third, a little way further along on the left, is decorated with medallions above its main windows featuring Krishna and Radha, and pastoral scenes.

If you continue ahead, the next haveli on your right is the *Bhanwar Niwas Hotel* (see p.301; the entrance is round the other side of the building). Instead, turn left (south) just before the third Rampuriya Haveli to emerge by the boarded-up 1918 **Golchha Haveli**, its three ground-floor windows topped with flowery rosettes. Continue roughly straight ahead, following the road as it makes two dog-legs to

the right, and you'll hopefully emerge after 100m onto a street full of ironmongers selling buckets, pots, pans and tiffin boxes. A left here would take you back to the City Kotwali. Instead, turn right and continue for 300m to reach the small square called **Rangari Chowk**, in the middle of which stands a neat white Hindu temple. Proceed along the right-hand side of the temple and straight ahead is the small, triangular square called **Kothrion ka Chowk**, where handsome havelis look down on you from both sides. Follow the road as it swings round to the left to reach the **Kothari Building** (on your right), with five wonderfully extravagant Art Nouveau balconies, surmounted by carvings including an elephant flanked by cherubs, two peacocks holding three strings of pearls, and George V between a lion and a unicorn. Beyond here is a little square called **Daga Sitya Chowk**. A house on the left still has fading murals of steam trains flanking its front door, while Diamond House, on the right with pretty tiles and a first-floor veranda, gets wider as it goes up, each storey overhanging the one below it.

Retrace your steps back to just before Kothrion ka Chowk, then turn left to reach the **Punan Chand Haveli** with its amazingly carved, almost psychedelic, floral facade – and while you're there, you might as well take a quick look at the decorative facade of the smaller and less spectacular building behind it too. Turn round again and head back towards Kothrion ka Chowk, then take the first left to reach the large square called **Daddho ka Chowk**, surrounded by fine havelis. Cross the square, to where the street ends at a T-junction; a left turn here takes you out of the old city at **Goga Gate** (straight on for 400m, then right at the end), passing more havelis on the way – in particular, check the one on the right after 200m, with lovely carving, cast-iron banisters on its upper-floor balcony, and murals round the side.

A right turn at the T-junction, on the other hand, leads after 400m to **Barah Bazaar**, centred on a large pillar painted in the colours of the Indian flag that appears to sprout out of a gaggle of auto-rickshaws. Follow the street round to the left and you'll eventually reach the **Bhandreshwar (Bhandasar) Temple**, unusual among Jain temples in being covered in a rich, almost gaudy, array of paintings. Porcelain tiles imported from Victorian England decorate the main altar, and steps lead up the unusually large tower, where you get a great view over the old city. Building started in 1468, before Bikaner itself was founded, but the temple wasn't finished until 1504. The mortar for the foundations was apparently made with ghee instead of water. Immediately to the rear on the edge of the high city wall lies the large Hindu **Laxminath Temple**, commissioned in the early sixteenth century by Lunkaran Singh, the third ruler of Bikaner. In a small park just beyond (follow the road between the Laxminath and Bhandreshwar temples) is a second Jain temple, the **Sandeshwar (Neminath) Temple** of 1536, also profusely but more soberly painted in dark greens and reds. A large model behind the temple shows the huge Jain religious complex at Palitana in Gujarat.

Lallgarh Palace and Ganga Golden Jubilee Museum

The sturdy red-sandstone **Lallgarh Palace** in the north of the town is home to the royal family of Bikaner, although parts now serve as a hotel (see p.301). It was built during the reign of Ganga Singh, who lived here from 1902, and despite some detailed carving, its modern aspect makes it fairly mundane compared to other Rajasthani palaces. The **Shri Sadul Museum** (Mon–Sat 10am–5pm; foreigners Rs40, Indian residents Rs20, camera Rs50, video Rs100) houses an enormous collection of old photographs showing various viceregal visits, pictures of Ganga Singh at the signing of the Versailles Treaty and royal processions that will fascinate Rajophiles. If you still have reserves left, you could go and see the small **Ganga Golden Jubilee Museum** (daily except Tues 10am–4.30pm; Rs5), east of the centre on NH-8, which offers much of the same, plus terracottas from the Gupta period (fourth and fifth centuries).

The camel farm

What claims to be Asia's largest camel-breeding farm, the **National Research Centre on Camels** (daily 3–6pm; foreigners Rs20, Indian residents Rs10, camera Rs20; camel ride Rs20, guided tour Rs100) lies out in the desert 10km south of Bikaner (around Rs120 round-trip by auto including 30min waiting time). Bikaner has long been renowned for its famously sturdy beasts – the camel corps was a much-feared component of the imperial battle formation – but the growing proliferation of motor vehicles has severely reduced the camel's traditional role as the staple means of rural transport. The main aim of the centre is to improve breeding stock; the best camels are sold to the Border Security Force, while others are auctioned off to villagers. It's best to take a guided tour of the farm; aim to be here for **feeding time** at 3.30–4pm, when you'll be wowed by the sight of three hundred stampeding dromedaries arriving from the desert for their daily chow. A new **museum** was under construction at the time of writing. There's also a kiosk selling camel milk and milk-based products such as lassis and kulfi – researchers at the farm are busy studying the properties of camel milk, which is purportedly effective in staving off tuberculosis and diabetes.

Devi Kund Sagar

Some 11km east of town on the Jaipur highway, **Devi Kund Sagar** (daily 9am–5pm; foreigners Rs10, Indian residents Rs5) is home to the royal cenotaphs of the rulers of Bikaner, a sequence of finely carved marble chhatris squeezed cheek-by-jowl inside a narrow walled enclosure. The burial ground was created by Rai Singh (r.1571–1612), the fifth raja of Bikaner, who also built Junagarh fort, and who lies here along with nineteen subsequent rajas and their assorted wives and consorts. There's also a small *sati* temple here which still attracts devotees (despite the fact that *sati* worship is now technically illegal), commemorating the fifty-odd ladies of the royal family who, at various times, cast themselves into the

Rajasthani crafts

Rajasthan is renowned for its abundance of exquisitely made crafts. The state is most famous for textiles and jewellery, but woodwork, metalwork, ceramics, and almost anything they make, has that distinctive Rajasthani touch of shimmering colour and delicate application. Whether it's sumptuous fabrics, fine paintings, beautiful enamelwork or bold jewellery, Rajasthan offers a feast of artistic creations you may find hard to resist.

Textiles and clothing

Rajasthani textiles are known for their vibrant colours, and they come in a splendid variety. The most characteristic are rich **brocades** with embroidery, appliqué, and sometimes gold and silver thread. Mirrorwork, with small mirrors stitched into the cloth, was originally a speciality of Jaisalmer, and is now found state-wide.

A very popular method of colouring textiles is **tie-dyeing**. Many Rajasthani fabrics are made this way, their faming colours making vivid saris and *dupattas*. Rajasthani tie-dyed fabrics are enlivened with huge splashes of bold dyes, especially reds, yellows and greens, and are regularly designed for specific festivals or times of the year. *Bandhani* fabric has lots of little dots on it, formed by impressing the fabric with a nail, then tying off and blocking the raised spot of material before dyeing. More sophisticated are *lehariya* tie-dyes, with long lines or bands of colour, the hues generally more subdued than those of *bandhani* fabrics.

Block printing is another common method of adding a pattern to a cloth. A pattern is carved into a wooden block, which is dipped into dye and impressed on the fabric. Most block-printed cloth will be printed on one side only, but the best is printed on both sides. Block printing may also be accompanied by resist printing in which a dye-resistant material such as wax or gum is painted onto the fabric, which is then dyed. Once dry, the resist is washed away with hot water leaving that part of the fabric undyed, ready to be block printed. Nowadays, much apparently block-printed fabric is in fact machine-printed, so check carefully.

Measuring fabric, Jaisalmer ▲

Block printing custom fabric ▼

Embroidered bag ▼

Textiles and clothing

Rajasthani textiles are known for their vibrant colours, and they come in a splendid variety. The most characteristic are rich **brocades** with embroidery, appliqué, and sometimes gold and silver thread. Mirrorwork, with small mirrors stitched into the cloth, was originally a speciality of Jaisalmer, and is now found state-wide.

A very popular method of colouring textiles is **tie-dyeing**. Many Rajasthani fabrics are made this way, their faming colours making vivid saris and *dupattas*. Rajasthani tie-dyed fabrics are enlivened with huge splashes of bold dyes, especially reds, yellows and greens, and are regularly designed for specific festivals or times of the year. *Bandhani* fabric has lots of little dots on it, formed by impressing the fabric with a nail, then tying off and blocking the raised spot of material before dyeing. More sophisticated are *lehariya* tie-dyes, with long lines or bands of colour, the hues generally more subdued than those of *bandhani* fabrics.

Block printing is another common method of adding a pattern to a cloth. A pattern is carved into a wooden block, which is dipped into dye and impressed on the fabric. Most block-printed cloth will be printed on one side only, but the best is printed on both sides. Block printing may also be accompanied by resist printing in which a dye-resistant material such as wax or gum is painted onto the fabric, which is then dyed. Once dry, the resist is washed away with hot water leaving that part of the fabric undyed, ready to be block printed. Nowadays, much apparently block-printed fabric is in fact machine-printed, so check carefully.

Measuring fabric, Jaisalmer ▲

Block printing custom fabric ▼

Embroidered bag ▼

Rajasthani crafts

Rajasthan is renowned for its abundance of exquisitely made crafts. The state is most famous for textiles and jewellery, but woodwork, metalwork, ceramics, and almost anything they make, has that distinctive Rajasthani touch of shimmering colour and delicate application. Whether it's sumptuous fabrics, fine paintings, beautiful enamelwork or bold jewellery, Rajasthan offers a feast of artistic creations you may find hard to resist.

Metalware and jewellery

The decorative metalwork most typical of Rajasthan is **meenakari**, made with enamel inlays on silver or gold. The technique was introduced from the Punjab in the eighteenth century, and is used to make pillboxes, caskets and jewellery, among other things. At its best, *meenakari* work is a feast of glowing colour, especially blues and greens. Jaipur in particular is a centre.

Jewellery is big in Rajasthan, in all senses. Earrings, nose-rings, finger rings, toe rings, anklets, bangles and necklaces are not just decorative, but can also indicate caste, religion, ethnic group or social standing. Along with *meenakari* enamelwork, the other main jewellery-making technique is *kundan*, which means embedding gemstones into precious metal, especially gold. Some pieces will have *kundan* on one side, and *meenakari* on the reverse. Very traditional in *kundan* are *navratan* pieces, which have nine gemstones (traditionally: ruby, pearl, coral, emerald, yellow sapphire, blue sapphire, diamond, cat's eye, and gomed, aka hessonite). These are supposed to correspond to the nine planets of Indian astrology, so they are auspicious on any occasion, no matter which planet rules. A very popular piece of jewellery among Rajasthani men is the *karanphool jhumka* ("flower of the ear") ear stud, made in the form of a flower, with different coloured petals.

Bangles are usually decorated with gold leaf and often studded with mirrors or glass *chatons*. They are made from lac (shellac), a red resin secreted by a plant-sucking bug (*Laccifer lacca*), known as the lac insect. Rajasthani women wear their bangles by the armload, and you can buy them in most towns, but the top place is Tripolia Bazaar in Jaipur.

▲ Green gemstone ring, Jaipur

▼ Bangles at craft market

▼ Jewellery boxes

Puppets, Jaisalmer market ▲

Potter, Pushkar ▼

Miniature paintings ▼

Other crafts to buy

Wooden furniture can be a real bargain, but heavy to cart around, let alone take home, though you could have it shipped. A lot of shops in Jodhpur sell reproduction antique carvings and chests.

Also typical are the **puppets** traditionally used in staging dramatizations of popular folk tales such as Dhola and Maru (see box, p.305) or Moomal and Mahendra (see box, p.293). The puppets have a wooden head and are clothed, and double as dolls. Udaipur and Jaipur are the best places to get them, but you'll find them in Jodhpur and Jaisalmer too. Udaipur is also known for its painted **toys**, made from a softwood called *doodhia* (the same techniques are used to make kitchen utensils). Bassi, near Chittaurgarh, is famous for special little wooden statues of Parvati, and for ingenious folded-in miniature wooden temples, painted with scenes from the Hindu epics. Once used by travelling bards, they gradually unfold to recount the story.

Rajasthan's finest **ceramic** work is the blue glazed pottery of Jaipur and Delhi. Unusually, the pottery itself is made with quartz and fuller's earth rather than clay. The vivid blue of the glaze is cobalt oxide, supplemented by oxides of copper (light blue), manganese (yellow) and chromium (green). Jaipur is the best place to buy (see p.203).

Rajasthani **leatherware** can be very cheap and well-made, though the leather doesn't normally come from cows. Camel-hide *mojadi* slippers in particular are extremely comfortable.

Miniature paintings, on cotton, silk or paper, are a tradition in Rajasthan, and at one time almost every Rajput principality had its own style of miniature painting. Udaipur and Kishangarh in particular are known for their miniatures, though almost every tourist centre in the state will sell them. Things to look out for are fineness and detail.

Dhola and Maru

The tale of Dhola and Maru is a typical Rajasthani romantic folk legend, and a favourite theme of miniature paintings, poems, ballads and puppet shows. Numerous versions of the tale exist, and every poet, singer or storyteller adds their own details, but the broad outline of the story usually runs something like this.

Once upon a time, the king of Pugal, near Bikaner, had a daughter called Maru. While she was still a little girl, as was then the custom, he married her to Dhola, the infant son of his good friend, the king of neighbouring Narwar. Unfortunately, the king of Narwar died before Dhola was old enough to learn that he had been married off, and so ended up marrying another woman, called Malwani. Maru, however, grew up knowing that she was married to Dhola, and remained faithful to him.

Dhola, meanwhile, continued to remain ignorant of his long-lost wife. Maru attempted to write to him, but her letters were intercepted and destroyed by Malwani. Finally, Maru arranged for a troupe of balladeers to visit Dhola and sing to him of their marriage. Hearing their tale, Dhola set off immediately for Pugal to see Maru for himself. Despite numerous obstacles and red herrings strewn in his way by Malwani – and by a bandit chief (or, in some versions, a Sindhi prince) who fancied Maru himself – Dhola reached Pugal and, seeing Maru, realized that she had always been his true love. In most versions of the tale, Malwani accepts the situation and they all live happily ever after. In some permutations, it is Dhola's faithful camel, a present to the king of Narwar from Maru's father, whose undaunting efforts bring the two lovers together – in paintings, the couple are invariably shown riding on a camel.

flames of their husbands' funeral pyres. Rai Singh himself can be found at the back of the enclosure, next to a lotus-covered lake, on the far side of which stands a secondary walled enclosure containing further chhatris.

The tombs can only be reached by tuktuk or taxi, but can easily be visited to or from a trip to the Deshnok temple.

Eating and drinking

Restaurants are thin on the ground and most visitors eat at their hotels, but there are a few good places to eat scattered around town should you need them. Bikaner's **sweets** are as ubiquitous as they're famous. Try *kaju katli*, made with cashew nuts (its taste and texture are somewhere between *barfi* and marzipan), and *tirangi*, a three-coloured sweet made with cashews, almonds and pistachios. A heavenly seasonal sweet if you're in town during December or January is *malai ghaver*, a fried honeycomb ring moistened with syrup and filled with saffron cream.

For a **drink**, the sleazy bar of the *Hotel Ankur*, down an alley opposite *Amber* restaurant, is not a place where women will feel comfortable, and neither is *King's Bar*, opposite the bus stand, but the bar of the RTDC *Dholamaru Hotel* at Pooran Singh Circle isn't too bad. Otherwise, you can drink without hassle at the bar of the *Lallgarh Palace Hotel*, but don't expect the cheapest beers in town.

Amber Station Rd. Simple but clean local restaurant popular with Westerners, with a long menu of Indian veg standards along with a few snacks. Most mains Rs50–70.

Bhikharam Chandmal Bhujiwala Just off Station Rd on the road to Kote Gate (the English sign is very small and easy to miss). Top *mithai* (sweet) shop, known for its excellent Bengali and Rajasthani confectionery, though it also has a good range of savoury snacks. *Haldiram's*, next door, is almost as renowned.

DFC (Dwarika Food Cuisine) Station Rd, by Silver Square mall. Clean and pleasant restaurant offering a big list of veg mains (most Rs60–80), thalis (Rs60–110) and even train tiffins (Rs90) to take with you on a rail journey.

Gallops Court Rd. Pleasant but seriously overpriced restaurant opposite the fort that has grown fat on the easy pickings of passing coach parties. The food's not bad, however, with a range of North Indian veg and non-veg standards, plus a few local specialities, served in big portions. Usually full of tour groups at lunchtime, but quieter and nicer in the evenings. Mains Rs175–450. Licensed.

Heeralal Opposite the train station. Clean and spacious veg restaurant serving up North and South Indian cuisine, including a good Rajasthani thali (Rs125) and other local specialities. Mains Rs100–140.

Moomal Tucked away behind the south side of Panch Shati Circle, this white linen restaurant serves sumptuous South Indian veg food that's popular with well-heeled locals. The punchy cashew and cherry Moomal Special alone is worth the trip. Prices around Rs100–180.

Shopping

Bikaner is famous for its skilled lacquer work and handicrafts, sold in the bazaar for a fraction of Jaisalmer's inflated "tourist prices", and for its hand-woven woollen shawls and blankets. The best place to buy the latter is the **Abhivyakti** handicrafts shop (closed Sun afternoon), established with the aid of funding from the local Urmul Trust and from Oxfam in Britain. There's a small outlet at the camel-breeding farm, but serious shoppers will want to visit the main store on Ganganar Road, near the bus stand. The store manager can even arrange visits to villages to see how the textiles are woven by the charity-supported women's co-ops. **Vichitra Arts**, at *Bhairon Vilas*, sells a fine range of vintage royal garb and miniature paintings.

Listings

Banks and exchange There are ATMs directly opposite the station, and another one 100m south, on Station Rd almost opposite the road from Kote Gate and between RTDC *Hotel Dhola Maru* and Panch Shati Circle. Thomas Cook (Mon–Sat 9am–6pm), inside the entrance to the fort, also changes cash and travellers' cheques.

Bicycle rental Available for Rs4/hr from a couple of shacks just south of the main post office, opposite the southwest corner of the fort.

Festival Bikaner's camel fair (Jan 18–19, 2011; Jan 8–9, 2012; Jan 26–27, 2013), though not as renowned, nor as touristed, as those of Pushkar or Jaisalmer, still has plenty of colour, with camel races, razor-cut camel hairstyle competitions, camel milking and camel acrobatics, not to mention Gair dancing, fire dancing and fireworks. Most of the

action takes place at the polo ground north of town near *Desert Winds* and *Harasar Haveli* hotels. Accommodation prices don't rocket like they do in Pushkar, but it's a good idea to book ahead.

Hospital PB Memorial Hospital by Ambedkar Circle ℡0151/222 6334.

Internet access Internet is widely available for around Rs30–40/hr but generally slow. There are lots of places around Kirti Stambh Circus; alternatively, try New Horizons behind the Amber Restaurant on Station Rd or Cyber World (just Rs10/hr), immediately south of the *Marudhar Heritage* hotel.

Police Station Rd ℡0151/252 2225.

Post office The main post office is just west of the fort (Mon–Fri 10am–3pm, Sat 10am–1pm).

Swimming pool The *Padmini Niwas Hotel* allows non-guests to use theirs for Rs100.

Moving on from Bikaner

Destinations served by **bus** include Ajmer (every 2hr; 7hr), Amritsar (1 daily; 12hr), Bundi, Kota and Chittaurgarh (1 daily; approximately 9hr, 10hr & 11hr respectively), Delhi (4 daily; 11hr), Fatehpur (hourly; 3hr), Jaipur (every 3hr, including several private overnight services; 7–8hr), Jaisalmer (4 daily, including one private overnight service; 7hr), Jodhpur (hourly; 5hr), Mandawa and Nawalgarh (hourly; 3hr–3hr 30min), Pushkar (every 2hr; 6hr) and Udaipur (3 daily; 12hr).

RSTRC government buses operate out of the main bus stand, near Lallgarh Palace on the north side of town (℡0151/252 3800). **Private buses** are run by a handful of firms, most of which have offices at the old bus stand, next to Junagarh Fort – shop around until you find a service that suits. Most private services depart

Recommended trains from Bikaner

The following trains are recommended as the fastest or most convenient; other services exist, but take longer or arrive at inconvenient times. Train timetables change frequently; check latest schedules either at your nearest station or online at ⓦ www.indianrail.gov.in before travel. There are no direct trains to **Ajmer** – it's much easier to take the bus. For Sawai Madhopur, Kota and Chittaurgarh, change at Jaipur.

Destination	Name	No.	Departs	Arrives
Abu Road	Ranakpur Express	4707	9.45am (daily)	7.55pm
	Ahmedabad Express	9224	12.25am (daily)	10.40am
Agra	Howrah Superfast	2308A	6.20pm (daily)	6.35am
Delhi	Assam Express†	5610	10pm (daily)	7.15am
Jaipur	Jaipur Intercity	2467	5.20am (daily)	11.55am
	Jaipur Special	0233	10.50pm (daily)	7am
Jaisalmer	Lallgarh–Jaisalmer Express†	4704	7.30am (daily)	1.20pm
	Bikaner–Jaisalmer Express	4702	11.25pm (daily)	5.30am
Jodhpur	Ranakpur Express	4707	9.45am (daily)	2.45pm
	Barmer Express	4887	10.45am (daily)	4pm
	Ahmedabad Express	9224	12.25am (daily)	5.30am

†From Lallgarh Junction

from outside these offices, though check when you book your ticket (there's also a new private bus stand 5km north of town along the Ganganagar road, though few operators were using it at the time of writing). The most comfortable long-distance buses are run by Chandra Travels, Sharma Travels and Milan Travels. Alternatively, most guesthouses should be able to book tickets for you. Buses to **Shekhawati** leave from Khatri Bus Stand, about 3.5km east of town along the Jaipur highway.

The **railway** station is on Station Road, just east of the old city, although a few services leave from **Lallgarh Junction**, on the northwestern edge of town. Recommended services are listed in the box above.

Deshnok and the temple of rats

The **Karni Mata temple** (daily 6am–10pm; free; Rs20 camera, Rs50 video; ⓦ www.karnimata.com) in **DESHNOK**, 30km south of Bikaner, is definitely one of India's more bizarre attractions. Step inside the Italian marble arched doorway and everywhere you'll see free-roaming rats, known as *kabas*, which devotees believe are reincarnated souls saved from the wrath of Yama, the god of death. Around the temple, bowls of milk are put out daily for the holy rodents. The innermost shrine, made of rough stone and logs cut from sacred jal trees, houses the yellow marble image of the folk hero turned goddess Karniji (see box, p.308). This in turn is encased by a much grander marble building, erected by Rao Bika's grandson after he defeated the Mughals. Pilgrims bring food offerings for the rats to eat inside the main shrine (they seem rather partial to *ladoo*), and it's customary to eat this *prasad* (conse-crated food) after it has been nibbled by the *kabas*. Ashes from a fire in the shrine are also daubed on pilgrims' foreheads. Some spend hours searching for a glimpse of the white rat, which is believed to be highly auspicious. It's also considered a blessing for a rat to run over your feet (this would require you to stand still for a while, and preferably next to some food), but whatever you do don't step on one, or you'll have to donate a gold model of a rat to placate the deity. Shoes have to be removed at the gate (a guardian looks after them for a small tip), leaving you to wander among the

The Deshnok Devi and the sacred rats

Members of the Charan caste of bardic musicians believe that incarnations of the goddess Durga periodically appear among them, sometimes as *sagats*, who are blessed with healing powers, and less commonly as more powerful *purn* avatars. **Karni Mata**, born into a Charan family at a village near Phalodi in 1387, exhibited from birth traits associated with this latter incarnation of the *Devi* (goddess). She went on to perform such miracles as water divination and bringing the dead back to life, eventually becoming the region's most powerful cult leader, worshipped by Jats and low-caste farmers.

According to legend, one of Karni Mata's followers, a Charan woman, came to her because her son was grievously ill, but by the time they got to him, he had died, so Karni Mata went to Yama, the god of the underworld, to ask for him back. Yama, however, refused. Knowing therefore that of all the creatures upon the earth, only rats were outside of Yama's dominion, Karni Mata decreed that all Charans would be henceforth reincarnated as rats, thus escaping Yama's power, and when they died as rats, they would be reincarnated into the Chamar caste again. It is these sacred rats (*kabas*) that inhabit the Deshnok Temple.

The rise in Karni's popularity, dating from her family's move north to Deshnok, mirrored the rise in power of the Rathore clan, whose constant raids were causing great instability in the region at the end of the fourteenth century. **Rao Bika**, the founder of Bikaner, realized that he and Karni could forge a formidable alliance to rid the area of the Rathores, and wooed her with promises of tax exemptions and tutelary deity status if she gave his clan her stamp of approval. When her eventual endorsement came it turned Bika's fortunes, quadrupling the size of his army. After he finally defeated the local warlords, Karni was accorded the honour of laying the foundation stone of Junagarh fort, and Bika regularly consulted her throughout his reign – a connection with the ruling family that has endured to this day. The Bikaner flag sports Karni's colours, and she is the patron goddess of the Bikaner camel corps, who still march into battle crying "Shree Karniji!".

rat droppings barefoot or in your socks. A net over the shrine protects the rodents from birds of prey, but it doesn't seem to keep out the "rats with wings" (pigeons), which are almost as prolific as their terrestrial counterparts.

Directly in front of the temple, the easily overlooked **Shri Karni Sixth Centenary Auditorium** contains a collection of oil paintings recounting the major events in Karniji's life, with English captions. A few kilometres away on the edge of town, the rarely visited **Nahrij Temple**, although lacking in rodents, has encased in marble the tree where Karniji in her last years came to make butter and await nirvana.

Buses for Deshnok from Bikaner leave roughly every fifteen minutes (journey time 45min) from the main bus stand, stopping on the east side of Ambedkar Circle near PB Memorial Hospital, and just south of Goga Gate Circle, near the southeast corner of the old city. There are also **trains** (1hr journey) at 9.45am and 10.45am, with return services from Deshnok at 2.54pm and 3.25pm.

Southwest of Bikaner: Gajner and Kolayat

You're unlikely to go to **Gajner wildlife sanctuary** (Rs150, vehicles Rs2000), 32km southwest of Bikaner, 5km off the main Bikaner–Jaisalmer highway, just to look at the wildlife, which is unexceptional for the hefty entrance price, though it does harbour a number of gazelle and antelope species, including chinkara (Indian gazelle), nilgai (bluebull) and blackbuck, as well as wild boar and desert foxes, and its lake attracts large numbers of waterfowl, especially in the winter. Most people come to stay at the *Gajner Palace Hotel* (℡01534/275061, 🌐www.eternalmewar .in; ❼, thirty percent discounts in summer), a rather grand affair in red sandstone, built in the early twentieth century as a hunting lodge for the maharajas of Bikaner. The hotel overlooks the lake, and can arrange jaunts around the sanctuary, which otherwise has no transport or accommodation.

Kolayat

Hardly any tourists make it to the beautiful little town of **KOLAYAT**, 55km west of Bikaner (4km off the main Bikaner–Jaisalmer highway). The second-holiest place of Hindu worship in Rajasthan after Pushkar, Kolayat grew up around the temple of the great Vedic sage Kapila (or Kapil Muni), locally considered to be the fifth incarnation of Vishnu, who is said to have worshipped here at the *peepul* tree which still stands close to his temple. As at Pushkar, the town is arranged around a large lake, almost entirely covered in lotuses and surrounded by 52 *ghats*, a similar number of temples and dozens of dharamsalas (pilgrims' resthouses). A bathe in the lake is said to wash away various sins, and the town attracts large number of pilgrims, including many colourfully attired sadhus, particularly during the **Kolayat Fair**, held at the same time as the Pushkar Fair on the full-moon day fifteen days after Diwali (late Oct/early Nov). As at Pushkar, the event also features a major camel and livestock fair.

Kolayat is an easy day-trip from Bikaner, with **buses** from the Government Bus Stand (every 30–45min; 1hr 30min). There's nowhere to stay here, unless you can find space in a dharamsala, although foreigners aren't generally accepted. There are a few simple *dhabas* in and around town, or just bring a picnic.

Nagaur

Almost equidistant between Bikaner, Ajmer and Jodhpur, the ancient city of **NAGAUR** (sometimes spelt Nagore, which is how it's pronounced) is dominated by the magnificent **Ahhichatragarh** (Fort of the Cobra's Hood; daily 9am–5pm; foreigners Rs50, Indian residents Rs15, camera Rs25, video Rs100, guide Rs100), a huge, rambling edifice surrounded by over 2km of ramparts. The fort was originally constructed around 1120 on the site of an earthwork predecessor dating back to the fourth century, and was subsequently added to by successive maharajas and Mughal emperors. It fell into disrepair during the eighteenth century, but has recently been spruced up thanks to a major conservation project.

The guided tour is worth taking to get an idea of what's what. Highlights include the **Hadi Rani Mahal** (Queen's Palace), with its wonderful murals of Krishna dancing (on the downstairs ceiling) and ladies desporting (upstairs in the queen's bedroom), and the **Amar Singh Mahal**, which has some beautifully restored murals and a water system that supplied a *hammam* with hot and cold water. The Mughal emperor Akbar had his own apartment in the fort, near the **Deepak Mahal** (Lamp Palace), where alcove-lined walls were furnished with a multitude of oil lamps. Outside the fort, Nagaur's sights include the sixteenth-century **Akbari Mosque**, east of Gandhi Chowk, its tapering minarets recalling the style of the Tughluqs of Delhi (see p.358), though it is in fact Mughal.

Nagaur's main event is its **cattle fair** (Ramdev Pashu Mela), held in late January or early February each year (Feb 10–13, 2011; Jan 30–Feb 2, 2012; Feb 17–20, 2013). Though not as big as the camel fair at Pushkar, Nagaur's event still brings in thousands of visitors, not to mention some seventy thousand steers, cows and bullocks to be bought, sold, raced or just shown off. The region's own breed of cattle is much sought-after, and the state government has moved in to protect it by banning the sale of animals under three years old to buyers from outside Rajasthan. The fair is enlivened by less commercial events such as moustache and turban-tying competitions, as well as cattle races and tug-of-war contests.

Practicalities

The **train station** and **bus stands** are at opposite ends of town, with the old city and fort in between. Six **trains** a day serve Bikaner (the best are the #4708 Ranakpur Express at 12.55pm and the #4888 Kolkata Express at 1.42pm, arriving in Bikaner at 4pm and 4.40pm respectively). There are also services to Jodhpur (5 daily; 3–4hr) and Jaipur (3–4 daily; 5–6hr). Frequent **bus** departures from the Roadways Bus Stand (for state buses) serve Bikaner, Jodhpur and Ajmer. Private buses, from a smaller stand just outside Delhi Gate, include an overnight sleeper service to Delhi. In Bikaner, the same buses that serve Deshnok continue to Nagaur, and can be picked up at the same stops (see p.308).

There's a limited choice of **accommodation** in Nagaur. You can stay in the fort itself in one of the twenty luxury tents at the *Royal Camp* (℡0291/257 2321, Ⓦwww.welcomheritagehotels.com; ❽, rising to ❾ during cattle fair). Two further upmarket choices, the *Khimsar Fort* hotel and *Khimsar Sand Dunes Village* (see box, p.271), are just 40km from Nagaur. Of the hotels in town, the best is *Hotel Bhaskar* on the Bikaner road near the train station (℡01582/240100; from Rs300 ❶), which has a variety of rooms at different prices, as does the more run-down but still respectable *Hotel Mahaveer International*, at Vijay Vallabh Chowk, near the bus stands (℡01582/243158; ❷). The *Bhaskar* is the best place in town to **eat**, though there are some reasonable *dhabas* between it and the station. Bicycles can be rented just across the square from the private bus stand outside Delhi Gate. There are two **ATMs** on Fort Road, southwest of Gandhi Chowk on the way to the train station.

Southern Rajasthan

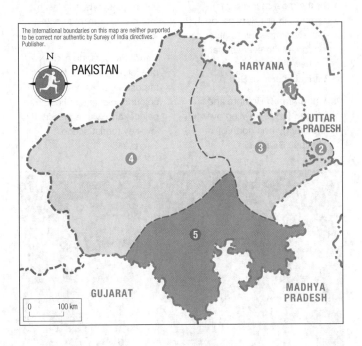

The International boundaries on this map are neither purported to be correct nor authentic by Survey of India directives. Publisher.

N

PAKISTAN

HARYANA

UTTAR PRADESH

GUJARAT

MADHYA PRADESH

0   100 km

CHAPTER 5 # Highlights

✳ **Udaipur** Rajasthan's – if not India's – most romantic city: a fairy-tale ensemble of lakes, floating palaces and sumptuous Rajput architecture ringed by dramatic green hills.
See p.314

✳ **Ranakpur** Home to one of the most magical Jain temples in the Subcontinent, a marvellous sculptural *tour de force* with every surface embellished in a riot of intricate carving. See p.330

✳ **Kumbalgarh** Remote and rugged fort, sprawling over the craggy hills north of Udaipur. See p.331

✳ **Mount Abu and Dilwara temples** Rajasthan's only hill station, with a scenic setting, a laidback holiday atmosphere and some of the finest Jain temples in India.
See p.333

✳ **Chittaurgarh** One of Rajasthan's most dramatic and historic forts, filled with a fascinating array of temples, towers and palaces. See p.340

✳ **Bundi** Picturesque and peaceful little town, full of atmospheric old havelis, colourful bazaars, a fine palace, and with a pleasantly low-key tourist scene.
See p.345

▲ Detail of temple in Chittaurgarh Fort

5

Southern Rajasthan

S outhern Rajasthan has a notably different flavour from the rest of the state. Shot through with the heavily forested southern outliers of the Aravalli hills, the region is markedly greener and cooler than the desert areas to the north, while its distance from Delhi and Jaipur lends it a pleasantly laidback atmosphere which can be bliss for those sated on crowds and traffic. Highlight of the region is the marvellous city of **Udaipur**, whose palace-fringed lake is Rajasthan's most romantic. Nearby, and easily visited as a day-trip from Udaipur, are the superb fort of **Kumbalgarh** and the eye-popping Jain temples at **Ranakpur**, while there are further lavishly embellished Jain shrines at breezy **Mount Abu**, Rajasthan's only hill station, thronging with cheerful Gujarati tourists and dreamy-eyed local honeymooners. Northeast of Udaipur, the picturesque little town of **Bundi** is becoming an increasingly popular destination among budget travellers, while nearby **Kota** is one of the few cities in southern Rajasthan to have experienced any kind of significant industrialization. Midway between Bundi and Udaipur, the legendary fort at **Chittaurgarh** is one of southern Rajasthan's most

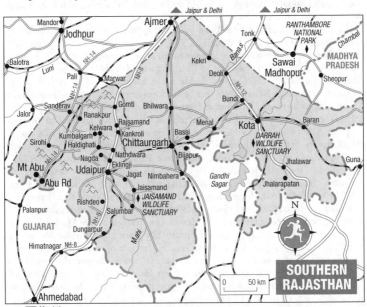

compelling attractions, whose glorious but ill-starred legacy of heroic defeats and ritual mass suicides encapsulates the region's history at its – depending on your point of view – goriest or most glorious.

Udaipur

The valley of Oodipur, the most diversified and most romantic spot on the continent of India

Col. James Tod, *Annals and Antiquities of Rajasthan* (1829)

Spreading around the shores of the idyllic Lake Pichola and backdropped by a majestic ring of craggy green hills, **UDAIPUR** seems to encapsulate everything that's most romantic about Rajasthan and India, with its intricate sequence of ornately turreted and balconied palaces, whitewashed havelis and bathing *ghats* clustered around the waters of the lake – or, in the case of the *Lake Palace* hotel and Jag Mandir, floating magically upon them. Not that the city is quite perfect. Insensitive lakeside development, appalling traffic and vast hordes of tourists mean that the city is far from unspoilt or undiscovered. Even so, Udaipur remains a richly rewarding place to visit, and although it's possible to take in most of the sights in a few days, many people spend at least a week exploring the city and the various attractions scattered about the surrounding countryside.

Some history

Udaipur is a relatively young city by Indian standards, having been established in the mid-sixteenth century by Udai Singh II (see p.316) of the **Sisodia** family, rulers of the state of **Mewar**. The Sisodias are traditionally considered the foremost of all the Rajput royal dynasties. The present maharana is the seventy-sixth in the unbroken line of Mewar suzerains, which makes the Mewar household the longest lasting of Rajasthan's royal families, and perhaps the oldest surviving dynasty in the world.

The state of Mewar was established by Guhil in 568 AD. His successors set up their capital first at Nagda and then, in 734, at the mighty fort of Chittaurgarh, from where they established control over much of present-day southern Rajasthan (for a brief history of the Sisodias at Chittaurgarh, see p.341). By the time **Udai Singh II** (see box, p.316) inherited the throne of Mewar in 1537, however, it was clear that Chittaurgarh's days were numbered. Udai began looking for a location for a new city, to be named Udaipur, eventually choosing a swampy site beside Lake Pichola, protected on all sides by outcrops of the Aravalli range. The Mughal emperor Akbar duly captured Chittaurgarh after a protracted seige in 1568, but by then Udai was firmly established in his new capital, where he remained unmolested until his death in 1572. His son, the heroic **Pratap Singh** (see box, p.323), continued to defy Akbar and spent much of his reign doggedly defending his kingdom's freedom against the overwhelming military muscle of the Mughal army.

As the city prospered, the arts flourished: Mewar became home to a flourishing school of miniature painting, while imposing palaces were constructed around and even on the lake. However, in 1736 Mewar was attacked by the **Marathas**, who gradually reduced the city to poverty until they were finally driven off by the British in the early eighteenth century. Yet the principle of refusing to bow down to a foreign power persisted and the maharanas never allowed the British to displace them. When Britain withdrew from India in 1947, the maharana of Udaipur spearheaded the movement by the princely states to join the new democratic and independent India. Congress was, however, determined to reduce

UDAIPUR

H (25km), Eklingji & Mount Abu

Clock Tower

Chand Pol

Raiba House

Footbridge — Gangaur Ghat

Heera Cycle Store

Bagore-ki Haveli

Mewar International

Jagdish Temple

Mayur Books

Lalghat

City Palace

ATM

0   100 m

Sahelion-ki-Bari

Nehru Park

Statue

Moti Magri

Jetty

Entrance

Fateh Sagar

Shilpgram

Bharatiya Lok Kala

Jet Airways

GPO

State Bank of India & ATM

Swaroop Sagar

State Bank of Bikaner and Jaipur

New Bridge

Rang Sagar

Hathi Pol

Delhi Gate

Indian Airlines

Sajjangarh "Monsoon Palace" & J

Clock Tower

See inset

City Palace

Jetty

Lake Palace

Bank of Baroda

Town Hall

Suraj Pol

Private Bus Stand

State Bus Stand

Udai Pol

Airport (20km)

Thomas Cook

Kamlesh Travels

Tibetan Market

Samode Bagh

Sajjan Niwas Garden & Zoo

Lake Pichola

Jag Mandir

City Railway Station

Ahar River

0   500 m

AHMEDABAD ROAD

T & Ahmedabad

ACCOMMODATION

Amet Haveli	O	Lake Pichola Hotel	N
Devi Garh	H	Lalghat Guest	
Dream Heaven	K	House	D
Fateh Prakash Palace	P	Laxmi Vilas Palace	I
Gangaur Palace	A	Mewar Haveli	C
Jagat Niwas	F	Panorama	L
Jaiwana Haveli	E	Shikarbadi	T
Kankarwa Haveli	F	Shiv Niwas	R
Kumbha Palace	Q	Udai Kothi	M
Lake Corner Soni	G	Udai Niwas	B
Lake Palace	S	Udaivilas	J

RESTAURANTS

Ambrai	O
Edelweiss	2
The Gallery	P
Jagat Niwas	F
Kankwara Haveli	F
Natraj	4
Queen Café	3
Savage Garden	1
The Whistling Teal	5

315

the Rajput princes to the status of normal citizens, and political recognition of royalty came to an end in 1969.

Centuries of loyalty between rulers and subjects have been kept alive by songs, stories and paintings; the maharana may now lack political power, but he remains as

Udai Singh II

The founder of Udaipur, **Udai Singh II** (1522–72, reigned from 1540), is one of the most intriguing of all Rajput rulers, alternately vilified as the leader who abandoned his kingdom's ancestral capital at Chittaurgarh (Chittor) to the Mughals, and celebrated as the founder of the new city which bears his name. Udai's accession to the throne of Mewar is itself the stuff of Rajput legend. The youngest of four brothers, it was never expected that he would succeed to the throne, but by the time Udai had reached the age of fifteen his three elder brothers had all met violent deaths – the last at the hands of Udai's cousin Banbir, who had determined to seize the throne for himself. Anxious to eliminate the final surviving brother, Banbir set out to murder the young Udai while he slept in the fort at Chittor. Udai's nurse, **Panna Dhai**, hid the young heir, put her own son in Udai's bed and looked on while he was murdered by Banbir, who promptly declared himself king of Mewar, believing that he had extinguished all rival claimants to the throne. Panna Dhai spirited the young Udai away from Chittor and, following an arduous journey of several weeks, eventually found refuge at the fort of Kumbalgarh, where Udai Singh lived incognito for the next two years until old enough to march upon Chittor and reclaim his rightful inheritance. Banbir was driven into exile, never to be heard of again.

Having seen off rival Mewari claimants to his kingdom, Udai Singh faced an even greater challenge to his rule in the form of the great Mughal emperor **Akbar** (1542–1605), who had determined to subjugate the various independent kingdoms of Rajasthan and bring them into the Mughal fold. Previous Mughal rulers had been unable to subdue the fiery Rajputs, but Akbar's more subtle approach – using intermarriage and the forging of alliances with the region's ruling families rather than attempts at outright military conquest – had already borne considerable fruit. All such attempts to coerce Udai Singh into an alliance with the Mughal empire, however, were steadily rebuffed, while Udai Singh poured scorn on those Rajput rulers (such as the Kachchwahas of Amber) who had come to terms with the Muslim invaders.

The scene for a decisive clash between Akbar, the ruler of Muslim India, and Udai Singh, the figurehead of Hindu resistance in the north, was thus set. Akbar determined to attack Chittor and bring the kingdom of Mewar to heel once and for all. Hearing of the planned attack, Udai Singh, instead of defending the fort against whatever odds in time-honoured Rajput-style, simply abandoned Chittor to the care of eight thousand soldiers and ran off to the fledgling city of Udaipur, in which he had already established a palace back in 1559. This act of apparently brazen cowardice called down the wrath of centuries of commentators upon Udai Singh's unsuspecting head. The British historian Colonel Tod, in his celebrated *Annals and Antiquities of Rajasthan* (1829), described Udai Singh as "a coward succeeding a bastard to guide the destinies of the Sesodias." Others echoed his view, characterizing Udai Singh as a "craven prince", "the unworthy son of a noble sire" and so forth. Modern historians have seen the matter somewhat differently, however. Realizing the impossibility of defending Chittor against the armies of Akbar, it is argued, Udai Singh made a strategic withdrawal to a more secure position from which the independence of the state of Mewar could be far more easily guaranteed. In this respect, history has proved him right. Chittor duly fell in 1568, after a protracted and bloody siege, though by that time Udai Singh was safely established in his new capital, from where he continued to defy Akbar up until his death in 1572. Udaipur itself has flourished since its foundation right up to the present day, while, interestingly, the city founded by his adversary Akbar at Fatehpur Sikri lasted barely two decades before falling into terminal decline.

respected by the people of Udaipur as were his forefathers. His personal funding and income from tourism are invested in the Maharana of Mewar Trust, which subsidizes local hospitals and educational institutions, and supports environmental projects.

Arrival, information and city transport

The **bus stand** is on the east side of the centre; pre-paid autos from the main entrance charge Rs32 to the City Palace area. Private buses drop you on the other side of Town Hall Road. **Trains** pull in at Udaipur City Station, southeast of the city centre. **Flights** arrive at **Dabok Airport** (☏0294/265 5453), 20km east of Udaipur, a Rs300 taxi ride from the city. The main **tourist office** (Mon–Sat 10am–5pm; ☏0294/241 1535) is in Fateh Memorial on Airport Road at Suraj Pol, on the east side of the city, with desks at the airport and railway station.

Auto-rickshaws are the usual means of transport; there are no cycle rickshaws in town. Renting a **bicycle** is another possibility (see p.326), although traffic around the city is bad. **Tours** to Ranakpur, Kumbalgarh, Nathdwara and Eklingji are offered by some of the innumerable **travel agents** dotted around the city centre (see p.327), as well as car rental with driver (usually around Rs1200/day for up to 300km).

Accommodation

Most accommodation is on the **east side of Lake Pichola**, although there are a growing number of places on the far more peaceful **northwestern side** of the lake, just across the bridge by Chand Pol.

East of Lake Pichola

Fateh Prakash Palace City Palace ☏0294/252 8016, ⓦwww.hrhindia.com. The best location in the city, right in the heart of the City Palace complex, with prices to match. Most of the rooms (Rs16,200) have superb lake views, although some are rather small and characterless for the price. ❾

Gangaur Palace Gangaur Ghat Marg ☏0294/242 2303, ⓦwww.ashokahaveli.com. Popular budget hotel in an atmospheric traditional haveli. There's a wide range of rooms of varying standards (fan and a/c), including some with lake views, though prices for the smarter rooms can be a bit steep – try bargaining. Facilities include in-house palmist, painting lessons and German bakery. ❷–❺

Jagat Niwas 23–25 Lalghat ☏0294/242 2860, ⓦwww.jagatniwaspalace.com. Beautifully restored seventeenth-century haveli right on the lakeside, with pleasant a/c rooms (some with lake views) and a good restaurant (see p.325), though not as peaceful or as good value as the nearby *Kankarwa* and *Jaiwana* havelis. ❺–❻

Jaiwana Haveli 14 Lalghat ☏0294/241 1103, ⓦwww.jaiwanahaveli.com. Good-value lakeside haveli accommodation with a range of spotless modern rooms; some have a/c, and the more expensive ones have fine lake views, as does the good rooftop restaurant. ❺

Kankarwa Haveli 26 Lalghat ☏0294/241 1457, ⓦwww.indianheritagehotels.com. Romantically restored haveli right on the waterfront. Not quite as pristine as the nearby *Jagat Niwas*, but more atmospheric and much better value, with colourful, antiquey rooms (all a/c; some with superb lake views). There's also excellent veg food (see p.325). ❺–❻

Kumbha Palace 104 Bhatiyani Chohatta ☏0294/242 2702, ⓦwww.indianheritagehotels .com. Friendly, Dutch-owned guesthouse hidden under the east walls of City Palace and backed by a bougainvillea-strewn garden. Rooms (a few with a/c) are simple but bright and clean, and the whole place is refreshingly peaceful. ❷–❹

Lake Corner Soni Paying Guest House Lalghat ☏0294/252 5712. This simple little guesthouse, run by a charming elderly couple, offers some of the cheapest lodgings in Udaipur. Rooms (some with shared bathroom) are basic but clean and peaceful, and there are fine lake views from the rooftop terrace and some rooms. ❶

Lake Palace Lake Pichola ☏0294/252 8800, ⓦwww.tajhotels.com. One of India's most famous and romantic hotels, sailing in magnificent isolation on its own island amid the serene waters of Lake Pichola. Accommodation is in a selection of rooms and suites, which range from the merely luxurious to the opulently theatrical, while facilities include a spa, pool, butler service and limousine rental. Service in the restaurant is impeccable. The full rate for a standard room is Rs51,150, but check the website for discounts. **⑨**

Lalghat Guest House Lalghat ☎0294/252 5301, ✉lalghat@hotmail.com. One of the oldest guesthouses in Udaipur, and still going strong thanks to its superb lakeside position and cheapish rates. There's a mix of rooms (all attached, some a/c, and some with lakeside views), plus a nicer-than-average ten-person dorm (Rs100). **①–④**

Mewar Haveli 34–35 Lalghat ☎0294/252 1140, ⓦwww.mewarhaveli.com. Spotless and well-run modern mid-range hotel in a very central location. Rooms (some with a/c and lake views) are chintzy but comfortable, and there are further lake views from the attractive rooftop restaurant. **③–⑤**

Shiv Niwas City Palace ☎0294/252 8016, ⓦwww.hrhindia.com. This upmarket heritage hotel trades on its superb location inside the City Palace complex, with grand public areas, a dreamy pool (non-guests Rs300) and a brand-new spa. The viewless standard ("palace") rooms are disappointingly small and ordinary given the Rs12,960 price tag; suites (from Rs25,920) are far more memorable, with genuine old-world atmosphere and marvellous lake views. twenty percent discounts in summer. **⑨**

Udai Niwas Gangaur Ghat Marg ☎0294/241 4303, ⓦwww.hoteludainiwas.com. Bright modern high-rise hotel with a range of smart rooms in various price categories (the more expensive ones with a/c), although road noise and the periodic outbursts of massively amplified music from the nearby Jagdish Temple mean that it's not particularly peaceful. **③–⑤**

Northwestern side of Lake Pichola

Amet Haveli Chand Pol ☎0294/243 4009, ✉ametchaveli@sify.com. This fine old white haveli is one of the best lakefront properties in town. All rooms are beautifully decorated with traditional touches and come with a/c, TV and fine lake views, though you might want to spend a little bit extra to get one of the superb suites, with big windows right over the water. Also home to the excellent *Ambrai* restaurant (see p.325). **⑦**

Dream Heaven Chand Pol ☎0294/243 1038, ✉deep_rg@yahoo.co.uk. Deservedly popular (book ahead) with a good range of clean, cheap and competitively priced rooms; some have superb lake views, as does the rooftop restaurant. **①–④**

Lake Pichola Hotel Chand Pol ☎0294/243 1197, ⓦwww.lakepicholahotel.com. This long-established

hotel won't win any design awards, but the lakeside location and City Palace views are just about perfect, and prices quite reasonable. Don't bother with the viewless standard rooms, though. All rooms with a/c and TV. **⑤–⑥**

Panorama Chand Pol ☎0294/243 1027, ✉krishna2311@rediffmail.com. Excellent budget hotel, efficiently run and with cheap, cosy and excellent-value rooms (some with slight lake views; a few with a/c). There's also a nice rooftop restaurant with superb lake views and better-than-average food. Book ahead. **①–③**

Udai Kothi Chand Pol ☎0294/243 2810, ⓦwww.udaikothi.com. Smart and spotless modern hotel in traditional style, with lots of flowery murals and chintzy little architectural touches. Rooms all come with TV, a/c and plenty of slightly twee furnishings; there's also a pool (non-guests Rs300) and a lovely garden. **⑦–⑧**

Outside the city centre

Laxmi Vilas Palace Off Fateh Sagar Rd ☎0294/252 9711, ⓦwww.thelalit.com. Luxury hotel occupying a nineteenth-century hilltop guesthouse above Fateh Sagar Lake. It's strong on creature comforts, with well-equipped rooms and a huge pool, although less atmospheric than the similarly priced hotels in the City Palace. **⑨**

Udaivilas ☎0294/243 3300, ⓦwww.oberoihotels.com. Udaipur's most opulent hotel, occupying a sprawling palace, embellished with acres of marble and a novel "moated pool" which flows around the outside of the main building. Suites come with their own infinity swimming pools and private butler, and the spa is pure indulgence. **⑨**

Around Udaipur

Devi Garh Delwara Village, 25km north of Udaipur ☎02953/289211, ⓦwww.deviresorts.com. Hidden away in the Aravalli Hills a 40min drive north of Udaipur, this luxury hotel occupies the magnificent seventeenth-century Devi Garh palace, mixing traditional Rajasthani palace opulence with contemporary style to memorable effect. Facilities include a superb spa and a spectacular pool. Suites only, starting at Rs27,000 in high season. **⑨**

Shikarbadi Goverdhan Vilas, 5km south of Udaipur on the NH-8 ☎0294/258 3201, ⓦwww.hrhindia.com. Former royal hunting lodge with its own pool, lake, deer park and stud farm – less ostentatious (and significantly cheaper) than the palaces in town. Suites in the old 1930s block have more character than the newer a/c rooms. Rooms Rs6480, suites Rs7560. **⑦**

The City

The original sixteenth-century old city of Udaipur grew up around the grand **City Palace**, on the east shore of **Lake Pichola**, and the **old city** maze of tightly winding streets still spreads eastward from the palace. North of here stretches the second of Udaipur's two major lakes, **Fateh Sagar**.

Lake Pichola

Udaipur's idyllic **Lake Pichola** provides the city's most memorable views, a beautiful frame for the City Palace buildings, havelis, *ghats*, temple towers and other structures which crowd its eastern side – best seen from a boat trip around the lake (see below). The lake's two **island palaces** are among Udaipur's most famous features. **Jag Niwas**, now the *Lake Palace* hotel, was built in amalgamated Rajput–Mughal style as a summer palace during the reign of Jagat Singh (1628–52), after whom it was named. Unfortunately, for fear of a terrorist attack, it is now closed to all except hotel guests. The larger **Jag Mandir** (for access, see below), on the island to the south, has changed little since its construction (which was begun by Karan Singh in 1615, and finished by Jagat Singh, who, once again, named it after himself). The main building on the Jag Mandir, the **Gol Mahal**, has a domed roof with detailed stone inlay work on the inside, and houses a small exhibition on the history of the island. In front of it a green marble chhatri carved with vines and flowers stands at the centre of a garden guarded by stone elephants. Karan Singh offered refuge here to the Mughal Prince Khurram (later Emperor Shah Jahan), who had been exiled by his father, Emperor Jahangir, in the 1620s. Khurram succeeded his father while still in Udaipur, and the Mughal gathering for the occasion defied the established code of Rajput–Mughal enmity. According to tradition, Prince Khurram was so impressed by the architecture of the Gol Mahal that he later used elements of its design in the Taj Mahal, although it's difficult to see much resemblance between the two buildings. During the 1857 uprising the island once again served as a safe haven, this time for European women and children, when Maharaja Swaroop Singh offered them sanctuary here, remarking that "war is only for men". Today, Jag Mandir's only inhabitants other than flocks of birds are three royal servants who tend the gardens and grow flowers for the maharana's celebrations.

Boat rides around the lake depart from the jetty towards the south end of the City Palace complex, offering unforgettable views of the various palaces. Choose between a quick thirty-minute circuit of the lake (Rs200) or the same trip with an additional stop at the Jag Mandir (Rs300). Both tours depart hourly on the hour from 10am to 6pm. To make the most of them, sit on the side of the boat facing the palace (they usually run anticlockwise around the lake). You can also hire your own boat (seating up to 7 people) here for Rs3000. Alternatively, on the water-front between the *Jaiwana* and *Kankarwa* havelis, you can rent pedalos (2-seater Rs125/30min) or motorboats (from Rs700/30min), or be taken on a sunset jaunt around the lake in a group boat (Rs200/person).

City Palace

Udaipur's fascinating **City Palace** stands moulded in soft yellow stone on the northeast side of Lake Pichola, its thick windowless base crowned with ornate turrets and cupolas. The largest royal complex in Rajasthan, it is made up of eleven different *mahals* (palaces) constructed by successive rulers over a period of three hundred years. Part of the palace is now a **museum** (daily 9.30am–4.30pm; Rs50, camera Rs200, video Rs200, audioguide Rs250, guides Rs150 for up to five people). Narrow low-roofed passages connect the different *mahals* and courtyards, creating a confusing, labyrinthine layout designed to prevent surprise intrusion by

▲ City Palace, Udaipur

armed enemies – fortunately visitors are directed around a clearly signed one-way circuit, so your chances of getting lost are limited.

Toran Pol to the Badi Mahal

To reach the palace museum, first buy your ticket at the kiosk at the main entrance then walk across the massive courtyard bounding the eastern side of the palace where elephants once lined up for inspection before battle. At the far end of this courtyard, head to the right through a large gate, the **Toran Pol**, and then turn right again across the **Moti Chowk** courtyard (look out for the large portable tiger trap in the middle of the courtyard). The entrance to the museum is on the far side of the courtyard, past the palace's small **armoury**.

Go in, past propitious statues of Ganesh and Lakshmi set amid rich wall tiling, and head up some steep stairs to reach the first of the palace's myriad courtyards, the **Rajya Angan**. A room off on one side is devoted to the exploits of Pratap Singh (see p.323), including some of his own weapons, as well as a model of his famous horse, Chetak.

Steps lead up to the **Nav Chowki Palace** and past a small railed shrine ("fire pit") dedicated to Goswami Prem Giri, who in 1559 advised Udai Singh to build his new palace on this spot. Further steps lead up to the **Chandra Mahal**, home to a huge basin carved from a single block of marble that was filled with one hundred thousand silver coins to celebrate the wedding of Maharana Karan Singh (reigned 1620–28). The coins were subsequently distributed among the citizens of Udaipur. A finely carved balcony with the remains of stained glass overlooks the

---

Note that to reach certain parts of the City Palace, including the *Fateh Prakash Palace* and *Shiv Niwas* hotels, the Durbar Hall, Crystal Gallery and the jetty for boats around Lake Pichola and over to the *Lake Palace* hotel, you'll have to fork out Rs25 for a **general entrance ticket** to the City Palace complex. You don't have to buy this ticket if you are just visiting the City Palace Museum or the courtyard outside, or if you're actually staying at any of the three hotels.

lake from here. More steps lead up to pleasantly sylvan **Badi Mahal** (Garden Palace; also known as Amar Vilas after its creator, Amar Singh II, who reigned 1695–1755), its main courtyard embellished with finely carved pillars and a marble pool and dotted with trees which flourish despite being built some 30m above ground level.

The Dilkushal Mahal to the Surya Choupad

From the Badi Mahal, a twisting passageway leads down to the **Dilkushal Mahal**, whose rooms house a superb selection of small- and large-scale paintings depicting festive events in the life of the Udaipur court and portraits of the maharanas, as well as the superb **Kanch ki Burj**, a tiny chamber eye-catchingly walled with red zigzag mirrors and capped with a reflective dome. The mirrors are nineteenth-century, but the room dates from the reign of Karan Singh II (1620–28), who was responsible for many of the palace's most striking buildings, including the Chandra Mahal, Mor Chowk and Zenana Mahal, as well as the Jag Mandir in Lake Pichola. Immediately past here, the courtyard of the **Madan Vilas** (built by Bhim Singh, who reigned 1778–1828) offers fine lake and city views; the lakeside wall is decorated with quaint inlaid mirrorwork pictures.

Stairs lead down to the **Moti Mahal** (Pearl Palace), another of Karan Singh's diminutive futuristic-looking mirrored chambers, flanked by a pair of old ivory doors. The walls are entirely covered in plain mirrors, with the only colour supplied by its stained-glass windows. Steps lead around the top of the Mor Chowk courtyard (see below) to the **Pitam Niwas** (built by Jagat Singh II, who reigned 1734–90) and down to the small **Surya Choupad**, dominated by a striking image showing a kingly-looking Rajput face enclosed by a huge golden halo – a reference to the belief that the rulers of the house of Mewar are descended from the sun.

Mor Chowk to Laxmi Chowk

Next to here, the wall of the fine **Mor Chowk** courtyard is embellished with one of the palace's most flamboyant artworks, a trio of superb mosaic peacocks (*mor*), commissioned by Sajjan Singh in 1874, each made from around five thousand pieces of glass and coloured stone. On the other side of the courtyard is Karan Singh's opulent little **Manek Mahal** (Ruby Palace), its walls mirrored in rich reds and greens.

From here a long corridor winds past the kitsch apartments of Rajmata Shri Gulabkunwar (1928–73) and through the **Zenana Mahal** (women's palace), whose long sequence of rooms now houses a huge array of paintings depicting royal fun and frolics. Continue onwards to emerge, finally, into the last and largest of the palace's internal courtyards, **Lakshmi Chowk**, the centrepiece of the Zenana Mahal. The exit is at the far end.

The rest of the City Palace complex

The small **Government Museum** (daily 10am–4.30pm; Rs10; closed for refurbishment at the time of writing), opposite the entrance to the City Palace Museum, is mainly of interest for its impressive sculpture gallery of pieces from Kumbalgarh, including some outstanding works in black marble, along with various stone inscriptions and the inevitable assortment of miniature paintings, weapons and faded bits of cloth, along with stuffed animals, including a pair of conjoined calves and a monkey which for some reason is holding a chandelier lantern.

More interesting in many ways – and certainly far more atmospheric – is the vast **Durbar Hall** in the Fateh Prakash Palace immediately behind the main City Palace building, which now houses the *Fateh Prakash Palace* hotel. This huge, wonderfully time-warped Edwardian-era ballroom was built to host state banquets, royal functions and the like, and remains full of period character, complete with huge chandeliers, creaky old furniture and fusty portraits. You can have afternoon tea here as part of a visit to *The Gallery* café (see p.325). In a gallery overlooking the hall is the eccentric **Crystal Gallery** (daily 9am–6.30pm; Rs525), housing an array of fine British crystal ordered by Sajjan Singh in the 1880s and featuring outlandishly kitsch items including crystal chairs, tables and lamps – there's even a crystal hookah and a crystal bed. The extortionate entrance charge is a bit of a turn-off, though it does include a free audioguide and also gets you a drink at *The Gallery* café.

Jagdish Temple

Just north of the City Palace, **Jagdish Temple** is one of Udaipur's most popular and vibrant shrines. Built in 1652 and dedicated to Lord Jagannath, an aspect of Vishnu, its outer walls and towering *shikhara* are heavily carved with figures of Vishnu, scenes from the life of Krishna and dancing *apsaras* (nymphs). The circular *mandapa* leads to the sanctuary where a black stone image of Jagannath sits shrouded in flowers, while a small raised shrine in front of the temple protects a bronze Garuda. Subsidiary shrines to Shiva, Ganesh, Surya and Durga stand at each corner of the main temple.

Bagore-ki-Haveli

North of Jagdish Temple, a lane leads to Gangaur Ghat and the **Bagore-ki-Haveli**, a 138-room lakeside haveli of 1751. A section of the building has been converted into a worthwhile **museum** (daily 10am–5pm; Rs25, camera Rs10, video Rs50), arranged on two floors around one of the rambling haveli's several courtyards. The upper floor has several immaculately restored rooms with original furnishings and artworks, plus some fine murals. The lower floor has rooms full of women's clothes, musical instruments, kitchen equipment and – the undisputed highlight – what is claimed to be the world's largest turban. Traditional **music and dance** shows (Rs60, camera Rs50, video Rs50) are staged here nightly at 7pm.

Bharatiya Lok Kala

Just north of Chetak Circle in the new city, the hoary old **Bharatiya Lok Kala** museum (daily 9am–5.30pm; foreigners Rs35, Indian residents Rs20, camera Rs10, video Rs50) is home to a mildly interesting collection of exhibits covering the folk traditions of Rajasthan and India, with dusty displays of colourful masks, musical instruments and models of folk dances, plus some interesting photos of Rajasthani and other Indian indigenous tribes such as the Bhils and Garasias, and an entertaining roomful of quaint puppets from around the world. Short, amusing **puppet shows** (tip expected) are staged throughout the day on demand (the performers will probably hunt you down and drag you into the theatre shortly after your arrival), while there's an hour-long show, with music, dancing and more puppets, daily at 6pm (foreigners Rs50, Indian residents Rs30, camera Rs10, video Rs50).

Moti Magri

The northeast side of the city is bounded by the expansive **Fateh Sagar** lake, connected to Lake Pichola by a canal built in the early 1900s, and fringed with rugged hills. On the eastern side of the lake is the pleasantly peaceful **Moti Magri** (Pearl Hill; daily 9am–6pm; Rs20, camera Rs10, video Rs25), a steep-sided hillock covered in a mix of light woodland and ornamental gardens, and offering fine views over Fateh Sagar. Paths lead up to the ruins of the modest **Moti Mahal**, the original palace of Udai Singh, where he and his family lived while the City Palace was under construction. Close by, at the highest point of the hill, stands a large equestrian statue of **Pratap Singh** (see box opposite) astride his famous mount Chetak, decorated with friezes showing scenes from the battle of Haldighati, scene of his greatest triumph. Further Pratap Singh memorabilia can be found in the **Hall of Heroes Museum** (Rs5), a short distance back down the hill, featuring a few dull paintings of various rulers of Mewar and scenes from the state's history (Hindi signs only), along with a couple of big models of Chittaurgarh Fort and the battlefield at Haldighati.

Just past the entrance to Moti Magri, a small jetty marks the departure point for boats to **Nehru Park**, on an island in the centre of the lake (daily: March–Oct 8am–7.30pm; Nov–Feb 8.30am–6.30pm; foreigners Rs125, Indian residents Rs30, including return boat trip to park) – nothing special, but a pleasant enough escape from the bustle of the town. You can also hire pedaloes, rowing boats, water scooters and motor boats at the jetty for trips out onto the lake.

Sahelion-ki-Bari

Northeast of Moti Magri, **Sahelion-ki-Bari** (daily 8am–7pm; Rs5), the "garden of the maids of honour", was laid out by Sangram Singh (1710–34) as a summer

Pratap Singh: Rajput freedom fighter

There is not a pass in the alpine Aravalli that is not sanctified by some deed of the great freedom fighter, Maharana Pratap Singh, some brilliant victory or, more often, more glorious defeat.

Colonel James Tod, *Annals and Antiquities of Rajasthan*

The first son and successor of the founder of Udaipur, Udai Singh (see p.316), the feisty **Pratap Singh** (1540–97, reigned from 1572) is still revered as the original Mewari freedom fighter who defied the odds to take on the might of the Mughal empire and emerge bloody but unbowed. Born at Kumbalgarh in the year in which Udai Singh officially recaptured the mantle of King of Mewar, Pratap Singh continued his father's lifelong struggle against the forces of the Mughal emperor Akbar. Following his father's example, Pratap Singh met all of Akbar's numerous attempts to reach a diplomatic compromise with stubborn resistance, refusing to cede sovereignty to the Mughals and constantly rebutting their envoys – the last of the Rajput rulers to hold out against the might of the Mughals. Anticipating the inevitable attack, Pratap Singh put the kingdom on a war footing, in whose austerities he took full part, promising to eat off nothing but plates of leaves, to sleep on straw mattresses and not to shave his beard until the war was finished.

The promised attack finally arrived in 1576. Akbar massed an army of some eighty thousand soldiers at Ajmer, which marched into Mewar under the command of the rival Rajput ruler, Man Singh of Amber. On June 18, 1576, a short but intense pitched battle was fought at the narrow mountain pass at **Haldighati** between Pratap Singh's modest forces and the numerically far superior Mughal army. The outcome was inconclusive, though the encounter has been celebrated ever since as a moral triumph for the hopelessly outnumbered Mewari forces. Pratap Singh himself led from the thick of the action, saved only by his legendary steed **Chetak**, who bore him to safety before succumbing to his own wounds, and by his own previously estranged brother Sakta, formerly in the pay of the Mughal forces, who switched sides at the last minute to save Pratap from pursuing horsemen.

Following the battle of Haldighati, Pratap Singh retired to the Aravalli hills where, in time-honoured guerrilla fashion, he continued to harry the forces of Akbar over the following years until the Mughal emperor finally gave up the pursuit of Mewar in 1587 in order to concentrate on new campaigns in the Punjab. Pratap Singh was thus able to spend the final years of his reign unmolested, the ruler of a kingdom which, though still independent, had been largely bankrupted by continual warfare.

retreat for the diversion and entertainment of the ladies of the royal household – though the eye-catching fountains weren't installed until the reign of Fateh Singh (1884–1930). The gardens are centred on a peaceful courtyard enclosing a large pool and surrounded by attractive formal walled gardens, at the back of which four elephant statues surround Udaipur's most striking fountain – a fanciful tiered creation which looks a bit like a huge, multicoloured cake stand.

South of the Old City

Vintage car enthusiasts might care to cast an eye over the Maharana's **Vintage and Classic Car Collection** at the Garden Hotel on Garden Road in the southeast corner of the old city (daily 9am–9pm; Rs100 with free soda pop; Rs150 with veg thali served 11am–3pm & 7–10pm). Models on display include a Rolls-Royce used in the film *Octopussy*. Directly opposite, **Sajjan Niwas Gardens** is a park with a zoo and its own miniature railway, which children might appreciate.

Shilpgram

The road running around the south of Fateh Sagar leads to the rural arts and crafts centre of **Shilpgram** (daily 11am–7pm; Rs25, camera Rs10, video Rs50), near the village of Havala, 5km out from town. Shilpgram was set up by Rajiv Gandhi as a crafts village to promote and preserve the traditional architecture, music and crafts of the tribal people of western India, and holds displays dedicated to the diverse traditional lifestyles and customs of the Subcontinent's rural population. Around thirty replica houses and huts in traditional style are arranged in a village-like compound, with examples of buildings from various states. Musicians, puppeteers and dancers – hijras (see p.67) among them – hang out around the houses and strike up on the approach of visitors (tip expected), while you may also see people weaving, potting and embroidering as they would in their original homes – though most of the actual handicrafts on sale are fifth-rate, if that. Despite its honourable intentions, many tourists find the atmosphere contrived and resent the hustling by musicians and their ilk. Even so, it's well worth a visit if only for the scenic journey out along the road around Fateh Sagar Lake, best done by bicycle. Alternatively, the return journey by auto-rickshaw costs around Rs150 including waiting time.

Sajjangarh (Monsoon Palace)

High on a hill 5km west of the city, the so-called "Monsoon Palace", **Sajjangarh**, was begun in 1883 by Maharana Sajjan Singh to serve as a summer retreat, complete with a nine-storey observatory from which the royal family proposed to watch the monsoon clouds travelling across the countryside below. Unfortunately, the maharana's untimely death the following year put paid to the planned observatory, and although the palace itself was finished by Singh's successor, Maharana Fateh Singh, it was found to be impossible to pump water up to it, and the whole place was abandoned shortly afterwards. The large though rather plain building is now a somewhat melancholy sight, but the views over Udaipur, more than 300m below, are unrivalled. The journey up to the palace takes a good fifteen minutes by rickshaw or taxi (around Rs300 for the round trip); the climb is too steep to tackle comfortably by bicycle, though some people try. The palace is located inside the **Sajjangarh Wildlife Sanctuary** (foreigners Rs80, Indian residents Rs10, plus Rs25 for an auto-rickshaw or Rs65 for car). It's open daily from 8am, with last entry at 5.30pm, although you can come down after sunset.

Royal cenotaphs and Ahar museum

Across the narrow River Ahar, 2km east of Udaipur, domed **cenotaphs** huddle together on the site of the royal cremation ground. The cenotaphs are raised on platforms, some of which are decorated with shiva lingams, although many of the chhatris are falling into disrepair and the site is pretty dirty. Even so, it's a good place to pick up on local history, featuring an ornate memorial to the prodigious builder Jagat Singh (1628–52) and the cenotaph of Amar Singh (d. 1620) who contributed so much to the City Palace, embellished with friezes depicting the immolation of his wives.

Less than 1km south of here, archeological exhibits at the **Ahar Museum** (daily except Fri 10am–5pm; Rs5) include locally unearthed pottery from the Ahar Civilization, which is believed to have come into existence around 2000 BC, making it one of India's earliest cultures. Among more recent statues is a handsome tenth-century Surya image.

Eating, drinking and entertainment

The place to eat in Udaipur has long been the *Lake Palace's* romantic dining terrace. The closest most visitors get to it, however, are the rooftop **restaurants** stacked behind Lalghat and Gangaur Ghat, whose gastronomic shortcomings and generally inflated prices are more than offset by spellbinding views over Lake Pichola to the distant Aravallis. Many of them screen the James Bond movie *Octopussy*, with its manic boat and auto-rickshaw chases around the city's landmarks, every evening at 7pm. Many of them serve beer, but the best place in town for a **drink** is *Ambrai* (see below), though it closes around 10.30pm. Alternatively, *Jagat Niwas* (see below) does an impressive array of cocktails at Rs235 a go.

Live music can be found at many of the more expensive restaurants in town and every day at 7.30pm at the Sunset View Terrace overlooking the boat jetty on Lake Pichola below the *Fateh Prakash Palace* hotel. Bagore-ki-Haveli (see p.322) also has nightly dance performances, while Shilpgram (see opposite) routinely invites out-of-town performers. If you can get together a group, or coincide with one, Rajasthani **folk dances** are staged (usually at 7pm) at the Meera Kala Mandir, Meera Bhawan, Sector 11, on the Ahmedabad Road – call ☎0294/258 3176 to ask about watching a performance.

Restaurants and cafés

Ambrai *Amet Haveli*, Chand Pole. In a super-lative setting facing the City Palace, this is one of the few lakeside restaurants where the cooking lives up to its location. The menu features an extensive selection of North Indian veg and non-veg dishes (including top-notch tandooris), as well as a few Chinese and European offerings. Or just come for a sundowner and watch the sun set over the lake. Non-veg mains Rs165–210.

Edelweiss 71 Gangaur Ghat Marg, next to *Gangaur Palace*. Excellent hole-in-the-wall bakery and pastry shop that receives a steady stream of customers thanks to its tasty home-baked apple pie, chocolate cake and fresh ground coffee.

The Gallery City Palace. Buried away in the innards of the *Fateh Prakash Palace* hotel (just finding it is half the fun), this is Udaipur's most memorable spot for a classic English-style high tea (daily 3–6pm), served either on a sunny terrace overlooking the lake or in the grandiose Durbar Hall (see p.321). Cream teas cost Rs325, or just come for a tea or coffee.

Jagat Niwas 23–25 Lalghat. Popular restaurant in the hotel of the same name, serving up well-prepared North Indian standards (non-veg mains Rs170–235), with nice views over the lake from its comfy window seats and discreet live sitar music.

Kankarwa Haveli 26 Lalghat. The low-key rooftop restaurant at this excellent hotel offers a welcome alternative to your average tourist menu, with a choice of three thalis (Rs200–450) featuring authentic and delicious home-cooked dishes such as sweet aubergine and pumpkin curries. Cold beer and panoramic lake views complete the ambience.

Natraj New Bapu Bazaar (behind Town Hall Rd's Ashok Cinema). Udaipur's top thali joint for over twenty years, but off the tourist trail and hard to find (from Suraj Pol gate, head north up Bapu Bazaar, turn right after 30m, then left, and it's 20m up on your right). Easily the best cheap meal in town – just Rs60 for unlimited portions of veg curries, soups, dhal, curd and chapatis.

Queen Café Chand Pol. This homely and unpreten-tious little café offers a refreshing alternative to Udaipur's mainstream tourist restaurants, with an authentic taste of home-style vegetarian Indian cooking including coconut-flavoured banana, mango and pumpkin curries – all at giveaway prices, with most mains at Rs55–60.

Savage Garden Chand Pol. Stylish restaurant set in an old haveli given a funky modern makeover, with loads of blue and white paint and minimalist decor. Food is Middle Eastern and European, with slight gourmet pretensions, and the menu is short but well chosen. Pasta Rs150–180, mains Rs160–550.

The Whistling Teal *Raj Palace* hotel, 103 Bhattiyani Chohatta. Attractive, tented garden restaurant serving well-prepared North Indian and Rajasthani veg and non-veg dishes from around Rs125 veg, Rs225 non-veg – pricier than average, but worth it. There are also hookah pipes with fruit-flavoured tobacco (Rs250), plus good coffee.

Shopping

Udaipur rivals Jaipur, Pushkar and Jaisalmer as one of Rajasthan's top shopping destinations, with an extremely eclectic array of crafts by artisans from the city and across the state. The city's particular speciality is **miniature painting**, with numerous shops selling traditional Mewari-style works on paper and silk (while a few galleries around town stock more contemporary Indian artworks). Many places also do a good local line in attractive leather- and cloth-bound **stationery** using handmade paper – diaries, notebooks, photo albums and the like. Udaipur is also well known for its **silver jewellery** – Bara Bazaar, running east from the clock tower, is a good place to explore. Generic **Rajasthani crafts** can be found all over town, including plenty of Jaisalmer-style patchwork fabrics, block-printed cloth, wood and stone carvings, and cheap, colourful clothes, while you'll also find plenty of little shops devoted to spices, perfumes and jewellery. The city also has the best selection of **bookshops** in the state (see below).

The obvious place to start looking is the area **around the Jagdish Temple and City Palace**, whose streets are stuffed with hundreds of little shops offering a bewildering array of colourful merchandise, often at bargain prices, especially if you haggle. Outlets become progressively more upmarket as you head south down **Bhattiyani Chohatta** and along **Lake Palace Road** – the latter, in particular, is home to a string of emporiums selling heirloom-quality Hindu bronzes and wood carvings, among many other things. It's also a significantly more relaxed and less traffic-plagued place to shop, and you'll generally suffer less hassle and sales patter. The main courtyard outside the **City Palace** also has a good, though expensive, range of shops, including a small branch of the excellent Jaipur-based Anokhi clothes shop (see p.203), tucked away opposite Toran Pol.

Listings

Airlines Indian Airlines, Sahelion-ki-Bari Rd ⌖0294/241 0999; Jet Airways, airport ⌖0294/265 6288; Kingfisher Airlines, Chetak Circle ⌖0294/510 2468.

Banks and exchange There are ATMs all over the new city, plus a particularly handy 24hr machine on the street leading to the City Palace. Lots of places around Jagdish Temple offer forex. Mewar International (daily 9am–11pm), on Lalghat, changes cash and all brands of travellers' cheques, as well as giving cash advances on Visa and MasterCard. Thomas Cook on Lake Palace Rd (Mon–Sat 9am–6pm) changes cash and travellers' cheques.

Bicycle and motorbike rental Heera Cycle Store at 86 Gangaur Ghat Marg near Jagdish Temple (⌖0294/513 0625; daily 7.30am–9pm), rents out basic bicycles for Rs50/day, and mountain bikes for Rs100/day. They also have mopeds (Rs200/day), Vespas (Rs350/day) and Enfields (Rs450/day); you'll need to bring your passport and leave a hard-currency deposit.

Bookshops Mewar International, on Lalghat behind the Jagdish Temple, has new and secondhand books. Mayur Book Paradise, on another branch of the same alley, is particularly good for secondhand titles, while OK books, a few doors away, isn't bad either. All three sometimes buy or exchange used books.

Cooking lessons Available at numerous places around town. Good options include the *Panorama Guest House* (see p.318; Rs500 for 3hr classes) or, more expensive, the homely little *Queen Café* (see p.325; Rs900 for 3hr).

Horseriding Various places around town offer horseriding expeditions into the surrounding countryside. The reputable *Hotel Kumbha Palace* (see p.317; ⓦ www.krishnaranch.da.ru) runs half- and full-day excursions (Rs950/1800), as well as longer trips. Princess Trails (☎ 0294/309 6909, ⓦ www.princesstrails.com) specializes in more extended, 4- to 8-day safaris on thoroughbred Mewari mounts.

Hospital Aravalli Hospital (private), 332 Ambamata Rd ☎ 0294/243 0222.

Internet access Dozens of places around Lalghat and Gangaur Ghat (going rate currently Rs30/hr). Try Mewar International, on Lalghat near the Jagdish Temple, or the cybercafé on the ground floor of *Udai Niwas* hotel.

Music The enthusiastic Rajesh Prajapat at the Prem Musical Instrument shop (☎ 0294/243 0599), opposite the *Gangaur Palace* hotel, offers sitar and tabla lessons (Rs350 for 90min) and can also arrange flute lessons with his brother, or musical appreciation classes if you just want to learn more about Indian music.

Painting lessons Lessons in traditional Indian painting are offered by many places around town; the *Gangaur Palace* is a reliable option (Rs100/hr).

Palm readings The resident palmist at the *Gangaur Palace* charges Rs300 for a 20min reading.

Photography Mewar International, on Lalghat behind the Jagdish Temple, burn CDs and DVDs, sell memory cards and have equipment to download photos from most types of digital cameras; they also offer back-up and photo recovery from defective memory cards.

Post office Parcels are best sent from the GPO at Chetak Circle (Mon–Sat 10am–4pm).

Travel agents Virtually every shop and guest-house around the Jagdish Temple seems to offer bus and rail ticketing. Reliable agents include Mewar International, on Lalghat behind the Jagdish Temple; Gangaur Tour 'n' Travels, close by on Gangaur Ghat Marg; and the travel agency inside the *Udai Niwas* hotel.

Volunteer work The Animal Aid Society, Badi Village, Across from T.B. Hospital. Main Road ☎ 0294/251 3359, ⓦ www.animalaidunlimited .com, run by a friendly American expat couple, maintains a pet hospital where volunteers and visitors are encouraged and no special skills are required – just a willingness to work with animals, usually including street dogs, cows, donkeys, cats and monkeys.

Yoga Ashtanga Yoga Ashram (aka "Raiba House"), Chand Pol (☎ 0294/252 4872). Daily 90min hatha yoga classes for all standards at 8.30am. Free, but donations appreciated – proceeds go to a local animal charity. Individual lessons also available.

Moving on from Udaipur

By bus

Government buses leave from the main RSTRC bus stand at Udai Pol, with services to Agra (2 daily; 14hr), Ahmedabad (roughly hourly; 7hr), Ajmer (roughly hourly; 7hr), Bikaner (1 nightly; 12hr), Bundi (5 daily; 7hr), Chittaurgarh (roughly half-hourly; 2hr 15min), Delhi (3 daily; 15hr), Jaipur (roughly hourly; 10hr), Jodhpur (10 daily; 9–10hr), Kota (8 daily; 6hr), Mount Abu (4 daily; 7hr) and Pushkar (1 daily; 6hr 30min). Make sure when you buy your ticket that you're booked on an express bus, not a slow passenger service.

Private buses depart from across Town Hall Road, and are a better option for longer and (especially) overnight journeys – most night buses are sleepers. Destinations include Agra (2 nightly; 14hr), Ahmedabad (5 daily; 4–6hr), Ajmer (2 daily; 6hr), Delhi (3 nightly; 13hr), Jodhpur (3 daily; 6hr; one connecting for Jaisalmer), Mount Abu (2 daily; 5hr) and Mumbai (3 nightly; 13hr 30min–15hr 30min). It's easiest to book **tickets** for private buses through one of the many travel agents in town (usually for a modest surcharge of around Rs20). If you want to book your own ticket you'll need to make a reservation with one of the bus-company offices around Udai Pol – try the reliable Kamlesh Travels (☎ 0294/248 5823).

Local buses to destinations such as Nagda, Eklingji, Nathdwara and Kankroli leave regularly from the RSTRC bus stand.

Recommended trains from Udaipur

The following trains are recommended as the fastest or most convenient. Other services may also exist which may take longer, or arrive at inconvenient times, or not run every day. Train timetables change frequently; check latest schedules either at your nearest station or online at ⑭www.indianrail.gov.in before travel.

Destination	Name	No.	Departs	Arrives
Ajmer	Ajmer Express	2991	6.15am daily	11.40am
	Chetak Express	2982	5.20pm Mon/Wed/Fri	10.35pm
Ahmedabad	Ahmedabad Fast Passenger	431	9.35am daily	9.05pm
	Ahmedabad Express	9943	7.45pm daily	4.25am
Bundi	Mewar Express	2964	6.15pm daily	10.46pm
Chittaurgarh	Mewar Express	2964	6.15pm daily	8.30pm
Delhi (Hazrat Nizamuddin)	Mewar Express	2964	6.15pm daily	6.30am
Kota	Mewar Express	2964	6.15pm daily	11.40pm
Sawai Madhopur	Mewar Express	2964	6.15pm daily	1.06am

By train

Train services from Udaipur are surprisingly poor; those listed above are the best of a very bad bunch. There are currently no direct services to Jaipur or Jodhpur (change at Kota), or Mumbai (change at Ahmedabad). You can save a trip to the station by booking tickets through travel agents in town (see "Listings", p.327) for a surcharge of around Rs50–75, which is about what you'd pay for a rickshaw to the station and back.

By air

At the time of writing, flights were being operated out of Udaipur's Dabok Airport by Jet Airways (9W), JetLite (S2), Indian Airlines (IC) and Kingfisher Airlines (IT), with services to **Delhi** (4–5 daily; 1hr 10min–2hr 30min; 9W, IC, IT); **Mumbai** (2–4 daily; 1hr 15min–1hr 55min; 9W, S2, IT, IC); **Jaipur** (1–2 daily; 45min–4hr 30min; 9W, IC, IT, with 9W the fastest, and IT routed via Delhi, making it slow and impractical) and **Jodhpur** (1–2 daily; 40min–1hr; IC, IT). One-way fares usually start at around US$55 to Jodhpur, US$65 to Jaipur, US$70 to Delhi and US$75 to Mumbai – it's worth checking latest fares online with all the relevant airlines. Local contact details are given in the Listings on p.326.

Around Udaipur

North of the city are the historic temples of **Nagda**, **Eklingji**, **Nathdwara** and **Kankroli**, while to the northwest, en route to Jodhpur, lie the superb Jain temples of **Ranakpur** and the rambling fort at **Kumbalgarh**. Renting a car or motorcycle saves time, though local buses serve both routes.

Nagda and Eklingji

Dating back to 626 AD, the ragged remnants of the ancient capital of Mewar, **NAGDA**, stand next to a lake 20km northeast of Udaipur. Buses from Udaipur travelling north along the main road to Eklingji set passengers down at the turn-off for Nagda, conveniently next to a small bicycle rental shop. Nagda itself is a further 1km away down this side-road. Most of the buildings here were either destroyed by the Mughals or submerged by the lake, which has expanded naturally over the centuries. All that survives is a fine pair of tenth-century Vaishnavite temples known as **Saas–Bahu** – literally "mother-in-law" and "daughter-in-law". The more impressive mother-in-law temple has lost its *shikhara* (tower) but preserves a wealth of carving inside, while within the *mandapa* a marriage area is marked by four ornate pillars, bearing images of the gods Brahma, Vishnu, Shiva and Surya to which couples are supposed to pay homage. On the northeast pillar you can make out representations of Sita's trial by fire, a favourite episode from the Ramayana, while scenes from the Mahabharata cover the ceilings. The outer walls of both temples display images of the entire Hindu pantheon, nubile *apsaras* (heavenly maidens), and even a few couples engaged in erotic acts.

Returning to the main road, you can continue to **EKLINGJI** via the road or along a path that leads behind the old protective walls and downhill. Ask for directions at the bike shop. The god **Eklingji**, a manifestation of Shiva, has been the protective deity of the rulers of Mewar ever since the eighth century, when Bappa Rawal was bestowed with the title *darwan* (servant) of Eklingji by his guru. To this day, the maharana of Udaipur still visits the 108-temple complex every Monday evening, the day traditionally celebrated all over India as being sacred to Shiva, when the whole place is usually full of local pilgrims seeking his blessings. The milky-white marble main temple (daily 10.30am–1.30pm & 5–7.30pm) is crowned by an elaborate two-storey *mandapa* guarded by stone elephants; inside, a four-faced black marble lingam marks the precise spot where Bappa Rawal received his accolade. Frequent **buses** leave for Eklingji from Udaipur's main bus stand, dropping passengers off close to the temple. Images of Shiva and his fellow deities, *apsaras* and musicians are etched into the walls both outside and within. The temple had to be rebuilt under Maharana Raimal at the end of the fifteenth century, and again two hundred years later after the ravages of the iconoclastic forces of the Mughal emperor Aurangzeb.

Nathdwara

The temple dedicated to Krishna – known also as **Nath**, the favourite avatar (incarnation) of Vishnu – at **NATHDWARA**, "Gateway to God", is one of the richest temples in India, and gets incredibly crowded during major religious festivals. It dates from the seventeenth century when a chariot laden with an image of Krishna – being carried from Mathura to Udaipur to save it from destruction by Aurangzeb – became stuck in the mud here. Its bearers interpreted the event as a divine sign, establishing the new **Shri Nathji Temple** where it had stopped.

The temple lies about 1km south of the town's bus stop, surrounded by a fascinating tangle of narrow streets where stalls display incense, perfumes and small Krishna statues. The temple opens for worship eight times daily, when the image is woken, dressed, washed, fed and put to bed. Don't miss the radiant *pichwai* paintings in the main sanctuary, made of hand-spun cloth and coloured with strong vegetable pigments. You could also ask a guide to show you the "footsteps of Krishna", a process that requires rubbing rose petals on the marble floor. Nathdwara is on NH-8, and sees a constant flow of buses en route north and south.

Kankroli and Rajsamand

Northeast of Nathdwara, NH-8 winds through another 17km of undulating scrub before reaching **KANKROLI**, 65km from Udaipur. This dusty little market town stands on the shores of the vast **Rajsamand Lake**, whose construction was commissioned by Maharana Raj Singh in the seventeenth century after a terrible drought swept Rajasthan. On the lake's western shore, a few kilometres out of town, is **Nauchowki**, a collection of nine *chowks* (pavilions) erected by Raj Singh on platforms above the steps leading to the water. The **Dwarkadish Temple** overlooking the southern shore houses an image of Krishna installed by Raj Singh in 1676, and has a sanctuary similar to that at Nathdwara. You can buy grain to feed the local flocks of pigeons beside the lake. The best views of the lake are to be had from the **Digambara Jain Temple**, dedicated to Adinath, which crowns a steep hill between Nauchowki and the bus stand. From here you can see the Dwarkadish Temple, Nauchowki, scattered old palaces on the nearby hills, and the Aravalli landscape rolling south as far as the eye can see.

With your own car or a lot of patience (local buses are painfully slow), it's possible to travel from here for two hours on empty country roads to **Kumbalgarh** (see opposite).

Ranakpur

Some 90km north of Udaipur, the spectacular **Jain temples** at **RANAKPUR** boast marble work on a par with that of the more famous Dilwara shrines at Mount Abu (see p.337). The temples are hidden away in a beautiful wooded valley, deep in the Aravalli hills, that was originally given as a gift to the Jain community in the fifteenth century by Rana Kumbha, the Hindu ruler of Mewar.

Arrival and information

Ranakpur is a bumpy **bus** ride from Udaipur (6 daily; 3hr), or from Jodhpur (6 daily; 4–5hr) via the market town of Falna (the nearest railway station) on the NH-14; there are also two daily buses to Abu Road (5–6hr). Buses stop right outside the Jain temples, which are 2–4km from the hotels; if you're lucky, you might find an auto or Jeep at the bus stop – if not, you'll have to ring your hotel and ask to be picked up, or (worst-case scenario) walk.

Ranakpur can also be visited as a day-trip from Udaipur, either on its own or in combination with nearby Kumbalgarh; count on around Rs1200 for the round trip by **car**. If you're intending to visit Kumbalgarh as well, though, think

▲ Jain temple, Ranakpur

about **trekking** between the two sites, a beautiful hike through an unspoilt section of the Aravalli hills. As Kumbalgarh is on the top of the range, it's much easier to hike from there down to Ranakpur (for more on this route see p.333), but guides may be arranged at the hotels listed below for the six-hour uphill climb in the other direction.

Accommodation and eating

You can stay with the Jain pilgrims at the temple complex for a Rs10 donation, but don't expect anything more than a mattress on a cold, cement floor. Other **accommodation** in Ranakpur is relatively expensive. There are no restaurants outside the hotels and guesthouses, and virtually everyone **eats** where they are staying.

Aranyawas 11km from Ranakpur on the Kumbalgarh road ☎02956/239029, ⓦwww .aranyawas.com. Small jungle lodge with rustically elegant rooms and cottages overlooking a watering hole sometimes frequented by leopards – an ideal place to recharge your batteries in complete isolation. Rates include breakfast. ❻

Fateh Bagh 4km south of the temples ☎02934/286186, ⓦwww.hrhindia.com. Ranakpur's best accommodation, a 200-year-old palace transported piece by piece for 50km, and rebuilt here. Rooms are comfy and characterful, and facilities include a pool, spa and Ayurveda centre. Rooms from Rs6600. ❼

Maharani Bagh Orchard 3.5km south of the temples ☎02934/285105, ⓦwww .jodhanaheritage.com. Pleasantly low-key resort, with attractively furnished rooms (all a/c) in

red-brick cottages around rambling gardens. There's also a pool. ❼

Ranakpur Hill Resort 3km south of the temples ☎02934/286411, ⓦwww.ranakpurhillresort.com. Chintzy pink little resort with a range of rooms (air-cooled and a/c) of varying standards, and some less appealing tents (available Oct–March only). Also has a decent-size pool and a small Ayurveda centre, and can arrange half-day horse safaris. Rooms ❺–❻

Shivika Lake Hotel 2km south of the temples ☎02934/285078 or 09929 918419, ⓦwww .shivikalakehotel.com. The only real budget option in Ranakpur, although the cheaper rooms are disappointingly basic given the price; the more expensive rooms (some with a/c) are relatively better value. Local treks (Rs350pp) and Jeep safaris (Rs650pp) can be arranged here. ❸–❹

The temples

The **main temple** (noon–5pm; free, camera or mobile phone with camera Rs50, video Rs100) was built in 1439 according to a strict system of measurement based on the number 72 (the age at which the founder of Jainism, Mahavira, achieved nirvana). The entire temple sits on a pedestal measuring 72 yards square and is held up by 1440 (72 x 20) individually carved pillars. Inside, there are 72 elaborately carved shrines, some octagonal in shape, along with the main deity (a 72-inch-tall image of the four-faced Adinath, the first *tirthankara*) encased in the central sanctum. The carving on the walls, columns and the domed ceilings is superb. Friezes depicting the life of the *tirthankara* are etched into the walls, while musicians and dancers have been modelled out of brackets between the pillars and the ceiling.

Three smaller temples nestle among the trees in the enclosure in front of the main temple. The most impressive is the **Parshwanath Temple**, around 100m from the main temple, with a small but finely carved shrine, while a further 100m walk brings you to the simpler **Neminath Temple**. Close by (a short walk across the car park) is a contemporary Hindu temple dedicated to **Surya**.

Kumbalgarh

The remote hilltop fort of **KUMBALGARH** (daily 8am–5.30pm; foreigners Rs100, Indian residents Rs5), 80km north of Udaipur, is the most formidable of the 32 constructed or restored by Rana Kumbha of Chittaurgarh in the fifteenth

▲ Kumbalgarh Fort

century. Protected by a series of monumental walls and bastions, it was only successfully besieged once, when a confederacy led by Akbar poisoned the water supply. Aside from the fort itself, Kumbalgarh is worth a visit to experience the idyllic Aravalli countryside, dotted with tribal villages, and magnificent views.

The most memorable panorama of all is from the pinnacle of the rather plain **palace** building, crowning the summit of the fort, with striking bird's-eye views over the numerous Jain and Hindu **temples** clustered around the main gate and scattered over the hills below. The oldest are thought to date from the second century; the **tombs** of the great Rana Kumbha himself (murdered by his eldest son) and his grandson Prithviraj (poisoned by his brother-in-law) stand to the east. Some 36km of crenellated ramparts wind around the rim of the hilltop, and it's possible to walk around them in two comfortable days, sleeping rough midway around. You won't need a guide, but be sure to take food and water.

Lining the deep valley that plunges west from the fort down to the plains, the **Kumbalgarh Wildlife Sanctuary** comprises a dense area of woodland that offers a refuge for wolves and leopards. With a local guide, you can trek through it to Ranakpur, a rewarding and easy hike of between four and five hours (the alternative is a long journey on an infrequent country bus). Entry **permits** (foreigners Rs80, Indian residents Rs10, camera Rs200) are obtainable from the District Forest Officer at **Kelwara**, 7km down the road, though local guides – contactable through the hotels listed below, at local shops, or at the café just inside the fort gates – can obtain permits for you, and will charge around Rs600–1000 to do the walk with you, or Rs1500 including entry fees to go round in a Jeep.

Practicalities

Kumbalgarh and Ranakpur can easily be visited as a (longish) day-trip from Udaipur (around Rs1200 for the round trip by taxi for up to four people). Otherwise, take a shared Jeep from Chetak Circle to **Kelwara**, 7km down the road, from where you should be able to pick up a Jeep or rickshaw to Kumbalgarh.

Accommodaton

There's no budget accommodation in Kumbalgarh.

Aodhi 1km below the fort ☏02954/242341, ⓦwww.eternalmewar.in. Peaceful and welcoming heritage hotel with accommodation in stylishly furnished rooms in a cluster of attractive little thatched granite buildings. There's also a big pool and Jeep safaris to local villages (2hr, Rs1550). Rooms cost Rs6600. ❼
Club Mahindra Fort Kumbalgarh 5km along the Kelwara road ☏02954/242625 or 6,

ⓦwww.clubmahindra.com. Recently renovated upmarket modern hotel with superb views from its garden terrace and pool, and marbled a/c rooms. Rates include breakfast. ❼
Kumbhal Castle 1.5km below the fort ☏02954/242171, ⓦwww.thekumbhalcastle.com. Pleasant modern hotel, with spacious and nicely furnished air-cooled and a/c doubles, plus a pool. You can also arrange Jeep and car hire here. ❹–❻

Mount Abu

Rajasthan's only bona fide hill station, **MOUNT ABU** (1220m) is popular with honeymooners who flock here during the winter wedding season (Nov–March), and with holiday-makers from Gujarat, a short distance south across the state border, whose importance to Mount Abu's economic health is evidenced by the signs in Gujarati script which adorn virtually every restaurant and hotel in town. Mount Abu's hokey commercialism is aimed squarely at local vacationers rather than foreign tourists, but the sight of lovestruck honeymooners shyly holding hands and jolly parties of Gujarati tourists on the loose lends the whole place a charmingly idiosyncratic holiday atmosphere quite unlike anywhere else in Rajasthan – and the fresh air is exhilarating after the heat of the desert plains.

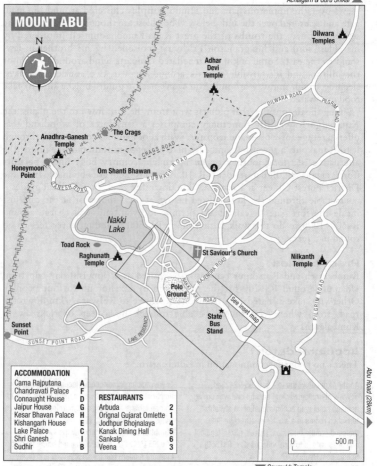

MOUNT ABU

Achalgarh & Guru Shikar ▲

Dilwara
Temples ▲

N

Adhar
Devi
Temple ▲

DILWARA ROAD

PILGRIM ROAD

Anadhra-Ganesh
Temple ▲

The Crags

CRAGS ROAD

Honeymoon
Point ●

Om Shanti Bhawan

SUBHASH ROAD

A

GANESH ROAD

Nakki
Lake

Toad Rock ●

St Saviour's Church ✝

Nilkanth
Temple ▲

Raghunath
Temple ▲

RAJENDRA ROAD

▲

NAKKI LAKE ROAD

Polo
Ground

See inset map

PILGRIM ROAD

Sunset
Point ●

LAKE RESIDENCY

State
Bus
Stand ★

SUNSET POINT ROAD

Abu Road (28km) ▶

ACCOMMODATION
Cama Rajputana	A
Chandravati Palace	F
Connaught House	D
Jaipur House	G
Kesar Bhavan Palace	H
Kishangarh House	E
Lake Palace	C
Shri Ganesh	I
Sudhir	B

RESTAURANTS
Arbuda	2
Orignal Gujarat Omlette	1
Jodhpur Bhojnalaya	4
Kanak Dining Hall	5
Sankalp	6
Veena	3

0   500 m

▼ Gaumukh Temple

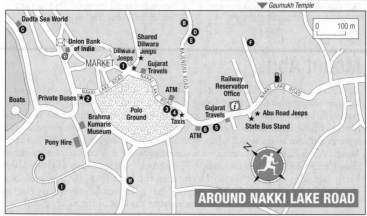

Dadta Sea World ●
C

0   100 m

Union Bank
of India ✉
@

Shared
Dilwara
Jeeps

B
D
E

F

MARKET

Dilwara
Jeeps ★
1

Gujarat
Travels

RAJENDRA ROAD

Railway
Reservation
Office

Boats

Private Buses ★ 2

NAKKI LAKE ROAD

NAKKI LAKE ROAD

ATM

Polo
Ground

3 4 ★
Taxis

NAKKI LAKE ROAD

Gujarat
Travels ⓘ

★ Abu Road Jeeps

Brahma
Kumaris
Museum

6 5 ★
ATM

State Bus Stand

Pony Hire

G

I

H

N

AROUND NAKKI LAKE ROAD

According to Hindu mythology, the focal point of Mount Abu, **Nakki Lake**, was formed when the gods scratched away at the mountain with their fingernails (*nakh*). These days, the waterside is cluttered by far more pedaloes and ice-cream parlours than pilgrims, but the temple marking the site of the famous *yagna agnikund* – a powerful fire ceremony conducted in the eighth century AD, to which Rajasthan's ruling caste, the "twice-born" Rajputs, trace their mythological origins – at Gaumukh, 7km south of Mount Abu, still sees streams of devotees. In addition, around Mount Abu itself, you'll come across many white-clad **Brahma Kumaris**, members of an international spiritual movement whose headquarters are situated in a quiet valley behind the lake.

Note that during the peak months of April to June, and at almost any major festival time (especially Diwali in Nov) the town's population of thirty thousand mushrooms, room rates skyrocket, and peace and quiet are at a premium.

Arrival and information

Mount Abu is accessible only by road. Aim to spend as little time as possible in the grim bazaar town of **Abu Road**, the nearest railhead, where travellers pick up buses for the 45-minute ascent from the plains. Entering Mount Abu itself, you have to pay a Rs10 fee (plus Rs10 for a car or Jeep). Passengers arriving at the main **bus stand**, on Nakki Lake Road in the southeast of Mount Abu, are greeted by hotel touts and luggage porters.

The **tourist office** (Mon–Sat 10am–1.30pm & 2–5pm) is opposite the main bus stand; there's also information online at ⓦ www.mountabu.com. To **change travellers' cheques** the best bet is the Union Bank of India, hidden away in the bazaar near the **post office**. The State Bank of India has an **ATM** in front of the tourist office, and there are two more between there and the polo ground. For **internet** access, the Yani-Ya Cyber Zone, just south of the post office, or the Shree Krishna Cybercafe in the lane just behind Yani-Ya, charge Rs30 per hour.

Horse and pony rides are available from next to the Brahma Kumaris Museum (Rs300/hr), or you can hire various types of boat for a cruise around Nakki Lake from around Rs30 per person for 30 minutes. *Shri Ganesh* guesthouse (see p.336) runs **Jeep tours** (Rs400 for the vehicle for a half-day trip) out to places like Achalgarh and Guru Shikar. *Shri Ganesh* and RSRTC (at the bus stand) both offer tours of the town at Rs80 per head.

Accommodation

The steady stream of pilgrims and honeymoon couples ensures that Mount Abu has plenty of **hotels**, lots of them offering luxuries for newlyweds in special "couple rooms". Checkout time in most places, however, is a chippy 9am. Prices rocket in **high season** (April–June & Nov–Dec), reaching their peak during Diwali.

Cama Rajputana Adhar Devi Rd ☏ 02974/238205, ⓦ www.camahotelsindia.com. Attractive resort-style place occupying a neatly refurbished colonial building in sprawling grounds. Rooms (all a/c) are cool and spacious, while the extensive facilities include a gym, massage centre and a big pool (guests only). Popular with tour groups. ❾

Chandravati Palace 9 Janta Colony ☏ 02974/238219. Excellent and very good-value little guesthouse on a quiet side-road. The small, bright modern rooms are impeccably maintained and have good-sized balconies and hill views. ❶

Connaught House Rajendra Rd ☏ 02974/238560, ⓦ www.jodhanaheritage .com. Mount Abu's most memorable accommodation option, occupying a time-warped colonial-era retreat set in a flower-filled garden with sweeping views. Rooms (all a/c) in the old house are beautifully preserved, with period furniture and decor;

those in the modern block on the hill above are much less atmospheric. ⑦

Jaipur House South of the lake ☎02974/235176, ⓦwww.royalfamilyjaipur.com. A fine old summer palace perched on a hilltop above town, with some of the town's best accommodation in tastefully decorated suites with wooden furnishings – although the "deluxe" rooms, in an ugly modern block halfway down the drive, are dull and overpriced. ⑥

Kesar Bhavan Palace Sunset Rd ☎02974/238647, ⓦwww.kesarpalace.com. Functional modern hotel rather than the promised "palace", though rooms (some with a/c) are pleasantly spacious and sunny, with views over the treetops from large individual verandas. The rooms in the new annexe (same price) are darker and less appealing. ⑥

Kishangarh House Rajendra Rd ☎02974/238092, ⓦwww.royalkishangarh.com. Not as memorable as the neighbouring *Connaught House*, but still offering a modest helping of colonial-era charm. Accommodation is in neatly furnished rooms (mostly a/c) in the old building itself, or in cheaper but fairly characterless "cottage" rooms in a new block outside. ⑥–⑦

Lake Palace Nakki Lake Rd ☎02974/237154, ⓦwww.savshantihotels.com. One of the town's best mid-range options, in a scenic position facing Nakki Lake, with good service and a range of well-maintained modern rooms (all a/c, the more expensive ones with lake view and balcony). ⑥

Shri Ganesh Southwest of the polo ground, near Sophia High School ☎02974/237292, ⓔlalit_ganesh@yahoo.co.in. Easily the best budget hotel in town, and the only one geared to foreign backpackers. There are plenty of simple, clean rooms (some attached, some with very hard beds) plus dorm beds (Rs60–100/person), plus Indian cooking lessons (Rs200), guided walks, Jeep tours (see p.335), reliable internet access, and free pick-up from the bus stand. ①–②

Sudhir Opposite *Connaught House*, Rajendra Rd ☎02974/235120, ⓔhotelsudhir@gmail.com. Functional modern hotel with bright and spacious rooms: choose between the rather bare "semi-deluxe" and the significantly nicer "deluxe" categories. ⑥

The town and around

At the centre of town, **Nakki Lake** is popular in the late afternoon for pony and pedalo rides. **Dadta Sea World**, on the lakeshore by the Lake Palace Hotel (daily 9am–9pm; foreigners Rs50, Indian residents Rs20), contains a few tanks of guppies and goldfish, and an unlabelled collection of seashells, and is worth neither time nor money.

Of several panoramic viewpoints on the fringes of town above the plains, **Sunset Point** is the favourite – though the hordes of holiday-makers and hawkers also make it one of the noisiest and least romantic. **Honeymoon Point**, also known as Ganesh Point (after the adjacent temple), and **Anadhra Point** offer breathtaking

---

Hiking in Mount Abu

Down in Mount Abu's market area, you gain little sense of the wonderfully wild landscape enfolding the town, but head for a few minutes up one of the many trails threading around the sides of the plateau, and it's easy to see why the area has inspired sages, saints and pilgrims for centuries. Unfortunately **hiking alone** is not recommended, as there have been robberies and even murders of unaccompanied visitors, and police will turn back anyone spotted heading out alone. There's also a chance of running into bears and leopards – bears, in particular, can be dangerous if surprised, or when with young.

Two good local **guides** are Lalit Kanojia at the *Shri Ganesh* hotel, who leads 5-hour treks every morning (Rs100/person); and Mahendra Dan, better known as "Charles" (ⓦwww.mount-abu-treks.blogspot.com), who runs a range of half-day (from Rs380) and full-day (from Rs610) walking tours focusing on village life, wildlife spotting and local Ayurvedic plants, as well as overnight camping expeditions. He can be contacted via the *Lake Palace Hotel* or on ☎09414 154854, or emailed on ⓔmahendradan @yahoomail.co.in.

views over the plain at any time of day, and tend to be more peaceful; 4pm is a good time to visit, but don't take clifftop paths between Sunset and Honeymoon points, as tourists have been mugged here.

The **Brahma Kumaris Museum** (daily 8am–8pm; free), between the polo ground and the lake, is devoted to the spiritual ideals of the Brahma Kumaris ("children of Brahma"), whose headquarters are situated nearby. The Brahma Kumaris preach that all religions reach for the same goal, but label it differently. Once through the "Gateway to Paradise", you'll be greeted by freakish, life-sized mannequins including blue monsters wielding long knives. Each personifies a vice such as greed or lust, vestiges of the current "iron age" from which temple leaders promise deliverance. The Brahma Kumaris Spiritual University at Om Shanti Bhawan (☎02974/238268) to the north of Nakki Lake aims to foster awareness, tolerance, love and "God-consciousness" in a meditative atmosphere where smoking, alcohol, meat and sex are avoided. Classes range from three-day raja yoga camps to advanced six-month courses. If it all sounds somewhat cultish you'll understand why many locals try to keep foreigners from entering into the sect's clutches.

Dilwara temples

Jains consider temple-building to be an act of devotion, and their houses of worship are always lovingly adorned and embellished, but even by Jain standards the **Dilwara temples** (daily noon–6pm; free, but donation requested; no photography, leather, phones, radios, tape recorders, or menstruating women), 3km northeast of Mount Abu, are some of the most beautiful in India. All five are made purely from marble, and the carving, especially in the two main shrines, is breathtakingly intricate, unparalleled in its lightness and delicacy. For sheer aesthetic splendour, only the main temple at Ranakpur comes close. Entrance is by guided tour only – you'll have to wait until sufficient people have arrived to make up a

▲ Interior, Vimala Vasahi temple

group – though once inside it's easy enough to slip away and look around on your own and at your own pace.

The oldest temple, the **Vimala Vasahi**, named after the Gujarati minister who funded its construction in 1031, is dedicated to Adinath, the first *tirthankara*. Although the exterior is simple (as, indeed, are the exteriors of all the temples here), not one wall, column or ceiling within is unadorned, a prodigious feat of artistry which took almost two thousand labourers and sculptors fourteen years to complete. There are 48 intricately carved pillars inside, 8 of them supporting a domed ceiling arranged in 11 concentric circles alive with dancers, musicians, elephants and horses, while a sequence of 57 subsidiary shrines runs around the edge of the enclosure. In front of the entrance to the temple the so-called "Elephant Cell" (added after the construction of the temple itself in 1147) contains ten impressively large stone pachyderms. A more modest pair of painted elephants, along with an unusual carving showing stacked-up tiers of *tirthankaras*, flanks the entrance to the diminutive **Mahaveerswami Temple**, built in 1582, which sits by the entrance to the Vimala Vasahi.

The **Luna Vasahi Temple**, second of Dilwara's two great temples, was built in 1231, and is dedicated to Neminath, the 22nd *tirthankara*. It follows a similar plan to the Vimala Vasahi, with a central shrine fronted by a minutely carved dome and surrounded by a long sequence of shrines (a mere 48 this time). The carvings, however, are even more precise and detailed, especially so in the magnificently intricate dome covering the entrance hall. Friezes etched into the walls depict cosmological themes, stories of the *tirthankaras* and grand processions, while sculptures near the entrance porch commemorate the temple's patrons, the two brothers Vastupala and Tejapala. Said in legend to have discovered a huge treasure, they were advised by their wives – also portrayed here – to build temples, and funded many on the holy hill of Shatrunjaya in Gujarat.

The remaining two temples, both fifteenth-century, are less spectacular. The **Bhimasah Pittalhar Temple** houses a huge gilded image of the first *tirthankara*, Adinath, installed in 1468, which measures nearly 2.5km high and weighs in at around 4.5 tonnes. The large three-storey **Khartar Vasahi Temple** (near the entrance to the temples) was built in 1458 and is consecrated to Parshvanath. The temple is topped by a high grey stone tower and boasts some intricate carving in places, though overall it's only a pale shadow of the earlier temples.

To **get to Dilwara**, you can charter a Jeep (Rs50 one way or Rs150 return including waiting time) from the junction at the north end of the polo ground, or take a place in a shared one (Rs5) from just up the street. The hour-long walk up there is also pleasant, though many prefer to save their energy for the downhill walk back into town.

Hindu temples

On the north side of town, en route to the Dilwara temples, a flight of more than four hundred steps climbs up to the **Adhar Devi Temple** (dedicated to Durga). The small main shrine is cut into the rocky hilltop and entered by clambering under a very low overhang. There are fine views from the terrace above, where there's another tiny shrine cut out of solid rock. The milk-coloured water of the **Doodh Baori** well at the foot of the steps is considered to be a source of pure milk (*doodh*) for gods and sages.

A further 8km northeast, the temple complex at **ACHALGARH** is dominated by the **Achaleshwar Mahadeo Temple**, believed to have been created when Lord Shiva placed his toe on the spot to still an earthquake. Its sanctuary holds a yoni with a hole in it that is said to reach into the netherworld. Nearby, the **Jamadagni Ashram** is site of the *yagna agnikund*, where the sage Vashishtha presided over the fire ritual that produced the four Rajput clans (the Parmars, Parihars, Solankis and Chauhans).

The lesser visited, but more dramatically situated, **Gaumukh Temple** lies 7km south of the market area. Reached via a steep flight of 750 steps, the small pool inside the shrine – which continues to flow even during times of drought – is believed to hold water from the sacred Sarawati Ganga River. Pilgrims come here to perform puja, to invoke the blessings of India's two greatest *rishis* (sages), Vashishtha and Vishwamitra, who are thought to have meditated and debated here.

The last important Hindu pilgrimage site on Mount Abu is the Atri Rishi Temple at **Guru Shikar**, 15km northeast of town, which at 1772m above sea level marks the highest point in Rajasthan. You can enjoy superb panoramic vistas either from the temple itself, or from the drinks stall at the bottom of the steps leading up to it. There's no public transport there, however, so you'll have to hire a Jeep (around Rs400).

Eating and drinking

Mount Abu's predominantly middle-class Gujarati visitors are typically hard to please when it comes to food, so standards are exceptionally high and prices low. Meat is fairly rare in Mount Abu; if you get carnivorous cravings, there are a couple of non-veg Punjabi restaurants in the bazaar.

Arbuda Nakki Lake Rd. Perennially popular spot with a huge veggie menu ranging from pizzas, burgers and sandwiches through to Chinese and Indian (mains Rs50–80), as well as good fresh juices. Lightning-fast, friendly service and a popular, airy terrace.

Jodhpur Bhojnalaya Nakki Lake Rd. The best place in town for authentic Rajasthani veg food. It's famous for its *dhal bati churma* (Rs90), but also has the usual list of Indian veg dishes.

Kanak Dining Hall Nakki Lake Rd. Friendly place offering the best Gujarati thalis in town – a superb array of subtly spiced veg delicacies for a very modest Rs90/head. Come hungry – portions are literally limitless. They also have a Punjabi thali (Rs100) and a range of veg dishes.

Orignal Gujarat Omlette Nakki Lake Rd. If you need an eggy snack, omelette sandwiches are Rs30 a go at this little shack opposite the northern tip of the Polo Ground.

Sankalp Nakki Lake Rd. Branch of a South Indian chain offering the usual fare (*iddlis, dosas, uttapams* and the like) in comfortable, modern surrounds, with specialities such as veg pulao (Rs80) or tomato masala uthappa (Rs100), or if you really want to go to town, a 3m-long *dosa* (Rs500).

Veena Nakki Lake Rd. Open-air seating next to the main road. Brightly lit and can be kind of tacky when it's got the latest *filmi* hits blaring out, but the fast food is second to none and they have a welcome open fire on the terrace most evenings. Try a tangy *pau bhaji* (Rs50–70) or melt-in-the-mouth *dosas* (Rs50–85).

Moving on from Mount Abu

Government buses run from the State Bus Stand on Nakki Lake Road. **Private buses** are run by a string of operators along Nakki Lake Road west of the State Bus Stand (Gujarat Travels is a reliable option). There are currently private services to Ajmer (1 nightly; 7hr), Ahmedabad (3 daily; 6hr), Jaipur (1 nightly; 11hr), Jodhpur (1 daily; 6hr) and Udaipur (3 daily; 5hr).

There's a computerized **train booking office** (daily 8am–2pm) upstairs at the tourist office. Buses leave Mount Abu for **Abu Road**, the nearest railhead, every hour until 9pm; Jeeps leave when full (from next to the bus stand), and taxis can be hired at the corner by the *Jodhpur Bhojnalaya* restaurant for Rs300.

Recommended trains from Abu Road

Destination	Name	No.	Departs	Arrives
Ahmedabad	Ahmedabad Express	9224	11am (daily)	3.30pm
	Ahmedabad Mail	9106	12.47pm (daily)	6.40pm
Ajmer	Aravalli Express	9707	10.10am (daily)	4.05pm
	Haridwar Mail	9105	2.15pm (daily)	8.20pm
Delhi	Rajdhani Express*	2957	8.33pm	7.25am
	Ashram Express	2915	9.13pm (daily)	10.10am
Jaipur	Aravalli Express	9707	10.10am (daily)	6.40pm
	Haridwar Mail	9105	2.15pm (daily)	10.40pm
Jodhpur	Jammu Tawi Express	9223	3.20pm (daily)	8pm
Mumbai	Aravalli Express	9708	5.20pm (daily)	6.45am
	Surya Nagri Express	2479	11.07pm (daily)	11.45am

Chittaurgarh, Kota and Bundi

The belt of hilly land east of Udaipur is the most fertile in Rajasthan, watered by several perennial rivers and guarded by a sequence of imposing forts perched atop the craggy ridges that crisscross the region. Heading east, the first major settlement is the historic town of **Chittaurgarh**, capital of the kingdom of Mewar before Udaipur and site of one of Rajasthan's most spectacular and historic forts. Further east, the tranquil town of **Bundi** boasts another atmospheric fort and picturesque old bazaars and havelis, while an hour away by bus, **Kota** is home to another impressive palace, if not much else.

A prime crop in this area for centuries has been **opium**. Although grown for the pharmaceutical industry according to strict government quotas, the legal cultivation masks a much larger illicit production overseen by Mumbai drug barons. An estimated one in five men in the area are addicts.

Chittaurgarh and around

Of all the former Rajput capitals, **CHITTAURGARH** (or Chittor), 115km northeast of Udaipur, was the strongest bastion of Hindu resistance against the Muslim invaders. No less than three mass suicides (*johars*) were committed over the centuries by the female inhabitants of its **fort**, whose husbands watched their wives, sisters and mothers burn alive before smearing ash from the sacred funeral pyres over their bodies and riding to their deaths on the battlefield below. An air of desolation still hangs over the honey-coloured ramparts, temples, towers and ruined palaces of the old citadel. It seems impossible that such an imposing structure, towering 180m over the Mewar valley on a rocky plateau, could have ever been taken, but it fell three times. As a symbol of Rajput chivalry and militarism only Jodhpur's Meherangarh Fort compares.

Below the fort, the modern **town**, spread over both banks of the River Ghambiri, holds little to detain travellers beyond the narrow bazaars of its old quarter, and some tourists choose to squeeze a tour of Chittaurgarh into a day-trip, or en route between Bundi and Udaipur. A one-night stop, however, leaves time for a more leisurely visit to the fort and a stroll through the town.

Some history

The origins of Chittor fort are obscure. According to legend it was founded by Bhim, one of the Pandava heroes of the Mahabharata, although it probably

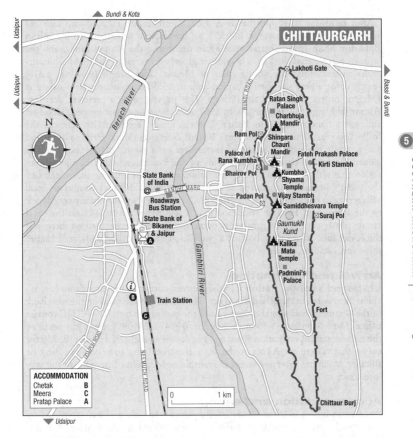

Map labels (Chittaurgarh):

Bundi & Kota

Udaipur

Udaipur

Udaipur

CHITTAURGARH

Bassi & Bundi

Lakhoti Gate

Ratan Singh Palace

Charbhuja Mandir

Bundi Road

Ram Pol

Shingara Chauri Mandir

Fateh Prakash Palace

Palace of Rana Kumbha

Kirti Stambh

Bhairov Pol

Kumbha Shyama Temple

Padan Pol

Vijay Stambh

Samiddhesvara Temple

Gaumukh Kund

Suraj Pol

Kalika Mata Temple

Padmini's Palace

Fort

Chittaur Burj

State Bank of India

GANDHI MARG

Roadways Bus Station

State Bank of Bikaner & Jaipur

Berach River

Gambhiri River

N

Train Station

NEEMUCH ROAD

LALGARH ROAD

ACCOMMODATION
Chetak   B
Meera   C
Pratap Palace A

0   1 km

Udaipur

actually dates from around the 7th century. The fort was seized by **Bappa Rawal**, founder of the Mewar dynasty, in 734, and remained the Mewar capital thereafter for the next 834 years, bar a couple of brief interruptions.

Despite its commanding position and formidable appearance, however, Chittor was far from invincible, as proved by the three catastrophic attacks that blighted the city's later history and led to its eventual abandonment. The first sack of Chittor occurred in 1303, during the reign of **Rana Ratan Singh**, a devastating attack launched by **Ala-ud-Din Khalji**, the fiercest of the Delhi sultans. Having besieged the city, he offered to withdraw on condition that he be allowed a glimpse of Ratan's famously beautiful queen, **Padmini**. After he was admitted alone into the palace to view the queen's reflection in a lake, however, the sultan contrived to have Ratan ambushed just as he was showing him out of the door. Padmini devised a plan to recapture her husband. Sending word that she would give herself up to the sultan, the queen left the fort accompanied by troops disguised as maids of honour. Once inside the Muslim camp the sari-clad commandos unveiled themselves and managed to rescue Rana Ratan, but seven thousand of them were killed in the process. As a result, the defence of the fort foundered and the Rajputs lost the ensuing battle. Thirteen thousand women, led by Padmini, committed *johar* by throwing themselves and their children onto a huge funeral pyre, whereupon the angry sultan destroyed most of the fort's temples and palaces.

After returning to Rajput hands in 1326, Chittaurgarh enjoyed two hundred years of prosperity. However, in 1535, an unexpected onslaught led by **Sultan Bahadur Shah** from Gujarat once again decimated the Rajput ranks, and the women surrendered their lives in another ghastly act of *johar*. Aware of Chittaurgarh's vulnerability, the young ruler of Mewar **Udai Singh** (see box, p.316) searched for a new site for his capital and, in 1559, established a new palace at Udaipur on the shore of Lake Pichola. This proved to be a prescient decision. **Akbar** laid siege to Chittaurgarh in 1567 and, after one of the longest, bloodiest and most famous sieges in Indian history, finally breached its defences the following year. Once more the fort's Rajput defenders sallied forth to death and glory, while the women sacrificed themselves on a raging pyre. Having finally gained the fort, Akbar devastated many of the buildings within it, and – in an action that rather undermines his reputation as the most humane and tolerant of the great Mughals – massacred at least twenty thousand non-combatant local villagers who had sought refuge within it. Chittaurgarh was eventually ceded back to the Rajputs in 1616 on condition that it was never refortified, but the royal family of Mewar, by now firmly ensconced in Udaipur, never resettled there, and the entire fort, which once boasted a population of many thousands, now houses just a few hundred people.

Arrival and information

Chittaurgarh's **railway station** is in the western corner of the city. From here it's about 2km north to the **Roadways** (aka "**Kothwali**") **Bus Stand** on the west bank of the Ghambiri, and a further 2km east to the base of the fort. The RTDC **tourist office** (Mon–Sat 10am–1.30pm & 2–5pm; ☎01472/241089) stands just north of the railway station on Station Road and has details of registered guides (Rs230 for up to 4hr). There are **ATMs** at the State Bank of India and the State Bank of Bikaner & Jaipur. **Internet** access is available at Megavista Internet, on the way into town.

Accommodation and eating

Accommodation in Chittor is relatively pricey; the only really cheap places are the slightly grim hotels around the train station and in the middle of town, though there are a couple of good heritage hotels nearby at Bassi, 24km to the east (see p.345). You'll probably end up **eating** where you're staying, unless you fancy trying one of the rough-and-ready *dhabas* in the town centre or around the train station.

Chetak Neemuch Rd, immediately outside the railway station ☎01472/245192. Passable budget option, with spotless modern rooms (though avoid the noisy ones next to the main road) and a busy little restaurant downstairs. ❸–❹

Meera Neemuch Rd ☎01472/240266. The best budget option in town, with a wide selection of fan and a/c rooms, a dorm (Rs150) and some very quirkily decorated suites; facilities include an inexpensive restaurant and a good bar. ❷–❸

Pratap Palace Opposite the GPO on Shri Gurukul Rd ☎01472/240099, ✆www.bijaipurhotels.com. Functional mid-range hotel – a bit shabby in places, but with an attractive garden and good food. The smarter deluxe rooms are the nicest in town (though rather expensive); the cheaper rooms are relatively unappealing and overpriced. They can also arrange countryside tours starting from *Castle Bijaipur* (see p.345). ❺–❻

The fort

The entire fort is 5km long and 1km wide, and you could easily spend a whole day up here nosing around the myriad remains, although most visitors content themselves with a few hours. **Tours** of the fort are most easily made by auto-rickshaw (Rs200 for around 3hr); many hang out at the bus station awaiting tourists, though note that drivers tend to take visitors to only the most famous monuments rather than around the entire fort, unless specifically requested. An alternative is to just take an auto up to the entrance, and then explore on foot or, perhaps best, to rent a **bike** from the shop on the road leading west from the crossroads outside the station. It's a long, steep climb up to the fort, but most of the roads on the plateau itself are flat.

The Palace of Rana Kumbha to the Kumbha Shyama temple

The ascent to the fort (daily 7am–6pm; foreigners Rs100, Indian residents Rs5; plus Rs5/rickshaw), protected by massive bastions, begins at **Padan Pol** in the east of town and winds upwards through a further six gateways.About 100m uphill from the second gateway, Bhairov Pol, stand the memorial chhatris of Jaimal and his cousin Kalla, who carried the injured Jaimal piggyback into battle in the final sacking of 1568. The houses of the few people who still inhabit the fort are huddled together near the final gate, Rama Pol, where you buy your ticket.

Entering the fort, you first reach the slowly deteriorating fifteenth-century **Palace of Rana Kumbha** (reigned 1433–68), built by the ruler who presided over the period of Mewar's greatest prosperity on the spot where Padmini (see p.341) is said to have committed *johar* in 1303. The main palace building still stands five storeys high, though it's difficult now to make much sense of the confusing tangle of partially ruined walls, cupolas and towers which surround it, the general dereliction concealing a few finely carved balconies, pillars and friezes. Opposite the palace stands the intricately carved fifteenth-century **Shingara Chauri Mandir**, dedicated to Shantinath, the sixteenth *tirthankara*, a small but lavishly adorned Jain temple, though many of the faces around the main door have been obliterated, possibly by Islamic iconoclasts. Another, even smaller, Jain temple stands directly behind.

Nearby, the modern **Fateh Prakash Palace**, a large, plain edifice built for the maharana in the 1920s, is home to a small **archeological museum** (daily except Fri 10am–5pm; Rs10), filled with a forgettable display of weapons, costumes and pictures, plus a fine array of Jain and Hindu carvings recovered from various places around the fort.

A couple of hundred metres further on lies the imposing **Kumbha Shyama Temple**, the first of several superb Hindu temples which dot the fort and another creation of Rana Kumbha, after whom it's named. Crowned by a pyramidal roof and lofty tower, with every interior and exterior surface embellished in a riot of carved decoration, this marvellously ornate structure wouldn't look out of place among the famous temples of Khajuraho in Madhya Pradesh, and its sinuous, purely Indian outlines offer a striking architectural contrast to the more Islamic-influenced styles of the fort's palace buildings. A black statue of Garuda stands in its own pavilion in front of the shrine, while an image of Varaha, the boar incarnation of Vishnu, occupies a niche at the rear of the temple, surrounded by an open-side ambulatory from where there are fine views back to Rana Kumbha's palace. A second shrine stands close by within the small walled enclosure, also constructed by Rana Kumbha and dedicated to **Meerabai**, a Jodhpur princess and poet famed for her devotion to Krishna – smaller but almost equally finely decorated, with a similarly delicate curved tower.

The Vijay Stambh and beyond

The main road within the fort continues south to its focal point, **Vijay Stambh**, the soaring "tower of victory", erected by Rana Kumbha to commemorate his 1440 victory over the Muslim Sultan Mehmud Khilji of Malwa. This magnificent sand-coloured tower, whose nine storeys rise 36m, took a decade to build; its walls are lavishly carved with mythological scenes and images from all Indian religions, as well as Arabic inscriptions in praise of Allah. You can climb the dark narrow stairs to the very summit for free.

The area around the Vijay Stambh is littered with an impressive number of further remains, including a pair of monumental gateways and a number of florid temples, including the superb **Samiddhesvara Temple**, its *shikhara* tower honeycombed with deeply incised, geometrical carvings, while a frieze of busty celestial nymphs runs around the walls and a statue of a lion sits guard on the roof. The shrine inside houses an image of the three-headed *trimurti*, a composite, three-headed image of Shiva, Brahma and Vishnu. A path leads from here down to the **Gaumukh Kund**, a large reservoir fed by an underground stream that trickles through carved mouths (*mukh*) of cows (*gau*) and commands superb views across the plains. On the other side of the enclosure, clusters of small chhatris and red-painted stones commemorate some of the acts of *sati* performed by women of the fort.

Buildings further south include the **Kalika Mata Temple**, originally dedicated to Surya in the eighth century, but rededicated to the Mother Goddess, Mahadevi, after renovations in 1568. Carvings on the outer wall include a frieze depicting the churning of the ocean by the gods and demons, a popular creation myth, and (next to it) another image of Varaha, the boar-headed incarnation of Vishnu. Some 200m beyond the Kalika Mata Temple lies **Padmini's Palace**, its rather plain buildings enclosing a series of attractive little walled gardens leading to a tower overlooking the small lake in which Ala-ud-Din Khalji was allegedly allowed to glimpse the reflection of the beautiful princess after whom the palace is named (see p.341).

The road continues south past the deer park to the point once used for hurling traitors to their deaths, and returns north along the eastern ridge to **Suraj Pol** gate, with spectacular vistas across a patchwork of farmland. Several temples line the route, but the most impressive monument is **Kirti Stambh**. The inspiration for the tower of victory, this smaller "tower of fame" was built by Digambaras as a monument to the first *tirthankara* Adinath, whose unclad image appears throughout its six storeys.

Moving on from Chittaurgarh

There are **buses** to Ajmer (7 daily; 5hr), Udaipur (roughly hourly; 2hr 30min) and Kota (2 daily; 4hr 30min), but no direct buses to Bundi – to get there (and usually to Kota), take a bus to Bhilwara, and another one from there. Recommended **trains** are listed in the box below.

Recommended trains from Chittaurgarh

Destination	Name	No.	Departs (daily)	Arrives
Ajmer	Udaipur–Ajmer Express	2991	8.42am	11.40am
	Ratlam–Ajmer Express	9653	10.10am	1.55pm
Bundi	City Link Express	9019A	2.55pm	5.10pm
	Mewar Express	2964	8.50pm	10.46pm
Delhi (Hazrat Nizamuddin)	Mewar Express	2964	8.50pm	6.30am
Jaipur	Gwalior Superfast	2966	12.35am	6am
Kota	Nimach–Kota Express	9019A	2.55pm	6.05pm
Udaipur	Mewar Express	2963	5.05am	7.20am
	Ajmer–Udaipur Express	2992	7.15pm	9.20pm

Bassi and around

The small town of **BASSI**, 24km east of Chittaurgarh, doesn't have much in the way of tourist sights, but is known for its *kavads* – little painted boxes that unfold to make a miniature temple with a shrine in the middle and illustrated scenes from Hindu mythology (usually the Ramayana or the Mahabharata) on the surrounding panels. Originally used by itinerant storytellers to illustrate their tales, they make novel and colourful souvenirs, and are sold all over Rajasthan, though best bought, of course, at source. Bassi's fort has been transformed into the *Bassi Fort Palace* (T01472/225321, Wwww.bassifortpalace .com; ➏), a heritage hotel with sixteen comfortable rooms and spacious grounds where a sacred tree is believed to grant wishes. There's another attractive heritage hotel in a 350-year-old castle in a tranquil and unspoilt rural location 18km south in Bijapur, *Castle Bijaipur* (T01472/240099, Wwww .bijaipurhotels.com; bed and breakfast ➏–➒), whose rooms are decorated with traditional Rajasthani wooden furniture and artefacts, and there's a pool, Ayurvedic massages, daily group yoga and meditation sessions (and individual tuition on request), plus cycle, Jeep and horse safaris to nearby villages. They also have tented accommodation (➐) a few kilometres away in an even more remote rural location at Pangarh Lake. Both Bassi and Bijapur are connected with Chittor by regular local bus services.

Bundi

The walled town of **BUNDI**, 37km north of Kota, lies in the north of the former Hadaoti state, shielded by jagged outcrops of the Vindhya Range. The site was the capital of the Hadachauhans, but although settled in 1241, 25 years before Kota, Bundi never amounted to more than a modest market centre, and remains relatively untouched by modern developments. The palace alone justifies a visit thanks to its superb collection of **murals**, while the well-preserved **old town**, crammed with crumbling havelis, makes this one of southern Rajasthan's most appealing destinations – a fact recognized by the ever-increasing numbers of foreign tourists.

Arrival and information

Buses arrive in the southeast part of town near the post office, from where it's around Rs30 by auto-rickshaw to the palace and guesthouses; the train station is around 5km south of town (Rs50 or so by auto-rickshaw). Bundi's **tourist office** (Mon–Fri 9.30am–6pm; T0747/244 3697) is south of town near the Circuit House. You can **change money** at Pandey Forex, about 100m south of the palace, and at the *Kasera Heritage* guesthouse; there are also several **ATMs** in the southern end of town (see the map on p.346 for locations). Dozens of places offer **internet** access for around Rs40 per hour, while lots of places also rent out **motorbikes** (around Rs250/day), and a few also have **bicycles** (around Rs30/day; try GM Cycle Repairs in the bazaar).

If you're in the area around mid-November try to arrive for the annual **Bundi Festival**, a celebration of Hadaoti heritage with a very local, country-fair feel.

Accommodation and eating

Much of Bundi's **accommodation** is in old havelis, with a wide range of standards and prices. Most people **eat** where they're staying. To eat out, the *Bundi Haveli* (see p.346) has a good rooftop restaurant (non-veg mains Rs175–260) and real coffee in a stylishly laidback setting, while the terrace at the *Royal Retreat* (see p.347) has fine town views and is a great spot for a sundowner.

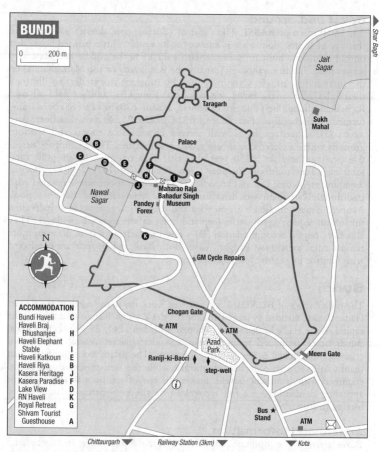

BUNDI

▶ *Shar Bagh*

Jait Sagar

Taragarh

Sukh Mahal

Ⓐ Ⓑ
Ⓒ Ⓓ Ⓔ Ⓕ Ⓖ
Ⓗ Ⓘ
Ⓙ

Palace

Maharao Raja Bahadur Singh Museum

Nawal Sagar

Pandey Forex

Ⓚ

GM Cycle Repairs

Chogan Gate

ATM

ATM

Azad Park

Ranjit-ki-Baori ♦

step-well

Meera Gate

ⓘ

Bus ★ Stand

ATM

N

0   200 m

ACCOMMODATION

Bundi Haveli	C
Haveli Braj Bhushanjee	H
Haveli Elephant Stable	I
Haveli Katkoun	E
Haveli Riya	B
Kasera Heritage	J
Kasera Paradise	F
Lake View	D
RN Haveli	K
Royal Retreat	G
Shivam Tourist Guesthouse	A

Chittaurgarh ▼   *Railway Station (3km)* ▼   ▼ *Kota*

Bundi Haveli ⓣ 0747/244 6716, ⓦ www .bundihotel.com. Traditional old haveli given a stylish contemporary makeover, with beautifully furnished rooms (most with a/c), a good restaurant and facilities including internet access and money exchange. Excellent value at current rates. ④–⑥

Haveli Braj Bhushanjee ⓣ 0747/244 2322, ⓦ www.kiplingsbundi.com. Wonderfully atmospheric 150-year-old haveli, with original murals, antiques and assorted artworks adorning virtually every surface. Rooms (some with a/c and TV) are similarly engaging, and immaculately maintained. ④–⑦

Haveli Elephant Stables ⓣ 09928 154064, ⓔ elephantstable_guesthouse@hotmail.com. Accommodation in the palace's former elephant stables, a pretty and very peaceful spot underneath the fort's huge walls. Rooms are fairly basic, but at this price and in this location you can't really complain. ①–②

Haveli Katkoun ⓣ 0747/244 4311, ⓦ havelikatkoun.free.fr. Former budget guesthouse, now revamped with marble floors and a range of spacious and smart modern rooms, the best of which have a/c and palace views. ③–⑤

Haveli Riya ⓣ 0747/244 4211. Friendly family guesthouse with a selection of rooms at bargain prices, some a little basic, but all neat and clean, and there's a nice little rooftop café. ①–②

Kasera Paradise ⓣ 0747/244 4679, ⓦ www .kaseraparadise.com. Tucked away in a peaceful little lane just behind the *Braj Bhushanjee*, this attractive guesthouse occupies a meticulously restored sixteenth-century haveli with a range of variously priced a/c rooms, all nicely furnished and decorated with traditional murals. There's a slightly wider variety of rooms in the same owner's *Kasera Heritage* (②–⑥), just over the road. ②–⑤

Lake View ☎0747/244 2326, ✉lakeviewbundi
_@yahoo.com. Scruffy guesthouse in an old lakeside
haveli, not the cleanest place in town, but compensates with cheap rates and a fine terrace overlooking
Nawal Sagar. The cheap garden rooms are pretty
basic; the more expensive ones in the haveli itself
have faded old murals and lake views. ❶–❷

RN Haveli ☎0747/512 0098, ✉rnhavelibundi
@yahoo.co.in. Friendly, homely and deservedly
popular female-run guesthouse in a 200-year-old
haveli, where the rooms are simple but decent, and
the home-cooked meals are excellent. ❶–❷

Royal Retreat ☎0747/244 4426, ✉royalretreat
bundi@yahoo.com. Just four comfortable rooms
(all air-cooled) in a superb and peaceful location in
the lower part of the palace complex – although
the place can feel a mite lonely after dark,
especially if there's no one else staying. There's
decent food in the terrace restaurant. ❷–❸

Shivam Tourist Guesthouse ☎0747/244 7892,
✉shivam_pg@yahoo.com. Extremely sociable little
family guesthouse with friendly management, six
clean and pleasantly decorated attached rooms,
and good home cooking. ❶–❹

The Palace

Soaring over the northern end of the bazaar, Bundi's **palace** (daily 8am–6pm;
Rs60; camera Rs50, video Rs100) was one of the few royal abodes in Rajasthan
untouched by Mughal influence, and its appearance is surprisingly homogeneous
considering the number of times it was added to over the years. If you want a
guide, the extremely informative Keshav Bhati (☎09414 394241, ✉bharat_bhati
@yahoo.com) charges around Rs250 for a tour of the entire palace, and also offers
visits to local rock-painting sites and of Kota.

A short steep path winds up to the main gateway, **Hathi Pol**, surmounted by
elephant carvings, beyond which lies the palace's principal courtyard. On the
right-hand side, steps lead up to the **Ratan Doulat**, the early seventeenth-century
Diwan-i-Am, or Hall of Public Audience, an open terrace with a simple marble
throne overlooking the courtyard below.

At the far end of the Ratan Daulat, further steps lead up to the *zenana* (women's
quarters), entered via the **Chhatra Mahal**, centred on a small courtyard with a
marble pool at its centre and fine views over the town and its numerous blue
houses, which looks a bit like a miniature Jodhpur from this angle; you can also
make out the **Nawal Sagar** tank with its half-submerged temple. Go through the
open-sided turquoise-painted pavilion on the southern side of the courtyard and
the room beyond to reach a superb little **antechamber** (usually described as a
"dressing room"). This is one of the most beautiful rooms in the palace, every
surface covered in finely detailed murals from the 1780s, embellished with gold
and silver leaf, including scenes showing Krishna playing his flute amid cows and
gopis; a spectacular procession with hundreds of horses, soldiers and some superb
elephants; scenes of courtly life; and (in a niche by the window) a stirring battle
scene. The opposite side of the courtyard is flanked by a pavilion with columns
supported on the backs of quaint black trumpeting elephants, at the back of which
you'll find a well-preserved old squat toilet (still in occasional use, judging by the
smell), offering possibly the best view from any public convenience in Rajasthan.

From the Chhatra Mahal courtyard, a narrow flight of steps leads up to the
Phool Mahal (1607, though the murals date from the 1860s), with an even smaller
courtyard flanked by another superbly decorated room, its murals including a vast
procession featuring regiments of soldiers in European dress, a camel corps and yet
more elephants and horses. From here further narrow steps ascend to the **Badal
Mahal** (Cloud Palace; also built 1607, though the murals date from the 1640s),
home to what are often regarded as the finest paintings in Bundi, if not the whole
of southern Rajasthan. A vividly coloured ring of Krishnas and Radhas dances
around the highest part of the vaulted dome, flanked in the two subsidiary domes
by murals showing Krishna being driven to his wedding by Ganesh, and Rama
returning from Sri Lanka to Ayodhya following the battle against Ravana

described in the Ramayana; the god is shown travelling through the sky in his air-chariot, borne on the shoulders of four winged angels, while Hanuman looks on, brandishing a palm frond. The ten human and animal avatars (incarnations) of Vishnu are shown around the base of the dome.

The Chhitra Sala

There are further outstanding murals in the **Chhitra Sala** (sunrise–sunset; free), just above the palace (to reach it, exit the palace, go downhill for 20m then head up the signed ramp on your left, up the hill and in past the sign saying VEDIOGRAPHY PROBIBIRED). At the rear left-hand corner of the garden inside, steps lead up to a small courtyard embellished with an outstanding sequence of murals painted in an unusual muted palette of turquoises, blues and blacks. The main panels are devoted to scenes from the life of Krishna, with successive murals showing the divine young shepherd boy dancing in a ring with the *gopis* (while various deities hover overhead in floating palanquins); lifting Mount Goverdhan with the little finger of his fourth arm while simultaneously playing the flute and brandishing a lotus; and sitting in a tree playing his flute after having stolen the clothes of the *gopis*, who splash around in the river below. On the opposite wall is a fine mural showing a panorama of eighteenth-century Bundi, with a stylized map on the right.

A steep, twenty-minute climb up from the Chhitra Sala, the monkey-infested **Taragarh** offers even more spectacular views over Bundi, its palace and the surrounding countryside.

The rest of the town

Right in the centre of town, the recently opened **Maharao Raja Bahadur Singh Museum** (daily: April–Sept 9am–1pm & 2–6pm, Oct–March 9am–1pm & 2–5pm; Rs50, camera Rs50) houses a skull-crackingly tedious collection of self-congratulatory portraits of assorted maharajas of Bundi, plus a gallery of

▲ Shopping in Bundi

stuffed tigers and other dumb animals massacred in the name of sport by notables ranging from Lord Mountbatten to Haile Selassie. Save your cash.

On the south side of town is the much more rewarding **Raniji-ki-Baori** (no set hours), one of Rajasthan's most spectacular step-wells. Built in 1699, the well is reached by a flight of steps punctuated by platforms and pillars embellished with sinuous S-shaped brackets and elephant capitals. As you descend, look for the beautifully carved panels showing the ten avatars of Lord Vishnu, which line the side walls. A **second step-well** sits next to the road immediately to the east – impressively deep, but now choked with rubbish.

Northeast of the town on the southern shore of Jait Sagar tank is the pretty but now rather neglected **Sukh Mahal** – Rao Raja Vishnu Singh's summer palace – where Rudyard Kipling (who stayed here for a few months at the invitation of the raja) wrote parts of *Kim* and the *Jungle Book*. The building itself is closed to visitors but it's a pleasant spot, and you can walk for a short distance along the lakeshore on either side of the palace. Some 1.5km further along the side of the lake, **Shar Bagh** encloses sixty crumbling royal cenotaphs. If the door is locked, ask for the key at the chowkidar's hut on your left just after the gateway over the main road some 100m north of the cenotaphs. Count on around Rs80 return by auto from town to Sukh Mahal, or Rs120 to Shar Bagh.

Moving on from Bundi

Heading south, there are regular buses to **Kota** (every 30min; 45min–1hr), and two evening trains: 39019A Kota Express (departs 5.12pm, arrives 6.05pm) and #1771 Haldighati Passenger (departs 5.50pm, arrives 7.30pm). The same trains run the other way to **Chittaurgarh** in the morning at 7.15am (#1772 Haldighati Passenger, arriving 10.35am) and 9.38am (#9020A Dehra Dun Express, arriving 12.05pm). No buses run direct to Chittaurgarh, but there are plenty to Bhilwara, and from there to Chittor. There are four buses daily to Udaipur (7–8hr), but the only train is the #2963 Mewar Express, which currently passes through Bundi at 2.02am nightly, arriving in Udaipur at 7.20am.

Heading north, there are buses to **Sawai Madhopur** (for Ranthambore National Park; 4 daily; 4hr 30min); alternatively, take a bus to Kota and a train from there (see p.352 for details). Buses are the best way of reaching **Ajmer** (every 20min; 4hr), **Jaipur** (every 20min; 5hr) and **Jodhpur** (5 daily; 10hr).

Kota

KOTA, 230km south of Jaipur on a fertile plain fed by Rajasthan's largest river, the Chambal, is one of the state's dirtier and less appealing cities. With a population nudging 700,000, it is one of Rajasthan's major commercial and industrial hubs, with hydro, atomic and thermal power stations lining the banks of the Chambal, alongside Asia's largest fertilizer plant, whose enormous chimneys provide a not-very-scenic backdrop to many views of the town. Kota is worth a visit if only for its city palace, which houses one of the better museums in Rajasthan, while the old town has a commercial hustle and bustle which makes a nice contrast to somnolent Bundi, just down the road.

Greatly prized **saris** from the village of **Kaithoon**, 20km southeast of Kota, are sold in all the bazaars. Made of tightly woven cotton or silk, and often highlighted with golden thread, they are known here as *masooria* and elsewhere as *Kota doria* saris.

Arrival and information

Kota's **railway station** is in the north of town, a few kilometres from the central **bus stand** on Bundi Road. The **tourist office** (Mon–Fri 9am–5pm; ☎0744/232 7695) is in the RTDC *Chambal Hotel*, just north of the Kishor Sagar. The best place for

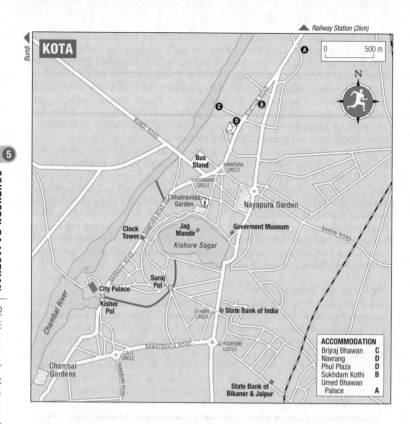

Railway Station (2km)

KOTA

0   500 m

N

Bundi

BUNDI ROAD

STATION ROAD

Bus
Stand

NAYAPURA
CIRCLE

VIVEKANAND
CIRCLE

Chhatravilas
Garden

Nayapura Garden

Clock
Tower

Jag
Mandir

Goverment Museum

BARAN ROAD

Kishore Sagar

Suraj
Pol

City Palace

Kishor
Pol

CHAWNI
CIRCLE

State Bank of India

Chambal River

RAWATBHATA ROAD

AERODROME
CIRCLE

C.A.D
CIRCLE

RANPUR ROAD

Chambal
Gardens

State Bank of
Bikaner & Jaipur

ACCOMMODATION	
Brijraj Bhawan	C
Navrang	D
Phul Plaza	D
Sukhdam Kothi	B
Umed Bhawan Palace	A

changing **travellers' cheques** is the inconveniently located State Bank of Bikaner &
Jaipur in the south of town. There are several **ATMs** scattered around the road intersection by the *Navrang* hotel.

Kota is a surprisingly large and sprawling city, and you'll need a rickshaw to
cover the sights, especially if arriving at the train station, on the far northern side
of town. Arriving at the bus station, it's a long but feasible walk through the
bustling main bazaar to the City Palace.

Accommodation and eating

Kota's **hotels** cater mainly for passing business travellers, if you can't afford to
stay in one of the places below, it's better to base yourself in Bundi. For **eating**,
the modern *Venue* pure-veg restaurant, attached to the *Navrang* hotel, has a good
selection of North Indian veg mains (mains Rs50–80) plus *dosas*, pizzas and
Chinese dishes.

Brijraj Bhawan Civil Lines ☎0744/245 0529,
Ⓦwww.indianheritagehotels.com. An idyllic retreat
in the heart of noisy Kota, occupying a fine old
colonial mansion set in a peaceful spot overlooking
the river. Rooms are pure Victorian period pieces, all
scrupulously maintained and very comfortable. Ⓖ
Navrang Station Rd ☎0744/232 3294. The nicest
cheap hotel in town, with a mix of simple

air-cooled and more attractively furnished a/c
rooms, all with TV. The adjacent *Phul Plaza* is
reasonable too, but not quite as appealing. ❷–❹
Sukhdham Kothi Civil Lines ☎0744/232 0081,
Ⓦwww.sukhdhamkothi.com. Marvellously
atmospheric guesthouse located in a hundred-
year-old stone mansion set amid extensive
gardens. Comfy and atmospheric rooms with old

wooden furniture and assorted nineteenth-century bric-a-brac. **6**
Umed Bhawan Palace Station Rd, Khelri Phatak ☏ 0744/232 5262,

Ⓦ www.welcomheritagehotels.com. Occupying a huge and rather ugly former royal residence, this fancy hotel offers upmarket comforts (and a fair bit of chintz) at a reasonable price. **7**

The City Palace

The huge walls of Kota's **fort**, built in 1264 by Rajkumar Jait Singh of Bundi, rise above the flat eastern bank of the Chambal, encircling the old town centre (although they've now been largely swallowed up by modern buildings). At the southern end of the fort, around 2km from the bus station, lies the **City Palace**, a well-preserved cluster of royal residences painted an incongruous mixture of very pale sky-blue and fleshy salmon pink; construction on them began in 1625 and continued sporadically until the early years of the twentieth century. The palace now houses the excellent **Maharao Madho Singh Museum** (daily except official holidays 10am–4.30pm; combined entrance to museum and palace foreigners Rs100, Indian residents Rs10, camera Rs50, video Rs100). The first room is filled with a selection of the usual luxury items that were considered *de rigueur* by any status-conscious Indian ruler, including elaborate *howdahs* and palanquins, silver hookah pipes, a gem-studded chair and a magnificent silver painted throne. Walk diagonally across the courtyard to reach the dazzling **Raj Mahal**, built by Rao Madho Singh (ruled 1625–49), though the lavish paintings and mirrorwork date from the nineteenth and twentieth centuries, which served as the ruler's public audience hall. An attached room is decorated with religious miniatures and further mirrors.

From the Raj Mahal, a corridor leads into a further sequence of rooms. These begin with a well-stocked **armoury**, home to an unusual golden fish emblem, the Mahi Maratib, awarded by the Mughals to high-ranking rajas and carried aloft in procession. Beyond here a large room is filled with rather dull photos of the rulers of Kota and their nearest and dearest, along with the occasional Brit. The next room contains a small art gallery containing a few fine (but poorly displayed) **miniatures**, mainly of various maharajas on horseback, complete with shiny little halos, a visual combination designed to emphasize both their military prowess and kingly virtues. The depressing **wildlife gallery** downstairs is mainly filled with the mothy remains of various leopards and tigers.

Exit the museum then follow the steps up past the Raj Mahal to reach a series of finely painted palace buildings. Two storeys up, the red-pillared **Barah Dari** offers good town views. A storey above is the **Barah Mahal**, one of whose rooms is richly decorated with dozens of square miniatures placed together on the wall like tiles and depicting a range of religious and contemporary scenes, from Krishna lifting Mount Goverdhan to exotic-looking European ladies and gentlemen.

The rest of the city

Kishore Sagar, an artificial lake built in 1346, gives some visual relief from the city's grim industrial backdrop; the red-and-white palace in its centre, **Jag Mandir**, was commissioned by Prince Dher Deh of Bundi in 1346. On the northern edge of the lake the dusty **Government Museum** (daily 10am–5pm; Rs10) serves as the dispiriting home for an excellent collection of local stone carvings (signs in Hindi only, if at all), including a few voluptuous heavenly nymphs and four-armed Vishnus carved in a dark, coppery stone, plus a fine sequence of miniatures showing scenes from the life of Krishna.

On the edge of the river a few kilometres south of the fort, crocodiles and gharial sometimes sun themselves in a shallow pond in the **Chambal Gardens** (Rs5); boats from here offer brief jaunts (Rs30) on the crocodile-infested River Chambal.

Recommended trains from Kota

Destination	Name	No.	Departs	Arrives
Agra (Agra Fort)	Avadh Express	9037	2.50pm (Mon/Wed/Thurs/Sat)	9.50pm
	Haldighati Passenger	1771	9pm (daily)	6am
Bundi	Dehra Dun Express	9020A	9.05am (daily)	9.36am
Chittaurgarh	Dehra Dun Express	9020A	9.05am (daily)	12.05pm
Delhi (Hazrat Nizamuddin)	Kota Jan Shatabdi	2059	6am (daily)	12.30pm
	Golden Temple Mail	2903	11.20am (daily)	6.30pm
	Mewar Express	2964	11.55pm (daily)	6.30am
Jaipur	Dayodaya Express	2181	8.15am (daily)	12.30pm
	Jaipur Express	2955	8.50am (daily)	12.55pm
	Ranthambore Exp	2465	12.40pm (daily)	4.45pm
Mumbai (Central)	Jaipur–Mumbai SF	2956	5.35pm (daily)	7.50am
Sawai Madhopur (for Ranthambore National Park)	Dayodaya Express	2181	8.15am (daily)	9.50am
	Golden Temple Mail	2903	11.20am (daily)	12.30pm
	Ranthambore Exp	2465	12.40pm (daily)	2.25pm
	Dehra Dun Express	9019	7.40pm (daily)	9.20pm

Moving on from Kota

Buses leave regularly from the stand near Nayapura Circle to Bundi (every 30min; 45min–1hr), Ajmer (every 30min; 6hr), Chittor (5 daily; 4hr 30min), Jaipur (every 30min; 6hr) and Udaipur (7 daily; 6hr). Kota also has good **train** connections; see the box above.

Contexts

Contexts

History

Northwestern India – the region comprising modern Rajasthan, Delhi and Agra – has played a crucial role in the history of the Subcontinent. South Asia's first great civilization developed in the valley of the Indus River, just west of Rajasthan in what is now Pakistan, and the region also bore the brunt of the waves of invaders who swept down from the mountains of Central Asia into the Subcontinent over the succeeding centuries. These invaders – ranging from the first Indo-Aryans through successive waves of Greeks, Persians, Huns, Scythians, Parthians, Afghans, Mongols and Mughals – each helped shape the history, culture and ethnic make-up of the region, sometimes in ways which are now so buried in the past that they have become almost impossible to decipher.

It's no coincidence, therefore, that India's most historically important city, **Delhi**, should be located at this cultural crossroads between Central Asia and the wide-open plains of the Subcontinent. The city has been home to a remarkable array of dynasties, ranging from the semi-legendary heroes of the Mahabharata through to twentieth-century British imperialists, and also served for centuries as the principal cultural watershed between India's Hindu majority and roving Muslim empire builders. The latter were also responsible for the most glorious days of nearby **Agra**, the Mughal capital *par excellence* and home to its most memorable monuments, including the unforgettable Taj Mahal. Interlopers from Central Asia are also central to the early history of **Rajasthan**, though for much of its subsequent history the region has remained somewhat isolated and introspective, protected by its expanses of desert and craggy fortresses and enjoying a political and physical separation which has fostered the development of one of India's most colourful and staunchly Hindu cultures.

Prehistory and the Vedic Age

Around 2500 BC, one of the world's earliest civilizations – roughly contemporary with those of Sumer and ancient Egypt – began to develop around the Indus Valley (now in Pakistan) and its tributaries. Known variously as the **Indus Valley Civilization** or the **Harappan Civilization**, this first great Subcontinental culture spread across a sizeable proportion of what is now southern Pakistan and the periphery of western India. Archeological remains of Harappan-style culture have been discovered as far afield as Lothal in Gujarat and at several places in Rajasthan, including the extensive finds at **Kalibangan**, in a remote spot in northern Rajasthan close to the Pakistan border (some 200km from Bikaner), where remains of an entire town have been uncovered, built on a grid plan, with temples devoted to the worship of fire, and relics of a well-developed agricultural society, including what is claimed to be the remains of the world's oldest ploughed field.

The written history of India begins with the arrival of the charioteering **Indo-European** or **Aryan** tribes, who emerged from the steppes of Central Asia at around the start of the second millennium BC and proceeded to raid and conquer their way across the length and breadth of the Eurasian continent, eventually settling in Europe, the Middle East and the Indian Subcontinent. The epic migrations of these early Central Asia peoples can be traced through the spread of the early Indo-European languages they disseminated in their wake, which lay the foundations for tongues as diverse as modern Spanish and Bengali – and which also provide an ancient and unexpected linguistic bridge between English and Hindi, both of which ultimately derive from a common, if exceedingly remote, source.

Arriving in India, the Aryans rapidly overwhelmed what was left of the Indus Valley civilization. This period of Indian history is usually known as the **Vedic Age**, after the earliest Indian literature, the **Vedas**, collections of Aryan religious hymns composed in Sanskrit. By 1000 BC, the Aryans had become integrated with the indigenous inhabitants of India, establishing a fourfold division of society based on the **varnas** (see p.374), the origin of the caste system which persists to this day.

The first Aryan settlements were concentrated in northwest India and the Punjab, though during the later Vedic period, between 1000 and 600 BC, the centre of Aryan culture and power shifted to the Doab, the region between the Ganges and Yamuna rivers in modern Uttar Pradesh (including the area around modern Agra), whence their influence continued to spread eastwards and southwards. Many **sacred texts**, including the Upanishads, Mahabharata and the Ramayana (see p.374 & p.375), date from this period.

Though they are unreliable as historical sources, being overlaid with accretions from later centuries, it's possible to extract some of the facts entwined with the martial myths and legends. The great battle of **Kurukshetra** – the central theme of the Mahabharata – is certainly historical, and took place near modern Delhi some time in the ninth and eighth centuries BC, while archeological evidence has been found of the two main settlements mentioned in the epic: Indraprastha (Delhi) and Hastinapura, further north on the Ganges.

Invaders from the west

For the thousand years following the arrival of the Aryans, the regions which would later become Rajasthan and Delhi remained at the periphery of northern Indian history, which largely developed along the fertile **Ganges valley**, where a string of important new cities such as Magadha, Ayodhya and Pataliputra (modern Patna) was established, and where the new Buddhist and Jain religions first emerged. This period of steady internal development was interrupted by further invaders arriving in the northwest, most importantly, **Alexander the Great**, who crossed the Indus in 326 BC, and overran the Punjab. He stayed in India for just two years, and although he left garrisons and appointed satraps to govern the conquered territories, his death in 323 BC made their position untenable.

The ensuing political vacuum was quickly exploited by Chandragupta Maurya, who around 321 BC seized control of the city of Magadha, in the Ganges valley, and rapidly overran large portions of north India, thus establishing the **Mauryan Empire**, the first great Indian dynasty. From about 297 BC onwards, Chandragupta's son Bindusara and grandson **Ashoka** successively extended the empire south to Mysore, east to Assam and west to Afghanistan, though it appears to have had little influence on Rajasthan, which remained a peripheral area of small kingdoms contested by local tribes such as the Bhils and Minas, who still survive in isolated pockets of the state to this day.

After Ashoka's death in 232 BC, the empire began to fall apart and India became politically fragmented. Successive **invasions** followed as different ethnic groups from Central Asia poured down into the Subcontinent, fighting with and displacing one another in turn. This is one of the most confusing and least understood periods in Indian history, but also one of the most significant in the development of Rajasthan, since it seems likely that at least some of the colourful Rajput clans which loom so large in the later history of India are directly or partly descended from these Central Asian invaders.

The Bactrian Greeks of Gandhara (in what is now northern Afghanistan) were the first to arrive, followed by Parthians from Iran, Yueh-Chi Central Asian nomads and the Scythians, or **Shakas**, from the Aral Sea area. This chaotic period was interrupted by the emergence of the **Guptas** (320–550 AD), during which north India was once again reunified into a single empire. The first great Gupta ruler, Chandra Gupta I (no relation to the Mauryan Guptas), established a powerful kingdom centred on Magadha in the Ganges valley in central northern India. His son and heir, Samudra Gupta (c.335–376 AD), expanded the empire from the Punjab to Assam and, according to an inscription in Allahabad, "violently uprooted" nine kings of northern India and temporarily incorporated parts of Rajasthan into the Gupta empire.

By the mid-fifth century, however, western India was again threatened by invasions from Central Asia. The last major Gupta ruler, Skanda Gupta (reigned 455–467 AD), managed to repel repeated raids by the **Huns**, another nomadic people who had wandered into India from Central Asia, but after his death their disruption of Central Asian trade seriously destabilized the empire. By the end of the fifth century, the Huns had wrested the Punjab from Gupta control, and further incursions early in the sixth century dealt the deathblow to the empire, which had completely disintegrated by 550 AD. At around the same time, another wave of Central Asian tribes, the **Gurjaras**, also arrived in west India, and established themselves in Gujarat and parts of what is now southern Rajasthan.

The emergence of the Rajputs

During the sixth and seventh centuries, a new warrior class began to take control of large parts of northern and western India, describing themselves as **Rajputs** (a corruption of *Raj-puteras*, meaning "son of a raja" – raja being translated variously as "prince" or "king"). Exactly where this new ruling class came from remains something of a mystery, although it seems most likely that the Rajputs were largely or entirely of foreign origin, the descendants of the waves of invaders who poured into northwest India from Central Asia between the third and sixth centuries AD, and who were gradually integrated into Indian society. The Huns, Shakas (Scythians) and Gurjaras have all been named as possible progenitors, and quite possibly all three (and probably quite a few other) ethnic groups all played a part in establishing this new bloodline in Indian society. It's worth noting that the name originally had no particular ethnic or geographical connotations, and that even today self-professed Rajputs can be found not only in Rajasthan, but also in several other states in India, as well as in Pakistan and Nepal. Only in the Mughal era did the name Rajput come to be applied to the warlike inhabitants of the area which later became the modern state of Rajasthan. The Rajputs also formed a minority of the overall population (and still make up under ten percent of the population of contemporary Rajasthan) – a ruling aristocracy bound, like the medieval European knights to which they are frequently compared, by strict codes of honour and ties of loyalty to the family clan.

The theory that the Rajputs are descended from people of foreign origin is supported by the efforts that were made to give them a suitably grandiose royal lineage and to incorporate them within India's caste system – and by their own unusually dogged insistence on their *kshatriya* (warrior) status. The various Rajput clans can be divided into three main groups. The four clans of the **Agnikula** ("Fire Family", comprising the Chauhans, Solankis, Paramaras and Pratiharas), claiming descent from a mythical figure who emerged from a vast fire pit near Mount Abu, were the dominant force in early Rajput affairs. Later clans subsequently emerged belonging to the **Suryavansa** or **Chandravansa** Rajput branches and claiming descent from either the sun or moon respectively – these included the Guhilas (later the Sisodias) of Mewar in southern Rajasthan and the Chandellas of Khajuraho in modern Madhya Pradesh. By the tenth century, Rajput clans could be found controlling many parts of northern India – not only in present-day Rajasthan, but also in Gujarat, Madhya Pradesh and Haryana. Some of the best known include the Chauhans of Ajmer, the Sisodias of Chittaurgarh, the Chandellas of Khajuraho, and the Tomars of Haryana, who (according to tradition) founded the modern city of Delhi in 736.

The Delhi Sultanate

Despite their military prowess and newly acquired genealogical credentials, incessant Rajput infighting fatally undermined their ability to counter a powerful new threat from the northwest. Between 1000 and 1027 the Turkish chieftain **Mahmud of Ghazni**, founder of the **Ghaznavid** dynasty in Afghanistan, launched no less than seventeen raids into northwest India in search of plunder – the first of the incessant Muslim raids from Central Asia which were to convulse northwest India right through until the eighteenth century. A long period of calm followed Mahmud's demise, though Mahmud's descendants were subsequently ousted by another Afghan Turk, **Muhammad of Ghor**, who seized Ghaznavid possessions in the Punjab at the end of the twelfth century and then turned towards the wealthy lands further east. Prithviraj III, ruler of the Chauhans of Ajmer, the most important of the early Rajput dynasties, patched together an alliance to defeat the Turkish warlord at Tarain (near Thanesvar) in 1191, but Muhammad returned the next year with a superior force and defeated the combined Rajput forces. He had Prithviraj executed before returning home, leaving his generals to complete the conquest of northern India and seize Delhi from the Chauhans (who had themselves wrested it from the Rajput Tomars barely a decade earlier).

Muhammad of Ghor was assassinated in 1206 and his empire rapidly disintegrated. The Turkish slave general **Qutb-ud-Din Aiback**, whom Muhammad had left behind in Delhi to look after the newly conquered Indian territories, thus suddenly found himself the independent ruler of a sizeable kingdom. These fortuitous events led to the creation of one of north India's most important and enduring states, the **Delhi Sultanate**, which would prove to be the major political force in the region from the thirteenth to the sixteenth century, and under which Delhi would become the most important city in north India.

Aiback's son-in-law **Iltutmish** (1211–36) extended the sultanate's territories from Sind in Pakistan to Bengal, though shortly after his death another and even more deadly Central Asian force, the **Mongols**, arrived on the Indian scene, sending raiding parties into the Punjab and even laying siege to Delhi for two months in 1303 before being decisively beaten off by the implacable **Ala-ud-Din Khalji** (1296–1316), generally regarded as the greatest – or at least the most single-mindedly brutal – of the Delhi Sultans. Ala-ud-Din went on to energetically enforce Islamic rule over the northern Hindu states, conquering Gujarat and assorted Rajput fortresses in a series of expeditions between 1299 and 1311 – including, most famously, the sack of Chittaurgarh in 1303 (see p.341) – before turning his attention to the Deccan and the south, although his hopes of building a stable empire were subsequently dashed by rebellions in Gujarat and Chittaurgarh.

A fresh imperial impetus came from the **Tughluq** dynasty, which succeeded the Khaljis in 1320. Under Muhammed Tughluq (1325–51), the sultanate reached its maximum extent, although the end of his reign was marred by a series of revolts sparked by burdensome taxes exacted to finance his endless military campaigns, and an aborted attempt to relocate the capital to Daulatabad in the Deccan. Firoz Shah Tughluq (1351–88) re-established the capital at Delhi and reasserted Tughluq control, though the degeneracy of his successors made the sultanate increasingly vulnerable to external predators. When **Timur**, the Central Asian conqueror known to the West as Tamerlaine, sacked Delhi in 1398, the Delhi Sultanate was reduced to just one of several competing Muslim states in northern India.

The Sultanate experienced a modest revival under the energetic rule of the Afghan **Lodis**, especially Sikandar Lodi (1489–1517), who established a new, subsidiary capital at the hitherto relatively unimportant city of **Agra**, a move whose full significance would only be realized under the subsequent Mughal dynasty. His successor, Ibrahim (1517–26), however, was unable to overcome the dissension among his Afghan feudatories, and eventually fell victim to yet another Central Asian invader, Babur, the first of the Mughals (see below), at the Battle of Panipat.

The rise of Mewar, Marwar and Amber

The fluctuating efforts of the Delhi sultans to subdue the independent kingdoms of northern India made little lasting impression on Rajasthan, where a trio of important Rajput Hindu statelets had emerged during the centuries of Islamic rule in the north. The kingdom of **Mewar** in southern Rajasthan had become increasingly powerful, despite the sack of its capital, Chittaurgarh, by Ala-ud-Din-Khalji in 1303. Chittaurgarh itself had been retaken by the ruling **Sisodia** family in 1326 and subsequently refortified by **Rana Kumbha** (reigned 1433–68), traditionally regarded as one of the greatest of Mewar's rulers. Kumbha also established a massive new citadel at Kumbalgarh (north of Udaipur), as well as refortifying existing settlements throughout Mewar, consolidating the Sisodias' hold over southern Rajasthan – one which would survive largely intact, despite ferocious Mughal challenges, until Independence.

Meanwhile, in northern Rajasthan, the **Rathore** clan had established themselves as rulers of the state of **Marwar** (the area around Jodhpur). The Rathores were originally from Kanauj, near Kanpur in Uttar Pradesh. Having lost control of that city to Muhammad of Ghor in 1193, they established themselves as rulers of Pali, south of Jodhpur, before ousting another local dynasty, the Parihars, from Mandor, to the north, in 1381. In 1459 Rao Jodha (reigned 1438–89) moved his capital to a new site at Jodhpur, where he built the virtually impregnable Meherangarh fort. His second son, Bika, subsequently established himself as ruler of the desert city of **Bikaner**.

The Rathores' near neighbours, the **Kachchwahas of Amber**, originally hailed from Gwalior in Madhya Pradesh. In 1128 a prince named Dulha Rai had married a daughter of the Rajput chief of Dausa, east of Jaipur, whose throne he subsequently inherited, thus founding the Kachchwaha dynasty. Around 1150 a descendant of Dulha Rai wrested Amber from the Susawat Minas clan, who had previously controlled it, and it was here that the Kachchwahas constructed the imposing fort and palace that would serve as the Kachchwaha capital for six centuries until Jai Singh II moved it to Jaipur in 1727.

Babur and the arrival of the Mughals

The fall of the Delhi Sultanate was to usher in an even more famous dynasty – indeed probably the most famous in Indian history: the **Mughals**. The founder of the Mughal dynasty, **Babur** (reigned 1526–30), was a descendant of the ferocious Mongol adventurers Timur and Genghis Khan (his dynastic name, "Mughal", being simply a variant of "Mongol") – indeed it was Timur's sack of Delhi in 1398 which gave Babur his extremely tenuous claim to sovereignty in north India. The ruler of Kabul in Afghanistan, Babur spent much of his life attempting to recapture his ancestral home of Samarkand, in modern Uzbekistan – India appears to have been something of an afterthought. In 1526, his small but battle-hardened and well-armed forces descended on the squabbling remnants of Ibrahim Lodi's Delhi Sultanate and, despite being outnumbered ten to one, routed them at the **Battle of Panipat**, during which Ibrahim, the last of the Delhi Sultans, was killed.

Babur thence claimed control of Delhi, while his son Humayun rode off to take control of the Lodi's new fort and treasury at **Agra**. Despite having gained control of Delhi and Agra, Babur found his position threatened by a Rajput confederacy led by Rana Sanga of Mewar and the Afghan chiefs, who had united under the Sultan of Bengal – the first of innumerable Rajput–Mughal clashes. Babur reacted vigorously by declaring a religious war (*jihad*) against the rana and annihilating the Mewar forces at the **Battle of Kanwaha** (close to Fatehpur Sikri) in 1527, before turning his attention to the Afghan uprisings in the east. Although he crushed the allied armies of the Afghans and the Sultan of Bengal in 1529, his failing health forced him to retire to Agra, where he died in 1530.

Humayun (reigned 1530–56), Babur's son and successor, was a volatile character, alternating between bursts of enthusiastic activity and hedonistic indolence. He subdued Malwa and Gujarat, only to lose both while he took his pleasure in the harem in Agra. Humayun's empire was soon threatened by the redoubtable Afghan warrior Sher Khan (also known as **Sher Shah Suri**), based in south Bihar, and after two resounding defeats at his hands, Humayun was forced to seek refuge in Persia in 1539. A much cleverer politician than Humayun, Sher Khan later subjugated several of the Rajput dynasties which had proved troublesome for the Mughals, though it was during a siege against one of these dynasties, at Kalinjar in modern Uttar Pradesh, that the Afghan was killed, when a rocket rebounded off the fort's walls and exploded a pile of weapons next to him.

Akbar

After Sher Khan's death in 1545 Humayun took advantage of the ensuing chaos to stage a return. His armies, led by the redoubtable general Bairam Khan, crushed Sher Khan's successor, Sikander Suri, at Sirhund in 1555; but Humayun died the following year after a fall in the Purana Qila in Delhi, leaving his young son **Akbar** as the new emperor. Akbar, aged only thirteen, faced an immediate crisis when Delhi was briefly stormed and occupied by the brilliant Hindu general **Hemu** (a remarkable figure who despite his tiny stature and feeble physique had risen from hawking saltpetre in a bazaar to commanding the united armies of northern India in a sequence of 23 consecutive victories). Akbar's own generals favoured a retreat to Afghanistan, but Bairam Khan encouraged Akbar to stand firm. The advice bore fruit when Akbar and Hemu's forces met at a second Battle of Panipat, the site of Babur's earlier victory over Ibrahim Lodi, in 1556, during which Hemu was killed and his army put to flight. Bairam Khan subsequently recovered Gwalior and Jaunpur, and handed over a consolidated north Indian kingdom to Akbar in 1560.

It was during Akbar's reign that the Rajputs – or at least almost all the Rajputs – were finally brought into the Mughal fold (Akbar, coincidentally, was actually born in a Rajput fort not far from Jaisalmer, at Umarkot, just over the border in present-day Pakistan). Akbar succeeded where his predecessors had failed, thanks to a notable change of tactic, introducing a carrot-and-stick-style strategy based on a combination of military might and diplomatic overtures. Establishing a large garrison in Ajmer, Akbar set out to woo the Rajputs. His first notable "conquest" was his **marriage**, in 1562, to Mariam, the daughter of the maharaja of Amber (Mariam, in turn, would become the mother of the next Mughal emperor, Jahangir, thus binding the Mughals and Amber even closer). The maharaja of Amber and his progeny were inducted into the Mughal hierarchy and given high offices – indeed the raja's grandson, **Man Singh**, would become one of Akbar's most trusted generals and headed many campaigns on behalf of the emperor, including several against fellow Rajputs, such as that against Pratap Singh which led to the Battle of Haldighati (see p.323). Subsequent treaties were soon brokered with many of Rajasthan's other rulers, signalling a new and peaceable alliance between the empire's Islamic centre and the Hindu hinterlands. Mughals would thenceforth be able to count on the Rajput loyalty and military assistance, while the Rajputs were able to reap the rewards of holding high offices within the mighty Mughal empire – by 1580, 43 of the 222 Mughal *umrah* (nobility) were Rajput.

Unfortunately for Akbar, the Sisodia rulers of the pre-eminent Rajput state, Mewar, still holed up in the mighty fort at **Chittaurgarh**, were unpersuaded by Akbar's advances or promises of elevated official Mughal status – and indeed publicly derided the maharaja of Amber for his perceived sell-out. The carrot having failed, Akbar resorted to the stick, launching a huge offensive against Chittaurgarh (see p.342), which he finally captured after a long and brutal siege in 1568. The siege marked the end of Chittaurgarh's illustrious history – although by then the ruler of Mewar, Udai Singh II (see p.316), had absconded to his newly founded capital of **Udaipur**, from where he and his successor Pratap Singh (see p.323) continued to defy Akbar.

Akbar, meanwhile, was indulging in his own spate of city building. In 1565 he had the small fort built by Sikander Lodi in **Agra** demolished and replaced by the magnificent new Agra Fort, the centrepiece of a revitalized city that would rival Delhi as the major centre of Mughal power. Not content with this, in the early 1570s he embarked on the creation of an entire new city, the remarkable but short-lived **Fatehpur Sikri**, which served for a brief period as the capital of the empire, before the court's return to Agra, and thence, ultimately, back to Delhi.

Akbar possessed the personal magnetism of his grandfather and was a brilliant general, and by the end of his reign in 1605 he controlled a broad sweep of territory from the Bay of Bengal to Kandahar in Afghanistan. Akbar was as clever a politician and administrator as he was a successful general. In addition to involving Hindu landowners and nobles in economic and political life, Akbar adopted a conscious policy of religious toleration aimed at widening his power base, abolishing the despised poll tax on non-Muslims (*jizya*) and tolls on Hindu pilgrimages. A mystical experience in about 1575 inspired him to instigate a series of discussions with orthodox Muslim leaders (*ulema*), Portuguese priests from Goa, Hindu Brahmins, Jains and Zoroastrians at his famous Diwan-i-Khas in Fatehpur Sikri. The discussions culminated in a politico-religious crisis and a revolt, organized by the alienated *ulema*, which Akbar ruthlessly crushed with customary efficiency in 1581.

Jahangir and Shah Jahan

The reign of **Jahangir** (1605–27) was a time of brisk economic and expansionist activity conjoined with artistic and architectural brilliance – as well as some notable imperial excesses. Jahangir was a contradictory character: an alcoholic and a sadist, but also a notable connoisseur of art and loving husband of his famous queen, **Nur Jahan** (see pp.168–169). He was also an able and determined military commander who succeeded in extending the bounds of the already very considerable domains bequeathed to him by Akbar. One of his principal targets was the recalcitrant state of Mewar, against which he launched repeated expeditions. The new ruler of Mewar, Pratap Singh's son **Amar Singh**, continued to fight for as long as he could, but sheer weight of Mughal offensives gradually rendered him helpless. In 1615 he was finally forced to sign a treaty recognizing Mughal overlordship. His son, Karan Singh, presented himself at the Mughal court, where he was showered with honours and became firm friends with Prince Khurram (the future Shah Jahan) – who would himself later seek refuge in Udaipur (see p.319), an ironic turnaround in Mughal-Mewari relations.

Shah Jahan (1628–57) came to power in 1628 after the by now traditional military contest between rival brothers, followed by the exile or (if they could be caught) execution of the losing party. The bloodbath which generally preceded the emergence of a new emperor at least ensured that only the fittest were able to survive and claim the Mughal throne, and in this respect Shah Jahan – who had already proved himself an outstanding military commander during his father's reign – was no exception, displaying all the traditional Mughal qualities of administrative and military élan. It is, however, as perhaps the greatest patron of architecture the world has ever known, that Shah Jahan is best remembered. In 1648 he officially moved the Mughal capital from Agra back to Delhi, celebrating the translocation with the construction of the new city of **Shahjahanabad** (now better known as Old Delhi), complete with its huge new Red Fort and Jama Masjid, though it was in Agra that he left his greatest mark, with his myriad embellishments to the city's fort and, pre-eminently, in the creation of the **Taj Mahal**, arguably the most beautiful building on the planet.

Aurangzeb

Shah Jahan's reign witnessed the entry of a new force into Indian history: the **Marathas**, a potent new military power which would loom large in the later history of north India in general and Rajasthan in particular. A group of militant Hindus from Maharastra in central India, the **Marathas** had carved out a kingdom of their own under their inspirational chief, **Shivaji**, and soon began to turn their attentions northwards. Shah Jahan had responded to the Maratha threat by sending his third son, an ambitious young prince named **Aurangzeb**, to the Deccan to take charge of Mughal interests in the region, although his military successes were repeatedly undermined by Shah Jahan's oldest son and preferred heir **Dara Shikoh**, who was anxious to destabilize Aurangzeb's military exploits lest they create a threat to his own prestige. The anticipated struggle between the two brothers erupted in 1657 when Shah Jahan fell suddenly and seriously ill with acute constipation (bowel problems appear to have been a recurrent feature of Mughal rule – Akbar himself apparently perished of acute diarrhoea). Shah Jahan recovered, but not before Aurangzeb had seen off Dara Shikoh, wiping out his army in a series of encounters that culminated in a rout at Ajmer. The thirty-year reign of the ailing emperor ended ignominiously. Aurangzeb had him incarcerated in Agra Fort, where he lived out his remaining days in an opium-induced stupor gazing wistfully down the Yamuna at the mausoleum of his beloved Mumtaz.

Though lacking the charisma of Akbar or Babur, Aurangzeb (reigned 1658–1707) evoked an awe of his own and proved to be a capable administrator who retained a firm grip on the increasingly unsettled empire until his death at the age of 88. In contrast to the extravagance of the other Mughals, Aurangzeb's lifestyle was pious and disciplined. However, his religious dogmatism ultimately alienated the Hindu community whose leaders had been so carefully cultivated by Akbar. Hindu places of worship were again the object of iconoclasm, the *jizya* tax on non-Muslims was reintroduced and discriminatory duties were imposed on Hindu merchants. The Jats of the Agra–Delhi region rebelled, and elsewhere peasant farmers rallied behind Maratha and Sikh leaders.

Disintegrating relations between the Hindu populace and Muslim rulers across the empire were mirrored by events in Rajasthan. In 1678 the ruler of the leading Rajput state of **Marwar** (Jodhpur) died without leaving an heir. Pending the election of a successor, Aurangzeb seized control of the state and garrisoned it with Mughal troops, who passed the time by vandalizing local Hindu temples, an activity hardly calculated to please local Rajput sensibilities. By the time the succession had been decided, two of the deceased ruler's wives had given birth to male heirs (although one soon died), though ignoring the surviving infant's claims, Aurangzeb conferred the throne on an unpopular relative, whereupon revolt erupted. The infant's mother decamped posthaste to Udaipur, whereupon the rulers of Mewar joined the fray, launching their army against various Mughal targets. Aurangzeb was forced to dispatch a large military expedition to the region in 1680. An inconclusive series of battles ensued, before a tenuous peace was reimposed, but not before Udaipur had been sacked by Mughal troops, who followed up their conquest with a further spate of temple bashing.

Aurangzeb's attention, however, was turning steadily south. In 1681 he transferred his base to the Deccan, where he spent the rest of his extremely long life overseeing the subjugation of the Bijapur and Golconda kingdoms and trying to contain the Maratha rebellion. In 1689, he succeeded in capturing and executing Shivaji's son, and by 1698 the Mughals had overrun almost the whole of the peninsula. The Rajputs had been left in peace and the Marathas had been temporarily suppressed – though they would increasingly re-emerge in the next century to harass the remnants of Mughal and Rajput power.

Maratha threats and the rise of Jaipur

Aurangzeb's death was followed by the rapid disintegration of the empire, and although a succession of Mughal "emperors" continued to rule in Delhi right through until the uprising of 1857, their actual powers were increasingly limited. By the 1720s Hyderabad, Avadh and Bengal were effectively independent, while closer to Delhi the **Jats** succeeded in creating their own independent statelet in Bharatpur out of a slice of previously Mughal territory. In 1737 the Marathas raided Delhi and the following year overwhelmed the rich province of Malwa (in Madyha Pradesh). Two years later, **Nadir Shah** of Persia dealt a fatal blow to the Mughal empire's prestige when he invaded India, defeated the Mughal army and sacked Delhi in 1739.

In the midst of the general chaos, one forward-looking development was occurring in Rajasthan. In 1727, the Kachchwaha ruler Jai Singh had taken the momentous decision to relocate his capital from the hoary old fortress of Amber to a brand-new city to be named (after himself) **Jaipur**. Major Rajput towns and fortresses had hitherto always been sited in places which offered the greatest defensive security – the summits of craggy, sheer-sided hills, for example, as at Chittaurgarh, Meherangarh (Jodhpur) and, indeed, Amber itself. For his new capital, however, Jai Singh, for the first time in Rajasthan's history, put mercantile above military considerations, locating his new city on the plains in a commercially strategic position directly beside the major highway between Ajmer and Agra and inviting tradesmen and craftspeople to settle in it – a far-sighted decision which largely explains why Jaipur, rather than Udaipur (the capital of the pre-eminent Rajput kingdom of Mewar), is now the most important city in Rajasthan.

The city immediately flourished, though Jai Singh's failure to provide an heir meant that his death in 1743 and subsequent arguments over the royal succession, opened the door to **Maratha interference**, with disastrous consequences. The rival pretenders to the throne each enlisted Maratha mercenaries to back up their claims, though the successful contender, Madho Singh, upon attaining the throne found himself at the mercy of the Maratha troops who had put him there. In 1753 the Marathas returned in numbers and were only bought off with a substantial bribe, a pattern which continued on and off for the next forty years. Attempts to take on the Marathas on the battlefield met with mixed results. In 1787 Madho Singh's successor, Pratap Singh narrowly defeated a combined Mughal–Maratha force at the Battle of Tunga by bribing the Mughal contingent to switch sides at the beginning of the fighting, though Pratap's subsequent attempt to engage a purely Maratha force, at the Battle of Malpura in 1800, backfired when 27,000 Rajputs were put to flight by a far smaller but superior force of Maratha troops.

Similar events unfolded at Jodhpur and Udaipur, and at many other places around Rajasthan, during the second half of the eighteenth century, with Maratha armies roaming the countryside demanding huge amounts of tribute from whoever they felt was vulnerable to attack, until they had effectively bled the various rulers' treasuries dry. Things were little better in **Delhi**. Following Nadir Shah's murderous spate of looting in 1739, the city was again ransacked in 1757, this time by an independent Afghan force led by Ahmad Shah Durrani. Mughal ministers enlisted the services of the Marathas, who succeeded in driving the Afghans back to the Punjab. Ahmad Shah returned in 1761, however, and overwhelmed the Marathas at the third battle of Panipat, although any designs he had on the imperial throne were dashed when his soldiers mutinied over arrears of pay.

The rise of the British

The scourge of the Marathas was finally arrested, not by any of the royal houses of Rajasthan, but by an entirely new breed of interlopers: the British. India's trading potential had attracted European interest ever since 1498, when Vasco da Gama landed on the Malabar coast. During the ensuing century Portuguese, Dutch, English, French and Danish companies had all set up coastal trading centres. British interests in India were formalized by the creation of the **East India Company**, granted a royal charter by Elizabeth I in 1600, whose representatives arrived at Surat in Gujarat in 1608, quickly establishing 27 trading posts around the country, including those at the nascent cities of Bombay, Madras and Calcutta.

The War of the Austrian Succession in Europe in 1740 led to armed conflict between the French and English trading companies along the South Indian coast, which soon developed into a minor war over the succession of the Nizam of Hyderabad. Sporadic fighting continued until the end of the Seven Years' War in Europe and the Treaty of Paris in 1763 put an effective end to French ambitions in India. Meanwhile, **Robert Clive**'s defeat of the rebellious young nawab of Bengal at Plassey in 1757 had decisively augmented British power; by 1765 the enervated Mughal emperor legally recognized the Company by granting it the revenue management of Bengal, Bihar and Orissa.

For the next thirty years, the British in India contented themselves with developing trade and repulsing Indian offensives against their three provinces in Calcutta, Bombay and Madras, though by the end of the century the defeat of Tipu Sultan of Mysore, the Company's best-organized and most resolute enemy, and the subjugation of the Nizam of Hyderabad resulted in the annexation of considerable territories, and by 1805 nearly all the other rulers in India recognized British suzerainty. A long-drawn-out series of conflicts between the British and Marathas (the so-called three "Marathas Wars" of 1774–1818) finally extinguished the Marathas as an effective military threat.

Following the subjugation of the Marathas, the British established a series of treaties with the rulers of Rajasthan – or **Rajputana**, as it became known during the colonial era. In **1818**, treaties were signed between the British and all the leading Rajput rulers – Jaipur, Udaipur, Jodhpur and Bikaner – while the city of Ajmer was purchased from the Marathas for fifty thousand rupees. Under these treaties, the various kingdoms of Rajputana retained their autonomy more or less intact and received a guarantee of military protection in exchange for pledging their loyalty to the British Crown and agreeing to certain political, mercantile and financial concessions. Similar arrangements were reached with most of India's other surviving independent kingdoms, collectively known as the so-called "**princely states**", stretching from Hyderabad in the south to Kashmir in the north; although some were gradually swallowed up and incorporated into British-ruled India, many were to survive until Independence. The war-torn city of Delhi, the traditional capital of north India, fared less well, as the British established their capital at the burgeoning new city of Calcutta.

The 1857 uprising

The new British colony, however, was in a state of social and economic collapse as a result of the almost incessant conflicts of the previous hundred years. The controversial "Doctrine of Lapse", whereby autonomous states were gradually annexed, caused widespread resentment. In addition, the Company's policy, after 1835, of promoting European literature and science (with English replacing Persian as the official state language), the suppression of local customs such as *sati* and child marriage, and the deployment of Indian troops overseas (causing them to lose caste) all created resentment and were increasingly perceived as part of a covert but systematic British attack on traditional Hindu and Muslim religious and cultural practices.

The final spark which ignited a full-blown uprising by the Indian army was supplied when troops were issued with cartridges for a new Enfield rifle smeared in cows' and pigs' grease (polluting to both Hindus and Muslims). The resultant **1857 uprising** (traditionally referred to by the British as the Indian Mutiny or Sepoy Rebellion, and by Indian historians as the First War of Independence) began with a rebellion at Meerut on May 10, 1857. Delhi was seized the next day. The last Mughal emperor Bahadur Shah, in Delhi, the dispossessed court at Lucknow, and the exiled members of the Maratha court at Kanpur all supported the cause (albeit possibly under duress) and some landlords participated in the rebellion – though, crucially, the Sikh regiments in the Punjab chose to side with the British. The rebellion quickly spread across most of central northern India, where mutineers seized Lucknow and Kanpur and threatened Agra, whose rebellious citizens forced the European community to flee into the city's fort for safety. The states of Rajasthan, which remained nominally independent and had benefited more than other parts of the country by the British presence, remained relatively unaffected, with the maharajas of Jaipur and Udaipur both remaining loyal.

The British authorities were caught by surprise, though control was gradually reasserted. Delhi and Kanpur were both retaken in September, Agra was relieved soon afterwards, and the final recapture of Lucknow in March 1858 effectively broke the back of the Mutiny.

The Raj and Indian nationalism

The uprising had important consequences for subsequent British rule in the Subcontinent. The governing powers of the East India Company were abolished and the British Crown assumed the direct administration of India in the same year. Henceforth, British India was no longer merely a massive trade operation, but a fully-fledged independent kingdom, or **Raj**. As a British colony, India assumed a new position in the world economy. Its trade benefited from the railways developed by the British, and Indian businessmen began to invest in a range of manufacturing industries, including textiles, iron and steel – among them the remarkable Marwari trading families from Rajasthan (see p.367) who would come to dominate Indian manufacturing in the twentieth century. However, India subsidized the British economy as a source of cheap raw materials and as a market for manufactured goods, while its own economy and agriculture remained underdeveloped.

British civil servants dominated the higher echelons of the administration, imposing Western notions of progress on the indigenous social structure and often introducing policies contrary to Indian interests. At the same time, the propagation of the English language and the Western knowledge to which it gave access resulted in the emergence of a new **middle class** of civil servants, landlords and professionals, whose consciousness of an Indian national identity steadily increased. Public demonstrations eventually forced the British to sanction the creation of the **Indian National Congress** party (usually known simply as "Congress") in 1885, and by 1905 Congress had adopted self-government as a political aim – while in 1906, concerns about the predominantly Hindu Congress led to the foundation of the **All-India Muslim League** to represent the country's Muslims. The Morley–Minto Reforms of 1909 paved the way for Indian participation in provincial executive councils and made allowance for separate Muslim representation.

At the **Great Durbar** of 1911, held in honour of the new king, George V, the capital was moved back to **Delhi**, with the construction of yet another imperial city, so-called "New" Delhi, to celebrate (though it wasn't completed and officially inaugurated until 1931). A few years later, the Royal Proclamation of 1917 promised a gradual development of dominion-style self-government; and two years later the Montagu–Chelmsford Reforms attempted to implement the declaration. At this point an England-educated lawyer, **Mohandas Karamchand Gandhi** – better known as the Mahatma, or "Great Soul" – took up the initiative, espousing a political philosophy based on non-violence (*ahimsa*), the pursuit of truth (*satyagraha*) and the championing of the untouchables (see p.374), whom he renamed the Children of God (*Harijan*). Gandhi began by organizing India-wide one-day strikes and protests, though these were mercilessly crushed by the government – as in the infamous incident in 1919 when General Dyer dispersed a meeting at Jallianwalla Bagh Amritsar by firing on the unarmed crowd, killing 379 and wounding 1200.

By 1928 Congress was demanding complete independence. The government offered talks, but the more radical elements in Congress, now led by the young **Jawaharlal Nehru**, were in a confrontational mood. Gandhi, in turn, led a well-publicized 240-mile "salt march" from his ashram in Sabarmati to make salt illegally at Dandi in Gujarat in defiance of a particularly unpopular British tax. This demonstration of nonviolent civil disobedience (*satyagraha*) fired the popular imagination, leading to more processions, strikes and mass imprisonments.

The idea of a **separate Muslim state** was first raised in 1930 by the celebrated Indian Muslim poet and writer Muhammad Iqbal. **Mohammed Ali Jinnah**, a lawyer from Bombay who assumed the leadership of the Muslim League in 1935, initially promoted Muslim–Hindu cooperation, but he soon despaired of influencing Congress and by 1940 the League passed a resolution demanding an independent Pakistan.

Another problem faced in the run-up to Independence was the question of what was to become of the numerous **princely states** scattered over many parts of India – nowhere more so than in Rajputana – which were still technically independent and autonomously run. The states still covered two-fifths of the country's total area and represented a huge potential stumbling block to future independence should their rulers (most of whom were deeply suspicious of Congress) choose not to join the newly independent country. The question was never to be properly solved and even at Independence rulers of several of the major states had yet to decide which country they were going to join (with enduringly disastrous consequences in the case of Kashmir).

Confrontations between the government, Congress and the Muslim League continued throughout World War II, despite the promise, in 1942, by a Britain increasingly reliant on Indian troops, of postwar Independence (an offer which Gandhi compared to "a post-dated cheque on a failing bank"). British attempts to find a solution that would preserve a united India and allay Muslim fears after the war, disintegrated in the face of continued intransigence from both sides, and they gradually realized that the division – or so-called **Partition** – of the existing country of India into separate Muslim and Hindu states was inevitable.

Independence

India achieved **Independence** (and the newly created state of Pakistan came into official existence) on August 14 and 15, 1947. The celebrations were overshadowed, however, by events in the newly partitioned Punjab, where five million Hindus and Sikhs from Pakistan and a similar number of Muslims from India fled from India to Pakistan or vice-versa, accompanied by an enormous outbreak of reciprocal communal atrocities which cost half a million lives. The fighting even spread as far as **Delhi**. Most of the city's Urdu-speaking Muslims who had lived there since the time of the Mughals, fled to Pakistan, while numerous Punjabi Sikhs travelled in the opposite direction, dramatically altering the city's ethnic demographic, while post-Partition, towns like Jaisalmer and Bikaner suddenly found themselves marooned at the country's western extremity and severed from traditional trans-Thar trading routes which had previously connected them to places in what had suddenly become Pakistan.

The modern state of **Rajasthan** was slightly longer in the making. Following Independence, the rulers of the region's princely states finally agreed to merge with India, and the new state – the largest in the country – was formally inaugurated on March 30, 1949 (though it didn't reach its current extent until November 1956, when Ajmer and a few areas in the south were added). Jaipur was named the new capital, and its maharaja, Man Singh II, given the honorary title of *Rajpramukh*, a kind of ceremonial head of state. Many centuries of proud independence were thus erased at a single administrative stroke. Their rulers – who had suddenly become ex-rulers – were allowed to retain their titles and property, and were to be solaced by generous allowances, the so-called "privy purses", to be funded in perpetuity by the national government.

The Marwaris: business warriors of Rajasthan

One of Rajasthan's major contributions to modern India has been the business skills of its **Marwari merchant** community. Originally hailing from the region around Jaipur – Shekhawati in particular – Marwari merchants have long been famous as traders in Rajasthan, and have been venturing further afield since perhaps as far back as the sixteenth century, accompanying local princes who had been appointed as governors to distant provinces by the Mughals. In the nineteenth century, many Marwari merchants left Rajasthan and moved out to India's burgeoning new cities, Bombay and Calcutta in particular, where they established commercial dynasties which in many cases have survived to this day – most notably the great **Birla** group in Calcutta, one of India's largest industrial conglomerates, which was established (and is still owned) by a Marwari family from Pilani in Shekhawati. Marwari businessmen such as G.D. Birla were also closely associated with the Independence struggle, and gave generous financial support to Congress and other opponents of British rule – and also played a vital role in the country's rapid industrialization following Independence in 1947.

Nehru and Indira Gandhi

Jawaharlal Nehru, India's first and longest-serving prime minister, proved a dynamic and popular leader, establishing a democratic, secular nation and overseeing the first stages of its agricultural and industrial development, while the country's first elections, in 1951, involving 173 million voters, made India the **world's largest democracy**. Many of the Rajput rulers who had lost their hereditary powers at Independence now began to enter the democratic fray, often with considerable success thanks to the esteem in which they continued to be held by their former subjects.

On the economic front, Nehru engineered the first three of India's Five-Year Plans, inaugurating a programme of rapid industrialization whose productive (if unaesthetic) results can be seen in the massive factories and chimney stacks which ring cities like Agra and Kota. In foreign policy, Nehru became closely associated with the widespread postwar pan-Asian policy of **nonalignment**, which sought to keep a healthy distance from both the US and USSR, though this had to be speedily abandoned (and replaced with desperate appeals for US military aid) in 1962 following a brief Chinese invasion of Assam. Nehru died in 1964, which prevented him from witnessing the restoration of India's military prestige in the **Indo–Pakistan War** of 1965, during which Indian tanks advanced to within 5km of a virtually defenceless Lahore before a UN ceasefire was agreed.

Nehru's daughter **Indira Gandhi** succeeded her father as leader of Congress in 1966 and continued his policy of rapid industrialization and agricultural development – the latter, the so-called "Green Revolution", led to the enviable position of India becoming entirely self-sufficient in food production by the 1970s. She also introduced a series of socialist reforms that included abolishing the generous annual allowances that had been granted to the rulers of the princely states, such as the maharajas of Rajasthan, at Independence. In a final indignity, the state's increasingly impoverished former masters were thus forced to either sell off their assets or convert their superb ancestral palaces into luxury hotels in order to get by.

After widespread unrest against the rate of inflation and corruption within the Congress in 1975, Mrs Gandhi declared a **State of Emergency**, which suspended all civil rights and silenced all opposition, using strict press censorship. Her administrative and economic reforms had the desired effect of cutting inflation and curbing corruption, but the enforced sterilization of men with two or more children, and brutal slum clearances in Delhi supervised by her son Sanjay, created a widespread legacy of bitterness. When she finally released her opponents and called off the Emergency in January 1977, the widespread anger she had engendered resulted in her ignominious defeat in the March elections. The ensuing **Janata** coalition fell apart within two years and Mrs Gandhi, who had rebuilt her Congress (I) Party with Sanjay's help, swept back into office in 1980. Their joint triumph was short-lived, however. Sanjay died in a plane crash soon afterwards, and in 1984 **Mrs Gandhi was assassinated** in Delhi by her Sikh bodyguards in retaliation for her decision to send the Indian Army into Amritsar's Golden Temple to flush out Sikh militants holed up in the shrine. Delhi was subsequently convulsed by another wave of communal rioting during which thousands of Sikhs were murdered.

The rise of the BJP

Mrs Gandhi's other son, **Rajiv Gandhi**, a former airline pilot, came to power in 1984 on a wave of sympathy boosted by his reputation as "Mr Clean". The honeymoon was short-lived, however, and allegations of corruption soon tarnished his image. In December 1989 elections, V.P. Singh's ousted Janata Party formed a coalition government with the support of the "Hindu first" **Bharatiya Janata Party** (BJP), led by L.K. Advani. Founded in 1980, the BJP was to prove a massive new force in Indian politics, and the only nationwide challenger to Congress. The BJP has been widely criticized for being anti-Muslim and for stirring up communal tensions, though its formidable electoral success is based on a wide-ranging appeal to India's more traditional voters. The party has done particularly well in Rajasthan, breaking the virtual monopoly of power that Congress had enjoyed in the state since Independence.

Singh's government lasted less than a year thanks to the first and most controversial of all the BJP's policies, led by Advani, who argued that the Babri Masjid mosque in **Ayodhya**, built by Babur in the sixteenth century on the supposed site of the birthplace of Rama, god-hero of the epic Ramayana, should be torn down and replaced with a Hindu temple. The building rapidly became a deeply contentious symbol of the increasingly rocky relationship between India's two largest religious groups. Singh, utterly committed to secularism, pleaded with Advani to desist but, undeterred, Advani set off towards Ayodhya in October 1990. Singh had Advani arrested before he could reach Ayodhya, but saw his own coalition immediately collapse as a result. Fresh elections were called, in the lead-up to which Congress were doing well, promising a return to power for Rajiv Gandhi, until he was assassinated by Tamil Tigers seeking revenge for India's intervention in the civil war in Sri Lanka.

It was left to **P.V. Narasimha Rao** to steer Congress to electoral victory, though the BJP also increased its parliamentary representation, with Advani becoming leader of the opposition. Simmering tensions at Ayodhya final boiled over in December 1992, when extremists incited crowds of fanatical devotees to tear down the Babri Masjid in a blaze of publicity. Nationwide riots ensued, and the BJP-led state governments (including those of Rajasthan and Delhi) were suspended. Subsequent elections in these states in late 1993 showed that the popularity of the BJP, and its call for the creation of **Hindutva**, a Hindu homeland, was fading. They reasserted control of Delhi, which has always been a stronghold of the Hindu right, barely hung on in Rajasthan, and lost the rest.

National morale during this post-Ayodhya period was shaky. After a year blighted by riots and the rise of religious extremism, it seemed as if India's era as a secular state was doomed. Against this backdrop of uncertainty, the rise of right-wing Hindu-fundamentalist parties gathered pace. Temporarily cowed by the Babri Masjid debacle, the BJP took advantage of the power struggle in the Congress Party to rekindle regional support. Expediently sidelining the contentious Hindutva agenda, the new rallying cry was **Swadeshi** – a campaign against the Congress-led programme of economic liberalization and, in particular, the activities of multinationals such as **Coca-Cola**, **Pepsi** and **KFC** (one of whose branches was forced to close by the BJP-controlled Delhi municipality).

After the general election of May 1996, the BJP emerged as the single largest party and attempted to form a government but was unable to muster a majority and was ousted by the hastily formed Unified Front coalition. Another general election followed in March 1998, after which the BJP struggled to power as the head of a new conservative coalition government under **Atal Behari Vajpayee**. The BJP had promised change and the restoration of national pride, and one of its early acts in government was to conduct five underground **nuclear tests** in May 1998 in Pokaran near Jaisalmer (see box, p.295), provoking Pakistan to respond in kind.

Following its defeat in the 1998 elections, the Congress Party emerged as a stronger political force with **Sonia Gandhi**, the Italian-born widow of Rajiv Gandhi, at the helm. Congress helped to bring about the downfall of the BJP in

April 1999, but was unable to form a coalition government. As a consequence, India faced a third **general election** in as many years. At the start of the campaign, Congress hopes were high that, with a Gandhi once again as party leader, it could revive the popular support lost after years of infighting and corruption scandals. However, a decisive victory against Pakistan in a border conflict at Kargil was a godsend for Vajpayee. Riding high on the feel-good factor, his party inflicted the biggest defeat Congress had sustained since Independence.

The new millennium

Figures from the **millennium census** revealed that the population of India stood at around 1.1 billion (with a literacy rate of 66 percent and an average life expectancy of 68 years – a significant increase on those of 1947). This measure of national progress, however, was eclipsed by a succession of catastrophic natural disasters which wracked the country in mid-2000, including a savage **drought** in parts of Rajasthan and Gujarat, during which high summer temperatures and the third failure of the monsoon in as many years forced tens of thousands of poor farming families off their land in search of fodder and drinking water.

Elections in 2004 brought Congress back to power under the leadership of Sonia Gandhi, although constant BJP sniping over her foreign origins led to the appointment of former finance minister **Manmohan Singh** as prime minister. Despite opposition carping, Singh's low-key leadership, concentrating on economic fundamentals, the alleviation of poverty and improving relationships with Pakistan, proved surprisingly popular in a country which had enjoyed more than its fair share of big-talking but ineffective politicians. Singh was also India's first ever Sikh prime minister, while in July 2007 the then Governor of Rajasthan, **Pratibha Patil**, was sworn in as India's first ever female president.

Despite improving relationships with Pakistan, Delhi continued to be targeted by **Islamic militants**. In September 2008 a series of five explosions killed around thirty people in Delhi (with another bomb attack later the same month killing three more). More surprising – and even more deadly – were the blasts that rocked the normally peaceful city of **Jaipur** in May 2008, when seven bombs exploded in various busy streets around the Pink City, killing 63 people – various militant Islamic organizations including the Bangladesh-based Harkat-ul-Jihad-al-Islami, the Student's Islamic Movement of India and the Pakistan-based Lashkar-e-Taiba were implicated in the attacks. Further **elections in 2009** saw an unexpected landslide victory for Manmohan Singh's Congress-led coalition. Congress even suceeded in wresting back control of Rajasthan from the BJP, while Singh himself became the first Indian leader to be immediately returned to power after a five-year term since Nehru in 1952.

Meanwhile, in Rajasthan, **water**, or the lack of it, remains a chronic problem, with the persistent failure of the monsoon in many parts of the region. Substantial underground water reserves remain, although they are being exhausted at an alarming rate. The Rajasthani economy has been boosted by another liquid asset, however, with a discovery of large **oil reserves** around the remote desert city of Barmer, thought to be worth around $1.5 billion per year, with the first barrels rolling off the production line in mid-2009.

Delhi and Rajasthan thus continue to symbolize many of the jarring paradoxes of modern Indian life – between oil millionaires on the one hand, and those who cannot even afford clean drinking water on the other. The coca-colonization of the urban middle classes continues apace, with smart modern residential and commercial developments springing up on a weekly basis in Jaipur and, especially, Delhi, as the Indian capital underwent a massive urban face-lift in preparation for

You don't have to be long in Rajasthan to realize that **women** are rarely seen or heard. As part of the state's feudal legacy, the purdah system, by which married women are kept isolated and under veil by their husbands, is still widespread in rural areas. Ditto for the dowry system and the age-old practice by which girls are denied an education. Women living in the state's rural areas are arguably the most repressed in all of India. By one account half are forced into marriage by the age of fifteen, and despite the intense work of internationally supported NGOs like the Urmul Trust and Barefoot College (see p.259), which work to valorize the contributions of women to rural life, economic independence remains at best a distant dream for most.

But it's not all chauvinism and second-class status. In India's male-dominated political system, where women have an abysmally low representation, it's striking that, under the conservative BJP regime which held power in Rajasthan from 2003 to 2008, the state's top three political offices – Chief Minister, Governor, and Speaker of the Rajasthan Assembly – were all women. The BJP's Chief Minister, **Vasundhara Raje**, hails from a politically powerful family that has long monopolized power in the state. Key to her 2003 election victory was her marriage to the former ruler of Dholpur. Her decision to play the role of maharani during the campaign – trading in her chiffons for bright ethnic garb and a *rath* (chariot) – certainly endeared her to a local populace nostalgic for Rajputana's glorious past. But many feminists were uncomfortable with Raje's actions and asserted that she, along with Governor **Pratibha Patil** and Assembly Speaker **Sumitra Singh**, rose to the top of their field by playing as rough and dirty as the boys and carefully avoiding the suicidal tag of "feminist".

Raje and Singh both lost office following the BJP's defeat by Congress in the 2008 state elections, but Governor Patil – who belongs to the Congress Party – moved on to higher things: in 2007 she became India's first woman President of the Republic. Gender equality is obviously still a long way off, but Patil's achievement does demonstrate that, despite everything, a Rajasthani woman can break through the glass ceiling.

C

CONTEXTS | History

its role as host of the **2010 Commonwealth Games**. And meanwhile, just a few hundred kilometres away, impoverished Rajasthani villagers continue to eke a living out of the soil using technology that has hardly changed in centuries. Whether or not future governments can simultaneously satisfy the burgeoning social and economic aspirations of India's urban middle classes, while also providing for the basic needs of its rural poor, remains to be seen.

Religion

T he region encompassing Delhi, Agra and Rajasthan is one of India's most religiously diverse areas, predominantly **Hindu**, though also including a large **Muslim** community, as well as a considerable number of **Sikhs**. **Delhi** and **Agra** have traditionally been among India's most Islamicized cities thanks to their history as the seat of power of the country's two most important Muslim dynasties (although many of Delhi's Muslims left the city during Partition in 1947, their places taken by incoming Sikhs from the Punjab). **Rajasthan**, by contrast, has always been staunchly Hindu, though its people have espoused a variety of gods, ranging from the ruling Rajputs' devotion to the cult of Krishna through to the flourishing array of local deities worshipped in the state's rural villages. The **Jain** religion has also added another small but colourful thread to the region's cultural fabric.

Hindu gods and goddesses

Vishnu

The chief function of **Vishnu**, "**the preserver**", is to maintain the balance of the universe. He is typically depicted as blue-skinned with four arms, holding a conch, discus, lotus and mace, and often shaded by a serpent, or resting on its coils, afloat on an ocean. He is usually seen alongside his half-man-half-eagle vehicle, **Garuda**. His consort is **Lakshmi**. According to tradition, Vishnu has descended to earth nine times in various forms (avatars) in order to fight the forces of evil and chaos and preserve the harmony of the cosmos: as a fish (Matsya), tortoise (Kurma), boar (Varaha), man-lion (Narsingh), dwarf (Vamana), axe-wielding Brahmin (Parsuram), Rama, Krishna and Buddha (though some claim that Krishna's brother, Balaram, was also an avatar of Vishnu, and some even reckon Jesus an avatar). The most important of the nine avatars are Rama (the hero of the Ramayana; see p.375) and Krishna (a character in the Mahabharata; see p.375). Vishnu's tenth appearance on earth as Kalki, the saviour who will come to restore purity and destroy the wicked, is eagerly awaited. Followers of Vishnu, or **Vaishnavites**, are often recognizable by two vertical lines of paste on their foreheads.

Shiva

Shiva, unlike Vishnu, has never been incarnate on earth, but is presented in many different aspects, such as **Nataraja** (Lord of the Dance), **Mahadev** (the Great God), **Maheshvar** (the source of all knowledge), and the terrible **Bhairav**, the god of the Shaivite ascetics who renounce family and caste ties and perform extreme meditative and yogic practices. Though he does have terrifying aspects, his role extends beyond that of destroyer, and he is revered as the source of the whole universe. He is typically depicted holding a trident, draped with serpents, and bearing a third eye in his forehead. In temples, he is identified with the lingam, or phallic symbol, resting in the yoni, a representation of female sexuality. Shiva is guarded by his bull-mount, **Nandi**, and often accompanied by his consort, **Parvati**, who also assumes various forms, and is looked upon as the vital energy, **shakti**, that empowers him.

Other gods and goddesses

Chubby and smiling, **Ganesh** acquired his unmistakeable elephant head when he was mistakenly beheaded by his father, Shiva. The first son of Shiva and Parvati, Ganesh is invoked before every undertaking (except funerals). Seated on a throne or lotus, his image is often placed above temple gateways, in shops and houses; in his four arms he holds a conch, discus, bowl of sweets (or club) and a water lily, and he's

Hinduism

Contemporary **Hinduism** – the religion of over 85 percent of Indians – permeates every aspect of life, from commonplace daily chores to education and politics. It has no founder or prophet, no single creed, and no single prescribed practice or doctrine; it takes in hundreds of gods, goddesses, beliefs and practices, and widely variant cults and philosophies. Some deities are recognized by only two or three villages, others are popular right across the Subcontinent. Hindus (a term derived from the name of the Indus River, the cradle of South Asian civilization) call their beliefs and practices **dharma** – a way of living righteously and in harmony with the natural order.

Early developments

The foundations of Hinduism were laid by the **Aryans**, who are believed to have migrated into northwest India during the second millennium BC. They brought a

always attended by his vehicle, a rat. Credited with writing the Mahabharata as it was dictated by the sage Vyasa, Ganesh is regarded by many as the god of learning, the lord of success, prosperity and peace.

The great mother goddess, or **Mahadevi**, is represented in various forms. The most important is **Durga**, the fiercest of the female deities, an aspect of Shiva's consort **Parvati** (also known as Uma), typically shown with ten arms, riding a tiger. Parvati, associated with beauty and fidelity, is her gentler aspect, but she may also appear as the fearsome **Kali**, goddess of destruction, depicted with a garland of skulls round her neck, and her tongue hanging from her mouth, dripping with blood.

Vishnu's consort **Lakshmi**, usually shown sitting or standing on a lotus flower, and sometimes called Padma (lotus), is the embodiment of loveliness, grace and charm, and the goddess of prosperity and wealth (and thus enduringly popular with India's commercial classes). Lakshmi appears in different aspects alongside each of his avatars; the most important are Sita, wife of Rama, and Radha, Krishna's favourite *gopi*. In many temples she is shown as one with Vishnu, in the form of the composite male-female Lakshmi Narayan.

India's great monkey god, **Hanuman**, features in the Ramayana as Rama's chief aide in the fight against the demon-king of Lanka. Depicted as a giant monkey clasping a mace, Hanuman is the deity of acrobats and wrestlers, but is also seen as Rama and Sita's greatest devotee, and an author of Sanskrit grammar. As his representatives, monkeys find sanctuary in temples all over India.

Brahma, the creator, shown with four faces, has diminished in importance since Shiva and Vishnu took over as the main Hindu gods, but he still has a major temple at Pushkar (see p.263). His consort is **Saraswati**, the goddess of music, creativity and learning, who is usually shown with a flawless milk-white complexion, sitting or standing on a water lily or peacock, playing a lute, sitar or *vina*.

Mention must also be made of the **sacred cow**, Kamdhenu, who receives devotion through the respect shown to all cows, left to amble through streets and temples all over India. The origin of the cow's sanctity is uncertain; some myths record that Brahma created cows at the same time as Brahmins, to provide ghee (clarified butter) for use in priestly ceremonies. To this day cow dung and urine are used to purify houses (in fact the urine keeps insects at bay), and the killing or harming of cows by any Hindu is a grave offence. The cow is often referred to as mother of the gods, and each part of its body is significant: its horns symbolize the gods, its face the sun and moon, its shoulders Agni (god of fire) and its legs the Himalayas.

number of gods with them, including **Agni**, the god of fire and sacrifice, **Surya**, the sun-god, and **Indra**, the chief god. Most of these deities subsequently faded in importance, though Indra is still regarded as the father of the gods, and Surya, widely worshipped until the Middle Ages, still has particular significance in Rajasthan, as some ruling families (including the Sisodias of Udaipur) claim direct descent from the sun.

Aryan religious beliefs were set out in the **Vedas**, a collection of hymns, prayers and directions for ceremonial rituals, transmitted orally for centuries, and written down in Sanskrit between 1600 BC and 1000 BC. The second group of core Hindu religious writings, the **Upanishads**, written between 800 BC and 400 BC, describe in beautiful verse the mystic experience of unity of the soul (*atman*) with **Brahma**, the supreme god, ideally attained through asceticism, renunciation of worldly values and meditation. The Upanishads also introduce the concepts of **samsara**, a cyclic round of death and rebirth characterized by suffering and perpetuated by desire, and **moksha**, liberation from *samsara*. These fundamental aspects of the Hindu world view are accepted by all but a handful of Hindus today, along with the belief in **karma**, according to which one's present position in society is determined by one's actions in past lives.

Caste

Hindu society is divided into four hierarchical classes, or **varnas**, each assigned specific religious and social duties. In descending order the *varnas* are: **brahmins** (priests and teachers), **kshatriyas** (rulers and warriors), **vaishyas** (merchants and cultivators) and **shudras** (menials). Below the four *varnas* are the casteless **untouchables** or **dalits**, whose jobs involve contact with dirt or death (such as undertakers, leather-workers and cleaners). Though discrimination against *dalits* is now illegal, thanks in part to the campaigns of Gandhi (who rechristened them the "Harijans", or "Children of God"), their social disadvantage has by no means disappeared.

Within the four *varnas*, social status is further defined by **jati**, in which each individual is classified according to family and occupation (for example, a *vaishya* may belong to any one of hundreds of groups – anything from a jewellery seller or cloth merchant to a cowherd or farmer). Although the *varnas* are sometimes referred to as castes, a person's *jati* is their true **caste**, and restricts them in many ways, from the food they can eat to their religious obligations and their relations with other castes. It also determines possible marriage partners, since Hindus generally only marry members of the same *jati*, and marrying someone of a different *varna* often results in social ostracism. There are almost three thousand *jatis*; the divisions and restrictions they have enforced have repeatedly become the subject of reform movements and the target of critics – though, equally, they also ensure a valuable but easily overlooked degree of social cohesion and economic support. Your caste, and thus your rank in society, is held to be based on *karma* from your previous lives, and gaining good *karma* through righteousness in this life is believed to give you a higher caste in the next one.

The principal Hindu deities

Surpassing even the Vedas and Upanishads in cultural influence and popularity, Hinduism's two great epics, the **Mahabharata** and **Ramayana** (see box opposite), are thought to have been written by the fourth century AD, and helped crystallize the basic framework of Hindu religious belief which survives to this day, based on

The Mahabharata

Eight times as long as the *Iliad* and *Odyssey* combined, the **Mahabharata** tells of a feuding *kshatriya* family in northern India during the fourth millennium BC. The chief character is **Arjuna**, who, with his four brothers, represent the **Pandava** clan, supreme fighters and upholders of righteousness. The Pandava clan are resented by their cousins, the evil **Kauravas**, led by Duryodhana, the eldest son of Dhrtarashtra, ruler of the Kuru kingdom.

When Dhrtarashtra hands his kingdom over to the Pandavas, the Kauravas are understandably less than overjoyed. The subsequent battle between the Pandavas and Kauravas is described in the sixth book, which includes the famous **Bhagavad Gita**. This consists of the words of Arjuna's friend and advisor **Krishna**; when Arjuna feels unable to kill his own kin, even in pursuit of a rightful kingdom, Krishna reveals himself to be an incarnation of the god Vishnu, and reminds Arjuna that earthly life is only transient, and that as an immortal being, Arjuna must fulfil his dharma, which in this case means his duty as a warrior for a just cause.

The Pandavas finally win the battle and Yudhishtra, eldest of the five Pandava brothers, is crowned king. Eventually Arjuna's grandson, Pariksit, inherits the throne, and the Pandavas trek to Mount Meru, the mythical centre of the universe and the abode of the gods.

The Ramayana

The Ramayana tells the story of **Rama**, the seventh of Vishnu's eight incarnations (Krishna is the eighth). Although possibly based on a historic figure, Rama is essentially a representation of Vishnu's heroic qualities. Rama is the oldest of four sons born to Dasaratha, the king of Ayodhya, and heir to the throne. When the time comes for Rama's coronation, Dasaratha's scheming third wife Kaikeyi has her own son Bharata crowned instead, and has Rama banished to the forest for fourteen years. In a show of filial piety, Rama accepts the loss of his throne and leaves the city with his wife Sita and brother Laksmana.

One day, Suparnakhi, the sister of the demon **Ravana**, spots Rama in the woods and instantly falls in love with him. Being a virtuous, loyal husband, Rama rebuffs her advances, while Laksmana cuts off her nose and ears in retaliation. In revenge, Ravana kidnaps Sita, who is borne away to one of Ravana's palaces on the island of **Lanka**.

Determined to find Sita, Rama enlists the help of the monkey god **Hanuman**, and the two of them gather an army and invade Lanka. After much fighting, Sita is rescued and reunited with her husband. On the way back to Ayodhya, Sita's honour is brought into question. To prove her innocence, she asks Laksmana to build a funeral pyre and steps into the flames, praying to Agni, the fire god. Agni walks her through the fire into the arms of a delighted Rama. They march into Ayodhya guided by a trail of lights laid out by the local people. Today, this illuminated homecoming is commemorated by Hindus all over the world during **Diwali**, the festival of lights. At the end of the epic, Rama's younger brother gladly steps down, allowing Rama to be crowned as the rightful king.

---

a triumvirate of supreme deities. **Brahma**, the original Aryan godhead, or "creator", was joined by two gods who had begun to achieve increasing significance in the evolving Hindu worldview, **Vishnu** ("the preserver") and **Shiva**, "the destroyer" (a development of the Aryan god Rudra, who played a minor role in the Vedas). The three supreme gods are often depicted in a trinity, or *trimurti*, though Brahma's importance has long since declined relative to Shiva and Vishnu – the famous Brahma temple at Pushkar (see p.262) is now one of the few in India dedicated to this venerable but rather esoteric god.

Local Rajasthani deities

In addition to the major Hindu gods (see box, pp.372–373), most of Rajasthan's tribal people and rural villagers worship various deities associated with the natural world; there are sacred trees in every village, while animals including cows, monkeys, peacocks, deer and snakes – as well as the famous rats of the Deshnok temple near Bikaner – all have various religious associations. Another remarkable example of how local agricultural and environmental concerns have merged with the religious is supplied by the tree-worshipping **Bishnois** of the Jodhpur region, who under their inspirational guru Jambeshwar Bhagavan espoused a pantheistic creed in which all forms of natural life are considered sacred – for their full story, see p.278.

A number of folk heroes have also achieved quasi-divine status and are widely worshipped throughout the state (and in other parts of India), the pre-eminent

Krishna

Krishna, the penultimate incarnation of Vishnu (see box, p.372), takes a pre-eminent place in the affections of maharajas and commoners alike. The Chandravansa (moon-descended) Rajput dynasties (see p.357) claim direct descent from him, and he is also considered the tutelary deity of the rulers of Jaipur, as well as occupying an important place in the religious worship of the house of Mewar, the rulers of Udaipur.

Krishna was probably originally a historical figure who lived around 3200–3000 BC. According to legend, he was born into the ruling family of the kingdom of **Mathura**, between Agra and Delhi. It was ruled by a tyrant named Kansa, who had usurped his own father and, according to a prophecy, would meet his death at the hands of his sister's eighth son, Krishna. Luckily, before Kansa could have him killed, the boy was spirited away and brought up in secret as the adopted son of a cowherd in the countryside of **Vrindavan**, Mathura's hinterland. The young Krishna spent his time sporting with the local maidens, or **gopis**, in particular his favourite, **Radha** (considered an incarnation of Vishnu's consort, Lakshmi).

In due course Krishna grew to manhood and, fulfilling the prophecy, returned to Mathura, slew Kansa, and placed his father back on the throne. He also became friendly with his cousins, the **Pandavas**, the heroes of the Mahabharata (see box, 375), serving as Arjuna's charioteer during the epic's climactic battle and offering him the advice which forms the core of the celebrated **Bhagavad Gita**. He later established a kingdom at **Dwarka**, on the coast of modern Gujarat, where he eventually died, accidentally shot by a hunter while meditating in the forest.

Part of the reason for Krishna's local importance is geographical. The proximity of the sacred region of Vrindavan meant that certain Rajput rulers (particularly the Kachchwahas of Amber) became directly involved in preserving temples and religious artefacts in the area – the images worshipped by the rulers of Udaipur at Nathdwara (see p.329) and the rulers of Jaipur at the city's Govind Devji temple were both rescued from Vrindavan during the time when Aurangzeb was attacking non-Muslim religions. In addition, Krishna's military ethos, as expressed in the Bhagavad Gita, is very much of a piece with Rajput warrior values.

It is Krishna's amatory exploits as the young flute-playing cowherd Govinda, however, that continue to inspire the greatest devotion in his followers, and he is most often depicted dancing with the *gopis*, or playing his flute to them. Their love for Krishna equates physical and spiritual love – a form of personal devotion, or **bhakti**, which makes it possible to achieve union with the divine without the ritualized intercession of Brahmin priests or the asceticism and renunciation which had previously been considered essential elements in traditional Hindu worship, and which lies at the heart of Krishna's enduring appeal, both to Indians and to Krishna devotees worldwide.

being Gogaji and Pabuji. **Gogaji** (or Gugga, also revered by Muslims, who call him Jahar Pir) was an eleventh-century Chauhan Rajput from the Churu region in Shekhawati. According to legend he was chasing bandits who had stolen a relative's cows when he was confronted by a hostile snake. Gogaji pleaded with the snake to allow him to pass, promising to return later. The snake granted this wish, and Gogaji – having bested the dacoits – returned to the snake as promised. The snake, impressed by the warrior's honesty, promised that Gogaji would henceforth have the power to cure his followers of snakebite, and many villages have shrines to him, to which victims of snakebite are taken. Like Gogaji, the medieval Hundu reformer **Ramdevji** (see p.296) is also revered by Hindus and Muslims alike.

Rajasthan's other principal folk deity, **Pabuji**, was another warrior-like figure who has achieved immortality thanks to his devotion to cows. The historical Pabuji appears to have been a minor fourteenth-century noble belonging to the Rathore clan of the Jodhpur region, although he has since become embroiled in a tangled skein of legend, existing in various confusing versions (in one he even travels to Lanka and, Rama-like, kills the demon king Ravana). The various Pabuji legends are all characterized by his superhuman fighting prowess and his long struggles to prevent the cattle-rustling villain Khici from making off with the herds of Deval (perhaps a form of the mother goddess Devi), during which Pabuji is assisted by his magical horse, Kesar Kalami (who, it turns out, is a reincarnation of his own mother). Interestingly, Pabuji's divine status is not accepted by higher-caste Hindus, and his shrines are attended not by Brahmins, but by low-caste Nayaks.

Female deities and folk heroes also have an important place in the Rajasthan pantheon; most are considered manifestations of the Mother God, or Mahadevi. Various local incarnations of the Devi (or, according to other interpretations, Durga) are widely worshipped, most famously **Karni Mata** (see p.308), the miracle-working medieval divine whose bizarre rat temple just outside Bikaner still attracts hordes of pilgrims. Women who have voluntarily performed **sati** are widely venerated – most famously at the immensely popular Sati Mata temple at Jhunjhunu in Shekhawati, though shrines to *satis* can be seen throughout the region, most famously at Chittaurgarh Fort.

Hindu religious practice

The primary concern of most Hindus is to reduce bad karma and acquire merit by honest and charitable living in the hope of attaining a higher status of rebirth. Strict rules address purity and pollution, the most obvious of them requiring high-caste Hindus to limit their contact with "polluting" lower castes. All bodily excretions are polluting (hence the strange looks Westerners receive when they blow their noses and return their handkerchiefs to their pockets). Above all else, **water** is the agent of purification, used in ablutions before prayer, and revered in all rivers, especially Ganga (the Ganges).

In most Hindu homes, a chosen deity is worshipped daily in a shrine room, and scriptures are read. Outside the home, worship takes place in temples, and consists of **puja**, or devotion to god – sometimes a simple act of prayer, but more commonly a complex process when the god's image is circumambulated, offered flowers, rice, sugar and incense, and anointed with water, milk or sandalwood paste (which is usually done on behalf of the devotee by the temple priest). The aim in puja is to take **darshan** – glimpse the god – and thus receive his or her blessing. Whether devotees simply worship the deity in prayer, or make requests – for a healthy crop, a son, good results in exams, a vigorous monsoon or a cure for illness – they leave the temple with *prasad*, an offering of food or flowers taken from the holy sanctuary.

Communal worship and get-togethers en route to pilgrimage sites are celebrated with the singing of hymns. Temple ceremonies are conducted in Sanskrit by *pujaris* who tend the image in daily rituals that symbolically wake, bathe, feed and dress the god, and finish each day by preparing the god for sleep during the elaborate evening ritual, or *aarti*. In many villages, shrines to *devatas* – village deities who function as protectors and may bring disaster if neglected – are more important than temples.

Festivals and pilgrimages

The Hindu year is marked by **festivals** devoted to deities, re-enacting mythological stories and commemorating sacred sites. The grandest festivals are held at places made holy by association with gods, goddesses, miracles, and great teachers, or rivers and mountains; throughout the year these are important **pilgrimage** sites, visited by devotees eager to receive *darshan*, glimpse the world of the gods, and attain merit. Important Hindu pilgrimage sites in Rajasthan include the Karni Mata temple near Bikaner (see p.307), the town of Pushkar and its Brahma temple (see p.259), the Sati Mata temple in Jhunjhunu (see p.222), and the Ramdev Mandir near Pokaran (see p.296).

For a full list of religious festivals see pp.53–55.

Islam

Muslims – making up nearly nine percent of Rajasthan's population, just over ten percent in Agra, and just under twelve percent in Delhi – form a significant presence in almost every town, city and village, and the majority in Ajmer. The belief in only one god, Allah, the condemnation of idol worship, and the observance of their own dietary laws and festivals set Muslims apart from their Hindu neighbours. Since Partition, Delhi and Rajasthan have largely avoided the communal fighting which has engulfed other parts of the country, most notably the neighbouring state of Gujarat.

Islam (literally, "submission to God") was founded by **Mohammed** (570–632 AD), to whom God transmitted the **Koran** (Qur'an), his final revelation to mankind. The Islamic era is dated from 622 AD, when Mohammed and his followers made the *hijra*, or migration from the holy city of Mecca to Medina, from where they attacked and defeated the Meccan pagans in 630, removing the idols from the city's sacred shrine, the Kaaba, and making it the centre of Islamic worship.

Muslim traders reached India in the seventh century, but it was the arrival of the **Ghaznavids** (see p.358) and the onset of Islamic rule that really established a Muslim presence in Delhi and Agra. The Muslim presence in Rajasthan also dates from this time: Ajmer became part of the Ghaznavid empire, and Muslims also established a subsidiary statelet further north at Jhunjhunu in Shekhawati, where they continue to live in considerable numbers. The fruits of Islamic rule include the superb Islamic monuments of Delhi, Agra, Fatehpur Sikri and Ajmer – the finest architectural legacy of Islam anywhere in the Subcontinent.

Many Muslims who settled in India intermarried with Hindus and Jains, and the community spread. A further factor in its growth was missionary activity by **Sufis**, who emphasized abstinence and self-denial in service to God, and stressed the attainment of inner knowledge of God through meditation and mystical experience. Sufi teachings also spread among Hindus – their use of music (particularly *qawwali* singing) and dance, shunned by orthodox Muslims, appealed to Hindus, for whom *kirtan* (singing) played an important role in religious practice. Some of India's most important Sufi **shrines** are located in Delhi, Agra and Rajasthan, including (most famously) the shrine of Khwaja Muin-ud-Din Chishti in Ajmer, along with the shrines of his successors, Sheikh Nizamuddin Aulia in Delhi and Sheikh Salim at Fatehpur Sikri.

Sikhism

Sikhs, originally from the Punjab, are less than one and a half percent of the Rajasthani population, but around four percent in Delhi, largely thanks to the influx of refugees from Pakistani Punjab in 1947.

Sikhism was founded by **Guru Nanak** (1469–1539) and combines elements of both Hinduism and Islam. Nanak declared that "God is neither Hindu nor Muslim" and regarded God as **Sat**, or truth. In common with Hindus, Nanak believed in a cyclic process of death and rebirth, but he asserted that liberation (*moksha*) was attainable in this life by anyone, regardless of caste. He opposed ancestor worship, astrology, caste and sex discrimination, auspicious days, and Brahmin rituals, but did not attack Islam or Hinduism, regarding their deities as names for one supreme God, and encouraging his followers to shift religious emphasis from ritual to meditation.

Following Nanak's death, nine successive Sikh gurus acted as leaders of the faith. Guru Arjan Dev became Sikhism's first martyr when he was executed in 1606 by Jahangir, while Guru Teg Bahadur was beheaded by Aurangzeb in 1675. In 1699 Teg Bahadur's son and successor, the last Sikh guru, **Gobind Singh**, founded the Sikh brotherhood known as the **Khalsa**, designed to protect the faithful from persecution and fight oppression. The Khalsa requires members to renounce tobacco, halal meat and sexual relations with Muslims, and to adopt the **five Ks**: *kesh* (unshorn hair – hence the distinctive Sikh turban), *kangha* (comb), *kirpan* (sword), *kara* (steel bracelet) and *kachcha* (short trousers). This code, together with the replacement of caste names with Singh ("lion") for men and Kaur ("princess") for women, created a distinct cultural identity. Guru Gobind Singh also compiled a standardized version of the Adi Granth, which contains the hymns of the first nine gurus as well as poems written by Hindus and Muslims, and installed it as his successor, naming it **Guru Granth Sahib**. This became the Sikhs' spiritual guide, while political authority rested with the Khalsa.

Sikh **worship** takes place in a **gurudwara** ("door to the guru") or in the home, providing a copy of the Guru Granth Sahib is present. There are no priests, and no fixed time for worship, but congregations often meet in the mornings and evenings, and always on the eleventh day of each lunar month, and on the first day of the year. During **Kirtan**, or hymn singing, a feature of every Sikh service, verses from the Guru Granth Sahib or Janam Sakhis (stories of Guru Nanak's life) are sung to rhythmic clapping. The communal meal, *langar*, following prayers and singing, reinforces the practice laid down by Guru Nanak that openly flaunted caste and religious differences. *Gurudwaras* – often schools, clinics or hostels as well as houses of prayer – are usually whitewashed and surmounted by a dome, and are always distinguishable by the *nishan sahib*, a yellow flag introduced by Guru Hargobind (1606–44). As in Islam, God is never depicted in pictorial form. Instead, the representative symbol Ek Onkar is etched into a canopy that shades the Guru Granth Sahib, which always stands in the main prayer room.

Jainism

Jains form less than one percent of India's population, but a relatively high 1.2 percent in Rajasthan, where Jain traders have played an important economic role, and the state is home to two of the world's finest Jain temple complexes (at Ranakpur and Mount Abu). Similarities to Hindu worship, and a shared respect for nature and non-violence, have contributed to the decline of the Jain community through conversion to Hinduism, but there is no antagonism between the two sects.

Focused on the practice of **ahimsa** (non-violence), Jains follow a rigorous discipline to avoid harm to all living substances – including humans, animals, plants, water, fire, earth and air. Like Hindus, they believe in *karma* and reincarnation. Jainism was founded by **Mahavira** (c.599–527 BC), the last of 24 **tirthankaras** ("crossing-makers") said to appear on earth every three hundred million years. Like his contemporary, Buddha, Mahavira spent years as an ascetic, and after achieving enlightenment, began preaching about the means required for *moksha* (release from the cycle of rebirth).

His teachings were written down in the first millennium BC, and Jainism thrived, but then came a schism between the **Digambaras** ("sky-clad"), who believed that nudity was an essential part of world renunciation, and that women are incapable of achieving *moksha*, and the **Svetambaras** ("white-clad"), who wore clothes and incorporated nuns into monastic communities, even acknowledging a female *tirthankara*. Today the two sects worship at different temples, but the number of naked Digambaras is minimal. Many Svetambara monks and nuns wear white masks to avoid breathing in insects, and carry a "fly-whisk", sometimes used to brush their path; none will use public transport, and they often spend days or weeks walking barefoot to a pilgrimage site.

Jain **temples** are wonderfully ornate, with pillars, brackets and spires carved into voluptuous maidens, musicians, saints, and even Hindu deities; the *swastika* symbol commonly set into the marble floors is central to Jainism, representing the four states of rebirth as gods, humans, "hell beings", or animals and plants. Worship in temples consists of prayer and puja before images of the *tirthankaras*; the devotee circumambulates the image, chants sacred verses and makes offerings of flowers, sandalwood paste, rice, sweets and incense. It's common to fast four times a month on *parvan* (holy) days, the eighth and fourteenth days of the moon's waxing and waning periods.

Art and architecture

The area covered by Rajasthan, Delhi and Agra boasts an extraordinary wealth of art and architecture, exemplified by world-famous monuments such as the Taj Mahal, the lake palaces of Udaipur, the desert citadel of Jaisalmer and Jodhpur's doughty Meherangarh Fort. Two distinct strands run through the region's artistic history: the Islamic monuments of the Delhi Sultanate and their Mughal successors, and the great forts and palaces of Hindu Rajasthan, and it is these two diverse traditions – and the constant interactions between them over the centuries – which have shaped almost all the region's artistic achievements.

Early Islamic architecture

The region's first great architectural monuments date from the beginning of Islamic rule in the Subcontinent, starting with the **Qutb Minar** complex in Delhi, built following the founding of the Slave Dynasty by Qutb-ud-Din Aiback in 1206. The complex is a good example of the eclectic range of styles that went into the making of north Indian architecture. The Qutb Minar itself is similar in design to earlier Persian funeral towers, while the adjacent **Quwwat-ul-Islam** ("Might of Islam"), India's first mosque, shows an odd stylistic contrast between its beautiful Islamic-style screen, with finely pointed arches and delicate bands of Koranic calligraphy, and the interior courtyard, made out of recycled columns salvaged from the Hindu and Jain temples which formerly stood on the site (a combination which can also be seen in Ajmer's Adhai-din-ka-Jhonpra).

The subsequent **Tughluq** dynasty favoured a monumentally simple architectural style, epitomized by buildings such as the massive Begumpuri Masjid and the fortress-like Khirki Masjid (both in south Delhi), as well as the stikingly minimalist tombs of Ghiyas ud-Din Tughluq at Tughluqabad and the similar Lal Gumbad nearby. The buildings of the later **Sayyid** and **Lodi** dynasties tend to be smaller in scale and much more effeminate in style, such as the pretty octagonal tombs of Sikander Lodi and Muhammad Shah in the Lodi Gardens – early precursors to the great garden tombs of the later Mughals.

Mughal architecture

For many people, the great monuments of the Mughal period represent the pinnacle of Indian architecture, although to what extent they can be properly regarded as "Indian" at all remains a subject of considerable debate, and Hindu nationalists have always felt uncomfortable with the way in which Indian culture is often symbolized by the "Islamic" Taj Mahal rather than, for example, by the temples of Khajuraho or Tamil Nadu. Conversely, during Partition, some Muslim nationalists claimed that the Taj Mahal should have been taken to pieces and moved to the Islamic state of Pakistan, where – they claimed – it more properly belonged.

In fact, despite its Muslim provenance and superficially Persian-influenced design, the sources of Mughal architecture are surprisingly varied, and include not only the Islamic styles which they brought with them from their original Central Asian homelands but many Indian features as well, ranging from local Hindu sculptural traditions through to the important (but easily overlooked) influence of the numerous Indo-Islamic works already constructed in the Subcontinent by the Delhi Sultans. Different styles come to the fore in different buildings, ranging from the largely Persian-style **Humayun's Tomb** through to the almost entirely Hindu buildings constructed during Akbar's reign at **Fatehpur Sikri** and **Agra Fort** – a constant interaction between conflicting styles which only achieved a kind of synthesis towards the end of the great Mughal period during the reign of Shah Jahan.

The early Mughals

The first two Mughal rulers, Babur and Humayun, were more concerned with establishing their hold on the empire, and left little in the way of physical remains. **Babur** appears to have been happy to live in tents during his four brief years in power, and channelled his creative energies into commissioning a modest sequence of Persian-style gardens inspired by his Central Asian homeland, such as the much-modified **Rambagh** at Agra. **Humayun** spent most of his life in exile, and had only just begun work on a new citadel in Delhi, now known as the **Purana Qila**, when he was deposed by the Afghan warlord **Sher Khan** (reigned 1540–55). Sher Khan continued Humayun's building works at the Purana Qila, commissioning the **Sher Mandal** pavilion and **Qila-i-Kuhna** mosque. The elegantly simple designs of these two buildings, with large masses of red sandstone delineated by towering pointed arches and bands of white marble, are the first buildings to display the essential hallmarks of what would later be called the "Mughal" style – a notable irony, given that they were created by the man who very nearly extinguished Mughal rule in India before it had even properly begun.

Akbar and Jahangir

Following Sher Khan's death, Humayun briefly reclaimed his Indian empire before tumbling to his death down a steep flight of steps in the Sher Mandal – Sher Khan's architectural legacy wreaking an unintentional posthumous revenge on his former adversary. It was thus left to **Akbar** to initiate the golden era of Mughal architecture (and art; see p.384).

Akbar and his successors embarked on an unprecedented architectural spree, the lavishness of their buildings intended to symbolize the dynasty's imperial glory, and thus to buttress its legitimacy in the eyes of their Hindu subjects. The first great Mughal monument is a royal mausoleum, **Humayun's Tomb** in Delhi, a type of building with which the Mughals would become inextricably associated, and which would eventually reach its apotheosis in the peerless Taj Mahal – though the fact that the Koran expressly forbids the construction of extravagant funerary monuments suggests just how shaky the Mughals' Islamic credentials really were, and how much they owed to local Indian cultural circumstances, including those of the recently vanquished Delhi Sultans, whose own funerary monuments can still be seen scattered across Delhi.

Humayun's Tomb established a pattern which was followed in virtually all Mughal mausoleums, with a monumental square or rectangular tomb chamber (usually – but not always – topped by a dome) set on a raised plinth within a *charbagh*-style Persian garden, divided into four quadrants by walkways and water channels – a symbolic representation of the gardens and rivers of paradise. Some of the tomb's design features had already appeared in mausoleums erected by the Delhi Sultans, though never before on this epic scale, with a huge but simple sandstone tomb, its monumental mass artfully broken up by symmetrical arched portals (*iwans*) and decorative bands of coloured inlay work, the whole combining simplicity with subtlety on an epic scale – a classic example of the Mughal style.

Humayun's Tomb is, however, quite untypical of most of the architecture of Akbar's reign. Far more representative are the great abandoned city of **Fatehpur Sikri** and **Agra Fort**, which Akbar comprehensively remodelled. Both these sites are characterized by their extraordinarily eclectic medley of architectural styles – from the chastely Islamic to the exuberantly Indian – a physical expression of the emperor's famous cultural and political tolerance. Many of the buildings at both sites are architectural one-offs, such as the strange **Diwan-i-Khas** at Fatehpur Sikri and the flamboyant, Gujarati-influenced **Jahangiri Mahal** at Agra Fort – not to mention the great mosque at Fatehpur Sikri which, in an odd echo of the Quwwat-ul-Islam mosque in Delhi, uses Hindu-style temple columns to support the arcades of an otherwise traditional Islamic place of worship.

Akbar's successor, **Jahangir**, was more interested in painting (and opium) than architecture. The major monument from his reign is another tomb, the enormous mausoleum built for Akbar at **Sikandra** near Agra, though it suffers from a rather hotchpotch design – possibly the result of the emperor's own interference in ongoing designs. More successful is the exquisite **Itimad-ud-daulah** mausoleum commissioned for her father by Jahangir's remarkable wife, Nur Jahan (see p.167), the dynasty's first purely marble structure, beautifully decorated with inlay work – a combination that was to become one of the defining features of the culminating phase of Mughal architecture.

Shah Jahan

The pinnacle of Mughal architecture was reached during the reign of **Shah Jahan**, one of the greatest patrons of architecture the world has known, whose massive sequence of building projects in Delhi and Agra has done much, for good or ill, to colour foreign perceptions of the nature of Indian art and culture. Many of Shah Jahan's creative energies were expended in comprehensively remodelling the old imperial capital at **Delhi**, where he commissioned both the Red Fort and the new city of Shahjahanabad (now better known as Old Delhi) – a gargantuan undertaking with which the self-styled King of the World (as his imperial moniker translates) intended to thoroughly eclipse all the creations of his illustrious forebears and stamp his mark on posterity once and for all. Unfortunately, both have suffered major depredations since their construction, and the only part of the plan that survives intact is the magnificent Jama Masjid, a vast sandstone edifice whose masterfully proportioned ensemble of *iwans*, domes and minarets encapsulates the Mughal style at its most massively simple and severe.

It is with **Agra**, however, that Shah Jahan is now most closely associated, most obviously the Taj Mahal, though he also made significant embellishments to the city's fort, creating a fine new sequence of apartments within Akbar's original palace. Whereas previous Mughal architecture had been built largely in sandstone, Shah Jahan's new palace architecture employed pristine white marble, typically decorated with beautiful *pietra dura* inlay, in which semiprecious stones were inlaid into the marble in graceful floral patterns and abstract geometrical designs.

Besides the lavish use of marble and *pietra dura*, Shah Jahan's buildings at Agra Fort also exemplify a new phase in Mughal architecture. Compared to the stylistic free-for-all of Akbar's reign, the elegantly simple outlines of Shah Jahan's palace buildings appear, superficially at least, to represent a return to a purer and more obviously Islamic style of architecture. Despite their ostensibly Persian appearance, however, Shah Jahan's creations also incorporate many of the Hindu features – chhatris, *chajjas*, *bangaldar*-style roofs and Hindu temple-style columns – which had crept into Mughal architecture during the reign of Akbar, though they are now incorporated into the overall design in a more subtle and considered form, achieving a genuine synthesis of Islamic and Indian motifs which is perhaps the true definition of the Mughal style.

This new-found synthesis is also present in Shah Jahan's **Taj Mahal**. Most obviously, the Taj represents the culmination of the great Mughal tradition of tomb building – an etherealized version of Humayun's Tomb, its proportions reworked in a more satisfyingly compact form and clad in a translucent coat of white marble. Again, however, the overall Islamic design is blended with specifically Indian elements, such as the four chhatris which surround the main dome, while even the four minarets which flank the mausoleum are topped by decidedly Indian-looking cupolas.

Mughal painting

Although the Mughals are now best remembered for their architectural creations, they also oversaw a golden era in Indian painting thanks to their assiduous patronage of both local and foreign artists (although many of the finest Mughal-era artworks are now in foreign collections). Mughal art grew out of the traditions of Persian painting, though, as with their buildings, a host of foreign influences soon enriched the original style. The painting of Persian-style miniatures had already been encouraged by Muslim rulers in various parts of India since the fifteenth century, such as the sultan of Mandu, in modern Madhya Pradesh, who around 1500 had commissioned the celebrated *Ni'mat-nama* ("Book of Delectation"), an illustrated recipe book.

The second Mughal emperor, **Humayun**, probably had painters working for him before his exile from India in 1539 (the loss of several illustrated manuscripts while on campaign is recorded by his court biographer). The effective foundation of the school of Mughal painting, however, can be dated to 1549, when Humayun, in temporary exile in Kabul, recruited the painters Mir Sayyid Ali and Abd al-Samad. Both subsequently travelled to India with Humayan, where they oversaw a creative explosion of Mughal art, as well as giving painting lessons to both Humayun and his son Akbar.

Akbar greatly increased production and established a state atelier, employing around a hundred mainly Hindu artists working under the supervision of Mir Sayyid Ali and Abd al-Samad, who trained these local artists in the Persian manner – while the Indian painters in turn introduced aspects of their own pictorial traditions. Akbar-era paintings were predominantly historical or political in nature; many depict famous events from various legends, showing a sense of drama and action quite unlike the more sedate style of the traditional Persian miniature. Most of these paintings were found in the enormous illustrated books which the emperor commissioned, including the *Akbarnama*, the official court history of his reign, along with other works of Muslim history, poetry and legend, most famously the *Romance of Amir Hamza* (or *Hamza-nama*), an account of the legendary struggles of the Prophet's uncle, comprising around fourteen hundred large (over 60cm high) illustrations painted on pieces of cotton. Richly illustrated translations of the Hindu classics the Mahabharata and Ramayana were also produced – a typical example of Akbar's tolerance and curiosity.

The increasing presence of European diplomats and merchants at Akbar's court also introduced local painters to contemporary Western art (a selection of illustrated Bibles presented to the emperor by a Jesuit mission in 1580 proved particularly influential). Europeans subsequently began to crop up occasionally in Mughal painting, as did Western stylistic features such as halos, cherubs and angels. In addition, a new Western-style emphasis on realism and the greater use of perspective began to creep into Mughal art; figures become more three-dimensional, with the introduction of shading on faces (though these developments were perhaps also partly influenced by Indian artists, who had been brought up in the much more sculptural traditions of Hindu art).

Mughal painting reached its apogee during the reign of **Jahangir**, who had a particular passion for the pictorial arts. Jahangir reduced the number of artists working for him and encouraged a cult of technical excellence, whereby individual painters became fully responsible for particular works (many Akbar-era works had been produced on an assembly-line principle, so that different artists were responsible for colouring, outlines, the painting of figures and faces, and for overall composition). The emphasis shifted from the massive illustrated historical books and dramatic action scenes favoured by Akbar to a much more restrained style, with far fewer figures, often arranged in carefully stylized poses. The most frequent subject is, not surprisingly, the emperor himself, who features in a long line of hagiographic portraits, some of them featuring an outlandish array of allegorical symbols (perhaps influenced by Western mannerist art) intended to emphasize Jahangir's secular and spiritual credentials. Natural history was another of the emperor's pet themes, and there are dozens of paintings, such as those by the famous artist Mansur, showing pictures of exotic creatures which had been brought to court, ranging from turkeys to zebras.

The production of miniatures continued under Shah Jahan, though he was less interested in painting than in jewellery and architecture. The pious Aurangzeb had even less concern with artistic matters, and his declining patronage meant that most of the painters of the Mughal atelier left court to work for Hindu nobles – a considerable number appear to have ended up in Rajasthan.

Rajput secular architecture

Rajput architecture developed out of a completely different set of cultural traditions to those which informed Mughal art, and although Mughal stylistic innovations had an important influence on Rajput designs (just as Rajput styles, in turn, influenced Mughal craftsmen), the art and architecture of the state evolved in its own distinct way, and out of an essentially Indian, rather than Islamic, tradition.

Despite the state's strong Hindu culture, Rajasthan's major monuments are almost all secular, either the great Rajput forts or the lavish palaces that were often built alongside or within them, or the flamboyant havelis constructed by wealthy merchants. The finest expressions of Rajput architecture can be found in the region's sumptuous **palaces** (for more on which, see the *Rajasthan forts and palaces* colour section). Like their Mughal equivalents, these buildings were intended to symbolize the glory of the ruling dynasty, and were frequently expanded and embellished by subsequent rulers, as in the remarkable City Palace at Udaipur, where over a dozen individual mini-palaces created by successive Mewari maharanas are squeezed into a single, sprawling edifice. Rajput palaces also reflect the Indian traditions shared by both Indian and Mughal rulers, both in their division into male and female quarters (the *mardana* and *zenana*, respectively – a division also seen in the region's havelis), and by their configuration of private and public spaces, exemplified by the *diwan-i-am* and *diwan-i-khas* (private and public audience halls) found in Mughal and Rajput palaces alike. The region's remarkable collection of **havelis** (the best of which can be found in Jaisalmer and Shekhawati) also shares many of these features, with a similar division into *mardana* and *zenana* quarters, and a homespun version of the *diwan-i-khas*, known as the *baithak*, in which local merchants would meet to transact business and swap news.

Although Mughal architecture had a strong influence on Rajput styles – leading to the introduction of features like mirrored Sheesh Mahals and cusped arches – most features of Rajput architecture spring from Hindu architectural traditions, with features drawn from temple and vernacular architecture. These include the **jarokha**, or projecting balcony, often containing a small window seat, which is one of the classic features of Rajput architecture; **chajjas**, a type of large overhanging eave, designed to protect against monsoonal downpours, also found its way into many Mughal buildings, along with other elements such as finely carved stone screens (*jalis*), cusped arches fringed with stylized lotus buds, coloured tiles and traditional decorative patterns. Another characteristic architectural motif is the **bangaldar** pavilion, topped with a distinctively curved roof inspired by the roof of Bengali village huts (a notable pair of copper-roofed *bangaldar* pavilions can even be seen flanking the Khas Mahal in Agra Fort).

Perhaps the classic Rajasthani architectural feature, however, is the **chhatri** (literally "umbrella", though often described as "pavilions"), usually a simple dome supported by four columns, although far more lavish examples are common. These were originally erected as memorials to deceased royals or other notables (as at Royal Gaitor in Jaipur or Bada Bagh near Jaisalmer), though in time they also appeared as purely decorative features lining the rooftops of buildings across the region, as well as in numerous Mughal buildings – four octagonal chhatris even appear on the roof of the Taj Mahal, flanking the main dome.

One final notable Rajasthani architectural form is the **step-well** (*baori* or *baoli*). Examples of step-wells can be found throughout the region, especially in Shekhawati. Most are modest structures, surrounded by a raised plinth topped by a pair of pillars, though there are also a number of remarkably elaborate versions, such as the vast Chand Boari in Abhaneri: huge and lavishly decorated wells approached via grand flights of steps descending deep into the bowels of the earth, whose architectural splendour attests to the crucial role water has always played in this arid desert state.

Rajput temple architecture

Rajasthan's **Hindu religious architecture** is not particularly well known compared to other places in the country, though the state boasts plenty of fine examples of Hindu sacred architecture, such as those at the remote complex of Osian in western Rajasthan and the temples in the fort at Chittaurgarh, which rival those at more celebrated north Indian sites such as Khajuraho in the lavishness of their ornamentation.

There could scarcely be a greater contrast between the region's Hindu temples and Mughal mosques. Mosques are essentially places of communal worship, enclosing large open courtyards in which the faithful can gather to pray together. The Hindu temple, by contrast, is considered the home of the god whose image it enshrines, and its architecture emphasises the mysterious, personal encounter with god – a sense of being in the presence of the divine, known as *darshan*, which is central to Hindu worship. At the heart of every temple is the principal shrine, or *garbhagriha* ("womb chamber"), housing the image of the temple's principal deity. This main shrine is generally topped by a large stone tower, or *shikhara*, and fronted by a small pillared hall, the *mandapa*, while subsidiary shrines are placed into the exterior walls, the whole complex set on a raised plinth (a scheme which was copied in Indo-Islamic mosques and mausoleums).

If the state's Hindu temples remain relatively unappreciated, its **Jain temples** are among the most celebrated in the country – most obviously those at Ranakpur and Dilwara (at Mount Abu), though there are further outstanding examples at Jaisalmer, Osian and Chittaurgarh. Jain temples share many common features with Hindu places of worship, except that the shrines within are dedicated to one of the religion's various *tirthankaras* (see p.380) rather than a Hindu god. They are usually relatively small in scale, but compensate with the extraordinary detail of their decorative carving – the examples at Ranakpur and Dilwara are particularly remarkable, with fine white marble columns and vaults fretted into extraordinary three-dimensional sculptural design, while the larger examples also display some idiosyncratic architectural features, such as the richly carved domes supported on an octagonal arrangement of columns (a Jain variant of the classic Hindu *mandapa*) which front the main shrines in temples at both Ranakpur and Dilwara.

Rajasthani painting

Rajasthani painting is one of the most vivid expressions of the state's artistic heritage, and (unlike Mughal painting) many fine works remain *in situ*, with at least a few works of interest on display in virtually every major museum or palace in the region – the collections at the city palaces of Bundi, Kota and Udaipur are particularly fine. Despite the intermittent influence of Mughal art, painting in Rajasthan developed in a quite different manner to that of its Islamic counterpart. Whereas most Mughal art was more or less realistic, Rajasthani painting was essentially symbolic. Much of the reason for this is the far greater concentration on **religious subjects** – particularly those connected with the life of Krishna, an enduring source of fascination for local artists. Such paintings were one result of the popularization of religion and increasing emphasis on personal devotion to god (*bhakti*) rather than on formal Brahmin-led rituals, which for many Hindus took the form of ecstatic Krishna worship.

Unlike their Mughal contemporaries, Rajasthani painters were not usually looking to depict contemporary or historical events or to explore the personality of their subjects, but to create a poetic mood, and there is relatively little concern with realism, perspective or the three-dimensional modelling of figures. These qualities give many Rajasthani paintings a wonderfully fairy-tale, and often an also strangely modern, appearance – a kind of slightly surreal, magical realism which sometimes suggests the work of much later Western artists like Douanier Rousseau or Chagall. Part of this quality is created by the use of intense colours, which are sometimes used in an explicitly symbolic way – red for anger, brown for the erotic, yellow for the miraculous, and so on. Colour is also a key element in the remarkable Rajasthani **ragamala** ("garland of melody") pictorial style, in which individual paintings are designed to evoke the mood of one of the classical modes of Indian music (either the six "male" ragas or their five musical "wives", called raginis), with different colours used to represent specific musical notes from the raga or ragini.

Different schools of painting flourished in various parts of the region from the sixteenth to eighteenth centuries, each developing its own idiosyncratic characteristics (although many of the subtle nuances of style which distinguish the various schools are generally discernible only to the eyes of professional art historians). Rajasthani painting first flourished in **Udaipur**, which remains the state's largest contemporary producer of traditional-style miniatures. Early paintings from the state are marked by their simple designs and vivid colours, almost like folk art, though later paintings – such as the numerous examples on display at Udaipur's City Palace – tend to concentrate on courtly subjects. Rajasthani painting reached its apogee, however, in the relatively minor state of **Bundi**, whose painters showed an almost obsessive fascination with various aspects of the Krishna legend – the lifting of Mount Goverdhan is a popular subject, as are Krishna's dalliances with the *gopis*, whether in the celebrated scene showing Krishna making off with the *gopis'* clothes while they are bathing, or the popular round dance (the Mandalanritya or Rasamandala), showing a circle of *gopis* dancing in a ring around Krishna and Radha, most memorably depicted in the marvellous mural which crowns the Badal Mahal in Bundi's City Palace. A similar, if slightly cruder, style flourished at nearby **Kota**, while another striking regional school of painting emerged at **Kishangarh**, whose artists specialized in elegantly elongated figures with huge eyes.

A later and hugely idiosyncratic development of Rajasthani painting occurred during the nineteenth and early twentieth centuries in the towns of **Shekhawati**, whose magnificent havelis were decorated by local artists in a vast assortment of colourful murals depicting both traditional and contemporary themes – a remarkable kind of public street-art designed for the entertainment and edification of the masses, rather than for the private delectation of a cultured elite. Although technically amateurish compared to earlier Rajasthani paintings, the engagingly naive style of these Shekhawati murals, with their fantastical depictions of modern European inventions like planes, trains and motor cars, is hugely entertaining, and adds a final, quaint flourish to the region's remarkable artistic traditions.

Wildlife

R ajasthan's wide-open spaces are home to a plentiful array of wildlife, ranging from magnificent tigers and leopards through to local curiosities such as the nilgai (bluebull) and four-horned chowsingha (swamp deer) – not to mention a rich selection of colourful birdlife. The relatively low population density (by Indian standards) and the presence of numerous nature reserves – some first established as hunting grounds by former rulers – have helped conserve wildlife, as have the attitudes of traditional rural communities closely attuned to the natural world, exemplified by the celebrated Bishnois of the Jodhpur region (See p.278), India's original eco-warriors. Habitat loss due to human encroachment remains a problem, however, as does the often catastrophic attentions of wildlife poachers, who have succeeded in reducing Rajasthan's tiger population to the verge of extinction, as well as targeting species ranging from sambar deer to birds such as the great Indian bustard.

Rajasthan's wildlife highlights are the world-famous **Keoladeo National Park** at Bharatpur and **Ranthambore National Park**. The former is one of Asia's most celebrated ornithological destinations, home – recent periods of drought excepted – to an extraordinary array of aquatic (and other) birdlife. Ranthambore is one of India's – indeed the planet's – foremost tiger-spotting destinations, offering excellent odds of seeing these magnificent beasts in the wild. The state's other main park, the peaceful **Sariska Tiger Reserve**, is home to pretty much every sort of wildlife found in the region; tigers were poached out of existence there in the first decade of this century, but are now being reintroduced.

Elephants

The Indian **elephant**, distinguished from its African cousin by its long front legs and smaller ears and body, and the fact that not all male elephants have tusks, is still widely used as a beast of burden throughout Rajasthan. Elephants have worked and been tamed in India for three thousand years, but it is through the battle legends of the sixteenth and seventeenth centuries that they earned their loyal and stoic reputation, both as great mounts in the imperial armies of the Mughals and as bejewelled bearers of rajas and nawabs. Elephants are also of great religious significance – they're a common sight in temple processions and ceremonies, often sporting a brightly painted trunk and forehead, and throughout the Subcontinent, stone elephants stand guard with bells in their trunks as a sign of welcome in medieval forts and palaces.

Wild elephants are now no longer found in Rajasthan, though captive elephants are a common sight around the region, especially at Amber and during the famous elephant festival in nearby Jaipur.

Tigers

India – including Rajasthan – is one of the very few places where **tigers** can still be glimpsed in the wild. As recently as the beginning of the last century, up to one hundred thousand tigers still roamed the Subcontinent, even though *shikar* (tiger hunting) had long been the "sport of kings". An ancient dictum held it auspicious for a ruler to notch up a tally of 109 dead tigers, and nawabs, maharajas and Mughal emperors all indulged their prerogative to devastating effect. But it was the trigger-happy British who brought tiger hunting to its most gratuitous excesses. Photographs of pith-helmeted, bare-kneed *burra-sahibs* posing behind mountains of striped carcasses became a hackneyed image of the Raj. Even Britain's Prince Philip (who subsequently served as president of the Worldwide Fund for Nature) couldn't resist bagging one during a royal visit in 1961.

In the years following Independence, demographic pressures nudged the Indian tiger perilously close to extinction. As the human population increased in rural districts, more and more forest was cleared for farming, depriving large carnivores of their main source of game and of the cover they needed to hunt. Forced to turn on farm cattle as an alternative, tigers were drawn into direct conflict with humans; some animals, out of sheer desperation, even turned man-eater and attacked human settlements. **Poaching** has taken an even greater toll. The black market has always paid high prices for live animals – a whole tiger can fetch up to US$100,000 – and for the various body parts believed to hold magical or medicinal properties. The meat is used to ward off snakes, the brain to cure acne, the nose to promote the birth of a son and the fat of the kidney – applied liberally to the afflicted organ – as an antidote to male impotence.

By the time an all-India moratorium on tiger shooting was declared in the 1972 Wildlife Protection Act, numbers had plummeted to below two thousand. A dramatic response geared to fire public imagination came the following year, with the inauguration of **Project Tiger** (⨈projecttiger.nic.in), created at the personal behest of Indira Gandhi. Nine areas of pristine forest were set aside for the last remaining tigers, displaced farming communities were resettled and compensated, and armed rangers employed to discourage poachers. Demand for tiger parts did not end with Project Tiger, however, and the poachers remained in business, aided by organized smuggling rings.

One of the problems facing conservationists is that even if poachers are caught, they are unlikely to be adequately punished – the maximum fine for tiger poaching is US$125, or one year in prison. Well-organized guerrilla groups thus operate with virtual impunity out of remote national parks, where inadequate numbers of poorly armed and paid wardens offer little more than token resistance. Project Tiger officials are understandably reluctant to jeopardize lucrative tourist traffic by admitting that sightings are getting rarer, but the prognosis looks very gloomy indeed.

Tigers on the web

⨈**www.savethetigerfund.org**
Homepage of the Save The Tiger Fund, with everything you ever wanted to know about tigers, in India and elsewhere.

⨈**www.wwfindia.org**
Home page of the Worldwide Fund for Nature, India, dedicated to conservation and environmental protection in the Subcontinent. Useful source of volunteer work opportunities and news.

⨈**projecttiger.nic.in**
Home page of Project Tiger.

⨈**www.tigersincrisis.com**
US-based tiger conservation group.

⨈**www.wpsi-india.org**
Wildlife Protection Society of India, set up to provide support in the struggle against poaching; the site has a wealth of information, links and news on everything connected to tigers in India.

Today, though there are 27 Project Tiger sites in India – including Ranthambore in Rajasthan – numbers continue to fall. Official figures optimistically claim a national **population** of over 3500, but independent evidence is less encouraging, still putting the figure at under two thousand. It was estimated in 1996 that one tiger was being poached every eighteen hours and the situation is believed to be just as depressing today. In 2005 it was discovered that there was no longer a single tiger left in the Sariska Tiger Reserve, in eastern Rajasthan, presumably due to poaching, and the resultant national scandal prompted a government enquiry and has cast a long shadow over Project Tiger's activities and credibility. There have been suggestions that park wardens at both Sariska and Ranthambore National Park have been implicated in poaching, and although such allegations have been vehemently denied (indeed one of Ranthambore's park trackers was murdered in 1992, possibly in a confrontation with poachers), suspicions remain. Tigers are now being reintroduced at Sariska (see p.232), but the most pessimistic experts are still claiming that, at the present rate of destruction, India's most exotic animal could face extinction within the next decade.

Other wild cats

Some of India's other **big cats** have fared even worse than the tiger. The Asiatic lion is now found only in one tiny patch of Gujarat and not at all in Rajasthan, while the Asiatic **cheetah** became extinct in India at the end of the 1960s and now exists only in Iran; the good news there, however, is that cheetahs are now being reintroduced in four Indian states, including Rajasthan. **Leopards** (panthers) survive, favouring forested areas near human settlement where domestic animals make easy prey. In Rajasthan they are mainly confined to hilly districts, such as the forested slopes around Mount Abu, and sightings are uncommon, although they can sometimes be spotted in Ranthambore National Park. Other indigenous felines include the **fishing cat** (occasionally spotted at Keoladeo National Park), the miniature **leopard cat**, the **jungle cat** (with a distinct ridge of hair running down its back), and a kind of lynx called the **caracal**. All these species are present in Rajasthan, though very rarely seen.

Deer and antelope

Deer and antelope, the larger cats' prey, are abundant throughout Rajasthan. The often solitary *sambar* is the largest **deer**, at up to 300kg and with antlers known to reach 120cm long (for which they are sometimes targeted by poachers). Smaller and more gregarious are *chital* (spotted deer), usually seen in herds skulking around langur monkey or human habitats looking for discarded fruit and vegetables. In Ranthambore you may hear the high-pitched call of the *chital* and the gruff reply bark of the langur warning of the presence of a tiger in the vicinity. Other deer include the elusive mountain-loving *muntjac* (barking deer) and the *para* (hog deer), which fall victim annually to flooding in the low grasslands. The smallest Indian deer, the nocturnal *chevrotain*, is known from its size (only 30cm high) as the mouse deer.

Antelopes include the endangered blackbuck, or "Indian antelope", revered by the Bishnoi (see p.278), along with the *nilgai* (bluebull; a curious creature halfway between an antelope and a cow), and the unique forest-dwelling four-horned *chowsingha* (swamp deer) – the last two are most easily spotted at Sariska Tiger Reserve. The desert-loving gazelle is known as the *chinkara* ("the one who sneezes") due to its alarm call, which sounds like a sneeze.

Monkeys

The two most common monkeys found in Rajasthan are the feisty red-bottomed Rhesus macaque and the shyer and more skittish grey-furred, black-faced common (or "Hanuman") langur, often found around temples. Monkeys are protected by the Hindu belief in their divine status as noble servants of the gods, a sentiment that derives from the Ramayana (see p.375), where the monkey god Hanuman leads his simian army to assist Rama in fighting the demon Ravana. Wild monkeys live in large troupes in the forests.

Other mammals

Among other wild animals you might see in Rajasthan, the shaggy **sloth bear** is hard to spot in the wild, being shy and mainly nocturnal. You may see captive specimens being forced to "dance" at tourist spots, but this is illegal under the Wildlife Protection Act; Wildlife SOS (Ⓦwww.wildlifesos.com) are working to save bears from being captured and mistreated in this way, and can be contacted on ℡09871 963535 to report such incidents. Other bears include the black and brown varieties, distinguishable by the colour of their fur. Of the **canines**, the scavenging striped hyena, the jackal and the small Indian fox are all fairly common. The Indian wolf lives in both desert and forest (particularly in that around Kumbalgarh), though it is threatened due to vigorous culling by humans protecting their domestic animals. The wild **buffalo** has a close genetic relationship with the common domesticated water buffalo.

Asia's answer to the armadillo is a scaly anteater called a **pangolin**, whose tough, plate-like scales run the length of its back and tail; this armour is believed to contain magical healing properties, for which the pangolin is illegally hunted. The three-striped **palm squirrel**, common around towns, is said to have been marked as such by the gentle stroke of Rama. The **common mongoose** is frequently seen in Rajasthan's national parks and elsewhere, as is the snouty **wild boar**.

Reptiles

The 238 species of **snake** in India (of which fifty are venomous) extend from the 10cm-long worm snake to nest-building king cobras and massive pythons. Venomous snakes you might meet in the wild are the majestically hooded cobra, the yellow-brown Russell's viper, the small krait and the saw-scaled viper. Snake charmers remove the cobra's venom, and quite often cut out the snake's fangs, a cruel and illegal practice.

Crocodiles and **gharial** (a species of freshwater crocodile with a curious and instantly recognizable bump on the end of its snout) are common throughout the Subcontinent and can be seen in Rajasthan in locations ranging from Sariska National Park to the banks of the River Chambal on the edge of Kota. **Lizards** are also common – every hotel room seems to have a resident gecko to keep the place free of insects, while the colourful garden lizard and Sita's lizard are both found throughout the country.

Birds

You don't have to be an aficionado to enjoy India's abundant **birdlife**. Travelling around the country, you'll see breathtaking birds regularly flash between the branches of trees or appear on overhead wires at the roadside, and even complete novices will enjoy a visit to the superb Keoladeo National Park at Bharatpur (see p.238). Serious birders should consult ⓦ www.camacdonald.com/birding/asiaindia.htm, which has reviews of birdwatching spots in Rajasthan and around Delhi, although many of the links are dead.

The wealth of different aquatic feeding and nesting habitats at Keoladeo draws exotic waterfowl such as flamingoes, spoonbills and pelicans. Stately **eagles** soar on the thermals at Keoladeo, Desert National Park (see p.295) and Sariska (see p.232), and peacocks flounce around forts and palaces.

Three common species of **kingfisher** are frequently spotted, perched on telephone wires or on the branches of a tree. Other common and brightly coloured species include the grass-green, blue and yellow **bee-eaters**, the stunning **golden oriole**, and the **Indian roller**, celebrated for its brilliant blue flight feathers and exuberant aerobatic mating displays. **Hoopoes**, recognizable by their elegant black-and-white tipped crests, fawn plumage and distinctive "*hoo...po...po*" call, also flit around fields and villages, as do several kinds of **bulbuls**, **babblers** and **drongos**, including the fork-tailed black drongo – a winter visitor that, like local kingfishers, can often be seen perched on telegraph wires. If you're lucky, you may also catch a glimpse of the **paradise flycatcher**, which is among the Subcontinent's most exquisite birds, with a thick black crest and long silver tail streamers.

Paddy fields, ponds and saline mud flats often teem with water birds. The most ubiquitous of these is the snowy white **cattle egret**, which can usually be seen wherever there are cows and buffalo, feeding off the grubs, insects and other parasites that live on them. Look out too for the mud-brown **paddy bird**, India's most common heron, distinguished by its pale green legs, speckled breast and hunched posture.

Common birds of prey such as the **brahminy kite** – recognizable by its white breast and chestnut head markings – and the **pariah kite** – a dark-brown buzzard with a forked tail – are widespread around towns, where they vie with raucous gangs of house **crows** and **white-eyed jackdaws** for scraps. Gigantic pink-headed **king vultures** and the **white-backed vulture**, which has a white ruff around its bare neck and head, also show up whenever there are carcasses to pick clean, although in recent years a mysterious virus has decimated numbers.

Rajasthan's abundant **forest birds** include the magnificent **hornbill**, with its huge yellow beak with a long curved casque on top. Several species of **woodpecker** also inhabit the wooded ranges of the Aravallis, among them the rare Indian great black woodpecker, which makes loud drumming noises on tree trunks between December and March.

The secretive but vibrantly coloured **red jungle fowl**, the wild ancestor of the domestic chicken, sports golden neck feathers and a metallic black tail. You're most likely to come across one of these scavenging for food on the verges of forest roads.

Books

India is one of the most written-about places on earth, though fewer works concentrate specifically on Rajasthan, Delhi or Agra. Books marked ♣ are particularly recommended.

History

William Dalrymple *The Last Mughal* (Bloomsbury/Knopf). Dalrymple surpasses himself in this masterful account of Delhi's part in the 1857 uprising. Using Urdu as well as English sources, he tells us what it was like for the insurgents, the British, the Mughal court and – most importantly – the ordinary people of Delhi. A great read, and a great piece of historical research.

Saul David *The Indian Mutiny* (Penguin). Rip-roaring account of the 1857 uprising. Not nearly as insightful as William Dalrymple's *The Last Mughal*, but with particularly strong coverage of the uprising's military aspect, including blood-curdling accounts of events at Delhi, Lucknow and Kanpur.

Abraham Eraly *The Mughal Throne* (Phoenix). The most detailed survey of the great Mughal rulers currently available, from Babur to Aurangzeb, with over 500 pages crammed full of absorbing historical minutiae and period detail.

Bamber Gascoigne *The Great Moghuls* (Constable & Robinson). Concise, entertaining and eminently readable account of the lives of the first six great Mughals, offering a fascinating glimpse into both the imperial ambitions and private lives of India's most remarkable dynasty.

Kalyan Kumar Ganguli *Cultural History of Rajasthan* (Sundeep). A wide-ranging study of how Rajasthan came into existence, the ethnic groups who make it up, its religious development and its art. Very learned, but very dry.

Christopher Hibbert *The Great Mutiny* (Penguin). Account of the 1857 uprising, told entirely from the British point of view, in easy prose and with some excellent first-hand material from the British side, but little about how the uprising was seen by the insurgents, or by ordinary civilians caught up in it.

M.S. Jain *Concise History of Modern Rajasthan* (Wishwa). A history of Rajasthan in the nineteenth and twentieth centuries, analyzing the integration of the Rajput kingdoms into the British colonial regime, and their exposure as outdated anachronisms as India gained Independence.

H.K. Kaul (ed) *Historic Delhi: an Anthology* (Oxford India). Delhi as seen by writers from the Middle Ages to the twentieth century in this collection of excerpts about the city, its incarnations, its constructions, the events that shaped it and the lives of its people through the ages. Ibn Battuta, Timur the Lame, Edwin Lutyens, Mark Twain and Mirza Ghalib are among the observers quoted.

S.A.A. Rizvi *The Wonder That Was India: Part II* (Picador). Rizvi's book (a follow-up to a classic study of India by A.L. Basham) looks at Indian history and culture from the arrival of Islam until colonial times, with thorough coverage of the Delhi Sultanate and Mughal Empire, though relatively little on Rajasthan.

Francis Robinson *The Mughal Emperors and the Islamic Dynasties of India, Iran and Central Asia 1206–1925* (Thames & Hudson). Not only the

Mughals, but also the Delhi sultans and the dynasties that came before and after, well illustrated with maps, timelines and colour photos, showing them in the context of a wider regional history.

Giles Tillotson *Jaipur Nama: Tales from the Pink City* (Penguin India). Engaging portrait of Jaipur through the ages, entertainingly presented using extensive eyewitness accounts from past visitors.

James Tod *Annals and Antiquities of Rajasthan* (Roli). The East India Company's political agent in Rajasthan, Tod originally published his monumental survey of Rajput history and folklore in two volumes in 1829 and 1832, and reprints of early editions are usually available, but for the modern reader, E. Jaiwant Paul's abridged, one-volume edition is far more accessible, condensing Tod's original and adding explanations where necessary.

Travel and reportage

William Dalrymple *City of Djinns* (Flamingo/Penguin). Dalrymple's award-winning account of a year in Delhi sifts through successive layers of the city's past. Each is vividly brought to life with a blend of inspired historical sleuth work and encounters with living vestiges of different eras: Urdu calligraphers, Sufi clerics, eunuchs, pigeon fanciers and the last surviving descendant of the Mughal emperors.

Robyn Davidson *Desert Places* (Penguin). Absorbing account of Davidson's long and difficult journey through Rajasthan and neighbouring Gujarat in company with the nomadic, camel-herding Rabari tribe, giving a rare insight into a way of life that has now virtually disappeared.

Royina Grewal *In Rajasthan* (Lonely Planet). Interesting contemporary travelogue exploring Rajasthan's folk music, architecture, feudal traditions and regional cuisine through encounters with a range of interviewees ranging from maharajas to itinerant snake charmers.

Justine Hardy *Scoop-wallah: Life on a Delhi Daily*. Entertaining account of roving reporter Justine Hardy's year in Delhi as a freelance writer on the *Indian Express*, featuring an absorbing cast of disaffected Rajasthani aristocrats, cocktail-swilling Delhi teens and migrant slum dwellers.

Tim Mackintosh-Smith *The Hall of a Thousand Columns* (John Murray). Quirky, learned and entertaining travelogue following the footsteps of the famous fourteenth-century Moroccan traveller Ibn Battuta through the Delhi of the Tughluq sultan Muhammad Shah and on to South India, with lashings of offbeat Subcontinental Islamic (and other) history en route.

Sam Miller *Delhi: Adventures in a Megacity* (Cape). Quirky travelogue whose sometimes rather random snapshot accounts take a look at places in Delhi that a tourist may rarely notice, from slums to suburbs, lively, and full of poignant little stories.

Fiction

Aravind Adiga *The White Tiger* (Harper Collins). Adiga's brilliantly dark satire on the state of India is largely set in Delhi, though the protagonists – a wealthy employer and

his impecunious servant – are both immigrants from Bihar.

Ahmed Ali *Twilight in Delhi* (New Directions). The author's love of his native city shines through in this portrait of Muslim Delhi, written in 1940 but set at the beginning of the twentieth century. Ironically, the very Independence for which the author so staunchly campaigned tore apart the community he portrays, and forced him into exile in Pakistan.

Anita Desai *Clear Light of Day* (Vintage). A touching exploration of the family issues revived when a woman who has been living abroad returns to visit her sister, left behind in the family home in Old Delhi from which her older siblings have managed to escape.

Tarquin Hall *The Case of the Missing Servant* (Hutchinson). Amusing and engrossing whodunnit set in Delhi and Rajasthan, involving a dapper but rather podgy gourmand private detective, a prosperous client and, as the title says, a missing servant.

Rudyard Kipling *Kim* (Penguin). Partly written at Bundi in southern Rajasthan, this classic Raj tale can be cringingly colonialist at times, but the atmosphere of India and Kipling's love of it shine through in this subtle story of an orphaned white boy.

Rama Mehta *Inside the Haveli* (Penguin). A free-thinking young Bombay woman marries into a conservative Rajput family from Udaipur and finds herself confined by purdah inside a Rajasthani haveli. As she gradually comes to terms with her environment, she starts to impose her own ideas upon it, which leaves her with the dilemma, now that she can, of how much she ought to try to change it.

Salman Rushdie *Midnight's Children* (Vintage). This story of a man born at the very moment of Independence, whose life mirrors that of modern India itself, won Rushdie the Booker Prize and the enmity of Indira Gandhi, who had it banned in India.

Khushwant Singh *Delhi: a Novel* (Penguin India). A jaded Delhiwallah and his hijra lover contemplate the accounts of characters from key moments in Delhi's past in this odd but compelling mix of serious history and bawdy humour by one of India's most distinguished and popular writers.

William Sutcliffe *Are You Experienced?* (Penguin). Hilarious novel sending up the backpacker scene in India (including the inevitable stint in Pushkar). Wickedly perceptive and very readable.

Women

Lucy Moore *Maharanis: The Lives and Times of Three Generations of Indian Princesses* (Penguin). Rip-roaring saga following the lives and loves of the maharanis of Jaipur (the legendary Gayatri Devi), Cooch Behar and Baroda in the later days of the Raj.

Sakuntala Narasimhan *Sati: Widow Burning in India* (Anchor Books). Definitive and engaging exploration of *sati* and its significance throughout history, including an account of the infamous 1987 Roop Kanwar case, in which an eighteen-year-old Rajasthani woman committed *sati*, to applause from some religious fundamentalists.

Mala Sen *Death By Fire* (Phoenix). Later made into a controversial movie, this book uses the Roop Kanwar case (see p.222) as a springboard to explore some of the wider issues affecting women in contemporary Rajasthani and Indian society – a bleak read, but one that shows up the hollow triumphalism of the country's right-wing politicians in its true colours.

The arts and architecture

Milo Cleveland Beach *Mughal and Rajput Painting (New Cambridge History of India)* (Cambridge University Press). Definitive academic overview of the pictorial arts of the Mughals and Rajputs.

Rustom Bharucha *Rajasthan: An Oral History - Conversations with Komal Kothari* (Penguin). Jodhpuri folklorist and musicologist Komal Kothari never wrote his own book about Rajasthani culture and folklore, so Bharucha, a Bengali writer on culture and theatre, interviewed him and wrote it for him. In it, Kothari talks about expected topics such as folk songs and puppet theatre, but also about agriculture and irrigation, religion and people.

Ebba Koch *The Complete Taj Mahal* (Thames & Hudson). The ultimate book on the Taj, erudite but plainly written, by an art historian who's been personally involved in the Taj's conservation, looking at its design, its history and its symbolism, lavishly illustrated with plans, maps and lots of wonderful colour photos.

Sehdev Kumar *Jain Temples of Rajasthan* (IGNCA). The temples of Dilwara and Ranakpur examined in minute detail, with a series of nine essays about their art and symbolism, and the Jain philosophy which shaped them.

George Michell *The Hindu Temple* (Chicago University Press). A fine primer, introducing Hindu temples, their significance, and architectural development.

George Michell and Antonio Martinelli *Princely Rajasthan: Rajput Palaces and Mansions* (Vendome Press). George Michell provides a solid, if pedestrian, account of Rajasthan's royal history and architectural heritage, accompanied by Antonio Martinelli's evocative photographs.

Also published in hardcover by Frances Lincoln as *The Palaces of Rajasthan*.

Lucy Peck *Delhi: a Thousand Years of Building* (INTACH). A wonderful and extremely thorough-going examination of Delhi's architecture from the earliest times to the present, covering just about every building of interest, with excellent maps, site plans and detailed descriptions to help you find and explore them.

Giles Tillotson *Mughal India* (Penguin). Excellent architectural guide to the great Mughal monuments of Delhi, Agra and Fatehpur Sikri, academic but accessible, and with interesting snippets of historical and biographical information thrown in to flesh out the descriptions of the buildings themselves. The same author's *Taj Mahal* is a fascinating memoir examining that sublime building's history and enduring mystique.

Giles Tillotson *The Rajput Palaces* (Yale University Press). Definitive, though expensive, study of Rajasthan's palace architecture, with an erudite but readable blend of history and architecture.

Giles Tillotson (ed) *Stones in the Sand: the Architecture of Rajasthan* (Marg Publications India). Refreshingly original overview of Rajasthani architecture, edited by one of the foremost authorities in the field, examining a range of local creations from forts and palaces through to havelis, temples and tanks.

Pauline van Lynden *Rajasthan* (Editions Assouline). Attractive coffee-table book showcasing photographs of Rajasthan's arts, crafts and cultural traditions amassed over the author's fifteen years of travel throughout the region.

Biography and autobiography

Gayatri Devi *A Princess Remembers* (Rupa). The nostalgic reminiscences of the multi-talented Gayatri Devi, maharani of Jaipur and global style icon – widely regarded as one of the most beautiful women of her era – who later became an immensely popular Rajasthani politician.

Giles Tillotson (ed) *James Tod's Rajasthan* (Marg Publications). Essays on different aspects of the life, ideas and legacy of James Tod, Company agent, and author of *Annals and Antiquities of Rajasthan* (see p.395). The essays cover Tod's work as a geographer and historian, the cultural significance of his collections of art, coins and manuscripts, and his opposition to direct British rule in India.

Religion

Krishna Dharma *Mahabharata: The Greatest Spiritual Epic of All Time* and *Ramayana: India's Immortal Tale of Adventure, Love and Wisdom* (Torchlight). There are numerous translations and retellings of the great Hindu epics (see p.375), including two published by Penguin, and some available for free online, but Krishna Dharma's are widely reckoned to be the most compelling reads.

Asghar Ali Engineer (ed) *Islam In India: The Impact Of Civilizations* (Shipra). Essays by different scholars on the history, impact and practice of Islam on the Indian Subcontinent.

Jeffery D. Long *Jainism: An Introduction* (I.B. Tauris). A clear and succinct introduction to the Jain religion, its tenets, origins and philosophy.

Kennath Morgan (ed) *The Religion of the Hindus* (Motilal Banarsidass). A good layperson's introduction to Hinduism, in the form of essays by different scholars covering aspects such as the history of Hinduism, the Hindu concept of God and Hindu religious practices, followed by excerpts from Hindu religious scripture.

Photographs

Tito Dalmau and Maka Abraham *Rajasthan: Houses and Men* (Contrasto). Beautiful colour shots of palaces, city streets, villages and people, all taken with a good eye for detail.

Bruno Morandi, Carisse Busquet and Gerard Busquet *Impressions of Rajasthan* (Flammarion). Murals and *mandanas* (festive floor paintings), and the people who paint them, are the subject of the shots in this book, covering Shekhawati, Bundi, Jodhpur and desert villages – not comprehensive, but choosy.

Reiner Sahm *Rajasthan: Panoramic Photography* (NZVP). Thirty fold-out panoramic colour photos in this lavish coffee-table book, supplemented with lots of smaller scenic photographs.

Language

Language

Language

The principal language of the Rajasthan, Delhi and Agra region is **Hindi**, the most important of India's eighteen official languages, spoken by over two hundred million people across the north of the country. Hindi, like all the major north Indian languages, is derived from the ancient Indo-Aryan language of Sanskrit and is written using a modified form of Sanskrit's classic Devanagari script (variants of which are also used to write Bengali, Punjabi and other Indian languages). It first developed around the markets and army camps of Delhi during the establishment of Muslim rule at the start of the second millennium AD. Hindi is closely related to **Urdu**, the principal language of Pakistan, which developed at the same time and subsequently became the lingua franca of the Mughal Empire. Urdu later became culturally more closely associated with Islam, being written in its own Perso-Arabic script. Delhi boasted a sizeable Urdu-speaking population right up until Independence, when many native speakers migrated to Pakistan.

Many people in Rajasthan also speak one of the various **local Rajasthani languages**, such as Marwari, Mewari, Mewati, Shekhawati, Dhundhari, Bagri, Wagri and Harauti. All these are closely related to Hindi – indeed it is only fairly recently that they have been accepted as separate languages in their own right, rather than dialects of Hindi. Rajasthani languages are also spoken by a few people in the neighbouring states of Gujarat, Haryana, Madhya Pradesh and Punjab, and in the Pakistani provinces of Punjab and Sind. **Other languages** spoken in Rajasthan include Sindhi, Gujarati and Punjabi.

Not surprisingly, given India's linguistic diversity and colonial heritage, **English** still plays an important role as a link language between Indians from different areas, and is still the preferred language of law, higher education, much of commerce and the media, and to some degree political dialogue. Indeed for many educated Indians, not just those living abroad, English is actually their first language, and it's not unusual to hear Indians talking together in English, especially in the larger and more westernized cities, particularly Delhi and Mumbai.

Indian English

During the Raj, **Indian English** developed its own characteristics, which have survived to the present day. Many Indian words – such as veranda, bungalow, sandal, pyjamas, shampoo, jungle, turban, pundit and yoga – entered the **vocabulary** of everyday English, but travellers in India soon become familiar with other terms in common usage that have not spread so widely outside the Subcontinent, such as *dacoit*, *dhoti*, *lakh* and *crore* (see the Glossary on pp.407–410 for definitions) – a full list of Anglo-Indianisms can be found in the famous *Hobson-Jobson* dictionary.

Perhaps the most endearing aspect of Indian English is the way it has preserved forms now regarded as **old-fashioned** in Britain or America. Addresses such as "Good sir" and questions like "May I know your good name?" are commonplace, as are terms like "tiffin" and "cantonment". Newspapers feature headlines such as "37 perish in mishap", referring to a train crash, or passages like this splendid report of a bank robbery: "The miscreants absconded with the loot in great haste. They repaired immediately to their hideaway, whereupon they divided the iniquitous spoils before vanishing into thin air."

It's well worth attempting to pick up a bit of Hindi to use on your travels – the language is relatively straightforward compared to many others in Asia, at least at a basic level. There are plenty of **tutorial aids** available. Hugo's *Hindi in Three Months* by Mark Allerton is brilliantly direct and will get you talking (almost) like a native in no time at all. Rupert Snell's *Teach Yourself Beginner's Hindi* offers a rather more detailed, but still commendably practical, course of study, with excellent audio materials. *The Rough Guide Hindi & Urdu* **phrasebook** makes a good on-the-road companion, with an extensive dictionary, thematically presented vocabulary lists and scenarios, and a rundown of the grammatical basics. The scenarios can also be downloaded free as audio files from Ⓦ www.roughguides.com.

Useful Hindi words and phrases

Greetings

Hello (slightly formal; not used for Muslims)	Namaste/Namaskar As salaam alaykum (formal; to a Muslim) Alaykum as salaam (in reply)
Goodbye	Namaste
See you later	Phir mileynge
Goodbye (to a Muslim)	Khudaa haafiz
How are you? (formal)	Aap kaise hai?

How are you? (familiar)	Kya hal hai?
brother (informal; not to be used to older men)	bhaaii
sister (informal; not to be used to older women)	diidi
sir	sahib
sir	hazur (Muslims only)

Basic words

yes (informal/ more formal)	haa or ji haa
no (informal/ more formal)	nahi or ji nahi
OK	acha or tiik hai
I/me	mai
you (formal)	aap
you (familiar; and to children)	tum
and/more	aur
how?	kaise?
How much?	Kitna?
thank you (formal; Indians don't usually say thank you during everyday transactions, eg when buying something. Note that there's also no direct Hindi equivalent to the English word "please".)	dhanyavad/shukriya

good	acha
very good	bahut acha
bad	buraa
big	barra
small	chhota
hot	garam
hot (spicy)	mirchi
cold	thanda
clean	saaf
dirty	gandaa
open	khulaa
expensive	mehngaa
come	aao
please come	aiiye
go	jaao
run (also "take a run" or "scram")	bhaago
enough	bus

Basic phrases

My name is…	Mera naam…hai	It is OK?	Tiika hai?
What is your name? (formal)	Aapka naam kya hai?	How much money?	Kitna paisa?
		How much is this?	Yeh kitne ka hai?
What is your name? (familiar, and to children)	Tumhara naam kya hai?	I don't need it (literally "not needed"); useful response to persistent touts	Nahi chai'iya
I'm from…	Mai…se hu		
We're from…	Hum…se hai		
Where do you come from?	Aap kaha se aate hai?	Do you have…?	…hai?
		I/we like it	Acha lagta hai
I understand	Samaj gayaa	How are you?	Kya haal hai?
I don't understand	Samaj nahin aayaa	I'm fine	Tiik hai
I don't know	Maluum nahi	What work do you do?	Kya kam karte hai?
I don't speak Hindi	Mai Hindi nahi bol sakta hu		
		Do you have any brothers or sisters?	Bhaai behan hai?
Please speak slowly	Dhiire se boliye		
Sorry	Ma'af kiijiye	Oh dear!	Arey!

Getting around

Where is the…?	…kaha hai?	What time does the train leave?	Gaarii kab jayegi?
I want to go to…	Mai…jaana chaata hu		
Where is it?	Kaha hai?	Stop!	Ruko!
How far?	Kitna duur?	Wait!	Thehero!
Which is the bus for Agra?	Agra ki bus kaun si hai?		

Accommodation

I need a room	Mujhe kamra chai'eeya	I am staying for one night	Mai ek raat ke liiye theheroonga
How much is the room?	Kamra kitne ka hai ?		

Medicinal

I have a headache	Sir me dard hai	medicine	dawaaii
I have a pain in my stomach	Mere pate me dard hai	ill	bimar
		pain	dard
The pain is here	Dard yaha hai	stomach	pate
Where is the doctor's surgery?	Daktar ka clinic kaha hai?	eye	aank
		nose	naakh
Where is the hospital?	Haspital kaha hai?	ear	kaan
Where is the pharmacy?	Dawaaii khana kaha hai?	back	piith
		foot	paao

Numbers and time

zero	shunya	sixty	saath
one	ek	seventy	sattar
two	do	eighty	assii
three	tiin	ninety	nabbe
four	char	one hundred	ek sau
five	paanch	one thousand	ek hazaar
six	che	one hundred thousand	ek lakh
seven	saat	ten million	ek crore
eight	aat	today	aaj
nine	nau	tomorrow/yesterday	kal
ten	das	day	din
eleven	gyaarah	afternoon	dopahar
twelve	baarah	evening	shaam
thirteen	terah	night	raat
fourteen	chaudah	week	haftaah
fifteen	pandrah	month	mahiinaa
sixteen	solah	year	saal
seventeen	satrah	Monday	somvaar
eighteen	ataarah	Tuesday	mangalvaar
nineteen	unniis	Wednesday	budhvaar
twenty	biis	Thursday	viirvaar
thirty	tiis	Friday	shukravaar
forty	chaaliis	Saturday	shanivaar
fifty	pachaas	Sunday	ravivaar

Food and drink

Basics

khaana	food	garam	hot
chawaal	rice	thanda	cold
chamach	spoon	(botal vaala) paani	(mineral) water
chhoori	knife	chai	tea
kanta	fork	kavhaa or kaafi	coffee
plate	plate	doodh	milk
namak	salt	chini (nahi)	(no) sugar
(kali) mirch	(black) pepper	paan	betel nut; (see p.48)
mirchi	chilli/hot	bill laiye	Can I have the bill/
mirchi kam	less hot		check?

Menu reader

alu	potatoes
appam	South Indian-style rice pancake speckled with holes, soft in the middle
baingan	eggplant (aubergine)
barfi (or burfi)	traditional sweet made with milk; a bit like fudge
bhaji (or bhajia)	pieces of vegetable deep-fried in chickpea batter, served as a main course or a street snack
bhatura	soft bread made of white flour and traditionally accompanying *chana*; common in Delhi
bhel puri	mix of puffed rice, deep-fried vermicelli, potato, crunchy puri with tamarind sauce; a Mumbai speciality, though now popular nationwide
bhindi	okra (ladies' finger)
bhujia	Bikaneri namkeen consisting of thin, vermicelli-like sticks made from gram and lentil flour
bhuna	roasted and then thickened-down medium-hot curry sauce
biriyani	rice baked with saffron or turmeric, whole spices, and meat (sometimes vegetables), and often hard-boiled egg; rich
brinjal	eggplant (aubergine)
chaat	snack
chana	chickpeas
chapati	unleavened bread made of wholewheat flour and baked on a round griddle-dish called a *tawa*
chingri	prawns
chop	minced meat or vegetable served with breaded mashed potato
cutlet	patty fried in batter

dahi	curd (a type of yoghurt)
dhal	lentils, usually reduced to a kind of soup
dhal bati churma	classic Rajasthani dish comprising dhal, *bati* (a baked wheatflour ball with a tough crust) and *churma* (a sweet made of coarse-ground wheat flour cooked with ghee and sugar)
dhansak	curry sauce made from reduced lentils; usually medium-hot
dopiaza	onion-based sauce; medium-mild
dosa	crispy South Indian rice pancake; can be served in various forms, the best known of which is the *masala dosa*, when the *dosa* is wrapped around a filling of spicy potato curry
dum	steamed in a casserole; the most common dish is *dum aloo*, with potatoes
falooda	traditional Muslim drink, made with milk, ice, cream, nuts and sweets
gaajar	carrot
garam masala	hot spice mix
gatta	small dumplings of gram flour cooked in a masala sauce
ghee	clarified butter; often used instead of cooking oil
gobi	cauliflower
gosht	meat, usually mutton
gravy	curry sauce
gulab jamun	classic Indian sweet made from deep-fried dough balls served in syrup
halwa	gelatinous sweet, typically flavoured with cardamom and nuts
iddli	South Indian steamed rice cake, usually served with *sambar*

jaggery	unrefined sugar
jalebi	deep-fried whorls of brightly coloured orange sugar-syrup
jalfrezi	dish cooked with tomatoes and green chilli; medium-hot to hot
jeera	cumin
kachori	small thick cakes of salty deep-fried bread
kadi	curd gravy
kadi pakora	pakora with curd and spices, a speciality of Jaisalmer
kair	caper-like fruit of a Rajasthani shrub
kaju katli	barfi-like sweet made with cashew nuts
karahi	cast-iron wok which has given its name to a method of cooking with dry spices to create dishes of medium strength
karhi	dhal-like dish made from *dahi* and gram flour
keema	minced meat
kheer	delicate, Mughal-style rice pudding
kofta	balls of minced vegetables or meat in a curried sauce
korma	mild sauce made with curd (and perhaps cream)
kulfi	Indian-style ice cream, often flavoured with pistachio
ladoo (or ladu)	sweets made from small balls of gram flour and semolina
lal maas (or laal maans)	literally "red meat": a spicy dish of lamb marinated in chilli
lassi	yoghurt drink, served plain, sweet (with sugar), salted, or with fruit, even occasionally with bhang (cannabis)
macchi	fish

makhania	with cream (often in fact butter or ghee)
malai kofta	vegetable balls in a rich cream sauce; usually medium-mild
mangodi	lentil-flour dumpling
masala	mixture, especially of spices
mawa samosa	sweet samosa filled with milk fudge and drizzled with syrup
methi	fenugreek (often the leaf)
mirchi bada	large chilli fried in a thick batter of wheatgerm and potato; a speciality of Jodhpur
mithai	traditional Indian sweets
mughlai masala	Mughal-style mild, creamy sauce
mughlai paratha	paratha with egg
murg	chicken
murg makhani	butter chicken
muttar	peas
naan	white leavened bread kneaded with yoghurt and baked in a tandoor
namkeen	dry savoury snacks ("Bombay mix")
nimbu	lemon
pakora	pieces of vegetable deep-fried in chickpea batter; a popular street snack
palak	spinach
paneer	a type of light, unripened cheese, usually eaten in small cubes as part of a curry
papad or poppadum	crisp, thin, chickpea flour cracker
paratha or parantha	wholewheat bread made with butter, rolled thin and griddle-fried; a little bit like a chewy pancake, sometimes stuffed with meat or vegetables.
pathia	thickened curry with lemon juice; hot
penda (or peda)	smooth barfi-like sweet, usually sold in small discs

phulka	a chapati that has been made to puff out by being placed directly on the fire	sambar	soupy lentil and vegetable curry with asafoetida and tamarind
piaz	onions	samosa	parcels of vegetable and potato (and sometimes meat) wrapped up in triangles of pastry and deep-fried
pilau	rice, gently spiced and pre-fried		
puri	crispy, puffed-up, deep-fried wholewheat bread	sangri	pods of the khejri tree
raita	curd with herbs and vegetables (usually mint and cucumber)	seekh kebab	minced lamb grilled on a skewer
		shahi paneer	"royal" paneer; slightly more elaborate version of standard paneer curry, sometimes including fruit and nuts
raj kachori	a crisp puri usually filled with chickpeas and doused in curd and sauce		
rogan josh	deep-red lamb curry, a classic Mughlai dish; medium-hot	shami kebab	small minced lamb cutlets
		sula (or maas ka sula)	Rajasthani tandoori kebab
rasam	South Indian-style spicy soup	tamatar	tomato
		tarka dhal	lentils with a masala of fried garlic, onions and spices
rasgulla	cheese balls flavoured with rosewater		
rasmalai	Bengali sweet consisting of cheese balls in sweet cream	thali	combination of vegetarian dishes, chutneys, pickles, rice and bread served as an all-in-one meal
roti	loosely used term; often just another name for chapati, though it should be thicker, chewier, and baked in a tandoor		
		tikki	"cutlet" (patty fried in batter)
		uttapam	thick, South Indian-style rice pancake often cooked with onions
sabji	vegetables (literally, "greens")	vada	doughnut-shaped, deep-fried lentil cake

Glossary

ahimsa non-violence

apsara heavenly nymph

arak liquor distilled from rice or coconut

ashram centre for spiritual learning and religious practice

avatar reincarnation of Vishnu on earth, in human or animal form

Ayurveda ancient system of medicine employing herbs, minerals and massage

baba respectful term for a sadhu

bagh garden, park

baithak reception area in house or palace

baksheesh tip, donation or alms

bandhani tie-dye

baoli (or **baori**) step-well

begum Muslim princess; Muslim woman of high status

betel leaf chewed in paan, with the nut of the areca tree, which is thus known as "betel nut"

bhakti religious devotion expressed in a personalized or emotional relationship with the deity

bhang pounded marijuana leaf, often mixed in lassi

bhawan (or *bhavan*) building, house, palace or residence

bhojanalaya diner; cheap restaurant (see p.45)

bidi Indian-style cigarette, with tobacco rolled in a leaf

bindu seed, or the red dot (also *bindi*) worn by women on their foreheads as decoration

brahmin the priestly *varna* (caste grouping)

burj tower or bastion

burra-sahib colonial official, boss or a man of great importance

cantonment area of town occupied by military quarters

chajja sloping dripstone eave

chandra moon

chappal sandals or flip-flops (thongs)

charas hashish

charbagh Persian-style garden divided into quadrants

charpoi Indian bed consisting of a wooden frame with cords stretched across it

chhatri domed stone pavilion, often erected over a tomb (see p.386)

chillum cylindrical clay or wood pipe for smoking *charas* or ganja

chowk crossroads or courtyard

chowki police post

chowkidar watchman/caretaker

coolie porter/labourer

crore ten million

dacoit bandit

dalit outcaste (the term, introduced by caste equality activist Dr B.R. Ambedkar, is preferred by so-called "untouchables" as a description of their social position)

dargah tomb of a Muslim saint

darshan vision of a deity or saint; receiving religious teachings

darwaza gateway; door

deva god

devi goddess

dhaba diner; cheap restaurant (see p.45)

dham important religious site, or a theological college

dharamshala rest house for pilgrims

dharma sense of religious and social duty (Hindu); the law of nature, teachings, truth (Buddhist)

dhobi laundryperson

dhoti white ankle-length cloth worn by males, tied around the waist, and sometimes hitched up through the legs

dhurrie woollen rug

digambara ("sky-clad") Jain sect originally distinguished by nudity among its monks (see p.380)

diwan-i-am public audience hall

diwan-i-khas hall of private audience

dowry payment or gift offered in marriage

durbar royal audience or council of state

eve-teasing sexual harassment of women, either physical or verbal

fakir ascetic Muslim mendicant

finial capping motif on temple pinnacle

ganj market

ganja marijuana bud

garbhagriha temple sanctuary, literally "womb-chamber"

garh fort

ghat mountain, landing platform, or steps leading to water

ghazal Urdu poetic form, often used in sad songs

ghee clarified butter

gopi young cattle-tending maidens who feature as Krishna's playmates and lovers in popular mythology

gurudwara Sikh place of worship

haj Muslim pilgrimage to Mecca

hajji Muslim engaged upon, or who has performed, the *haj*

hammam sunken Persian-style bath

haveli elaborately decorated mansion

hijra eunuch or intersexual person (see p.67)

howdah bulky elephant-saddle, sometimes made of pure silver, and often shaded by a canopy

idgah area laid aside in the west of town for prayers during the Muslim festival Id-ul-Zuha

imam Muslim leader or teacher

imambara tomb of a Shi'ite saint

IMFL Indian-made foreign liquor

Indo-Saracenic overblown Raj-era architecture that combines Muslim, Hindu, Jain and Western elements

iwan large central arch, very typical of Mughal buildings, especially mosques jali latticework in stone, or a pierced screen

jama or jami Friday, as in Jama masjid, or "Friday mosque"

jarokha small canopied balcony, often containing a window seat

jat North Indian ethnic group; particularly numerous in eastern Rajasthan around Bharatpur

jati specific caste (see p.374)

jhuta soiled by lips: food or drink polluted by touch

-ji suffix added to names as a term of respect

johar old practice of self-immolation by women in times of war

karma weight of good and bad actions that determine status of rebirth

katcha the opposite of pukka

kavad small decorated box that unfolds to serve as a travelling temple

khadi home-spun cotton; Gandhi's symbol of Indian self-sufficiency

khan Muslim (originally Central Asian) title for a ruler

khana dwelling or house

khejri small tree found throughout the desert regions of Rajasthan

kirtan hymn-singing

kohl black eyeliner

kot fort

kothi residence

kotla citadel

kshatriya the *varna* (caste grouping) of warriors and rulers

kund tank, lake, reservoir

kurta long men's shirt worn over baggy pyjamas

lakh one hundred thousand

lingam phallic symbol in places of worship representing the god Shiva

liwan prayer hall or covered area of a mosque

madrasa Islamic school

maha- great or large

mahadeva literally "great god", and a common epithet for Shiva

maharaja (maharana, maharawal) king

maharani queen

mahal palace; mansion

mahout elephant driver or keeper

maidan large open space or field

mandala religious diagram

mandapa hall, often with many pillars, used for various purposes: eg *kalyana mandapa* for wedding ceremonies and *nata mandapa* for dance performances

mandi market

mandir temple

mardana area for use of men in a haveli or palace

marg road

masjid mosque

mata goddess

mayur peacock

mela festival

memsahib respectful (colonial) term for a European woman

mihrab niche in the wall of a mosque indicating the direction of Mecca. In India the mihrab is thus in the west wall

minaret high slender tower, characteristic of mosques

minbar pulpit in a mosque from which the Friday sermon is read

moksha blissful state of freedom from rebirth aspired to by Hindus, Jains, Sikhs (who call it *mukti*) and Buddhists (who call it nirvana)

mor peacock

muezzin man behind the voice calling Muslims to prayer from a mosque

muqarna a style of Islamic moulded vaulting

nawab Muslim prince or provincial governor

nilgai bluebull (a type of large antelope; see p.391)

NRI non-resident Indian, someone entitled to Indian nationality but resident abroad

om (or aum) symbol denoting the origin of all things, and ultimate divine essence, used in meditation by Hindus and Buddhists

paan betel nut (usually wrapped in a betel leaf and chewed as a digestive, see p.48)

padma lotus; another name for the goddess Lakshmi

paise there are a hundred paisa in a rupee

parikrama ritual circumambulation around a temple, shrine or mountain

pietra dura inlay work, traditionally consisting of semiprecious stones set in marble; particularly associated with Agra

pir Muslim holy man

pol fortified gate

prasad food blessed in temple sanctuaries and shared among devotees

puja worship

pujari priest

pukka proper; correctly so-called

purdah literally "curtain"; the enforced segregation and isolation of women within a haveli or palace or, more figuratively, within society in general. General term for wearing a veil

qawwali Sufi devotional chanting

qibla wall in a mosque indicating the direction of Mecca

qila fort

raj monarchy, in particular the period of British imperial rule 1857–1947

raja king

Rajput class of rulers, making up around ten percent of the population of Rajasthan (see p.357)

rawal chieftain or ruler of a minor principality

rishi Hindu sage; divinely inspired poet of Vedic hymns

sadar main; principal

sadhu Hindu holy man with no caste or family ties

sagar lake

sahib respectful title for gentlemen, especially (in colonial times) European men

salwar kameez long shirt and baggy ankle-hugging trousers worn by Indian women

sambar a small Asian deer

samsara cyclic process of death and rebirth

sangeet music

sarai resting place for caravans and travellers who once followed the trade routes through Asia

sari usual dress for Indian women: a length of cloth wound around the waist and draped over one shoulder

sati one who sacrifices her life on her husband's funeral pyre in emulation of Shiva's wife. No longer a common practice, and officially illegal

satyagraha (literally "embracing truth") honesty in thought and deed as part of Gandhi's campaign of non-violent resistance to injustice

scheduled castes official name for "untouchables"

sepoy infantry private, an Indian soldier in the British army during the colonial period

shaivite follower of the Hindu god Shiva

shastra treatise

sheesh mahal "glass palace"; usually a small room or apartment decorated with mirrorwork mosaics

sheikh Muslim (particularly Sufi) holy man or saint

sri respectful prefix

Surya the sun, or sun god

svetambara ("white-clad") the main branch of Jainism (see p.380)

swami title for a holy man

tandoor clay oven

tank water pool, usually for ritual bathing

tempo three-wheeled taxi, much like an auto-rickshaw

tiffin light meal

tiffin carrier set of stainless-steel tins used for carrying meals

tirthankara enlightened Jain teacher, of whom 24 have appeared in the last 300 million years (see p.380)

tola the weight of a silver rupee: 180 grains, or approximately 11.6g

tonga two-wheeled horse-drawn cart

trimurti the Hindu trinity (Brahma, Shiva and Vishnu)

untouchables members of the lowest strata of society, considered polluting to all higher castes

urs Muslim saint's day festival

vaishya the *varna* of merchants and farmers

varna (literally "colour") caste grouping (brahmin, kshatriya, *vaishya* or *shudra*; see p.374)

vedas sacred texts of early Hinduism

-wallah ("man") suffix often implying occupation, eg: rickshaw-wallah, chai-wallah, but also Congress-wallah, Delhiwallah

wazir chief minister to the king

yoni symbol of the female sexual organ, set around the base of the lingam in temple shrines

zamindar landowner

zenana women's quarters; segregated area for women in a mosque, haveli or palace

Small print and
Index

A Rough Guide to Rough Guides

Published in 1982, the first Rough Guide – to Greece – was a student scheme that became a publishing phenomenon. Mark Ellingham, a recent graduate in English from Bristol University, had been travelling in Greece the previous summer and couldn't find the right guidebook. With a small group of friends he wrote his own guide, combining a highly contemporary, journalistic style with a thoroughly practical approach to travellers' needs.

The immediate success of the book spawned a series that rapidly covered dozens of destinations. And, in addition to impecunious backpackers, Rough Guides soon acquired a much broader and older readership that relished the guides' wit and inquisitiveness as much as their enthusiastic, critical approach and value-for-money ethos.

These days, Rough Guides include recommendations from shoestring to luxury and cover more than 200 destinations around the globe, including almost every country in the Americas and Europe, more than half of Africa and most of Asia and Australasia. Our ever-growing team of authors and photographers is spread all over the world, particularly in Europe, the US and Australia.

In the early 1990s, Rough Guides branched out of travel, with the publication of Rough Guides to World Music, Classical Music and the Internet. All three have become benchmark titles in their fields, spearheading the publication of a wide range of books under the Rough Guide name.

Including the travel series, Rough Guides now number more than 350 titles, covering: phrasebooks, waterproof maps, music guides from Opera to Heavy Metal, reference works as diverse as Conspiracy Theories and Shakespeare, and popular culture books from iPods to Poker. Rough Guides also produce a series of more than 120 World Music CDs in partnership with World Music Network.

Visit www.roughguides.com to see our latest publications.

Rough Guide credits

Text editor: Rosalyn Belford
Layout: Jessica Subramanian
Cartography: Rajesh Mishra
Picture editor: Chloë Roberts
Production: Rebecca Short
Proofreader: Jan McCann
Cover design: Dan May, Chloë Roberts
Photographer: Simon Bracken
Editorial: London Andy Turner, Keith Drew, Edward Aves, Alice Park, Lucy White, Jo Kirby, James Smart, Natasha Foges, Róisín Cameron, James Rice, Lara Kavanagh, Emma Traynor, Emma Gibbs, Kathryn Lane, Monica Woods, Mani Ramaswamy, Harry Wilson, Lucy Cowie, Alison Roberts, Eleanor Aldridge, Ian Blenkinsop, Joe Staines, Matthew Milton, Tracy Hopkins, Ruth Tidball; **Delhi** Madhavi Singh, Lubna Shaheen, Jalpreen Kaur Chhatwal
Design & Pictures: London Scott Stickland, Dan May, Diana Jarvis, Mark Thomas, Nicole Newman, Sarah Cummins, Emily Taylor; **Delhi** Umesh Aggarwal, Ajay Verma, Ankur Guha, Pradeep Thapliyal, Sachin Tanwar, Anita Singh, Nikhil Agarwal, Sachin Gupta

Production: Liz Cherry
Cartography: London Ed Wright, Katie Lloyd-Jones; **Delhi** Rajesh Chhibber, Ashutosh Bharti, Animesh Pathak, Jasbir Sandhu, Karobi Gogoi, Alakananda Roy, Swati Handoo, Deshpal Dabas
Online: London Faye Hellon, Jeanette Angell, Fergus Day, Justine Bright, Clare Bryson, Aine Fearon, Adrian Low, Ezgi Celebi; **Delhi** Amit Verma, Rahul Kumar, Narender Kumar, Ravi Yadav, Debojit Borah, Rakesh Kumar, Ganesh Sharma, Shisir Basumatari
Marketing & Publicity: London Liz Statham, Jess Carter, Vivienne Watton, Anna Paynton, Rachel Sprackett, Laura Vipond; **New York** Katy Ball, Judi Powers; **Delhi** Ragini Govind
Digital Travel Publisher: Peter Buckley
Reference Director: Andrew Lockett
Operations Assistant: Becky Doyle
Operations Manager: Helen Atkinson
Publishing Director (Travel): Clare Currie
Commercial Manager: Gino Magnotta
Managing Director: John Duhigg

Publishing information

This second edition published October 2010 by
Rough Guides Ltd,
80 Strand, London WC2R 0RL
11 Local Shopping Centre, Panchsheel Park, New Delhi 110017, India
Distributed by the Penguin Group
Penguin Books Ltd,
80 Strand, London WC2R 0RL
Penguin Group (USA)
375 Hudson Street, NY 10014, USA
Penguin Group (Australia)
250 Camberwell Road, Camberwell, Victoria 3124, Australia
Penguin Group (Canada)
195 Harry Walker Parkway N, Newmarket, ON, L3Y 7B3 Canada
Penguin Group (NZ)
67 Apollo Drive, Mairangi Bay, Auckland 1310, New Zealand
Cover concept by Peter Dyer.

Typeset in Bembo and Helvetica to an original design by Henry Iles.
Printed in Singapore
© Daniel Jacobs and Gavin Thomas, 2010
Maps © Rough Guides
No part of this book may be reproduced in any form without permission from the publisher except for the quotation of brief passages in reviews.
424pp includes index
A catalogue record for this book is available from the British Library
ISBN: 978-1-84836-555-1
The publishers and authors have done their best to ensure the accuracy and currency of all the information in **The Rough Guide to Rajasthan, Delhi and Agra**, however, they can accept no responsibility for any loss, injury, or inconvenience sustained by any traveller as a result of information or advice contained in the guide.

1   3   5   7   9   8   6   4   2

Help us update

We've gone to a lot of effort to ensure that the second edition of **The Rough Guide to Rajasthan, Delhi and Agra** is accurate and up-to-date. However, things change – places get "discovered", opening hours are notoriously fickle, restaurants and rooms raise prices or lower standards. If you feel we've got it wrong or left something out, we'd like to know, and if you can remember the address, the price, the hours, the phone number, so much the better.

Please send your comments with the subject line "**Rough Guide Rajasthan, Delhi and Agra Update**" to ✉mail@roughguides.com. We'll credit all contributions and send a copy of the next edition (or any other Rough Guide if you prefer) for the very best emails.

Have your questions answered and tell others about your trip at ⓦwww.roughguides.com.

Acknowledgements

Gavin: In Jaipur, massive thanks, once again, to the mighty Satinder Pal Singh for all his help and kindness, and to everyone at the *Pearl Palace Hotel* for making my stay so comfortable (particularly Bidyut Tarafdav for driving my passport all the way to Nawalgarh). Grateful thanks also to Abhinav Wadhwa at the *Sundar Palace Hotel* for further information, insights and assistance, and for providing such enjoyable company during my visits to the city. Elsewhere in Rajasthan, a big thank-you to Indar Ujjawal at Adventure Travel in Jaisalmer; Jaggi and Sohel at the *Govind Hotel* in Johdpur; Rahul and Abher at the *Tiger Safari Hotel* in Ranthambore; and to Sanjay Sain, for driving me from Jaipur to Ranthambore with unfailing patience and courtesy, despite my frequently incomprehensible meanderings.

At Rough Guides, thanks to Chloë Roberts for cracking pictures, and to my editor, Ros Belford, for running the whole show with exemplary skill and efficiency and for making this second edition such an enjoyable experience. Thanks also to Dave Abram for long-term moral support (and unacknowledged contributions to the previous edition) and to fellow author Dan Jacobs for all his work on the book and unstinting assistance during this and previous collaborations. And, last but not least, love and thanks to Allison, with whom I once travelled the length and breadth of the Subcontinent, and to Laura and Jamie, who I hope will one day see a tiger for themselves.

Daniel: Mahendra Dan, Ramesh Wadhwa, Rajesh, Anil, Ashok, Sabir and everyone at the *Tourists Rest House*, Agra.

ROUGH GUIDES

SMALL PRINT

Readers' letters

Thanks to all the readers who have taken the time to write in with comments and suggestions (and apologies if we've inadvertently omitted or misspelt anyone's name):

Erika Abrams; Anna Adam; Elaine Almén; Sam Barfoot; Wolfgang Bartels; Derek Bedlow; Pippa Behr; Sophie Broadbent; Beth & Steve Brown; Andre Burney; Eric & Sylvia Castaldi; Karein Davie; Theresa Durso; Mylene Evered; Stuart Forster; Aaron Fox; Peter Frank & Meryl D'Souza-Frank; Janet Giaretta; Geoff Hill; Geoffrey Kremer; Anne-Flore Laloë; Roger & Denise Lawrence; Ryan Leeward; Lynne Le Gros; Emil Malmborg; Amy Marsh; Carol Miller; Clare Mooney; Sophie Morris; Julia Morton; Rose Murphy; Andrew Mutter; Clare Oakland; Karyn Olden; Stephen Phelps; Dawn Richardson; Anthony Schlesinger; Minesh Shah; Natasa Stankovic; Tom Stuart; Roland Weilguny; Bradley Young.

Photo credits

All photos © Rough Guides except the following:

Title page
Flock of pigeons, Jaipur © Scott Stulberg/Corbis

Full page
The blue houses of Jodhpur © Jean du
Boisberranger/Corbis

Introduction
Elephant with face paint, Jaipur © Scott Stulberg/
Corbis
Signs bazaar, Bundi © Gavin Thomas
Market, Pushkar © Peter Adams/Corbis

Things not to miss
01 Taj Mahal and reflection with two Indian
women in foreground © Suzanne and Nick
Geary/Getty
02 Camel traders at the annual Pushkar fair
cooking dinner © Jill Gocher/Photolibrary.com
03 Ranakpur Jain temple © Frédéric Soltan/Corbis
04 Low angle view of a tower, Vijay Stambha,
Chittorgarh Fort © Photosindia/Corbis
06 Humayun's Tomb, Delhi © Jon Hicks/Corbis
07 A young Bengal tiger in the water, Ranthambore
National Park © Theo Allofs/Corbis
09 Mughlai cuisine © Simon Reddy/Alamy
10 Shekhawati havelis, Ramgarh © Gavin Thomas
11 Bahai Temple, Delhi © Gavin Hellier/Getty
12 Panch Mahal Palace, Fatehpur Sikri © Steven
Vidler/Corbis
13 White breasted kingfisher © Jan Baks/Alamy
14 Pink City, Jaipur © Gavin Thomas
16 Diwan-I-Am, Red Fort, Delhi © Tibor Bognár/
Corbis
17 Women socializing at Lake Pichola, Udaipur
David Sutherland/Corbis

Forts and palaces colour section
Lake Pichola, Jag Mandir Palace, Udaipur
© Wojtek Buss/Photolibrary.com
Mural painting in Chitra Shala area of Bundi
Palace © Tolo Balaguer/Photolibrary.com
Hawa Mahal (Palace of the Winds), Jaipur
© Robert Harding/Photolibrary.com
Meherangarh Fort outer walls, Jodhpur © Walter
Bibikow/Photolibrary.com
View from walls of Jaigarh Fort, Amber, near
Jaipur © Richard Ashworth/Photolibrary.com
Meherangarh Fort, Jodhpur © Robert Harding/
Photolibrary.com
City Palace, Udaipur © P Narayan/Photolibrary
.com

Rajasthani crafts colour section
Woman drying freshly dyed and printed sarees
on elevated bamboo racks © Jeremy Horner/
Corbis
Man measuring fabric, Jaisalmer © Hugh Sitton/
Corbis
A young man block printing custom fabric
© Win Initiative/Getty
Ring bearing a green gemstone, Jaipur
© Fernando Bengoechea/Corbis
Multicolored bangles at a craft market, Jaipur
© Martin Harvey/Corbis
Puppets in an outdoor market, Jaisalmer
© Jim Zuckerman/Corbis
Potter's hands on piece of pottery, Pushkar
© Ric Ergenbright/Corbis

Black and whites
p.97 India Gate © Scott Stickland
p.103 Cow in Paharganj © Daniel Jacobs
p.112 The Lahore Gate at the Red Fort, Delhi
© Simon Bracken
p.150 Sikandra Akbar Mausoleum, Agra
© Pictures Colour Library/Alamy
p.153 Elderly passenger awaits train, Agra
© Jeremy Horner/Corbis
p.159 Silhouette of man walking at entrance of
Taj Mahal, Agra © Gavin Gough/Getty
p.164 Multifoil arches in pavilion, Agra Fort
© Blaine Harrington III/Corbis
p.175 Fatehpur Sikri Fort © Fabian von Poser/
Photolibrary.com
p.184 City Palace, Jaipur © Tibor Bognár/Corbis
p.201 Pink City, Jaipur © Gavin Thomas
p.207 Window in Amber Fort, Jaipur © Bob Krist/
Corbis
p.242 Langur monkey at a temple, Ranthambore
National Park © Mary Ann McDonald/Corbis
p.248 Meherangarh Fort, Jodhpur © Gavin
Thomas
p.262 Pushkar © Gavin Thomas
p.312 Architectural sculpture on temple in
Chittorgarh Fort © Frédéric Soltan/Corbis
p.320 City Palace by the lake, Udaipur © Keren
Su/Corbis
p.330 Ranakpur © Gavin Thomas
p.337 Interior of Vimal Vasahi Temple, Mount Abu
© John Henry Clause Wilson/Corbis
p.348 Shopping in Bundi © Gavin Thomas

Index

Map entries are in colour.

I

Map symbols

maps are listed in the full index using coloured text

- - - Chapter boundary
- - - · International boundary
- - · · State boundary
—— Main road
—— Minor road
—■— Railway
- - - - - Track/trail
——— Coastline/river
—— Wall
⊠—⊠ Gate
≍ Bridge
ⁿᵘᴴ⁴ᵘ Rocks
⚞ Mountains
▲ Peak
/||\ Hill
⚹ Swamp
⚵ Viewpoint
Ⓜ Metro station
★ Bus stop
♦ Point of interest

- Petrol station
- @ Internet café
- ⓘ Tourist office
- ⊠ Post office
- ⊞ Hospital
- ◉ Accommodation
- ♟ Fortress
- ▯ Haveli
- 🏛 Palace
- ∴ Ruin/Archeological site
- ▬ Boat
- ⚑ Golf course
- ☪ Mosque/Muslim monument
- ⚶ Hindu/Jain temple
- ▤ Ghat
- ◯ Stadium
- ▮ Building
- ⊞ Church
- ⊡ Cemetery
- ▨ Park

So now we've told you about the things not to miss, the best places to stay, the top restaurants, the liveliest bars and the most spectacular sights, it only seems fair to tell you about the best travel insurance around

WorldNomads.com
keep travelling safely

Recommended by Rough Guides